Laurence W. Schwartz
158-50-9382
699-0002
Cambridge Hall D 206

SPORT AND AMERICAN SOCIETY: SELECTED READINGS

SPORT AND AMERICAN SOCIETY: SELECTED READINGS

Second Edition

GEORGE H. SAGE
University of Northern Colorado

ADDISON-WESLEY PUBLISHING COMPANY

Reading, Massachusetts
Menlo Park, California · London · Don Mills, Ontario

This book is in the
ADDISON–WESLEY SERIES IN PHYSICAL EDUCATION

ISBN 0-201-06703-X
ABCDEFGHIJ-CO-787654

PREFACE

At the time the first edition of this book was published in 1970 there were only one or two books available dealing with the social aspects of sport in America, despite the fact that there was some research and considerable writing on the subject scattered throughout a variety of publications, from popular magazines to quite scholarly journals. During the past four years this subject has gained enormous appeal. A number of sociology of sport and psychology of sport conferences have been held at the national and international levels; several anthologies on this subject have been published; and textbooks which attempt to treat the subject more or less systematically are beginning to appear.

As with the first edition, this volume is intended as a selective survey of the interdisciplinary literature on the general subject of the social aspects of sport in American society. I make no claim to have "covered the field." Many readers will discover that certain dimensions of this subject have been omitted. With such a broad subject there is probably no other alternative. Any single volume can only hope to have a sampling of the studies and writing on this topic. My aim has been to present readings which illuminate the very broad social science parameters of American sport.

The organization of topics in this edition is different than the first edition and about three-fourths of the readings are new to the book. The rationale for making so many changes is based upon the frank reactions of my students and professional colleagues to the first edition and to the rapidly expanding literature in this field of study. Approximately one-fourth of the readings in this edition are my own work and consist of research studies and conference presentations completed in the past few years. The other authors of selected articles are sociologists, psychologists, historians, anthropologists, and physical educators. Although they are scholars in their own particular field, they share one common interest—sport. They have studied sport from various points of view and they write about it with expertise in their own areas of specialization.

The readings in this volume are not restricted to the realm of theoretical concerns. In selecting readings I was guided by a belief that a book of this type might be used by instructors and students with widely diverse interests and should therefore not be limited to a narrow scope of the literature on sport. Certainly the theoretical and so-called "scientific" sources have important information to offer, but so do speculative and interpretive writings. Many times the questions and problems posed in speculative and interpretative writing serve to stimulate research into a particular area. I have also purposely included materials on widely different levels of writing. I had two basic reasons for such a procedure. First, I felt that any single writing style or format would be too narrow. While academic scholars may be able to describe sports phenomena that are significant at the .05 level of confidence, they frequently cannot provide us with as comprehensive an overview as can the essayists. My second reason for incorporating stylistic variety was for the sake of readability. I felt that a variety of materials would be much more exciting for readers of this book.

The study of sport is a puzzling paradox. While sports, games, and other play forms have been a prominent part of almost every culture, scholars have shown little inclination to undertake theoretical and scholarly studies of these phenomena. Historians have been curious about every conceivable part of societies of the past, but have virtually ignored the role of sport in the growth, development, and decline of civilizations. Except for several cursory efforts, few systematic histories of sport have been attempted.

Psychologists have exhaustively studied the behavior of man and lower animals, but have displayed a blissful unconcern with the psychosocial parameters of sport. Recently, one psychologist admitted that few psychologists care much about sports qua sports. This has been the prevailing attitude of psychologists—the scholars who study behavior. Such an attitude is rather bewildering in view of the enormous amount of human behavior that is devoted to sports and games.

Sociologists have shown even greater disdain for studying sports. It is true that this discipline has only recently established itself as truly a distinct subject; nevertheless the systematic study of sports has not appeared as a prominent topic for sociological investigation. Although sports take place in social settings, and sports have a profound influence on the social life of great numbers of people, sociologists apparently find other social phenomena more interesting to study.

American physical educators have, by contrast, shown an inordinate amount of interest in sport and its social-psychological dimensions. Indeed, the basic curricular structure of American physical education since 1900 has been firmly based on the belief that physical education and sports experiences provide a rich environment for the socialization of the individual and the modification of behavior. Unfortunately, very few physical educators have verified these beliefs with good solid social or psychological research. Instead, physical education researchers have traditionally been more concerned with the physiology of exercise and mechanical analysis of sports movements.

It is encouraging to observe, however, that the academic fashions of the past are changing and contemporary scholars are discovering sports as a legitimate field of study. Scholars from various disciplines are beginning to undertake serious investigations of the subject. For example, the field of physical education is giving emphasis to history, psychology, and sociology of sport as special academic sub-fields within the study of human movement, and these new academic specialties are beginning to appear in undergraduate and graduate curricula. Whether the marriage between these specialties and professional physical education will endure or whether the disciplines from which the basic subject matter is derived will expand to include these specialties is still to be ascertained. In any case, the upsurge of interest is beginning to produce some significant research.

What is emerging from all of these studies is a body of knowledge emphasizing the significance of sport as a social phenomenon. However, it is difficult for the interested person to gain a comprehensive view of the literature because many of the relevant writings are widely scattered among the writings of various disciplines. The purpose of this book is therefore to bring together in one volume some of the pertinent literature on the social aspects of American sport.

In selecting and organizing the material, I had in mind several groups of potential readers. First, the book should be particularly appropriate for physical education courses in sociology of sport, psychology of sport, introduction to physical education, and foundations of physical education. Second, this volume might be used as a supplemental text for certain courses in departments of sociology and psychology.

Undoubtedly, the greatest appeal will be directly to physical educators, for it is within this field that the most concentrated study and investigations of sport are taking place. Furthermore, physical educators from ancient Greece to modern America have affirmed psychological and social values for sports and games participation. The Greek paidotribe (the teacher of physical exercise) believed that the character development of the body was as important as his athletic skill. The Battle of Waterloo was supposed to have been "won on the fields of Eton." The "new physical education" of Thomas Wood and Clark Hetherington in the early 20th century provided an eminent place in its objectives for psychosocial development. American physical education programs have been the nursery for sports in this society. It would seem, then, that the content of the book is particularly pertinent for physical educators and aspiring physical educators. Sociologists and psychologists are beginning to offer courses on sport and this book would also be appropriate for these courses.

The readings are grouped under eight major headings. The topical headings may seem arbitrary and without purpose, but any attempt to organize this subject into neat packages is arbitrary and reflects more on the orientation of the organizer than any other single factor. There is no single organizing concept or theoretical frame of reference which could be used to select and arrange the readings in a way that would satisfy all instructors and students. I hold no brief for the topic headings I have chosen. I realize that categories such as sport as a social institution, sport as a social process, etc., might have been used, but in many ways these organizational frameworks are no less arbitrary than the ones I have chosen.

The readings are not mutually exclusive, and certain ones clearly overlap my classifications. Each chapter of readings is preceded by an introduction. In each introduction I have attempted to describe and clarify the importance of that particular dimension of sport and its social significance; I have also written a brief explanatory note on the contents of each reading.

I would like to express appreciation to my colleagues at the University of Northern Colorado for providing interest and constructive criticism while the book was taking form. Also, I am indebted to students and colleagues throughout the United States who used the first edition and contributed helpful suggestions for this second edition.

I would be remiss if I did not extend a grateful "thanks" to two able and dependable secretaries, Gertrude Fillinger and Sue Rich, for their painstaking typing of the manuscript.

Finally, I wish to thank the many editors and authors who gave permission to use their published materials in this book.

Greeley, Colorado   G.H.S.
February 1974

CONTENTS

1 / THE SOCIAL STUDY OF SPORT IN AMERICAN SOCIETY

The sociologist, James S. Coleman (1961), observed that a stranger to an American high school "might well suppose that more attention is paid to sports by teenagers, both as athletes and as spectators, than to scholastic matters [p. 34]." A comparable statement might be made with regard to American society; thus, a stranger to this country might well suppose that more attention is paid to sport than to almost any other activity. Indeed, some foreign observers have claimed that the United States is "sports crazy" —that we are obsessed with sport.

While there are claims that Americans overdo sports, we are periodically criticized, by both foreign and domestic observers, as being "soft Americans." Thus, we are frequently characterized as "unfit" and we are accused of having a dread disease called "spectatoritis." Although periodic reports do indicate that the average American, youth and adult, lacks the kind of physical fitness that physical educators and physicians consider reasonable for proper health maintenance, Americans of all ages do participate in a wide variety of sports activities. Community sponsored programs of sports are offered to persons of all ages: from Little League baseball for elementary school age boys to shuffleboard for senior citizens. Schools devote enormous resources to inter-school sports programs. Professional sports, which collectively constitute a major form of entertainment in American society, employ a great many athletes. At the informal level, millions of Americans participate in skiing, boating, tennis, golf, and a great many other sports for recreation. Indeed, facilities for most of these recreational activities cannot meet the needs of the participants.

Most sport involvement takes place within a social context; that is, typically sports participants (athletes) and sports consumers (spectators) engage in sport in the company of other persons. Sports which are organized on a team basis require that the participants band together and coordinate their efforts to overcome the opponent. Sports which are considered "individual," such as golf or tennis, do not require teammates but they do require an opponent and they are frequently played before spectators, so they may correctly be considered "social" in nature. Attendance by spectators at sports contests is a major form of entertainment in the United States. Support for the high school sports teams is considered a public duty in many communities. In collegiate sports, the practice of student support for the institution's teams is carried over from high school, and the only connection which most college graduates have with their alma mater is through attendance at its athletic events. Finally, professional sports depend upon spectators for their very livelihood, and sports fans all over the nation identify with the professional team nearest their residence. "Spectating," whether it be for the hometown high school or the New York Mets, is a social event, and anyone who has ever attended a sports event between two rivals was probably aware of the interesting social dynamics of the situation as fans booed the opponents, cheered the home team, and heckled the referee for what was considered a "bad" call.

The prominent position which sport has attained in American society in recent decades has not only affected the lifestyle of many persons, as broader and more diverse sports involvement impinges upon their daily experiences, but it has ushered in a scholarly interest on the part of social scientists. New courses in sport sociology, sport psychology, and sport history have been introduced in colleges throughout the country within the last decade, and there are signs that empirical and theoretical work on the social aspects of sport will become quite popular in the coming years.

In the first reading, Sage emphasizes that sports permeate American society and that, from infancy throughout adulthood, Americans find sport involvement a dominant activity in their lives. This involvement ranges from active participation to viewing sports via television. It is noted that sport is visible within all of the major cultural institutions. Thus we find: schools promoting and supporting interschool sports programs; the founding of big businesses upon the manufacturing of sports equipment, the provision of facilities, and the establishment of franchises, etc.; and even the use of sport for personal gain by politicians. However, despite the pervasiveness of sport, Sage points out that only recently have social scientists begun to bring sport into the mainstream of social analysis and research.

In the second reading, Kenyon discusses the criteria for and content of the emerging field of study called sport sociology. He describes the place of sociology of sport in terms of its academic origin, which he considers to be within the discipline of sociology. He contrasts the approach of physical educators to the "social development" objective with the approach of the sociologists who attempt to "understand" and extend knowledge about sport. Kenyon then identifies the three factors essential to the development of a field of study — a workable conceptual system, a value-free orientation, and a theoretical-empirical balance — and applies them specifically to the development of sport sociology. Kenyon's concluding remarks indicate how a sociology of sport subject-matter will have many implications for the field of physical education.

Martens, in the next reading, describes a field of study which focuses upon the social psychology of physical activity. He differentiates this area of study from the other sciences and discusses how sociology and social psychology are related to each other. A social psychology of physical activity, Martens claims, is concerned with the application of social psychological theory and methods to the study of social behavior in a physical activity context. Several of the major topical areas for analysis and research in this field are identified and discussed. They are: social influences on motor performance, influence of sports experiences on social behavior, attitude development, personality development, cultural transmission via sport, and group dynamics within sport settings.

In the final reading, Lüschen discusses the interrelatedness of sport and culture. The author is critical of those approaches to study in this field which have led to a research emphasis on the cultural diffusion of sports and games rather than on the social structure which determines their particular significance within various cultures. After showing that there is a structural interdependence between sport and culture, the author identifies and discusses several underlying cultural values which are related to sport involvement. Modern industrialization and technology are suggested as cultural variables which form a basis for sport. The relationship between sport and Protestantism is examined and several examples are cited which suggest that where Protestantism is strong, organized sport is prominent. Societal achievement orientations also seem to be related to the sport involvement of a country. Subsystems within a society tend to promote sports differentially. Thus we see the prominence of sport in the American adolescent age-group as well as the differential involvement in sport among persons from different social classes. Lüschen next deals with the influence of sport on the sociocultural system and discusses the basic functions of sport around Talcott Parsons' four societal functions: pattern maintenance, integration, adaptation, and goal attainment. He also identifies several dysfunctions of sport. Lüschen's last topic is concerned with the role of sport in cultural change and evolution.

REFERENCES

Coleman, J.S., "Athletics in High School," *Annals of the American Academy of Political and Social Science,* **338**: 33-43, 1961.

SPORT IN AMERICAN SOCIETY: ITS PERVASIVENESS AND ITS STUDY

George H. Sage

THE PERVASIVENESS OF SPORT IN THE UNITED STATES

Sport is such a pervasive human activity that to ignore it is to overlook one of the most significant aspects of contemporary American society. It is a social phenomenon which extends into education, politics, economics, art, the mass media, and even international diplomatic relations. Involvement in sport, either directly as a participant, or indirectly as a spectator, is almost considered a public duty by many Americans. It has been observed that if there is a religion in America today, it is sport.

Even an unbiased stranger to America would soon realize that sport is one of the most pervasive activities in our culture. Primary involvement in sport begins for most boys while they are still in elementary school. The Little League baseball program initiates boys to the world of organized sport at seven or eight years of age, and if a boy shows a little interest and aptitude for the sport, he will likely pass through the Pony League, Babe Ruth League, and American Legion baseball programs on his way to adulthood. Pop Warner football programs capture the efforts of young boys who are inclined toward rough, contact activity. Bitty Basketball, Pee Wee Hockey, age-group swimming and track also are available to youngsters in most communities who wish to participate in sports.

The programs mentioned above are sponsored by community, club, or service groups, but the school also provides abundant opportunity for sports involvement. Most states have legislation requiring the teaching of physical education through high school, and sports activities form the basic curriculum of American physical education programs. In addition to the required physical education classes, most schools throughout the country sponsor interschool athletic programs beginning in the junior high school and continuing through college. The significance of these programs in the high school life of students is best exemplified in Coleman's statement that a visitor to a typical American high school "might well suppose that more attention is paid to athletics by teenagers, both as athletes and as spectators, than to scholastic matters. He might even conclude . . . that the school was essentially organized around athletic contests and that scholastic matters were of lesser importance to all involved" [Coleman, 1961, p. 34].

Professional sports undoubtedly produce the greatest amount of sports involvement in American society of any other single sports enterprise. During the past 15 years professional sports teams have multiplied at a bewildering rate, thus providing job opportunities for an increasing number of professional athletes. The growth of professional sports may be exemplified by noting that the National Hockey League began the 1960's with six teams and the 1970's with fourteen; also during the 1960's professional basketball proliferated from one league to two and from 12 teams to a total of 28 teams; major league baseball broke the long-standing sixteen team tradition and went to twenty-four teams; professional football witnessed the birth of a new league, the merger of that league with the NFL and a new twenty-six team league, thus more than doubling the teams which existed in 1960. The growth of other professional sports could be described but the pattern is the same.

The major form of involvement with professional sport is through watching the contests, either by actually attending the contests or by viewing them on television. Television viewing is probably the single way in which most adults are involved in sport, especially professional sport. Up to twenty hours of professional sports are beamed into home television sets per week and it is not unusual for six to eight hours of professional sports to be aired on a single Sunday. Television contracts with professional sports is a billion dollar a year business, and few professional sports franchises could exist today without television revenue. Television virtually is professional sports and professional sports is television.

The economic impact of sport in the United States is awesome. In American society sport is big business. It is a commercial interest with a commanding position in the entertainment industry. Professional sports comprise one of the most successful and expanding industries in the United States. As has already been noted, in the past ten years the number of professional football, baseball, and hockey teams has more than doubled. Horse racing, golf, and bowling have moved into the big business arena, and sundry other sports give evidence of capturing more sports dollars in the future. Professional athletes' salaries reflect the value placed on sports. A minimum salary of over $15,000 is guaranteed in several sports and annual salaries of over $75,000 are not uncommon. A few of the so-called "super stars" have received salaries in excess of $200,000. The average salary in the National Football League in 1972 was over $25,000, while professional golfers compete for over 5 million dollars in prize money each year. Professional sports franchises are worth anywhere from five million to twenty million dollars.

Big business is not confined just to professional sports. In the process of fostering wholesome recreation, high school and college sports have unwittingly entered the field of professional entertainment. Over 150,000 student-athletes participate in NCAA-sponsored competitions in 30 different sports each year at a dollar investment of 2 billion dollars. Sport, in the form of participant recreation, is promoted by companies for their employees to the extent that industry buys more sports goods and equipment than United States schools and colleges combined, and it schedules more entertainment than the nation's night clubs. Americans spend about 50 billion dollars on recreation annually. This money is primarily spent in the purchase of equipment, supplies, and memberships, in the payment of dues, and in other necessities of active engagement in sports. Even gambling on sports is a major economic activity; estimates of the amount of money that Americans wager on sports range from 15 billion to 50 billion dollars per year. Of course, very little is known about the network of bookies, oddsmakers, etc. who are involved in sports gambling.

Many factors account for the burgeoning sports phenomena, but undoubtedly industrialization is of major importance. The industrial revolution secured leisure and affluence for the masses. Leisure naturally led to an increase in sports activities, so leisure ushered in big business in sport. The American appetite for sports pursuits seems to increase as weekly work hours decrease.

Sport is very visible in American politics. In their own way, of course, politicians realize the pervasiveness of sport and make every effort to use it for political gain. Presidents are well aware of the political potential of big-time sports, and this is why they never miss an opportunity to publicly associate themselves with sports. Nixon's telephone calls to the locker rooms of sports victors garnered publicity for him as well as for sport. This linking of politics and sport by Nixon earned him the reputation of a "football freak" in some quarters, however. But the President is only the most visible politician to be linked with sport. Politicians from the local level to the national level capitalize as much as possible on sport for political self-promotion.

The linking of politics and sport extends beyond the local, state, and national levels and into international affairs. Today, most countries of the world use sport as an instrument of international policy to some extent. Communist countries make quite clear their motive for supporting and promoting national and international sports: Sport is used as a visible example of the success of the ideological political system. As Morton (1963) says: "The Soviets have made serious business out of sport competition. . . . They have forged a direct propaganda link between sport triumphs on one hand and the validity of a social system on the other" [p. 82]. The Communist countries are not, of course, the only countries who practice sports diplomacy. The United States supports international level competitors and teams largely through the U. S. State Department and the military services. Although the federal government does not directly support American participation in the Olympic Games, untold millions of dollars are spent to indirectly assist the Olympic team so that the United States may field teams to impress other nations throughout the world.

Sport is even making a considerable impact on the literary and art fields. Although sport has occupied a prominent place in the newspapers for the past 70 years, serious writers have tended not to use sport to any extent. Palmer (1973) notes that "sports can hardly be said to constitute the focal metaphor of a single adult novel, nor does a single adult novel focus on an athletic hero" [p. 49]. However, with the rise in mass sport interest, there is a trend toward serious writing about sport. The greatest impact of sport in the literary field, however, is not coming from novelists, but from former athletes and sports journalists. Within the past four years there has been a virtual deluge of books published by professional athletes (most are actually ghost written) who describe their experiences in sports. A number of former athletes have written "kiss and tell" books which have either mocked their sports experiences or have been highly critical of them. The underpaid, unheralded sport journalist has also gotten into the publishing windfall of sports books in recent years, and several have written what might be called the exposé or muckraking type of books.

Sport has even invaded Broadway and shows evidence of making a happy marriage with drama. Several years ago, the story of Jack Johnson, the first black heavyweight boxing champion, came to life in the play *The Great White Hope* and became an immediate success. This has been followed up with several other dramas about sport. Jason Miller's grimly funny account of a high school basketball team's 20th reunion, *The Championship Season,* was voted the best play of 1972 by the Drama Critics Circle. In 1973, *The Jockey Club Stakes,* and *The Changing Room* became two of the most popular plays in New York. There are definite indications that sport will become increasingly used in serious stage plays and motion pictures.

Even everyday language reflects the influence of sport. One who goes beyond normative behavior is said to be "off side" or "out-of-bounds." A person who begins an activity before the agreed-upon time is said to have "jumped the gun" or engaged in "foul play." Politicians and businessmen frequently sprinkle such euphemisms as "taking a cheap shot," "laying the ground rules," "game plan," and "fumbled the ball" into their professional conversations. The swain can gain nods of appreciation among his friends by saying he "scored" or gestures of sympathy if he admits he "struck out."

James Reston wrote in *The New York Times:*

> Sport in America plays a part in our national life that is probably more important than even the social scientists believe. Sports are now more popular than politics in America, increasingly so since the spread of television. The great corporations are now much more interested in paying millions for sports broadcasts than they are for all political events except for the nominations and inaugurations of Presidents, because the general public is watching and listening.

He appears to possess great insight as an observer of American society.

STUDY OF THE SOCIAL ASPECTS OF SPORT

Since sports involvement consumes so much of the daily activity of American people, it seems logical that it should be of major importance to our understanding of their behavior. It would seem that social scientists would probably have devoted a great deal of their scholarly energy to it. Loy (1972) says, in this regard:

> One would think that the sheer magnitude of the public's commitment to sport would attract the attention of a number of social observers of human conduct. Moreover, sport seems to be an ideal proving ground for the testing of many social theories, and it also appears to offer several suitable settings for the development of formal theories of social behavior [p. 229].

Unfortunately, the serious study of sport has been virtually nonexistent in the social sciences until the past decade. Thus a body of knowledge, from a social science perspective, is in its infancy.

In surveys conducted by the American Sociological Association in 1950 and 1959 (Riley, 1960) each member of this association was asked to list three sociological fields in which he felt qualified to teach or to do research. The sociologists were free to describe their competencies in their own terms, thus the categories which emerged were not predetermined. Sport as a topic for teaching or research did not appear in enough cases to be classified as a topic.

By 1970 the American Sociological Association classified its membership into 33 areas of competence, and area #14 was entitled "Leisure, Sports, Recreation, and the Arts" and, according to a survey of its membership (Stehr and Larson, 1972) 60 sociologists out of 8,350 who returned the questionnaires marked this area as an area of personal competence. This represents 0.7 percent of the total group and places this area as the 30th out of 33 categories, in terms of rank position. Loy (1972) reports that the actual specialization of sociologists within this "grab bag" area divides up something like this: ". . . approximately one-third identify the arts as their special area of competence, another one-third leisure, while a final one-third cite sport as their specific domain of interest and expertise" [p. 50]. Comparable conditions exist in the other social sciences. In psychology, the American Psychological Association does not have a separate section on sport psychology, although it has a multitude of sections for the various specialties within the field of psychology. Historians, anthropologists, economists, etc. have not given much recognition to sport as a special topic for study.

There may be several reasons why the study of sport has not been in the mainstream of any of the social sciences. First, there has been a prevailing notion that playful activity, and therefore sport, is for children; that is, sports are appropriate for children, but adults are certainly not expected to pursue an interest in them to any extent. Thus, sport has been looked upon as something one engaged in as a child but placed behind himself as an adult. Secondly, and this is related to the first reason, the proper scholar in a given field was expected to study topics that scholars in that field were studying because it was by following this path that one gained recognition, rewards, and prestige in a field of study. Although there are certainly exceptions to this pattern in every discipline, it is easy to find a few topics that are well mined by the majority of workers in that field. The scholar who chose to study sport was not only isolating himself from the "proper" topics for study in his field but he was also laying himself open to the ridicule of studying a frivolous children's pastime. A third reason for the reluctance to study sport may be related to the same reluctance to studying the sociology of education which Gross (1959) identified, namely the quality of the literature is poor, consisting mainly of essays, and the scant research has little or no relevance to existing social science theory and research.

Another reason that sport has not been seriously studied until recently may be related to its recent rise to omnipresence. Until recent years, sports participation was primarily a recreation of the upper classes, when it was engaged in by adults. Long working hours, physically exhausting labor, and limited income made sports prohibitive for the working class. Except for major league baseball, professional sports were not prominent until after World War I. Even in baseball, since only sixteen major league teams existed throughout the United States and transportation was rather cumbersome, very few persons actually got to see the games. It was not until the 1920's that radio began reporting live-action baseball games, and while this was an improvement over newspaper accounts of games, it could not compare with the impact that television had on the development of professional sports. College football has been popular since the late 19th century with the college students and alumni but mainstream America was not really a part of the college scene until after World War II, and even here TV had the greatest impact on popularizing college sports. So, although sports interests certainly existed prior to television, this particular mass media has had the most dramatic effect on the sports mania of today, and television is a phenomenon of the past twenty years.

Although it is surely not a major reason that social scientists have not pursued the serious study of sport, Stone (1972) humorously describes the difficulty a scholar has had in getting a piece of research on this topic published in the scholarly journals. He says: "When sociologists speak of play, those ghosts who control and patrol the journals strike terror into their hearts! . . . it is very difficult to find a resting place for an article on play in the graveyards staked out by major journals of sociology. Consult the gravestones—I mean, of course, the table of contents" [pp. 3-4].

Although study of the social aspects of sport is in its infancy, recent trends indicate that progress in developing a cogent body of knowledge is increasing at an accelerating rate. Physical education departments throughout the United States are now offering courses in sport sociology, sport psychology, social foundations of physical education, and other courses with a social science perspective. This general field has become a favorite area for specialization among graduate students in physical education. A few sociology departments now have professors within the department who are making sport their primary interest. Page (1969) notes that "a handful of sociologists, ever growing in size, are discovering, so to speak, that sport is a large and significant area of action, of human activity" [p. 191]. Several sociology departments are cooperating with physical education departments by employing a sports sociologist on a dual appointment basis; that is, the faculty member is assigned to both physical education and sociology departments. Another evidence that interest in the study of sport is growing is that national and regional professional social science associations are including sessions in their conventions devoted to research papers and seminars on sport.

Although it is always difficult, as well as risky, to identify a given incident or piece of writing as being the first of its kind, Steinitzer's (1910) book, *Sport and Kultur* published in Germany in 1910, may be identified as one of the pioneer works in the social science of sport because it was concerned with the relationship of sports and culture. A more well-known book entitled *The Sociology of Sport* written by Risse in 1921 and published in Germany is often referred to as the first treatise on the sociology of sport. Both of these books lacked systematic and theoretical research data for the ideas which were discussed. They were, Wohl (1966) says, "reflections on social phenomena and social consequences of sports, inspired by the fact that this subject was particularly thrown into relief at that time. Thus ... we can safely consider both belonging to the type of publicistic works, based only on one's own suggestions, that are the outcome of generally accepted opinions and prejudices about sports" [p. 5]. However, Risse did discuss various social issues related to sports and recommended that these phenomena be given systematic scientific study.

These books did not stimulate any immediate substantive study of sport but they did trigger a number of publications, especially in Europe, concerned with the relationship between sport and various social issues. Although most of these publications were not empirically based, the social sources and consequences of sport were thoroughly analyzed.

Few physical educators have devoted their careers to a study of the social aspects of sport. While the early 20th century leaders of the so-called "new physical education" such as Thomas Wood, Clark Hetherington, Jesse Feiring Williams, and Rosalind Cassidy gave a privileged position to "social development," the term went largely undefined and the social outcomes of physical education and interschool sports programs went unmeasured. These physical educators were not researchers; they did not document the claims they made with regard to the social outcomes of physical education. Actually, they were more interested in justifying programs of physical education than they were of studying the broad scope of social behavior in sport contexts, and they did not attempt to develop a basic subject matter on the social science of sport. Charles Cowell (1937, 1959), a physical educator at Purdue, published a few empirical studies between 1935 and 1960 but it was not until the publication of an article in the *Journal of Health, Physical Education, and Recreation* in 1965 by Gerald Kenyon and John W. Loy (1965) entitled "Toward a Sociology of Sport," that physical educators began to seriously pursue this subject. It should be mentioned, however, that a book by two physical educators, Frederick Cozens and Florence Stumpf, in 1953 must be considered as a pioneer effort to discuss the social role of sport in American society.

Play and sport within cultures has been on the periphery of anthropological study and rarely has more than description analysis been done. However, empirical cross-cultural research on children's play and sports activities was reported by Roberts, Sutton-Smith, and their coworkers (1959, 1962) in the 1950's and early 1960's. Their research, in addition to adding to the literature on games and sports of children from various cultures was also a test of their hypothesis that games and sports model the basic maintenance functions of a given society.

In the 1950's studies such as Weinberg and Arond's (1952) report on the subculture of the boxer and Riesman and Denney's (1951) presentation of football as an avenue of cultural diffusion provided pioneer work in the social science of sport in the United States. Subsequently Stone (1957) and Grusky (1963) offered interesting studies related to sport involvement and its relation to socioeconomic status and the application of social organizational theory to sport teams.

In the post-World War II period, two books published in England have had a marked impact on the development of the study of the social aspects of sport in America. These books, *Sport in Society* (McIntosh, 1963) and *Sport and Society* (Natan, 1958) were basically descriptive accounts of the social dimensions of sport, but they were well-written and illuminated the potential for the study of sport.

Sports journalists have provided the most extensive literature on sports during the 20th century. Their contribution to sport has been considerable; although most have done reportorial work primarily, some have written on the sociological, historical, economic, and political aspects of sport. One professional sociologist said that "sports writers are among my favorite list of sociologists" [Page, 1969, p. 196]. While those who work in the social science of sport might agree with Professor Page, they would undoubtedly emphasize that there is need for exhaustive empirical research to support or refute the essay-type writing of the journalist.

Two of the most significant events for the promotion and development of a social science of sport occurred in the mid-1960's. In 1964, the International Committee for Sport Sociology was founded as an affiliate of two

UNESCO organizations, the International Council of Sport and Physical Education and the International Sociological Association. This Committee sponsored its first conference in Cologne, Germany in 1966, with an invited group of around 50 participants. The second conference sponsored by this Committee was held in 1968 in Vienna, Austria, and the third conference occurred in 1971 at Waterloo, Ontario, Canada. An outgrowth of the first conference held in Cologne was the establishment of the *International Review of Sport Sociology* which is published in Poland and which carries essays and research articles. One issue has been published each year, beginning with 1966. The second major event in the advancement of the social aspect of sport occurred in 1965 with the founding of the International Society of Sport Psychology. This organization has sponsored three international conferences (Rome, 1965; Washington, D.C., 1968; Madrid, 1973) and began publishing the *International Journal of Sport Psychology* in 1970. Both of these groups have encouraged scholars from all of the social science fields who have an interest in studying sport.

The future is promising. Undoubtedly physical educators and social scientists who are currently concentrating their efforts on the social dimensions of sport will attract others. Indeed events of the past two years in graduate schools of physical education give evidence that a "bandwagon" effect is occurring toward this subject, as students are electing to specialize in the sociology, or psychology, or the history of sport instead of the old standbys, physiology and mechanical analysis. Sociology, psychology, history, and anthropology departments will certainly begin turning out Ph.D's with sport as their specialty. The prospects are very exciting.

REFERENCES

Coleman, J. S., "Athletics in High School," *Annals of the American Academy of Political Science,* **338** (November): 33-43, 1961.

Cowell, C. C., "Physical Education as Applied Social Science," *Educational Research Bulletin* (Ohio State University), **1**: 147-155, 1937.

Cowell, C. C., "Validating an Index of Social Adjustment for High School Use," *Research Quarterly,* **29**: 7-18, 1958.

Cozens, F., and Stumpf, F., *Sports in American Life,* Chicago: University of Chicago Press, 1953.

Gross, N., "The Sociology of Education," in R. K. Merton, *et al.* (eds.), *Sociology Today,* New York: Basic Books, 1959.

Grusky, O., "Managerial Succession and Organizational Effectiveness," *American Journal of Sociology,* **69** (July): 21-31, 1963.

Kenyon, G. S., and Loy, J. W., "Toward a Sociology of Sport," *Journal of Health, Physical Education, and Recreation*, **36** (May): 24-25, 68-69, 1965.

Loy, J. W., "Toward a Sociology of Sport," in R. N. Singer, *et al., Physical Education: An Interdisciplinary Approach*, New York: The Macmillan Company, 1972, pp. 229-236.

Loy, J. W., "A Case for the Sociology of Sport," *Journal of Health, Physical Education, and Recreation*, **43** (June): 50-53, 1972.

McIntosh, P. C., *Sport in Society*, London: C. A. Watts Company, 1963.

Morton, H. W., *Soviet Sport*, New York: Collier Books, 1963.

Natan, A., *Sport and Society*, London: Bowes & Bowes Publishers, 1958.

Page, C. H., "Symposium Summary, with Reflections upon the Sociology of Sport as a Research Field," in G. S. Kenyon (ed.), *Aspects of Contemporary Sport Sociology*, Chicago: The Athletic Institute, 1969, pp. 189-209.

Palmer, M. D., "The Sports Novel: Mythic Heroes and Natural Men," *Quest*, Monograph XIX, January, 1973, pp. 49-58.

Riley, M. W., "Membership in the ASA, 1950–1959," *American Sociological Review*, **25**: 914-926, 1960.

Riesman, D., and Denney, R., "Football in America: A Study of Cultural Diffusion," *American Quarterly*, **3**: 309-319, 1951.

Risse, H., *Soziologie des Sports*, Berlin, 1921.

Roberts, J. M., Arth, M. J., and Bush, R. R., "Games in Culture," *American Anthropologist*, **61** (August): 597-605, 1959.

Roberts, J. M., and Sutton-Smith, B., "Child Training and Game Involvement," *Ethnology*, **1**: 166-185, 1962.

Stehr, N., and Larson, L. E., "The Rise and Decline of Areas of Specialization," *The American Sociologist*, **7** (No. 7): 3, 5-6, 1972.

Steinitzer, H., *Sport and Kultur*, München, 1910.

Stone, G., "Some Meanings of American Sport," *60th Proceedings of the College Physical Education Association*, Washington, D. C.: American Association for Health, Physical Education, and Recreation, 1957, pp. 6-29.

Weinberg, S. K., and Arond, H., "The Occupational Culture of the Boxer," *American Journal of Sociology*, **57** (March): 460-469, 1962.

Wohl, A., "Conception and Range of Sport Sociology," *International Review of Sport Sociology*, **1**: 5-15, 1966.

A SOCIOLOGY OF SPORT:
ON BECOMING A SUB-DISCIPLINE

Gerald S. Kenyon

Although not a new idea, the sociology of sport has at present neither a substantial body of knowledge, nor a clearly defined domain of inquiry. Questions of definition, orientation, and method have hardly been raised, let alone answered. However, recent developments suggest that there is a mounting interest in the sociology of sport which promises to be more than fleeting. The quantity of literature has been increasing steadily during the past few years. There have been discussions at several professional meetings. In Europe, where there is the greatest activity, the International Committee for Sport Sociology was recently formed as an affiliate of two UNESCO organizations—the International Council of Sport and Physical Education, and the International Sociological Association. The Committee, which held its first international seminar in April, 1966, in Cologne, represented interest from a wide range of countries; from the Soviet Union to the United States, from Japan to Cuba. The English language *International Review of Sport Sociology*[1] became a reality in 1966. Insofar as they will encompass the social psychology of sport, the recently formed International and North American Societies for the Psychology of Sport could make additional contributions. Moreover, it is now possible in the United States to pursue the Ph.D. degree with a specialization in the sociology of sport.

Such an upsurge of interest in a relatively undelineated subject area calls for the consideration of certain conceptual and methodological issues that invariably confront workers in any new field. With this in mind, the purpose of this chapter is to identify, illustrate, and comment upon a few of such issues, with the hope that, if nothing else, some much-needed debate will be stimulated. The discussion is divided into three parts: first, an attempt to place the sociology of sport in a particular frame of reference; second, to consider some prerequisites to the development of a substantial sociology of sport; and third, to discuss some implications for physical education. The treatment of each of these questions will necessarily be brief.

Gerald S. Kenyon, 'A Sociology of Sport: On Becoming a Sub-Discipline,' in Roscoe C. Brown and Bryant J. Cratty (Eds.), *New Perspectives of Man in Action* © 1969. Reprinted by permission of Prentice-Hall, Inc., Englewood Cliffs, N. J.

A FRAME OF REFERENCE—THE LOCUS PROBLEM

Any new field has as its origin some already established field or fields. To date, interest in sport sociology has come from both sociology and physical education. However, physical educators, particularly those writing a decade or two ago, seemed to conceive of sport sociology as the study of ways to increase the efficiency of "social development," that is, the development of certain "desirable" social behaviors through school physical education programs. This "mission-oriented" approach is certainly an understandable one, since it came from dedicated members of a *profession*. The outlook of sociologists, particularly those in the Western countries, as members of a *discipline*, has been somewhat different. Thus, a choice can be made between the two approaches based on the direction of one's sympathies. Unfortunately, the issue is not as clear-cut as this.

Recently an old debate was revived by Henry (1964), namely, the question of whether physical education ought to be a discipline, a profession, or both. In the fact of the complexity of this issue, and, admittedly, on a somewhat authoritarian note, the following statements are presented for the readers' consideration.

To be a discipline implies among other things, having as an objective the *understanding of some portion of reality*—that is, *its description, its explanation, and sometimes its prediction.* A profession, on the other hand, has as its fundamental goal, the *altering of some aspects of reality* with a view to *improving the lot of mankind.* If the motivation of a discipline is curiosity, that of a profession is service, the welfare of humanity. It is simply a matter of "what is" vs. "what ought to be." It follows, therefore, that arguing that a given field can be simultaneously a profession and a discipline is little else save a logically invalid contradiction of terms. The only solution to this dilemma would be to recognize that, while it is possible for the same phenomenon to serve as the focal point of both a profession and a discipline (subject matter for one, a medium for the other), it is there that the similarity ends. Thus, the expression "physical education" with its obvious professional connotations, is not a suitable label for both the professional *and* disciplinary aspects of human physical activity. However, because of its widespread currency, and despite the semantic difficulties long alluded to, the term might be retained, but in a restricted sense. Those who would use physical activity to change behavior—whether it be cognitive, affective or psychomotor—we may term *physical educators.* On the other hand, those whose objective is to understand the phenomenon, we may consider members of a discipline, the name of which is still a topic of much debate.[2]

Regardless of the label that meets with the greatest favor, there is no logical reason why the study of all the various manifestations of sport, exercise, and dance cannot be put under a single umbrella, one that could include the traditional approaches, whether they be scientific or humanistic. It is conceivable that certain subfields would emerge, based primarily on different approaches to truth, and perhaps to some extent, on interest in particular forms of physical activity. Thus, one major classification may be the *sport sciences,* which in turn could be subdivided into the physical science of sport, the biological science of sport, and the social science of sport. Most existing scientific approaches could logically be placed within one of these subfields without doing too much damage to their traditional characteristics.

It follows that the *sociology of sport* would be subsumed under the social science of sport and as such may be defined as the study of the underlying regularity of human social behavior within situations involving sport. Such a definition places the field within the confines of a discipline; in this case one committed to the extension of knowledge about a phenomenon as old as man, his physical activity or movement.[3] Whether sport sociology becomes part of an already emerging sport sciences field,[4] or, as more sociologists become interested in the phenomenon, as part of sociology, perhaps closely related to the sociology of leisure, it is too early to say. So long as it continues to attract scholars and researchers with a wide variety of backgrounds the "locus" of sport sociology is not a crucial issue. Its orientation is crucial, however. Thus, for reasons already stated I cannot conceive of sport sociology and physical education as one and the same thing. I firmly believe that, if we seek a social scientific understanding of sport, we cannot play two roles at the same time. Just as sociology is not social work, neither is sport sociology motor therapy.

In the present context the question arises as to whether the subject matter of the sociology of sport is simply a part of sociology or some other social science, or whether it is sufficiently independent to warrant separate attention. For example, Henry (1964) has argued that exercise physiology is not *applied* physiology, but physiology *per se.* I would argue that it is neither, rather it is *exercise physiology.* This apparent tautology can be understood if we consider that the distinction between two fields of inquiry is based primarily on the nature of the phenomenon to which workers in those fields devote their attention. I would suggest that the exercise physiologist seeks to understand the physiology of exercise stress, while the goal of the physiologist is not to understand physical activity as such, but to understand the function of the organism or one of its systems. Similarly, the sociologist, insofar as he might wish to study the social aspects of sport, hopes to be able to understand the structure and function of social systems in general, using sport as a means, not an end.[5] The sport sociologist, on the other hand, has the understanding of sport per se as his goal, albeit with the help of sociological theory and method. Borrowing from set theory, the various subfields, each with human physical activity as its subject of inquiry, are not *subsets* of existing disciplines, but *intersect* with them.

Thus it follows that research in sport sociology could contribute to both an understanding of sport as a particular social phenomenon, and, at the same time, to knowledge about social systems in general.

> In short, questions initially restricted to a particular institutional sphere have a double objective. On the one hand, they direct attention to what may be distinctive to the particular class of institutions or organizations under study. These distinctive characteristics are not at once swallowed up in generalities that deliberately neglect them. On the other hand, these questions of restricted scope can often be extended to wider classes of situations. Neither the more general nor the more specific version of the originating questions claims exclusive value; each has its use in augmenting knowledge of differing kind. The focus on a particular institutional sphere, with its characteristic statuses, social structure, and value-system, results in findings that illuminate its distinctive character; it curbs that kind of premature generalization that loses sight of what is peculiar to an institution by attending only to what it shares with other institutions. (p. xvii)[6]

PREREQUISITES TO A SOCIOLOGY OF SPORT

Given a frame of reference, there remains a need to establish some more or less mutually acceptable principles upon which a meaningful body of knowledge can be based. Three of these appear critical: first, the need for a *workable conceptual system;* second, the need for, and implications of, a commitment to *value-free inquiry;* and third, the need for a *theoretical-empirical balance.* Obviously, the application of such principles, and the subsequent development of the field, depends on the availability of well prepared investigators together with adequate media for the dissemination of current thought and research. These will not be considered here, however.

A Workable Conceptual System

No science can proceed without a clearly formulated set of theoretical and operational terms.[7] They are essential prerequisites to clear and unambiguous communication, and thus permit the formulation and testing of useful hypotheses and theories. What is needed at the outset is the identification of those concepts and constructs that reflect the structure of, and processes within, various phenomena of concern to the sociologist of sport. We must begin by selecting, defining, and organizing our basic terms of reference—the precursors of both good description and adequate explanation. For example, at the descriptive level, biology has been greatly aided by the classification of organisms into phyla, classes, orders, families, genera, species, etc. More recently, the development of a Taxonomy of Educational Objective[8,9] promises to serve as an important catalyst to successful inquiry into learning and socialization.

Fortunately, the bastardized nature of sport sociology permits the use of many already well defined and well understood concepts—those already well established within existing social sciences. But there remains a need for the identification and clear definition of the concepts peculiar to sport as a social phenomenon. The task is not a simple one, however. For example, the word "sport" itself still lacks a generally accepted definition.[10] Certainly the operational definition, "Sport is that which is reported in the sport pages," is hardly adequate. The word "game" is another term difficult to define once and for all. We are not alone, of course, in having to deal with such problems; for example, exercise physiologists have been forced to deal with such concepts as "second wind" and "physical fitness," the definitions of which are still the subject of much debate.

However tentative the definitions of concepts useful for inquiry in sport sociology may be, it is important also to show how they are related to each other. The result is a conceptual framework or paradigm which should permit far greater precision in communication, and consequently, a clearer context within which research problems may be cast.

For example, suppose a sport sociologist is interested in explaining *involvement in sport.* Early in the process of developing a definitive statement of the problem, and certainly before he can formulate testable hypotheses, he would require some conceptual framework.[11] Hopefully an existing one is available. If not, he would need to develop one, a major project in itself. Since sport per se is too gross and complex a concept, it would need breaking down into its elements. One such paradigm is as follows:

Sport may be considered institutionalized, competitive, gross physical activity. Its major elements are its *form,* its *participants,* its *facilitators,* and the *situation* in which it occurs. (See Fig. 1.)

Any sport has a *form,* the details of which distinguish it from other sports. It has an *explicit form* including specified goals (the object of the

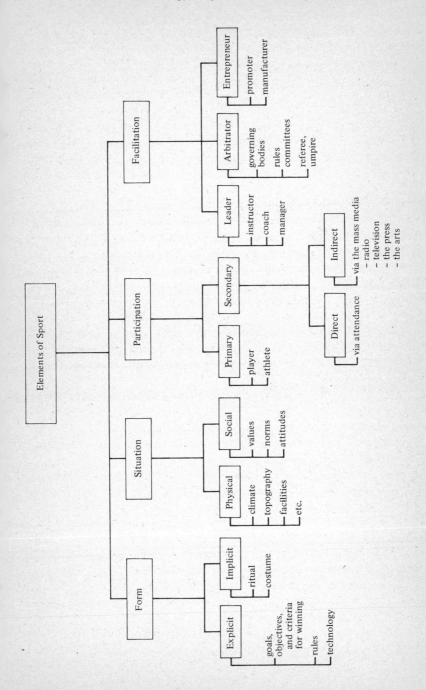

game and the criteria for winning), and the specified rules governing the pursuit of such goals; and an *implicit form,* including the acquired characteristics of the particular sport that help to give identity to the activity—such as the ritual of player dress and of behavior.

Obviously, any particular form of sport requires *participants.* These are of two types. The *primary participant* is actively involved in the activity as a player or athlete. The *secondary participant's* involvement can be either direct through attendance as a spectator, or indirect through the consumption of one or more forms of the mass media, such as radio, television, the press, or the arts.

Any particular form of sport requires a setting or milieu—its *situation,* which possesses both physical and social characteristics. The prevalence or incidence of the activity frequently depends on or is related to environmental factors ranging from climate and topography to social values and attitudes.

Although a particular *form* of sport may be established, its *situation* receptive, and a variety of *participants* ready to become involved, an additional impetus is required for a particular form of the activity to become operational. A *facilitator* is required to cause an event to occur. Facilitators are usually nonparticipating decision-making persons who are one of three types: the *leader,* who for the most part is the instructor or coach for a particular sport; the *arbitrator,* the rule-maker—the rules committee of sports governing bodies, and the rule enforcer—the referee or umpire; and the *entrepreneur,* the person whose primary interest in the activity is commercial, but nevertheless may facilitate the activity itself or some form of it. Such persons include the manufacturers of sporting goods and sporting goods dealers, the promoters of sport for entertainment or for the consumption of secondary participants, and the various ancillary enterprises that surround a given physical activity, from the sale of food and drink to the publication of newspapers, magazines, and books.

Given the elements of sport, and at least within the context of the above paradigm, *involvement* can be of several types. It can be as a primary or secondary participant or as one type of facilitator. All are involved but in different ways. Moreover, involvement can be further differentiated on the basis of its level, degree, and pattern. There are three gross phases of involvement in sport: the period of socialization, the period of sustained involvement, and the period of withdrawal. Obviously, to research the phenomenon of involvement in sport calls for a consideration of many concepts together with their operational definitions.

In general, if we wish to explain one or more *patterns* of involvement an important first step would be the identification of various existing patterns, followed by their careful description.

Upon an adequate identification and description of certain patterns of involvement any attempt to *explain* these would call for a careful consideration of sociological and social psychological theory, which in turn would lead to the introduction of new concepts, greater in number and complexity than those considered thus far. Some might be borrowed, some would need to be specially formulated. In any case, a conceptual system suitable for the study of sport would begin to emerge. It follows that the greatest impetus comes from the need created by research. Thus, however handy some well developed conceptual systems might be for the growth of sport sociology, their appearance, at least in a satisfactory form, will depend upon those able and willing to generate data called for by carefully conceived research problems.

As concepts are chosen and constructs invented, lurking in the background is the related question of whether those employed by sociologists should be reduced to those of psychology, which in turn should be reduced to those of biology, and so on, until ultimately the entire realm of social reality is explained in terms of certain subatomic particles—the so-called *problem of reduction.* Social reality however is not necessarily physical reality. Although it could be argued that any object, whether it be a large stone to a 250-pound tackle, is almost entirely space, approaching either head-first with considerable momentum is likely to suggest something otherwise. Moreover, a consequence of reducing one field to another, is that the constructs of the former field are eliminated. Are we ready to eliminate the several useful social and psychological concepts such as attitude, self-esteem, achievement motivation, mobility, social system, socialization, stratification, etc.?[12]

If social reality is considered to have some uniqueness and therefore can be distinguished from physical or biological reality, it follows, then, that the time is long overdue for challenging the long-held myth that exercise physiology is the primary source of explanation of sport, i.e., the queen of sport sciences. The writer is yet to be convinced that any amount of physiology will fully explain sport. Luckily, for both sides, many physiologists feel the same way.

Value-Free Inquiry

My business is to teach my aspirations to conform themselves to fact, not to try to make facts harmonize with my aspirations.   Thomas Huxley

However worthwhile dance, games, aquatics, or calisthenics might be, it is not the role of the sport sociologist to promote them, for his inquiries are not based upon the assumption that physical activity is *a priori* "good." Sport sociology, if conceived of as a value-free social science, does not endeavor to influence public opinion or behavior, nor attempt to find support for the so-called "social development" objective of physical education. Thus, the sport sociologist is neither a spreader of gospel, nor an evangelist for exercise. His function is not to shape behavior, attitudes, and values, but to explain them.[13]

More specifically, an argument for a value-free or value-neutral stance for the sport sociologist has three aspects to it. First, is the basic question of a value-free method. Here the researcher who allows his personal values or social philosophy to influence his observation (he sees what he wants to see) or color his interpretations is simply engaging in bad science, by definition. Since the goal of science is to achieve a semblance of lawfulness or agreement about the nature of physical and social reality, this goal can be greatly delayed by the use of contaminated methods, since it would be largely by chance that any consistency would be reported among observers of the same phenomenon.

A second aspect of the value-free argument concerns the choice of subject matter. Regardless of the "freedom" enjoyed by the investigator, certainly many factors, from the desires of a funding agency to those of the investigator's wife, may influence his choice of phenomena for study. However, if he is limited to problems reflecting current social problems or some practical need, the development of the very knowledge upon which social action depends could be greatly delayed. This is simply the old "basic" vs. "applied" research argument. Experience, in the United States at least, has shown that the large-scale "crash program" has not been particularly successful despite large expenditures in federal funds.

A third dimension of the concept of value-free inquiry is the restrictions placed on the theoretical frame of reference which provides a basis for formulating hypotheses and for explaining the findings. Limiting the researcher to a single social, religious, or political philosophy could prevent the discovery of new and often more elegant explanatory systems. If Darwin and his supporter Huxley had yielded to the pressures of the Christian church of their time, the world would have been deprived of some ideas that have since proven to be far-reaching.

That the researcher commits himself to a value-neutral attitude while conducting research does not imply that he is free of opinions, values, or aspirations. Indeed, he may be highly active in one or more ideologically based social movements. However, the degree to which his research is fruitful, that is, to which his findings are capable of replication by others, will depend in no small degree upon the extent to which he can hold in abeyance his personal values and perhaps even prejudices. This is particularly true when dealing with social phenomena, since there is often considerable emotional content in both the observer and the observed.

It would be well to acknowledge the fact that every scientist, prior to conducting a particular investigation, *has* made a value judgment, over and above his choice of subject matter. He has committed himself to a particular logic for ascertaining the "truth," namely, the scientific method. Beyond this point on, however, the objectivity of research becomes crucial for the discovery of new and valid explanatory principles. The point in belaboring this issue stems from the fact that sport in many of its manifestations is highly value-charged, and as such becomes most difficult to study objectively. Moreover, there is ample evidence in the research literature of studies that were obviously contaminated by researcher bias.

One of the first consequences of embracing a value-free approach for sport sociology is the casting aside of some long-held "self-evident truths" in the realm of sport. Among these is the intuitive belief that sport is sport regardless of who is perceiving it. Closer to the truth is that sport is seen differently by different people; that is, it depends on, in Thomas' terms, one's "definition of the situation." It is unrealistic to believe that the athlete, his parents, his coach, his principal, the local newspaper reporter, the sporting goods manufacturer and dealer, the promoter, or network television announcer all view the game in quite the same way. As Berger points out, in a deterministic sense, "Most of the time the game has been 'fixed' long before we arrived on the scene" (p. 87).[14] Accepting a "situation-dependent" hypothesis raises questions about the other long-held intuitive truths, for example, the often-heard suggestion that sport, in and of itself, is a prophylaxis to deviant behavior.

As a value-free science, then, sport sociology has as its objectives to describe, to explain, and even to predict. Descriptions, explanations, and predictions of what?

Description. The widespread prevalence of sport in all of its manifestations in American society is hardly news to anyone. Clearly, we have entered the era of *megasport*. However, despite the appearance of the obvious, together with the availability of certain gross information, good descriptive data are not always available. Statistics describing the distribution of sport and physical activity by region, sex, age, social class, religious preference, education, occupation, etc., are not readily available. Nor has the relative interest in, and attitude toward, sport been clearly enumerated. Although gathering such information is a somewhat pedestrian task, the data acquired could be a useful adjunct to the generation and testing of theories explaining the significance of sport.

Explanation. However interesting or dull a particular collection of facts may be, to stop at this point is to be vulnerable to the frequently-voiced criticism of sociologists, namely, that their efforts merely substantiate the already obvious, probably at considerable expense to a Federal grant-giving agency. Much more interesting questions are, "How is it that someone thinks such 'trivia' are important?" "What needs are met for individuals through actual or vicarious participation in sport?" or "What function does sport serve in a given society or subsociety?" Questions in this vein are only now being adequately formulated. In spite of some excellent thinking on such subjects during the past two decades, notably by Huizinga (1960), Riesman and Denny (1954), Stone (1957), Caillois (1961), and McIntosh (1963), relatively few empirical studies have been reported. An important exception, of course, is the work of Roberts and Sutton-Smith (1962), who have postulated, and to some extent verified, their "conflict-enculturation hypothesis." Other studies, on a lesser scale, show promise as well (Anderson *et al.*, 1956; Helanho, 1957; Lüschen, 1962; and Vlot, 1964).

Prediction. The final test of scientific explanation, and closely connected with explanation, is, of course, prediction. Thus far, the social sciences do not have an enviable record in this regard. Without raising the difficult question of *causality* at this point, it seems important that, difficult as it is, the notion of prediction should not be dismissed too quickly. By this it is not meant that five or six quick studies will enable us to predict the name of the winning pitcher in the third game of the 1984 World Series two years before the game is played. It is believed, however, that through an imaginative combination of theory and empirical findings, prediction, at least in a gross and statistical sense, is in the realm of possibility, particularly if we employ certain mathematical models, some of which are already available.

A Theoretical-Empirical Balance

Students of social phenomena fall somewhere on a methodological continuum whose extremes are occupied by either strict theorists or strict empiricists. Insofar as they compete with one another, we have the rationalist vs. the positivist. It would be valuable to distinguish between the two, in the context of sport sociology.

The empiricist often seems preoccupied with methods and techniques, despite Claude Bernard's observation of many years ago, "Method itself gives birth to nothing." Nevertheless, empirical observation is fundamental to science. By empirical, we do not mean the sudden seizing upon what one can remember of his past experiences, but rather, the careful acquisition of sense-data, capable of verification with other sense-data, acquired under similar circumstances. This method, although not an end in itself, often determines both the conditions under which observations are made, and the nature of the conclusions ultimately drawn. For example, to begin to appreciate the multidimensionality of small group behavior requires not only the development of adequate tools or instruments to make all the necessary observations, but also a knowledge of procedures of organizing and processing data. Fortunately for the social sciences, powerful tools are now becoming available for the empirical testing of hypotheses about social phenomena. Several mathematical models, such as multiple discriminant analysis and improved factor analytic procedures, are available for handling many variables simultaneously. Stochastic models permit the study of the dynamics of various individual and social phenomena. These, together with now readily available computers, for the first time provide the investigator with a capacity to deal with the mountains of data necessary for adequate tests of social theory.[15]

In the final analysis, however, it is not finding the techniques, but finding the problem that is most difficult.[6] Yet those who have studied exercise and sport frequently have been long on technical sophistication and short on adequate reasons for making their careful observations in the first place. For the most part the results have only increased the chaos in an already-chaotic brickyard.[16] As has been pointed out on several occasions, we hardly need further evidence that during vigorous exercise the heart rate often increases. Moreover, there must be a more imaginative strategy for studying the isometric phenomenon than by observing, almost at random, all possible combinations of load, joint angle, number of repetitions, and duration of rest periods. Such an approach is theoretically empty. Despite great toil, it is likely that nothing of significance will be found.[17]

Theory, then, can help in finding the problem by giving rise to the right questions—not trivial ones, but questions of some scientific consequence.[18] Our theories will need to be modest, and perhaps only partial at first, whether they be borrowed or whether they be specially created. For an example, if certain units or modules of a social system can be adequately understood, eventually it may be possible to put these together into a larger, more inclusive system that would provide a more general explanation.[19] In this regard, one potentially useful approach is the linking of mathematical models with discursive theory. For example, McPhee (1963) has postulated a model showing how the concept of addiction can be applied to a wide variety of human activities, including involvement in sport.

Returning to the phenomenon of involvement in sport, existing social psychological and sociological theory, together with a variety of available observational and data-processing techniques, could be expected to aid immeasurably in getting research underway, leading ultimately to the formulation of new propositions unique to sport. For example, social learning theory could be expected to be useful in studying the period of socialization; role theory, conformity-deviance theory and certain theories of motivation would be relevant for understanding sustained involvement; and theories of social change and of attitude change would certainly be pertinent in researching the period of withdrawal.

Given a firm theoretical base, viable hypotheses could be deduced that would begin to explain the particular aspects of involvement that may be of interest. By way of illustration, suppose that *patterns* of involvement are the focus of attention. Such a situation is one involving choice.[20] We can set out to discover the properties of the choosing organism, or we can inquire into the environment of choice. Since both are likely to generate factors influencing the pattern of involvement, the best strategy would be to include both. As a result, we are confronted with a system in which there is a continuous interplay among several variables—some providing stimulation to consumption ("stimulants") and others providing resistance ("resistants").

Although verbal theories may be useful in identifying appropriate constructs and hypothetical relations among them, mathematical models can be employed to increase the precision with which statements can be made, and to gain power in the analysis and interpretation of data. Traditionally *static models* have been chosen to describe the various aspects of human physical activity. For example, when several variables are to be considered simultaneously, a common practice is to study their interrelationships using various multivariate statistical models, such as discriminant functions, multiple regressions, and factor analysis. Since the problem here is concerned with changing amounts of involvement (or "levels of consumption" in McPhee's [1963] sense) over time, whether a few weeks or a lifetime, a *dynamic model* would be more appropriate. Of the several models[20,21,22] in contemporary use, which one might fit our data best? Strictly deterministic approaches such as the generation of a set of differential equations or the employment of game theory are probably not suitable for our purposes. The former is unsuitable because it is doubtful that we would have any high correlations among our determinants. Consequently, there is likely to be considerable error. Since game theory assumes the presence of rational choice for each decision made, this doesn't seem to be appropriate either.[23] If we accept the argument that the choice to participate is based on a combination of both rational and nonrational decisions, it would follow that a stochastic model would be most appropriate for our purposes. Models of this type allow us to attach probability values to each hypothesized variable at various points in time. Insofar as the probability of an event at one point in time has some influence upon the probability of that event occurring sometime later, a Markoff chain approach is called for. In the final analysis, determining the best techniques, whether they be for collecting of data or for treating them, will depend upon considerable trial and error.

Clearly then, for a meaningful contribution to knowledge in sport sociology as in any other science, research must be characterized by sophistication in both theory and method. After first rejecting authoritarianism and mysticism, the sociologist of sport should strive for a judicious combination of the rational and the empirical. He can afford neither soft theory nor soft procedure.

Researchers plod on, often ignoring the complexity of behavior, in their task of finding simple, isolated relations, while discursive theory soars even higher, constructing more and more elaborate verbal systems to describe behavior. At best, these verbal systems have provided us with a vivid heuristic image of a system of behavior in operation. At worst, they have led us into flights of fancy, and even further into a morass of words. In any case, they are hardly translatable into research terms. Yet, if our discursive theory is often too broad to be usable, our research is often so pedestrian that it offers no aid to the theorist. Ordinarily, concerned with single relations, inferred from correlations, most social research fragments behavior, leaving it like Humpty Dumpty, never to be put together again. (p. 92)[22]

IMPLICATIONS FOR PHYSICAL EDUCATION

Lest the sport sociologist be accused of an unconscious or conscious desire to ignore reality, I would like to make some reference to the implications of sport sociology for physical education, keeping in mind that for purposes of this paper and hopefully beyond, one is not a subset of the other. As the sport sociologist seeks to understand the situation as it really is, it is conceivable that some of his findings might well be useful to the physical educator who, in practicing a profession, needs to be armed with as much of the latest knowledge as he can possibly muster. For example, if people tend to behave the way they are expected to behave, it is conceivable that their motor behavior, that is, how, or even whether they play the game, is largely determined by those social norms embraced by the members of his reference group. A clear understanding of this and other relevant sociopsychological phenomena could assist the physical educator in meeting the goals of contemporary American education. It's not that Gulick or Wood or Hetherington or Williams were wrong; it's just that times have changed. As McCormack (1966) has observed, it's no longer "survival of the fittest," but "survival of the brainiest." Today, in answering the question, "Who needs fitness?" sociological factors are likely more important than any other.

Thus, it seems to me that the physical educator needs substantial knowledge of the social significance of sport, at least to the same extent that he has a grasp of its biological, or physical, aspects. To suggest that physical educators need sport sociology as one of their foundational subjects is nothing new, with the possible exception that in former times the suggestion implied a sport sociology in a more value-oriented or "social development" sense. Regardless of the orientation, few professional schools have had available qualified personnel. What is needed are more graduate programs providing academic opportunities in the social science of sport. Such programs might be offered by departments of sociology or academically oriented departments of physical education. At present, probably the best arrangement would be a joint program in which both departments in a given institution would cooperate to provide the best set of experiences possible. Although the need has prevailed for many years, only recently has it become possible to pursue a graduate degree with a concentration in the social science of sport.[24] To some extent the sport sociologist cannot help but benefit from an exposure to a wide array of physical activities and sport. There is a limit, however. If through such exposure one becomes a devoted apologist for exercise, as appears to be the objective of some professional preparatory programs for physical educators, there is a danger of contaminating one's objectivity—a fundamental prerequisite to scientific inquiry.

SUMMARY

In summary some attempt has been made to place the sociology of sport in a particular frame of reference—a subdiscipline pursuing knowledge in the tradition of the social sciences. In addition, comments upon what is considered to be three of several factors upon which the development of the field depends have been advanced, namely, a value-free orientation, a workable conceptual system, and a theoretical-empirical balance. The list was not meant to be exhaustive. For example, no reference has been made to the important question of what constitutes the best preparation for the sport sociologist. Finally some implications for physical education were touched upon briefly.

In conclusion, if we want to become serious about the sociology of sport we need to go beyond such interesting reflections as the observation that some churches sponsor extensive sport programs while others do not, and begin to consider what the church does to sport, what sport does to religious practice, and even preference, and ultimately, the place of church sport in a theory of sport. Work of this kind requires both vigor and rigor, particularly rigor—we need to be rigorous in our definitions, in the formulation of our constructs, hypotheses, and theories, in selecting measuring devices that have some semblance of validity, in treating our data, and in interpreting our findings.

As sport sociology becomes more fashionable, it is possible that we will witness a "bandwagon" effect. That is, in a Parkinsonian sense, orchestra size increases to meet tune popularity. If excellence is our goal, pursuing it is one thing, achieving it another. Pursuing mediocrity, however, and achieving it are the same thing. If we fail, at least we should have given rise to a successor—the sociology of sport sociology.

NOTES

1. *International Review of Sport Sociology* (Vol. 1, 1966, 265 pages) distributed by "ARS POLONA", Krakowskie Przedmiescie 7, Warsaw, Poland. Edited by Andrzej Wohl, Akademia Wychowania Fizycznego, ul. Marymoncka 34, Warsaw, Poland.

2. If "physical education" is to designate a profession—or better—a component of the teaching profession, what term should be used to designate the discipline? Several labels have been offered, but there appears to be little agreement at the moment. The point of departure for Morehouse and the group at UCLA has been "kinesiology." Larson has suggested "the activity sciences." The University of Illinois is developing a curricular option in "exercise science." At Laval University in Quebec their science of man in motion is "kinanthropology." Although in a more limited sense, Hubbard (1960) talks about "Homokinetics." Stish (1963) and others, avoiding the mixing of Latin and Greek roots, have used the term "anthropokinetics." Since "ology" is the Greek suffix meaning "the study of", the study of moving man actually should be "anthropo-kineticology" (an-throp´-o-kin-et-i-col´-o-gy).

3. It should be clear then, that a *sociology of physical education,* is closely akin to the already established *sociology of education* and as such has not too much in common with the sociology of sport.

4. An International Congress of Sport Sciences was held in conjunction with the 1964 Tokyo Olympics. In 1967, the Canadian Association for Sport Science was formed.

5. The orientation found in much of the published research in sport sociology.

6. Merton, R. K., "Notes on Problem-Finding in Sociology," in Merton, *et al.* (eds.), *Sociology Today,* New York: Basic Books, 1959.

7. For a discussion of the role of concepts in the sociology of sport, see "The Sociology of Sport as an Area of Specialization," a report of the Sub-Committee for the Sociology of Sport, Western Conference Physical Education Meetings, Chicago, 1966.

8. Bloom, B. S., *et al., Taxonomy of Educational Objectives—Handbook I: Cognitive Domain,* New York: David McKay, 1956.

9. Krathwohl, D. R., *et al., Taxonomy of Educational Objectives— Handbook II: Affective Domain,* New York: David McKay, 1964.

10. For an analysis of what constitutes sport, see Loy and Kenyon (1968).

11. An investigator must decide whether to use existing conceptual frames of reference or to develop new or modified ones. For example, if sport is taken to be a social institution, or a social system, the nomenclature and theory associated with institutions or social systems in general could be extremely useful as a basis for analysis, if the objective is to determine the degree to which sport as a social system can be explained (serves the same function) in terms consistent with other social systems. If, however, the object is to dwell upon the phenomenon itself, then regardless of the utility of existing knowledge of other social phenomena, that which is unique to the phenomenon must be taken into account.[6] I would argue that both approaches are legitimate for the sport sociologist, so long as the worker using one approach does not overlook work employing the alternative approach.

12. Consider your instructor's chair. If a specialist in the branch of physics called mechanics were to study it, he would see it as a combination of weights and balances; a biologist specializing in anatomy would see it as a receptacle for the human form and might assess its effect on the spinal column; an economist might see it as a product of mass production, a unit cost and price; the psychologist might see it as a part of the perceptual frame of the student; and the sociologist might see in the chair a symbol of status. Like any field of inquiry, sociology is selective in its approach." (p. 3).[26]

13. For a position somewhat opposed to that presented here, see Trogsch, Friedrich, "Forschungsergebnisse im Bereich der Körperkultur und der Formierungsprozess von Sportgruppen," *Kölner Zeitschrift für Soziologie und Sozialpsychologie,* X (1966), 268-72; and Erbach, Günther, "The Science of Sport and Sport Sociology—Questions Related to Development—Problems of Structure," *International Review of Sport Sociology,* I (1966), 59-73.

14. Berger, P. L., *Invitation to Sociology,* Garden City, N.Y.: Doubleday (Anchor), 1963.

15. A word of caution is appropriate at this point, however. In this electronic age, now more than ever before, there is a danger of becoming pre-occupied with technique, but of a special kind. It is rather easy today to hide in or near a university's sleek, air-conditioned computing center, amusing oneself with punched cards, magnetic tapes, and the latest version of Fortran. The danger lies in allowing the sterility of such an environment to create a situation wherein the objectives of research are lost by confusing technology with science. We must not lose sight of the fact that measuring instruments and data-reducing procedures are tools, not ends. Never before have so many investigators been in a position to make so many mistakes so fast.

16. Forscher, B. K., "Chaos in the Brickyard," *Science,* **CXLII** (1963), 2590.

17. Or as Berger has put it, in science as in love, a concentration on technique is quite likely to lead to impotence.[14]

18. Just as our emphasis upon technique may hamper discovery, so does our reliance upon the arm chair. Those who theorize need to know what the empiricist is up to, even if he never dirties his hands with raw data. To theorize in a vacuum is to risk arriving at a situation whereby "explanations are sometimes provided for things that never were"[6] Skinner (1963), not one to get overly excited when it comes to theory, argues that they can create a false sense of security, an unwarranted satisfaction with the status quo, with a failure to recognize that most theories are eventually overthrown, resulting in the greater part of the associated research being discarded.

19. Zetterburg, H. L., *On Theory and Verification in Sociology,* Totowa, N.J.: Bedminster Press, 1963.

20. Simon, H. A., *Models of Man,* New York: John Wiley and Sons, 1957.

21. Bush, R. M., and Mosteller, F., *Stochastic Models for Learning,* New York: John Wiley and Sons, 1955.

22. Coleman, J., *Introduction to Mathematical Sociology,* Glencoe, Ill.: The Free Press, 1964.

23. Game theory might be useful for describing certain aspects of the system, however. For example, the competition among entrepreneurs for clients is a complex *n*-person game.

24. Although several universities in the United States are offering course work in the social science of sport, only a few, such as the Universities of Illinois and Wisconsin, and Michigan State University, have inaugurated Ph.D. programs designed to prepare sociologists of sport.

REFERENCES

Anderson, Helge, *et al.,* "Sports and Games in Denmark in the Light of Sociology," *Acta Sociologica,* **II** (1956), 1-28.

Broom, L., and Selznick, P., *Sociology,* Evanston, Ind.: Row, Peterson, 1958.

Caillois, Roger, *Man, Play, and Games,* Glencoe, Ill.: The Free Press, 1961.

Helanko, R., "Sports and Socialization," *Acta Sociologica,* II (1957), 229-40.

Henry, F. M., "Physical Education: An Academic Discipline," *Journal of Health, Physical Education, and Recreation,* LXIX (1964), 32-33.

Hubbard, A. W., "Homokinetics: Muscular Function in Human Movement," in Johnson, W. (ed.), *Science and Medicine of Exercise and Sports,* New York: Harper and Row, Publishers, 1960.

Huizinga, J., *Homo Ludens,* Boston: Beacon Press, 1960.

Kenyon, G. S., and Loy, J. W., "Toward a Sociology of Sport," *Journal of Health, Physical Education, and Recreation,* XXXVI (1965), p. 24.

Larson, L. A., "Professional Preparation for the Activity Sciences," *The Journal of Sports Medicine and Physical Fitness,* V (1965), 15-22.

Loy, J. W., and Kenyon, G. S., *Sport, Society and Culture,* New York: The Macmillan Co., 1968.

Lüschen, G., "Sport et Stratification Sociale," *Revue de l'Education Physique,* II (1962), 1-6.

McCormack, T., "Changing Social Structure and the Concept of Fitness," paper read at YWCA Consultation on Fitness for Women, Geneva Park, Ontario, January 4-8, 1966.

McIntosh, P. C., *Sport in Society,* London: C. A. Watts & Co., Ltd., 1963.

McPhee, W. N., *Formal Theories of Mass Behavior,* Glencoe, Ill.: The Free Press, 1963.

Riesman, E., and Denney, R., "Football in America: A Study in Culture Diffusion," in David Riesman (ed.), *Individualism Reconsidered,* Glencoe, Ill.: The Free Press, 1954.

Roberts, J. M., and Sutton-Smith, B., "Child Training and Game Involvement," *Ethnology,* Vol. I (1962), 166-85.

Skinner, B. F., "The Flight from the Laboratory," in Marx, M. H. (ed.), *Theories in Contemporary Psychology,* New York: The Macmillan Co., 1963.

Stish, E. E., "Anthropokinetics and Physical Education," *Newsletter: The Wisconsin Association for Health, Physical Education and Recreation,* XXXIII (1963), 1-4.

Stone, G. P., "Some Meanings of American Sport," *Sixtieth Annual Proceedings,* College Physical Education Association, Columbus, Ohio, 1957, 6-29.

A SOCIAL PSYCHOLOGY
OF PHYSICAL ACTIVITY

Rainer Martens

Within this century, physical educators have begun to search for the complex physiological, psychological, and social factors that interrelate and act as antecedents and consequences of involvement in physical activity. Such areas as exercise physiology and kinesiology have made initial contributions to the understanding of these antecedents and consequences. More recently, psychology and sociology of sport have emerged as sub-disciplines of considerable importance. Just beginning to emerge as an area in its own right is social psychology. This paper delineates the relationship of social psychology with physical activity, and distinguishes between social psychology and its parent sciences—psychology and sociology. In addition, some of the concerns of a social psychology of physical activity are outlined.

SOCIAL PSYCHOLOGY AND THE OTHER SCIENCES

The sciences are commonly categorized into three main bodies: the physical sciences, the biological sciences, and the social sciences. Within this scheme, psychology is a hybrid being partly a biological and partly a social science. This paper is concerned with the social science aspect. Where psychology is concerned with the behavior of human beings in relationship to their environments, social psychology is concerned with human behavior in relationship to the social parts of those environments. Social psychology as a behavioral science may be defined as the "study of how human behavior is influenced by the presence, behavior, and products of other human beings, individually and collectively, past, present, and future."[1]

   Social psychology has been viewed as a special field within sociology. In fact, some behavioral scientists consider social psychology to be "micro-sociology." Regardless of the terminology, the relationship between sociology and social psychology is important. General sociology is concerned with the forms and processes of collective behavior. Social psychology, however, deals

Rainer Martens, "A Social Psychology of Physical Activity," *Quest*, Monograph XIV, June, 1970, pp. 8-17. Reprinted by permission.

with the articulation between the individual as an actor and as a target of effects, and with larger social entities as they affect and are affected by individuals. Thus, social psychology may be considered an interdisciplinary field of study analogous to biophysics and biochemistry. Similarly, social psychology has attained some maturity and independence from its parent disciplines and is considered as a distinctive field. This distinctiveness rests in two major factors: (1) its interest in the *individual* as a participant in social relationships, and (2) its emphasis on *understanding* the "social-influence processes" underlying these relationships.

Social psychology is primarily concerned with the process of social influence. Social influence occurs whenever one individual responds to the actual or implied presence of one or more other individuals. It may occur in the reciprocal effect of one person upon another in social interaction, or between a group and an individual, or in the relationship between two or more groups. The goal of the social psychologist is to understand these social-influence processes and to predict the behavior of individuals on the basis of these understandings. Consequently, the social psychologist assumes that social behavior is not capricious but has some recurring order—or cause and effect. Obviously, every individual has some social experiences that are unique, associated with particular moments; whereas, other experiences recur again and again in much the same order or with much the same cause or effect. Social psychology attempts to understand the influences producing regularities and diversities in human social behavior through objective study and the use of scientific methods.

A SOCIAL PSYCHOLOGY OF PHYSICAL ACTIVITY

A social psychology of physical activity may be defined simply as the application of social psychological theory and methods to the study of human social behavior while involved in physical activity. Physical activity, in this definition, is a somewhat more general term encompassing a large variety of vigorous activities ranging from highly competitive sports to more simple forms of human movement as found in games and calisthenics. Involvement refers to the relationship an individual has with physical activity. As Kenyon[2] notes, involvement may refer to actual participation or *primary involvement*, and also to such forms as the observance of sporting events or *secondary involvement*.

Most readers will quickly recognize that the study of human social behavior while involved in physical activity is not really any new development. Physical education literature has examples of social psychological research appearing as early as the 1940's.* The purpose of this paper therefore is not to propose that physical educators begin investigating a new field. Physical educators have long been aware that social psychology has considerable application to physical education. What is proposed here as "new" is the *approach* to investigating social psychological phenomena as related to physical activity.

Approaches to Social Psychology

Historically, three distinct approaches for studying social behavior have influenced modern social psychology. The oldest is *social philosophy* characterized by conjecture and speculation, usually in the absence of any systematic gathering of factual information. The next stage known as *social empiricism* arose in rebellion against the social philosophy approach. A nineteenth-century development, social empiricism is characterized by systematic data-gathering not related to theory. This stage, while going beyond conjecture, is often guided by it. The third and most advanced stage, a twentieth-century development, is known as *social analysis* and focuses on theory development in conjunction with the controlled testing of theoretically derived hypotheses. The major feature of this approach is to go beyond simple descriptive data to the level of verifying relationships between variables.

Research by physical educators pertaining to social psychological phenomena can best be described as exemplifying the social empiricism approach. Most has been oriented toward the investigation of practical problems rather than the resolution of broader theoretical problems. Unfortunately, most of this empirical research has not evolved from any systematic research program or from theory. This unsystematic testing of relationships between variables has been termed the "shot gun" approach. This term describes not only social psychological research related to physical activity but much of the research conducted by physical educators in general. Consequently, the social psychological research related to physical activity has derived few, if any, significant generalizations.

One other deficiency in previous social psychological research is noteworthy. Many investigations were conducted oblivious to existing theory and empirical observations formulated by social psychologists. Upon careful examination of the social psychological literature, considerable research can be found that is quite relevant to physical activity. Physical educators can

---

* It is interesting to note that the first social psychological study ever completed (Triplett, 1898) was concerned with the facilitating effects of competition and co-actors on bicycle riding and fishing-reel winding.

certainly draw upon these findings to increase their understanding of social-influence processes occurring during physical activity. These social psychological investigations provide valuable information by suggesting alternative hypotheses and procedural refinements. Fortunately, this shortcoming has come to the attention of some dedicated researchers. As a result, physical educators today have a greater awareness of the research developments in the behavioral sciences. Hopefully, the time is past for near-replication of experiments completed 20 years previously without utilizing the refinements suggested by these studies.

THE SOCIAL ANALYSIS APPROACH

The "new" approach advocated here is the development of a social psychology of physical activity which abandons both the social philosophy and the social empiricism approaches. Rather than research guided by conjecture and speculation and aimed solely at the description of social phenomena, "new" research should be directed at understanding the relationships underlying these social phenomena. Previously, the social empiricism approach provided a description of human characteristics and attributes associated with physical activity. Social analysis represents an extension of social empiricism toward establishing a scientifically valid foundation for what is described. The new social psychology of physical activity needs to probe beneath the descriptive data to understand the nature of causal relationships. Social psychology of physical activity research needs to strive for the development of theory and the testing of relevant hypotheses derived from these theories.

To alleviate the possibility of confusion, the term "theory" needs precise definition. For present purposes, theory is defined according to Kerlinger as:

> ...a set of interrelated constructs (concepts), definitions, and propositions that presents a systematic view of phenomena by specifying relations among variables, with the purpose of explaining and predicting the phenomena.[3]

In these terms, theory may be considered the ultimate aim of science. Also, it is visibly evident that theory development in most subdisciplines of concern to physical educators has progressed very little. This failure is perhaps attributed to the applied nature of these fields and their heavy reliance upon the parent discipline. Because a social psychology of physical activity has no theories of its own, it is suggested that it is appropriate and parsimonious to borrow social psychological theories and determine their applicability to physical activity. Systematic testing to determine the appropriateness of these theories can lead in one of two directions: (1) support may be found for these theories, or (2) they may be found inappropriate for physical activity. If the latter is the case, the theory can either be abandoned and a search made for another, or it may be modified based on theory-testing research. If no social psychological theories are found to be adequate, physical educators must attempt to construct their own.

The diversity and complexity of behavioral science research is nowhere manifested to any greater extent than in social psychological research. The complex social processes occurring between individuals, individuals and groups, and between groups themselves form much of the substance of physical activity. The final section of this paper discusses some of these social processes and attempts to show the relationship between them and physical activity.

SOME CONCERNS OF "A SOCIAL PSYCHOLOGY OF PHYSICAL ACTIVITY"

In studying social-influence processes, social psychologists commonly refer to the constructs that they investigate as variables. A variable is an attribute or condition which can vary in one or more ways and which can be systematically shown to affect or be affected by other attributes or conditions. Many social psychological variables can be either "dependent" or "independent" and are not permanently fixed as one or the other with regard to the direction of effect when applied to the study of human behavior involved in physical activity. In other words, interest may be either in the effects that social psychological variables have on various aspects of physical activity, or in the effects that physical activity have on social psychological variables. In experiments using the former paradigm, the social psychological variable would be the independent variable and that aspect of physical activity measured would be the dependent variable. In the latter experimental arrangement, the independent variable becomes some aspect of physical activity and the dependent variable is some social psychological variable.

Social Influences on Motor Performance

A primary concern of a social psychology of physical activity is with an individual's behavior as influenced by other individuals when involved in physical activity. This problem is an example of the social psychological variable as the independent variable and some aspect of physical activity as the dependent variable. Several recent studies have investigated the effects of passive and active audiences as well as co-actors on one component of physical activity—motor behavior. For example, the presence of a passive audience has been shown to impair motor skill acquisition but to facilitate the performance of a well-learned motor skill.[4] Co-actors (other individuals performing the same task at the same time) have also been shown to facilitate performance on a simple muscular endurance task.[5] The influence of an active audience providing praise and reproof (social reinforcement) on motor skill acquisition is another social process not yet clearly understood.[6] Observational learning or imitation, cooperation, and competition are other basic social influence processes requiring further investigation.

Influence of Physical Activity on Social Performance

In contrast with the above research, a social psychology of physical activity is also concerned with how various facets of physical activity influence social performance. Problems in this area are exemplified by such questions as:

What are the effects of involvement in physical activities on social performance?

What are the consequences of successful competitive experiences on social performance?

What, if any, social skills are acquired during participation in physical activities?

Are certain social skills more effectively acquired while engaging in intensive physical activity?

What is the effect of physique on personal perception and how does body image influence social performance? Answers to these questions would bring physical educators much closer to realizing and functionally assessing the attainment of the social objective so often claimed.

Paradoxically, this line of research probably has been less explored than any other. It is not difficult, however, to understand why. Manipulation of the independent variable has been difficult enough, but the dependent variable—i.e., social performance or social skills—has often seemed beyond measurement. Recently, however, social psychologists have made substantial progress in measuring social performance.[7] Therefore, with the operational measurement of social performance being more feasible and with the methodological advances in the behavioral sciences, the effects of participation in physical activities on social performance should in the near future receive more experimental attention.

Attitudes

Among the important social-influence processes with which a social psychology of physical activity is concerned are such variables as attitudes, personality, and culture. Probably, the most widely studied social-influence process in physical education research has been the construct of attitude. The study of attitudes is most useful in accounting for individual differences in reacting to a given situation. In large measure, attitudes conveniently sum up the past history of the individual's social experience to allow differential prediction of individual social behavior.

Attitude research in physical education probably offers the best example of using the social empiricism rather than the social analysis approach. This research has typically assessed attitudes toward various sports, athletes, physical education programs at every level, and competition. As a whole, these studies have not been theory oriented, but directed toward practical ends. The variety of methods employed and the diversity of attitudes assessed have made it virtually impossible to reach any generalizations. The value of these studies lies in a cataloguing of attitudes for a small sample of the population at one particular point in time. They do not probe beneath the surface to discover how the attitudes are formed or why they change.

A recent exception to the strictly empirical approach in the study of attitudes toward physical activity, however, is noteworthy. Kenyon[8] has used the social analysis approach by constructing a model to characterize physical activity as a social psychological phenomenon. His proposed model is based upon empirical data from which hypotheses may be derived for the study of attitudes toward physical activity. Even though, as Kenyon suggests, his model is only a crude beginning, it should be recognized as a big step in the right direction. Future attitude research in physical education needs to investigate the underlying reasons for the formation of attitudes toward physical activity and how and why these attitudes change. Anecdotally, a most fascinating problem is to discover why such a discrepancy exists between positively expressed attitudes toward physical activity and actual behavior!

Personality

Deeply entrenched in the sciences is a desire for parsimonious explanation of behavior. This desire is commonly bought at the price of grossly imprecise general statements about social behavior. It is apparent that persons differ markedly in their orientations to the social environment. General statements about the reaction of persons to a particular situation must all too often be modified. Therefore, adequate development of a social psychology of physical activity will ultimately depend on the integration of personality constructs into the explanation of social behavior of individuals engaged in physical activity.

Personality constructs refer to an individual's unique characteristics. The contemporary view of personality focuses on dispositions that lead individuals to typical responses rather than focusing on the responses alone. Dispositions are considered to function within the individual's psychological field and to intervene between experience and responses to social stimuli. A social psychology of physical activity is concerned with personality in two ways. First, it is concerned with the interaction of personality dispositions and situational variables on individual behavior while involved in physical activity. Second, it is concerned with the impact of the social environment surrounding physical activity on personality development.

Physical educators have been interested in personality dispositions for some time, but the research to date typifies the "shot gun" approach. Investigation of such dispositions as anxiety, need achievement, risk taking, authoritarianism, and internal and external locus of control by physical educators suffers from the same weaknesses identified in attitude research. Again, personality research offers a good example of the social empiricism approach. Any generalizations reached are extremely tenuous as a result of the diversity of methods used and samples studied. These descriptive data are not without use, but only by employing the social analysis approach can the nature of causal relationships between personality dispositions and components of physical activity be understood. Finally, it is apparent that the consideration of situational variables alone, without respect to the interaction of situation and personality, is a fruitless quest.

Culture

Another important influence on physical activity and sport is culture. A society's culture consists of the relationships and social arrangements passed on and institutionalized to routinely handle the characteristic problems of that society.[9] By providing social reality, the basic psychological effect of culture is to influence a society's members toward distinctive ways of thinking and acting. It should be important for physical educators to understand the effects of cultural norms on individual participation in physical activity. In social psychological terms, norms and roles are in the nature of social expectancies which individuals share in their psychological fields. Roles refer especially to those particular expectancies regarding appropriate behavior for a person occupying a position in a given situation.

From a social psychological point of view, physical educators need to be concerned about the cultural influences on individual behavior while involved in physical activity and the role of sport as a transmitter of cultural expectancies. The importance of physical activities as a medium for such transmissions is becoming increasingly recognized as an integral part of the socialization process.

Although some researchers in the area of sociology of sport have demonstrated interest in culture as a variable of study, few have explored cultural effects on physical activity from a social psychological or individual point of view. Answers to such questions as the following will increase our understanding of the relationship between culture and physical activity:

What effect does role variation have on individual motor performance?

What behavior is expected from individuals occupying various roles in sports?

Is the establishment of roles into a hierarchical order detrimental to certain individuals occupying lower roles?

What is the relationship between sport participation and such culturally affected variables as social class, social mobility, and ethnic affiliation?

Many more questions can be asked, but the point is that little is known about the array of cultural influences affecting involvement in physical activity.

The subcultural influences affecting individual involvement in physical activity are also of vital concern to the physical educator. Subcultures are divisions of society represented in social class, community, and ethnic differences. They are important in social psychology because of their influence on the values and behaviors of individuals identified with them in a reference group sense. Social class, for example, is a major subculture variation based on the qualities valued in a society such as family standing, income, and education. Physical educators can find the importance of subcultural influences on physical activity in such questions as:

What is the influence of the peer group, the family, a sibling, and the school on participation in and involvement with physical activity?

Do these early experiences affect an individual's disposition toward involvement in physical activity?

How does social class influence individual involvement in physical activity?

What influences do ethnic distinctions based on racial, religious, and national origins have on individual involvement in physical activity?

Group Dynamics

Social psychology of physical activity is also deeply concerned with the structure and processes of groups involved in physical activity. The study of groups, commonly referred to as group dynamics, is dedicated to increasing knowledge about the nature of groups, the laws of their development, and their interrelationships with individuals, other groups, and larger institutions. The affiliations individuals have in groups formed for purposes of involvement in physical activity possess the potential for affecting the individual's actions and psychological states. Even though considerable research has appeared in the field of group dynamics, physical educators as well as social psychologists know very little about the dynamics of sport groups and the effects they may produce.

Some of the variables included in the study of the structure and processes of groups formed for the purpose of involvement in physical activity are: group productivity, group cohesiveness, cooperation and competition, communication, leadership, and the power structure within the group. Another important variable is the relationships that exist between groups. For example, what effect does competition have on intergroup relations? What is the basis for intergroup conflict and how can it be managed? If direct conflict does not occur, intergroup tension usually takes the form of hostility and prejudice. What methods then can be employed to relieve such tensions? These and many other questions indicate some of the variables and problems of concern in the study of the structure and processes of groups involved in physical activity.

Extensive reference to the completed social psychological research related to physical activity has not been made in this paper. It should be noted, however, that a few physical educators have employed the social analysis approach to investigate social psychological phenomena related to physical activity. This research is noteworthy, but unfortunately has not been very extensive and is overshadowed by the strictly empirical investigations. Today, as never before, physical educators and coaches alike are seeking greater understanding of man's relationship with his social environment. Thus, the need for a concerted social analysis research program investigating the social psychology of physical activity on a much larger scale is warranted.

CONCLUSION

Thus far, the field of social psychology has been defined, distinguished from its parent disciplines, and the concerns of a subdiscipline called social psychology of physical activity outlined. Social psychology was defined in terms of both its content and its method. Simply stated, its content deals with the individual's relationships with his social environment. Its method is that of modern psychology as an empirical science. A social psychology of physical activity is concerned with how human behavior is influenced by the presence, behavior, and products of other human beings individually and collectively, while involved in physical activity. A social analysis approach rather than a social empiricism approach was advocated for this field of study. The social analysis approach is a three-step process which involves: (a) the collection of carefully made observations, (b) the ordered integration of these observations to permit the statement of general principles describing the logical patterns into which they fall, and (c) the utilization of these general principles to predict future observations.

Physical educators have long claimed a social objective in their programs. Over the years, however, little tangible evidence has been found to support the achievement of this objective. Failure to rigorously study the social nature of man while involved in physical activity has been partially due to the complexity and limitations of behavioral science research techniques. With improvements in these techniques and the development of high speed computers, the ability to experimentally investigate the social concomitants associated with physical activity has greatly increased.

Today, more than ever, research in the behavioral sciences seems particularly challenging. It is now generally recognized that physical activity plays no small role in the social life of man. Therefore, the need to understand social behavior while involved in physical activity increases as we spend ever-increasing amounts of time in such pursuits. For the creative and dedicated scholar, the world of social phenomena is waiting to be explained.

NOTES

1. McGrath, J. E., *Social Psychology: A Brief Introduction*, New York: Holt, Rinehart and Winston, 1965, p. 1.

2. Kenyon, G. S., "Sport Involvement: A Conceptual Go and Some Consequences Thereof," paper presented at Sociology of Sport Symposium, University of Wisconsin, November, 1968.

3. Kerlinger, F. N., *Foundation of Behavioral Research*, New York: Holt, Rinehart and Winston, 1967, p. 11.

4. Martens, R., "Effect of an Audience on Learning and Performance of a Complex Motor Skill," *Journal of Personality and Social Psychology*, **12**, 252-260, 1969.

5. Martens, R., and Landers, D. M., "Coaction Effects on Muscular Endurance," *Research Quarterly*, **40**, 733-737, 1969.

6. Roberts, G. C., and Martens, R., "Social Reinforcement and Complex Motor Performance," *Research Quarterly*, **41**, 175-181, 1970.

7. Argyle, M., and Kendon, A., "The Experimental Analysis of Social Performance," *Advances in Experimental Psychology*, Vol. 3, edited by L. Berkowitz, New York: Academic Press, 1967.

8. Kenyon, G. S., "A Conceptual Model for Characterizing Physical Activity," *Research Quarterly,* **39**, 96-105; "Six Scales for Assessing Attitude Toward Physical Activity," *Research Quarterly,* **39**, 566-574, 1968.
9. Hollander, E. P., *Principles and Methods of Social Psychology,* New York: Oxford University Press, 1967, p. 239.

THE INTERDEPENDENCE OF SPORT AND CULTURE

Günther Lüschen

INTRODUCTION

Sport is a rational, playful activity in interaction, which is extrinsically rewarded. The more it is rewarded, the more it tends to be work; the less, the more it tends to be play.[1] If we describe it in an action system frame of reference, this activity depends on the organic, personality, social, and cultural systems. By tradition, physical education has tried to explain this action system largely on the grounds of the organic system, sometimes making references to the personality system. Only on rare occasions has it been approached systematically from the social and cultural systems as well. Yet it seems obvious that any action going on in this system is to be explained with reference to all of the subsystems of the action system.

Even such a simple motor activity as walking is more than a matter of organic processes initiated by the personality system. It is determined by the social and cultural systems as well, as is most evident in the way the Israelians from the Yemen walk. Since in their former society, in the Yemen, the Jews were the outcasts, and every Yemenite could feel free to hit a Jew (whenever he could get hold of one), the Yemenitic Jew would always run in order to escape this oppression. This way of walking finally became an integrated pattern of his culture. And though the environment in Israel no longer is hostile to him, the Yemenitic Israelite still carries this pattern with him as part of his culture and walks in a shy and hasty way.

Günther Lüschen, "The Interdependence of Sport and Culture," *International Review of Sport Sociology,* Volume 2, 1967, pp. 127-139. Reprinted by permission.

This example shows in addition that the different subsystems of action are not independent from one another, they are structurally related. Thus, in dealing with the cultural system of sport and its interdependence with general culture, we will not always be able to explain the culture of sport and that of its environment in terms of the cultural system, and therefore should refer as well to the social and personality system to describe and explain what we call culture. It was Radcliffe-Brown who stressed the point that culture should be explained through its social structure. Furthermore, one should discuss the function of a unit within general culture, as well as cultural process and change.[2]

CONCEPTS OF CULTURE AND REVIEW OF RESULTS

Culture as a concept does not refer to behavior itself. It deals with those patterns and abstractions that underlie behavior or are the result of it. Thus culture exists of cognitive elements which grow out of everyday or scientific experience. It consists of beliefs, values, norms, and of signs that include symbols of verbal as well as nonverbal communication.[3]

Anthropologists have sometimes held a broader view of culture and given more attention to the material results of human behavior. Leslie White in a critique of the above-stated concept of culture has called for more attention to "acts, thoughts and things dependent upon symboling." These would include not only the study of the above-mentioned elements, but also those of art, tools, machines, fetishes, etc.[4] As attractive as White's critique may be, especially for cultural anthropology as an independent science, this approach as related to the cultural study of sports has led more to mere curiosity about things than to theoretical insights. This methodological approach has also dealt more with the cultural diffusion of sport and games than with the social structure of which they are a part. For decades we have learned about all types of games in all types of societies (especially primitive ones), which may well lead to the conclusion that we know more about the games and sports displayed by some Polynesian tribe than those of our own children and ancestors. For an understanding of sport it is less important to find the same games in different cultures as Tylor did.[5] It is more important to analyze for example the different meaning of baseball in the United States and Lybia, which in the one culture has ritualistic functions, while it has also economic functions in the other.[6]

Another concept of culture, mainly held in Central Europe, has almost led to the same results for sport. In this concept "higher" culture was separated from civilization and expressed itself significantly in the arts and sciences. On the basis of values attributed to sport *a priori*, it was related either to "Zivilisation" or to "Kultur".[7] Physical educationalists through Huizinga's theory on the origin of culture in play saw in the latter approach their main support.[8] Thus defining sport as a special form of play, physical educationalists felt safe in their implicit attempt to justify sport for educational purposes. Yet Huizinga's theory has not only been criticized on the basis of ethnological findings,[9] but he himself was very critical about the play-element in sport.[10] Those that believed in the role of sport within higher culture were hardly able to prove their hypothesis. So, as recently as René Maheu,[11] they often expressed their hope that sport in the future would contribute to "Kultur."

One can hardly deny that sport has indeed some impact on "higher" culture, as may be shown by symbolic elements from sport to be found in script and language. In an analysis of the cultural meaning of the ball-game of the Aztecs and Maya, Krickeberg found that in their script there were elements related to this game. The symbol for movement, for example, was identical with the I-shape of the ball-court.[12] "To get (take) a rain-check" refers to baseball, but has now become in American English symbolic for any situation where you get another chance. "That's not cricket" refers to a dishonest procedure in everyday life. And though German is not as idiomatic as English, it contains elements which originated in sport and games as well. "Katzbalgerei," and the phrase "sich gegenseitig die Bälle zuspielen," refer to a game which today is still known in the Netherlands as "Kaatsen" and perhaps appears in the New York children's game of one-o-cat. As did football in Shakespeare's King Lear, so appeared this game and its terminology in the 16th century poetry of J. G. Fischart.[13]

How weak the relationships of sport to "higher" culture indeed are, may be shown by the relatively unsuccessful attempts to establish, through special contests in modern Olympics, a relationship between sport and the arts. Sport only rarely expresses itself in the material aspects of culture. It is, what I would like to call a momentary activity.

It is just on a certain level that an event may have its appearance as a short-range cultural element, such as on the sports page of the next day's newspaper.[14] This appearance of sport in the media of mass communication, in language, poetry, and the arts is significant for the overall meaning of sport within society, but these manifestations tell us little about sport itself and its interdependence with general culture as we define it.

It may also be interesting to discuss cognitive elements such as scientific insight coming out of sport. Also religious beliefs and ritual found in sport would be an interesting point of analysis. Yet showing how sport is indeed bound to society and structured by general culture, we will mainly discuss our problem on the level of cultural values and their related social structure.

SPORT AS PART OF CULTURE AND SOCIETY

That sport is structurally related to culture and society has sometimes been questioned. Yet it is quite easy to show how strong this relationship is. Sport is indeed an expression of that sociocultural system in which it occurs. David Riesman and Reuel Denny describe how American Football was changed through the American culture from rugby to a completely different game. It is now well integrated and quite obviously shows, in its vigor, its hard contact, and greater centrality on the individual, the basic traits of the culture of American society.[15]

On the level of the so-called primitive societies we see the same dependence of sport and games on culture and its underlying social structure. The Hopi Indians had 16 different terms for foot races which nearly all referred to one aspect of the social organization of that tribe.[16] A recent socio-historical study on three Illinois subcultures finds the same close relationship between sociocultural system and sport.[17] And Käte Hye-Kerkdal outlines the tight structural relation between the log-races of the tribe of the Timbira in Brazil and their sociocultural system. This ritualistic competition between two teams has symbolic meaning for nearly every aspect of the dual-organization of this tribe. It refers to all kinds of religious and social polarities and is so strongly imbedded in this religious-dominated system that winning or losing does not have any effect on the status of the team or individual, nor are there any other extrinsic rewards. Yet these races are performed vigorously and with effort.[18]

Now that we have proven that there is a structural relationship between sport and culture, the first question is that of sport's dependency on culture. What factors make for the appearance of sport? Or more specifically, what are the underlying cultural values?

CULTURAL VALUES AND SPORT

By values we mean those general orientations in a sociocultural system that are not always obvious to its members, but are implicit in actual behavior. On the level of the personality system they are expressed partly in attitudes. Values should be separated from norms which are derived from values and are actual rules for behavior. For instance, health is a high value in the American culture as it seems to be in all young cultures, while death is higher in the hierarchy of values in old cultures like India.[19] On this continuum we may explain why sport as an expression of the evaluation of health is more important in American than Indian society. The whole emphasis on physical fitness in the United States may well be explained by this background, and the norm "run for your life" is directly related to it.

Sport, Industrialization and Technology

In comparing the uneven distribution and performance level of sport all over the world, one widely accepted hypothesis is that sport is an offspring of technology and industrialization. The strong emphasis on sport in industrialized societies seems to show that industrialization and technology are indeed a basis for sport. This would be a late confirmation of Ogburn's theory of social change, as well as of the Marxian theory that society and its structure depend on its economic basis. However, there are quite a number of inconsistencies. Not all sport-oriented societies or societal subsystems show a relation to technology and industrialization, and historically games and sport have been shown to have existence prior to industrialization. Yet it can hardly be denied that certain conditions in the later process of industrialization have promoted sport; and technology has at least its parallels in modern sport. The above-stated hypothesis may, despite its obvious limitations, lead us to the independent variable.

Sport, a Protestant Subculture?

In an investigation that because of its methodological procedure turned out to be a profound critique of Marxian materialism, Max Weber studied the interrelationship of what he called "The Protestant Ethic and the Spirit of Capitalism."[20] This investigation about the underlying values of capitalism in Western societies quoted data on the overrepresentation of Protestants in institutions of higher learning, their preference for industrial and commercial occupations and professions, and the stronger trend towards capitalism in Protestant-dominated countries (most obvious in the United States). Weber found that not the material basis but Protestant culture, with achievement of worldly success and asceticism held as the basic values, caused industrialization and capitalism. In accordance with the Calvinistic belief in predestination the Protestant felt that he was blessed by God once he had achieved success. Thus, need for achievement became an integrated part of his personality and a basic value in Protestantism. Together with the value of asceticism this led to the accumulation of wealth and to Western capitalism. If we turn to sport, we find the same values of achievement and asceticism. Even the Puritans, generally opposed to a leisurely life, could therefore justify sport as physical activity that contributed to health.[21]

Today we find significance for this relationship in the YMCA, in a group like the American Fellowship of Christian Athletes, and also in the Protestant minister who in Helsinki became an Olympic medal winner in the pole vault. He showed the consistency between Protestantism and sport in his prayer right after his Olympic winning vault. Max Weber's findings about the relationship between the Protestant ethic and the spirit of capitalism may thus well be extended to the "spirit" of sport. Not only was Weber aware of this relationship but also Thorstein Veblen, who described the parallels in religious and sport ritual.[22]

The relationship between sport and Protestantism is not only to be observed in the emphasis on sport in the Scandinavian and other Protestant countries. A rough compilation of the probable religious preference of Olympic medal winners on the basis of the percentage of different religious groups in their countries also shows the dominance of Protestantism up to 1960. Protestantism accounted for more than 50 percent of the medal winners, while its ratio among the world population is less than 8 percent.[23] Furthermore, in 1958 a survey of young athletes in West Germany showed the following distribution according to religious preference (in percent):[24]

	Whole population West Germany	Sport club-members 15-25	Track, swimming	High achievers, track/swimming
Protestants	52	60	67	73
Catholics	44	37	31	26
Others	4	3	2	1
n =	universe	1,880	366	111

These figures indicate the overrepresentation of Protestants in German sport. Moreover, they indicate a higher percentage in individual sports, and an even higher percentage of Protestants among those that have achieved a higher level of performance. Thus it may be concluded that there is a correlation between Protestantism and sport and the culture of both. This was obvious for individual sports, but less for team sports where, in the German sample, Catholics appeared quite often. Since in Catholicism collectivity is highly regarded, this inconsistency is to be explained by the value of collectivity in team sports. It is consistent with this hypothesis that Catholic Notre Dame University has been one of the innovators of football in America. At present, it is a leading institution in this discipline. And internationally Catholic-dominated South America is overall rather poor in individual sports, but outstanding in team sports like soccer and basketball.

This result on the overall, strong relationship between sport and Protestantism is, despite support by data, theoretically insufficient. As was the case with sport in its relationship to industrialization, there are many exceptions.

The high achievement in sport of the Russians, the Poles, the Japanese, the Mandan Indians, the Sikhs in India, or the Watusi in Africa cannot be related to Protestantism, though in Japanese Zen-Buddhism there are parallels.

The Centrality of the Achievement-Value

Since again Protestantism cannot be specifically identified as being the independent variable, we may hypothesize that there is a more general system of values as the basis for Protestantism, capitalism, and sport. In his critique of Max Weber, D. C. McClelland has considered the ethic of Protestantism as a special case of the general achievement orientation of a system, this being the independent variable. Achievement orientation (or, as he puts it on the personality-system-level, need achievement) precedes all periods of high cultural achievement in ancient Greece, in the Protestant Reformation, in modern industrialism[25]—and, as we may conclude, in modern sport. He referred in his analysis also to the related social structure of the achievement value (such as family organization), which should also be studied in its relation to sport.

If we turn again to the cross-cultural comparison of those systems that participate and perform strongly in sport, we find that in all of these societies achievement-orientation is basic. In Russia this value is expressed in the norm that social status should depend only on achievement. The Sikhs and the Watusi are both minority groups in their environment. In order to keep their position, they have to achieve more than the other members of the societies they live in. The Japanese[26] and the Mandan Indians[27] also place a heavy emphasis on achievement.

Similar results appear in cross-cultural investigations of different types of games as related to basic orientations in the process of socialization. Roberts and Sutton-Smith find in a secondary analysis of the Human Relation Area Files of G. P. Murdock that games of chance are related to societies that emphasize routine responsibility in the socialization process. Games of strategy are found in societies where obedience is stressed, games of physical skill in those where achievement is stressed.[28] Individual sports would mainly qualify as games of physical skill and again show achievement as their basic cultural value. Team sports as well are games of strategy. Their relation to training of obedience would support exactly what we called earlier the value of collectivity.

It remains an open question, for further research into the value structure of sport, as to which other values are related to this system. It is to be expected that the structure of values will be more complex than it appears on the basis of our limited insight now. Roberts and Sutton-Smith briefly remark that games of physical skill are related to occupational groups that exert power over others.[29] Thus, power orientation may be another value supporting sport. This would cross-culturally be consistent with power-oriented political systems that strongly emphasize sport. Here we could refer to countries like Russia or the United States, as well as to tribes like the Mandan Indians.

The Culture of Societal Subsystems and Its Relation to Sport

Within a society we find subsystems that have their own subculture, which will be another influence on sport. The female role in modern societies still depends on a culture that stresses obedience as the main value-orientation, while the male culture is strongly oriented towards achievement. Thus we find a disproportionately high participation of men in sport which in most of the disciplines is a male-culture. One of the most male-oriented sports however is pool, a game supported mainly by the subculture of the bachelor; it has, with the general change in the number of people marrying, lost its main supporting culture.[30]

Another subsystem which in its culture shows a strong relationship to sport is that of the adolescent age-group.[31] Sport is dependent more on the culture of the adolescent than on that of any other age-group. Helanko raises the point, referring to his studies of boys' gangs in Turku, that sport has its origin in the gang-age and boys' gangs. The fact that there are no rules for early sports to be found is seen as one of the supporting factors.[32] Generally speaking, achievement is again more central as a value in adolescence and early adulthood than later, where the main response to sport goes not so much toward achievement but toward values of health and fitness.

The different social classes have a culture of their own. The greatest emphasis on achievement and thus the highest sport participation, is to be found in the upper-middle class. It is considerably less important in the lower class where routine responsibility is valued. The notion that there is no way to gain higher status accounts for the high regard for games of chance or those sports where one may just have a lucky punch, as in boxing.[33] Loy has related the different types of games and the passive and active participation in sport to different modes of adaptation and to the members of social classes.[34] His theoretical analysis as to "innovation" found in the lower class, ritualism in the lower-middle class, and conformity in the upper-middle class is supported by data that show the same ways of adaptation in sport.[35] However, in responding to the social class system and its culture as related to sport one should have in mind that class-determined behavior may not follow the traditional class lines in sport. Sport may indeed show or promote new orientations in the class system.[36]

Finally sport is organized within, or relates to, different institutions whose cultures sometimes have a profound influence on sport itself. This is especially true for physical education in schools where, with the same skills and rules, we may find a completely different culture as compared to sport in the military establishment. And while intercollegiate and interscholastic athletics are overall a surprisingly well integrated subculture within American schools and universities, the different values held by an educational (the school or university) and a solely success-oriented unit (the team) may well lead to strong value-conflicts. This could result in a complete separation of school and athletics.[37]

FUNCTIONS AND DYSFUNCTIONS

The Functions of Sport within Culture and Society

After we have found achievement, asceticism in individual sports, obedience (collectivity) in team sports, and exertion of power the basic value orientations that give structure to this activity, we may then proceed to the second question: How does sport influence the sociocultural system at large? Though we have little evidence through research, we may on the basis of structural-functional methodology be able to outline the basic functions of sport for pattern maintenance, integration, adaptation and goal attainment.

As in the case of the Timbira, Hye-Kerkdal states that through the log-race the basic values of that culture were learned. Furthermore, the participants were functionally integrated into the social system.[38] Thus we may hypothesize that the main functions of sport are for pattern maintenance and integration.

Since sport implies (as we saw) basic cultural values, it has the potential to pass these values on to its participants. We know at least from studies of the process of socialization that the exposure of children to competitive sport will cause these children to become achievement-motivated; the earlier this exposure occurs, the more achievement-motivated they become.[39] And the child's moral judgment may, for instance, be influenced through games such as marbles. Again, according to Piaget, the child not only becomes socialized to the rules but he at a later age also gets an insight into the underlying structure and the function of the rules of a game, and thus into the structure and function of social norms and values as such.[40] Overall, from the level of primitive societies to modern societies, sport does not only socialize to the system of values and norms. In primitive societies it socializes toward adult and warfare skills as well.[41]

Since we mentioned that sport is also structured along such societal subsystems as different classes, males, urban areas, schools, and communities, it functions for integration as well. This is obvious also in spectator sport, where the whole country or community identifies with its representatives in a contest. Thus, sport functions as a means of integration, not only for the actual participants, but also for the represented members of such a system.

Sport in modern societies may as well function for goal-attainment on the national polity level. Sport in primitive societies functions besides for goal-attainment also for adaptation, since the sport skills of swimming, hunting, and fishing are used for the supply of food and mere survival.

Possible Dysfunctions of Sport and Social Control

A question that should be raised at this point is whether sport is dysfunctional for culture and society as well. Th. W. Adorno has called sport an area of unfreedom ("ein Bereich der Unfreiheit"),[42] by which he obviously referred to the differentiated code of rules which earlier led Huizinga to his statement that excluded sport from play.[43] Both seem to overlook what Piaget called the reciprocity and mutual agreement on which such rules rest.[44] And they may also be considered as an expression of a highly structured system.

Another dysfunctional element for culture and for the system of sport itself could be the centrality of achievement. It has such a high rank in the hierarchy of values of sport that, by definition, the actual objective performance of a member of this system will decide the status he gets. In the core of sport, in the contest on the sportsfield, there is only achieved status. It seems that there is no other system or any societal subsystem with the exception of combat where achievement ranks that high. It may create conflict once this value-orientation is imposed on the whole culture, and it may create conflict within the system of sport itself since its members bring other values into this system as well.

M. Mead in an investigation of competition and cooperation (the first concept of which is related to achievement) of primitive peoples, however, finds that there seems to be no society where one of these principles existed alone.[45] And on the microsociological level, small groups seem to control this value by discrimination against those that deviate from the group norm of a fair performance.[46] Thus one would notify some kind of a mechanism built into a social system that keeps it in a state of balance. Exactly this seems to happen within sport where the sporting groups themselves and their differen-tiated organizational and institutional environment perform social control in regard to those participants whose achievements surpass a certain level.

In a survey of sport club members in Germany, it was found that the norms expressed for the behavior of an athlete referred surprisingly less to the achievement-value, but very often to a value of affiliation, which is to be defined as a positive orientation toward other group members or opponents. Fair play was the one mentioned most frequently. The value of affiliation expressed by the respondents was found the more in normative statements the higher their level of performance. On the basis of the hypothesized mechanism of social control they are under stronger pressure to affiliate with others.[47] Similar results were found in a field experiment with two school classes.[48] This may explain (on the basis of this structural relationship) why in the culture of sport, we find not only the value of achievement but also that of fair play and other affiliative orientations.

However, achievement and affiliation may not necessarily be related. It depends on the amount of social control imposed on sport from the internal as well as external system, whether this relationship will be strong or weak. In professional boxing these controls are very weak, while in golf with the handicap-rule they seem to be comparatively strong.

How much this pattern would influence the culture as such is an open question. Yet it seems not so mis-oriented as Litt and Weniger thought when Oetinger stated that sport would provide a good model for political partner-ship.[49] We may on the basis of our findings hypothesize that also on the political level the amount of social control will decide whether two or more systems will coexist or not.

CHANGE AND EVOLUTION

Sport and Sociocultural Change

After we have discussed the culture and underlying social structure of sport and its function, we are left with Radcliffe-Brown's third programmatic point—that of social and cultural change. We know little about the role of sport in sociocultural change, though we hypothesized earlier that it may have a function of innovation, or at least structural relationship to changes in the system of social classes. Sport has also functioned as an initiator for the diffusion of technical inventions, such as the bicycle or the automobile.[50] The same holds true to a degree for conduct in regard to fashion and a healthy life. Typically, this question of change has been highly neglected so far.

Sport and Cultural Evolution

If we finally try to explain the different cross-cultural appearance of sport on the basis of an evolutionary theory it is hard to justify, on the basis of our present knowledge about the appearance of sport, that there are such things as primitive and developed cultures of sport. The Mandan Indians had a highly developed sport culture, the Australian aboriginals as perhaps the most primitive people known to us today knew quite a variety of recreational activities and physical skills, and the variety of competitive games in Europe and America in the past was probably richer than today.

An evolution can only be seen on a vertical level which on the one hand shows in a state of mechanic solidarity rather simple rules in sport and games, while in a state of organic solidarity as in modern industrialized societies the code of rules and the structure of games get more differentiated.

What we may furthermore state is, that on the level of primitive cultures sport's function is universal, often religious, collectivity-oriented, and in the training of skills representative and related to adult and warfare skills, while modern sport's function may be called specific for pattern maintenance and integration, is individual-oriented and in the training of skills nonrepresentative. The rewards are more intrinsic in primitive cultures, while they are more extrinsic in the sport of modern cultures. Thus, referring to our definition at the beginning, one may well differentiate between physical and recreational activities of primitive cultures and sport in modern cultures.[51]

NOTES

1. I owe much of this definition to a discussion with my colleague, G. P. Stone, University of Minnesota.
2. A. R. Radcliffe-Brown, *Structure and Function in Primitive Society*, The Free Press, Glencoe, Ill., 1952.
3. This refers to a concept held by Kluckhohn/Kroeber and Talcott Parsons. For a general reference as to culture and the action frame of reference within structural-functionalism see H. M. Johnson, *Sociology: A Systematic Introduction*, Harcourt, Brace and World, New York, 1960.
4. L. White, "The Concept of Culture," *American Anthropoligist*, **61**, 1959, p. 227-251.
5. Cf. E. B. Tylor, "On American Lot-Games," *Internationales Archiv für Ethnographie*, supplement 9, Leiden, 1896, p. 55-67.
6. C. Gini, "Rural Ritual Games in Lybia," *Rural Sociology*, **4**, 1939, p. 283-299.
7. Most significantly to be found in an unpublished lecture of C. Diem, *Sport und Kultur*, 1942 at the University of Halle.

8. J. Huizinga, *Homo Ludens,* The Beacon Press, Boston, 1955.

9. Cf. A. E. Jensen, "Spiel und Ergriffenheit," *Paideuma,* **3**, 1942, p. 124-139.

10. J. Huizinga, *op. cit.,* p. 196.

11. R. Maheu, "Sport and Culture," *International Journal of Adult and Youth Education,* **14**, 1962, 4, p. 169-178.

12. W. Krickeberg, "Das mittelamerikanische Ballspiel und seine religiöse Symbolik," in *Paideuma,* **3**, 1944.

13. Cf. articles "Katzball and Katzenspiel," in J. Grimm and W. Grimm, *Deutsches Wörterbuch* 5, Hirtz, Leipzig, 1873, p. 279 and 302.

14. For one of the few content-analyses of the special jargon of sport language see P. H. Tannenbaum and J. E. Noah, "Sportugese: A Study of Sports Page Communication," *Journalism Quarterly* **36**, 1959, 2, p. 163-170.

15. D. Riesman and R. Denney, "Football in America," in D. Riesman, *Individualism Reconsidered,* Glencoe, Ill., 1954, p. 242-251.

16. S. Culin, *Games of the North American Indians. 24th Annual Report,* Bureau of American Ethnology, Washington, D.C., 1907, p. 801.

17. Ph. J. Hill, *A Cultural History of Frontier Sport in Illinois 1673-1820.* PhD thesis, University of Illinois, 1966.

18. K. K. Hye-Kerkdal, "Wettkampfspiel und Dualorganisation bei den Timbira Brasiliens," in J. Haekel (ed.), *Die Wiener Schule der Völkerkunde,* Wien, 1956, p. 504-533.

19. Cf. T. Parsons, "Toward a Healthy Maturity," *Journal of Health and Human Behavior,* **1**, 1960, 3, p. 163-173.

20. M. Weber, *Die protestantische Ethik und der Geist des Kapitalismus,* Gesammelte Aufsätze zur Religionssoziologie, Tübingen, 1920, 1.

21. Cf. P. C. McIntosh, *Sport and Society,* Watts, London, 1963, p. 35-45.

22. Th. Veblen, *The Theory of the Leisure Class,* University of Chicago Press, Chicago, 1899.

23. G. Lüschen, "Der Leistungssport in seiner Abhängigkeit vom soziokulturellen System," *Zentralblatt für Arbeitswissenschaft,* **16**, 1962, 12, p. 186-190.

24. Unpublished, investigation of German Sport's Youth by Lüschen, 1958. Data obtained by random sample of sportsclub members 15-25 in West Germany and West Berlin.

25. D. C. McClelland, *The Achieving Society,* Van Nostrand, New York, 1961.

26. R. N. Bellah, *Tokugawa Religion: The Values of Pre-Industrial Japan,* Free Press, Glencoe, Ill., 1957, p. 57.

27. D. C. McClelland, *op. cit.,* p. 491.

28. J. M. Roberts and B. Sutton-Smith, "Child Training and Game Involvement," *Ethnology,* **1**, 1962, 2; p. 166-185.

29. B. Sutton-Smith, J. M. Roberts, R. M. Kozelka, "Game Involvement in Adults," *Journal of Social Psychology*, **60**, 1963, 1, p. 15-30.

30. N. Polsky, "Poolrooms and Poolplayers," *Trans-action*, 1967, 4, p. 32-40.

31. J. S. Coleman, *The Adolescent Society*, The Free Press, Glencoe, Ill., 1961.

32. R. Helanko, "Sports and Socialization," *Acta Sociologica*, **2**, 1957, 4, p. 229-240.

33. S. K. Weinberg and R. Arond, "The Occupational Culture of the Boxer," *American Journal of Sociology*, **57**, 1952, 5, p. 460-463.

34. J. W. Loy, *Sport and Social Structure*, paper at the AAHPER Convention, Chicago, 1966.

35. G. Lüschen, "Soziale Schichtung und soziale Mobilität," *Kölner Zeitschrift für Soziologie und Sozialpsychologie*, **15**, 1963, 1, p. 74-93.

36. G. Kunz and G. Lüschen, *Leisure and Social Stratification*, Paper at International Congress for Sociology, Evian/France, 1966.

37. This institutional influence is so strong that it may well be advisable to treat informal (recreational), formal (organized for sport purpose only) and institutional sport (physical education and athletics in school) separately.

38. K. K. Hye-Kerkdal, *op. cit.*

39. M. R. Winterbottem, *The Relation of Childhood Training in Independence to Achievement Motivation*, PhD thesis, University of Michigan, 1953.

40. J. Piaget, *The Moral Judgement of the Child*, The Free Press, New York, 1965.

41. F. Stumpf, F. W. Cozens, "Some Aspects of the Role of Games, Sports and Recreational Activities in the Culture of Primitive Peoples," *Research Quarterly*, **18**, 1947, 3, p. 198-218 and **20**, 1949, p. 7-30.

42. Th. W. Adorno, *Prismen*, Suhrkamp, Frankfurt, 1957.

43. J. Huizinga, *op. cit.*

44. J. Piaget, *op. cit.*

45. M. Mead, *Competition and Co-operation Among Primitive Peoples*, University of California Press, Berkeley, 1946.

46. F. J. Roethlisberger, W. J. Dickson, *Management and the Worker*, Harvard University Press, Cambridge, Mass., 1939.

47. G. Lüschen, *Soziale Schichtung...*, *op. cit.*

48. G. Lüschen, *Leistungsorientierung und ihr Einfluß auf das soziale und personale System*, G. Lüschen (ed.), *Kleingruppenforschung und Gruppe im Sport*, Köln und Opladen: Westdeutscher Verlag, 1966, p. 209-223.

49. F. Oetinger, *Partnerschaft*, Stuttgart, 1954. Litt and Weniger in "Die Sammlung," Göttingen, 1952, attacked the concept of partnership as a mode of political conduct which would not provide a way of socialization towards political power.

50. A. L. Kroeber, *Anthropology*, Harcourt, Brace and World, New York, 1963, p. 163-165.

51. Cf. H. Damm, "Vom Wesen sogenannter Leibesübungen bei Naturvölkern," *Studium Generale*, **13**, 1960, p. 3-10.

2 / THE HERITAGE OF SPORT
IN AMERICA

A review of the past helps to explain current conditions and may even provide a basis for the prediction of future events; it enables us to understand why things are as they now are and to predict what might reasonably be expected in the future. The study of any social phenomena which is based entirely upon the present is bound to reveal a very incomplete picture of reality. Current social circumstances are related to events of the past. Social institutions, organizations, and processes of the past have, after all, produced the present.

Contemporary sport in the United States owes its structure and functions to the past. The major historical forces which have molded American sport are the religious influence of the colonial Puritans, industrialization and urbanization in the nineteenth century, the growth and development of universal public education, and the emergence of mass media during this century.

In the past 200 years the United States has grown from a small number of widely scattered and disunited settlements located along the eastern seaboard of North America into the most modern and industrially powerful nation in the world. It has also become the most advanced nation in sports. Americans are sports enthusiasts, and their natural love for sports, fostered by a variety of historical, social, and economic institutions, has generated sports into a tremendous national pastime. From a nation of farmers who had little time for games and sports, except for special occasions, the United States has developed into a nation of urbanites who watch ten to twenty hours of sports on television each weekend and almost consider it a duty to participate in some form of sport for recreation. Social, religious, economic, and geographic factors have all contributed to this development. Therefore, to understand the character of sport in American society, we must examine the factors responsible for molding American sport from a historical perspective.

Colonial America was divided into three distinct geographic regions. The New England colonies were settled by religious dissenters who were, ironically, often intolerant of the views of others. Religion dominated the lives of these people, and the prevailing attitude toward games and sports was one of condemnation. The reward for toil and hard work was salvation; games and sports were a temptation that was the handiwork of Satan. In the Middle Atlantic colonies there was no religious uniformity. A variety of religions—Catholicism, Lutheranism, and Quakerism—were prominent. Strong religious prohibition of games and sports, while not absent in this region, was not as dominant as it was further north. In the early Southern colonies subsistence living left little time for leisure activities, but the plantation system which emerged changed lifestyles. With their one-crop economy and social structure of aristocrats at one extreme and slaves at the other, the Southern colonists exhibited a very heterogeneous sport pattern. Since many of the plantation owners were members of the liberal Anglican Church or other tolerant groups, games and sports were enjoyed by these Southerners without church disapproval.

In the first selection in this section, Foster Rhea Dulles outlines the attitudes toward games and sports in colonial America, with an emphasis on Puritanism in the New England colonies. He notes that even the Puritan oppression of sports was incapable of eradicating the natural urge to play. He concludes that the Puritan attitude has affected America's play patterns and still permeates our recreation attitudes.

Sports retained the form of informal games up to the late 1880's, when there was a virtual explosion of organized sports. Sports clubs, college and professional sports, and sports fads all combined to plunge Americans into an obsession with sports. In the second reading, Frederic Paxson discusses the sports activities of that era and probes into the various social influences that were responsible for this new burst of interest in sports. His article is an excellent work of social history, accentuating the influence of sport on society and vice versa.

In the last reading in this section Frederick Cozens and Florence Stumpf recount the evolution of American school sports. Until the beginning of this century, interschool sports at the high school and collegiate levels were organized and administered by the students themselves. The physical education programs of the latter nineteenth century were primarily calisthenics and gymnastic activities in content, with little provision for games and sports participation. By the early years of the twentieth century two trends produced the beginnings of elaborately organized interschool sports programs. The foreign gymnastic systems were rejected by physical educators and games and sports became the core of the physical education curriculum. The informal interschool sports programs of the nineteenth century gradually came under the direction of school authorities. These two developments laid the foundation for the sports programs in American schools. Cozens and Stumpf emphasize the societal environment in which school sports grew, and they stress how educators of the early twentieth century promoted sports for their potential for developing desirable citizenship traits. The authors also discuss some of the excesses and abuses of school sports, particularly college sports.

IN DETESTATION OF IDLENESS
Foster Rhea Dulles

The settlers who planted the first English colonies in America had the same instinctive drive for play that is the common heritage of all mankind. It suffered no sea change in the long and stormy crossing of the Atlantic. Landing at Jamestown, Sir Thomas Dale found the almost starving colonists playing happily at bowls in 1611.[1] The first Thanksgiving at Plymouth was something more than an occasion for prayer. Edward Winslow wrote that among other recreations the Pilgrims exercised their arms and for three days entertained and feasted the Indians.[2]

Against the generally somber picture of early New England life may also be set the lively account of those gay and wanton festivities at Merry Mount. To the consternation of "the precise separatists, that lived at new Plymouth," the scapegrace followers of Thomas Morton set up a May-pole, brought out wine and strong waters, and invited the Indians to join them:

Drinke and be merry, merry, merry boyes,
Let all your delight be in the Hymens joyes,
Joy to Hymen now the day is come,
About the merry Maypole take a Roome.
Make greene garlons, bring bottles out
And fill sweet Nectar freely about.
Uncover thy head and fear no harme,
For hers good liquor to keepe it warme.[3]

From Foster Rhea Dulles, *A History of Recreation: America Learns to Play,* 2nd ed. (New York: Appleton-Century-Crofts, 1965), Chapter 1. Copyright © 1965, Meredith Corporation. Reprinted by permission of Appleton-Century-Crofts, Educational Division, Meredith Corporation.

They spent several days, in William Bradford's disapproving phrase, "dancing and frisking togither, (like so many fairies or furies rather,) and worse practises."[4]

It was from these beginnings that American recreation grew to the varied and full activities we know today. They naturally open any record that would attempt to trace its growth and expansion under the changing conditions of American life. But it would be placing a greatly exaggerated emphasis on these simple sports and festivities to imagine that they were everyday occurrences. The first settlers actually had very little time or opportunity to play. Harsh circumstances fastened upon them the necessity for continual work. In the strange and unfamiliar wilderness that was America, "all things stared upon them with a weather-beaten face." The forest crowded against their little settlements along tidewater, and they felt continually menaced by its lurking dangers. None knew when the eerie war-whoop of the Indians might break the oppressive silence. Starvation again and again thinned their ranks, and disease was a grim specter hovering over each household. Merely to keep alive in a land which to their inexperience was cruel and inhospitable demanded all their energy.

The ruling powers, whether north or south, Puritan or Anglican, consequently found it at once necessary to adopt the strictest regulations "in detestation of idleness," to the end of enforcing work and prohibiting all amusements. Sir Thomas Dale sternly forbade further bowling at Jamestown and decreed that any tradesman unfaithful and negligent in daily attendance upon his occupation should be "condemned to the Galley for three years."[5] Governor Endicott of the Massachusetts Bay Colony cut down the May-pole at Merry Mount, gravely warning the revelers for the future "to looke ther should be better walking," and prepared rigorously to enforce the General Court's law that "no person, householder or other, shall spend his time idly or unprofitably, under paine of such punishment as the Courte shall thinke meet to inflict."[6]

It was the paramount need of a primitive, pioneer society for the whole-hearted cooperation of the entire community that fastened upon the first Americans a tradition of work which still weighs heavily upon their descendants. The common welfare in those difficult and perilous days could not permit any "mispense of time." Those who would not work of their own volition had to be driven to it under the lash of compulsion. Religion provided the strongest moral sanction for every law suppressing amusements. It was one of the vital forces making for a life in which recreation for long played hardly any part. But in all the colonies there was this basic fact: if the settlers did not direct all their energy to their work, they could not hope to survive.

Virginia originally enacted laws fully as restrictive as those of New England.[7] The Assembly in 1619 decreed that any person found idle should be bound over to compulsory work; it prohibited gaming at dice or cards, strictly regulated drinking, provided penalties for excess in apparel, and rigidly enforced Sabbath observance.[8] There was, for example, to be no admission of actors "because we resolve to suffer no Idle persons in Virginia."[9] Court records show that offenses against these laws were dealt with severely.[10] It was only as conditions of life became somewhat easier that enforcement grew lax. Once the colony was firmly established and the need for incessant work began to lessen, Virginians were more generally permitted to make the most of whatever opportunities for recreation their expanding life presented.

In New England, where the stern rule of Calvinism condemned idleness and amusements for their own sake, the tradition that life should be wholly devoted to work ("that noe idle drone bee permitted to live amongst us"[11]) held its ground more firmly. The magistrates attempted to suppress almost every form of recreation long after the practical justification for such an unrelenting attitude had disappeared. The intolerance of Puritanism was superimposed upon economic necessity to confine life in New England within the narrowest possible grooves. Massachusetts and Connecticut banned dice, cards, quoits, bowls, ninepins, "or any other unlawful game in house, yard, garden or backside," singling out for special attention "the Game called Shuffle Board, in howses of Common Interteinment, whereby much precious time is spent unfruitfully."[12] They listed "common Coasters, unprofitable fowlers, and Tobacko takers" as idlers subject to immediate punishment. No smoker in Connecticut could "take any tobacco publiquely in the street, nor shall any take yt in the fyelds or woods." His indulgence in a habit generally condemned as time-wasting was limited to the "ordinary tyme of repast commonly called dynner."[13]

Throughout New England, local ordinances further ordered the constables to "search after all manner of gameing, singing and dancing" and to report "disordered meetings" even when they were held in private homes.[14] John Cotton had condoned dancing under certain circumstances, reserving his disapproval with possible justification for "lascivious dancing to wanton ditties, and in amorous gestures and wanton dalliances," but his successors admitted no such subtle distinctions. The Devil was responsible for all dancing, and especially "Gynecandrical Dancing or that which is commonly called Mixt or Promiscuous Dancing of Men and Women."[15] When the Massachusetts General Court learned that the custom of dancing at weddings was growing up, it flatly decreed that there should be no more of it, then or at any other time.[16]

The theatre was of course absolutely prohibited. Connecticut was prepared to adjudge as common rogues and serve fifteen stripes on the bare back to anyone who should attempt to "set up and practice common plays, interludes, or other crafty science." Boston on one occasion refused permission for an exhibition of tight-rope walking "lest the said divertisement may tend to promote idleness in the town and great mispense of time."[17]

These laws represented a determination to promote industry and frugality; they also reflected the Puritan concept of the evil inherent in any frivolous waste of time. In one instance there was a curious conflict between these two motives. Toward the close of the period of the Great Migration, the popularity of the midweek church meeting, known as the Great and Thursday, began keeping many of the country people from their work. "There were so many lectures now in the country," John Winthrop wrote in 1639, "and many poor persons would usually resort to two or three in the week, to the great neglect of their affairs, and the damage of the public."[18] Here was one of the few breaks in the harsh routine of daily life that the early settlers experienced, a social function when there were no others. And while the lecture itself might be wearisome and dreary, at least for those to whom Calvinistic theology was not always completely absorbing, it offered a chance for neighborly gossip after the service and for the pleasure of seeing offenders against the Puritan code properly punished—placed in the stocks or whipped at the cart's tail. Consequently the colony's theocratic rulers found themselves in a difficult quandary. Attendance at these meetings could not be prohibited: it hardly fell under the head of idle or frivolous amusement. Nonetheless it represented, from a utilitarian viewpoint, a serious "mispense" of time.

It was first ruled, to prevent waste of a whole day, that lectures should not begin before one o'clock. Then the ministers were urged to hold fewer midweek meetings. And finally the order went out that the church assemblies should ordinarily break up in time to enable people who lived a mile or two off to get home before dusk. Nothing could be permitted that in any way would impair the spirit expressed in William Wood's dictum that aside from everything else "all New England must be workers in some kind."[19]

No such reason could be advanced to justify the vehement efforts of magistrates and elders to compel that strict observance of the Sabbath which they had made one of the cardinal articles of their stern faith. Religion stood its ground without economic support. The Lord's Day was to be wholly devoted to pious reflection upon the bounties of an all-wise Providence. Puritanism did not admit the idea that this one day free of work might possibly be enjoyed for itself.

Virginia had forbidden Sunday amusements in the early years of settlement. The laws of that colony, as applied by Governor Argall in 1618, made the penalty for failure to attend church service imprisonment in the guardhouse ("lying neck and heels on the Corps of Gard ye night following and be a slave ye week following") and strictly banned any Sabbath-day dancing, fiddling, card-playing, hunting, or fishing.[20] But while these laws soon fell into abeyance, New England's holy zeal in trying to turn the day into one of vacuous melancholy was not abated.

The strict prohibition of any Sunday labor, travel, or recreation was supplemented by specific bans on "all unnecessary and unseasonable walking in the streets and fields."[21] Application of this law was graciously limited to children over seven, but the Massachusetts General Court gave warning that this by no means implied that "we approve of younger children in evil."[22] In Connecticut the town of New London found occasion to hale John Lewis and Sarah Chapman into court "for sitting together on the Lord's Day, under an apple tree in Goodman Chapman's Orchard."[23] And there is the well authenticated case, cited by Charles Francis Adams, of the New England minister who refused to baptize children born on the Sabbath in the belief that they had been conceived on the Lord's Day, only to be confounded when his wife gave birth to Sabbath-day twins.[24]

Why had Puritanism developed such an intense disapproval of sports and games, popular amusements? Where had its stern insistence upon the sanctity of the Sabbath come from? In part these ideas stemmed from the religious dissenters of fourteenth-century England. The revolt of Wycliffe and the Lollards against the worldliness of the Anglican Catholic Church had been directed against all those diversions which the Church of that day freely countenanced. They symbolized in the eyes of these reformers the triumph of evil impulses over truly spiritual values; they could have no place in consecrated lives. But there was also a social bias, a class-conscious protest, in this condemnation of pleasure. The Lollards came from the lower classes—poor, hard-working, struggling to improve their position. They resented the pleasures of the rich—the landed nobility, the dissolute court circle, and the wealthier classes in the towns. It was an easy rationalization of this natural feeling to condemn as sinful the amusements they could not themselves enjoy.[25]

Some two centuries later the Puritans found themselves in very much the same position. They too were a party of reform, condemning the worldliness of the Church and damning as sinful many of the pleasures that the Church countenanced. They too resented the amusements of the more wealthy, leisured classes, making a moral issue of their discontent. These two influences, spiritual reform and economic envy, can never be disentangled. They were both present in the sixteenth and seventeenth centuries, and they have been present in every later-day manifestation of the Puritan spirit. The popular conception of this attitude is expressed in Macaulay's often-quoted phrase that the Puritans forbade bear-baiting, not because of the pain it caused the bear, but because of the pleasure it afforded the spectators. But it was rooted in the belief of a people who could not afford to waste time (they were dominated by their middle-class ideals of money-making, getting ahead) that any frivolous use of it was inherently sinful.

There was nothing in the original Calvinistic creed to justify the stern attitude that the Puritans assumed. John Knox once came upon Calvin himself playing at bowls, on a Sunday. So sincere a Puritan as Milton expressed again and again the most lively appreciation of all the joyous aspects of life in Merry England—the sports and games, the holidays

> When the merry bells ring round,
> And the jocund rebecks sound,
> To many a youth and many a maid,
> Dancing in the chequered shade.

But as the Puritans struggled to bring about the reforms they thought essential, they grew more and more scornful of the way of life of those who opposed them. Their disapproval of the moral laxity of the leisured classes of society soon covered all their diversions. Their foes jeered at them. On the anvil of persecution, disapproval was hammered into fanatical intolerance.

One of the most bitter sources of conflict between the Puritans and James I revolved around sports and Sabbath observance. Compulsory church attendance was a general rule in the early seventeenth century—not a Puritan invention; but after service the day was often given over to recreation—rough-and-tumble sports, morris-dances, interludes. Obsessed by an Old Testament interpretation of the meaning of the Sabbath, the Puritans took it upon themselves to condemn utterly this carefree enjoyment on the Lord's Day. There should be no sports or games, no dancing or interludes, no amusements whatsoever. They ascribed to God rules for keeping His day holy which were entirely born of their own intolerance.[26]

King James took up this challenge. In 1618 he issued a pronouncement, since known as the Book of Sports, declaring it to be the royal pleasure "that after the end of Divine Service, our good people be not disturbed, letted, or discouraged from any lawfull Recreation; Such as dauncing, either men or women, Archeries for men, leaping, vaulting, or other harmless Recreation,

THE KINGS
MAIESTIES
Declaration to His
Subiects,

CONCERNING
lawfull Sports to
be vsed.

LONDON

Printed by BONHAM NORTON,
and IOHN BILL, Deputie Printers
for the Kings most Excellent
Maiestie.

M.DC.XVIII.

nor from having of May-games, Whitson Ales, and Morris-dances, and the setting up of Maypoles and other sports therewith used. . . . But withall We doe accompt still as prohibited all unlawfull games to be used upon Sundayes onely, as Beare and Bull-baiting, Interludes, and at all times in the meaner sort of people by Law prohibited, Bowling."[27]

These were among the pastimes that Englishmen, and among them many of the prospective settlers of Jamestown and Plymouth, Maryland and Massachusetts Bay, were accustomed to enjoy. King James would have encouraged them by annulling Sabbath bans. "For when shall the common people," he asked, "have leave to exercise if not upon the Sundayes and Holidays, seeing they must apply their labour, and winne their living in all working days?" Nevertheless, when their day of power came in England, the Puritans had the Book of Sports publicly burned by the common hangman.[28]

In America, as we have seen, the Puritans took an equally intolerant stand. They had sought out the New World to escape persecution, abandoning the program of reform at home to found a Utopia across the seas. They were determined that here there should be no trace of worldliness. "God hath sifted a nation," William Stoughton declared, "that he might send choice grain into this wilderness."[29] Among these chosen people the pagan festivities, the licentious plays and spectacles, the violations of the Sabbath, the generally dissolute ways which were bringing ruin on England, would not be tolerated. There could be no evil in Zion. From the moment of their first landing on the shores of New England, the leaders of this seventeenth-century exodus set themselves implacably against the slightest infringement of their austere code.

So long as these ideals were allied with the practical necessities of life, so long as the condemnation of idle sports and games conformed to that paramount need for day-long labor on which the very survival of the early settlements depended, Puritanism served the colonies well. The strict rule of magistrates and ministers, for which they generously acknowledged the inspiration of God, emphasized the importance of work during a period when any turning aside toward an easier life might well have doomed New England. This debt to Puritanism is a primary fact in American history. But the rulers of Massachusetts Bay and Connecticut, unlike those of the other colonies, became more and more strict in their insistence upon these rigid rules of conduct as their economic justification gradually lessened.

Suppression became a fetish of the Calvinist mind in the New World. Having convinced themselves that all idle pursuits were a Satanic trap to lure the godly from the path of duty, strict followers of the New England way could no more tolerate frivolity than heresy. Their conscience would not let them enjoy worldly pleasures themselves; it would not let them permit others such enjoyment. The compulsion was equal in either instance. On Christmas Day of 1621, when the greater number of Plymouth colonists had gone about their usual tasks, Governor Bradford was shocked to discover a group of newcomers to that godly community "in the streete at play, openly; some pitching the barr and some at stoole-ball, and such-like sports." He promptly took away their "implements," telling them that while it might be against *their* conscience to work on Christmas, it was against *his* conscience that they should play.[30] New England's magistrates took it upon themselves to control with conspicuous zeal every activity of the people given over to their moral and spiritual guidance. When an opportunity to interfere in any way with other people's lives presented itself, they joyfully answered the still, small voice of duty.

The attitude of one member of this ruling hierarchy is graphically portrayed in the intimately self-revealing diary kept by Samuel Sewall in the last decade of the seventeenth century and opening years of the eighteenth.[31] Magistrate and elder, Judge Sewall was continually busy with moral problems, counseling others on what they should do and sorrowing over their departure from the narrow path of righteousness. "I was grieved," we find him writing a friend on one occasion, ". . . when I heard and saw you had drunk to excess; so that your head and hand were rendered less useful than at other times. . . . I mention this that you may believe I write not of prejudice, but kindness; and out of a sense of duty as indeed I do." Another time, when a party of revelers were drinking the Queen's health with too much enthusiasm, he went out in the middle of the night to remonstrate with them. They refused to go home. He took down their names in his little book—or rather, as he tells us, "not knowing how to spell their names, they themselves of their own accord writ them."[32]

Sewall thoroughly approved when Cotton Mather "struck at the Root, speaking against mixt Dances." He maintained an obdurate stand against the scandalous suggestion of allowing play-acting in Boston and vigorously combated the idea of any holiday festivities: "I took occasion to dehort mine from Christmas-keeping and charged them to forebear." When a dancing-master named Francis Stepney attempted to hold classes, he took a leading part in seeing that they were immediately prohibited. With testy ill-humor he noted "the great disorder in the town" when the English introduced the old sport of cock-skailing, or throwing sticks at a cock. "Jos. Mayhem carries a cock at his back, with a Bell in's hand, in the Main Street," he wrote scornfully; "several follow him blindfold, and under pretence of striking him

or's cock, with great cart whips strike passengers, and make great disturbance."[33]

Nevertheless he had his own simple pleasures. He thoroughly enjoyed
good food and wine: his diary bears frequent witness to his fondness for "rost
Beef and minc'd Pyes, good Cheese and Tarts," and he had a special liking for
black-cherry brandy with a lump of sugar in it. His appreciation of nature was
surprising. We find him noting happily that "the Singing of Birds is come,"
and of seeing "Six Swallows flying together and chipering very rapturously."
Another time he speaks of walking in a friend's orchard and getting quiet
enjoyment out of "pushing Catterpillars off the Appletrees." It is also
suddenly revealing to find in the memorable account of his courtship of
Madame Winthrop the passage where he tells his lady that he came to see her
only every other night for fear he would drink too deep draughts of
pleasure—"She had talk'd Canary, her kisses were to me better than the best
Canary."[34]

Other diversions more generally centered about the good judge's religious
life. He often went to service, gladly riding several miles to the Great and
Thursday at some outlying town, taking his wife, or perhaps his mother-in-
law, on the pillion behind him. He led what went for singing at his own
meetinghouse. There were only a few mournful repetitive tunes in the Puritan
repertory, to which were sung such strange distortions of the Psalms as

> Within their mouths doe thou their teeth
>   break out O God most strong,
> Doe thou Jehovah, the great teeth
>   break, of the lions young.

"I set York tune and the congregation went out of it into St. David's in the
very 2nd. going over," Sewall wrote in his diary one day. "This seems to
me an intimation and a call for me to resign the precentor's place to a better
voice. I have through the Divine long suffering and favor done it for 24
years."[35]

This upright man found real enjoyment in seeing punishments properly
administered, whether it was a whipping or a hanging, and he had that morbid
preoccupation with death which was one of the most unpleasing of Puritan
characteristics. He took a melancholy pleasure in serving as a pall-bearer at
funerals, making a great collection of the gloves and rings with which custom
decreed the pall-bearer should be rewarded. He was always happy to undertake this congenial task—unless he disapproved of the deceased's morals. But
the obsession with death found most startling expression in his account of
how he spent one Christmas. One of his daughters had recently died. Sewall

passed the day in the family tomb: "I was entertained with a view of, and converse with the coffins. . . . 'Twas an awful yet pleasing Treat."[36]

In these varied pleasures—spying upon one's neighbors, upholding public morals, going to church meetings, morbidly contemplating death—the Puritan leaders might find some compensation for the amusements of which they deprived themselves. But they could not possibly satisfy the needs of the humbler members of the community whose instinct for play could not so easily be eradicated. Even when these men and women in the ordinary walks of life were wholly in sympathy with the rule of the church, it was not enough for them to attend service and go to funerals. And increasingly large numbers of New Englanders were not Puritans. During the Great Migration even, between 1630 and 1640, only some four thousand out of sixteen thousand arrivals in Massachusetts Bay were church members. The rigid requirements for membership made it entirely possible for a majority even of the nonmembers to be in sympathy with the church, but nevertheless there was a dissident element in the colony from the very first. And it steadily grew as more and more people poured into New England whose motives for seeking the New World had nothing to do with religion.

In their zeal to maintain godliness, to enforce general conformity with their own principles of conduct, the magistrates failed signally to take this group into consideration. Whatever may be said for the first generation of Puritan leaders, their successors' inability to recognize the need of the people as a whole for a freer outlet to the normal urge for recreation was continually adding fuel to the discontent of the non-Puritans. They began to consider the restraints imposed upon them an intolerable burden. Worn out by the endless work on their little farms, discouraged by poor harvests, fearful of famine, plague, or Indian attack, they had to have some release for pent-up emotions, some way to forget the world.

Many of them—and this was true not only in New England but in all the colonies—found it in drinking. The tavern sprang up as naturally as the meeting-house, and the conviviality of the tap-room met a genuine need. They came of good drinking stock, these New World pioneers, and the early lack of malt and spirituous liquors had been for a time a great cause for complaint. It is revealing to find how proud one godly minister was because he had learned to drink water, and to note another worthy writing home that while he did not yet prefer water to good beer as some professed to do, "any man would choose it before Bad Beere, Wheay, or Buttermilk."[37] Nevertheless the Puritans did not allow any pernicious habit of water-drinking to take hold. Beer and cider were soon plentiful; rum became a New England staple. The taverns and ordinaries everywhere offered an engaging selection of drinks to gratify every taste.[38]

Drunkenness was a frequent consequence of their growing popularity. The early records show many cases of fines, confinement in the stocks, and public whippings for an overindulgence which the lower classes (the indentured servants, the apprentices, the laborers) could hardly avoid with rum at two shillings a gallon. Sometimes the penalty of public scorn was administered. "Robert Cole, having been oft punished for drunkenness," John Winthrop reports in his history of Plymouth (an anything but isolated case even for that sober community), "was now ordered to wear a red D about his neck for a year."[39]

The increase in drinking and its attendant evils was largely due to the lack of other entertainment and to the promotion by tavern-keepers of what was a very profitable business. By the middle of the seventeenth century the General Court was compelled to recognize that it had created a serious social problem. "How has Wyne and Cider, but most of all Rum debauched Multitudes of People," exclaimed the redoubtable Increase Mather. Viewing the fearful circumstances into which Connecticut had been brought, Cotton Mather somewhat later declared somberly that "the consequences of the affected Bottel, in that Colony, as well as in ours, are beyond Imagination."[40]

Many other instances might be cited to show the extent to which tavern drinking took the place of other amusements in these days of Puritan repression. One law deplored the growing custom whereby on pretext of going to midweek church meetings, men and women rode from town to town "to drinke and revell in ordinarys and tavernes." An irate clergy thundered the warning that "the Riots that have too often accompanied our Huskings have carried in them fearfull Ingratitude and Provocation unto the Glorious God."[41]

It may well be noted, however, that it was not in New England but in what has so often been called Cavalier Virginia that an attempt was made in the seventeenth century to enforce prohibition. For all his alarms, even Increase Mather accepted the need for taverns to sell liquor. "No sober Minister," he declared, "will speak against the Licensing of them."[42] But an Assembly dominated by Nathaniel Bacon passed a law, in 1676, taking their licenses from all taverns in Virginia except those at Jamestown and at the two main ferries on the York. These privileged ordinaries were permitted to sell beer and cider, but otherwise a fine of one thousand pounds of tobacco was to be imposed on anyone who sold "any sorte of drinke or liquor whatsoever to be drunke or spent in his or their house or houses, upon his or their plantations."[43]

It was not only in drinking that New England was breaking through the bonds of Puritan restraint. The diary of Samuel Sewall itself affords graphic evidence of the revolt against repression. Its accounts of the pageantry of Joseph Mayhew, parading through the streets of Boston with cock and bell; of attempts to stage plays and hold dancing-classes; of the celebration of Christmas festivities, all reveal a departure from the original severity of life in New England.

This is shown also in many of the laws that the magistrates found it necessary to pass after the middle of the seventeenth century. They are fully as indicative of what certain elements in the growing towns of New England were actually doing as of what their rulers were determined they should not do. Laws on the statute books often have this paradoxical significance. The future student of twentieth-century legislation will be quite justified in assuming that our prohibition laws reflected the popularity of drinking quite as much as they represented an authoritarian attempt to impose a dry régime. In the same way, much of the legislation of early New England forbidding tavern sports, card-playing, and dancing throws a penetrating light on how a very considerable number of the people were spending such free time as they had. Not the rulers and magistrates, but the everyday people of the Puritan world.

This is illustrated in successive edicts with respect to observance of the Sabbath. We learn from the statute books that on Saturday and Sunday young people were more and more freely taking "liberty to walk and sport themselves in the streets and fields ... and too frequently repair to public houses of entertainment and there sit drinking."[44] Finally it even became necessary to forbid, on Sunday and in the neighborhood of meeting-houses, "all shouting, hollowing, screaming, running, riding, singing, dancing, jumping, winding horns or the like."[45] Here are glimpses of a Puritan Sabbath oddly at variance with copy-book and historical legend. Some of the youths and maidens of old New England, for all the insistence of the godly that the Sabbath should be a day of peace and quiet, appear to have utilized it for a little restrained hell-raising in vociferous protest against the laws.

Indeed, at no time after the very first years of settlement was the New England scene actually as devoid of all amusements as it is so often said to have been. The Puritans have been depicted as a "crowd of sad-visaged people moving duskily through a dull gray atmosphere"; there social life has been termed "bare and spiritless beyond the possibility of description."[46] But this is to take at their face value the repressive edicts of the magistracy. It ignores the place in New England's life of the large number of its settlers who were non-Puritan in their sympathies and who could hardly be compelled by magisterial fiat to accept the idea that pleasure was synonymous with sin.

Those two stern guardians of public morals, Increase and Cotton Mather, had no doubts as to what was happening in the closing years of the seventeenth century. The iniquities of the younger generation were causing the glory of the Lord to depart from New England. "How many there are amongst us whose Fathers in coming into the Wilderness, designed nothing but Religion," declared Increase. "But *they* are for another Interest. Their Hearts are not but for the World. . . . That there is a general defection in New England from Primitive Purity and Piety in many respects is so plain that it cannot be denied." Cotton labored under no such restraints in characterizing the age. "Some of our Rising Generation," he stated, "have been given up to the most abominable Impieties of Uncleaness, Drunkeness, and a Lewd, Rude Extravagant sort of Behaviour. There are the Children of Belial among them, and Prodigies of Wickedness."[47]

The Mathers often found evil in what another age would freely condone. Many of their "prodigies of wickedness" would today go unrecognized under such a description. Their fierce onslaughts against the rising generation reflected a bitterness at their own departing glory as well as at the departing glory of the Lord. At the same time it was inevitable that reaction to the stern rule Puritanism attempted to impose should in some cases lead to extremes. For in forbidding so many forms of normal recreation the elders and magistrates had only served to confuse moral values. When they instituted such strict laws as to forbid, according to one traveler in Connecticut, "even a harmless Kiss or Innocent merriment among Young people,"[48] they were asking for trouble. Human nature could not be flouted with impunity, even by professed men of God.

Puritanism failed to eradicate the early Americans' natural urge for play. It brought on the inevitable revolt against attempted suppression of human impulses. Nevertheless it left a deep imprint on the mind of New England. And for all the growth of more liberal ideas as the power of the clergy and magistrates declined, some part of the old intolerance lingered on. The northern colonies were always more restricted in their diversions than the middle colonies or the South.

The spirit of Puritanism still has an important influence on our recreational life. Conditions have so greatly changed that our whole idea of leisure-time activities has been completely transformed. The suspicion with which church and state three centuries ago viewed all diversions in their common "detestation of idleness" has given way to the active encouragement and promotion of every form of healthful amusement. But there is certainly more than a trace of the old Puritanism, whatever other factors in a capitalistic society may enter the picture, in an attitude which so often views the increase in present-day opportunities for recreation as the "problem of leisure."

NOTES

1. Ralph Hamor, *A True Discourse of the Present Estate of Virginia*, London, 1615; reprint Richmond, 1860, 26.

2. Edward Winslow (December 11, 1621), quoted in Alice Morse Earl, *Child Life in Colonial Days*, New York, 1899, 217.

3. Thomas Morton, *The New English Canaan*, London, 1637; reprint *Prince Society Publications*, XIV, Boston, 1883, 279.

4. William Bradford, *History of Plymouth Plantation*, in J. F. Jameson (editor), *Original Narratives of Early American History*, New York, 1908, 238.

5. Peter Force, *Tracts and Other Papers*, 4 vols., Washington, 1836-46, III, 2, 16.

6. Bradford, *loc. cit.*, 238; *Records of the Court of Assistants of the Colony of Massachusetts Bay*, Boston, 1904, II, 37.

7. Alexander Brown, *The Genesis of the United States*, Boston, 1890, I, 70.

8. Edward Channing, *A History of the United States*, 6 vols., New York, 1905-25, I, 200.

9. Quoted in George C. D. Odell, *Annals of the New York Stage*, New York, 1927–, I, 3.

10. Philip Bruce, *Institutional History of Virginia in the Seventeenth Century*, New York, 1910, I, 528.

11. *Records of the Governor and Company of Massachusetts Bay*, Boston, 1853, I, 405.

12. *Ibid.*, II, 195; *Public Records of the Colony of Connecticut*, Hartford, 1850, I, 527.

13. *Records of the Court of Assistants ... of Massachusetts Bay*, II, 37; *Public Records of ... Connecticut*, I, 528.

14. See *Records of the Governor ... of Massachusetts Bay*, II, 70, 180; William B. Weeden, *Economic and Social History of New England*, Boston, 1890, I, 224-25; *Documents and Records Relating to the Province of New Hampshire*, Concord, 1867, I, 391; Walter F. Prince,

"An Examination of Peter's 'Blue Laws,' " *American Historical Association Annual Report*, 1898, 97ff.

15. *Massachusetts Historical Society Collections*, Ser. 2, Vol. X, 183-84,

16. *Records of the Governor . . . of Massachusetts Bay*, III, 224.

17. Gustavus Myers, *Ye Olden Blue Laws*, New York, 1921, 211; Arthur A. Hornblow, *History of the American Theatre*, Philadelphia, 1919, I, 24.

18. John Winthrop, *History of New England*, in J. F. Jameson (editor), *Original Narratives of Early American History*, New York, 1908, I, 325-27.

19. *Records of the Court of Assistants . . . of Massachusetts Bay*, II, 37; Alexander Young, *Chronicles of the First Planters of the Massachusetts Bay Colony*, Boston, 1846, 413.

20. Force, *Tracts*, III, 2, 10; Alexander Brown, *The First Republic in America*, Boston, 1898, 278; Bruce, *Institutional History of Virginia*, I, 37.

21. *Records of the Court of Assistants . . . of Massachusetts Bay*, III, 316-17; *Public Records of . . . Connecticut*, II, 280; *Documents . . . of New Hampshire*, I, 388.

22. *Records of the Court of Assistants . . . of Massachusetts Bay*, III, 316-17.

23. Frances M. Caulkins, *History of New London*, New London, 1895, 250.

24. Charles Francis Adams, "Some Phases of Sexual Morality and Church Discipline in Colonial New England," *Proceedings of the Massachusetts Historical Society*, Ser. 2, Vol. VI, 1891, 496.

25. See Thomas Cuming Hall, *The Religious Background of American Culture*, Boston, 1930, Chap. I.

26. Edward Eggleston, *The Beginnings of a Nation*, New York, 1897, 124-34.

27. *The King's Majesties Declaration to his subjects concerning Lawful Sports to be used*, London, 1618; reprinted Philadelphia, 1866.

28. H. D. Traill (editor), *Social England*, London, 1895, IV, 167.

29. See Cotton Mather, *Magnalia Christi Americana*, Hartford, 1820, I, 240, quoted in Thomas J. Wertenbaker, *The First Americans (A History of American Life, II)*, New York, 1929, 92.

30. Bradford, *loc. cit.*, 126-27.

31. Samuel Sewall, *Diary, Massachusetts Historical Society Collections*, Ser. 5, Vols. V-VII (1878-82), and in abridged form, Mark Van Doren (editor), New York, 1927. See also N. H. Chamberlain, *Samuel Sewall and the World He Lived in*, Boston, 1897.

32. Sewall, *Diary* (Van Doren edition), 218.

33. *Ibid.*, 24-25, 27, 46.

34. *Ibid.*, 22, 177, 209, 255-56, 263.

35. *Ibid.* (Massachusetts Historical Society edition), VII, 171.

36. *Ibid.* (Van Doren edition), 151, 138.

37. Alice Morse Earle, *Customs and Fashions in Old New England,* New York, 1893, 164*ff.*

38. *Ibid.,* 168*ff.;* Wertenbaker, *The First Americans,* 200*ff.*

39. Winthrop, *loc. cit.,* I, 120.

40. Cotton Mather, *Diary* (March 18, 1710-11), *Massachusetts Historical Society Collections,* Ser. 7, Vols. VII-VIII (1911-12), VII, 51.

41. *Records of the Governor ... of Massachusetts Bay,* V, 63, quoted in James Duncan Phillips, *Salem in the Seventeenth Century,* Boston, 1933, 244.

42. Quoted in Wertenbaker, *The First Americans,* 196.

43. *The Statutes at Large of Virginia, 1619–1792,* Philadelphia, 1823, II, 361. See also John A. Krout, *Origins of Prohibition,* New York, 1925, 6-7.

44. Quoted in Myers, *Ye Olden Blue Laws,* 147.

45. *Ibid.,* 158.

46. Earle, *Customs and Fashions,* 256; Weeden, *Economic and Social History,* I, 294.

47. Quoted in Wertenbaker, *The First Americans,* 196-97.

48. Sarah Kemble Knight, *Private Journal,* Albany, 1865, 50. For further discussion of this point see John Dunton, *Letters from New England,* Prince Society Publications, IV; Edward Ward, *A Trip to New England,* London, 1699; Charles Francis Adams, *loc. cit.,* 477-516; and Wertenbaker, *The First Americans,* 196-200.

THE RISE OF SPORT

Frederic L. Paxson

No people has passed through greater changes in a single lifetime than did Americans in the generation which saw the closing of the old frontier. Social groups that had been nearly homogeneous were broken up, and out of them were selected and combed specialized industrial colonies to be moved to town and driven before the machinery of economic change. The fathers of this

Frederic L. Paxson, "The Rise of Sport," *The Mississippi Valley Historical Review,* 4:144-168 (September 1917). Reprinted by permission.

generation had been a sober lot, unable often to bend without a break, living a life of rigid and puritanical decorum, interspersed perhaps with disease and drunkenness but unenlivened, for most of them, by spontaneous play. When Barnum started upon his long career as showman in 1835 he introduced Joice Heth, "nurse of General George Washington" and now "arrived at the astonishing age of 161 years;" but he was careful to add that she had been "a member of the Baptist church for upwards of one hundred years" and took pleasure in the conversation of the clergy.[1] Amusement was under suspicion of wickedness unless disguised as instruction; and sport was hard to find.

"I idled away the morning on Mr. Daniel Greenleaf's wharf," wrote Charles Francis Adams in his diary in 1843, after playing with his boys for a few hours; "perhaps this consumption of time is scarcely justifiable; but why not take some of life for simple enjoyments, provided that they interfere with no known duty?"[2] A few years later the genial Autocrat scolded at a portion of his fellow-countrymen: "I am satisfied that such a set of black-coated, stiff-jointed, soft-muscled, paste-complexioned youth as we can boast in our Atlantic cities never before sprang from loins of Anglo-Saxon lineage. . . . We have a few good boatmen, no good horsemen that I hear of, nothing remarkable, I believe, in cricketing, and as for any great athletic feat performed by a gentleman in these latitudes, society would drop a man who should run around the Common in five minutes."[3] Farther south, or farther west, if an Adams had criticized himself or a Holmes his neighbour, the showing might, in spots, have been less doleful; but neither in east nor west did America esteem the human body.[4] "The taste for athletic sports in America is not over fifteen years old," wrote a shrewd observer in 1869.[5] In 1886 some of our journals could still find "news" in Dr. Peabody's baccalaureate upon the text, "The temple of God is holy, which temple ye are."[6] But before the boys who heard this sermon reached middle life their world had changed.

On the first of March, 1909, there gathered in the White House without rebuke—almost without comment—a group selected not for purposes of state but for play alone.[7] An ambassador was there, a scout, a scientist, a soldier, and even a president of the United States, who addressed his guests as "men with whom at tennis, or hunting, or riding, or walking, or boxing, I have played; with whom I have been on the round-up, or in the mountains, or in the ranch country." Proctor's stealthy cougar, in bronze,[8] that the "tennis cabinet"[9] left behind them for their host, was a fair type of the new work and the newer play; of the art of Frederic Remington and the tales of Owen Wister, of a generation that had appraised the spiritual values of its play and that had settled itself into a new environment. Today a president dismisses an ambassador and goes off to golf, with all approving,

And, while studying closely his putts, to explore
The obscurity shrouding the roots of the war. [10]

So late as Arthur's day a vacation trip to the Rockies was a luxury, if not an indiscretion.

The various stages in that disappearance of the frontier that brought one American cycle to an end have been portrayed by various scholars, and Mr. Turner's part in that portrayal is, perhaps, the most distinguished feat in American historical scholarship in the last half century. The free lands were used up. The cow country rose and fell. The social safety valve was screwed down. But the explosion did not come. The reason for continued bearable existence under the increasing pressure generated in industrial society cannot yet be seen from all its sides; but one side is already clear: a new safety valve was built upon the new society. The rumblings and premonitory tremblings were not followed by disaster. The strikes of 1877 seemed to many to presage a revolution, and the anarchistic riots of 1886 appeared to be the first blow. But American society learned to give instead of crack. Perhaps its sense of humor helped to save. *Puck* began in 1877 its career as weekly emollient, cartoonists multiplied in every editorial shop, and *Life* in 1883 found it possible to combine knight-errantry and humor. Mark Twain was at his crest of popularity; not yet a sage, but always sane. Saved by its temper from immediate explosion, American society went to work to provide new outlets.

Between the first race for the America's Cup in 1851 and the first American aeroplane show of February last, the safety valve of sport was designed, built, and applied. Between the organization of the oldest of the major leagues—the National league of baseball clubs—in 1876, and the earliest golf tournament in the United States, in 1894, the progress and development were rapid. Between the first meet of the League of American Wheelmen in 1880, and the first national tournament of the United States Lawn Tennis Association in 1881, on one hand, and the interdict launched in 1888 by the Amateur Athletic Union against amateurs who dared participate in unauthorized games or meets, the growing pains of a society which was entering almost monthly upon a new pastime were mingled with the soreness of its muscles as it undertook, on ever broader scale, baseball, cricket, bicycling, tennis, and roller skating; polo, racing, coaching, field sports, and canoeing; gymnastics, curling, boxing, hunting, and archery. To enumerate them all would take the space of a sporting cyclopedia; to describe them all would emphasize the fact that in nearly every one wholesale participation and adoption came between the years of the centennial in Philadelphia and the world's fair in Chicago. [11] Together they constitute the rise of sport.

Spectators' sports found lodgment in American society earlier than did those in which participation is the price of enjoyment. Racing and boxing can be traced through the first years of the republic with a train of admirers behind each champion. In his old age Diomed, who had won the initial Derby at Epsom Downs in 1780, came to America[12] to breed a great family of racing horses on a Virginia stock farm; other victors followed him to re-invigorate the strain, and from time to time Americans aroused one side of national pride as they endeavored to grasp the Derby stakes. Iroquois did this at last in 1881, for Pierre Lorillard,[13] his owner; and in 1907 Richard Crocker's Kentucky-bred Orby[14] did it again. Racing that could produce such finest flowers developed an American establishment that grew almost beyond control.

The opening of the American Jockey Club[15] at Jerome park, on the old Bathgate farm at Fordham in 1866, was an epoch for the American turf.[16] Through the next decade it seemed as though the horses were coming to own America. Trotting for the humbler at the county fairs, and running races over the great courses near the cities, drew mighty audiences. But the spectators who had made possible this high exploitation killed it in the end. The gamblers and the cheap sports brought racing into disrepute, and before the Coney Island Jockey Club[17] held its inaugural meeting in 1879 the game was outlawed by conservative society. Yet its evil profits kept it alive during the eighties—through six hundred and one races run in the vicinity of New York in ninety-five days in 1888[18]—until at last the legislature and the constitution[19] were invoked against it. But Maud S. and her successors,[20] and Nancy Hanks before her pneumatic-tired sulky,[21] made a place in the American imagination that called for something else to fill it when the race course had run through its day.

Trotting and racing had gathered their crowds and stirred the blood, but they produced no sentimental symbol equal to the America's Cup, with which, wrote Caspar Whitney, "there is no trophy in all the world of sport to compare . . . in point of age or distinction."[22] The American clipper ship knew no superior in the forties of the last century,[23] and one of its fleet took away the Queen's Cup from Cowes and the royal yacht squadron[24] in the year of the London exposition, 1851.[25] This feat quickened a nation's feelings on either side of the Atlantic, though no challenger came to America to take it back for nineteen years. Then, with the *Cambria* in 1870 a series of adventurers began to seek the trophy guarded by the New York Yacht Club, its custodian.[26] On the eve of the great war, Sir Thomas Lipton was arranging for the fourth time to try to take the prize. Dunraven had preceded him; and he the *Thistle* (1887), and the *Galatea* (1886), and the *Genesta* (1885), and the *Atlanta* (1881), and the *Countess of Dufferin* (1876), and the *Livonia* (1871), in a gallant succession of vain attempts. Four times in the eighties and thrice each in the seventies and nineties did the autumn races off New York renew the interest, with an ever-widening circle acquainted with the skipper, learned on the points of sail and beam, and ready to debate measurement, centerboard, or keel. And in the intervals between the races they could turn to wrangle over the prospects for Richard Fox's diamond belt.

This diamond belt was designed to adorn the heavyweight champion of the world, and was the donation of Richard K. Fox, editor of the *Police Gazette*. It followed a precedent that had, in another sport, uncovered the financial possibilities behind the promotion of great spectacles. All through the seventies there had been occasional matches between professional long-distance pedestrians; but these had grown into disrepute through the quarrels of promoters and the trials of referees, who fell foul of the question. What is a walk? In a single issue, in 1879, the *New York Sun* noted that Miss Lulu Loomer, clad in black silk tunic and sky-blue hose, was walking 3000 quarter miles in 3000 quarter hours in a public hall; that Van Ness and Belden were at work on a six-days' race in the Fifth regiment armory; and that in Cooper Hall, Jersey City, a similar test was under way.[27]

Sir John Astley had already tried to reduce pedestrian chaos to matters of record by offering, in 1878, a purse of £500 and a championship belt worth £100 more to the winner of a six-days' test, go-as-you-please. In the Agricultural Hall at Islington this was first walked off and won by one O'Leary, a Chicago Irishman, already well-known, who now established a six-day record of five hundred and twenty miles.[28] The trophy was contested again in October, 1878, and three times in the following year. An English walker named Rowell captured it in March, 1879; Edward Payson Weston, an American, took it from him in the following June, and defended it in Madison Square Garden for six days in the following September.[29] Weston had raised the record to five hundred and fifty miles, but Rowell won back the belt this time in a field of thirteen contestants. No new record was made, but for the whole week crowds gathered round the course to smoke and bet and encourage the various entries, and similar contests continued to draw their throngs for many years. Only recently Weston, hearty still on his seventy-first birthday,[30] walked from New York to San Francisco in one hundred days, though the Astley belt has left the sporting recollection.

The Fox diamond belt indicates a revival of the manly art after two decades of well-deserved oblivion. The last great fight that Americans of the centennial decade could remember was fought in a meadow at Farnboro, near London, for thirty-six rounds, on April 17, 1860. Here Heenan, the American, and Sayers, the English champion, fought to a draw in a turf ring, with twenty-one London "pugs" as ringkeepers, who let the ring break in before the American could knock out his opponent.[31]

The recollection of the Heenan-Sayers fight endured through years when pugilists failed to hit each other, until a new slugger with a genius for advertising appeared within the ring. This was John L. Sullivan, born in Boston in 1858, who emerged as a driving fighter about 1881. In February, 1882, he won from Paddy Ryan the title of champion of America,[32] and for the next ten years was as popular a sporting character as the world possessed. The leather football that Mike Donovan,[33] boxing instructor of the New York Athletic Club, had adapted to new use as a punching bag spread its vogue once it had trained this champion.[34] Audiences repeatedly crowded Madison Square Garden when Sullivan was announced to box, and the paragraphers treasured his words uttered in his cups or sober. "The worship of brute force," wailed Leslie's newspaper, had filled the boxing schools of New York. "Let prize-fighters be once more regarded as outlaws, and not as public 'entertainers,' "[35] it urged; but when Sullivan went to England in 1887, he and Buffalo Bill and the Prince of Wales competed on easy terms for space.

The reluctance of fighters to fight was well dispelled by 1887. In this year Jake Kilrain fought Jem Smith for one hundred and six rounds in France, but only to a draw which left the ownership of the new diamond belt in doubt, since this was offered for a finish fight.[36] Sullivan, who had been boxing to huge audiences in the English music halls, and who had been received by the Prince of Wales,[37]—much, it is said, to the mortification of the queen, then celebrating her jubilee—trained now at Windsor, and in March, 1888, fought Charley Mitchell to a thirty-six-round draw near Chantilly. It was a single-handed bout, for the American broke his right arm in the fifth round, and could only defend himself with his left for the rest of the fight.[38] "There is hardly a more disreputable ruffian now breathing than this same Sullivan," commented the *New York Tribune,* "but with all his brutality, his coarseness, and his vices, he certainly is not afraid of meeting any living man with bare fists."[39] Early in 1889 he and Kilrain agreed to fight for $20,000, the title, and the belt; and this time there was no draw, for Sullivan battered his way to a knockout at Richburg, Mississippi, on July 8.[40] They talked of running him for congress on the Democratic ticket now; but he went on a boxing tour to Australia instead, and came back to lose his title to a new winner, James J. Corbett, in 1892.

How Corbett's science won the title and maintained it until Robert Fitzsimmons ended his reign; how Fitzsimmons was finally worsted by Jim Jeffries; and he by Johnson, and he in turn by Willard would bring the boxing story down to date. But none of his successors has equalled Sullivan in his popular appeal, and it was his gold-mounted rabbit's foot, for luck, that Colonel Roosevelt carried through his African trip in 1909.[41] Sport had a new appeal to the city crowds of the eighties, and the promoters catered to it. The periodic crises of the races and the fights were interspersed by the meetings of the national game, baseball.

The major leagues and the shoal of minor leagues that today control the formal side of baseball, with permanent million dollar parks,[42] with a president of the United States to throw the first ball of a season, with over seven million paid admissions to the major leagues alone within a single year,[43] represent an institution that is far removed from the game of ball as it was played by a few private clubs after the Mexican war, and from the earliest of its organizations, the national association of baseball players, of 1858.[44] It seems to have been the Civil War that brought potential nines together and nationalized the game. Men who might have joined the militia regiments for exercise or recreation before the war played baseball around the cities, after it. The Cincinnati Red Stockings, a strictly professional team, discovered the financial possibilities of the game in 1869. A national association of professional baseball players emerged in 1871, but its base of organization was faulty, and no financially successful scheme appeared for five years more.[45]

In February, 1876, William A. Hulbert of Chicago, and A. G. Spalding, a prominent professional of Boston, having signed up a strong team for the approaching season made a workable machine for the furtherance of their profits and the game. At the Grand Central Hotel, in New York, they organized the National League of Baseball Clubs, the parent league of today, with eight member teams: Boston, Hartford, Chicago, St. Louis, Louisville, Cincinnati, the Mutuals (New York), and the Athletics (Philadelphia).[46] The transition from an association of players to a league or partnership of managers gave a firm basis to the sport. It was, indeed, only a spectators' sport. With only changes in detail the scheme continues workable. A second league branched off in 1882 as the American Association; a Federal league and various brotherhoods or fraternities have followed it. But baseball as a producer's business in the larger cities has not been shaken. Spalding's Chicago team won the pennant year after year. The pitched ball changed from a toss to a throw, an arsenal of mitts, shields, and masks evolved, and in 1888-1889 Spalding's baseball tour around the world introduced the full-grown national game to other countries.[47] The umpire became a recognized butt for the comic papers. And at last the sedate editor of the *Atlantic Monthly Almanac,* confident that all his readers can understand the lingo, adorns the opening baseball date of 1917 with the alleged oriental maxim, "There are no fans in Hell."

Baseball succeeded as an organized spectators' sport, but it did also what neither racing nor boxing could do in turning the city lot into a playground and the small boy into an enthusiastic player. The cigarette pictures of leading players that small boys of the eighties collected by scores indicate at once their interests and their naughty habits. Like cricket in England, baseball became a game for everyone.

Cricket, indeed, had been played around Boston and New York and chiefly Philadelphia, since the English factory hands had brought it to Kensington and Germantown in the middle forties. The late Dr. S. Weir Mitchell remembered to have played a full-fledged game in 1845[48]; and ever after this there was at least one Newhall to play in Philadelphia,[49] and a growing list of cricket clubs. From time to time an inter-city game enlivened the mild sport; then a visit from Canadian players; then an imported English team that with eleven ordinary veterans could retire an American team of twenty-two without batting out its second innings. But in September, 1885,[50] though cricket was "still an exotic in the United States," a team of eleven Philadelphians beat eleven Britishers for the first time at their own game. The interest of the spectator was being translated into proficiency in sport.

Indoors and out-of-doors city growth and changing habits lured more men to exercise. The notion of participation for the fun there was in it, or for the physical advantage entailed, was more widely spread before the Civil War than the existing records would indicate; but it was scant enough. The Young Men's Christian Association, an importation of the early fifties, had begun to group its charges and to see the various sides of the new problem they raised. Their city buildings, undertaken in the later sixties, included room for gymnasiums[51] as well as chapels and class rooms; and their directors taught gymnastics, upon a basis resembling that of the German immigrants, exhibited through their turner societies a dozen years before.

Father Friedrich Ludwig Jahn and his gymnastic educational revival had done much for German nationalism and democracy before the revolutionary movements of 1848 brought it under suspicion and drove many of its leaders into more or less involuntary exile. Into America the Germans came with common resentments and with familiarity with this bond that might hold them together and cheer their hearts as they struggled against nativistic critics in a strange land.[52] Singing, playing, exercising, drinking their beer together on Sunday evenings, they had immediately started turner societies and had formed a turnerbund with more than one hundred and fifty member societies before the Civil War.[53] Many of these societies marched to the front with ranks almost untouched by failure to enlist, and more than one German regiment paid for shelter and hospitality with all it had to give. In the winter of 1864-1865 the league reorganized as the Nordamerikanischer Turner-bund,[54] and since that day its athletic festivals and congresses have at once broadened the influence of comradeship and kept the German-Americans in contact with their common past. A team of Milwaukee turners invaded the fatherland in 1880 and carried off the trophies of a general meet at Frankfort-on-Main[55]; while the twenty-third festival at St. Louis[56] opened the next year with 20,000 people on the fairground.

The growing wealth of cities, the appearance of a class of men with leisure, and the consequences of sedentary life could not have failed to develop organized provision for play nor to induce young men to start athletic clubs in increasing numbers. The greatest of the clubs was organized in 1868 in New York, and rented a field for athletic games that soon gave fame to Mott Haven, on the Harlem River. This was the New York Athletic Club,[57] whose growth and expansion would alone illustrate and typify nearly the whole of modern sport. For almost twenty years it flourished on the stern diet of athletics, and only athletics. Its boathouse, its track, and its field became the center of general sport, while at its various annual games young athletes accumulated records that ought to have gladdened the heart of Dr. Holmes.

In 1876, after the New York Athletic Club had held its own seventh annual spring meet, it devised a novelty and held the first open amateur handicap field meeting in America.[58] Already the Intercollegiate Athletic Association had been organized to regulate the play of college boys, and had conducted its first games at Saratoga.[59] But the New York open games represented a new principle possible only because sport was becoming universal, and necessary because definitions and standards were so unsettled as to imperil sport itself. Out of these open games there grew, under the patronage of the New York Athletic Club, the National Association of Amateur Athletics of America, an organization without a plant of its own, and aspiring to govern sport. In 1888, after a dispute in this association,[60] from which the New York Athletic Club had withdrawn its countenance, and which the Intercollegiate Athletic Association was ready to desert,[61] the greatest of the Philadelphia clubs, the Athletic Club of the Schuylkill Navy, took steps to create the Amateur Athletic Union.[62] The new union held a first meet at Detroit in September, 1888,[63] and was a success from the beginning. In its first summer, August 25, 1888, it faced the country courageously—insolently, some thought—and resolved that any amateur participating in unauthorized games should thereby disqualify himself as entry in games controlled by the Amateur Athletic Union.[64] This union and other governing bodies are still defining the amateur and adjusting the terms of his competitions; but this interdict of the athletic protestant—or infidel—is a high mark in the rising tide.

Long before the Amateur Athletic Union had been conceived, its parent outgrew its primitive athletic plant and, stimulated by its own needs and the rivalry of eager imitators, had come into town with a great athletic club house. In 1885, with William R. Travers as president and Herman Oelrichs as financial backer, the New York Athletic Club opened its own building at Sixth avenue and Fifty-fifth street; three years later it opened a country home on Travers Island; and in 1896 it moved up Sixth avenue to a larger city palace on Fifty-ninth street.[65] Meanwhile its development had been paralleled in Philadelphia by the Athletic Club of the Schuylkill Navy, whose rowing had grown into general athletics and produced the Arch street club house in 1889.[66] In Boston the athletic club boasted among its members Henry L. Higginson and John Boyle O'Reilly, and opened modern quarters in 1888.[67] In Chicago the building on Michigan avenue was regarded as the last word in athletic architecture when it opened in 1893.[68] In smaller towns and among poorer athletes, where marble palaces were out of question, where the Young Men's Christian Association or the turnverein or the local school or college might be the agency, the athletic club was extending its stimulation deep into the social body.

The increasing organization of sport tells one side of the story; the invention of new activities the other. The mechanical genius of one Plimpton, about 1863,[69] made roller skating possible and bred a mania that first infected Australia, then Europe, then America, and that raged, an intermittent epidemic, for a generation. Tools of the game were cheap; skill was not hard to acquire; but the rinks in which to skate controlled the sport. The Brooklyn rink, long to be famous as a political meeting place, was opened in 1877. On the future site of the Auditorium Hotel, Chicago had one in 1880; and A. G. Spalding opened another in the same city in 1884.[70] There was a great Olympia rink in New York, on Fifty-third street, in 1885. At this time, according to one estimate, there was $20,000,000 of skating rink property in America,[71] and the capacity of these was supplemented many fold by the new concrete sidewalks and the asphalt pavements that invited the small boy to "hitch behind" and risk his neck. A six-day skating race in New York in 1885 produced a record of 1,090 miles.[72] Women and girls adopted the pastime, while their elders "viewed with alarm" the demoralization of the growing generation. Boxwood, the material for skate wheels, in the preferable three-inch growth, rose from thirty-eight to one hundred and twenty dollars a ton under the demand of manufacturers, and far-off Persia and Turkey, where this wood grew, benefited by the craze.[73]

Nearly twenty years before skating thus literally carried its devotees off their feet, another epidemic had "swept over our land," "the swiftest and most infectious" yet, croquet.[74] To the rules and definitions of this game the *Nation* devoted a long article in 1866. In England three years later, writes Alfred Austin, it was "in the heyday of its popularity."[75] Like roller skating, its paraphernalia was simple and readily set up anywhere, and as a courting game few have surpassed it. It produced in time its experts who, in 1879, gathered in Chicago at "the first national convention of croquet players ever held in this country,"[76] to debate "loose" against "tight" methods and to formulate its laws. Such a useless gathering, regretted the *Chicago Times,* was a "severe commentary upon our civilization;" but whether because of the prize tournament mallet offered by A. G. Spalding or because the game had merit of its own, croquet declined to disappear. At Norwich, Connecticut, the National Croquet Association built its tournament grounds, and here year after year a handful of persistent players reduced the game to one of nice skill, similar to nothing less than billiards.[77] And everywhere croquet, like roller skates, became part of the education of the child.

The wooden-wheeled, iron-tired "bone-shaker" bicycle of the Civil War decade brought zest to life at yet another spot. Charles de Drais[78] had experimented with his "draisena" early in the century, and Pierre Lallement[79] had built and ridden a bicycle in Paris in 1863. Thereafter where roads and nerve permitted the old high bicycle gained its advocates and, with velocipede and tricycle, tempted even an occasional girl to learn to ride. A clipping from a scrap book of 1869 celebrates the early sporting girl:

> But I am of the Yankee sort,
> A gutta-percha lady sport,
> Fair and tough, and fast and strong
> And hold to my paces all day long. . .
> Stir the dust and take the shoot,
> Pantalettes and gaiter-boot.
> Houp la! houp la!—needn't try
> To find a lovelier wretch than I.

As the seventies advanced the bicycle became a tool of delicate grace, with a fifty-one-inch wheel weighing thirty pounds,[80] although the general public still found interest in articles telling how to pronounce the word.[81] Colonel A. A. Pope, of Hartford, imported several of the English machines in 1878 and then began to build his own Columbia bicycles[82]; and here and there enthusiasts began to organize clubs to ride together, and even held their race meets by 1879. Riding academies multiplied,[83] often using armories or skating rinks, and park commissioners were exasperated by appeals to permit citizens astride their wheels to use the public drives. Horses started upon the long course of nervous education that the motor car has finished. And on May 31, 1880, there met at Newport delegates from twenty-nine bicycle clubs who there organized the League of American Wheelmen and held their first parade.[84]

Bicycling is unique among the sports in the extent to which participation was on an individual basis and in the degree to which individuals joined in the national organization. The annual meets of the League of American Wheelmen were of increasing interest for twenty years, both as sporting events with fast and furious racing, and as social gatherings to which members and their families went as for a sporting vacation. *Wheeling*, a monthly magazine, appeared as organ of the sport in 1882, and still continues, with enlarged scope, as *Outing*. Thomas Stevens crossed the continent a-wheel in 1884,[85] and soon after made his memorable trip recorded in *Around the world on a bicycle.*[86] There were supposed to be thirty thousand bicycles in the United States in 1885[87] and twelve thousand members of the league by 1889; and this while the old high wheel was the one most generally used.

The safety bicycle—chain driven, with wheels of equal size—appeared in the catalogs of 1887, and with the pneumatic rubber tire[88] that was soon devised, opened new worlds to be conquered. By 1898 the league had over one hundred thousand paying members[89] and women had taken their great step toward equal treatment by free participation with the men. After 1900 the league collapsed, but it had widened the effective radius of life, quickened sluggish blood for both sexes and all ages, and reawakened a love for out-of-doors that city dwellers had begun to lose.

Contemporary with wheeling was lawn tennis, fit for both sexes, anywhere and at all ages, and invented at about the same time. In 1881 the United States Lawn Tennis Association[90] was organized and held its first national tournament at Newport, under conditions resembling those which surrounded the Wimbledon grounds of the All England Lawn Tennis Club, then five years old. The game was first played in America not earlier than 1875,[91] but its conquest was sweeping and complete. On private lawns, in newly-organized clubs, on the commons by the country schoolhouse, even on the unused side of at least one burying ground, the nets were stretched and the game begun. By 1890 the women had a national championship tournament of their own[92] and in another decade an American girl invaded England and there held her own against all comers. International matches were an annual feature of the game, and city, state, sectional, and national championships covered the country with their nets. Three hundred tournaments authorized[93] for 1916 by the United States Lawn Tennis Association give a measure for the most perfect of the participating sports.

The love of outdoor sports, spreading each year into new regions and new classes, worked on whatever materials it could find. Florida became a playground, opening its west coast to the rich in winter when the Plant system completed its line to Tampa in 1885.[94] Theodore Roosevelt, of an active family whose name is to be found in the initial lists of nearly every sport that I have seen, bought his ranch on the Little Missouri in the early eighties.[95] Here he rode the roundup and hunted outlaws, and less dangerous wild game, consciously building a frame to carry burdens. Here he saw the cow country in its final phase, and hence he went to write *The Winning of the West*. In December, 1887, at a private dinner, he and his outdoor friends organized the Boone and Crockett Club[96] for the study and conservation of big game, naming it for the great pathfinders for whom game was no luxury and hunting not a sport. The saving of the Yellowstone Park[97] was one of the early public services of this club, the founding of the New York Zoological Society was another. The love of open country for hunting, camping, hiking, and the respect for common interests that all this entailed were not accidental products of our decade. They came directly from the swelling national interest.

Not every American could take time to hunt big game, or watch it, or to commune with remote nature, but the opportunity for something out of doors was demanded and provided. The rise of the country club is a feature of the later eighties. The institutions that were competent to grow into the country club where the environment was right for evolution were already provided. Here and there an older club could be made over. The old Staten Island Cricket and Baseball Club built a new home with full outdoor equipment in 1886.[98] The Essex County Hunt opened the Essex County country club in 1888.[99] The New York Athletic Club, always partially out-of-doors, finished its complete home and playground on Travers Island in the same year. A Boston country club, with grounds near Brookline, emerged from a racing group in 1887. But the country club that served as text for the most discussion was opened in 1886 on Pierre Lorillard's ancestral estate on Ramapo mountain under the control of the Tuxedo club.[100] At Tuxedo was a resident suburban colony club, where members could build their own cottages and use a clubhouse more elaborate than the old casino at Newport, and with "an aggressively English air" that suggested the country life of a society that wealthy Americans liked to imitate. It was socially exclusive and highly expensive, and novel enough to furnish paragraphs for many years. It represented one of the three clear types toward which the country clubs tended to standardize for thirty years.

"Fifteen years ago," wrote Robert Dunn in 1905, "country clubs seemed fads, were confined to the East, and associated with the somewhat un-American and unrelaxed atmosphere of what one hears called 'society,' "[101] but they served a need too broad to be so circumscribed. Some were the country toys of city men, who hurried out of town when work was done, who often slept at the club house, and who were as nearly unconscious of the local world around the grounds as possible. Such was Travers Island for the New York Athletic Club. Others became the foci for suburban colonies. Like Tuxedo, and in simpler imitations of it, their members chose to live and rear their children within walking and driving distance of the playground; and the ladies' clubhouse and the junior annex became as important as the club itself. Still others were acclimated in the country towns, used without pretense, recruited with little or no parade of society or exclusion, and became as true an organ of local life as the high school or the board of commerce. The community of 20,000 without a country club became an anomaly requiring explanation.

The roots of country clubs sprang from the older games, and were strengthened by tennis and bicycling that widened their opportunity and their availability. But most of all they multiplied from the impetus given by a new game that must be played over the open country if at all, the royal game of golf.

The beginnings of the game of golf, with the leather ball[102] stuffed with feathers, are doubtless based "upon the desire of the Anglo-Saxon to arm himself with a stick and drive a small round body with it,"[103] but they are lost in the antiquity that conceals, perhaps, the common parent of all games of ball. Old prints and casual references carry the game back for several centuries in England and Scotland,[104] but Americans are not known to have played it in the United States before the later eighties. A writer in *Harper's Weekly,* in 1891,[105] prophesied that it was likely to take foothold here, but had few facts of playing to produce. The nine-hole course at Southampton, in the Shinnecock Hills, was open to play in 1892,[106] while Mr. H. C. Chatfield-Taylor remembers to have played a game over a primitive private course at Lake Forest in the same year.[107] The attractions of the game distributed it from the cities out into the country, and middle age came into its own. The playing season of 1895 was memorable for the new courses over lumpy greens, and for the shoal of old clubs that added golf and new clubs that organized to play it. In Newport the casino acquired a healthy rival in the country club. Already, in 1894, five of the pioneer clubs had organized the United States Golf Association,[108] whose annual meetings and expanding membership brought the rules and players under firm control.[109] And the environs of the cities became embroidered with the turfs and costumes of the new adoption.

It would be easy to overstate the significance and influence of single factors in the change that has altered the old American life beyond recovery or reconstruction, but not the change itself. "The great development and wide diffusion and practice of athletic exercises among our people during the last quarter of a century (this diffusion taking place precisely among those classes where the need of it was greatest)," observed Colonel Roosevelt in 1893, "has been a very distinct advantage to our national type."[110] In proportion as inducement appeared for city folk to go afield mechanical devices speeded up their going. One decade saw the opening of the Brooklyn Bridge, and the beginnings of the perennial fight for rapid transit; the next saw the electric trolley quicken the circulation on city streets and gladden the hearts of promoters of suburban real estate additions; the third is memorable for the extended use of motor cars.

Today there are a few of us who own no Ford, but all are rapidly forgetting the time two decades back when only experimental cars existed, when the debate between steam and gasoline was real, and when the horseless carriage was a carriage, not a car. In January, 1900, New York held its first American automobile show, following the several years' precedent of the bicycle shows. And since that time the physical habits of society have undergone a revolution. Part of this change is chronicled and photographed in *Country Life in America,* appearing first in 1901; more of it is still a part of our unrecorded recollection. The body of man has been freed from the restrictions of space and time; his soul has occupied new realms of nature and of play. No earlier president[111] than Colonel Roosevelt would have denounced a tribe of "nature fakers,"[112] and no earlier generation would have cared or even understood.[113] Only the invention of a portable camera made it practicable for ordinary persons to see life as it really is.[114]

Such are the partial facts to illustrate the major currents in the rise of sport. They might be enlarged to include the college games, and football with its ups and downs. They might embrace the timely subject of marksmanship, and relate the facts about the Creedmoor range and the local and international matches of the National Rifle Association, which opened there in 1873.[115] They might tell of the coaching revival that paraded down Fifth avenue for the first time in 1876[116]; or of Bennett's introduction of polo[117] in the same year. They might mention the National Archery Association that tried to revive the Anglo-Saxon affection for the long bow, and that opened its series of national tournaments in Chicago, at the White Stockings park, before "quite a large and certainly a very select audience" in 1879.[118] They might recall the gathering of campers who had learned the charms of the Indian canoe, and formed the American Canoe Association at Lake George in 1880,[119] and continued for years, in camping meets, to profit by and popularize all water sports.

They might from a different angle record the interests of collectors and owners that turned the successive buildings at Madison Square Garden into the custody of sporting shows and gave to St. Gaudens's gold Diana on the tower a real significance as goddess of the newer chase. In 1895 a series of annual sportsmen's expositions was begun, to amuse the crowds and display the dealers' wares.[120] Already other shows had prepared the way for this. Greatest of all was the horse show, that began in 1883 to aid in defining classes and improving breeds of horses, and that took at least a decade to teach exhibitors and judges genuine types.[121] There had been a dog show— first of a long series—by the Westminster Kennel Club in 1877,[122] on whose benches the uninspiring pug gave way to the terriers and collies[123] of later preference, and in whose chambers exhibitors debated the merits of "bat" and "rose-bud" ears.[124] A poultry show appeared in these same precincts in 1887,[125] with a toy dog show in an annex[126]; and a cat show in the spring of 1895 was "an epoch in the history of the cat in America."[127]

There can be no question as to there having been this rise of sport. It obtrudes from the sources of the eighties, and had created in the daily press the clean-cut sporting page before 1890, giving sharp contrast to the papers of the seventies where sport was only general news, and thin at that. In nearly every game we play today there is evidence that between 1876 and 1893 playing expanded on a widening scale, and organization made its government quasi-national. A new generation appeared taking all this for granted, and living the rounded life unconscious of a change.

It was the open frontier that kept America young during its first century of national existence. Year after year the continuous pressure from the newer states, noisy, ill-informed, but irrepressible, had driven congress and the nation along the path of liberalism. The free ballot, the public school, the state university had kept America the land of opportunity; and however men despaired in their public utterances, their inner souls were conscious of this spark of youth and life. When the frontier closed in the eighties the habit of an open life was too strong to be changed offhand. The search for sport revealed a partial substitute for pioneer life. City congestion stimulated the need at this immediate moment, but without the cities the transition must any way have occurred. Baseball was already adopted in the small towns; the country club has produced its most numerous and typical examples away from the large cities and even in the remoter west whence the frontier has barely disappeared.

But the causes of the rise of sport, whether in the needs of city life, or in the automatic adaptation of a society whose old safety-valve, free land, was closing down, or in the aptitudes of a community inured to frontier conditions and now deprived of them, are of slighter consequence than its results upon America. No one can probe national character, personal conduct, public opinion of today without bringing out their difference from that which formerly prevailed. The hysteria of the period of the Spanish War and of Cleveland's Venezuela episode has sobered into better deliberation and balance, far enough from the ideal, but notably of higher tone. The moral indifference to methods of achievement, bred somewhat in our own great war and dominant when men smiled at the cipher dispatches or the star route frauds; or printed in their advertising pages the lying romances of quack doctors and patent medicines, is giving way to a real concern for honest methods; and those who would not of themselves reform are being squeezed by sheer force of public disapproval into a reluctant degree of compliance with the rules. Personal behavior, too, has changed. A cleaner living and a lessened indulgence in strong drink come with the sharpened intellect and the acuter soul. We know that we shall live to see a dry America, and one of equal rights for all. And who shall say that when our women took up tennis and the bicycle they did not as well make the great stride towards real emancipation; or that the quickened pulse, the healthy glow, the honest self-respect of honest sport have not served in part to steady and inspire a new Americanism for a new century?

NOTES

1. *New York Transcript*, August 8, 1835, advertisement, p. 3. The attempts to expose this hoax are in the *New York Herald*, September 8, 13, 1836, and are commented on in various editions of the Barnum autobiography. Phineas T. Barnum, *Life of P. T. Barnum*, New York, 1885; *Struggles and Triumphs*, 1873, 73.

2. *Charles Francis Adams, 1835-1915, An Autobiography, with a Memorial Address Delivered November 17, 1915, by Henry Cabot Lodge,* Boston and New York, 1916, 12.

3. Oliver W. Holmes in *Atlantic Monthly*, May 1858, p. 881.

4. In *Sports and Pastimes, a Magazine of Amusements for All Seasons,* Boston, Adams and Company, croquet, ring toss, angling, embroidery, and card and question games are described in July, 1871; and in April, 1875, dialogues, cricket, pet rabbits, magnetism, and "Silent Sam, the conjuror."

5. *The Nation,* September 2, 1869, p. 188, made this assertion while commenting upon the Harvard-Oxford boat race which had just been rowed.

6. *New York Tribune,* June 21, 1886, p. 2.

7. *Ibid.,* March 2, 1909, p. 2.

8. *Theodore Roosevelt, an Autobiography,* New York, 1913, 48.

9. There is a photograph of the famous White House tennis court, in use, in *Harper's Weekly,* March 6, 1909, p. 13; and another of the White House offices built on the same site by President Taft in *ibid.,* November 27, 1909, p. 30.

10. *Punch,* January 31, 1917, p. 75.

11. Gladys Miller, *Certain Aspects of Organized Recreations in the United States, 1876-1889,* Master's thesis, University of Wisconsin, 1916.

12. Edward Spencer, "The Classic English Derby," in *Outing,* June, 1902, p. 292; Francis Trevelyan, "Status of the American Turf," in *ibid.,* March, 1892, p. 469.

13. *Frank Leslie's Illustrated Newspaper,* June 18, 1881, p. 263; July 9, pp. 319, 321.

14. Photographs of Orby, Richard Crocker his owner, and "the foremost racing event of the world," in *Outing,* September, 1907, pp. 727-732.

15. Francis Trevelyan, "The American Turf. The race-courses of the East," in *Outing,* May, 1892, p. 129.

16. *New York Herald,* September 26, 1866, p. 7, devotes three columns to the opening of the club, comparing its equipment with that of Ascot, Epsom, and Longchamps.

17. *Coney Island Jockey Club, 1879* (pamphlet), gives an account of this new venture. Coney Island had now become famous as a New York resort, having been "discovered" about 1874 by William A. Engeman. *New York World,* January 12, 1884. The Ocean Parkway drive from Brooklyn was completed late in 1876.

18. *Frank Leslie's Illustrated Newspaper,* October 27, 1888, p. 167.

19. Betting rings were abolished by the New York constitution of 1894.

20. E. T. Riddick, "Robert Bonner's Stock Farm," in *Harper's Weekly,* July 23, 1892, p. 709.

21. There is a cut of this sulky in *Outing,* October, 1892, appendix 19.

22. *Outing,* November, 1907, p. 237.

23. A. J. Kenealy, "The New York Yacht Club, a Sea-dog's Yarn of Fifty Years," in *Outing,* August, 1894, p. 388.

24. *New York Daily Tribune,* September 8, 1851; *New York Evening Post,* September 9, 1851.

25. A. J. Kenealy, "The Racers for the America's Cup," in *Outing,* August, 1893, p. 381.

26. R. F. Coffin, "History of American Yachting," in *Outing,* August, 1886, p. 509. The New York Yacht Club was now established at Clifton, S. I., and was conducting regular regattas and fleet cruises in American waters. *Ibid.,* p. 402.

27. *New York Sun,* February 10, 1879.

28. *New York Herald,* March 18, 24, 1878; September 22, 1879.

29. *Chicago Inter-Ocean,* September 22, 1879.

30. *Harper's Weekly,* March 27, 1909, p. 31.

31. *New York Herald,* April 29, 1860, describes this fight.

32. The younger Bennett, consistently interested in racing, polo, yachting, and other sports, made the *New York Herald* the best source for sporting news in this period. Sketches of Sullivan are given in the issues for January 30 and February 8, 1882, and July 9, 1889.

33. Mike Donovan, "How to Punch the Ball," in *Outing,* April, 1902, p. 54.

34. A New York correspondent, after a visit to Sullivan's training quarters, described the superiority of the "leather football" over the sand pillow formerly used. *New York Herald,* January 29, 1882, p. 13.

35. *Frank Leslie's Illustrated Newspaper,* March 31, 1883, p. 86; November 29, 1884, p. 227.

36. *New York Herald,* December 20, 1887; *New York Tribune,* December 20, 1887.

37. *New York Sun,* December 10, 1887; *New York Tribune,* December 26, 1887; *New York Herald,* January 5, 1888. John Boyle O'Reilly asserted that "skill in pugilism has always been coincident with political freedom." *New York Tribune,* December 20, 1887.

38. "John L. Sullivan . . . has faced his last opponent in the ring, and it is doubtful if he will ever again do the knocking out act." *New York Herald,* March 12, 1888, p. 4.

39. December 30, 1887, p. 4.

40. *Milwaukee Sentinel,* January 8, 1889; *Idaho Avalanche,* July 13, 1889; *Chicago Inter-Ocean,* July 9, 1889.

41. *Theodore Roosevelt, an Autobiography,* 46.

42. Shibe Park, the home of the Athletics, and the grounds of the Pirates at Pittsburgh, both opened in 1909, are good specimens of the modern equipment. *Harper's Weekly,* May 1, 2, 1909.

43. Arthur B. Reeve, "What America Spends for Sport," in *Outing,* December, 1910, p. 300.

44. H. C. Palmer, J. A. Fynes, F. Richter, and W. I. Harris, *Athletic Sports in America, England, and Australia* (1889) 26.

45. Albert G. Spalding, *America's National Game; Historic Facts concerning the Beginning, Evolution, Development and Popularity of Baseball, with Personal Reminiscences of its Vicissitudes, Victories, and its Votaries*, New York, 1911, 64.

46. The text of the call for this meeting, and an account of its transactions, are in the *Chicago Tribune*, February 7, 1876.

47. "The Return of the Ball Players," in *Harper's Weekly*, April 6, 1889, p. 226.

48. *Harper's Weekly*, September 22, 1894, p. 908.

49. The numerous Newhall brothers, famous in cricket annals, are described in *ibid.*, June 22, 1889, p. 495.

50. *Chicago Tribune*, September 18-21, 1885.

51. *Physical Education in the Young Men's Christian Associations of North America*, 1914, p. 5. An international training school for directors was organized in Springfield, Massachusetts in 1885, while a series of annual conferences of the association of general secretaries was continuous from 1871. *Louisville Commercial*, May 6, 11, 1893.

52. Marion D. Learned, *The German-American Turner Lyric*, Baltimore, 1897, 40.

53. *Harper's Weekly*, September 20, 1890, p. 734.

54. Heinrich Metzner, *Geschichte des [Nordamerikanischen] Turner-Bunds*, Indianapolis, 1874, 85; *New York Tribune*, September 12, 16, 1864; *New York Herald*, April 6, 1865.

55. *Chicago Tribune, Milwaukee Sentinel*, September 11, 1880.

56. *Frank Leslie's Illustrated Newspaper*, June 25, 1881, pp. 281, 283, gives sketches of the festival; *Chicago Inter-Ocean*, June 6, 1881.

57. *Memorial History of New York*, edited by J. G. Wilson, 4:258; S. C. Foster, "The New York Athletic Club," in *Outing*, September, 1884, p. 403.

58. On July 29, 1876. *New York Herald*, July 16, 30, 1876.

59. Intercollegiate rowing, since the Harvard-Oxford race, had become a mild "mania." *Frank Leslie's Illustrated Newspaper*, July 15, 1876, p. 302. On the day after the annual Saratoga regatta, July 20, 1876, the Intercollegiate Athletic Association held its meet. *New York Herald*, June 17, July 21, 1876.

60. The Manhattan Athletic Club organized as a rival to the New York Athletic Club in 1878, was special patron of the National Association of Amateur Athletics of America in its later years, and occupied an imposing house at Madison avenue and Forty-fifth street between 1890 and 1893. *New York Sun*, February 19, 1893.

61. The resolutions embodying this desertion are in *Outing*, April, 1889, appendix, 1; June, 1889, appendix, 32.

62. The details of the breach are in *Outing,* November, 1888, p. 168, January, 1889, p. 363.

63. *New York Herald,* September 20, 1888.

64. The meeting that passed this resolution was held in the house of the New York Athletic Club. *Outing,* October, 1888, p. 81.

65. M. W. Ford, "The New York Athletic Club," in *Outing,* December, 1898, p. 247.

66. *New York Times,* September 23, 1889.

67. *New York Herald,* December 30, 1888.

68. *Chicago Inter-Ocean,* July 16, 1893.

69. *Annual Cyclopaedia and Register of Important Events of the Year 1884,* New York, 737.

70. *Spalding's Manual of Roller Skating,* 1884, 78; *Chicago Times,* May 18, 1864, p. 7.

71. *Frank Leslie's Illustrated Newspaper,* April 18, 1885, p. 139.

72. *New York Herald,* March 8, 1885.

73. *Scientific American,* March 28, 1885, p. 200.

74. *The Nation,* August 9, 1866, p. 113.

75. Alfred Austin, *Autobiography of Alfred Austin, Poet Laureate, 1835-1910,* London, 1911, 2:1.

76. *Chicago Times,* September 24, 1879, pp. 4, 8.

77. E. S. Martin in *The Nation,* September 3, 1898, p. 862.

78. *Wheelman,* March, 1883, p. 460.

79. Charles E. Pratt, "Pierre Lallement and his Bicycle," in *Outing and the Wheelman,* October, 1883, p. 4.

80. *Scientific American,* July 17, 1875, p. 39.

81. *Cincinnati Commercial,* November 22, 1879.

82. A. A. Pope, "The Wheel," in *Wheelman,* October, 1882, p. 69; an early Columbia advertisement, with cut, is in *Christian Union,* February 12, 1879, p. 168.

83. *New York Sun,* January 2, 1880, p. 1, describes the opening of a new academy in the American Institute Building.

84. *New York Tribune,* May 31, 1880; *Frank Leslie's Illustrated Newspaper,* June 19, 1880, p. 261.

85. His itinerary, via Humboldt Valley, Laramie City, and the old Platte trail is in *Outing,* May, 1887, p. 187.

86. Before appearing in book form, his journal ran as serial in *Outing,* October, 1885-June, 1888.

87. *Chicago Tribune,* November 7, 1885, "Wheeling as a Sport."

88. W. T. Farwell, "The Story of the Tire," in *Outing,* January, 1913, p. 472.

89. *Outing,* April, 1900, p. 95.

90. Wright and Ditson's *Lawn Tennis Guide,* 1897, p. 18; *New York World,* May 22, 1881, p. 2.

91. James Dwight, "Lawn Tennis in New England," in *Outing,* May, 1891, p. 157.

92. Miss Ellen C. Roosevelt won the first national championship on the Philadelphia Cricket Club grounds at Wissahickon. According to Alice Barber Stephens, as well as the illustrator for styles, girls played tennis in 1891 in long skirts, long sleeves, high collars, and trimmed hats. *Harper's Bazaar,* June 6, 1891, p. 443, July 18, 1891, pp. 557, 559.

93. *Chicago Tribune,* January 28, 1917, pt. 2, p. 1.

94. With a connecting link in a steel steamer to run to Havana. *Chicago Tribune,* July 28, 1885; G. H. Smythe, *Henry Bradley Plant,* 1898, 75.

95. *Theodore Roosevelt, an Autobiography,* 94.

96. George Bird Grinnell, *Brief History of the Boone and Crockett Club, with Officers, Constitution, and List of Members for the Year 1910,* New York, 1911, 3.

97. *Ibid.,* 10.

98. C. E. Clay, "Staten Island Cricket and Baseball Club," in *Outing,* November, 1887, p. 110; *New York Times,* July 5, 1886; *New York Herald,* July 6, 1886.

99. At Hutton Park on Orange Mountain. *New York Tribune,* December 5, 1887, January 3, 1888; *New York Sun,* December 23, 1887; *New York Herald,* May 6, 13, 1888, gives a description of country clubs near New York.

100. B. L. R. Dana, "An Original Social Experiment—Tuxedo," in *Cosmopolitan,* October, 1899, p. 547; J. N. Smith, "The Tuxedo Club," in *Munsey's,* November, 1891, p. 161; *Harper's Weekly,* December 18, 1886, p. 827; *New York World,* June 2, 1886.

101. "The Country Club," in *Outing,* November, 1905, p. 165.

102. "The Golf Ball," in *Harper's Weekly,* April 8, 1889, p. 351.

103. *The Nation,* August 26, 1869, p. 168.

104. *Country Life in America,* May, 1902, p. 35; Andrew Lang discusses the history of the game in H. G. Hutchinson, *Golf* (Badminton Library), 1902, 1.

105. E. N. Lamont, "The Royal Game of Golf," September 12, 1891, p. 695.

106. *Harper's Weekly,* August 27, 1892, p. 832; cf. *Outing,* September, 1894, appendix, 173; October, 1894, appendix, 22; August, 1898, p. 498.

107. H. C. Chatfield-Taylor, "The Development of Golf in the West," in *Outing,* August, 1900, p. 531.

108. The earliest American tournament was begun at St. Andrews, October 11, 1894. *New York Times,* October 12, 1894; *Outing,* August, 1895, appendix, 11, February, 1897, p. 502.

109. For the case of Francis Ouimet against the United States Golf Association, see *Chicago Examiner,* January 14, 1917.

110. Theodore Roosevelt, "Value of an Athletic Training," in *Harper's Weekly,* December 23, 1893, p. 1236.

111. Thomas Jefferson, indeed, while minister in France, had a costly private argument with M. de Buffon over the characteristics of the moose. Jefferson to Rutledge, September 9, 1788, *Writings of Thomas Jefferson* (Monticello edition), Washington, 1904, 7:137.

112. Edward B. Clark, "Roosevelt on the Nature Fakirs," in *Everybody's Magazine,* June 1907, p. 770. The immediate reply of W. J. Long is in *Boston Evening Transcript,* May 23, 24, 1907; he returned indirectly to the attack in "The Bull Moose as a Political Totem," in *Independent,* July 11, 1912, p. 85. When Colonel Roosevelt walked through New Forest on June 9, 1910 with Sir Edward Grey, they identified forty-one forest birds and heard the note of twenty-three. *Theodore Roosevelt, an Autobiography,* 334.

113. The struggles of Audubon to find subscribers for his *Birds of America,* and his final resort to a British publisher, give a measure for early American interest in natural science. Washington Irving to Martin Van Buren, October 19, 1836, in *The Life of John James Audubon, the Naturalist,* edited by his widow, New York, 1869, 394.

114. The followers of Daguerre made slow progress until, about 1878, the dry plate was perfected. *Outing,* December, 1889, p. 220. Immediately experimenters began to work towards series-photography and moving pictures. *San Francisco Chronicle,* in *Cincinnati Commercial,* August 21, 1879. Nine years later the Eastman Company brought out its roll-film cameras and began to advertise "You press the button, we do the rest." *Harper's Weekly,* July 20, 1889, p. 583; *Harper's Bazaar,* May 23, 1891, p. 407; *Encyclopaedia Britannica* (eleventh edition), 21: 503. A photographers' association of America completed its organization and held its first national convention in Chicago in 1880. *Chicago Tribune,* August 24-27, 1880. Portraits of living game were shown at the fourth annual sportsmen's show. *Harper's Weekly,* January 22, 1898, p. 101. And a little later A. R. Dugmore could describe "A Revolution in Nature Pictures," in *World's Work,* November, 1900, p. 83.

115. "The American Wimbledon," *New York Tribune,* June 23, 1873. General George W. Wingate, captain of the first international team, participated in the formation of a gigantic public schools athletic league in 1903. *Outing,* September, 1901, p. 616, May, 1908, p. 166. Luther H. Gulick, famous in Y.M.C.A. activities, and associate of General Wingate, became president in 1906 of the new Playground Association of America, with Colonel Roosevelt and Jacob A. Riis as honorary officials. *Playground,* April, 1907, p. 7.

116. Colonel De Lancay Lane expected to start his daily coach to Pelham Bridge on May 1, 1876. *New York Herald,* March 18, 1876.

117. His Westchester Polo Club built a house at Jerome Park, and played inside the track. "Polo in America," in *Wildwood's Magazine,* November, 1888, p. 10; *Frank Leslie's Illustrated Newspaper,* June 24, 1876, p. 261; *New York Herald,* May 12, June 2, 1876.

118. *Chicago Tribune,* August 14, 1879; Maurice Thompson, "Bowshooting," in *Scribner's Magazine,* July, 1877, p. 273.

119. *New York Herald,* August 5, 1880. Judge Nicholas Longworth, of Cincinnati, first vice-commodore, offered a tournament cup to the Western Canoe Association a few years later. Western Canoe Association, *Seventh Annual Yearbook,* 1891, 22.

120. George Bird Grinnell, editor of *Forest and Stream* and an active member of the Boone and Crockett Club, was connected with the management of the first exposition, May 13-18, 1895. *New York Times,* December 16, 1894, p. 20. Subsequent expositions became, to a great extent, dealers' sporting goods exhibits. *Harper's Weekly,* January 29, 1898, p. 100; March 18, 1899, p. 276.

121. *Topeka Commonwealth,* October 23, 1883; *New York Sun,* October 23, 1883. Alexander J. Cassatt, later president of the Pennsylvania Railroad, but now gentleman-farmer at Haverford, exhibited one of the first hackneys seen in America, a "general purpose" type whose period lies between the rise of the modern macadam road and the advent of the automobile. *Harper's Weekly,* April 9, 1892, p. 348; *World's Work,* July, 1901, p. 973; *Country Life in America,* December, 1901, p. 41.

122. The first dog show opened Tuesday, May 8, 1877, at the Hippodrome with some 1,300 dogs on exhibition. *New York Times,* May 8, 1877; *Frank Leslie's Illustrated Newspaper,* May 26, 1877, p. 203. In later years Madison Square Garden was utilized.

123. J. P. Morgan's collies, American-bred at his Cragston kennels, won the honors of 1894. *Harper's Weekly,* March 3, 1894, p. 215.

124. The introduction of the French bull-dog about 1897 raised the debate over the shape to which the ears should conform. *Harper's Weekly,* February 26, 1898, p. 214.

125. *New York Tribune,* December 15, 22, 1887.

126. The American Toy Dog Club was organized to conduct this show. *New York Tribune,* November 17, 1887, p. 5; *New York Herald,* May 26, 1888, p. 3.

127. *Harper's Bazaar,* May 11, 1895, p. 380; *New York World,* May 12, 1895.

THE ROLE OF THE SCHOOL IN THE SPORTS LIFE OF AMERICA

Frederick Cozens and Florence Stumpf

There are three significant reasons why any study of sports in American culture must necessarily give considerable space to the role of the school. First, it must be considered a training ground for the sports tastes and habits of future adults. Second, it is the actual locale for much of the sports and play life of a sizable group of the population, the students themselves. Third, the sports activities of the school often form an integral part of the recreational life of the rest of the community.[1]

A VIEW AT THE TURN OF THE CENTURY

The place of sports in the school curriculum at the beginning of the century is illustrated by the report of the famous Physical Training Conference of 1889.[2] In the entire discussion of thirty-three participants, mention was made of athletic sports only twice, once by Hartwell of Johns Hopkins and once by Hitchcock of Amherst. Sports were valued only as pastimes, and systematic gymnastics were considered to be the forms of exercise yielding the best results in the physical training of school children and college students. This represents a reasonably accurate point of view regarding the place of sports in the school curriculum just prior to the turn of the century, since it came from men who were considered *the* authorities.

It is a far cry from this point of view to one in which the program of sports is of paramount importance in the instructional program as well as in the so-called extracurricular aspects of competition—recognized by the school and presided over by schoolmen. It will be the purpose of this chapter to indicate how these changes came about and how cultural change and pressure were able to overcome the twin traditions of Puritanism and work.

Our early settlers needed no prodding to work because of their previous indoctrination in their homeland and because of the labor shortage in America. But the worship of work made it difficult for Americans to learn

From Frederick Cozens and Florence Stumpf, *Sports in American Life*, Chicago: University of Chicago Press, 1953, Chapter 6. Reprinted by permission.

how to play. "The first mitigation of the daily grind took the form of hunting, fishing, barn-raisings and log-rolling—activities that had no social stigma because they contributed to the basic needs of living."[3]

The beginnings of recreation (or play) as a serious business were laid in the middle of the nineteenth century. Americans played not for fun but to win "with all the fierce energy that once felled the forests and broke the prairies."[4] However, the idea of play as an integral part of life was difficult to assimilate, and it is little wonder that at the beginning of the twentieth century there were grave misgivings about making it a part of the school curriculum.

CULTURAL PRESSURES EVENTUATING
IN A SPORTS CURRICULUM IN THE SCHOOLS

Early twentieth-century educators emphasize the value of play. One of the cultural pressures which gradually exerted an influence on the school program in general and on physical education in particular was the wide dissemination of the idea of play as an educative process. The philosophy of secondary education around the turn of the century was away from the classical course of study, made up chiefly of Latin, Greek, and mathematics, designed primarily for those who were preparing for a college education. It gave consideration to the whole child, not just to the mental part of him. Whitton, for example, pointed out the common tendency of the schools to consider their duty done when the students left the classroom, when actually the function of the school had just begun.[5]

Prior to the opening of the century the reform philosophy of Horace Mann and that of the disciples of Pestalozzi remained largely in the realm of theory.[6] However, despite a great deal of conservatism, there appeared to be an awakening on the part of some educators to the narrowness of the traditional classical curriculum with its emphasis on mental discipline and mental power and one program for all.

Along with the new philosophy of education stressing the free activity of children came a very decided increase in enrollment in the secondary school. which helped to bring the play idea to more boys and girls. Drastic changes in the ideas of child-training, publicized by such magazines as the *Ladies' Home Journal,* were responsible for a revision of the previous attitude toward play. Widespread changes in the school curriculum were a part of the adjustment of the culture to the new ideas of play. School playgrounds, lessened homework loads, Montessori methods in the kindergarten, President Theodore Roosevelt's support of the idea of play in the school curriculum, and recess game periods were all evidences of cultural interaction which made way for a new philosophy of education in America.[7]

The periodical literature of the day stressed the point that participation in sports and games tended to influence young people toward better citizenship. Teamwork and good sportsmanship were associated with competition in vigorous athletic games. It was recognized that group behavior on the playground served as a powerful democratizing force, particularly in the big cities.

Some of the leaders in physical education recognize the potential value of sports. While it is true that gymnastics carried by far the major emphasis in any school program of physical education, a number of leaders recognized the potential values of sports and games despite well-founded objections to their manner of conduct. Sargent, one of the most discerning men of all time in the field, extolled the favorable effects of athletics (and by that he meant athletic competition).[8] George E. Johnson, a school superintendent and famous for his book on *Education by Plays and Games,* made a plea for the use of games in the school instead of gymnastics or at least giving games an equal opportunity with gymnastics.[9]

Much more was written in the early years of the century about college sports than about sports in the secondary school, but some idea of the place of sports at this level can be obtained from a survey made by McCurdy in 1905 embracing 555 cities in all parts of the country.[10]

It must be assumed from his report that the instructional program of physical education was almost exclusively one of gymnastics. He found, however, that the large majority of school superintendents approved of competitive athletics in high school and desired to place the supervision of the boys' sports in the hands of a regular teacher. While such a condition indicates no particular change for the class program, it does show a favorable attitude toward accepting interschool sports as a part of the school's over-all responsibility. However, it should not be inferred from McCurdy's report that all was "sweetness and light" insofar as interschool competition was concerned. Meylan, of Columbia University, characterized three sets of individuals holding general views on the question of intercollegiate athletics: (1) the extremists—nothing but good can come from athletics; (2) the dispensers—do away with athletics; and (3) the middle-grounders—athletics have many advantages as well as some bad features.[11] His concluding sentence would have been taken from any number of statements written fifty years later and merely illustrates the fact that social problems are never solved once and for all but remain to be reexamined in terms of changing cultural conditions. "The abuses of athletics are in the direction of excess, inordinate desire to win at any cost, the spirit of commercialism, and the tendencies to professionalism and to gambling." Though interschool competition forms a considerable part of the picture given to the public regarding the role of the school in the sports life of America, it must be regarded as only a small part, relatively, since only a small segment of the school population took part.

The content of the physical education programs in the early part of the century showed a cultural lag—gymnastics in the instructional program and sports in the afterschool program. This lag was undoubtedly due to a number of factors. In the first place, educators were still not fully willing to accept play (and hence sports) as a part of the school program. They recognized the necessity for a certain amount of vigorous physical activity in the school as a relief from the tension of continuous mental effort and were willing to include gymnastics because it afforded such relief, did not take much time, and could not be construed as play. There was little tendency to have fun in a gymnastics class.

Second, the vast majority of individuals who were available to serve as teachers of gymnastics had been trained in one of the European systems or had picked up their knowledge of gymnastics by themselves. McCurdy's survey of 1905 showed that about two-thirds of the teachers had some normal school training, while one-third had not. Very little sports instruction was given in such normal school courses, and it is probably safe to assume that teachers of gymnastics were not well prepared to handle a sports program.

Third, the time element, the size of classes, and the facilities available were not well adapted to instruction in a program of sports. Gymnastic classes of a hundred can be accommodated easily in a gymnasium sixty by one hundred feet, but such size is impossible for even one-third that number in basketball. The out-of-door facilities were either woefully inadequate or entirely lacking. As a consequence, gymnastic exercises were almost the only type of program which could be offered.

Over the years from the beginning of the century to World War I, little evidence of a sports program can be found in the physical education class period. Almost all the discussion in the literature was concerned with various aspects of interschool sports—aspects that were causing difficulties of one sort or another. One forward-looking fact was brought out in Lowman's study of physical training in the secondary schools of the United States and commented on by McCurdy's editorial.[12] The private high schools and academies were better equipped for physical education than the public high schools. Here was to be found a much higher percentage of both directors and participants. In all probability, much of the participation was of the intramural variety, and it could well be that a reasonable share of the "athletics for all" movement which gained prominence in the second decade of the century came from programs in the academies, a heritage from the private schools of England.

One of the great contributions to the fundamental idea of play in the education of the child was demonstrated by Hetherington in a summer program on the Berkeley campus of the University of California beginning in 1913. While it might seem to the casual observer a far cry from the play-school idea to sports in the physical education program of the secondary school, the point which needs to be stressed has to do with the necessity for the provision of skilled leadership in play activities in the early years of the child's life.[13]

The development of sports for women. Throughout the first decade of the century there was growing evidence of the right of girls and women to participate in sports both in and out of school, and it must be kept in mind that school sports are not and should not be limited to the boys' program. Sargent's voice in the pages of the *Ladies' Home Journal* was carried to the girls and women of the nation in answer to several articles decrying the desirability of freedom for girls and women in athletics.[14]

Early in the century attention was being given to the sports program for women in some of our leading colleges. At Vassar, for example, the introduction of athletics into the program of physical education did much to stimulate the interest of girls in their physical welfare. Apparently the girls were not satisfied with a program of mild gymnastics.[15] Lavinia Hart, writing on a girl's college life in the *Cosmopolitan,* indicated that open-air athletics were very popular the year around.[16] Among the sports mentioned were skating, tobogganing, rowing, tennis, golf, lacrosse, swimming, riding, cycling, and certain events in track and field.

The rise of intramural sports. [17] Perhaps the most persistent criticism leveled at the intercollegiate athletic program by both the public and educational administrators centers around the lack of opportunity for participation offered to the mass of the students. A partial response to this criticism is to be found in the rise of intramural sports. College boys who wanted to play on a team and were not good enough to make the varsity joined together and challenged another group which had done the same thing. Class teams were organized, and fraternity and living groups formed teams, originally without the help of varsity athletic or physical education administrators.

As the movement grew, it became apparent that an overall organization was needed to stabilize and centralize control. Michigan and Ohio State in

1913 took the lead and created a staff position in physical education, "Director of Intramural Sports." Aided by the success of mass competition on the playgrounds and in the War Training Camps, other institutions began to realize the value from such organization. Following World War I, the growth of men's intramural sports began to assume great proportions in the colleges, soon filtering into the women's program and into the high schools.[18]

National associations made a place for the discussion of intramurals at their yearly meeting,[19] and it was not long before the interest in afterschool play began to have an effect upon the class program where instruction in sport fundamentals could be given. Widespread attention to the new state requirements offered the opportunity of giving instruction to many thousands of boys and girls who had not hitherto been reached. Team play began to be recognized as a legitimate part of the instructional program, and provisions were made for a broadening of the scope of activities offered to the student in "required" physical education. As a consequence, the ideal physical education program for girls as well as boys now offers instruction as well as some competitive experience in a considerable number of sports activities designed to meet their needs.

SPORTS IN THE CULTURE PRODUCE
CHANGES IN THE SCHOOL PROGRAM

Beginning soon after the organization of the Playground and Recreation Association of America and with the establishment of playgrounds in many cities all over the country, the idea of out-of-door play in programs of physical education was stressed by play leaders.[20] Professional personnel through the leading journal of physical education *(American Physical Education Review)* came face to face each month with "propaganda" regarding many phases of the playground movement—the opening of new play facilities, the amount spent by various cities on playgrounds, data on playground legislation, the value of playgrounds in a community, the activities conducted on the playgrounds, municipal administration of play facilities, and the like.

The same children who were subjected to gymnastics in the school found delight in a play program on the playgrounds and often under the same leadership which was present in the school. It is not strange, therefore, that both the children and the leadership recognized a play or sports program as being infinitely more fun than one composed largely and sometimes exclusively of gymnastics exercises. Playground programs, particularly in the summer months, were reinforced by organized competitions in which large numbers took part. The Athletic Badge Tests, promoted by the Playground and Recreation Association of America beginning in 1913, were used as motivating devices to promote the physical efficiency of the boys and girls of the nation and were undoubtedly helpful in interesting hundreds of thousands of boys and girls in their physical skill status.

Prior to World War I there was a strong demand all over the country to use school facilities for play purposes in the evenings, on weekends, and in the summer. "The wider use of the school plant" became a slogan which caught the fancy of taxpayers and municipal officials, and, despite some objection from schoolmen, there was a gradual "opening-up" of school facilities for all types of recreation, and in gymnasiums and on playgrounds sports programs flourished.[21] Thus, early attempts to introduce sports into the class program of physical education were reinforced.

THE SCHOOLS APPLY THE PRINCIPLE OF ASSOCIATIVE ACTIVITY TO THE CONDUCT OF SPORTS

The movement for athletic competition in colleges which swept across the country in the last years of the nineteenth century spread to the public and private secondary schools of the nation, and the many problems of control arose as with the institutions of higher learning. Lack of interest on the part of school administrators and domination of partisan spectators were particularly condemned by leading physical educators.[22] The Society of Secondary School Physical Directors realized this, and part of its program was concerned with a careful study of many and varied athletic problems such as the organization by colleges of championships for high-school boys, competition outside of the school, the management of contests, the periods of training, the amount of participation, medical examination, and recruiting of high-school players by colleges.[23]

The New York Public School Athletic League. Early in his work as director of physical training of the New York City public schools, Luther Halsey Gulick saw the need for organizing athletic competition which would provide for the average boy rather than the one who was highly skilled.[24] He initiated a movement which resulted in the formation of the New York Public School Athletic League in 1903. One of the interesting things about this organization was that, although sanctioned by the board of education, it was not made a part of the work of the board but rather a separate organization set up through the cooperative efforts of the superintendent of schools, the presidents of the board of education and the City College of New York, the secretary of the AAU, the chairman of the Intercollegiate Athletic Association, and several prominent businessmen influential in the political and financial world.[25] Realizing the necessity for good publicity in this venture, Gulick secured the assistance of nine newspapers in metropolitan New York, and the league was dramatically launched in 1903.[26]

Because of the large number of entries and the fact that groups had to be handled rapidly, the program of the big meets consisted largely of running and relay racing with boys classified by weight rather than age. However, other activities involving team competition were approved and included baseball, basketball, football, soccer, cross-country, swimming, ice- and roller-skating, and shooting. Baseball was especially popular, and in 1907 there were 106 teams in competition, with fifteen thousand spectators for the final game.[27]

Rifle-shooting soon became a prominent activity of high-school boys, with seven thousand boys receiving instruction in 1908 and annual contests held between different high schools. Marksmanship badges were awarded and President Theodore Roosevelt, during his term of office, always wrote a letter of commendation to the boy showing the greatest proficiency during the year. Prizes were awarded by E. I. du Pont de Nemours Powder Company to the school team having the highest score. General Wingate, president of the PSAL, believed that none of the activities conducted by the league was "likely to have as important an influence upon the country at large as the system of instruction in military rifle shooting."[28]

The operation of the league program was supported by membership fees and contributions from citizens, among whom were to be found such prominent financiers as J. Pierpont Morgan, Andrew Carnegie, John D. Rockefeller, and Harry Payne Whitney.[29]

In 1905 the Girls' Branch of the league was established, not independent from the school system but as an integral part of the physical education department. The activity most successful in the girls' program was folk dancing, and, though there was no interschool competition, play days were arranged where thousands of girls took part.

In speaking of the Public School Athletic League, which he called the world's greatest athletic organization, Reeve stressed the work of the league in developing cleaner, better lives for thousands of boys and the fact that athletic competition had been instrumental in increasing scholarship.[30]

There can be little question that the New York Public School Athletic League served as a pattern for the formation of other city school athletic organizations.[31] Seventeen cities are reported to have formed similar leagues, and inquiries about league organization came from Chile, Argentina, India, and Turkey.[32]

The National Federation of State High School Athletic Associations. In the early part of the century high-school boys were just as eager for competition in sports as were college men, and, like the college situation, sports grew up in a very haphazard fashion.[33] They were ignored or tolerated until the school-men finally decided that, since they were fast becoming an integral part of the school's extracurricular program, something must be done about their regulation and control.[34] This led to a school organization or association for the purpose of establishing policies within a school, then to an association between two or more schools, and, finally, after a number of intermediate steps, to a state-wide organization charged with the responsibility of developing uniform regulations suitable for all. This development went on simultaneously in a considerable number of states in the years just preceding and just following 1900. Forsythe reports that by 1925 there were athletic associations in all states, though "not all state organizations are called athletic associations." [35] Prior to 1920 there was strong feeling that the control of all high-school contests should be in the hands of schoolmen and not representatives of colleges, clubs, and promotional organizations. In 1920 the secretary of the Illinois High School Athletic Association invited representatives from neighboring states to come together in Chicago for a discussion of the problems which had arisen. As a result of this meeting and another in 1921, involving four midwestern states, the 1922 conference, attended by representatives from eleven states, officially adopted the present name of the organization—The National Federation of State High School Athletic Associations. Forty-four states now hold membership in the federation, and over the years it has done much to stimulate member organizations to reach agreement on such matters as eligibility rules, elimination of national championships, regulation in regard to interstate meets and tournaments, the formulation of rules for high-school players, and national policies in regard to suitable equipment and sports adaptations.[36]

The National Collegiate Athletic Association. Reform in college athletics, particularly football, received a considerable amount of journalistic attention in the early years of the century.[37] As has been so well stated in the published literature on the subject,[38] school and college athletics had undergone an evolution from an "institution" that was almost universally opposed by schoolmen in the latter part of the nineteenth century to one which was tolerated as a more or less necessary evil to a final stage at the turn of the century where a considerable amount of recognition had been given athletics as an established part of the educational program. However, school and college administrators were faced with serious problems when the decision was made to "take over" their control, since within educational institutions an almost innumerable number of variations of faculty and/or alumni, student, and trustee committees or boards had been set up.

Because intercollegiate competition in sports was inevitable from the start, it was logical that colleges of similar size, ideals, and geographical location should effect an association for intercollege control as each had done for intracollege organization. Similarly, when competition commenced to go outside of a rather narrowly defined geographical area, some organization of a national character was equally inevitable.

The number of fatalities and serious injuries during the football season of 1905 served as a spark to touch off widespread indignation regarding the conduct of sports in general and football in particular. In an attempt to save football, a game he loved, President Theodore Roosevelt called a conference of college representatives at the White House and urged immediate action. In December, 1905, a national football conference of college and university presidents and faculty members was called by Chancellor McCracken of New York University. Among the thirty institutions represented, a number favored immediate abolition of football, but constructive suggestions in regard to the elimination of mass play and unnecessary roughness saved the game and provided for vast improvement.[39]

The McCracken conference resulted in the organization of the Intercollegiate Athletic Association of the United States, later (1910) to become the National Collegiate Athletic Association, the first body actually to be established for the purpose of regulating and supervising college athletics throughout the United States. It is primarily an educational body and at first served only in an advisory and consultative capacity, but since World War II its policies have changed. Now membership in the NCAA can be retained only if institutions adhere to the principles which have been established.[40]

Thus, in keeping with the regulations which have been set up from time to time for the control of other aspects of our culture, it was found necessary to bring to task those colleges violating the spirit of a program which, because of its connection with institutions of higher learning, had appeared to be unassailable. It is worthy of more than passing note to point out that the lay public has taken an active and at times a vociferous part in the condemnation of aspects of college sports which appeared to be out of control. If education belongs to the public, any phase of it may also come under public scrutiny.

The formation of intercollegiate athletic conferences in the past half-century has played no small role in the standardization and stabilization of competitive sports in the schools and colleges of the nation. This movement began with the formation of the Western Intercollegiate Conference in 1895 and since that time has embraced more than seventy-five groups[41] composed of colleges of similar size and academic standards located in a particular geographical area.[42]

Other groups apply the principle. The principle of associative activity in the conduct and control of sports was not limited to the formation of athletic conferences. Among the national organizations which have had a vital interest in such programs are the American Association for Health, Physical Education and Recreation, the College Physical Education Association, the Society of State Directors of Health, Physical Education and Recreation, and the National Association of Physical Education for College Women.[43]

In the field of sports for women the National Section on Women's Athletics has had a tremendous influence on the development of standards in competitive athletics for girls and women. Organized originally by a group of professional women in physical education for the purpose of establishing a set of basketball rules for girls and women, it developed into a very strong section of the American Association for Health, Physical Education and Recreation. Nor can we neglect small professional groups which gave intensive study to the development of basic principles in the conduct of physical education and athletics. Among these was the Athletic Research Society, which, despite its brief existence of twelve years (1907-18), contributed materially to the acceptance of competitive sports as an integral part of the school and college program.[44]

The National Amateur Athletic Federation. Another organization deserves specific mention, not for what it actually did, but for what it tried to do. The National Amateur Athletic Federation, organized in 1922, attempted to bring together all national groups and agencies in any way promoting athletics and physical training in the United States. There was a general awareness that the promotion of athletics for all boys and girls, young men and young women, would be a stepping-stone to the physical fitness of a nation found comparatively unfit in the medical examinations for armed service personnel in World War I. The development of high ideals in amateur sport and the raising of American citizenship to a higher plane were stressed as fundamental in the federation's platform.[45]

Because of the vision of representatives of the founding organizations, it became clear that girls and women were as vitally interested in nation-wide athletic participation as boys and men. As a result, there was formed, almost immediately, a Women's Division of the NAAF which grew and prospered but was finally merged with the American Association for Health, Physical Education and Recreation and became in 1940 the National Section on Women's Athletics of that body.[46]

Several of the independent forces which were brought together to make up the NAAF (Men's Division) were too strong to submerge their special interests, and the organization was not successful for more than a few years. However, the attempt to set up a body devoted to the "unity of sport," wherever found in America, indicates a desire on the part of many groups to work toward the ideal of national health and soundness through a program of universal participation in athletics, sports, and games.[47]

The junior colleges organize. With the growth of the junior college in the early part of the century, it was quite natural that here too athletics should become an integral part of the educational program. Some fears were expressed almost immediately regarding the manner in which athletics should develop. Men of experience insisted that athletics should be controlled and made a part of the educational program. [48] Community pressures for successful athletic teams undoubtedly gave rise to an emphasis which resulted in the organization of junior-college athletic conferences throughout the country. As early as 1930 a questionnaire sent to 320 junior colleges of the nation indicated that twenty such conferences, embracing a total membership of 120 schools, had been formed.[49] In California the junior-college athlete made good when he transferred to the university,[50] indicating a high type of training in the junior college or superior ability as a high-school player. But it is well known that, more often than not, the junior-college athlete does not have the scholastic entrance requirements to come immediately to the state or private university of his choice.

The principle operates at mid-century. In sports the principle of associative activity has taken various forms, from the organization of student associations in particular institutions to the cooperative efforts of a number of schools and colleges and, finally, to the banding-together of educational institutions from all parts of the nation.

These national organizations were well established by 1930, but their work had only just begun. Though many devious ways have been found to evade the regulations of associative groups, school and college sports leaders are still pinning their faith on this typically American principle. Today we see the rise of the conference commissioner in college sports and the formation of various associations of coaches. In mid-century we have top-level educational bodies, notably the American Council on Education through its

Committee of College Presidents, seeking to set up further regulatory measures which will attempt to insure the stability of a phase of college life which has almost universal appeal to the American public.

The proper conduct of school and college sports must be regarded as a social problem and, like many other social problems, cannot be solved by laws alone. One possible solution would appear to be an attempt to get each institution to assume full responsibility for the conduct of its sports program as an educational project rather than as a business enterprise. Essentially, then, the problem becomes one of the downright, homely honesty of each institution.

WAR BRINGS COMPULSORY PHYSICAL EDUCATION PROGRAMS

Wars, terrible as they are, do cause an acceleration in development in many fields of human endeavor—in medicine, in industrial production, and certainly in sports. It may be that professional educators would have succeeded *eventually* in setting up compulsory physical education programs in American schools had there been no World War I. It is a matter of record, however, that a direct result of the preparation for and participation in World War I produced cultural pressures which resulted in the passage of such state legislation.

Four distinct pressures finally culminated in the passage of state legislation regarding the teaching of physical education in the public schools: (1) the movement toward preparedness which began more than two years before the United States declared war on Germany in April, 1917; (2) the fear that the Congress would pass federal legislation requiring universal military training perhaps extending into the elementary schools, or that federal legislation requiring universal physical training would be enacted; (3) the invocation of the states' rights doctrine on matters pertaining to the prerogatives of individual states; and (4) the deplorable physical condition of the youth of the nation as revealed by statistics from the Selective Service Act of 1917.

No one thing or no one set of circumstances produced the sports program in the school. Rather, such programs came from a combination of circumstances sparked by almost universal physical education requirements throughout the nation. In other words, had it not been for the requirement, the millions of boys and girls of school age six to eighteen (possibly twenty-five million) would not have had the exposure to the program which was afforded them. This statement should not be presumed to mean that, as soon as a compulsory program started to function in a state, immediately a sports program was instituted. A considerable number of other factors were involved. Schools found themselves lacking in personnel, equipment, and facilities. But almost immediately a number of states followed the example of California in introducing into the programs of physical education sports skills and tests for these skills to motivate progress in their acquisition. [51] Thus a gradual change from a gymnastics to a sports program developed in the years between World War I and the early thirties.

The need for teachers. The enactment of legislation in many states following World War I presented a number of problems. In order to comply with requirements, school systems had to have teachers immediately and could not wait until colleges and universities instituted teacher-education programs. As a result, many men and women were recruited who were not well prepared. Men particularly were selected from the ranks of college athletes who had a Bachelor's degree, many of whom had attained officer status in World War I. These men knew their sports, and it was logical that they should use this knowledge in their programs of physical education. As a consequence, more and more attention was given to this aspect than ever before. The class program became the seasonal major sport program on a less intensive basis. During the football season, football fundamentals were taught; next came basketball, then track, and finally baseball, where softball was substituted for hardball.

Later the demand for teachers of physical education and sports coaches was met by four-year Bachelor's degree curriculums in state and private institutions supplemented by summer courses including coaching schools and clinics for both men and women, where the emphasis was almost entirely on technique and strategy in team games. While not organized in such great numbers as in the twenties, these coaching schools and clinics have continued to thrive as a means of in-service training. However, comparatively little attention was given to activities other than the traditional major sports, or to the class program, despite some emphasis on the organization of intramural sports.

THE YEARS BETWEEN WORLD WARS I AND II

There is no question about the effect which various aspects of World War I had on sports in schools and colleges during the years between World Wars I and II. The emphasis placed upon sports as a most valuable preparation for conditioning and morale of soldiers, the tremendous spectator interest developed in France as a result of the sports competition placed before the armed forces during and after World War I, the indignation of the people at home in regard to the physical unfitness of draftees—all of these became pressures in American culture to set the stage for the great boom in sports participation and interest which developed in the nineteen-twenties. This was the period in which the public created a demand for the erection of huge stadiums on the campuses of colleges and universities and to a lesser degree on high-school campuses of the nation. Sports became available to out-of-school youth and adults as well as to those in school. Owing in part to war experiences, the in-school program gradually changed from gymnastics to sports.

Pressures for the enactment of state laws regarding the teaching of health and physical education in public school systems did not end with the cessation of hostilities and the return to civilian life of armed service personnel. From 1921 through 1929 ten additional state legislatures had passed such compulsory laws, thus making twenty-seven states which had enacted public school health and physical education legislation as a result largely of World War I.

School sports in the depression. The financial crash of 1929 did not immediately affect the school situation, but by 1932 the schools were hard hit. Budgets were cut, teachers' salaries were lowered, and teaching loads were heavier due to the increase of student enrollment as a result of unemployment.[52] Physical education, along with other so-called "frills" as, for example, art and music, experienced some difficulty.[53] Equipment and facilities were drastically curtailed, and the dollar was wrung dry. Interschool competition involving out-of-town trips was often eliminated. Smaller schools, in order to economize, adopted a new type of football—six-man football. Competition in this activity spread rapidly, and by 1941 it was played in forty-five states.[54] Intercollegiate football attendance reached its lowest level in 1932 but thereafter started to increase. The sale of sports goods declined 57 per cent from 1929 to 1933, partly due to export and partly to the financial condition of the nation as a whole.

However, out of the depression came some things favorable to the development of sports in the schools. A considerable share of WPA and PWA funds was used for the building of school sports facilities—gymnasiums, swimming pools, tennis courts, and athletic fields. By 1937 it was estimated that $75,000,000 had been spent for such projects.[55] In Michigan alone sixty gymnasiums were under construction.[56] The WPA Recreation Projects instituted for the community affected the sports program of the school. There was a demand for the teaching of sports for which the community was providing facilities—golf, tennis, badminton, and swimming. It appears to be a reasonable assumption that the inclusion of many individual sports in the school program of physical education came as a direct result of cultural pressures during the nineteen-thirties. Intramural activities developed at all levels of education. Schoolmen had become increasingly aware of the inadvisability of interscholastic competition at the junior high school level and were substituting intramural activities to meet the demand for competition.

In the field of interscholastic and intercollegiate competition for girls and women there was a steady growth of playdays during the depression. Following the ideal of "sports for all" rather than for the few, the professional women of the nation went all-out for the encouragement and promotion of sports and games for all, to be wisely chosen, wisely promoted, and wisely supervised. The National Section on Women's Athletics in 1937 set up important standards for the guidance of girls and women in their competitive programs which were described by a male member of the profession as a contribution destined to be of far-reaching importance in the field of health and physical education.[57]

The value of sports in the use of leisure time by both youth and adults was given serious and detailed study by many organizations, and in the middle of the depression (1935) the newly-created American Youth Commission gave its undivided attention to the consideration of the needs of youth and plans for the development of programs most helpful in solving their problems.[58] In its recommendations the commission stressed the close relationship between education and recreation and emphasized the major responsibility of the school in this regard and the importance of establishing a program which would offer every school boy and girl "the opportunity to cultivate physical fitness through games, sports and outdoor activities."[59] Because there was no place on the economic market in the depression years for young people of school and college age, enrollments increased. Since society virtually said to the schools, "Keep our boys and girls happy and out of mischief," opportunity was given to educational institutions to expose more young people to a program of sports than ever before.

THE PREPAREDNESS PROGRAM

The early armed services rejection statistics caused even more concern to the nation than those of World War I. High government officials and members of the medical profession and of physical education attempted, early in our serious consideration of war, to persuade the Congress to vote national legislation which would attempt to remedy the condition of our national fitness by providing federal aid to states. The famous Schwert Bill (10606), which died in committee with the close of the Seventy-sixth Congress, and its successor (H.R. 1074), though vigorously supported by such organizations as the American Legion, the Benevolent and Protective Order of Elks, and the National Congress of Parents and Teachers, did not come to a vote of the Congress but did do much to direct the attention of the people toward preparedness through physical fitness.[60] Another bill was introduced which called for a survey of the nation's facilities and personnel for the purposes of improving our efforts in the field of physical education and athletic participation and the preparation of a program of physical activities to meet the needs of youth.[61]

Physical fitness emphasized. To meet the demands of the armed services for men in better physical condition, teams of experts toured the country in 1942 holding institutes and demonstrations for educators particularly in regard to wartime programs of school physical education which would emphasize vigorous and rugged activities. Sponsored by the United States Office of Education, the personnel of the institutes included representatives from the armed forces and the American Association for Health, Physical Education and Recreation.[62] To supplement the work of these institutes, the United States Office of Education, Federal Security Agency, published two handbooks on physical fitness, one for high schools and one for colleges and universities.[63] Both publications stressed the necessity for emphasis on sports where large numbers participate (intramural) and where the element of endurance as well as that of skill was prominent. Another publication, a Navy manual, adapted for the use of schools and colleges, came as the result of many requests from educators to set forth the program of sports developed at the preflight schools and training bases.[64]

Unquestionably, the almost universal emphasis placed on physical fitness did much to strengthen school and college *class* programs of physical education. Particular attention was given to those sports which had the possibility of developing endurance. Among these were included football, boxing, wrestling, basketball, ice hockey, lacrosse, water polo, soccer, speedball, handball, squash, track and field, and swimming. Since many colleges and universities were concerned with programs for men in service, the type and extent of the activities offered depended to some degree on the approval of commanding officers. Many intercollegiate athletic teams were made up largely of armed services personnel, in some instances almost exclusively of Navy students. In intramural competition, however, the other armed services permitted sports participation. It seems fair to say, however, that the general emphasis in school and college programs was on so-called physical fitness activities rather than sports requiring a considerable area for competition. Competitive areas required for a large number of teams in such sports as football, baseball, soccer, and speedball were seldom available either at colleges or at high schools. Daily participation at a given hour had to be limited to those sports requiring a minimum of space and hence the stress on boxing, wrestling, tumbling, and mass exercises of various kinds. Swimming was, of course, a must. Obstacle courses were built on many school and college campuses, and, when inclement weather drove participants indoors a variety of gymnasium obstacle courses was devised. The flair for obstacle courses during World War II resembled that for miniature golf courses during the depression years. As the war ended, their demise was just as rapid.

Despite the emphasis given to physical fitness in school programs of physical education during World War II, it is apparent that this emphasis produced no lasting effects. The impetus given to sports in school programs during the twenties as a result of World War I and the state legislation which followed, the attention given to sports as valuable assets in the use of leisure time during the depression years, both within and without the school, seem to indicate an American point of view which could not be changed by expedient adaptations. Here, then, is a reaffirmation of the philosophy that physical fitness is only one outcome of physical education as an educational means and that the program, to be lasting, must contain the element of fun to be found in sports.

WORLD WAR II AND ITS EFFECT ON THE SPORTS PROGRAM IN SCHOOLS AND COLLEGES

With the advent of World War II, the talk of physical fitness centered around the value of sports in the building of morale as well as in the building of physical stamina necessary to its successful prosecution. Educational leaders turned their attention to the matter of what should be done with sports in schools and colleges, both in the class program and in the competitive program.

Two schools of thought emerged. One school believed sincerely that physical condition was the primary requisite for induction into the armed services: Give the boys (all of them) strenuous, all-out exercises and get them into condition quickly so that when they are called they will be ready! The proponents of this school were not antagonistic to the values inherent in athletic competition but were insistent that the time element was of the utmost importance and that to condition all men and boys by means of athletic sports alone required facilities and personnel far beyond available resources.[65]

The other school of thought believed that the values to be gained in sports participation should not be discarded because of the expediency of condition and that to subject men to drudgery would produce disadvantageous results.[66] Although there was some rather sharp debate in the professional literature, the extent of the feeling as a national issue would be difficult to discover. When leaders disagree as to what ought to be done, the "little people" often wonder where to turn,[67] but, despite the confusion, by and large school physical education people as well as those in the armed services did the best possible job under existing conditions.

Interscholastic and intercollegiate competition. Interscholastic and intercollegiate competition were very definitely handicapped during the war period. The depletion of manpower in many colleges and universities resulted in the abandonment of competitive schedules. Other institutions, particularly those which were training Navy personnel, played a limited schedule with due consideration for long trips and time given to practice.

Most state departments of education vigorously encouraged interschool competition for high-school boys even though it was necessary to limit schedules because of gas rationing and the lack of athletic supplies. In many instances the lack of trained personnel caused difficulties, but volunteers from the teaching staff were able to replace temporarily those who had gone into the various services. Brace, in reviewing this phase of the program (1944), says:

> Interschool athletics are probably now being conducted on at least 80 per cent of the prewar basis. Regrouping of competing schools has reduced length of trips. ... As regards intercollegiate athletics the present picture appears to be one in which college coaching staffs have struggled to keep some kind of team in the field. Many colleges have been forced to give up intercollegiate athletics for the duration and still others will probably have to follow suit. Nevertheless the value of athletics is probably more clearly recognized now than ever before.[68]

WAR'S END AND THE AFTERMATH

Long before the end of World War II, leaders in all aspects of our culture were giving serious consideration to what should be done in postwar America. The type of physical education program which should be carried on or instituted in schools and colleges was widely discussed and widely publicized. Physical fitness continued to receive a considerable share of attention; swimming programs were emphasized; the question was raised as to whether a games program was sufficient to obtain physical fitness; the needs of the veterans returning to college were considered to be of particular importance; the old question of too much time spent on the stars to the neglect of the masses was given attention; the broadening of the competitive athletic program for both boys and girls received special consideration. These and many other problems, including the professional preparation of teachers of health education, physical education, and recreation, were treated at length in the professional literature and discussed in conferences and institutes.

The work of the Athletic Institute since 1947 in promoting and financing five national conferences under the sponsorship of leading organizations in physical education, health education, and recreation is highly significant.[69] A nonprofit organization subsidized by more than a hundred and fifty producers of athletic equipment, the Athletic Institute endeavors to develop a community consciousness of the need for providing better facilities, programs, and leadership to the end that more wholesome living will result. Its publications have been well received and include not only a body of literature resulting from the conferences which represents the best national thinking but printed aids in learning and teaching sports skills, in addition to motion pictures and slide films in archery, badminton, baseball, basketball, bowling, boxing, fishing, football, golf, hunting, softball, tennis, track, tumbling, volleyball, and wrestling. The institute's board of directors includes fourteen national leaders in athletics, physical education, and recreation, two of whom are women.

It would appear, however, that World War II has changed the school program but little, except in the matter of emphasis on interschool and intercollegiate competition. At the college level, particularly, war's end produced problems which were to have serious repercussions in the early nineteen-fifties. The immediate eligibility of athletes returning from service in the armed forces, together with government subsidy under the G. I. Bill, caused spirited bidding for players—"shopping around" of players and the old problems of recruiting and subsidization. War breeds a certain amount of delinquency among servicemen. They were out to get whatever they could, and this applied equally to the college as to the armed services. The problems, however, were not much different from those of the early nineteen-hundreds, except that in the late forties and early fifties athletics were supposed to be under the control of the colleges.

Mid-century "athletic" scandals. The basketball gambling scandals of 1950 and 1951, followed by the West Point cheating affair, brought indignation to sport lovers throughout the country. They started a flood of scathing denunciations against school and college sports in rather wholesale fashion, some justified, some unjustified. The rotten apples must be removed from the barrel lest the entire lot be contaminated; but, in writing about the rotten apples, the good apples must not be forgotten, nor should we overlook the nourishing food they provide. It is most unfortunate for sports that some filth has been discovered in their conduct as well as among the players, but the answer to the rottenness in athletics, as it is in government, is not "do away with athletics or government" but "clean them up." Cultural pressures have been exerted to produce unfortunate conditions, but, by the same token, pressures will be exerted in the other direction.

Two issues of the *Saturday Evening Post* of October, 1951, offer frank accounts of college football as a big-business enterprise and the pressures exerted on the big-time coach and are indicative of the tremendous and often morbid interest which thousands of fans have in the game.[70]

The pressures exerted on athletes, at least in some institutions, are brought out by John Lardner, veteran sports writer. [71] It is his contention that college sports are today performed by specialists, hand-picked from the high schools. Their function is to increase revenue, bring glory to the college via the sports page, and thereby attract more specialists to keep the cycle in operation. He further contends that the varsity becomes the athlete's life, overpowering him to such an extent as to subject him to fears, tensions, and hypocrisies.

Lardner would have us believe that all big-time college sport is rotten, and he is undoubtedly sincere in his condemnation of what he has seen and heard, but he has not conducted a nation-wide survey, and there are big-time teams which can refute everything he has said.

Clair Bee's article in the *Saturday Evening Post* is an excellent exposition of the way in which some colleges get into big-time athletics. [72] He explains why the recruiting system used in many places, coupled with overemphasis and the need of money to support a bigger program, can backfire when gambling pressures are put on the players.

In all likelihood, the events of 1950 and 1951 brought pressure to bear on the American Council on Education that led to the appointment of the famous committee of eleven college presidents. This committee, charged with the responsibility of recommending remedies for college athletics out of control, set forth, early in 1952, a ten-point program which was to be administered by the six powerful accrediting agencies throughout the country. The hope was that the "code" would be enforced by the refusal to accredit schools which violated it.

Reactions to the report were varied. There was some sentiment in favor of every item in the report, and there was considerable opposition to a number of items. Spokesmen for the NCAA, which was holding its annual meeting during the time press releases of the ACE committee's action were made, indicated that changes should be made by working through the NCAA, a body already sanctioned by college presidents in general. There were sharp differences of opinion on at least two points, namely, the ban on bowl games and out-of-season practice. However, it was the opinion of the president of the NCAA that, if colleges as a whole approved the ACE report, then, in essence, it would become the code of the NCAA.

Within two months two eastern college-accrediting agencies, the Middle Atlantic States Association and the New England States College and Secondary Schools Association, had met and announced that they could not enforce the ACE code because it was impractical and beyond their function.

The newspaper publicity which was given to the entire situation is an indication of the apparent importance of intercollegiate competition in the minds of both college administrators and the general public.

So long as educational institutions operate without centralized government control, solutions to their problems, including the problem of competitive athletics, must be sought through the medium of voluntary associative activity. This is the time-honored principle which America has used for a hundred and seventy-five years in business, in politics, and in education. It is often a slow process, because democracy is a slow process; it makes mistakes, and some corruption appears, but it offers the only acceptable means within the framework of our American culture. Solutions to social problems become acceptable only when a majority of the cultural forces involved cooperate to make such solutions effective. Thus when the public and the press, as well as our educational leaders, are agreed on a plan of action even though it be a compromise, the distressing problems of competitive athletics will be minimized.

NOTES

1. Lundberg, George A., Komarovsky, Mirra, and McInerny, Mary Alice, *Leisure: A Suburban Study,* Chapter 8, New York: Columbia University Press, 1934, pp. 396.
2. Barrows, Isabel C. (ed.), *Physical Training Conference of 1889,* Boston: Press of George H. Ellis, 1890, pp. 135.

3. Schlesinger, Arthur M., *Paths to the Present,* p. 9, New York: Macmillan Co., 1949, pp. 317. (Quotation used with the permission of the Macmillan Company.)

4. *Ibid.*

5. Whitton, Fred, "Higher Ideals in Secondary Education," *School Review,* 8 (April, 1900), 261-67.

6. Dewey, John, *The Educational Situation,* pp. 50-80, Chicago: University of Chicago Press, 1906 (Contributions to Education, No. III), pp. 104.

7. Elsson, Jay P., "What Really Is the Montessori Method?" *Ladies' Home Journal,* 29 (November, 1912), 30.

   Nearing, Nellie, and Seeds, Scott, "Fitting the Public School to the Children," *Ladies' Home Journal,* 30 (March, 1913), 20.

   Harrison, Elizabeth, "What the Kindergarten Has Done," *Ladies' Home Journal,* 28 (April, 1911), 23.

   Irwin, Edward P., "Luther Burbank and Child Culture," *Overland Monthly,* 45 (July, 1905), 265-70.

   Angell, Emmett D., "New Games in the School and Playground," *Ladies' Home Journal,* 21 (September, 1904), 9.

   [Roosevelt, Theodore]. "The President's Objections to Modern School Methods," *Ladies' Home Journal,* 23 (January, 1907), 19.

8. Sargent, D. A., "The Place for Physical Training in the School and College Curriculum," *Amer. Phys. Educ. Rev.,* 5 (March, 1900), 9.

9. Johnson, George E., "Children's Games in the Andover Public Schools, as Means for Avoiding Over-Pressure," *Amer. Phys. Educ. Rev.,* 6 (June, 1901), 160-69.

10. McCurdy, J. H., "A Study of the Characteristics of Physical Training in the Public Schools of the United States," *Amer. Phys. Educ. Rev.,* 10 (September, 1905), 202-13.

11. Meylan, Geo. L., "Harvard University Oarsmen," *Amer. Phys. Educ. Rev.,* 9 (June, 1904), 124.

12. Lowman, G. S., "The Regulation and Control of Competitive Sport in Secondary Schools of the United States," *Amer. Phys. Educ. Rev.,* 12 (September, 1907), 241-55; *ibid.,* December, 1907, pp. 307-23.

    Editorial, *Amer. Phys. Educ. Rev.,* 12 (December, 1907), 348.

13. Hetherington, Clark W., "The Demonstration Play School of 1913," *Amer. Phys. Educ. Rev.,* 20 (May, 1915), 282-94; *ibid.,* June, 1915, pp. 373-80; *ibid.,* October, 1915, pp. 429-45.

14. Sargent, Dudley A., "Are Athletics Making Girls Masculine?" *Ladies' Home Journal,* 29 (March, 1912), 11.

15. Ballintine, Harriet I., "The Value of Athletics to College Girls," *Amer. Phys. Educ. Rev.,* 6 (June, 1901), 153.

16. Hart, Lavinia, "A Girl's College Life," *Cosmopolitan,* 31 (June, 1901), 188-95.

17. The rise of intramural sports is particularly well developed in three books:

Mitchell, Elmer D., *Intramural Sports,* New York: A. S. Barnes & Co., 1939, p. 324.

Brammell, P. Roy, *Intramural and Interscholastic Athletics,* Office of Education, Bulletin No. 17, 1932, National Survey of Secondary Education, Monograph No. 27, Washington, D.C.: Government Printing Office, 1933, p. 143.

Means, Louis E., *The Organization and Administration of Intramural Sports,* St. Louis: C. V. Mosby Co., 1949, p. 442.

18. Throughout the issues of the *American Physical Education Review* for 1916, 1917, and 1918 there are many evidences of the growing tendency to institute competition for all.

19. Particularly is this trend shown in the announced programs of the College Physical Education Association, the Athletic Research Society, and the American Physical Education Association. For a rather detailed report see Wilce, J. W., "Report of the Committee on Intramural Sports, Athletic Research Society, December 27, 1918," *Amer. Phys. Educ. Rev.,* 23 (April, 1918), 199-212; *ibid.,* May, 1918, pp. 279-86.

20. Curtis, Henry S., "The Relation of the Playgrounds to a System of Physical Training," *Amer. Phys. Educ. Rev.,* 13 (May, 1908), 248-49.

21. Articles and editorials in the issues of *Playground, American City,* and *American Physical Education Review* just prior to World War I offer ample evidence of the fact that many forces were advocating the wide use of the school plant for play purposes.

22. Hetherington, Clark W., *School Program in Physical Education,* Yonkers, N.Y.: World Book Co., 1922, p. 132.

23. DeGroot, E. B., "President's Address," *Amer. Phys. Educ. Rev.,* 8 (March, 1903), 40-46.

Meylan, Geo. L., "Athletics," *Amer. Phys. Educ. Rev.,* 10 (June, 1905), 157-63.

24. Dorgan, Ethel J., *Luther Halsey Gulick, 1865-1918,* New York: Bureau of Publications, Teachers College, Columbia University, 1934 (Contributions to Education. No. 635), p. 180.

25. Wingate, George W., "The Public Schools Athletic League," *Outing,* 52 (May, 1908), 165-75.

26. Dorgan, *op. cit.*

27. Wingate, *op. cit.*

28. *Ibid.*

29. *Ibid.*

30. Reeve, Arthur B., "The World's Greatest Athletic Organization," *Outing,* 57 (October, 1910), 106-15. The list of cities which patterned their public school athletic leagues after the New York organization included New Orleans, Seattle, Baltimore, Newark, Buffalo, Cleveland, Birming-

ham, Tacoma, Philadelphia, Chicago, Troy, San Francisco, Kansas City (Kan.), Oakland, and Helena.

31. McKenzie, R. Tait, *Exercise in Education and Medicine,* Philadelphia: W. B. Saunders Co., 1923 (3d ed.), p. 601.

32. Reeve, *op. cit.*

33. Wagenhorst, Lewis H., *The Administration and Cost of High School Interscholastic Athletics,* New York: Teachers College, Columbia University, 1926 (Contributions to Education No. 205), p. 134.

34. A news note in the *American Physical Education Review* for December, 1904, voiced the concern of the Massachusetts Teachers Association for the way in which athletic competition was developing and urged that organization to "do something about it."

35. Forsythe, Charles E., *The Administration of High School Athletics,* New York: Prentice-Hall, Inc., 1948, p. 440.

    See also "A Review of Athletics in the High Schools," *Athletic Journal,* 10 (June, 1930), 42-69.

36. *Ibid.*

37. Between 1905 and 1910 *Outlook* printed more than thirty articles on the control of college athletics in general and football in particular.

38. Ryan, W. Carson, Jr., *The Literature of American School and College Athletics,* New York: Carnegie Foundation for the Advancement of Teaching, 1929 (Bulletin No. 24), p. 305.

39. Pierce, Palmer E., "The Intercollegiate Athletic Association of the United States," *Proceedings,* 1907, pp. 27-32.

    Pierce, Palmer E., "The Intercollegiate Athletic Association of the United States," *Amer. Phys. Educ. Rev.,* 14 (February, 1909), 76-81.

    Pierce, Palmer E., "The Intercollegiate Athletic Association of the United States," *ibid.,* 15 (February, 1910), 82-87.

40. Luehring, Frederick W., "Affiliated Organizations: XIV. The National Collegiate Athletic Association," *Jour. of Health & Phys. Educ.,* 18 (December, 1947), 707-9, 751-53. An excellent bibliography of twenty-six references is appended.

    Scott, Harry A., *Competitive Sports in Schools and Colleges,* New York: Harper & Bros., 1951, p. 604.

41. Scott, *op. cit.*

42. A partial list of the conferences in existence in 1929 is to be found in "A Review of Athletics in the College Conferences of 1929-1930," *Athletic Journal,* 10 (June, 1930), 25-42, 69. In this particular article only twenty-seven conference reports are listed.

43. These and other organizations have worked diligently for the proper organization and control of athletic competition and have made their influence felt in all sections of the country.

44. Scott, *op. cit.*

Babbitt, James A., "Present Condition of Gymnastics and Athletics in American Colleges," *Amer. Phys. Educ. Rev.,* 8 (December, 1903), 280-83.

45. "The Fifth Annual Meeting of the National Amateur Athletic Federation—Report of Colonel Henry Breckenridge, President," *Amer. Phys. Educ. Rev.,* 32 (January, 1927), 49.

Griffith, John L., "The Function of the National Amateur Athletic Federation," *Amer. Phys. Educ. Rev.,* 32 (May, 1927), 378.

Griffith, John L., "National Amateur Athletic Federation," *ibid.,* October, 1927, p. 632.

46. "A Merger: The Women's Division, NAAF, Becomes an Integral Part of the AAHPER," *Jour. of Health & Phys. Educ.,* 12 (January, 1941), 36-37.

47. Britt, Albert, "On the Sidelines," *Outing,* 80 (July, 1922), 161. Griffith, John L., "The National Amateur Athletic Federation," *Athletic Journal,* 6 (August, 1925), 3-13, 46-47.

48. Proctor, Wm. M. (ed.), *The Junior College,* Stanford University: Stanford University Press, 1927, p. 226. Merton E. Hill, who has an article in this volume on the rural junior college, should be credited with the quote.

49. Vande Bogart, G. H., "Physical Education and Athletics in Junior Colleges of the United States," *Athletic Journal,* 10 (April, 1930), 14-17, 54.

50. Eells, Walter C., and Davis, Harold M., "The Junior College Transfer in University Athletics," *School Review,* 37 (May, 1929), 371-76.

51. In connection with the publication of the *California State Manual of Physical Education,* a decathlon chart was prepared for teachers of physical education in California which popularized the testing of various sport skills.

52. Educational Policies Commission, *Research Memorandum on Education in the Depression,* New York: Social Science Research Council, 1937 (Bulletin No. 28), p. 173.

53. Rogers, J. F., "What's Happening to Physical Education," *Jour. of Health & Phys. Educ.,* 4 (November, 1933), 17.

Scott, Harry A., "A Comparative Study of the Effects of the Financial Depression on Certain Vocational Aspects of College Physical Education," *Research Quarterly,* 5 (October, 1934), 97-106.

Steiner, Jesse F., *Research Memorandum on Recreation in the Depression,* New York: Social Science Research Council, 1937 (Bulletin No. 32), p. 124.

Rogers, J. E., "How Has the Depression in Education Affected Physical Education?" *Jour. of Health & Phys. Educ.,* 5 (January, 1934), 12-13.

54. Larson, A. W., "Six Man Football," *Athletic Journal,* 18 (June, 1938), 40.

55. See *School and Society*, 46 (August, 1937), 177.

56. Mitchell, E. D., "Physical Education Utilizes CWA and FERA Help," *Jour. of Health & Phys. Educ.*, 5 (March, 1934), 20.

57. Mitchell, E. D., "Great Day for Women's Athletics," *Jour. of Health & Phys. Educ.*, 8 (April, 1937), 218.

58. Wrenn, C. Gilbert, and Harley, D. L. *Time on Their Hands*, Washington, D.C.: American Council on Education, 1941, pp. 266. A report on leisure, recreation, and young people, prepared for the American Youth Commission.

Reeves, Floyd W., "Youth—in the War Crisis and After," *Recreation*, 36 (November, 1942), 459.

59. "Recommendations of the American Youth Commission," *Jour. of Health & Phys. Educ.*, 11 (September, 1940), 339.

60. "A Plan for National Preparedness," *Jour. of Health & Phys Educ.*, 11 (September, 1940), 397-99, 453-54. Gives the detail on the early consideration of the Schwert Bill.

"An Open Letter from Dr. Jones," *Jour. of Health & Phys. Educ.*, 11 (November, 1940), 523-27. The Schwert Bill details; the consideration of a new bill H.R. 1074, the text of which will be found in *Jour. of Health & Phys. Educ.*, 12 (February, 1941), 70-73.

61. "National Association News—Federal Bill Calls for Survey," *Jour. of Health & Phys. Educ.*, 12 (March, 1941), 157. H.R. 1798, introduced January 10, 1941.

62. "The High School Victory Corps" (editorial), *Jour. of Health & Phys. Educ.*, 13 (December, 1942), 590-91.

63. *Physical Fitness through Physical Education*, Washington, D.C.: Government Printing Office, 1942, pp. 102.

Physical Fitness for Students in Colleges and Universities, Washington, D.C.: Government Printing Office, 1943, pp. 140.

Both of these manuals were published by the Federal Security Agency, U.S. Office of Education.

64. *Physical Fitness Program for High Schools and Colleges*, Washington, D.C.: U.S. Navy, Training Division, Bureau of Aeronautics, 1942, pp. 57.

65. Schrader, Carl L., "Education of or through the Physical," *Jour. of Health & Phys. Educ.*, 14 (February, 1943), 87.

McCloy, C. H., "A Common Denominator of Physical Condition," *Jour. of Health & Phys. Educ.*, 14 (February, 1943), 87.

66. Two editorials decry the gymnastic conditioning program and point out that our objectives cannot be achieved by such procedures:

Oberteuffer, Delbert, "An Open Letter to Mr. McCloy and Mr. Schrader," *Jour. of Health & Phys. Educ.*, 14 (June, 1943), 310-11.

Williams, Jesse F., "Who Are Our Friends," *Jour. of Health & Phys. Educ.*, 14 (June, 1943), 311.

These two editorials are answered by McCloy, C. H., "A Reply to Our Critics," *Jour. of Health & Phys. Educ.*, 14 (December, 1943), 526-27.

67. Pieh, Robert, "The Little People," *Jour. of Health & Phys. Educ.*, 15 (May, 1944), 260. Pieh points out that if our leaders are squabbling over what to do, what course shall the little people take? Which way shall they go?

68. Brace, David K., "Physical Fitness in Schools and Colleges," *Jour. of Health & Phys. Educ.*, 15 (November, 1944), 490. Dr. Brace was at that time principal specialist in physical fitness, U.S. Office of Education.

69. Publications of the Athletic Institute (209 S. State St., Chicago 4, Ill.) resulting from national conferences include:
Planning Facilities for Athletics, Recreation, Physical and Health Education, 1947; *Undergraduate Professional Preparation in Health Education, Physical Education and Recreation*, 1948; *Graduate Study in Health Education, Physical Education and Recreation*, 1950; *Physical Education for Children of Elementary School Age*, 1951; *Recreation for Community Living (Guiding Principles)*, 1952.

70. Guthrie, Hunter, "No More Football for Us," *Saturday Evening Post*, 224 (October 13, 1951), 24-25, 115, 117-18.

Cherry, Blair, "Why I Quit Coaching," *Saturday Evening Post*, 224 (October 20, 1951), 40-41, 145-47, 149.

71. Lardner, John, "My Case against Sport," *American*, 152 (October, 1951), 24-25, 111-13.

72. Bee, Clair, "I Know Why They Sold Out to the Gamblers," *Saturday Evening Post*, 224 (February 2, 1952), 26-27, 76-78, 80.

3 / SOCIALIZATION AND SPORT

Socialization is the process by which an individual learns the cultural attitudes, values, and roles of his group and thus acquires a unique personality
and becomes a member of society. The activity of socialization is called
cultural transmission, which is the means by which a society preserves its
norms and perpetuates itself. Every society provides for socialization of its
norms and roles, and every society expects its new members to learn the
standard rules of conduct and assigns someone the role of teaching these. The
primary agents and agencies for socializing the young are the family, peer
groups, schools, churches, and the mass media.

Socializing experiences begin at birth and continue throughout life, but
the critical years in which the primary and lasting socialization occurs is in
childhood and adolescence. For the individual, the socialization process
produces attitudes, values, knowledges, and behaviors which are related to
cultural norms and the roles which the individual plays in the society.

Each society uses informal as well as formal techniques for cultural
transmission. The family, peer groups, and the mass media constitute
informal experiences for socialization, while schools and churches provide
deliberate institutional means of bringing about socialization. Regardless of
the extent of formal agencies for cultural transmission, socialization always
depends to a large extent upon informal face-to-face contacts in small groups
because culture is not merely conveyed by the written or spoken word—it is
acted out in daily activities and becomes an important part of those who are
involved.

Out of the infinite array of socializing stimuli in any society, one individual can only experience a few. The individual is given only one set of parents, and, assuming he lives with them, he is socialized by them and not by other parents. A specific set of individuals serve as "significant others" from which the individual learns and whose behavior he emulates. Most individuals live out their lives in a limited geographical part of society—perhaps in a rural or urban area and perhaps in the Midwest, Southwest, or the Pacific Northwest. In any case the residence, or residences, provide the individual with a unique environment in which his socialization takes place. Thus, for each individual, a specific set of socializing agents impinge upon him and draw him into certain activities and away from others. The social experiences into which he is introduced produce social consequences in the form of attitudes, values, and behaviors.

Very little is known about the social dynamics by which persons are socialized into sports. Undoubtedly, the family, peers, the school, and the mass media all are influential social sources in drawing the great numbers of American youth into sport involvement. Certainly, a great deal of interest and effort is devoted to sports by American youth. Social experiences have their consequences, or outcomes, for the participants and there is a popular belief that sports experiences provide an excellent medium for fostering personal-social qualities which are desirable for and functional in the accepted societal norms and roles in America. The readings in this chapter are concerned with two aspects of socialization: socialization into sport and socialization via sport.

In the first reading, Roberts et al. describe how ethnological research has been used in examining the role of games in society. After defining "a game," they classify games according to their distinctive pattern of play. Thus there are games of physical skill, of strategy, and of chance. The authors then proceed to describe the salient characteristics of each class of game and provide examples. Using the Cross-Cultural Survey materials at Yale University, they found that each type of game is widely but unevenly distributed throughout the world. The authors then identify two general characteristic human needs which games meet and which are related to societal needs. They are the expressive and model characteristics. Applying their three-category classification of games to 50 tribal societies, the authors report that their results suggest that games of strategy are related to complex social systems, games of chance are associated with religious activities, and games of physical skill are related to natural environmental conditions. In essence, this research suggests that a multitude of psychological and societal factors socialize persons into a specific type of game involvement. Although the authors examined only relatively primitive cultures, perhaps some extrapolation can be made by the reader with regard to American society and the ways in which American children are socialized into sport.

There is little social research on the family and its role in sport socialization. Presumably, though, the family figures prominently in socializing youth into sport involvement. Parents and siblings may encourage and serve as models for drawing children into sports, but anecdotal accounts are about all that exists with regard to familial influence. One exception to this state of affairs is the second reading. In this reading, Nisbett relates one aspect of family structure—birth order—to sports participation. Drawing upon other research which shows that later-born children will endure more pain stimuli than first-born children and inferring from this research that later-born children will more likely be found in dangerous sports—sports involving physical contact and risk of bodily injury—Nisbett tested this proposition. Using a sample of collegiate students, he found that later-born children are indeed overrepresented in dangerous sports, such as football, soccer, and rugby, and that the probability of sport participation in a dangerous sport increases with family size.

Sport involvement socializes members to the specific norms and roles of the activity, but there is a prevailing belief that sport also produces desirable attitudes, values, and behaviors for performing in the diffuse roles of parent, employee, employer, citizen, etc. Snyder reviews the notion about socialization via sport—that is, whether socialization which occurs in sports results in the development of situational role-specific characteristics or general and diffuse personal-social characteristics. He suggests that there is a considerable body of sociological literature which supports situational role-specific socialization as not carrying over to other situational contexts unless there are similarities in the situational expectations. He suggests that the analysis of the dimensions of social interaction in the socialization process is necessary to understand the influence of sport for developing specific or diffuse role behavior, and he further points out that the dimensions vary with the situational context within which the experience takes place. He identifies five dimensions and discusses each one with regard to sport. He concludes that although sport may develop only role-specific behavior traits it is no different than many social experiences. In fact, he argues that this is just as well since some behaviors accepted and sanctioned in a sport context might be dysfunctional in the broader society.

In the next reading, Sage identifies briefly the possible ways in which American children may be socialized into sport and then discusses at greater length the social outcomes of sport. He emphasizes that little data exist to clearly delineate the extent to which socialization occurs via sport. The effects of sport involvement on personality development, self-concept development, social status, value orientations, and sportsmanship attitudes are examined from the standpoint of the speculations and research which have been completed on this subject. Sage concludes with a discussion of potential dysfunctional effects of youth sports programs on the participants. Kids' sports programs have been damned and praised; whether they minimize the potential dysfunctional aspects depends to a great extent upon the leadership in such programs, Sage suggests.

Mandel and Vander Velden, in the next reading, describe a research project into the relationship between the professionalization of attitude toward play of boys who had participated in organized sports and that of boys who had not. Extending research by Webb, who found that attitude toward play moved from a high priority on "fairness" and "equity" to "skill" and "victory" as the children got older, Mandel and Vander Velden hypothesized that participants in organized sports programs would place greater emphasis on skill or victory while nonparticipants would emphasize fairness as the most important attitude toward play. The findings supported their predictions. Although it is difficult to credit (or discredit) sports participation entirely for the greater professionalized attitudes toward play, since so many socializing agents and agencies are influencing the individual, it seems that sport for fun, enjoyment, fairness, and equity are sacrificed at the altar of skill and victory as children move toward adulthood.

Sage, in the next reading, reports on a research project concerned with the relationship between personality and sport. The subject of this relationship has been a central interest of physical educators and coaches for many years. It has been suggested that certain personality traits are developed by sports participation. Although an extensive body of literature exists which is concerned with the relationship of personality and sport, the literature is contradictory and confusing. The notion that personality traits are actually modified through sports experiences has not been verified because the research strategies which have been employed are actually incapable of producing findings of a cause-effect nature. The notion that athletes in various sports possess unique and specific personalities has also been widespread, and occasional studies that have found personality differences between athletes from different sports have tended to perpetuate this idea. However, recent research, using more sophisticated research tools, has generally found no differences. Sage presents a study of personality profiles on over 500 collegiate athletes from eight different sports. He found no significant differences between athletes from the various sport groups. On the basis of his study and other recent research, Sage cautions about accepting notions about a sport-specific personality.

The final two readings are concerned with the personality and value orientations of athletic coaches. Personality and value orientations of coaches may be important factors in socializing the young athletes who play under them because these qualities may influence the personal and social development of the athletes. In recent years critics have attacked coaches, claiming that their personality and values are brutalizing and dehumanizing to their athletes. Sage investigated the Machiavellian trait among high school and college coaches and found that coaches were no more Machiavellian than a national sample of college students. In the final reading, Sage reports on the value orientations of coaches compared to college students and businessmen. As Sage predicted, he did find that coaches tend to be more conservative than college students, but not as conservative as some critics have suggested. However, in comparison to businessmen, coaches tended to be more liberal in value orientation.

GAMES IN CULTURE

John M. Roberts, Malcolm J. Arth, and Robert R. Bush

Recreational activities have been classic ethnographic concerns, and sophisticated questions about the distributions of games were asked early in the history of anthropology.[1] Still, the science has yet to produce a general theory which deals with such anthropological problems as the description and explanation of the historical development of games, their world distribution, and their functional significance in various societies. This paper suggests a line of inquiry which might lead to the construction of such a theory.

In the extensive ethnographic literature on the subject, a wide range of recreational activities has been called "games," but this general category is too broad for the purposes of this article. Here, a game is defined as a recreational activity characterized by: (1) organized play, (2) competition, (3) two or more sides, (4) criteria for determining the winner, and (5) agreed-upon rules. Other recreational activities which do not satisfy this definition, such as noncompetitive swimming, top-spinning, and string-figure making, are considered "amusements." It is relevant to note that most games reported in the ethnographies are activities in which adults can participate.

The games of the world may be classified in terms of distinctive patterns of play. Some outcomes are determined primarily by the physical abilities of the players, some by a series of moves, each of which represents a player's choice among alternatives, and others either by nonrational guesses or by reliance on the operation of some mechanical chance device such as a die;

John Roberts, Malcolm J. Arth, and Robert R. Bush, "Games in Culture," *American Anthropologist*, 61:597-605 (August 1959). Reprinted by permission of the American Anthropological Association.

some are determined by combinations of these patterns. All these ways of determining outcomes are widely distributed among the societies of the world, and it is therefore possible to offer the following general classification of games: (1) physical skill, (2) strategy, and (3) chance.

Each of these three categories requires further definition. Games of physical skill as herein defined must involve the use of physical skill, but may or may not involve strategy or chance; examples are marathon races, prize fights, hockey, and the hoop and pole games. In games of strategy, physical skill must be absent and a strategy must be used; chance may or may not be involved. Chess, go, poker, and the Ashanti game of *wari* are examples. Finally, games of chance are so defined that chance must be present and both physical skill and strategy must be absent; examples are high-card-wins, dice games, and the moccasin games. We should note that there are three defining attributes for games of chance (chance, strategy, and physical skill), two for games of strategy (strategy and physical skill) and one for games of physical skill (physical skill).

Games of each type are widely but unevenly distributed. Although we did not conduct a comprehensive survey, data on games were sought both from the literature and from the Cross-Cultural Survey files[2] on approximately 100 tribes. These tribes displayed a wide geographical distribution and great cultural variability, but they did not represent either a stratified sample or a random sample of the tribes of the world; the recorded materials on games were so uneven that this was impossible.

In 82 instances the tribal literature contained some information on games. In the literature on 19 tribes explicit statements were found that either a complete description of the games was being given or that no games existed. We refer to these tribes as well-covered: Baiga, Chagga, Chukchee, Copper Eskimo, Hopi, Kababish, Lepcha, Lesu, Macheyenga, Menomini, Murngin, Nauru, Siriono, Siwa, Tanala, Wapishana, Warrau, Yaruro, and Zuni. With 31 additional societies, it was inferred either from similar reports by independent observers or from the extensive treatment by a single writer that the descriptions were intended to be complete. We refer to these tribes as apparently well-covered: Achewa, Ainu, Aleut, Alor, Arikara, BaVenda, Bena, Buka, Dahomey, Euahlayi, Gros Ventre, Jukun, Kansa, Kiwai, Korea, Kwakiutl, Lakher, Lamba, Malekula, Maricopa, Masai, Mbundu, Navaho, Papago, Rwala Bedouin, Sema Naga, Vietnam, Witoto, Woleaian, Yap, and Yungar. The materials on the remaining societies were inadequate; although games were noted in some of them, there was no reason to infer that the descriptions were complete. It is plain that while widespread interest in games can be easily documented, the systematic description of all the games played by the members of a tribe is by no means common in the ethnographic literature.

Among the 50 tribes that were either well-covered or apparently well-covered, 19 had games of strategy, 19 had games of chance, and 44 had games of physical skill (see Table 1). Five were reported as having no games at all. It is clear that games, as here defined, are widely distributed, but that no single type is universal.

Table 1 Distribution of Game Types in Fifty Societies

Societies	Number of societies	Physical skill	Chance	Strategy
Achewa, Aleut, Chagga, Hopi, Korea, Nauru, Vietnam, Zuni	8	+	+	+
Ba Venda, Jukun, Lakher, Lamba, Masai, Mbundu, Tanala, Woleaian, Yap	9	+	–	+
Dahomey	1	–	+	+
Siwa	1	–	–	+
Baiga, Chukchee, Copper Eskimo, Gros Ventre, Kansa, Kwakiutl, Maricopa, Menomini, Navaho, Papago	10	+	+	–
Ainu, Alor, Arikara, Bena, Buka, Euahlayi, Kiwai, Lesu, Macheyenga, Malekula, Rwala Bedouin, Sema Naga, Siriono, Wapishana, Witoto, Yungar	16	+	–	–
Kababish, Lepcha, Murngin, Warrau, Yaruro	5	–	–	–

Games occur so widely that it is an easy inference that they meet general human needs. They are integrated into tribal cultures in many ways. For example, in some societies games are linked with religion; elsewhere, they are associated with hunting or war. The relationships between games and needs of any single society must be complex and generalizations about them cannot be made easily, but consideration of two general characteristics of all games points the way toward further inquiry. These are the expressive and the model characteristics.

The expressive character of games is plain. They do not directly satisfy the biological needs associated with survival. There are few obvious environmental and technological limitations on them. Indeed, the artifacts for most games can be made by peoples with quite simple technologies. Go, a Japanese game of strategy, requires only two sets of "stones" and a rectangular board on which 19 equidistant lines are drawn parallel to one edge and 19 lines at right angles to them. This simple equipment could easily be duplicated by almost any group, but the game itself is equal in complexity to any in the world. Everything suggests that games are expressive, much as are folk tales, dramatic productions, music, and paintings. If such is the case, games should be related to other expressive behaviour, some of which has already been explored cross-culturally.

It is also evident that most games are models of various cultural activities. Many games of physical skill simulate combat or hunting, as in boxing and competitive trap shooting. Games of strategy may simulate chase, hunt, or war activities, as in backgammon, fox and geese, or chess. The relationship between games of chance and divining (ultimately a religious activity) is well known. In instances where a game does not simulate a current cultural activity, it will be found that the games ancestral to it were more clearly models. The characteristics of such models have not been systematically studied, but they are related to problems in abstract thought and cognitive mapping.

If games are expressive models, they should be related to other aspects of culture and to the variables which figure in expressive or projective mechanisms. More specifically, games of strategy which are models of social interaction should be related to the complexity of the social system; games of chance which are models of interaction with the supernatural should be linked with other expressive views of the supernatural; and there is a possibility that games of physical skill may be related to aspects of the natural environment. This paper examines these possibilities in the hope of stimulating further inquiry.

GAMES OF STRATEGY

Games of strategy do appear to be models of social interactive systems. Chess, for example, as described in an early classic,

> ... must be classed as a game of war. Two players direct a conflict between two armies of equal strength upon a field of battle, circumscribed in extent, and offering no advantage of ground to either side (Murray 1913:25).

The role structure of the two "armies" is quite complex. Both the structure and the terminology of such a game of strategy may offer clues to the nature of the interactive system it represents. Pieces are called "men"; they capture or kill, they attack or defend, they race, and so on.

Let us consider the hypothesis, then, that since games of strategy simulate social systems, those systems should be complex enough to generate such needs for expression. Simple societies should not possess games of strategy and should resist borrowing them.

In his world sample, G. P. Murdock provided various ratings on 565 tribes (Murdock 1957). Two of his ratings—on levels of political integration, and on levels of social stratification—may be used as indices of social system complexity. Some of Murdock's ratings were combined to produce the breakdown shown on Table 2. The ratings "No political integration" and "Autonomous local communities" were classed as low political integration; "Minimal states," "Little states," and "States" were classed as high political integration. The categories "Absent," "Formal age groups," and "Wealth distinctions," were classed as social stratification absent. "Hereditary aristocracy" and "Complex stratification" were classed as social stratification present. Forty-three of the 50 tribes found to be adequately covered in our study received ratings on these two dimensions. The results given below confirm the expected relationship between games of strategy and social complexity, but this relationship does not hold for games of chance and physical skill.

With political integration, 52 tribes supported the hypothesis while 11 did not. With social classes, 31 tribes fitted the hypothesis and 12 did not. Among societies with either low political integration and no social classes or high political integration and social classes, 25 societies supported the hypothesis and five did not.

The association between games of strategy and complexity of social organization is supported also by the fact that among the adequately-covered tribes, the four hunting and gathering groups lacked games of strategy, only one out of five fishing groups had such a game, and only one out of three pastoral groups. On the other hand, no truly complex society appears to have lacked them.

Table 2 does not list the most complex American tribes, but among the inadequately-covered tribes, games of strategy were reported for the Aztec, Inca, Ashanti, and Tiv. According to Murdock, three of these tribes were politically integrated and socially stratified, but the Tiv had local autonomy and incipient social stratification with slavery. The presence of the Aztec and Inca in this group would indicate that the hypothesis also holds for the New World.

Table 2   System Complexity and Games of Strategy

	Games of strategy present	Games of strategy absent
Low political integration		
Social classes absent	3 (Hopi, Woleaian, Zuni)	13 (Baiga, Copper Eskimo, Kiwai, Lesu, Murngin, Navaho, Papago, Siriono, Wapishana, Warrau, Witoto, Yaruro, Yungar)
Social classes present	2 (Aleut, Nauru)	5 (Alor, Buka, Chukchee, Kwakiutl, Malekula)
High political integration		
Social classes absent	2 (Achewa, Masai)	4 (Ainu, Gros Ventre, Maricopa, Menomini)
Social classes present	12 (Ba Venda, Chagga, Dahomey, Jukun, Korea, Lakher, Lamba, Mbundu, Siwa, Tanala, Vietnam, Yap)	2 (Kababish, Rwala Bedouin)

A few cases are worthy of special note. In Africa, the Bushmen do not have a game of strategy and the Hottentot do. The Tanala may be divided into two distinct groups, one of which is hierarchically organized while the other is not, and of these only the first has a game of strategy.[3]

GAMES OF CHANCE

Unlike games of strategy, games of chance appear to be associated with religious activities. It is commonly thought by many peoples that the winners of games of chance have received supernatural or magical aid. Even in the European tradition, religious beliefs conditioned views of games of chance:

> The Greeks and the Romans (so far as one can make summary statements about races whose members held such differing views) seem, on the whole, to have regarded the world as partly determined by chance. Gods and goddesses had influence over the course of events and, in particular, could interfere with the throwing of dice; but they were only higher

beings with superhuman powers, not omnipotent entities who controlled everything. And the vaguer deities—Fortuna, the Fates, and Fate itself—appear to modern eyes more in the retributive role of a personified guilty conscience than as masters of the universe. The situation was radically changed by Christianity. For the early fathers of the Church, the finger of God was everywhere. Some causes were overt and some were hidden, but nothing happened without cause. In that sense, nothing was random and there was no chance. . . . Thomas Aquinas, arguing that everything is subject to the providence of God, mentions explicitly the objection that, if such were the case, hazard and luck would disappear. . . . He reflected the spirit of his age, wherein God and an elaborate hierarchy of His ministers controlled and foreordained the minutest happening; if anything seemed to be due to chance that was our ignorance, not the nature of things (Kendall 1956:11).

Although games of chance, as found over the world, are "fair" games, perhaps as a result of long trial and error, explicit theories of chance do not appear in primitive cultures. Again and again, outcomes are attributed to the intervention of magical or supernatural forces.

It is plausible, then, to argue that games of chance should be linked to the larger expressive system of religious beliefs and that they are exercises in relationships with the supernatural. These hypotheses were not tested extensively, but the use of three scales developed by Lambert, Triandis, and Wolf[4] provided some interesting results. Here a sample of tribes was scaled in terms of (1) the frequency of benevolent actions by gods or spirits, (2) the frequency of aggression by gods or spirits, and (3) the frequency of coercion of gods or spirits. The first two scales had seven points ranging from "always benevolent or aggressive" to "never benevolent or aggressive." The mid-points were defined as being "benevolent or aggressive about one-half of the time." Table 3 combines these two independent scales. The coercion scale ran from "continuous, every day or more often" to "never," and the midpoint was "once a month." The hypothesis that games of chance will occur in societies high in benevolence, low in aggression, or high in coercion is supported by Table 3 and Table 4 (only tribes appearing on the Lambert scale are cited). However, the relationships shown did not hold either for games of strategy or for games of physical skill.

In the case of the benevolence measure, 16 out of 19 cases supported the hypothesis; with aggression, 15 out of 19 supported the hypothesis; and with coercion, 14 out of 15 cases supported the hypothesis. In keeping with the hypothesis, it might be conjectured from the lack of reference to gambling games in the latest concordance of the Bible that the God of the ancient Hebrews was neither benevolent more than 50 percent of the time nor was he easily coerced.

Table 3   Frequency of Benevolence and Aggression by Gods, and Games of Chance

	Games of chance absent	Games of chance present
Benevolent less than 50%		
Aggressive more than 50%	7 (Alor, BaVenda, Buka, Lakher, Lamba, Lepcha, Siriono)	1 (Kwakiutl)
Aggressive less than 50%	1 (Lesu)	
Benevolent more than 50%		
Aggressive more than 50%	1 (Bena)	1 (Navaho)
Aggressive less than 50%	1 (Mbundu)	6 (Baiga, Chagga, Dahomey, Hopi, Papago, Zuni)

Table 4   Frequency of Coercion of Gods or Spirits, and Games of Chance

Frequency of coercion	Games of chance absent	Games of chance present
Low	9 (Alor, BaVenda, Bena, Buka, Lakher, Lamba, Lesu, Siriono, Tanala)	1 (Hopi)
High		5 (Baiga, Dahomey, Navaho, Papago, Zuni)

GAMES OF PHYSICAL SKILL

There is no apparent relationship between the presence or absence of games of strategy and the number of games of physical skill, but there does appear to be relationship between the presence or absence of games of chance and the number of games of physical skill (see Table 5). Societies having five or more games of physical skill frequently have games of chance but this may be a consequence of the varying completeness of descriptions in the literature.

Table 5   Number of Games of Physical Skill and Games of Chance

Games of physical skill present	Games of chance present	Games of chance absent
0 to 4	4 (Achewa, Baiga, Dahomey, Kansa)	26 (Alor, Ainu, BaVenda, Bena, Buka, Jukun, Kababish, Kiwai, Lakher, Lamba, Lepcha, Lesu, Macheyenga, Malekula, Masai, Mbundu, Murngin, Sema Naga, Siriono, Siwa, Tanala, Wapishana, Warrau, Witoto, Yaruro, Yungar)
5 to 20	15 (Aleut, Chagga, Chukchee, Copper Eskimo, Gros Ventre, Hopi, Korea, Kwakiutl, Maricopa, Menomini, Nauru, Navaho, Papago, Vietnam, Zuni)	4 (Arikara, Euahlayi, Rwala Bedouin, Yap

There was also a relationship between geographical location and the number of games of physical skill in a society. Of 23 tribes living within 20 degrees latitude of the equator, 18 had fewer than five games of physical skill, while of 24 tribes living more than 20 degrees north or south, only nine had fewer than five games of physical skill. Tentative work with mean annual temperature and protein and fat in the diet suggests some correlation. There may be a relationship between environment and activity as expressed in numbers of games of physical skill, but the data were inadequate for an extensive analysis.

DISCUSSION

The foregoing suggests that games of strategy are related to social systems, games of chance are related to religious beliefs, and that games of physical skill may be related to environmental conditions. The social system, the religion, and the environment are three important foci of anthropological interest, and further study of these relationships appears to be warranted.

Psychological inquiries are also indicated. In general, this paper supports the psychoanalytic notion that games are exercises in mastery. Certainly the area of child socialization, which has often been linked with expressive phenomena, should be considered. Exploratory work with unpublished data provided by Whiting, Lambert, and Child suggests that the presence of games of strategy is positively associated with low permissiveness in child training, high severity of bowel training, and high reward for obedience behavior. Games of chance appear to be related to none of the foregoing, but rather to high frequency of responsible behavior and high frequency of achievement behavior. Games of physical skill seem to be positively associated with low permissiveness and high conflict over nurturant and self-reliant behavior. Thus, we can speculate that further inquiry will show that games of strategy are linked with the learning of social roles, games of chance with responsibility and achievement, and games of physical skill with self-reliance. Alternatively stated, games of strategy may be related to mastery of the social system; games of chance may be linked with mastery of the supernatural; and games of physical skill are possibly associated with the mastery both of self and of environment.

This paper has advanced a three-category classification of games and has reviewed the distribution of these game types in 50 societies. It has suggested that games may be exercises in the mastery of environment or self, social system, and of the supernatural. We have not intended to say that the already well-recognized functions of games should be ignored, but rather have intended to suggest some new ways in which such expressive behavior might be viewed. If all the relationships suggested in this paper do not ultimately hold, it is still hoped that enough evidence has been presented to warrant further comparative studies of games. An anthropological theory of games could be the result.

NOTES

1. Cf. Tylor's famous articles on patolli and American lot-games (Tylor, 1879:116-129; 1896:55-67). The patolli problem stated by Tylor has continued to intrigue anthropologists and interest in this problem provided the initial impetus for the present investigation.

2. The authors are indebted to the Laboratory of Social Relations, Harvard University, for the support of this research and to the Cross-Cultural Survey, Institute of Human Relations, Yale University, and the Center for Advanced Study in the Behavioral Sciences for auxiliary aid. The authors are also grateful to John Champe, Franklin Fenenga, William Lambert, Kimball Romney, Richard Savage, Elizabeth Tooker, Leigh Minturn

Triandis, Gene Weltfish, John M. Whiting, Margery Wolf, and others, for useful suggestions and comments.

3. Personal communication from Elizabeth Tooker.

4. Use was made of the Lambert, Triandis and Wolf unpublished data which were subsequently reported in revised form in the *Journal of Abnormal and Social Psychology*.

REFERENCES

Kendall, M. G. (1956), "Studies in this history of probability and statistics. II. The beginnings of a probability calculus," *Biometrika,* 43:1-14.

Lambert, William W., Leigh Minturn Triandis, and Margery Wolf (1959), "Some correlates of beliefs in the malevolence and benevolence of supernatural beings—A cross-societal study," *Journal of Abnormal and Social Psychology,* 58:162-169.

Murdock, George Peter (1957), "World ethnographic sample," *American Anthropologist,* 59:664-687.

Murray, H. J. R. (1913), *A History of Chess,* Oxford, Clarendon Press.

Tylor, E. B. (1879), "On the game of patolli in ancient Mexico and its probable Asiatic origin," *Journal of the Royal Anthropological Institute,* 8:116-129.

_____(1896), "On American lot-games as evidence of Asiatic intercourse before the time of Columbus," *Internationales Archiv für Ethnographie,* 9:55-67.

Whiting, John W. M., and Irving L. Child (1953), *Child Training and Personality: A Cross-Cultural Study,* New Haven, Yale University Press.

BIRTH ORDER AND PARTICIPATION IN DANGEROUS SPORTS[1]

Richard E. Nisbett

It was found that firstborns are less likely than later-borns to participate in dangerous sports. The finding is consistent with evidence showing firstborns to be more frightened by the prospect of physical injury than later-borns.

Several findings reported by Schachter (1959) in *The Psychology of Affiliation* indicate that firstborns find physical pain more aversive or the prospect of it more frightening than do later-born individuals. When told that they were to receive severe electric shock, firstborn females reported more fear than did later-born females. In an experiment on toleration of electric shock, firstborn females asked the experimenter to terminate the shock earlier in the series than did later-born females. And an analysis of data obtained by Torrance (1954) indicated that in a situation involving considerable physical danger—piloting a fighter plane in combat—firstborns were less effective than later-borns.

If it is true that firstborns find pain or the prospect of it more aversive than do later-borns, one would expect them to avoid activities where the risk of physical injury is high. This paper examines the proportion of first- and later-born individuals who participate in one such activity—dangerous sports.

METHOD

Birth-order information was obtained from four samples: (a) A complete record of the intercollegiate athletic participation of the 2,432 undergraduates enrolled at Columbia in 1963 was obtained from the college files. Data on athletics or birth order were missing for fewer than 1% of the population; (b) reports of interscholastic participation in high school sports and birth-order information were obtained by questionnaire from 110 Pennsylvania State University freshmen enrolled in introductory psychology in 1964[2]; (c) similar reports were obtained from 384 Yale University students

Richard E. Nisbett, "Birth Order and Participation in Dangerous Sports," *Journal of Personality and Social Psychology*, 8(4):351-353, 1968. Copyright © 1968 by the American Psychological Association and reproduced by permission.

enrolled in introductory psychology in 1967; (d) birth-order reports were obtained by mailed questionnaire in 1964 from a professional football team—the New York Giants—and a professional baseball team—the New York Mets. Response to the mailed questionnaire was a little less than 50% in each club.

RESULTS

The proportion of Columbia students who participated in a dangerous intercollegiate sport at some point in their college career is presented in Table 1 as a function of birth order and family size. Dangerous sports were defined as those which a sample of 35 students rated as the three most dangerous played at Columbia. These were football, soccer, and rugby.

Two striking effects in Table 1 should be observed in passing: (a) Firstborns are markedly overrepresented in the sample. At every family size, the number of firstborns is greater than the number of children at every other position. This is consistent with Schachter's (1963) finding that firstborns are more likely to attend college; (b) the probability that an individual will play a dangerous sport increases with family size. This fact is consistent with

Table 1 Proportion of Columbia Undergraduates Who Play Dangerous Sports as a Function of Birth Order and Number of Children in Family

| Birth order | Family size | | | | | | |
	1	2	3	4	5	6 or more	Total
First	.088	.072	.096	.129	.206	.438	.091
N	(443)	(639)	(272)	(93)	(34)	(16)	(1497)
Second		.106	.130	.280	.400	.167	.130
N		(473)	(177)	(50)	(15)	(6)	(721)
Third			.121	.278	.111	.000	.150
N			(99)	(29)	(9)	(3)	(140)
Fourth				.250	.375	.000	.250
N				(20)	(8)	(4)	(32)
Fifth					.182	1.00	.308
N					(11)	(2)	(13)
Sixth						.143	.143
N						(7)	(7)
Total proportion	.088	.086	.111	.203	.247	.143	.110
N	(443)	(1112)	(548)	(192)	(77)	(7)	(2410)

Schachter's (1959) finding that large-family children were less frightened by the prospect of electric shock than small-family children, but since the family-size effect was observed only in the Columbia and Yale samples, it may be due to an idiosyncrasy of the Ivy League population.

Table 1 clearly shows the predicted birth order effect. At all but the very largest family sizes, firstborns are less likely to play a dangerous sport than later-borns.[3] Students from large families are more likely to play a dangerous sport than those from small families, and, on the average, later-borns are members of larger families than are firstborns. Thus, to examine the birth order effect it is necessary to control for family size. Of a variety of ways to do this, one of the more conservative is simply to compare players and nonplayers on the ratio of first- to *second*-borns from families with two or more children. This throws away much of the data, but completely circumvents the confounding effects of family size. The resulting χ^2 is 6.15, which for $df = 1$ is significant at the .02 level. The data on which this test is based are presented in Table 2.

Also presented in Table 2 are the comparable proportions for players and nonplayers for the Pennsylvania State and the Yale samples, and the proportions for the professional football and baseball teams. These differences are of the same magnitude and direction as that for the larger sample of Columbia students.

It may have occurred to the reader that football, rugby, and soccer are not only dangerous sports but team sports and that this latter similarity might account for the differential participation of firstborns and later-borns. A comparison of the participation of firstborns in nondangerous team[4] sports with their participation in nondangerous individual[5] sports renders this alternative unlikely. For the Columbia group, where the sample was large enough to perform the appropriate analysis, firstborns were nonsignificantly *more* likely to play a nondangerous individual sport: The ratio of first- to second-borns from families of two or more children among students playing team sports was .62, while the ratio for those playing only individual sports was .55. Finally, the underrepresentation of firstborns in the dangerous sports is not due to an avoidance of sports in general. At all three schools the proportion of firstborns among players of nondangerous sports was entirely similar to the proportion of firstborns among students who played no sports at all.

DISCUSSION

In summary, the evidence is in complete accord with the expectation that firstborns would avoid dangerous activity. Firstborns are as likely to play

Table 2   Ratio of Firstborns to Second Borns as a Function of Athletic Participation

	Columbia		Pennsylvania State		Yale		Professional teams	
	Students who play dangerous sports (college)	Students who do not play dangerous sports	Students who play dangerous sports (in high school)	Students who do not play dangerous sports	Students who play dangerous sports (in high school)	Students who do not play dangerous sports	Football	Baseball
Ratio of firstborns to second borns	.510	.603	.560	.660	.508	.581	.600	.727
N	(192)	(1583)	(25)	(53)	(124)	(260)	(15)	(11)

sports with low risk of injury as later-borns, but less likely to play those involving high risk. The underrepresentation of firstborns in the dangerous sports is not a pronounced effect but it is a consistent one. In high school, college, and professional athletics, firstborns are less likely to play the high-risk sports.

This type of evidence is of course subject to all the ills that correlational data are heir to. A variety of explanations could be marshalled to explain the finding that firstborns avoid dangerous sports. The fact that they do not avoid the safer sports eliminates many of the contending alternative explanations, however. In addition, the only empirically demonstrated birth order difference which can comfortably explain the finding is the observation that firstborns react with more anxiety to the prospect of physical harm than do later-borns.

Since Sampson, in his review of the birth-order literature (1965), gives the impression that there are no consistent birth order differences with respect to anxiety, a re-review of the evidence on this point is in order. It is correct to conclude that the evidence is contradictory and confused regarding chronic anxiety and situational anxiety where the threat is not physical. However, the evidence concerning reaction to physical danger is virtually uncontradicted. In addition to the studies cited in the introduction, Helmreich and Collins (1967) have replicated with a male population the finding that firstborns respond with more fear to the prospect of physical harm than do later-borns; and Helmreich (1966) has shown that firstborns express more fear than later-borns in a hazardous diving situation, and, as Torrance (1954) found with fighter pilots, perform more poorly. A reanalysis of data reported by Nisbett and Schachter (1966) again replicates the finding that firstborns respond with more fear to the prospect of physical harm than do later-borns. Following the fear manipulation, subjects in that experiment were given a jarring and unpleasant electric shock. Firstborns were judged by observers to react more strongly to it than later-borns ($p < .06$). The firstborn subjects also reported the shock to be more painful than did later-born subjects ($p < .05$). While it is possible that firstborns are in some way more sensitive to pain (and this conclusion was reached by Carman in 1899), a more cautious interpretation is to say that the reaction to the electric shock provides behavioral evidence that firstborns were more fearful than later-borns.

Only one study reviewed by Sampson failed to report significantly greater fear on the part of firstborns in response to physical danger (Weller, 1962). The writer is not aware of any other contradictory evidence. It seems safe to conclude that firstborns are more frightened by the prospect of physical harm than are later-borns, and it is plausible to infer that they avoid dangerous sports for this reason.

NOTES

1. This article is based on a paper presented at the Eastern Psychological Association meeting, Boston, April 1967. The author is indebted to Stanley Schachter for advice and help in all phases of this study.
2. Jerome E. Singer kindly provided this data.
3. The reversal for families of six or more children is not significant.
4. Baseball, basketball, crew.
5. Wrestling, track, swimming, tennis, fencing, golf.

REFERENCES

Carman, A., "Pain and strength measurements of 1,507 school children in Saginaw, Michigan," *American Journal of Psychology*, 1899, **10**, 392-398.

Helmreich, R. L., *Prolonged stress in Sealab II: A field study of individual and group reactions*, unpublished doctoral dissertation, Yale University, 1966.

Helmreich, R. L., and Collins, B. E., "Situational determinants of affiliative preference under stress," *Journal of Personality and Social Psychology*, 1967, **6**, 79-85.

Nisbett, R. E., and Schachter, S., "Cognitive manipulation of pain," *Journal of Experimental Social Psychology*, 1966, **2**, 227-236.

Sampson, E. E., "The study of ordinal position: Antecedents and outcomes," in B. A. Maher (Ed.), *Progress in Experimental Personality Research*, Vol. 2, New York: Academic Press, 1965.

Schachter, S., "Birth order, eminence, and higher education," *American Sociological Review*, 1963, **28**, 757-768.

Schachter, S., *The Psychology of Affiliation*, Stanford: Stanford University Press, 1959.

Torrance, E. B., *A Psychological Study of American Jet Aces*, paper presented at the meeting of the Western Psychological Association, Long Beach, California, 1954.

Weller, L., "The relationship of birth order to anxiety," *Sociometry*, 1962, **25**, 415-417.

ASPECTS OF SOCIALIZATION IN SPORTS AND PHYSICAL EDUCATION

Eldon E. Snyder

In a recent article Kenyon[1] considered the socialization process that takes place within the framework of sports and physical education programs. He pointed out that physical education and sports are valuable areas of social interaction for the analysis of the socialization process. Specifically, he focused on the goals of socialization; for example, does socialization in physical activity result in the development of generalized and diffuse characteristics or does it develop only the ability to play specific roles within the confines of the particular physical activity in question? Frequently, physical education and sports are cited as contributing to the development of desirable traits for playing diffuse roles, such as "democratic citizenship," "moral character," "adjusted personality," "respect for constituted authority," and "the ability to win and lose graciously."[2,3,4]

Kenyon presents a survey of research suggesting that various personality traits are associated with participation in physical activities. Recent research by Schafer and Armer[5] indicates that high school athletes may demonstrate higher academic performances than nonathletes. However, in many cases these studies do not hold constant the possible antecedent and intervening variables necessary to clarify the cause and effect relationships between these activities and the development of personality characteristics. Ulrich noted that, "Although there is always the hope that behavioral patterns can be taught in one place and used in another, it would seem that each behavioral response is specific to the situation, the time, and the place in which it is employed."[6] Sociological literature provides considerable support that situational role-specific expectations and behaviors may not carry over to other situational contexts unless the situational expectations are similar.[7,8,9]

THEORETICAL ASSUMPTIONS

Kenyon concluded with several propositions regarding the development of specific and diffuse roles through the media of physical education and sports.

Eldon E. Snyder, "Aspects of Socialization in Sports and Physical Education," *Quest,* Monograph XIV, June, 1970, pp. 1-7. Reprinted by permission.

He does not feel that instructional programs in physical education are particularly effective for socialization into diffuse roles; however, in inter-scholastic and intercollegiate athletics the increased frequency and intensity of social interaction is likely to socialize the athlete into both specific and diffuse roles.

Starting with these propositions, this article extends the discussion of the socialization process and the theoretical assumptions of specific-diffuse role learning. Specifically, the position taken is that by refining the analysis of the situational context within which physical education and sports take place, a greater understanding is likely of the specific-diffuse outcome.

Sociologists and social psychologists have developed a conclusive body of knowledge demonstrating that socialization involves past, present, and anticipated future interaction between the individual and significant others such as parents, siblings, girl friends, peer groups, coaches, teachers, religious educators, etc. These significant others represent the audiences, reference groups, or socializing agents that provide the cues and "feedback" for defining appropriate role behavior. The socialization influence of these groups varies temporally and situationally according to their primacy and control over rewards and punishment.[10] To understand the influence (rewards and punishment) of physical education and sports in developing specific or diffuse roles requires the analysis of the dimensions of social interaction in the socialization process. These vary with the situational context within which the physical activity takes place. Among the most important are:

1.*The degree of involvement in the activity by the participants.* Involvement includes an expressed desire and active engagement through a visible invest-ment of attention and muscular effort.[11] For example, the varsity coach, whose livelihood depends upon successfully carrying out his role as socializer of his players to the skills of the sport, usually is involved deeply in carrying out these expectations. A team captain is usually expected to demonstrate qualities of involvement greater than the other players through his actions in practice, game situations, and on trips. Team substitutes will usually show less involvement by sitting farther down the bench and standing aside from the most actively committed participants during time-outs.

Instructors and pupils in physical education classes are not usually as actively involved as are the participants in varsity sports. They meet fewer times a week and the range of interaction is narrow. Therefore, there is no heavy self-commitment. Playground recreational activities likewise would not ordinarily include a deep involvement. Little league sports, on the other hand, may take on a degree of involvement approximating a school sport. The heavy investment of community recreational resources, parental and coaching involvement, pep talks to get "psyched up," admonitions by the spectators, and auto-suggestions to "get serious" indicates something more than a superficial degree of involvement.

In complex societies, the reference groups and socializing agents may present conflicting demands on individuals. These conflicts help explain some lack of involvement in an activity. The demands of a girl friend may, for example, result in a team member giving little attention to the training rules of his coach; or the desire to spend more time with his friends or to work on a car may become more important than involvement.

In general, the degree of involvement in the socialization relationship would result in variations in acquisition of outcomes. Neither the development of specific nor diffuse traits would be possible, of course, without at least a moderate involvement.

2. Voluntary or involuntary selection and/or participation. Closely related to the degree of involvement is the consideration of voluntary or involuntary selection for, and participation in, an activity. [12] For example, participants in a physical education class are often meeting a requirement—their presence is involuntary (though they may in some cases select a particular activity or class section). Also, the instructor has little or no selection of the participants, but is assigned to an activity to be taught at a particular time and place. Conversely, the varsity coach selects the team members and the players voluntarily submit themselves to undergo the rigors of participation.

This discussion of voluntary or involuntary selection and participation could be extended to other forms of physical activity and recreation. The point is that the outcomes of the socialization process may vary depending on the combinations of these variables (the degree of control and discipline the socializer has over the pupil will differ also). We would expect that where both the teacher and pupil voluntarily select and participate in the activity there would be an in-depth involvement, high prestige associated with the activity, and a diffuse level of socialization. Where both the teacher and pupil have no choice but to interact together, we would expect less involvement, less prestige, and the transmission of role-specific skills for fulfilling the activity requirements.

This description has admittedly been overdrawn and is subject to qualification. The purpose here is not to argue that required participation is undesirable; but rather, to achieve an understanding of possible variations in the results.

3. Instrumental or expressive socialization relationship. This refers to the quality of the relationship between persons and their socializing agents. A purely instrumental socializing relationship imparts knowledge and skills functionally specific for the achievement of a desired end. The instrumental relationship is affectively neutral* since the relationship *per se* is not expected to be gratifying; the participants are expected to control their personal feelings, emotions, and attitudes lest they interfere with the specific task. In contrast, expressive relationships are affective and personally satisfying ends in themselves; they also allow for broader and deeper levels of communication. [13] Expressive relationships are broad and diffuse; for example, such a relationship with a childhood socializing agent would be "a person to whom the child has general feelings of attachment. Thus he becomes a model for the child, who tends to take over his values, his standards of taste, his fundamental philosophical or ethical outlook."[14]

If physical education and sports are to develop traits necessary for diffuse roles, the socialization process must involve some aspects of an expressive relationship between the teacher and pupil. Expressive relationships are unlikely to develop within the context of the usual school physical education classes; the best the teacher can hope for is the development of specific skills. On the other hand, the social interaction between a coach and his players will usually involve not only the learning of specific skills but a concern for the players' general physical and psychological well-being, their families, girl friends, style of hair, dress, and manners. The coach will often advise his graduating players on the selection of a college and future occupational possibilities. At least for some players the coach is often a consultant and advisor for many years after graduation. Recreational activities such as camping and youth hosteling likewise provide the opportunity for the development of expressive relationships and thus diffuse role characteristics.

A cross-cutting variable influencing the development of expressive relationships is the size of high school or college within which the physical education or sports activity takes place. Frequently, in the small rural community the high percentage of affective relationships both within the school and community will result in an entirely different school climate than in a large metropolitan school situation. Barker [15] found that in large high schools the kinds of extracurricular activities were twice as great as in small high schools, yet the proportion of participants was three to twenty times greater in the smaller schools. The differential influence of sports and physical education in differing school climates, i.e., large and small schools, junior high, high school, and college or university, private and public, needs further exploration.

* The terms "affectivity" and "affective neutrality" are attributed to Talcott Parsons, *The Social System*, Glencoe: The Free Press, 1951.

4. The prestige and power of the socializer. Physical educators and coaches vary in their knowledge, skill, success, and prestige. In general, we would expect that the educator or coach with the greatest professional and institutional prestige or esteem will have the greatest influence in developing both specific and diffuse roles. Power, while not conceptually the same as prestige, is closely related and involves the degree of control one person has over another. Usually, a person who is viewed with high esteem because of his knowledge, skill, and past successes will have considerable control and influence over others.

Studies indicate that the greatest likelihood of the inculcation of diffuse values occurs when the socializing agent is prestigeful, powerful, and the affective (expressive) rewards and punishment are great. [16] Childhood socialization usually involves relationships of this type, such as the relationship between parent and child. Conversely, most adult socialization takes place under conditions of low affectivity and little power differential. The most radical shifts of personality among adults usually occur when the socialization process includes conditions of high affectivity and an asymmetrical power relationship, e.g., prisoner of war camps, brainwashing, psychotherapy, religious conversion, intensive graduate programs, etc. Riley and Riley suggested that the "type of expressive relationship which makes for effective teaching is not one of equalitarian friendship, but one of admiration of the teacher as a superior and distant figure." [17] The eminent professional football coach, Vince Lombardi, who maintained a distance from his players and had a great deal of prestige and power in his position, said that his greatest satisfaction in coaching was not in winning but in the rapport and closeness he had with his team. [18] He reported that the essence of his career was that he was more parent than employer and more father than professional coach.

An important consideration for future research is to determine the point on the instrumental-expressive continuum which is optimal for the transmission of specific skills and/or diffuse values. Also, does the transmission of diffuse values interfere (is there a role conflict) with the development of specific skills (and in the case of sports, the winning of contests)? Obviously, there has been no interference in the case of Coach Lombardi but more empirical data is needed.

5. Personal and social characteristics. Numerous personal and social characteristics of participants in physical activities are potentially important in socialization. This range of characteristics is too broad to discuss in detail but some areas are suggested for additional analysis.

The participant's talent will be an important aspect of his behavior and self-perception. Self-perception can be an important motivator in the present and a determiner of future aspirations. The student who has the physical and mental abilities to be highly successful in physical education or sports is likely to be receptive to continued participation. Transmission of diffuse traits would seem to be more likely if the participant is talented than if he is not, although this characteristic will also be associated with the degree of involvement.

Social class, racial, and ethnic affiliation also represent important variables. If students see sports and physical education as a way of excelling and achieving social mobility, the possibility of transmitting diffuse traits would seem probable. However, one's racial affiliation and loyalties may present the participant with conflicting loyalties as was indicated by the threatened boycott of the 1968 Olympics and by discontent of black athletes in colleges and universities. Under these conditions of discontent, the socialization outcomes will be affected.

CONCLUSIONS

Kenyon raises some important questions—namely: (1) What are the contributions of sports and physical education as a socialization process? and (2) Does this socialization result in the development of traits suitable for diffuse as well as specific roles? Answers must be found lest physical educators delude themselves into assuming illusory outcomes for physical activities. This paper has attempted to extend the Kenyon discussion to a consideration of several dimensions of socialization seeming to contribute to an understanding of the development of specific and/or diffuse characteristics. It can be concluded that some physical activity results in the development of role-specific characteristics, some contribute to the learning of broader and diffuse roles, and some probably assume a median position. The dimensions outlined above seem to explain some of these differences.

Perhaps something should be said in defense of physical activities that seem to develop only specific skills. It may be that these activities are no different than many other courses. Does a math or foreign language course contribute more to the development of diffuse traits than a physical activity course? In fact, to some extent the development of diffuse role behavior may involve the incorporation of a number of specific roles; thus, "It is obvious that the more roles in an actor's repertoire, the better prepared he is to meet the exigencies of social life." [19] Furthermore, development of specific skills in an activity course may lead to more active participation in an intramural program or eventually into adult recreational activities of a more diffuse nature.

It should be noted that merely because some characteristics are diffuse they are not necessarily desirable. Some diffuse characteristics may be dysfunctional for individual adjustment to the society and for the society itself. For example, a player's behavior on the basketball floor is under constant supervision by the officials. The player is not expected to impose sanctions on himself if he violates the rules. If the player commits a violation he is expected to ignore it, continue playing, and "cover it up." Often, blame is placed on the officials for missing the violation rather than on the player for committing it. Is this socialization of a diffuse attitude toward rules and social control agencies functional to society? Perhaps, there is a relationship between our attitudes toward athletic officials and law enforcement officials.

By focusing attention on the socialization process within physical education and sports, one can better understand what is occurring and what is being achieved. This understanding is necessary to predict and achieve some control over the socialization outcomes. No other consideration is of more importance within the profession. Priority should be given to these matters.

NOTES

1. Kenyon, G. S., "Sociological Considerations," *Johper,* **39** (Nov.-Dec.), 1968, 31-33.

2. *Ibid.*

3. Reed, W. R., "Big Time Athletics' Commitment to Education," *Johper,* **34** (Sept.), 1963, 29-30, 64-65.

4. Singer, R., "Status of Sports in Contemporary American Society," *The Physical Educator,* **23**, 1966, 147-148.

5. Schafer, W. S., and Armer, J. M., "Athletes are Not Inferior Students," *Trans-Action,* **6** (Nov.), 1968, 21-26, 61-62.

6. Ulrich, C., *The Social Matrix of Physical Education,* Englewood Cliffs: Prentice-Hall, Inc., 1968, 124.

7. Lohman, J. D., and Reitzes, D. C., "Note on Race Relations in Mass Society," *The American Journal of Sociology,* **58**, 1952, 240-246.

8. Strauss, A., *Mirrors and Masks,* Glencoe: The Free Press, 1959, 89-109, 124-129, 144-147.

9. Yinger, J. M. *Toward a Field Theory of Behavior,* New York: McGraw-Hill Book Co., 1965, 103-115.

10. Brim, O. G., Jr., "Socialization Through the Life Cycle," in Brim, O. G., Jr., and Wheeler, S., *Socialization After Childhood,* New York: John Wiley and Sons, 1966, 3-49.

11. Goffman, E., *Encounters,* Indianapolis: Bobbs-Merrill, 1961, 105-110.

12. Barker, R. G., *et al., Big School-Small School: Studies of the Effects of High School Size Upon the Behavior and Expectations of Students,* Midwest Psychological Field Station, The University of Kansas, 1962.

13. Carlson, Richard O., "Environmental Constraints and Organizational Consequences: The Public School and Its Clients," *Behavioral Science and Educational Administration Yearbook,* Part II, edited by Daniel E. Griffiths, National Society for the Study of Education, Chapter 12, 1965. Discusses the variables of selectivity on the part of formal organizations and on the part of the client and their consequences.

14. Riley, J. W., Jr., and Riley, M. W., "Sociological Perspectives on the Use of New Educational Media," *New Teaching Aids for the American Classroom,* Washington, D.C.: Office of Education, U. S. Department of Health, Education, and Welfare, 1960, p. 32.

15. Barker, *op. cit.*

16. Brim and Wheeler, *op. cit.*

17. Riley and Riley, *op. cit.*

18. Johnson, W., "Ararararararargh! Vince Lombardi Puts a Legend on the Line," *Sports Illustrated,* **30,** 28-30, 33.

19. Sarbin, T. R., and Allen, V. L., "Role Theory," *The Handbook of Social Psychology,* Lindzey, G., and Aronson, E., Volume I, Reading, Mass.: Addison-Wesley Publishing Company, 1969, 491.

SOCIALIZATION AND SPORT

George H. Sage

For this symposium subject of "Kids in Sports" I have chosen to focus my attention on the specific topic of Socialization and Sports. Socialization is the process of learning and adapting to a given social system. In the context of society, the activity of socialization is called cultural transmission, which is the means by which a society preserves its norms and perpetuates itself. At birth an infant is certainly a living organism, but he is not a social being. A human raised in isolation develops only his animal nature, while one raised in

George H. Sage, "Socialization and Sport," revised edition of a presentation made at a Symposium of Colorado Sports, Intermountain Region College of Sports Medicine, February 1973.

human society demonstrates the human aspects which derive from social living. He also shows the impact of society by a particular behavioral pattern which is distinctly characteristic of his society and which varies widely from one society to another. Thus, the process of becoming a member of a social system is called socialization.

Socialization begins at birth and continues throughout the life cycle, but the years from birth to adolescence are considered the "critical" years for it is in these years that the basic cultural transmission takes place. The primary agents and agencies for socialization are the family, peer groups, schools, churches, and the mass media.

For the individual, socialization produces attitudes, values, knowledges, and behaviors which are related to the culture of which he is a part and the roles which he will play in it. Thus, as the child in a society interacts with others—through language, gestures, rewards, and punishments—he learns the attitudes, values, behaviors, and expectations of various individuals and the behavior appropriate to the various social situations of his life.

Now it is rather obvious that a human activity as pervasive as sport in our society is bound to impinge to some extent upon most children in the United States, so questions about the social sources and consequences of sport as a socializing agent for American children seems like a natural for the curious minds of social scientists. Remarkable as it may seem, unfortunately, social scientists—sociologists, psychologists, anthropologists, etc.—have been almost oblivious to sport as a topic for serious study. While conditions promise to change, as recently ago as 1970, only 60 out of 8,350 members of the American Sociological Association indicated Leisure, Sport, Recreation, and the Arts as their area of specialization (about .7%). Loy (1972) guessed that only about one-third of these 60 sociologists actually identify with sport. Thus, this leaves a dismal few who are toiling in the vineyards.

It can be correctly inferred from the preceding figures that very little empirical research has been done by social scientists on sport, so consequently the topic of socialization and sport is virtually untouched, with regard to hard data. I should hasten to add, however, that there is substantial essay-type literature on this topic. From the Ancient Greeks to the last Super Bowl, many claims have been made for the socializing function of sport. The Battle of Waterloo is supposed to have been won on the playing fields of Eton, and one of America's most famous generals coined the ditty: "Upon the fields of friendly strife are sown the seeds that on other days on other fields will bear the fruits of victory." American physical educators have all been weaned on "social development" as one of the objectives of physical education.

Now the topic of Socialization and Sport may be divided into two subtopics for analysis: Socialization into Sport and Socialization via Sport. In the former, an analysis is made of the agents and agencies which attract, or draw, children into sports—that is the way in which children become involved in sports. An analysis of Socialization via Sports focuses upon the consequences, or outcomes, of sports involvement. I want to touch only briefly on Socialization into Sports and give more attention to Socialization via Sports.

The family—its social class, its structure, and its patterning of activities—probably has a significant influence on socializing youngsters into sports. For example, the lower-class origins of many American sports performers is well-documented in the literature [Riesman and Denney's (1951) article on cultural diffusion in American football is a classic] and biographical work on famous American athletes frequently describes a lower social class background. Recently Nisbett (1968) has suggested that participation in dangerous sports is a function of birth order, with later-borns being over-represented in dangerous sports. In a master's thesis written at UCLA, Zeller (1968) found that parental attitudes toward physical activity and participation in sports were related to participation in sports of their offspring. Most studies of the type I have just mentioned used males as subjects. I have seen nothing which examines familial influence and sports involvement with girls.

The neighborhood and peer group serve as powerful socializing agents for sports involvement. Axthelm (1970) in his excellent book, *The City Game,* describes how playground basketball in Harlem captures the interest and energies of the young boys, and this phenomenon is duplicated in the inner city of most of our metropolises.

Of course, the school, with its physical education classes and interschool sports programs, serves a significant socializing role for American children. With universal education and state requirements for physical education, most American children are taught the rudiments of a variety of sports as they pass through the grades.

Community-sponsored sports programs for children exist throughout the country. Programs such as Little League, Pony League, Babe Ruth League, American Legion for baseball, and Pop Warner League for football, Bittie Basketball, age group swimming and track, practically engulf young boys, and increasingly girls, from 7 to 18 years of age. These programs serve as another source for socializing youth into sports.

Finally, I'll mention the mass media as a sports socializing agency. I'm sure that my suggestion that we are virtually inundated with sports via newspapers, magazines, and television, especially TV, does not need documentation. That the mass media brings sports to the attention of the young is obvious. Few boys do not know the names of the NFL, NBA, and professional baseball teams; a great many boys have idols among the current crop of professional athletes, and the typical wallpaper in boys' bedrooms today is sports posters of various types.

These, then, are the sports socializing agents and agencies which impinge on the youth of today. They are powerful influences, and it is a rare youngster who is not touched in some way by sports as he passes through childhood and adolescence.

The extent to which kids are socialized via sport is largely unknown. This is the case because few investigations have been undertaken on this topic. Furthermore, sport constitutes only one set of forces operating on children and youth. It must be recognized that there are multitudes of social experiences to which every youth is subjected which are not sport related. Thus much of what we "know" about the effects, or consequences, of sports participation is impressionistic, and this fact needs to be remembered in any discussion of this topic.

There are several principles of socialization theory, though, that probably hold true with regard to sports. For example, the degree of involvement (i.e., frequency, intensity, and duration) affects the amount of socialization. Second, whether the activity is undertaken voluntarily or involuntarily affects the extent of socialization. Third, the degree to which the activity is instrumental or expressive affects the socialization relationship. Fourth, the prestige and power of the socializer is an important factor.[1] With these factors in mind, let me identify some of the possible socializing effects via sport.

To some extent personality is developed through a process of socialization. Presumably, sports involvement might influence personality. Research on personality and sport is extensive, but contradictive. Some researchers have suggested that athletes have personalities which are different than nonathletes. Recent research, using more sophisticated statistical procedures than early studies, is not supporting the notion of an "athletic personality." It has even been suggested that athletes possess sport-specific personalities. A recent study by Sage (1972), using athletes from eight different sports, corroborates other recent research in showing no differences in personality profiles across sports groups.

Sports ability apparently does influence self-evaluation and esteem among peers. Sports provide innumerable opportunities to perceive the feelings of others and their judgments about you. Thus experiences in sports are instrumental in developing a self-image, or self-concept. Although with the firing of the first Sputnik, achievement began to replace adjustment as the highest goal of the American way of life, Biddulph (1954) 20 years ago reported better personal and social adjustment among school athletes. Recent investigations by Kay (1972) and his colleagues show that sports abilities and interests are related to a positive self-concept. Other research in the past 20 years has consistently shown that young sports participants score higher in a variety of tests which measure "mental health." With regard to esteem and sport involvement, Cowell once said, "much social interaction centers around physical skill. The child lacking motor skills is often barred or not accepted in social participation." Clarke and Green (1963), McGraw and Tolbert (1953), Coleman (1961), Broekhoff (1972), among others, have shown that athletes, or skilled sports performers, rate high among their classmates.

Before leaving this topic of personal-social development through sports, I must hasten to say that most of the literature to which I have alluded is correlational, and thus not causal. Therefore, differences which exist between athletes, or skilled performers, and the unskilled are not necessarily a consequence of sport involvement.

One major function of socialization is the transmission of values. Values refer to personal and social ideals, beliefs, or standards which may be used to evaluate and regulate one's own or others' behavior. These involve ideals or beliefs about what is good, right, desirable, or true. There are only a few studies which have looked at value orientations of youth athletes. Webb (1969) devised an instrument for measuring children's value orientations towards competition and found that as children grow older there is a shift from a high value on fairness and fun in participation to a greater emphasis on skill and victory as the paramount values in sport. Mandel and Vander Velden (1971) extended this work and assessed the values of preadolescent boys who participated in organized sports and found that boys who had played on organized sports teams placed higher emphasis on skill and victory than did the nonparticipants, who valued fairness more highly. Eldon Snyder (1971) has written an excellent paper entitled "Athletic Dressing Room Slogans as Folklore: A Means of Socialization" in which he shows how coaches attempt to socialize youngsters to the point where you find Heisman Trophy recipient Johnny Rogers say in *Life* (November 24, 1972), "Winnin' is everything to me, everything."

Kistler (1957) and Richardson (1962) have both reported studies which show that boys who have participated in organized sports have poorer sportsmanship value orientations than nonsportsmen. In a study not directly related to sports, but one which I think may have implications for socialization via sports, Pearlin and his colleagues (1967) found that parents whose aspirations are high for their children and who pressure them to achieve are contributing, probably unwittingly, to the learning of behavior that is undesirable. They found that cheating by children whose parents were this type was significantly more frequent. Although it is only a hunch, I think that the same consequence may be produced by "win at any cost" and "winning is the only thing" achievement criteria in sport.

Presumably, value orientations of coaches may influence the values of their athletes. Coaches have been characterized by recent radical writers as being highly conservative, even neofascistic. I (Sage, 1972) completed research which showed that coaches were indeed more conservative than college students in philosophical, political, economic, educational, social, personal-moral, and religious dimensions of value orientation (as is most of the adult population) but they are more liberal than businessmen.

I have only scratched the surface of the socialization consequences of sports, but before bringing this presentation to an end, let me just identify several potential dysfunctional social consequences of sports for kids. The subject of sports dysfunctions has become quite active the past two years and has been led by Jack Scott and a band of former professional athletes. Although the literature is rich with those who have axes to grind or converts to proselytize, they have made some very telling points, and only a head-in-the-sand ostrich, or possibly Woody Hayes, would believe that all is completely well in the sports world.

The first potential dysfunctional effect of kids' sports programs is the intrusion of adults on the play of youngsters.[2] The community, school, parents, and others make considerable emotional investment in the young athletes and they expect a payoff. The payoff is a win. Consequently, those who are emotionally invested in the youngster's performance attempt to manipulate the sports activity in order to maximize the likelihood of receiving a payoff. Thus, we see kids' sports programs which come to resemble the professionals. They are dressed as pros, coached as pros, have an admiring audience like pros, are taught that "winning isn't everything, it's the only thing," so by God they better win or else! Albinson (1972) used Webb's Professionalism Scale to assess the attitude toward play of volunteer amateur ice hockey coaches and found that overwhelmingly the coaches possessed a professional orientation toward playing the sport. The attitude undoubtedly is conveyed to the youth playing under these coaches. While I don't condemn all kids' sports programs, I do suggest that they are all suspect of taking the fun and other play-elements from the youngsters.

When someone is naive enough to inquire the reason behind this "professionalization" of kids' programs, the almost stock reply is that the kids need to prepare for the competitive dog-eat-dog world of adults. Three reactions come to my mind. First, apparently many adults haven't noticed that the American frontier closed over eighty years ago. The hard, physical struggle for survival against the elements does not exist today. Furthermore, with anti-trust legislation in effect and various other measures for restraining cutthroat business competition, the adult world "ain't" all that competitive. Indeed, in the field of economics there has been severe criticism of competition (Galbraith, 1968) by some while others have advocated a modified form of competition, with control and fair practices (Dewey, 1969). Second, there are many American youngsters who never partake of these organized sports programs and no one has ever documented that they are worse off for it in their occupational careers. Third, I would suggest that this "win at any cost" mentality may be dysfunctional in postindustrial society. What this world needs is not highly competitive societies going around trying to blow others up, but cooperative societies dedicated to sustaining and enriching life on this planet. Schickel (1972), writing in *The New York Times,* sums up the effects of sports as preparation idea. He says:

> Aside from their obviously healthy aspects, they [sports] were widely believed to prepare boys for the wins and losses of life—especially the former. And in a way they did, for so many of us are little Nixons, secret sharers of the lunatic notion that life is a succession of game-plans and games, a thing that can ideally be quantified in a won-and-loss column. We are prisoners, I think, of middle America's only universal metaphor and we have tried . . . to cram everything into it—politics, wars, careers— and it has stunted me, stunted us all [p. 26].

Adult intrusion into the world of kids' sports is dysfunctional for another reason. It robs the kids of one of the greatest potentials of sports— the opportunity to develop self-discipline and responsibility. George Sauer, former professional football player, "hit all the mumbo-jumbo about how sports programs develop an elite of self-disciplined and responsible adults. He said that '. . . coaches know damn well they have never given their jocks a chance to become responsible or self-disciplined. Even in the pros, they tell them when to turn off the lights, when to go to bed, . . . when to eat . . . [Hoch, p. 112] .' " The kids' programs are really adults' programs. The adult (coaches) make all the decisions—they decide who plays and what plays to run. The hired help (the youngsters) carry out the orders, and they do not ask questions, if they don't want to be labeled a "problem athlete." Although I don't have any facts, I suspect the imposition of adults into kids' programs drives some youngsters out of sports. The criterion for success—winning—

becomes a terrible burden to carry for some. To be labeled a "loser" is the epitome of criticism in our society. For some youngsters, it may be easier to withdraw from sports and just be a spectator. The former long-distance runner, Ron Clarke (quoted from Moore, 1973) eloquently summed up this idea by saying: "If youngsters are taught that losing is a disgrace, and they're not sure they can win, they will be reluctant to even try. And not trying is the real disgrace [p. 42]."

The second dysfunctional potential which I would identify with sport socialization has to do with norm learning. If one accepts the notion that children can learn normative behavior from sports, and if one agrees that social norm deviance is widespread in sport, it becomes clear that American kids' sports programs may be providing patterned reinforcement of attitudes, values, and behaviors which are at variance with our society's norms. I think that it is fair to say that deviation from ideal norms of sports frequently occurs in sports. Thus we see incidents like the 1972 Minnesota-Ohio State basketball game riot, the booing of officials, and even the incorporation of deviance as part of the strategy of the game, i.e., spearing in football, illegal use of body in basketball, etc. Most sports have well-planned deliberate violations of the norms to make it difficult for the opponent. The use of deviant normative behavior as acceptable is associated with, I think, the obsession to win. (I am not suggesting that winning should not be an objective of competitive sports. I hasten to add this, because any time someone suggests that winning is not the only thing in sport, there always are a few who will smugly conclude that the writer is one of those Commies who is trying to poison the minds of Americans.) When I say obsession, I'm talking about the mentality of those who put up locker room signs which read: "Defeat is worse than death because you have to live with defeat." While one might question the extent to which deviant normative patterns learned in sports are generalized to larger social relations, one certainly must consider the possible effects on athletes who play under coaches who encourage unethical behaviors. Moreover, Snyder (1970) has suggested that since it is approved behavior in sport to violate rules and attempt to conceal it from officials or if caught to use various ways of showing disrespect to the officials there may be "a relationship between our attitudes toward athletic officials and law enforcement officials [p. 6]."

A third dysfunctional potential which I fear lurks in many kids' programs is what I call the promotion of the Lombardi ethic, which is exemplified in the statement he is alleged to have made, to wit: "Winning isn't everything, it's the only thing." Now while this notion may have some validity for the big business of professional football, where coaches and players indeed are fired, or disposed of in other ways, if they do not win, I believe that this ethic is as lame as strict observance of the Protestant ethic in today's society. It is dysfunctional because it makes conditional persons out of the participants. They become defined by their won-loss records—the records become the basis for assigning "worthiness" to individuals. Winners are assigned prestige and honor; losers disdain and ridicule. As Jim Tatum, the late football coach, once said, "How can anyone be proud of a loser?" The expressive nature of sport—fun, joy, etc.—becomes strangled by the instrumental concerns. So joy, fun, excitement, and exhilaration in sport comes not from the movement, display of skill, and mastery of self, but from winning, and only winning. The Lombardian ethic separates groups into "our group" and "the enemy." Our group right or wrong must win and prevail; the enemy must be crushed. They are objects to overcome. It seems to me that this ethic is a carry-over from the "dog-eat-dog" eras of the past centuries and has become obsolete as we move rapidly toward the 21st century. Man has the capabilities of obliterating himself on this planet. What is needed is cooperative groups working toward mutual actualization of human potentialities. The old Nation State bickering over territory and natural resources is gradually becoming irrelevant as mankind realizes his destiny demands a new ethical ideal in human relations. If indeed ethical behavior learned in sport generalizes to more general role behavior, sport based upon optimizing expressive values and growth-promoting interpersonal relationships, has exciting possibilities.

Let me close on a positive note by saying that sports for kids have great functional benefits. Whether a given sports program has more functional than dysfunctional socialization effects depends primarily upon the leadership in the program. Anyone who really cares about kids' sports programs should become actively involved in some way with them.

NOTES

1. I am indebted to Eldon Snyder for this list of principles. See Eldon Snyder, "Aspects of Socialization in Sports and Physical Education," *Quest* Monograph XIV, June, 1970, pp. 1-7.

2. I am indebted to Emil Bend and his presentation "Some Dysfunctional Effects on Sports upon Socialization" for some of the ideas which follow.

REFERENCES

Albinson, J. G., "Professionalized Attitudes of Volunteer Coaches," paper presented at the Scientific Congress on Sport, Munich, Germany, August, 1972.

Axthelm, P., *The City Game*, New York: Harper & Row, 1970.

Biddulph, L., "Athletic Achievement and the Personal and Social Adjustment of High School Boys," *Research Quarterly*, 25:1-7, 1954.

Broekhoff, J., "Relationships between Social Status and Physical Measurements of Boys and Girls from the Fourth Through the Sixth Grade," paper presented at the Research Section of the National Convention of the American Association for Health, Physical Education, and Recreation, Houston, March, 1972.

Clarke, H. H., and Green, W., "Relationships Between Personal-Social Measures Applied to 10-year-old Boys," *Research Quarterly*, 34:288-298, 1963.

Coleman, J. S., *The Adolescent Society*, New York: The Macmillan Co., 1961.

Dewey, D., *The Theory of Imperfect Competition*, New York: Columbia University Press, 1969.

Galbraith, J. K., *The Industrial State*, New York: New American Library, 1968.

Hoch, P., *Rip Off the Big Game*, New York: Doubleday Co., 1972.

Kay, R. S., Felker, D. W., and Varoz, R. O., "Sports Interests and Abilities as Contributors to Self-Concept in Junior High School Boys," *Research Quarterly*, 43:208-215, 1972.

Kistler, J., "Attitudes Expressed About Behavior Demonstrated in Certain Specific Situations Occuring in Sports," *60th Proceedings of the National College Physical Education Association for Men*, 1957, pp. 55-58.

Loy, J. W., "A Case for the Sociology of Sport," *Journal of Health, Physical Education, and Recreation*, 43(6):50-53, 1972.

Mandel, R. C., and Vander Velden, L., "The Relationship between the Professionalization of Attitude Toward Play of Preadolescent Boys and Participation in Organized Sports," paper presented at the Third International Symposium of the Sociology of Sport, Waterloo, Canada, August, 1971.

McCraw, L. W., and Tolbert, J. W., "Sociometric Status and Athletic Ability of Junior High School Boys," *Research Quarterly*, 24:72-80, 1963.

Moore, Kenny, "But Only on Sunday," *Sports Illustrated*, 38 (February 26): 38-42, 1973.

Nisbett, R. E., "Birth Order and Participation in Dangerous Sports," *Journal of Personality and Social Psychology*, 8(4):351-353, 1968.

Pearlin, L. I., Jarrow, M. K., and Scarr, H. A., "Unintended Effects of Parental Aspirations: The Case of Children's Cheating," *American Journal of Sociology*, 73:73-83, 1967.

Richardson, D., "Ethical Conduct in Sport Situations," *66th Proceedings of the National College Physical Education Association for Men*, 1962, pp. 98-103.

Riesman, D., and Denney, R., "Football in America: A Study in Culture Diffusion," *American Quarterly*, 3:309-319, 1951.

Sage, G. H., "An Assessment of Personality Profiles between and within Intercollegiate Athletes from Eight Different Sports," paper presented at the Scientific Congress on Sport, Munich, Germany, August, 1972.

Sage, G. H., "Value Orientations of American College Coaches Compared to Male College Students and Businessmen," *75th Proceedings, National College Physical Education for Men,* 1972, pp. 174-186.

Schickel, R., "Growing Up in the Forties," *New York Times Magazine,* February 20, 1972.

Snyder, E. "Athletic Dressing Room Slogans as Folklore: A Means of Socialization," paper presented at the American Sociological Association Convention, Denver, Colorado, August, 1971.

Webb, H., "Professionalization of Attitudes toward Play Among Adolescents," in Gerald Kenyon (ed.), *Aspects of Contemporary Sport Sociology,* Chicago: The Athletic Institute, 1969, pp. 161-187.

Zeller, J., "Relationships between Parental Attitudes about Physical Education and their Children's Performance in Physical Tasks," M.A. Thesis, University of California at Los Angeles, 1968.

THE RELATIONSHIP BETWEEN THE PROFESSIONALIZATION OF ATTITUDE TOWARD PLAY OF PREADOLESCENT BOYS AND PARTICIPATION IN ORGANIZED SPORT

Richard C. Mantel and Lee Vander Velden

Democratic principles permeating the economic and political system in American society stress equality and achievement rather than ascriptive criteria in the race for success and the distribution of rewards. Individual

Richard C. Mantel and Lee Vander Velden, "The Relationship between the Professionalization of Attitude toward Play of Preadolescent Boys and Participation in Organized Sport," paper presented at the Third International Symposium on the Sociology of Sport, Waterloo, Ontario, Canada, August 1971. Reprinted by permission of the authors.

differences in ability, training, and motivation are emphasized in the pursuit of excellence and the quest for rewards which accrue to those who succeed in this competitive milieu. Institutions such as the school, the church, and the family serve to instill in our children the basic values of our achievement culture. Although often overlooked, sport, as an organized system of play, also operates as a means of imbuing economic and political culture. For example, games have been portrayed as cultural inventions rather than biological universals.[5] More specifically, Roberts and Sutton-Smith have depicted sport and games not only as products of culture, but also as cultural models in that they provide children practice in the cognitive operations involved in the competitive success appropriate for their levels of maturity, and which are not yet available to them in full-scale cultural participation.[4] The relationship between child-rearing and game involvement has been suggested in a conflict-enculturation hypothesis which holds that sport and games provide youth the opportunity to rehearse competitive roles without experiencing the adverse anxiety experienced by adults striving for success.[4,6]

Similarly, Webb[7] has described sport as providing a basis for attitudes and beliefs appropriate to adult participation in politics as well as in the economy. Particularly concerned with urban-industrialized societies, Webb pointed out that achievement criteria are presumed to have replaced ascriptive criteria as the basis for the organization of positions and the distribution of rewards. However, he qualified his position by asserting that sport provides in fact in one institution what is ideology in another, i.e., politics, economy. Describing his thesis in terms of the components of skill, equity, and victory, Webb associated equity with child's play in the sense that anyone can play and few rewards are based on differences in skill. Few rules or referees are needed because the notion of fairness is paramount. On the other hand, emphasis on achievement and success begins in early child training and is reinforced upon entrance into the formal institutions of school with its competitive framework. Furthermore, since skill may produce success and equity may actually inhibit it, a professionalization of attitude can be observed to parallel the structural change in play from simple child's play to more formalized sports and games. The professionalization of attitude is manifested by a greater emphasis on skill and victory over fairness as the admission policy to play activities changes from one of ascriptive to achievement criteria. For example, Webb pointed out that organized sport approaches the reality of achievement culture to a greater degree than do games. Moreover, Webb has supported his thesis with data which indicate that as a child grows older there is a shift from equity or fairness to skill as the paramount factor in play. Implied in this relationship is the assertion that as one advances in age his contacts with organized games and sport increase.

PROBLEM

Predicated on the suggestion that games and sport function as cultural models in the socialization process and the specific finding that with an increase in age the paramount factor in play shifts from a concern for fairness to an emphasis on success through skill, this investigation was designed to study the function of organized sport in the socialization of preadolescent boys. Specifically, it was hypothesized that the professionalization of attitude toward play among preadolescent boys is directly related to participation in organized sport. Moreover, it was predicted that:

1. Participants in organized sport emphasize skill or victory as the most important factor in play.

2. Nonparticipants in organized sport emphasize fairness as the most important factor in play.

SIGNIFICANCE

Whereas Webb implied that as the boy grows older he progresses from child's play to more formalized and complex games, it may also be that contact with other socializing institutions, both formal and informal, would likewise lead to a greater emphasis on achievement criteria. Hence, by limiting subjects to preadolescent boys—ten and eleven years old—the intent was to control for the effects of maturation and the continued, progressive socialization from other institutions. In addition, by controlling age it was possible to investigate the relationship between participation in organized sport, as distinct models of achievement, and the professionalization of attitude toward play. Although Webb demonstrated a relationship between the professionalization of attitude and increasing age, the function of particular kinds of play, games, and sport models involved was left to conjecture.

SAMPLE AND PROCEDURES

The sample consisted of 133 ten- and eleven-year-old boys from middle-class families living in a northern suburb of Washington, D.C. Participants in organized sport ($N = 73$) were selected from boys who had participated in at least one varsity sport—football or baseball—for a minimum of two years while members of either local Boys' Clubs or Catholic Youth Organizations (CYO); teams competed in highly structured leagues governed by a set of codified rules enforced by an elected commissioner. Each boy was issued his own uniform and was required to attend regular practice sessions directed by at least one adult coach. In addition, winning teams received trophies with a Super Bowl Championship shown on local television as the ultimate goal of each team. Nonparticipants were selected from those boys attending the same elementary schools as members of the participant sample, but who had never engaged in any form of organized sport ($N = 60$). Although it was assumed that nonparticipants took part in some form of sport and games, they were distinguished from participants by never having been members of teams competing in organized competition.

Each subject completed a questionnaire requesting specific information such as age, year in school, and the degree of participation in organized sport. In addition, each boy completed the following three-item play scale designed by Webb to measure items important in play.

What do you think is *most* important in playing a game?

Place a "1" next to the one you think is *most* important. Now place a "3" next to the one you think is *least* important.

_____   to play as well as you can
_____   to beat the other player or team
_____   to play the game fairly

The questions were intended to identify the components of play; namely, skill, victory, and equity.

Professionalization of attitude toward play was defined as the substitution of skill or victory for fairness as the paramount factor in play.

Finally, chi-square procedures were employed to assist in the interpretation of the data.

RESULTS AND DISCUSSION

Results shown in Table 1 support the hypothesis that the professionalization of attitude toward play among preadolescent boys is directly related to participation in organized sport. Specifically, participants in organized sport regard skill or victory as the most important factor in play while nonparticipants emphasize fairness. For example, whereas only one-third of those not involved in organized sport designated skill or victory as most significant, over one-half of the participant sample selected achievement criteria as paramount. Conversely, two-thirds of the nonparticipants regard fairness as the major factor in play. The emphasis placed on fairness within each group supports this conclusion (see Table 2).

Table 1   Skill or Victory Responses among Participants and Nonparticipants in Organized Sport

Rank skill or beat	Participants	Nonparticipants	Total
1	39	20	59
0	34	40	74
	73	60	133

Chi-square = 5.38591 with 1 df
$p < .05$

Table 2   Fair Responses among Participants and Nonparticipants in Organized Sport

Rank fair	Participants	Nonparticipants	Total
1	34	40	74
2	29	18	47
3	10	2	12
	73	60	133

Chi-square = 7.19233 with 2 df
$p < .05$

In contrast to Webb who reported that both skill and victory were strongly emphasized by fifth- and sixth-grade boys—the age level of subjects in this study—only four of the thirty-nine boys in the participant sample who held a more professional attitude toward play listed winning as most important; thirty-five reported that doing well was most important.

In general, these findings corroborate the observations of Webb and Roberts and Sutton-Smith who looked upon games and sport as cultural models ranging from the very simple games of children to the more complex, formalized sports and games. Roberts and Sutton-Smith[4] concluded that "as the models approach full-scale cultural participation they increase in scale becoming nearer in nature to the reality they copy" (p. 132). However, whereas Webb merely demonstrated a relationship between the professionalization of attitude and increasing age, he presumed that during the life of a child his play would progress from simple child's play to more formalized games and sport; the function of particular models was left to speculation. The findings reported here, namely, that emphasis on achievement criteria while concomitant with participation in organized sport is less evident among those engaged in the simpler and less organized forms of sport and games, suggest the function of a specific cultural model. This relationship is all the more striking when it is recalled that the subjects were selected from the same neighborhoods and all were either ten or eleven years old, in the pre-adolescent stage of development which Helanko[1] regarded as the crucial phase in the socialization process, when boys learn to behave in primary groups with their peers. The basic elements of this stage of development and of sport and games are the same; namely, interaction, control, and a system of values and norms. The selection of preadolescents was based in part on Helanko's regard for the significance of this period in the socialization of boys and also on the observation that during this age period boys are still relatively innocent of the realities of the adult world. Hence, it was expected that organized sport would have a considerable impact on preadolescents, an expectation which the data support. When these findings are compared with the relationship between attitude and age reported by Webb, it appears that organized sport is only one of several socializing agents operating. Neverthe-less, it has a strong influence on this age group. Kenyon[2] has indicated that even though sports and physical activities have generated highly influential models, and their influences as socializing agencies may be great, the degree to which such activity can shape behavior and values in some desired direc-tion may be no greater than any other group.

Unfortunately, the sports environment—including such phenomena as high stakes for winning, hero worship, publicity, mass audiences, and the attitudes of both coaches and parents—confounds the results of this study. For example, the professionalized attitudes of parents and coaches may be as important, if not more important, than the actual participation in the sport or game. For instance, a sample of ten- and eleven-year-old boys from the same neighborhoods as the original subjects, but who had participated in low organized sport, i.e., intramural programs sponsored by the Boys' Clubs ($N = 86$), was compared with the nonparticipant sample. There were no differences among skill, equity, and victory responses. Much of the sports environment stimuli do not reach those whose participation in sports is limited to sandlots, physical education classes, and intramural programs. In short, it is difficult to account for the relationships demonstrated in this study.

CONCLUSIONS

1. The attitude toward play among preadolescent boys is related to participation in organized sport; more specifically,

a)   Participants in organized sport emphasize skill or victory as the most important factor in play.

b)   Nonparticipants in organized sport emphasize fairness as the most important factor in play.

2.   Although a positive relationship between a professionalization of attitude toward play and participation in organized sport was demonstrated, it is not possible to identify the specific elements within the sports environment to account for this finding.

3.   Although the influence of sport as a socializing agency was demonstrated among preadolescent boys, it is but one of several forces shaping behavior and values.

NOTES

1. Helanko, R., "Sports and Socialization," *Acta Sociologica*, 2:229-240, 1957.

2. Kenyon, G. S., "The Contribution of Physical Activity to Social Development," *Report*, Symposium on Integrated Development, Lafayette, Indiana: Purdue University, 1964, pp. 48-54.

3. Loy, John W., Jr., "The Nature of Sport: A Definitional Effort," *Sport, Culture, and Society*, ed. John W. Loy, Jr. and Gerald S. Kenyon, London: Macmillan Co., 1969, pp. 56-71.

4. Roberts, John M., and Brian Sutton-Smith, "Child Training and Game Involvement," *Sport, Culture, and Society,* ed. John W. Loy, Jr. and Gerald S. Kenyon, London: Macmillan Co., 1969, pp. 116-136.

5. Sutton-Smith, Brian, "The Two Cultures of Games," *Aspects of Contemporary Sport Sociology,* ed. Gerald S. Kenyon, Chicago: The Athletic Institute, 1969.

6. Sutton-Smith, Brian, John M. Roberts and Robert M. Kozelka, "Game Involvement in Adults," *Sport, Culture, and Society,* ed. John W. Loy, Jr. and Gerald S. Kenyon, London: Macmillan Co., 1969, pp. 244-258.

7. Webb, Harry, "Professionalization of Attitudes toward Play among Adolescents," *Aspects of Contemporary Sport Sociology,* ed. Gerald S. Kenyon, Chicago: The Athletic Institute, 1969, pp. 161-187.

AN ASSESSMENT OF PERSONALITY PROFILES BETWEEN AND WITHIN INTER-COLLEGIATE ATHLETES FROM EIGHT DIFFERENT SPORTS

George H. Sage

In recent years psychologists and physical educators have become increasingly interested in assessing the personality of sports performers. There has been a general premise that athletes in a given sport possess unique and definable personality attributes which are different than athletes in other sports. Indeed, part of the folklore of the athletic world is that these personality differences exist — thus American football players are frequently characterized as being hyperaggressive and highly masculine. Athletes in other sports are stereotyped with other personality traits. If there are indeed personality traits capable of differentiating athletes in one sport from athletes in another sport, this information could be useful for diagnostic and prognostic purposes by coaches.

As one phase of a larger project investigating socialization and sport, the present study was concerned with personality profiles of university athletes who participated in eight different sports teams over a ten-year period. The purpose of this study was to assess the profiles of college athletes from eight sports at the University of Northern Colorado to determine if there were significant differences in team personality profiles between the various sports. A second purpose was to ascertain whether there were personality differences within sports when the sports team was divided into two groups on a time dimension.

REVIEW OF LITERATURE

Past research has produced equivocal results with regard to sport specific personality traits. Several investigators have found personality differences between various sports groups. H. Slusher (1964) reported differences

George H. Sage, "An Assessment of Personality Profiles Between and Within Intercollegiate Athletes From Eight Different Sports," *Sportwissenschaft* (West Germany), 2. Jahrgang, 1972/74, pp. 408-415. Reprinted by permission of Verlag Karl Hofmann.

between the various high school sports groups which he tested. W. Kroll and W. Crenshaw (1968) found that wrestlers and football players possessed similar personality profiles while gymnasts and karate performers differed from each other. On the other hand, some investigators have found no differences between sports groups. W. L. Lakie (1962) found similar personality structures for intercollegiate athletes in football, wrestling, basketball, golf, tennis, and track, while R. N. Singer (1969) reported no significant differences in personality profiles between collegiate tennis and baseball athletes. B. S. Rushall (1968) investigated personality variables of sports performers with different levels of achievement in baseball, basketball, swimming, and football and reported no systematic trends in personality difference for any of the groups studied. E. Darden (1972) assessed personality profiles of competitive body builders and weight lifters and reported no significant differences between the groups.

A few investigators have studied personality differences of athletes in a single sport who possess different levels of demonstrated achievement. Kroll (1967) studied the personality profiles of wrestlers classified into three levels of achievement and reported that there were no differences between wrestlers in the three groups. R. A. Berger and D. H. Littlefield (1969) found no significant differences between outstanding college football athletes and nonoutstanding football athletes on any of the 18 items of the California Psychological Inventory, nor on a composite score. However, W. F. Straub (1971) reported personality differences between Big Ten Conference intercollegiate football players and players from each of the other three conferences which he studied. Other studies could be cited to show the conflict in findings in this area of research.

Several possible reasons for the conflicting findings of the various researchers might be advanced, such as differences in assessment instruments, limitations on the number of subjects, variability in age and achievement level of the competitors, and the variety of analysis techniques.

Past research is so conflicting that it did not suggest the identification of any specific hypotheses for this study. Thus, this investigation must be considered exploratory in nature. However, from a broad inquiry into athletes' personalities, such as this study, subsequent investigators may be able to derive important hypotheses about personality and sports performers.

PROCEDURE

Intercollegiate lettermen athletes at the University of Northern Colorado between 1962 and 1971 in eight sports (football, basketball, baseball, wrestling, gymnastics, swimming, track, and tennis) constituted the population ($N = 646$) for this study. Athletes who had lettered in more than one sport were classified with the sport in which they earned the most letter awards. The Edwards Personal Preference Schedule (EPPS) was used to assess the personality of the athletes. The EPPS has been administered at the University of Northern Colorado since 1960 and EPPS scores were available for over 80 per cent ($N = 532$) of the lettermen athletes. The EPPS consists of 225 pairs of statements and the subject is forced to make a choice response to one of two statements which is most characteristic of himself. This instrument measures 15 relatively independent normal personality variables. Multiple discriminant function was used to make the between-group and within-group analyses. This statistic is a multivariate technique which determines whether criterion groups can be distinguished from each other using the entire profile simultaneously. This provides an important improvement in assessment of personality differences over statistics which employ analysis of profile components separately. The .05 level of confidence was selected for testing the null hypothesis in all statistical analyses in this study.

RESULTS

Multiple discriminant analysis comparisons were made between the athletes in the eight sports groups. Discriminant function analysis reduces multiple measurements to a single variable. Thus, in this case the 15 personality traits provided a profile score for each individual in each group, and group profiles were analyzed for significant differences. The results of the discriminant function analysis for between-groups are presented in Table 1 along with profile component means and separate univariate F tests. Wilks' lambda was .787 with an F ratio of 1.192, $p = 0.092$. Hence, using the customary .05 level of confidence, the multivariate generalized hypothesis that no differences existed in personality profiles between groups was regarded as tenable.

To determine whether there were personality differences within sports when a sports team was divided into two groups on a time dimension, each sports team was divided into a group of lettermen from 1962 to 1966 and a group of lettermen from 1967 to 1971. Group profiles were analyzed by discriminant function for significant differences. The results of the within-groups analysis are presented in Table 2. For football, Wilks' lambda was .783 with an F ratio of 1.903, $p = .03$. For wrestling, Wilks' lambda was .537 with an F ratio of 2.764, $p = .004$. Thus the multivariate generalized null hypothesis that no differences existed in personality profiles of football lettermen

Table 1 Means and Univariate F Tests of the EPPS Variables

Variable	Means								Univariate F	p
	Football $N=119$	Gymnastics $N=50$	Wrestling $N=64$	Tennis $N=28$	Basketball $N=44$	Track $N=93$	Baseball $N=69$	Swimming $N=65$		
Achievement	14.50	13.84	15.27	15.14	14.61	14.75	15.48	14.52	0.98	.55
Deference	11.79	11.82	12.14	11.71	11.45	12.15	12.16	11.17	0.65	.71
Order	10.62	10.24	10.06	10.21	10.18	10.21	9.69	10.08	0.33	.94
Exhibition	14.29	15.66	14.95	14.07	13.98	14.43	15.06	15.34	1.54	.15
Autonomy	13.31	14.08	13.06	14.04	14.00	13.97	14.25	14.00	0.69	.68
Affiliation	14.75	15.24	15.57	15.54	14.48	14.99	15.00	15.08	0.41	.90
Intraception	14.69	15.08	14.55	16.82	14.29	14.61	14.70	14.75	0.87	.53
Succorance	9.80	9.94	10.55	10.21	11.55	10.45	10.24	11.09	0.96	.54
Dominance	15.45	14.68	15.12	16.61	14.82	14.60	14.57	15.33	1.05	.39
Abasement	15.30	15.66	15.37	14.04	16.00	16.05	16.30	14.06	1.81	.08
Nurturance	13.81	13.20	14.28	14.79	14.43	14.09	14.35	14.03	0.52	.82
Change	15.88	15.92	15.67	13.96	14.55	16.14	14.77	17.28	2.93	.00
Endurance	13.56	14.10	12.81	13.29	13.20	13.75	12.12	12.51	1.22	.29
Heterosexuality	18.57	17.94	16.81	15.82	18.27	16.94	17.41	16.91	1.30	.24
Aggression	13.84	13.14	14.64	13.82	14.36	12.57	13.99	13.60	1.62	.13

Total Trace = .248, $\Lambda = .787$, $F = 1.19$ with 105 and 3274 df, $p = .092$

Table 2   Within Groups Wilks' Lambda Scores and Multivariate F Ratio

Sport	Wilks' lambda	Multivariate F ratio	F
Football	.783	1.903, df = 15 and 103	.03
Gymnastics	.757	.726, df = 15 and 34	.74
Wrestling	.537	2.764, df = 15 and 48	.004
Tennis	.491	.829, df = 15 and 12	.64
Basketball	.692	.831, df = 15 and 28	.64
Track	.867	.791, df = 15 and 77	.68
Baseball	.775	1.023, df = 15 and 53	.45
Swimming	.856	.549, df = 15 and 49	.90

from 1961 to 1966 and lettermen from 1967 to 1971 and wrestling lettermen divided in the same manner was rejected. The Wilks' lambda statistical approach could not be used when comparing the two tennis groups because of the small number of subjects in each group in relation to the number of variables tested, so the figures in Table 2 for tennis should be ignored. For lettermen in the other sports divided in the same yearly blocks, the null hypothesis that no differences existed in the personality profiles was regarded as tenable.

Univariate F tests were applied to the football and wrestling groups to ascertain the individual trait differences. Table 3 shows the means and univariate F ratios for the individual traits for these two sports.

Football lettermen from 1967 to 1971 were significantly (.05 level) higher in need for achievement, dominance, and aggression and significantly lower in need for nurturance than the 1961 to 1966 football athletes. Wrestlers from 1967 to 1971 were significantly lower in need for affiliation and abasement than the 1961 to 1966 wrestlers.

DISCUSSION

The generalized, multivariate, null hypothesis that intercollegiate athletes in eight different sports had similar personality profiles can be regarded as tenable, when using the .05 level of confidence. This finding is in accord with Singer's (1969) data, as he did not find differences between collegiate baseball and tennis players. It is also in accord with Rushall's (1968) study with various collegiate athletic categories with different levels of achievement, and it is in line with Kroll and Crenshaw's (1968) finding that college football players and wrestlers exhibited similar personality profiles. On the other hand, the present finding is at variance with research reported by B. Ogilvie (1968,a,b) and J. Kane (1966).

The finding of this study that no significant personality differences exist

Table 3   Means and Univariate *F* Tests of the EPPS Variables for Football and Wrestling

	Football means			Wrestling means		
	1962-1966 *N*=62	1967-1971 *N*=57	Univariate *F* ratio	1962-1966 *N*=22	1967-1971 *N*=42	Univariate *F* ratio
Achievement	13.66	15.42	6.30*	14.27	15.79	1.73
Deference	12.34	11.19	2.86	11.73	12.36	0.47
Order	11.08	10.12	1.90	10.18	10.00	0.04
Exhibition	13.76	14.86	2.45	15.00	14.93	0.01
Autonomy	13.56	13.04	0.41	12.68	13.26	0.29
Affiliation	15.44	14.00	3.81	18.23	14.19	11.78*
Intraception	15.08	14.26	0.81	13.68	15.00	1.08
Succorance	9.44	10.19	0.82	11.59	10.00	1.64
Dominance	14.48	16.51	6.28*	14.32	15.55	1.71
Abasement	15.82	14.74	1.40	17.09	14.48	4.52*
Nurturance	14.55	13.00	4.72*	14.68	14.07	0.27
Change	16.18	15.56	0.69	16.18	15.40	0.56
Endurance	14.02	13.07	1.27	12.73	12.86	0.01
Heterosexuality	18.39	18.77	0.12	15.05	17.74	2.59
Aggression	12.90	14.86	6.01*	15.41	14.24	1.08

* Significant at .05 level or better

for athletes in eight different sports suggests that attempts to generalize sport specific personality types from limited data, as some recent investigators have done, should be done with great caution. Although the University of Northern Colorado athletes in this study were not, as a total group, national or international level in achievement they must certainly be ranked as very highly skilled in their sport, so they may be viewed as representing an athletic elite. If indeed various sports either attract or develop sport specific personalities, these differences should have shown up in this study because all of the subjects have competed in their sport for at least four years and some have competed as many as ten years; all have attained a considerable measure of success in their sport.

It is suggested that claims such as those of Ogilvie (1968 b) and Ogilvie and T. Tutko (1966) that there are personality dimensions which are essential to sport success and which differentiate athletes in various sports must be viewed with suspicion. There is no attempt here to deny that these investigators and others may have found differences between athletes representing different sport groups which they studied, but it is suggested that the power of their findings for diagnostic and predictive purposes is weak.

The generalized multivariate, null hypothesis that intercollegiate athletes within different sports divided on a time dimension had similar personality profiles can be regarded as tenable for five of the sports (tennis was not included in this analysis). For two of the sports, football and wrestling, there were significant differences in the personality profiles within these sports. Thus, over a ten-year span there were no significant changes in personality profiles within most of the sports studied.

The findings with regard to football and wrestling do not lend themselves to easy interpretation. In the case of football, the fortunes of the teams have differed considerably during the two time periods studied. In the years from 1962 to 1966 the teams won 19 games and lost 26 and did not win any championships whereas from 1967 to 1971 the teams won 36 games and lost 8, winning three conference championships while playing about the same schedules as during the 1962-1966 period. That the 1967-71 teams were higher in need for achievement, dominance, and aggression and lower in nurturance, might be suggestive of differences in football performance, however a conclusion of this kind would be highly tenuous, particularly since Kroll (1967) with wrestlers, Kroll and B. R. Carlson (1967) with karate participants, D. R. Parsons (1963) with swimmers, Singer (1969) with baseball players, Bergen and Littlefield (1969) with football athletes, and Rushall (1968) with several sports groups reported no significant difference between higher- and lesser-skilled athletes in personality profiles. However, Kroll and K. Peterson (1965) did find significant differences between losing and winning football teams.

UNC wrestling teams have been Rocky Mountain Conference champions 29 of the past 30 years, and the skill level of the participants does not seem to have changed much in the past 10 years. The fact that the wrestlers from 1967 to 1971 possess lower needs for affiliation and abasement provides little meaningful data to add to the already substantial body of literature on the personality of wrestlers.

REFERENCES

Berger, R. A., and Littlefield, D. H., "Comparison Between Football Athletes and Nonathletes on Personality," *Research Quarterly*, **40** (1969), 663-665.

Darden, E., "Sixteen Personality Factor Profiles of Competitive Bodybuilders and Weightlifters," *Research Quarterly*, **43** (1972), 142-147.

Kane, J., "Personality Description of Soccer Ability," *Research in Physical Education*, Vol. 1, No. 1 (1966).

Kroll, W., "Sixteen Personality Factor Profiles of Collegiate Wrestlers," *Research Quarterly*, **38** (1967), 49-57.

Kroll, W., and Carlson, B. R., "Discriminant Function and Hierarchial Grouping Analysis of Karate Participants' Personality Profiles," *Research Quarterly*, **38** (1967), 405-411.

Kroll, W., and Crenshaw, W., "Multivariate Personality Profile Analysis of Four Athletic Groups," paper presented at the Second International Congress of Sport Psychology, Washington, D.C., 1968.

Kroll, W., and Peterson, K., "Personality Factor Profiles of Collegiate Football Teams," *Research Quarterly*, **36** (1965), 433-440.

Lakie, W. L., "Personality Characteristics of Certain Groups of Intercollegiate Athletes," *Research Quarterly*, **33** (1962), 556-573.

Ogilvie, B., "Psychological Consistencies Within the Personality of High Level Competitors," *Journal of the American Medical Assn.*, Special Report 1968 (a).

Ogilvie, B., "The Personality of the Male Athlete," Academy Papers, No. 1 (The American Academy of Physical Education, 1968), 45-52 (b).

Ogilvie, B., and Tutko, T., *Problem Athletes and How to Handle Them*, London, 1966.

Parsons, D. R., "Personality Traits of National Representative Swimmers – Canada 1962," Master's Thesis, University of British Columbia, 1963.

Rushall, B. S., "An Evaluation of the Relationship Between Personality and Physical Performance Categories," paper presented at the Second International Congress of Sport Psychology, Washington, D.C., 1968.

Singer, R. N., "Personality Differences Between and Within Baseball and Tennis Players," *Research Quarterly*, **40** (1969), 582-588.

Slusher, H., "Personality and Intelligence Characteristics of Selected High School Athletes and Nonathletes," *Research Quarterly*, **35** (1964), 539-545.

Straub, W. F., "Personality Traits of College Football Players Who Participated at Different Levels of Competition," *International Journal of Sport Psychology*, **2** (1971), 33-41.

MACHIAVELLIANISM AMONG COLLEGE AND HIGH SCHOOL COACHES

George H. Sage

INTRODUCTION

In recent years America's high school and college athletic coaches have been vigorously attacked by individuals from within and outside the field of education. These attacks have centered on the alleged ruthless methods that athletic coaches use in carrying out the tasks of coaching their teams. As American sports have developed, the role of the coach as the unquestioned authority in all matters pertaining to the team has become accepted. Not only is the coach the decision maker with regard to the teaching of skills and the implementation of strategy and tactics, but he is also the authority on modes of dress, grooming, and social behavior. In essence, when an athlete commits himself to a sports team, he commits himself to the will of the coach of that team on all matters which the coach thinks are important.

While Americans have never looked with great favor upon obedience to authority, they have been willing for many years to accept the authority of athletic coaches, perhaps because this obedience is associated with will-to-win, self-discipline, self-denial for the good of the team, etc.—all highly esteemed virtues in the field of sport. But recent years have witnessed a questioning of authority throughout the broad spectrum of American society—from the family to the political-economic structure. If one accepts the notion that sport is a microcosm of the larger society, it is not surprising that social change, in this case the questioning of coaches' authority, would appear.

George H. Sage, "Machiavellianism Among College and High School Coaches," *75th Proceedings of the National College Physical Education Association for Men*, 1972, pp. 45-60. Reprinted by permission.

One method of discrediting the authority of a position is to question the credibility of the persons who fill this position. This can be done by questioning the technical skills of persons filling the position. Another method, and one which is particularly appropriate where the activity involves education and/or interpersonal relations, is to question the genuine personal empathy, sincerity, affection, and humanism those in the position have for others. The critics of America's coaches have rarely used the first method. That is, they have not attacked coaches' technical knowledge of the sport. Indeed, if they have had any criticism in this regard, it was about coaches' overemphasis of the technical aspects of sports. It is the second method that has primarily concerned the critics. They see the coach as one who is not concerned with persons, not concerned with the players as humans; they see coaches as concerned only with winning games and using athletes as pawns, or as means, to this end. Ogilvie has stated: "Traditionally, you're going to find in the coaching profession men who are ... more interested in power and manipulation and less interested in humanistic approaches. They prefer control, organization, unquestioned commitment to their philosophy and so on."[1] One of the most outspoken of the recent critics of American coaches is Jack Scott. He characterizes the college coach in this way: "The typical ... coach is a soulless, back-slapping, meticulously groomed team-oriented efficiency expert—a jock's Robert MacNamara. ... Most coaches have as much concern for the welfare of their athletes as a general has for the soldiers he sends into battle. ... For most college coaches, the athlete is significant only to the extent that he can contribute to a team victory. ... For every relaxed, understanding coach ... there are one hundred rigid, authoritarian coaches who have so much ... character armor that they rattle."[2]

Ogilvie and Scott are only two of the many critics who have attacked high school and college coaches in the recent years. Sports journalists have written extensively about them. In the past four years, *Sports Illustrated* has published two major series of articles dealing with athletic coaches. The first series was entitled "The Black Athlete: A Shameful Story."[3] The second was entitled "The Desperate Coach."[4] Both series intimated that coaches' personalities tended to be highly oriented toward interpersonal manipulation.

The allegations which have been made about the personality structure of athletic coaches by the various critics is conspicuous by its lack of documentation. Indeed, although many professional occupational groups have been studied in recent years, no one has systematically studied athletic coaches. The purpose of this study was to examine the interpersonal manipulation trait of high school and college athletic coaches.

Although questions about how and why human beings manipulate other human beings by guile, deceit, illegal power, immorality, etc., have interested scholars for many centuries, only in recent years have psychologists turned specifically to studying whether conniving, manipulating strategies do indeed exist as personality syndromes, and, if they do exist, whether they are validly measurable. Using the writings of Machiavelli (*The Prince* and *The Discourses*) as an example of manipulatory tactics, Richard Christie and his associates[5] have developed an instrument to evaluate opportunism, guile, and duplicity in interpersonal relations, and their laboratory research with this instrument indicates that the tendency to respond in certain ways to the instrument is reliably related to interpersonal behaviors. That is, subjects who endorse guile, the use of illegal power, opportunism, and duplicity in interpersonal relations tend to engage more often and more readily in exploitive behaviors, presumably in an effort to implement their own desired ends. Christie[6] refers to this general class of attitudes and related behaviors as "Machiavellianism." Geis, one of Christie's associates, has stated: "Machiavellianism is associated with emotional detachment in interpersonal relations, a tendency to exploit situations and others for self-gain, and a tendency to take over control in small groups."[7]

The Machiavellian (Mach) scale in its current form (Mach V) has gone through several revisions. The Mach V scale is composed of twenty triads of items which are statements, paraphrases, and reversals of statements from *The Prince* and *The Discourses* of Machiavelli. A variety of laboratory studies by Christie and others have demonstrated that the Mach V instrument is reliable and consistent, and more important, that persons who score high on the scale actually behave in a more Machiavellian manner than those who score low.

Basically a score on the Mach scale may be interpreted as representing the degree to which a respondent believes that people in general are manipulatable, that is, that interpersonal manipulation is possible. Machiavellianism reflects a tough-minded and relatively affectless view of other persons. Christie and Geis suggest that a high-Machiavellian view might be, "People are no damn good. So what? Take advantage of it." And they report that the statement of one high Mach was, "Win by any means."[8]

A series of laboratory studies have confirmed the value of the Mach scale for successfully predicting interpersonal manipulative behavior in a variety of situations. High Machs manipulate more, win more, are persuaded less, persuade others more, and differ significantly from low-Machs. The experimental evidence indicates that high-Machs are markedly less likely to become emotionally involved with other people, or with sensitive issues. They are cold, amoral, and possess a detached personal unresponsiveness and a covertly aggressive willingness and ability to manipulate others. High-Machs have a generally unflattering opinion of others and a cynical view of people in general. Low-Machs, on the other hand, are more inclined towards valuing affective involvement with others and tending to believe that interpersonal relations should be governed by strict humanist, or ethical, norms.

Laboratory studies of Machiavellianism have involved a wide variety of experimental conditions. These studies of the interaction of individuals and situational conditions has led Christie and Geis[9] to propose an "interaction model" to characterize situations in which high-Machs are likely to be found and in which they will be successful. They suggest that high-Machs will be found in situational conditions in which there is:

1. Face-to-face interaction

2. Latitude for improvisation

3. Irrelevant affect

Situations in which there is face-to-face interaction refers to conditions in which activities are carried on with all the participants within talking distance of one another. That is, personal relations are conducted directly rather than indirectly. Christie and Geis state that, "Latitude for improvisation indicates that the structure of the social interaction is open-ended, not specifically predefined in terms of content or timing. . . . Improvisation implies both that subjects must improvise and that the improvisation can influence outcomes."[10] Most interpersonal situations involve some degree of affect, but situations in which affect may distract the person from concentrating on the operations which lead to success are situations in which high-Machs excel, since high-Machs tend not to invest affect in others.

Although no systematic attempt has been made to discover how Mach scores are related to various occupational groups, it seems possible that the choice of occupations and professions is related to Mach scores. A major problem of predicting occupational relationship and Mach scores, of course, is the need for a classification system for coding the relative variables in the "interaction model" for occupations. The few studies that are available "suggest that Strong Inventory scores related to feminine occupations are negatively correlated with Mach scores. In general professionals tend to score higher than businessmen who have similar numbers of years of education." Christie and Geis state: "We do not have representative samples of occupations but in general those unsystematic aggregates who have taken the Mach scales have scores consistent with our interpretation of the degree of structure imposed by the occupation."[11]

In applying the "interaction model" of relative degree of face-to-face contact, latitude for improvisation, and arousal of irrelevant affect to athletic coaching, it would appear that this occupation would attract persons who are high in Machiavellianism, since the situational conditions of coaching resemble the experimental situations in which high-Machs are more successful. Athletic coaching involves frequent face-to-face contact with players who are under the direction of the coach, and coaching generally involves a prolonged period of interpersonal interaction between the coach and his players. Furthermore, coaching permits rather wide latitude for improvisation. Although school coaches must conform to general school policy with regard to player treatment, and they must conform to game rules with regard to playing the sport, they are given broad latitude in teaching skills, strategies and tactics, and regulating the personal lives of their players. Certainly, methods of coaching vary widely. The third situational variable is the presence of irrelevant affect. Although affect is certainly an important aspect of athletics and coaches are seen as getting "emotional" for games, the critical question is whether this affect distracts the coach from concentrating on the operations of coaching which lead to success. Since standards of success in coaching are universally defined as winning, it would seem that someone attracted to the coaching occupation would not be likely to invest affect in others, since this could distract and interfere with effective pursuit of coaching goals—winning games.

Statements of criticism made in recent years about the behaviors of coaches suggests that they possess many of the traits of the high-Machiavellian. Statements that coaches are "more interested in power and manipulation," that they "prefer control and unquestioned commitment," that "for most coaches, the athlete is significant only to the extent that he can contribute to a team victory" characterize the high-Machiavellian.

We are led, then, to our first hypothesis, namely that high school and college coaches are characterized by high-Machiavellianism in comparison to a sample of male college students. More specifically the hypothesis is:

1. a) College athletic coaches will have a significantly higher Mach score than will a sample of male college students.
    b) College football coaches will have a significantly higher Mach score than will a sample of male college students.
    c) College track coaches will have a significantly higher Mach score than will a sample of male college students.
    d) College basketball coaches will have a significantly higher Mach score than will a sample of male college students.
    e) High school football coaches will have a significantly higher Mach score

than will a sample of male college students.

f) High school basketball coaches will have a significantly higher Mach score than will a sample of male college students.

Christie and Geis[12] found that agreement with Mach statements increases throughout adolescence, peaks around 20 years of age, and shows a gradual decrease in scores among older respondents. Although the trend toward a gradual reduction in Mach scores with age may occur with a general population, the reverse would seem to be true for a population that fits the "interaction model." In the case of a single occupational group, if the interaction model accurately applied, it would appear that the most successful in that occupation, and the ones who were most strongly attracted to the situational conditions of that occupation, would be selectively retained in that occupation.

Specifically, it is suggested that the Mach scores of coaches will increase with years of age, since many who are low in Machiavellianism will be screened out of the occupation and those who remain will increase their Machiavellianism due to the situational conditions associated with coaching. This leads to our second major hypothesis:

2. a) There will be a significant increase in Mach scores of college football coaches with years of age.
   b) There will be a significant increase in Mach scores of college track coaches with years of age.
   c) There will be a significant increase in Mach scores of college basketball coaches with years of age.
   d) There will be a significant increase in Mach scores of high school football coaches with years of age.
   e) There will be a significant increase in Mach scores of high school basketball coaches with years of age.

Our third hypothesis is that Machiavellianism among college coaches increases with years in coaching. Specifically, the hypothesis is:

3. a) There will be a significant increase in Mach scores of college football coaches with years in coaching.
   b) There will be a significant increase in Mach scores of college track coaches with years in coaching.
   c) There will be a significant increase in Mach scores of college basketball coaches with years in coaching.

A variety of laboratory research findings show that high-Machs win more in individual competition and in competition with groups when the situational conditions meet the "interaction model." These findings suggest that coaches who are successful at winning games are probably high in Machiavellianism. This prediction is based on consistent findings that high-Machs are not distracted by emotional involvement with others or getting carried away with personal sympathies which could distract them from evaluating resources and allocating tasks for optimal efficiency.

Our fourth hypothesis, then, is that coaches who have attained winning records will be high in Machiavellianism. More specifically:

4. a) College football coaches with a won-loss record of over 60% will have significantly higher Mach scores than those with a won-loss record of under 60%.

   b) College basketball coaches with a won-loss record of over 60% will have significantly higher Mach scores than those with a won-loss record of under 60%.

   c) High school football coaches with a won-loss record of over 60% will have significantly higher Mach scores than those with a won-loss record of under 60%.

   d) High school basketball coaches with a won-loss record of over 60% will have significantly higher Mach scores than those with a won-loss record of under 60%.

METHOD

Subjects. The college coaches were randomly selected from the 1970-71 Official Collegiate Guides for Football, Basketball, and Track which are published by the National Collegiate Athletic Bureau. One-hundred and fifty coaches were selected from each of the Guides. The high school coaches were randomly selected from the 1970-71 Colorado High School Coaches Directory. One-hundred football coaches and the same number of basketball coaches were selected. The Mach score for the sample of male college students is taken from Christie and Geis and is reported to be from "students in 14 different colleges." The colleges represented, they state, "are probably very close in student characteristics to a representative sample of colleges."[13] The total sample of both male and female students was made up of 1782 respondents.

Procedures. Mach V scales and a self-addressed envelope were sent to all of the coaches who had been selected. A letter accompanied the Mach V scale to encourage the coaches to complete and return the scales. No mention was made about the purpose and nature of the Mach scale. After several weeks, follow-up letters were sent to the coaches who had not returned the scale. The initial letter and follow-up yielded the following completed and correctly marked Mach scales (refer to Table 1): college football, 124 (83%); track, 115 (77%); basketball, 104 (69%); high school football, 69 (69%); and high school basketball, 84 (84%). The average age and years of head coaching experience for the various coaching groups were as follows: college football coaches, 41 years of age and 8 years of experience; college track coaches, 41 years of age and 10 years of experience; college basketball coaches, 39 years of age and 8 years of experience; high school football coaches, 32 years of age and 6 years of experience; high school basketball coaches, 32 years of age and 6 years of experience.

Coaches' responses to the Mach V scale were coded and computer cards for the respondents were punched. The computer cards were then processed by the IBM 360 model 30 computer in the University of Northern Colorado Computer Center for the statistical analyses.

Analyses of the data were performed through the use of Dunnett's "t" statistic, a method of comparing multiple means with a control, and analysis of variance simple randomized designs. Where significant F ratios were derived in the simple randomized designs, the Scheffe test of multiple comparisons was applied. The .10 level of significance was selected for the null hypothesis in all analyses in this study.

Table 1   Years of Age and Years as a Head Coach

Coaching group	Number of Respondents	Years of age (mean)	Std. dev.	Years as head coach (mean)	Std. dev.
College football coaches	124	41.19	7.25	7.54	6.21
College track coaches	115	40.61	10.19	9.52	7.96
College basketball coaches	104	39.42	7.41	3.11	7.00
High school football coaches	69	31.97	7.02	6.32	5.95
High school basketball coaches	84	32.01	6.40	6.12	5.60

RESULTS

Table 2 presents the numbers, means, and standard deviation on the Mach V scale for the sample of male college students which was reported by Christie and Geis.[14] This table also reports the numbers, means, and standard deviations on the Mach V level for college coaches of football, track, and basketball and for high school football and basketball coaches.

Table 2   Comparison of Coaches Mach V Scores with Male College Student Mach V Scores

Groups	Number	Mean	Std. dev.	Dunnet "t"*
Male college students	764	99.27	11.17	
College football coaches	124	98.14	7.42	0.04
College track coaches	115	97.26	7.16	0.06
College basketball coaches	104	97.65	7.86	0.05
High school football coaches	69	97.45	7.36	0.05
High school basketball coaches	84	97.22	8.67	0.06

* t = 2.34   Critical value for significance at .10 level

Dunnett has derived the sampling distribution for a "t" statistic which is appropriate when level of significance is desired for the set of all comparisons between several treatments and a control. In this study, the sample of male college students represents the control. The critical value for significance at the .10 level is 2.34. Since none of the observed values approached this, the null hypothesis was accepted. That is, there is no significant difference between Mach V scores of male college students and any of the coaching groups.

Table 3 presents the summary of the analysis of variance treatment of the data between age of college football coaches and Mach V scores. The three age levels were 25-35 years of age, 36-45 years of age, and 46 and over years of age. The computed F ratio is 1.044 and the critical value for significance at the .10 level is 2.35. Therefore, the null hypothesis is accepted. That is, there are no differences between age and Mach V scores for college and university football coaches.

Table 3   Analysis of Variance Summary for Treatment of Data on Mach V Scores and Age for College Football Coaches

College football coaches		Number		Mean		Std. dev.
25-35 years of age		29		99.59		7.684
36-45 years of age		62		98.15		7.759
46 years of age and over		33		96.85		6.462

Source of variation	df	SS	MS	F	F.10
Between groups	2	115.000	57.500	1.044	2.35
Within groups	121	6662.000	55.058		
Total	123	6777.000			

Table 4   Analysis of Variance Summary for Treatment of Data on Mach V Scores and Age for College Track Coaches

College track coaches		Number	Mean	Std. dev.
25-35 years of age		37	99.19	6.823
36-45 years of age		46	97.28	7.102
46 years of age and over		32	95.13	6.738
Source of variation	df	SS	MS	F	F.10
Between groups	2	284.00	142.000	2.971	2.39*
Within groups	112	5353.00	47.795		
Total	114	5637.00			

* Significant at the .10 level

Table 4 presents the summary of the analysis of variance treatment of the data between age of college track coaches and Mach V scores. The three age groups were the same as those used with college football coaches. The computed F ratio is 2.971 and the critical value for significance at the .10 level is 2.39. This significant F ratio is evidence of a difference among the three age groups and Mach V scores. To locate where the differences are found between age and Mach V scores, the Scheffe test of multiple comparisons was applied. The computer program contained an adjustment in the degrees of freedom whereby the values shown in the multiple comparisons tables are F ratios which may be judged against the critical value of 2.39. The comparisons of Mach V means are shown in Table 5. The comparison value of 2.965 between track coaches who are 35 to 45 years of age and those who are over 46 years of age indicates significant differences on Mach scores. Track coaches who are over 46 years old have significantly lower scores than those who are under 35 years of age on Machiavellianism.

Table 5   Multiple Comparisons of Mach V Means within Track Coaches

	Means	99.19	97.28	95.13
25-35 years of age	99.19	0.0	0.78	2.965*
36-45 years of age	97.28	0.0	0.0	0.919
46 years of age and over	95.13	0.0	0.0	0.0

* Significant at the .10 level

Table 6 Analysis of Variance Summary for Treatment of Data on Mach V Scores and Age for College Basketball Coaches

College basketball coaches		Number	Mean	Std. dev.
25-35 years of age		39	98.46	8.379
36-45 years of age		43	96.37	8.533
46 years of age and over		22	98.73	6.311

Source of variation	df	SS	MS	F	$F.10$
Between groups	2	121.375	60.688	0.934	2.39
Within groups	101	6562.188	64.972		
Total	103	6683.563			

Table 6 presents the summary of the analysis of variance treatment of the data between age of college basketball coaches and Mach V scores. The age groups are the same as those used for football and track. The computed F ratio is 0.934 and the critical value for significance at the .10 level is 2.39. Therefore, the null hypothesis is accepted. That is, there are no differences between age and Mach V scores for college basketball coaches.

Table 7 presents the summary of the analysis of variance treatment of the data between age of high school football coaches and Mach V scores. Data for only two age groups were analyzed for the high school coaches, due to the smaller number of high school coaches. The age groups were 25 to 35 years of age and 36 years of age and over. The computed F ratio is 1.743 and the critical value for significance at the .10 level is 2.79. Therefore, the null hypothesis is accepted. That is, there are no differences between age and Mach V scores for high school football coaches.

Table 7 Analysis of Variance Summary for Treatment of Data on Mach V Scores and Age for High School Football Coaches

High school football coaches		Number	Mean	Std. dev.
25-35 years of age		55	98.04	7.515
36 years of age and over		14	95.14	6.455

Source of variation	df	SS	MS	F	$F.10$
Between groups	1	93.438	93.438	1.743	2.79
Within groups	67	3591.688	53.607		
Total	68	3685.125			

Table 8   Analysis of Variance Summary for Treatment of Data on Mach V Scores and Age for High School Basketball Coaches

High school basketball coaches		Number	Mean	Std. dev.
25-35 years of age 36 years of age and over		62 22	97.94 95.18	9.176 7.109
Source of variation	df	SS	MS	F	F.10
Between groups Within groups	1 82	123.188 6197.063	123.188 75.574	1.630	2.79
Total	83	6320.251			

Table 8 presents the summary of the analysis of variance treatment of the data between age of high school basketball coaches and Mach V scores. The age group categories were the same as those used for high school football coaches. The computed F ratio is 1.630 and the critical value for significance at the .10 level is 2.79. Therefore, the null hypothesis is accepted. That is, there are no differences between age and Mach V scores for high school basketball coaches.

Table 9 presents the summary of the analysis of variance treatment of the data between years in coaching for college football coaches and Mach V scores. The three levels of years in coaching was 0-5 years, 6-12 years, and 13 years and over. The computed F ratio is 1.641 and the critical value for significance at the .10 level is 2.35. Therefore, the null hypothesis is accepted. That is, there are no differences between years in coaching and Mach V scores of college football coaches.

Table 9   Analysis of Variance Summary for Treatment of Data on Mach V Scores and Years of Experience as a Head Coach for College Football Coaches

College football coaches		Number	Mean	Std. dev.
0-5 years experience 6-12 years experience 13 years experience and over		60 39 25	99.13 98.00 95.96	8.031 6.775 6.611
Source of variation	df	SS	MS	F	F.10
Between groups Within groups	2 121	179.00 6598.00	89.500 54.529	1.641	2.35
Total	123	6777.00			

Table 10   Analysis of Variance Summary for Treatment of Data on Mach V Scores and Years of Experience as a Head Coach for College Track Coaches

College track coaches		Number	Mean	Std. dev.
0-5 years of experience		47	98.77	7.326
6-12 years experience		35	97.51	6.608
13 years experience and over		33	94.97	6.617
Source of variation	*df*	SS	MS	*F*	*F*.10
Between groups	2	282.00	141.000	2.949	2.39*
Within groups	112	5355.00	47.813		
Total	114	5637.00			

* Significant at .10 level

Table 10 presents the summary of the analysis of variance treatment of the data between years in coaching for college track coaches and Mach V scores. The three levels of years in coaching was the same as that used for football coaches. The computed F ratio is 2.949 and the critical value for significance is 2.39. This significant F ratio is evidence of a difference among the three levels of coaching experience and Mach V scores. To locate where the differences are found between coaching experience and Mach V scores, the Scheffe test of multiple comparisons was applied. The comparisons of Mach V means are shown in Table 11. The comparison value of 2.922 between track coaches with 0-5 years experience and those with 13 and over years of experience indicates significant differences on Mach scores. Track coaches with over 13 years of experience have significantly lower Mach scores than those with less than six years of coaching experience.

Table 11   Multiple Comparisons of Mach V Means within Track Coaches

	Means	98.77	97.51	94.97
0-5 years experience	98.77	0.0	0.329	2.922*
6-12 years experience	97.51	0.0	0.0	1.150
13 years experience and over	94.97	0.0	0.0	0.0

* Significant at .10 level

Table 12   Analysis of Variance Summary for Treatment of Data on Mach V Scores and Years of Experience as a Head Coach for College Basketball Coaches

College basketball coaches		Number	Mean	Std. dev.
0-5 years experience		51	97.84	3.484
6-12 years experience		28	96.71	8.679
13 years experience and over		25	98.32	6.498
Source of variation	*df*	SS	MS	F	F.10
Between groups	2	37.438	18.719	0.284	2.39
Within groups	101	6646.125	65.803		
Total	103	6683.563			

Table 12 presents the summary of the analysis of variance treatment of the data between years of coaching for college basketball coaches and Mach V scores. The three levels of years in coaching was the same as that used for football and track coaches. The computed F ratio is 0.284, and the critical value for significance at the .10 level is 2.39. Therefore, the null hypothesis is accepted. That is, there are no differences between years in coaching and Mach V scores for college and university basketball coaches.

Table 13 presents the summary of the analysis of variance treatment of the data between college and university football coaches with a won-loss record of over 60% with those whose won-loss record is under 60% on Mach V scores. The computed F ratio is 1.310 and the critical value for significance at the .10 level is 2.75. Therefore, the null hypothesis is accepted. That is, there is no difference between college football coaches with over 60% won-loss records and those with won-loss records below 60% on Machiavellianism.

Table 13   Analysis of Variance Summary for Treatment of Data on Mach V Scores and Won-loss Records for College Football Coaches

College football coaches		Number	Mean	Std. dev.
Won-loss record below 60%		81	97.58	7.352
Won-loss record above 60%		43	99.19	7.529
Source of variation	*df*	SS	MS	F	F.10
Between groups	1	72.000	72.000	1.310	2.75
Within groups	122	6705.000	54.959		
Total	123	6777.000			

Table 14 Analysis of Variance Summary for Treatment of Data on Mach V Scores and Won-loss Records for College Basketball Coaches

College basketball coaches		Number	Mean	Std. dev.
Won-loss record below 60%		67	98.69	8.221
Won-loss record above 60%		37	95.78	7.495
Source of variation	df	SS	MS	F	F.10
Between groups	1	200.813	200.313	3.160*	2.79
Within groups	102	6482.750	63.556		
Total	103	6683.563			

* Significant at the .10 level

Table 14 presents the summary of the analysis of variance treatment of the data between college and university basketball coaches with a won-loss record of over 60% with those whose won-loss record is under 60% on Mach scores. The computed F ratio is 3.160 and the critical value for significance at the .10 level is 2.79. This significant F ratio is evidence of a difference between these two groups. Thus basketball coaches with a won-loss record of over 60% have significantly lower scores than those with won-loss records under 60% on Machiavellianism.

Table 15 presents the summary of the analysis of variance treatment of the data between high school football coaches with a won-loss record of over 60% with those whose won-loss record is under 60% on Mach V scores. The computed F ratio is 0.001 and the critical value for significance at the .10 level is 2.79. Therefore, the null hypothesis is accepted. That is, there is no difference between high school football coaches with won-loss records of over 60% and those with won-loss records under 60% on Machiavellianism.

Table 15 Analysis of Variance Summary for Treatment of Data on Mach V Scores and Won-loss Records for High School Football Coaches

High school football coaches		Number	Mean	Std. dev.
Won-loss record below 60%		40	97.47	7.990
Won-loss record above 60%		29	97.41	6.533
Source of variation	df	SS	MS	F	F.10
Between groups	1	0.063	0.063	0.001	2.79
Within groups	67	3685.063	55.001		
Total	68	3685.125			

Table 16   Analysis of Variance Summary for Treatment of Data on Mach V Scores and Won-loss Records for High School Basketball Coaches

High school basketball coaches		Number	Mean	Std. dev.
Won-loss record below 60%		53	97.58	8.861
Won-loss records above 60%		31	96.58	8.598
Source of variation	df	SS	MS	F	F.10
Between groups	1	19.813	19.813	0.258	2.79
Within groups	82	6300.438	76.835		
Total	83	6320.250			

Table 16 presents the summary of the analysis of variance treatment of the data between high school basketball coaches with a won-loss record of over 60% with those whose won-loss record is under 60% of Mach V scores. The computed F ratio is 0.258 and the critical value for significance at the .10 level is 2.79. Therefore, the null hypothesis is accepted. That is, there is no difference between high school basketball coaches with won-loss records of over 60% and those with won-loss records under 60% on Machiavellianism.

DISCUSSION

Christie and Geis[15] have suggested that there is a relationship between kinds of occupations and Mach scale scores. They suggest that high-Machs will more likely be found in occupations in which the situational conditions resemble the experimental conditions under which high-Machs are more successful. In this study, it was hypothesized that college and high school athletic coaches would score higher on the Mach V scale because the situational conditions appear to be similar to those in which laboratory experiments found high-Machs to be successful and to occupations in which high Machiavellianism is characteristic. The results of this study showed no differences between the Mach V scores of a sample of male college students ($N = 764$) reported by Christie and Geis[16] and any of the college and high school athletic coaching groups.

How can we account for the findings that athletic coaches are no higher in Machiavellianism than a general college student group? One possibility is that some high-Mach coaches did not return the Mach V questionnaire. Laboratory studies have shown that high-Machs tend to be suspicious people—they are more suspicious of instructions and procedures in a situation. Although the percentage of returned Mach questionnaires was fairly high for all coaching groups, perhaps the high-Mach coaches refused to return the questionnaire because they were suspicious of the purpose and nature of it.

Another possibility in regard to the findings, and one that seems more tenable to this investigator, is that the degree of structure in athletic coaching does not meet the situational conditions in which high-Machs are attracted and are successful. Athletic coaching does provide a setting for frequent face-to-face interaction, so it seems that this situational condition is fully met in coaching. It is possibly in latitude for improvisation where coaching does not meet the situational conditions in which high-Machs are found. In many ways coaching permits little latitude for improvisation. The day-to-day tasks of athletic coaching are relatively standardized. The coach must function within the constraints of the policies of the institution for which he works, he must abide by the rules of the sport in which he coaches and he is regulated by conference and national athletic associations. The criterion for success in coaching is intimately related to objective performance—winning; this is another constraint to improvisation in that the situation is highly structured providing little room or latitude for improvisation. Any improvisation that occurs is primarily that of teaching skills and developing strategy and tactics for contests.

The third situational condition, that of irrelevant affect, seems to apply to coaching in most respects. Those who are less subject to the arousal of irrelevant affect would seem to function well in coaching. In general, the coach cannot become too affectively involved with those whom he is coaching, he must detach and depersonalize his relationships with the players in order to make effective decisions with regard to player selection, devising strategies, and a host of other decisions which require taking a hard line for the benefit of the team. On the other hand, high-Mach coaches, with a cool cognitive analysis of the needs of the team and a disregard for individual needs of their players, could perhaps produce a team with low morale, which may adversely affect individual and team performance.

It seems that we can agree with Christie and Geis with regard to attempting to relate coaching to Machiavellianism. They state that in attempting to generalize from the laboratory paradigm to the real world there is "simply not enough detailed information about the relative degree and kind of face-to-face contact, latitude for improvisation, and arousal of irrelevant affect in these situations to be precise in analyzing their influence."[17]

With regard to the statements made in recent years about the personality dynamics of coaches by critics such as Scott who said that "coaches as a group are rather insensitive in their interpersonal relationships, and . . . they will quite readily manipulate and exploit others,"[18] the results of this study do not support the charges that have been leveled at coaches in general. This is not to say that all coaches act with empathy, sincerity, affection, and humanism; of course they do not. There are very high Machiavellians in coaching just as there are in other occupational groups. Some coaches had Mach scores of over 115 but the average scores for the coaching groups were much less.

Many social practices essential to the welfare of an enterprise of some sort involve the control and manipulation of one person by another. To maintain the position that all control is bad, it is necessary to disguise useful practices for the accomplishment of many worthwhile goals. Although the goals of sports participation are (or should be) broader than merely winning contests, it is obvious that in American society winning is a primary goal in all sports competition, and winners are accorded high esteem and other rewards while losers are given little sympathy or are treated with disrespect. The athletic coach, then, has a well-defined social role—the production of a winner. Control of the conditions for producing a winning team becomes important. Coordination of many individual talents, and coordination of the strategy and tactics of the entire team makes certain forms of control necessary for achieving the objective of a successful team. Thus control is important in coaching. The problem is one of freeing athletes, not from control by the coach, but from certain kinds of capricious and unwarranted control exercised by a few coaches.

Even though Christie and Geis[19] found that Machiavellianism gradually decreases with age in adults, it was hypothesized that Mach scores of athletic coaches would increase with age and with years in coaching. Since the situational conditions of coaching appear to be similar to the conditions in which high-Machs are successful, it would seem that low-Machs will be screened out of the coaching occupation and those who remain will increase their Machiavellianism due to the situational conditions found in coaching.

The results of this study do not support the hypothesis that coaches increase in Machiavellianism with age and with years in coaching. For college football and basketball coaches there was no significant increase in Machiavellianism with years of age or with experience as a coach. For college track coaches, there was a significant difference in Mach scores between track coaches who were over 45 years old and those who were under 35 years of age, and there was a significant difference between track coaches with over 13 years of experience and those with less than six years of coaching experience. However, in both cases the differences were in the opposite direction from that which was hypothesized. Instead of an increase in Machiavellianism with age and years experience, there was a significant decrease in Machiavellianism.

The hypothesis that Machiavellianism increases with age and coaching experience for athletic coaches was based on the assumption that athletic coaching meets the situational conditions of the "interaction model" which Christie and Geis[20] proposed. Since the basic finding of this study suggests that athletic coaching perhaps does not fit the "interaction model," it seems that Machiavellianism among coaches would follow the same pattern of decline as reported by Christie and Geis.[21] The findings with college track coaches are in accordance with their findings.

The hypothesis that winning coaches are higher in Machiavellianism was based on previous findings (Geis,[22] Geis,[23] Christie and Geis[24]) that high-Machs are more competitive, organize and exploit whatever resources the situation provides more effectively, and consequently win more of whatever is being contested for than low-Machs. Furthermore, groups in which high-Machs are the leaders perform more effectively than those led by low-Machs.

The findings of this study do not support the hypothesis that winning coaches are higher in Machiavellianism than losing coaches. This finding is particularly puzzling because one of the most consistent findings of research on Machiavellianism is that high-Machs win more—they mobilize their resources to achieve task goals better than low-Machs. One possibility for explaining the present finding is that player ability is more important than the interpersonal manipulation traits of coaches. In other words, winning athletic contests depends more upon the athletic ability of the players than upon personal characteristics of coaches. A second possibility is that the high-Mach, with his detachment from emotional involvement with the personal needs of his players, may reduce the morale of his team. It is commonly believed, although not well documented, that low morale is associated with poor performance (Gellerman,[25] Vroom[26]). It is possible that because of the delicate nature of the interpersonal relations that appear to be necessary to get optimal effort from athletes, high Machiavellianism may be a deterrent rather than an asset in producing winning teams. The findings of this study, though, indicate that there are no differences between winning coaches, except in the case of college basketball coaches, and in this case the finding is in the opposite direction to that which was hypothesized.

CONCLUSIONS

Within the limitations imposed by the sample of subjects used in this study, the following conclusions are warranted:

1. There are no differences in Machiavellianism between college and high school athletic coaches and male college students.

2. There are no differences in Machiavellianism among college football, college basketball, high school football, and high school basketball coaches with regard to years of age or head coaching experience.

3. College track coaches who are over 45 years of age are lower in Machiavellianism than those who are under 35 years of age, and college track coaches with over 13 years of coaching experience are lower in Machiavellianism than those with less than six years of head coaching experience.

4. There are no differences in Machiavellianism between college football, college basketball, high school football, and high school basketball coaches with winning records (over 60%) and coaches with won-loss records under 60%.

NOTES

1. Bruce Ogilvie, quoted from J. Jares, "We Have a Neurotic in the Backfield Doctor," *Sports Illustrated*, Vol. 34 (January 18, 1971), p. 33.

2. Jack Scott, *Athletics for Athletes* (Hayward, California: Quality Printing Service, 1969), p. 7.

3. Jack Olsen, "The Black Athlete: A Shameful Story," *Sports Illustrated*, Vol. 30 (July 1, July 8, July 15, July 22, July 29, 1968).

4. John Underwood, "The Desperate Coach," *Sports Illustrated*, Vol. 31 (August 25, September 1, September 8, 1969).

5. Richard Christie and Florence L. Geis, *Studies in Machiavellianism*, New York: Academic Press, 1970.

6. *Ibid.*, pp. 1-9.

7. Florence L. Geis, "Machiavellianism in a Semireal World," *Proceedings of the 76th Annual Convention of the American Psychological Association*, Vol. 3, 1968, p. 407.

8. Christie and Geis, *op. cit.*, pp. 38, 133.

9. *Ibid.*, pp. 285-294, 350-354.

10. *Ibid.*, p. 287.

11. *Ibid.*, p. 354.

12. Richard Christie and Florence L. Geis, "Some Consequences of Taking Machiavelli Seriously," *Handbook of Personality Theory and Research*, eds. E. F. Borgatta and W. W. Lambert, Chicago: Rand McNally, 1968, pp. 959-973.

13. Christie and Geis, *Studies in Machiavellianism*, pp. 32, 314.

14. *Ibid.*, p. 32.

15. *Ibid.*, pp. 354-356.

16. *Ibid.*, p. 32.

17. *Ibid.*, p. 348.

18. Jack Scott, *The Athletic Revolution*, New York: The Free Press, 1971, p. 134.

19. Christie and Geis, "Some Consequences of Taking Machiavelli Seriously," pp. 966-969.

20. Christie and Geis, *Studies in Machiavellianism*, pp. 285-294, 350-354.

21. Christie and Geis, "Some Consequences of Taking Machiavelli Seriously," pp. 966-969.

22. Florence L. Geis, "The Con Game," in *Studies in Machiavellianism*, eds. Richard Christie and Florence Geis, pp. 105-160.

23. Geis, "Machiavellianism in a Semireal World," pp. 407-408.

24. Christie and Geis, "Some Consequences of Taking Machiavelli Seriously," pp. 949-973.

25. Saul W. Gellerman, *Motivation and Productivity*, American Management Association, 1963.

26. Victor H. Vroom, *Work and Motivation*, New York: John Wiley, 1964, pp. 211-270.

VALUE ORIENTATIONS OF AMERICAN COLLEGE COACHES COMPARED TO THOSE OF MALE COLLEGE STUDENTS AND BUSINESSMEN

George H. Sage

High school and collegiate sports have been a center of controversy in recent years, and athletic coaches have come under a great deal of criticism by persons within and outside the field of education. Scott,[1,2] one of the most

George H. Sage, "Value Orientations of American College Coaches Compared to Male College Students and Businessmen," *75th Annual Proceedings of the National College Physical Education Association for Men,* 1972, pp. 174-186. Reprinted by permission.

outspoken critics of athletic coaches, has suggested that many of the problems in sports are attributable to the behavior of coaches. He has indicated that the value orientations of coaches are so conservative as to be almost aberrant, and that these values are so incongruous with those held by their athletes that they produce a great deal of frustration and conflict between coaches and athletes. Ogilvie, another frequent critic of athletic coaches, also believes that coaches are conservatives in value orientation. He has said: "Traditionally, you're going to find in the coaching profession men who are socially and politically conservative."[3] John Underwood, in a series appearing in *Sports Illustrated* on the coaches' dilemma entitled "The Desperate Coach," said ". . . the student activists . . . regard the coach as a neofascistic racist."[4] Even some coaches view their colleagues as possessing extremely conservative values. Dr. David Nelson, athletic director at the University of Delaware and formerly the head football coach there, said: "Having been a coach . . . I know that most of us are almost Harding Republicans and three degrees to the right of Ghengis Khan."[5]

Although various persons have recently claimed that athletic coaches are out-of-step with the current times because they are much more conservative than other groups, no systematic research has been reported to support these assertions. The purpose of this study was to examine in an exploratory manner the values held by college athletic coaches and compare them with values which have been reported for college students and businessmen. Specifically, the purpose of the study was to determine:

1. What political, social, educational, economic, and personal-moral values are held by college football coaches, college track coaches, and college basketball coaches?

2. Do the values of the various coaching groups differ significantly from values held by college students?

3. Do the values of the various coaching groups differ significantly from values held by businessmen?

Most people would agree that values lie at the core of life and human behavior, and the concept "value" provides a focus for study in a variety of human endeavors, from theology to education. Each one of the disciplines which deal with the behavioral sciences employ this word, but with a great deal of diverse meanings.

For the purposes of this study, a value is considered as one's concept of an ideal relationship (or state of affairs), which he uses to assess the "goodness" or "badness," the "rightness" or "wrongness," of actual relationships which he observes or contemplates (Scott).[6] Furthermore, values refer to personal and social ideals, beliefs, or standards which may be used to evaluate and regulate one's own or others' behavior. These involve ideals or beliefs about what is good, right, desirable, or true. Kluckhohn has stated: "A value is a conception, explicit or implicit distinctive of an individual or characteristic of a group, of the desirable which influences the selection from available modes, means, and ends of action."[7]

It is assumed that values form the basis for behavior, but the possibility of inconsistency between the values held by an individual and the behavior of that individual is also recognized. Morris said: "As abstract possibilities, one can imagine an extreme case where every conceived value issued into an operative value and another extreme case where no conceived value influenced the system of operative values. But human beings seldom, if ever, find themselves at either extreme: some interaction and some incompatibility between conceived and operative values is the common state."[8]

Value orientations are frequently conceptualized as being on a conservative-liberal continuum. Conservatism refers to a set of values which give high priority to: loyalty to tradition, respect and obedience to established authority, normative standards of conduct, and strong religious commitment. Liberalism refers to a set of values which stress social change, equality in political, social, and economic affairs. Value orientations which lie between these two extremes are considered to be moderate.

Research on human values has been conducted for many years. Indeed the social psychology literature and the sociology literature is replete with studies about human values. However, very little research has been done to determine the values held by athletic coaches.

Numerous studies have been done to determine the values held by college students, using several different instruments to measure the extent to which students hold certain values. In the 1930's Vetter[9] and Nelson[10] conducted studies to determine conservatism-liberalism among college students at that time. Jacob[11] in 1957 reviewed the extensive data from related research on college-student values dating back to the 1920's. More recently Roscoe, [12] Teglovic,[13] Ritter,[14] Thayer,[15] Zehv,[16] and Elliott[17] have conducted studies on the values of college students using the *Polyphasic Values Inventory*.

Studies dealing with the values of educators have not been numerous, but Cox,[18] Norwalk-Polasky,[19] and White[20] have recently conducted studies concerned with the relationship between faculty and student values. McAllister[21] compared the values of several groups affiliated with education (school board members, school administrators, education professors, secondary school teachers, and counselors).

Formal research on the values of businessmen is not extensive. Clark[22] and Walter[23] studied the ethical standards and value orientations of selected groups of businessmen; White[24] and Elliott[25] compared the values of businessmen with values of college students and/or other adult groups.

METHOD

Subjects

The college athletic coaches were randomly selected from the 1970-71 Official Collegiate Guides for Football, Basketball, and Track which are published by the National Collegiate Athletic Bureau. One-hundred ten coaches were selected from each of the Guides. Data reported by Teglovic[26] about male college-student values and data reported by Elliott[27] about values held by businessmen were used in comparing the values held by these groups with the values held by college athletic coaches.

Teglovic reported that college students who took part in his study of American college student values were selected this way:

Figures published by the United States Office of Education were used in an analysis of the American college student population to determine the percentage of students enrolled in schools of various locations, affiliations, and sizes. The percentage figures were used in selecting the institutions used in this study. ... After the selection of the participating institutions, student directories were obtained from their research bureau, student personnel office, publications office, or college bookstore. A random sample ... was selected from each student directory.[28]

Teglovic reported a 68.31 percent total response of the 5,863 students sampled. Elliott reported that businessmen were selected in this way:

Members of the Junior Chamber of Commerce in one state from each of the five National Business Education Association geographical regions served as the sample of businessmen. State membership rosters were obtained from the national office of the Junior Chamber of Commerce in Tulsa, Oklahoma. ... These membership rosters provided a systematic random sample from each of the five states, in which every name was selected ...[29]

Elliott reported the following sample sizes in each of the five states:

Illinois	257
Kansas	158
Pennsylvania	266
Washington	100
West Virginia	50

Elliott reported a 57.6 percent total response of the 831 businessmen sampled.

Instrument

The Polyphasic Values Inventory (PVI) developed by Roscoe[30] was used to measure the values of college athletic coaches. This instrument was used by other investigators to measure the values of the other groups (college students and businessmen) with which the athletic coaches' values were compared. The PVI assesses value commitments using twenty multiple-choice items with the responses organized on a conservative-liberal continuum. The items cover selected philosophical, political, economic, educational, social, personal-moral, and religious dimensions of value difference. All of the items require the respondent to make value judgments rather than judgments of fact. Each item is treated as a separate piece of information, thus the respondent does not receive a total score. It was originally designed to be used with college students, but subsequent research has shown it to be applicable to adult populations.

Based upon his research with the PVI, Roscoe[31,32,33] reported that it had discriminant validity, content validity, and reliability.

Procedures

The PVI and a self-addressed envelope were sent to all of the coaches who had been selected. A letter accompanied the PVI to encourage the coaches to complete and return the inventory. After several weeks, follow-up letters were sent to the coaches who had not returned the PVI; a second follow-up letter was sent to those who had still not responded. The initial letter and follow-ups yielded the following completed and correctly marked PVI's: college football, 93 (84%); college track, 73 (67%); college basketball, 80 (73%).

Coaches' responses to the PVI were coded and computer cards for the respondents were punched. Data from Teglovic's[34] and Elliott's[35] research were added to the coaches' data. The data were processed by the IBM 360 model 30 computer at the University of Northern Colorado.

Analyses of the data were performed through the use of chi-square test of goodness-of-fit to determine whether coaches from each sport group were distributed in a fashion significantly different from the normative distributions.

RESULTS

The distribution of responses was recorded in terms of the number of percentage of respondents in each subsample choosing each response for each item in the inventory. There were a few respondents who gave no response to an item or whose response was uninterpretable, but these constitute a small proportion (less than 0.05%) of the total number of responses. Chi-squares were calculated from the number checking one of the five scaled responses (Table 1). In most cases where more than 20% of the expected frequencies in the cells of a group comparison were less than five the cells were collapsed. The degrees of freedom were changed accordingly and this is indicated in Table 1 when significant differences occur.

Each PVI item was treated as a separate source of information; thus no total score was given the respondents. Each item of the PVI has five responses which are arranged on a conservative to liberal spectrum; response #1 is the most conservative and response #5 is the most liberal. When a distribution of responses for an item showed a large proportion of responses at the lower end of the spectrum, the distribution was classified as conservative. When a distribution of responses for an item showed a large proportion of responses at the upper end of the spectrum, the distribution was classified as liberal. A larger proportion of responses in the central choices was interpreted as indicating more moderate value orientations toward that particular topic.

Response distributions were also classified as being either heterogeneous or homogeneous. If a larger proportion of the responses to an item was in one or two adjacent cells, the response distribution was interpreted as homogeneous, but if a response distribution had approximately the same proportion in all the cells or showed no particular distribution pattern this was interpreted as a heterogeneous distribution.

The data were organized into bivariate frequency tables for the purposes of comparing PVI responses to the other variables (these tables were used for working purposes only). The chi-square test of goodness-of-fit was used to determine whether coaches from each group were distributed in a fashion significantly different from the normative distribution. The .01 level of significance was selected for testing the null hypothesis in all statistical analyses of this study.

Table 1 Value Orientations of College Athletic Coaches Compared to Male College Students and Businessmen

| | Chi-square Goodness-of-Fit | | | | | | | |
| | Male college students | | | | Businessmen | | | |
Value orientations	Football coaches	Track coaches	Basketball coaches	All coaching groups	Football coaches	Track coaches	Basketball coaches	All coaching groups
Nature of science	6.56	7.25	12.24	17.88*(S)	2.38	6.42	10.49	12.29
Right-to-vote	43.09*(C)	6.13	20.23*(C)	54.56*(C)	13.35*(C)	4.70	5.77	8.20
Treatment of communists	12.65	4.20	4.66	10.93	16.50*(C)	45.31*(C)	29.44*(C)	70.12*(C)
Military action	7.39	14.42*(C)	7.94	27.10*(C)	4.98	11.02	4.27	17.23*(C)
International relations	5.85	6.97	13.05	23.09*(C)	14.77*(C)	9.19	9.65	29.93*(C)
Private enterprise	3.41	8.89	7.47	7.39	10.70‡(C)	3.22	19.65‡(C)	25.02‡(C)
Labor unions	9.50	8.64	7.77	17.79*(S)	5.09	6.07	7.09	15.45‡(B)
Citizenship education	35.26*(S)	9.42	22.59*(S)	60.41*(S)	24.11†(C)	6.31	7.69	29.34†(C)
Nation's schools	24.02*(S)	4.76	3.42	23.01*(S)	32.32*(C)	26.76*(C)	35.71*(C)	78.83*(C)
Academic freedom	88.46*(S)	57.15*(S)	65.76*(S)	208.52*(S)	45.21*(C)	25.30*(C)	46.29*(C)	114.01*(C)
Equality of man	8.70	3.82	4.84	13.87*(S)	6.84	2.63	1.81	6.89
Race relations	1.33	4.88	5.32	7.25	20.76*(C)	23.93*(C)	23.93*(C)	65.32*(C)
Treatment of criminals	4.99	3.90	8.00	14.32*(S)	17.27†(C)	10.64	7.82	33.05†(C)
Final authority for ethical conduct	32.42*(S)	15.91*(S)	15.32*(S)	54.91*(S)	4.34	9.36	14.03*(C)	22.01*(C)
Cheating on tests	11.16	14.72*(S)	8.67	31.97*(S)	2.36	1.11	5.85	7.19
Sexual behavior	31.27*(S)	22.12*(S)	30.40*(S)	82.61*(S)	8.85	6.08	9.07	22.53*(C)
Use of alcohol	16.93*(S)	19.89*(S)	19.23*(S)	48.88*(S)	60.15*(B)	51.16*(B)	63.92*(B)	169.39*(B)
Nature of God	38.25*(S)	13.62*(S)	16.32*(S)	62.71*(S)	7.40	1.60	4.97	7.90
The Bible	17.21*(S)	2.68	18.64*(S)	31.41*(S)	5.45	1.86	3.17	5.07
Man's responsibility for his deeds	15.12*(S)	8.11	20.15*(S)	35.22*(S)	8.23	8.26	3.72	13.90*(C)

* $df=4$; significant at .01 level
† $df=3$; significant at .01 level
‡ $df=2$; significant at .01 level

(S) = Students more liberal
(B) = Businessmen more liberal
(C) = Coaches more liberal

The distribution of responses regarding the purposes of science indicated that all the groups showed a moderately homogeneous, conservative pattern. Although none of the individual comparisons of coaching groups and college students was significantly different, the slightly greater conservatism on the part of track and basketball coaches produced a significant difference between the all-coaches group and college students, with the coaches showing greater conservatism than students. When comparing the values held toward science by coaches and businessmen the choices indicate that both groups hold moderately homogeneous, conservative values which suggests a strong tendency toward realism. Coaches did not differ significantly from businessmen regarding the purpose of science.

The distribution of responses regarding values held toward right-to-vote indicate that all groups displayed a homogeneous liberal viewpoint on this issue, and football coaches were the most liberal. Although college-student responses concerning the right-to-vote were on the liberal end of the continuum, football, basketball, and the all-coaches group expressed a significantly more liberal orientation than college students. Coaches and businessmen possess a very similar homogeneous, liberal viewpoint regarding right-to-vote, but football coaches were significantly more liberal than businessmen. The largest percentage of both groups felt the right-to-vote should be given to all adult citizens, whereas the largest percentage of college students felt a person should know and understand the rights and duties of citizenship and should meet basic literacy requirements.

The distribution of responses regarding attitudes toward communists in our country indicated that there was similarity between coaches and college students while businessmen were more conservative than any of the groups. Both coaches and college students displayed a moderate conservatism towards communists in our country, with some heterogeneity in the distribution of responses. Over half of the respondents in each of the groups believe that communists should be registered by the government and should not be allowed to hold positions critical to the defense of our nation. There were no significant differences between any of the coaching groups and students. Businessmen showed a significantly more conservative attitude toward communists than each of the coaching groups. This difference is most notable in the percentage of respondents who believed that communists are traitors and criminals and should be imprisoned or deported. Only 3.7 to 7.5 percent of coaches subscribe to this while over 18 percent of businessmen did.

The distribution of responses concerning beliefs about war indicated that there was an overall tendency toward heterogeneity and slight conservatism. All of the coaching groups showed a slight heterogeneity distribution on the moderate to conservative side of the continuum, and they strongly rejected pacifism. The college-student values on this topic were not significantly different than football and basketball coaches but they were significantly different than track coaches and all the coaches combined. Track coaches and the combined coaches group tended to express a more liberal viewpoint than college students. Each coaching group, when compared to businessmen, expressed similar value orientations, but when the responses of all the coaches were combined the result was a significant difference, with coaches showing more liberalism. This significant result was produced by each of the coaching groups having slightly more liberal opinion than the businessmen but not enough, individually, to show significance.

The distribution of responses regarding international relations policy showed that very few respondents from any of the groups selected the extreme choices for this item. The distribution of responses was moderate and homogeneous, indicating that the national interest should be subservient to mankind. Overall, about equal numbers of coaches felt that foreign policy should be administered without regard for nationality or form of government. The individual coaching groups differed enough with college students' viewpoints on this topic that there was a significant difference between the all-college coaching group and college students, with the coaches showing greater liberalism. The responses on this item indicated that football coaches and the combined coaches differ significantly from businessmen. The coaches expressed a greater liberalism, a greater willingness to see national interest subservient to the good of all mankind without regard to nationality or form of government.

Overall, a homogeneous, moderately conservative value orientation was expressed regarding the relationship between government and business enterprise. The coaches and college students expressed almost identical viewpoints about the values of free enterprise. The groups were all homogeneous and moderately conservative on this item; they believed that free enterprise should be encouraged but that some governmental regulation may be needed in certain circumstances. Football coaches, basketball coaches, and the all-coaches group were significantly different in value orientation on this item than businessmen, with the coaching groups expressing greater liberalism than businessmen. The coaches believed that private enterprise should be encouraged, but that government should ensure economic welfare for every citizen. Businessmen, on the other hand, believed that supply and demand should regulate economic matters and that government regulation should be minimal.

The distribution of responses about values and labor unions produced the most homogeneous pattern in all the groups of any other item in the inventory. Response #2 was chosen by between 78 and 83 percent of the coaches, 70 percent of college students, and 72 percent of businessmen. This choice affirms right-to-work laws which permit a worker to decide whether he wishes to belong to a union. The comparisons between individual coaching groups and college students and businessmen did not produce any significant differences. However, when the responses of all the coaching groups were combined there were significant differences with both the college students and the businessmen. In both cases, the coaches' value orientations were more conservative than the other two groups.

The distribution of choices regarding the value of certain educational approaches to the development of good citizenship indicated that all believed that teachers should guide and direct their students toward good citizenship; they rejected permissive methods of teaching citizenship. College-student responses to this item showed a homogeneous grouping, with the students tending to be moderately liberal. This pattern was similar for track coaches, but there were significant differences between the football and basketball coaches and the all-coaches group. In each case where significant differences occurred, the coaching groups expressed more conservative viewpoints. The coaching groups could be characterized as showing a homogeneous grouping, with a moderate conservatism. In comparing the choice distributions between coaches and businessmen, there were no differences between track and basketball coaches and the businessmen. However, although the businessmen also displayed moderate conservative values, there were significant differences between football coaches and the all-coaches group. In these two cases, the businessmen tended to express greater conservatism than the coaching groups.

The overall distribution of choices regarding values about the nation's schools is difficult to characterize because there were many significant differences between groups. Responses of college students showed that they were slightly heterogeneous and they tended to be relatively liberal in that they value an emphasis on practical applications of subjects, personal and social adjustment in school, and studies organized around pressing social problems. Track and basketball coaches showed similar value orientations but there were significant differences between college students and football coaches and the all-coaches group. Football coaches and the total coaching group exhibited greater conservatism, and this is particularly noticeable with regard to emphasizing studies organized around pressing social problems and initiating social change. On this choice less than 1 percent of the football coaches and 4 percent of the total coaching group responded, while over 10 percent of the college students responded. Businessmen displayed a moderate conservatism on this subject and their choices were significantly different from each of the coaching groups. The businessmen expressed a greater conservatism than each of the coaching groups.

The distribution of choices regarding values about academic freedom showed that college students tended to be quite liberal on this issue, all coaching groups tended to be moderately liberal, and businessmen tended to hold moderate views toward academic freedom. Each of the eight comparisons on this item is significantly different. College students were more liberal on this subject than the college coaches. Although coaches believed that professors should be free to express their ideas, they were not as willing to subscribe to permitting the expression of ideas that are disloyal to the government or the advocation of ideas without regard for the opinion of others as were students. Nevertheless, college coaches were more liberal than businessmen with regard to granting academic freedom. The differences show up remarkably in the comparisons in which college students and businessmen are compared with the all-coaches group.

The distribution of choices regarding values about the equality of man indicated that all groups expressed a quite homogeneous pattern favoring a moderately liberal viewpoint towards equality, supporting the belief that men are entitled to equal opportunity to develop their capacities to the fullest. The only comparison that was significant between students and coaches was the all-coaches group comparison. Here there was a significant difference, with the combined coaching group displaying a more moderate position than the more liberal students. Businessmen and coaches show a striking similarity in their responses to this item. None of the comparisons was significantly different.

The overall distribution of responses regarding values in race relations showed a rather homogeneous, liberal position on this item, indicating an undercurrent of general acceptance of racial equality. At the same time, it is evident that racial prejudice exists in all of the groups. The responses of coaches and students were remarkably similar, with a homogeneous and quite liberal position. College students and college coaches were more liberal on this item than on any other item in the PVI. Response five, the most liberal viewpoint, was chosen by over 38 percent of all coaching groups and by about 43 percent of the students, thus displaying a belief that the best way to overcome racial problems is through a maximum of personal contact, including intermarriage. There were significant differences in all the comparisons between college coaches and businessmen. Although businessmen showed a moderately liberal position on this topic, their position was not as liberal as the coaching groups. Businessmen were reluctant to support intermarriage between the races to the extent that coaches did.

The distribution of responses regarding values about the treatment of criminals indicated that the coaching and student groups hold a homogeneous and moderately conservative position on this topic. Businessmen showed a tendency toward more conservatism. About 60 percent of all the coaching groups and over 50 percent of the college students believe that the death penalty should be retained, but between 31 percent and 50 percent of students and coaches believe that the death penalty should be discarded. There was a significant difference between college students and the coaching groups combined, with more conservatism on the part of the coaches, especially in that more coaches tended to favor retaining the death penalty. There were no differences between track and basketball coaches and businessmen, but there were significant differences between football coaches, all coaches combined, and businessmen. In the cases where significant differences occurred, businessmen expressed greater conservatism, especially with regard to retaining the death penalty.

The distribution of choices regarding values held for authority and ethical conduct indicated that American male college students had a great heterogeneity in their views concerning what guidelines should be used in establishing patterns of conduct, with a slightly moderate outlook. Coaches showed a more homogeneous conservative pattern and businessmen tended to be even more conservative. There were significant differences between each of the coaching groups and the college students. The coaches were definitely more conservative on this subject, with a higher percentage of them believing that standards of ethical conduct are established by God or by universal laws, and a lower percentage believing that each individual must be free to determine for himself the rightness and wrongness of his deeds. There were no differences between football and track coaches and businessmen, but there were significant differences between basketball coaches, the coaching groups combined, and businessmen. In both cases where significant differences occurred, businessmen were more conservative than the coaches.

The distribution of responses for values about honesty in test-taking were more homogeneous and conservative than for any other item on the PVI for all groups. The value expressed by all groups was that one should refrain from cheating, with the percentage of responses among students about evenly divided between those who believed that one cannot be responsible for others, whereas coaches and businessmen more strongly support the belief that one should discourage others from cheating as well as refraining from cheating oneself. There were no significant differences in values on this topic for football coaches, basketball coaches, and college students. On the other hand, there were significant differences between track coaches, the all-coaches group, and college students. These two coaching groups displayed greater conservatism than the college students, feeling more strongly than students that one was obligated to discourage others from cheating. Businessmen and coaches showed an extraordinary uniformity in their value orientations to this topic. There were no significant differences between any of the coaching groups and businessmen.

The distribution of responses about values regarding sexual relations produced one of the most heterogeneous distributions in the entire inventory among all groups. The responses for the various groups can best be characterized as a great diversity of beliefs about this subject, with coaches showing greater conservatism than students and businessmen. There was a significant difference between each of the coaching groups and college students on this subject. Coaches tended to support the traditional values of sexual relations only in marriage—a marriage that is dissolvable by societal rules, however— whereas students expressed a more liberal view of sexual relations outside marriage. The individual coaching groups expressed similar values as businessmen on this topic. However, there was a significant difference between the responses of the combined coaches group and businessmen, with the businessmen having stronger conservative orientations.

The distribution of responses regarding values about the use of alcohol indicated a slightly heterogeneous moderately liberal value orientation on the part of college students and businessmen, whereas coaches showed slight heterogeneity with a more moderate value orientation. There were significant differences between each of the coaching groups and college students. Coaches subscribed to a more conservative view of the use of alcoholic beverages in moderation while students were more inclined toward drinking to excess on occasion. Also students were more supportive of drinking as an individual matter without regard to the opinion of others. There were significant differences between each of the coaching groups and businessmen. Here, too, coaches subscribed to a more conservative viewpoint on the use of alcohol.

The distribution of responses regarding beliefs about the nature of God indicated a homogeneous and quite conservative belief on this subject; all groups possessed a strong belief in a personal God, as indicated by between 68 and 92 percent of the responses in choices one and two. Although college-student responses displayed a conservative position, their distribution also showed considerable liberal orientation too. There were significant differences between college students and each of the coaching groups. The coaches expressed a more conservative position than the students. College coaches and businessmen expressed very similar values toward the nature of God. There were no significant differences between coaches and businessmen on this subject.

The total distribution of responses regarding beliefs about the Bible showed a homogeneous and moderately conservative pattern on this topic, with over 80 percent of the college students and over 90 percent of the coaches and businessmen choosing one of the first three choices on the continuum. There were significant differences between college students and three of the four coaching groups—football and basketball coaches and the combined coaches group. Although tending to be conservative in their viewpoint toward the Bible, the college students were not as extreme as these three coaching groups. Also the students expressed a more pronounced belief in the value of the Bible as merely a literary piece rather than a religious book with God's message to men. Businessmen and coaches showed very similar beliefs on this subject. There were no significant differences between the coaching groups and businessmen.

The distribution of responses regarding values held about man's responsibility for his own deeds is one of the most heterogeneous of all the items in the inventory. The general concentration of responses was more to the conservative side of the spectrum, but college students tended to be less conservative than either coaches or businessmen. Three of the four comparisons between coaches and college students showed significant differences—those with the football coaches, basketball coaches, and all coaches combined. In each case the coaches tended to be more conservative in their orientations. Although businessmen and the individual coaches groups held similar views with regard to this subject, the all-coaches group differed significantly from businessmen, with the coaches holding a more liberal value orientation than businessmen.

DISCUSSION

The cultural revolution in American society has penetrated into all spheres of American life including sports. Organized sports have been a center of controversy in recent years, and athletic coaches have come under considerable criticism. Much of this criticism has centered around allegations that coaches possess value orientations which are too traditional, dogmatic, and conservative for current American lifestyles, especially those relating to the younger generation. It has been claimed that conflicts over values have been responsible for the struggles which have taken place in recent years between coaches, their athletes, and other student populations. Unfortunately athletic coaches' value orientations had not been investigated, so it was the purpose of this study to ascertain their value orientations and compare them with those of male college students and businessmen.

It is commonly believed that college students possess the most liberal value orientations of any group in the population, and this belief has been reinforced in recent years as a result of student activism—even radicalism—on college and university campuses throughout the country. However, research on college-student values through several generations of students does not support this notion. Jacob in his *Changing Values in College* reviewed the research on this subject up to just over a decade ago and said that although students tend to take on the prevalent norms of their own colleges and become less dogmatic, less prejudiced, and more critical-minded, they tend not to become more liberal, except superficially in that they take on "a random collection of opinions in vogue during a particular generation." Jacob concluded that "college has a socializing rather than a liberalizing impact on values. It softens an individual's extremist views . . . increases the tolerance potential. It strengthens respect for the prevailing social order. . . . The weight of evidence indicates that actually very little change occurs during college in the essential standards by which students govern their lives. The values with which they arrive, and which are integral elements of their personality, are still there when most students leave."[36] Williams, writing about values and education in the United States, stated that in the area of values "it is certainly true that students are not radical, not rebels against their parents or their peers."[37]

In a more recent national study of college-student values, Teglovic's findings corroborate those of previous investigators. Teglovic found that, although student values varied from one institution to another and although students expressed strongly liberal tendencies on certain issues, overall college students hold rather moderate value orientations.[38]

Several studies suggest that coaches might be expected to possess greater conservatism than college students (Cox[39]; Norwalk-Polsky[40]; White[41]; McAllister[42]; Lipset and Ladd[43]; Campbell and Cooper[44]; Spaulding and Turner[45]), and the findings of these studies suggest that this conservatism is probably related to age and professional role.

There were 80 chi-square tests of significance made to test the null hypothesis of no differences between the values of various college athletic coaches groups and male college students. Significant differences were found at the .01 level of confidence in 43 of these comparisons of coaches and college students.

In comparing the value orientation of college football coaches with college students, the null hypothesis of no difference was rejected on 10 of the twenty PVI items. On 9 of these items the football coaches displayed a more conservative value orientation than the college students. The one item on which football coaches expressed more liberal tendencies was on the question of the right-to-vote. Football coaches tended to be more conserva-tive in value orientations to issues of educational approaches to teaching citizenship, educational methodology, academic freedom, authority for determining ethical conduct, sexual behavior, use of alcohol, the nature of God, the Bible, and man's responsibility for his actions.

In comparing the value orientation of college track coaches with college students, the null hypothesis of no difference was rejected on 7 of the twenty PVI items. On 6 of these items the track coaches expressed a more conservative position than the college students. These were issues about academic freedom, authority for determining ethical conduct, cheating, sexual behavior, use of alcohol, and the nature of God. The one item on which track coaches expressed more liberal tendencies was on the question of circumstances under which our country should take military action against another country.

In comparing the value orientation of college basketball coaches with college students, the null hypothesis of no difference was rejected on 9 of the twenty PVI items. On 8 of these items the basketball coaches expressed a more conservative viewpoint than the college students. Like football coaches, the only item on which basketball coaches expressed greater liberal tendencies was on the question of the right-to-vote. Basketball coaches expressed more conservative values on educational approaches to teaching citizenship, academic freedom, final authority for determining ethical conduct, sexual behavior, use of alcohol, the nature of God, the Bible, and man's responsibility for his actions.

In comparing the value orientations of all the coaching groups combined with college students, the null hypothesis of no difference was rejected on 17 of the twenty PVI items. On 14 of these items the total coaches expressed a more conservative orientation than the college students. These were: the purpose of science, labor unions, educational approaches to teaching citizenship, educational methodology, academic freedom, equality of men, criminal punishment, authority for determining ethical conduct, cheating, sexual behavior, use of alcohol, the nature of God, the Bible, and man's responsibility for his actions. As a total group, the coaches expressed greater liberalism on only 3 items—those dealing with the right-to-vote, justification for military actions, and governmental policy in international affairs.

The total response profile of the male college group can be characterized as moderate, although the students expressed some extreme liberal and conservative tendencies on certain topics. The total response profile of the college coaches showed them to possess moderate-conservative values, according to the responses they gave to the twenty PVI items. Although conservatism is not extreme among coaches, it is more pronounced than it is among college students.

The findings of this study support the notion that coaches possess greater conservatism than college students. But an item-by-item analysis of the response choices certainly does not support the assertions which have been made recently that coaches are extremely conservative—even reactionary—in value orientation.

However, the findings of this study do suggest that there is one set of value orientations which coaches possess that is a potential source of conflict between them and their young athletes. This set of value orientations might be classified as beliefs about "authority structure." Authority is an established right to make decisions and order the actions of others. All forms of social organization provide for orderly allocation of authority; i.e., an authority structure. As a result, authority is usually used in an orderly way to ensure performance of tasks and to facilitate attainment of collective goals.

The coaches' responses to items #8 and #14 indicate that they place higher value on obedience to authority and standards of good conduct which have been established by religious or societal norms than do college students. Furthermore, several other items on which coaches expressed greater conservatism than college students suggests that they manifest greater support for "authority structure" than students. The PVI was not designed to measure authoritarianism as such (Shils[46] and Rokeach[47] have pointed out that authoritarians may be found on either end of the conservative-liberal continuum), but response choices on certain items enables respondents to indicate their beliefs about "authority structure."

This high value for authority structure expressed by coaches will be evident in expectancies that their position culturally accords them the right to direct the actions of their athletes and that the athletes under their jurisdiction agree to accept as the premises of their behavior orders and instructions given to them by the coach. Recent upheavals in collegiate sports and the writings of Scott,[48] Underwood,[49] and others suggest that reliance upon authoritarian values by coaches is one of the most critical sources of conflict between coaches and athletes. They insist that the authoritarian nature of American sports is producing what Mills[50] calls an "insurgent-coercive" relationship between coaches and athletes. In an "insurgent-coercive" relationship, each party perceives the other as an aggressor. To the members, the leader (or authority figure) is powerful and dangerously oriented toward them; in turn, the leader may imagine that the group's desire is to unseat, or at least weaken, him. The result is that both parties share a mutual suspicion of the other. This condition does seem to exist in a substantive part of collegiate sports today.

The value orientations toward authority structure which were expressed by coaches does not seem to be occupation-related, as some writers have intimated, for the businessmen respondents expressed even stronger support for this set of values than coaches. The findings of this and other studies of value orientations suggest that orientations toward authority structure are basically related to generational factors rather than occupational.

Do athletic coaches possess values which are different than age-peers in other occupations? Several studies have shown businessmen to possess moderately conservative values (Clark[51]; Walter[52]; Elliott[53]). Except for some journalistic accusations that coaches are extremely conservative, there was no *a priori* reason to expect that coaches hold value orientations which are different than career businessmen.

There were 80 chi-square tests of significance made to test the null hypothesis of no difference between the values of various college athletic groups and businessmen. Significant differences were found at the .01 level of confidence in 36 of the comparisons of coaches and businessmen.

In comparing the value orientation of college football coaches with businessmen, the null hypothesis of no difference was rejected on 10 of the twenty PVI items. On 9 of these items the football coaches displayed a more liberal viewpoint. These items dealt with values regarding right-to-vote, treatment of communists, international relations, relationship between government and business, educational approaches to teaching citizenship, educational methodology, academic freedom, racial relations, and treatment of criminals. The only item on which coaches were more conservative than businessmen was on the use of alcoholic beverages; football coaches tended to value abstinence or moderation more than businessmen.

In comparing the values of college track coaches with businessmen, the null hypothesis of no difference was rejected on only 5 of the twenty PVI items. On 4 of the items the track coaches expressed a more liberal position. These were: treatment of communists, educational methodology, academic freedom, and racial relations. Again, the only item on which track coaches were more conservative was on the use of alcoholic beverages.

In comparing the values of college basketball coaches with businessmen, the null hypothesis of no difference was rejected on 7 of the twenty PVI items. On 6 of these items the basketball coaches expressed a more liberal position. Basketball coaches hold more liberal views regarding international relations, relationship between government and business, educational methodology, academic freedom, racial relations, and authority for determining ethical conduct. As with the other two coaching groups, the only item on which basketball coaches were more conservative was on the use of alcoholic beverages.

In comparing the values of all of the coaching groups combined with businessmen, the null hypothesis of no difference was rejected on 14 of the twenty PVI items. On 12 of these items the coaches expressed a more liberal viewpoint. The all-coaches group showed greater liberal tendencies on treatment of communists, justification for military action, international relations, relationship between government and business, educational approaches to teaching citizenship, educational methodology, academic freedom, racial relations, treatment of criminals, authority for determining ethical conduct, sexual relations, and man's responsibility for his actions. The coaches showed greater conservatism on questions regarding viewpoints about labor unions, and the use of alcoholic beverages.

The data on the values of businessmen which were used in this study were reported by Elliott and he stated: "Businessmen ... appear to be moderately conservative in their value orientations."[54] The total response profile of the various college coaching groups showed them to be moderately conservative also, but certainly tending less toward the conservative end of the continuum than businessmen. Overall, this study showed that coaches hold more liberal value orientations than businessmen from ten occupational categories.

Several critics of coaches have directly or indirectly accused them of racism. For example, Scott has said that "there is widespread racism in the coaching ranks. ... There are hundreds of racist coaches throughout the country. ..."[55] Although individual acts of racism have undoubtedly occurred, one of the most significant findings in this study shows that coaches hold a more liberal value orientation toward racial relations than businessmen and their value orientations are the same as college students. This is not to suggest that all coaches are equalitarians with regard to racial values, but it does suggest that stereotyping coaches as racists, as some have done, is as irrational as stereotyping the members of any large group. As a group, coaches appear to be seeking racial understanding, goodwill, and equality to a greater extent than the occupational peers with whom they were compared in this study.

NOTES

1. Jack Scott, *Athletics for Athletes,* Hayward, California: Quality Printing Service, 1969.

2. Jack Scott, *The Athletic Revolution,* New York: The Free Press, 1971.

3. Bruce Ogilvie, quoted from Jares, J., "We Have a Neurotic in the Backfield Doctor," *Sports Illustrated,* Vol. 34 (January 18, 1971), p. 33.

4. John Underwood, "The Desperate Coach," *Sports Illustrated,* Vol. 31 (August 25, 1969), p. 66.

5. David Nelson, quoted in *The Oregonian* (December 28, 1970), p. 1, Sports Section.

6. William A. Scott, *Values and Organizations,* Chicago: Rand McNally, 1965, p. 3.

7. Clyde Kluckhohn, "Values and Value Orientations in the Theory of Action," in Talcott Parsons and E. A. Shils, eds., *Toward a General Theory of Action,* Cambridge: Harvard University Press, 1951, p. 389.

8. Charles Morris, *Varieties of Human Value,* Chicago: University of Chicago Press, 1956.

9. G. B. Vetter, "The Measurement of Social and Political Attitudes and the Personality Factors, *J. of Abnorm. Soc. Psychol.,* Vol. 25, 149-189, 1930.

10. Erland Nelson, "Radicalism-Conservatism in Student Activities," *Psychol. Monog.,* Vol. 50 (No. 4), pp. 1-32, 1938.

11. Phillip E. Jacob, *Changing Values in College,* New York: Harper and Bros., 1957.

12. John T. Roscoe, "The Construction and Application of the Polyphasic Values Inventory," unpublished Ph.D. dissertation, Colorado State College, 1965.

13. Steve Teglovic, "American College Student Values: A Normative Study," unpublished Ph.D. dissertation, Colorado State College, 1968.

14. Carolyn Ritter, "American College Student Values: Their Relationships to Selected Personal and Academic Variables," unpublished Ph.D. dissertation, Colorado State College, 1968.

15. Jerome D. Thayer, "American College Student Values: Their Relationships to Philosophical and Sociological Variables," unpublished Ph.D. dissertation, Colorado State College, 1968.

16. William Zehv, "Values and Selected Variables of Colorado State College Students," unpublished Ph.D. dissertation, Colorado State College, 1968.

17. Thomas L. Elliott, "A Determination and Comparison of the Values of Various Student Groups, Secondary Business Teachers and Businessmen," unpublished Ed.D. dissertation, Colorado State College, 1969.

18. James B. Cox, "The Relationship Between Student Ratings of Teachers and Value Differences between Teachers and Students," unpublished Ph.D. dissertation, Colorado State College, 1968.

19. Zita Norwalk-Polsky, "A Preliminary Study of the Belief Systems and Selected Values and Attitudes of Faculty and Students in a State College for Teachers," unpublished Ph.D. dissertation, New York University, 1968.

20. Thomas R. White, "A Study of the Values and Attitudes of Distributive Education Teacher-Coordinators as Compared to Two Groups of Potential Teacher-Coordinators...," unpublished Ph.D. dissertation, Ohio State University, 1967.
21. B. J. L. McAllister, "Educators and Traditional–Emergent Values," unpublished Ed.D. dissertation, Stanford University, 1967.
22. John W. Clark, "A Preliminary Investigation of the Moral Standards of American Businessmen," unpublished Ph.D. dissertation, University of California at Los Angeles, 1965.
23. Louis W. Walter, "A Study of Business Ethics as Practiced by Businessmen," unpublished Ph.D. dissertation, University of Texas, 1964.
24. White, *op. cit.,* 1967.
25. Elliott, *op. cit.,* 1969.
26. Teglovic, *op. cit.,* 1968.
27. Elliott, *op. cit.,* 1969.
28. Teglovic, *op. cit.,* pp. 23, 25.
29. Elliott, *op. cit.,* 30-31.
30. Roscoe, *op. cit.,* 1965.
31. *Ibid.*
32. John T. Roscoe, "Report of First Research with the Polyphasic Value Inventory," *Journal of Research Services,* Vol. 1 (No. 1), pp. 3-12, 1965.
33. John T. Roscoe, "Test-Retest Reliability Study of the Polyphasic Values Inventory," Greeley, Colorado: Colorado State College, Bureau of Research (mimeographed), 1967.
34. Teglovic, *op. cit.,* 1968.
35. Elliott, *op. cit.,* 1969.
36. Jacob, *op. cit.,* p. 53.
37. Robin M. Williams, Jr., "Values and Modern Education in the United States," in *Values in America,* ed. Donald N. Barrett, South Bend: University of Notre Dame Press, 1961, p. 77.
38. Teglovic, *op. cit.,* 1968.
39. Cox, *op. cit.,* 1968.
40. Norwalk-Polsky, *op. cit.,* 1968.
41. White, *op. cit.,* 1967.
42. McAllister, *op. cit.,* 1967.
43. Seymour M. Lipset and Everett C. Ladd, Jr., "...and what Professors Think," *Psychology Today,* Vol. 4 (November, 1970), pp. 49-51.
44. A. Campbell and H. C. Cooper, *Group Differences in Attitudes and Votes,* Survey Research Center, Institute of Social Research, University of Michigan, 1956, pp. 28-30.

45. C. B. Spaulding and H. A. Turner, "Political Orientation and Field Specialization among College Professors," *Sociology of Education*, Vol. 41, pp. 247-262, 1968.

46. E. A. Shils, "Authoritarianism: 'Right' and 'Left'," *Studies in the Scope and Method of 'The Authoritarian Personality,'* Richard Christie and Marie Jahoda, eds., Glencoe, Illinois: The Free Press, 1954, pp. 24-49.

47. Milton Rokeach, *The Open and Closed Mind,* New York: Basic Books, 1960.

48. Scott, *The Athletic Revolution, op. cit.,* pp. 35-49, 187-202.

49. Underwood, *op. cit.,* 1969.

50. Theodore M. Mills, *The Sociology of Small Groups,* Englewood Cliffs, New Jersey: Prentice-Hall, Inc., 1967, pp. 123-124.

51. Clark, *op. cit.,* 1965.

52. Walter, *op. cit.,* 1964.

53. Elliott, *op. cit.,* 1969.

54. *Ibid.,* p. 117.

55. Scott, *op. cit.,* 1971, p. 134.

4 / SOCIAL STRATIFICATION AND SPORT

Social stratification is the arrangement of any social system into a hierarchy of positions which are unequal with regard to valued characteristics such as power, property, social evaluation, and/or psychic gratification. The stratification system is impersonal and involves only the ranking of positions or the assignment of status to them rather than the ranking of persons as individuals. Thus all occupants of a position with about the same value will be viewed as equal and occupants of positions of different value will be viewed as higher, lower, superior, inferior. Persons who occupy the highly-valued positions in a social system are considered to have high status. A commonly used label for strata power within the context of a society is *social class.* A social class is a set of persons who share similar valued characteristics of that society. The factors which show up most consistently in American social class differentiation are occupation, income, education, and race. The most commonly used indices in research on social class are occupational position and educational attainment (Hollingshead, 1957; Warner, et al., 1949; Blau and Duncan, 1967). Of course, while the terms upper and lower classes are used to designate positions in the social class structure, these are not meant by sociologists to reflect value judgments; they refer, for the most part, to power and prestige, and not to moral worth.

Every social system has rules, written or unwritten, which determine how power, property, social prestige, and psychic gratification are allocated and valued. Every social system has, therefore, a stratification system. Although there are no universal criteria for status differentiation, those positions which are functionally essential to a social system and which require special aptitudes and/or skills and which require relatively full-time participation are conferred with higher evaluation. Typically, greater rewards, both material and psychological, power, and prestige are associated with these positions.

Since its beginnings, Americans have cherished the notion that this is a classless society, and this belief has become known as the American creed of equality. Hodges (1964) emphasizes the extent of this belief:

> The creed of classlessness is imbedded in American folklore. It is part and parcel of the very American heritage, so much so, in fact, that to publically deny it is perilously close to blasphemy. Nor is this surprising. Much of our heritage and its accompanying ideology is premised on the compelling assumption that our worth is determined not by ancestry, but by what we, as individuals, accomplish in our own lifetimes by our own efforts. [p. 1]

Even a cursory review of American history vividly confirms the fact that this society has never been "classless" and the social ferment of the past decade has dramatically illustrated that we are indeed "class-bound" which in some respects even approaches caste characteristics, at least for a segment of our population.

If the American creed of equality is pervasive in our society, the notion of equalitarianism is even more pronounced in sport. The notion of social stratification in sport is anathema to many. Sport, many claim, is where you "make it on your own." You make it on your achievements. While there is no question that sports has many equalitarian aspects, social stratification is exemplified in various ways via sport.

The social class linkage is evident in many sports. It has been observed that sport, like fashion, tends to propagate downward in the social classes. Many sports were initially popularized by the upper classes and then adopted by the lower classes; i.e., tennis, baseball, golf, pool. School sports were started in England in the Great Public Schools, which were not public at all but instead were private and exclusively for the education of children of upper-class families.

There are a variety of ways in which social class is displayed through sport involvement. For example, while the upper classes purchase yachts and large cabin cruisers, the lower classes make do with small motor boats and row boats. The wealthy may own golf carts; the lower classes, if they can afford to golf at all, carry their clubs and walk. The wealthy wear expensive tennis, ski, golf, etc. sport clothing while the poor make do with the less extravagant apparel. The wealthy go on expensive hunting safaris or follow their favorite collegiate or professional team across the country while the less affluent are content to watch these events on television. Wealthy sports fans purchase box seats costing, sometimes, thousands of dollars while the poor watch on television or, if they attend the game, sit in the outfield or in the end zone.

Social stratification is evident within and between sports groups. Boxing is stratified by weight classifications; and the heavier the weight, the higher the status of the boxers. Judo has its system of "belts." Football has a neatly organized stratification system: the interior linemen play in "the pit" and are referred to as the animals. The backs, especially the quarterbacks, occupy the high-status positions—here is where the power, prestige, and rewards are in football. For anyone who doubts this, all he has to do is observe who wins the Heisman Trophy each year and which players are invariably chosen "most valuable." Social stratification is evident between sports teams since some sports are referred to as "major" and some as "minor." In some high schools the letter awards given are different for the so-called major and minor sports.

One important aspect of social stratification is the pattern of movement from position to position, and thus from one social class to a higher or lower one. Social systems differ in the processes by which movement, or social mobility, from one class to another occurs, the amount of such movement, and the different methods of institutional or internalized norms that influence these processes of mobility (Barber, 1957). Social systems are considered to be closed or open, in terms of social mobility, depending upon the extent to which positions in the system are available to its members. In a closed, or caste, system the positions of members are fixed for a lifetime because of the possession of hereditary traits of some kind. In an open system, positions are available to be filled by the best qualified and, theoretically, one can raise or lower his position in the status hierarchy by his achievements.

A part of the American creed is that the social class structure is open—that one may go from one stratum, or class, to another. This is manifested in the so-called "equality of opportunity" or "land of opportunity" principle. Wright (1951) selected "the Horatio Alger 'rags to riches' story" as one of the basic beliefs which forms the underlying faith of American democracy. Smith (1940) describes the Horatio Alger hero as:

A boy who was born in the slums of a great city with a very low social position, becomes a bootblack, works hard, applies himself to his studies, saves his money, and rises through sheer effort to a position of social, economic, and occupational importance. [p. 99]

It is often contended that sports participation is an important avenue for upward social mobility in the United States, and the "rags to riches" stories of some of the great athletes such as Joe Lewis, Willie Mays, and Mickey Mantle are often cited as examples of this process. Moreover, some sociologists have advanced the idea that sports serve as an avenue for mobility of lower social class boys. For example, Havighurst and Neugarten (1957) assert that "athletic prowess combined with education often provides a very good base for mobility in a lower class boy." [p. 45] In his text on social stratification, Hodges (1964) states that "college football has functioned as a highly effective status elevator for thousands of boys from blue collar ethnic backgrounds." [p. 167]

Aside from the examples of famous athletes from lower-class origins and the "off the cuff" statements of some sociologists, almost nothing is known about the actual extent to which sports participation facilitates upward social mobility, nor about the ways in which this occurs. Furthermore, there is a general impression that most athletes come from lower social class backgrounds but definite information on high school, college, and professional athletes is not plentiful.

In the first reading Burdge examines the social class factor of occupational prestige on involvement in leisure activities, especially sports activities. Though sports permeates American life, sports interest and participation are not identical in the various socioeconomic classes. Lifestyles—the kind of house and neighborhood one lives in, the kinds of books and magazines one reads, the cultural products one enjoys, and one's sports pursuits—vary from one social class to another. The author's basic proposition is that there is a relationship between occupational prestige and involvement in specific leisure activities. Although the concept "leisure activities" encompasses activities other than sports, a great deal of leisure activity is sport related, and, in fact, the author focuses specifically upon sports involvement as one prominent form of leisure activity. Burdge found several interesting relationships between sports activity involvement—both participant and spectator—and occupational prestige.

John Loy, in the second reading, articulately reviews the literature on sport and social mobility and then describes a study which he did using Life Pass award winners at UCLA. His study was concerned with assessing the social origins and present social class standing of these former collegiate athletes. One of his significant findings was that the idea that athletes in general come from lower social class origins is too simplistic. The athletes from several of the sports in Loy's study show a middle and even upper social class origin bias. Another significant finding of his study was that the athletes whose parents had the lowest social class status had experienced a remarkable degree of upward social mobility. Of course, the majority of all the former athletes were in occupations with relatively high social class standing. The paper by Loy was presented at a symposium and a discussion followed the presentation of the paper. This discussion is included in the reading. Perhaps the most important part of the discussion involves the materials presented by Harry Webb about his studies with Michigan State University athletes. His materials supplement nicely the study by Loy.

REFERENCES

Barber, B., *Social Stratification,* New York: Harcourt, Brace, & World, Inc., 1957.

Blau, P. M., and Duncan, O. D., *The American Occupational Structure,* New York: John Wiley & Sons, 1967.

Havighurst, R., and Neugarten, B., *Society and Education,* Boston: Allyn & Bacon, 1957.

Hodges, H. M., *Social Stratification – Class in America,* Cambridge: Schenkman Publishing Company, 1964.

Hollingshead, A. B., "Two-Factor Index of Social Position," New Haven: privately printed, 1957.

Smith, M. B., *Survey of Social Science,* New York: Houghton Mifflin Co., 1940.

Warner, W. L., Meeker, M., and Eels, K., *Social Class in America,* Chicago: Social Research Associates, 1949.

Wright, D. McC., *Capitalism,* Chicago: Henry Regnery, 1951.

LEVELS OF OCCUPATIONAL PRESTIGE AND LEISURE ACTIVITY

Rabel J. Burdge

Many sociological variables are related to leisure participation. For instance, people in high income brackets, young age categories, high educational levels, and having positions with paid vacations generally have been found to be the most active participants in structured leisure activity.[1]

For the purposes of this paper, leisure is defined as activity occurring during periods free from obvious and formal duties of a paid job or other obligatory occupation.[2] Occupational prestige is the variable here used to explain differences in the use of leisure. Membership in an occupation provides social recognition in the form of status. Society assigns higher status to individuals who are willing to acquire the necessary skill and education for complex occupations. The work experience also provides an opportunity for identity and meaningful life experience. Many of the experiences and associations gained during preparation for work and participation in it carry over to leisure time.

The general proposition guiding this study, then, is that a person's position in the occupational prestige structure is a determinant of how leisure is used. In short, the accruement of rewards—monetary and status—will determine the variety of leisure outlets.[3] Participation in leisure is designated as the dependent variable and occupational prestige as the independent variable. In keeping with previous research studies dealing with status evaluations the North-Hatt Occupational Prestige Scale was used as the empirical method of assigning prestige evaluations to specific occupations.

Rabel J. Burdge, "Levels of Occupational Prestige and Leisure Activity," *Journal of Leisure Research,* 1(3):262-274, 1969. Reprinted by permission of the National Recreation and Park Association.

PREVIOUS RESEARCH

The most influential study relating occupational prestige levels and leisure activity was completed by Clarke (1956, p. 301). This researcher studied the relationship between social status levels as measured by the North-Hatt Occupational Prestige Scale and participation in specific leisure activities. Clarke mailed questionnaires so as to obtain at least 100 completed schedules in each of the five occupational prestige categories. He found that most of the relationships were linear or near linear; that is, participation in specific forms of leisure were common to persons in either the highest or lowest occupational prestige level. Watching television, fishing, playing poker, attending drive-in movies, spending time in a tavern, and attending baseball games were activities common to persons in the lowest occupational prestige level. Working on automobiles was associated with level IV, playing golf with level III, and weekend trips, football games, and attending parties associated with persons in level II. Most other forms of leisure such as attending concerts, playing bridge, reading books, and working in a flower garden were found to be common to persons in prestige level I. Leisure activities found to be distributed among all prestige levels include hunting, bowling, gardening, listening to the radio, and picnicking. Reissman also found differences between occupational prestige groups on such items as reading and watching television (1965, p. 76).

Other investigations, which include the research of Outdoor Recreation Resources Review Commission (1962), White (1955, p. 145), Havighurst and Fiegenbaum (1959, p. 396), Burdge (1962), and Hollingshead (1949, p. 302) have found differences in the use of leisure time among occupational prestige groups and social class levels.

METHODOLOGICAL PROCEDURES

Data for use in this study come from a random, stratified sample of persons living in Allegheny County, Pennsylvania (which includes the city of Pittsburgh). This county typifies most metropolitan areas in that it is characterized by a large central city with a declining population, an expanding suburban area, and a hinterland of mixed rural and urban influences. The employment patterns of Pittsburgh may be classed as industrial, devoted predominantly to basic metal manufacturing.

A representative sample of 1,635 individuals was drawn from the 1,628,587 people in Allegheny County. The investigation was limited to individuals eighteen or older. Thus, for the age group selected, the sample includes about one in approximately 700 people eighteen and older living in Allegheny County. The sample was stratified utilizing a series of social, income, ethnic, racial, and residential variables taken from census data. From the 1,635 persons in Allegheny County selected for personal interview, 1,562 completed schedules were obtained. This represents a completion rate of 95.3 percent. Seventy-three people, including three persons who discontinued the interview, would not cooperate in completing the scheduled list of questions. No substitutions were permitted for those who refused to answer or were not at home.

In sampling validity checks reported in detail elsewhere, it was found that the sample of respondents obtained adequately reflected the racial, age, and occupational characteristics of Allegheny County (Burdge 1965, p. 27). It therefore appears reasonably safe to generalize the findings of this study to Allegheny County and perhaps to similar metropolitan areas in the Northeast. Although the inland Ohio Valley location of Allegheny County depresses the amount of participation in both deep water and mountaineering types of recreation, it is not anticipated that the basic relationships uncovered would be altered greatly at more favored locations.

North-Hatt Occupational Prestige Categories. The North-Hatt Scale was used as a measure of occupational prestige. This scale ranks occupations according to their relative prestige in relation to other occupations. The initial rating of occupational prestige was done by a nationwide sample of adults interviewed by the National Opinion Research Center (1947, p. 10). Respondents were instructed to assign scores from zero to one hundred to a series of occupations. The higher scores were to be assigned to the higher prestige occupations. The list of occupational prestige scores from the original study has been expanded to include most common occupations.

For purposes of analysis, the North-Hatt occupational prestige scale was divided into four broad categories—functionally labeled as levels of occupational prestige. Class I includes professional and high-level management; Class II includes other white-collar workers; Class III includes skilled workers; and Class IV includes unskilled workers. These levels of occupational prestige are similar to categories developed by Clarke from the North-Hatt Occupational Prestige Scale.[4]

In selecting occupational prestige as the measure of social class, such variables as income and education are explicitly excluded. Occupation, however, generally quite accurately reflects levels of income and education. There may be some deviant cases such as the high-status college professor drawing a low salary or the blue-collar truck driver making $17,000 a year, but the normative pattern suggests that occupation is a defensible choice.

Leisure Activity. The respondents were asked if they had participated in certain leisure activities within the past year. The responses were categorized as "participation" or "no participation." Information on annual frequency of participation was obtained for certain outdoor and urban recreation activities, but this analysis is not included in the present paper.

Outdoor recreation is here referred to as that activity taking place in an outdoor setting. Urban activities refer to types of leisure that generally are done at home or in an organized commercial setting.

ANALYSIS

Two important questions are explored in this section:

Are specific leisure activities associated with a particular occupational prestige level?

What, if any, clustering of leisure activities exists for a particular occupational prestige level?

The chi-square test for significant differences was used to determine if any significant disproportionality exists between participation in a specific leisure activity and levels of occupational prestige. The analysis examines six categories of leisure activity: outdoor recreation, urban recreation, playing sports, attending sports events, hobbies, and a collection of other recreation and activity orientations of interest to planners, developers, and administrators of recreation areas.

Outdoor Recreation Activities. Table 1 shows which occupational prestige level participated most frequently in sixteen types of outdoor recreation. With the exception of picnicking, canoeing, and hiking the analysis indicates that all the relationships were significant and that persons in prestige levels I and II were the most active in the listed sixteen forms of outdoor recreation. No outdoor recreation activities were found to be most common to persons in the class III and IV prestige levels. These data also indicate that winter sports and most water-related activities were more common to persons in prestige level I, while activities such as hunting and fishing were more common to prestige level II.

These findings disagree somewhat with those of other researchers. Fishing was found to be associated more with persons in the middle prestige groups than with the lower prestige groups as reported previously by Clarke (1956, p. 301) and Burdge (1965, p. 27). Hunting, which was previously reported to be associated with the lowest prestige category, was found to be more common among persons in Class II. Picnicking appears to be common to all prestige levels. Clarke and Burdge may have reached different conclusions due to the nature of their sampling procedures. Both used mailed questionnaires which yielded low return rates and required extensive remailings. It is suggested that persons responding to a mailed questionnaire about

Table 1   Outdoor Recreation Activities by Prestige Level Participating Most Frequently*

| Activity | Prestige level participating most frequently | | | | Level of significance |
	I (N = 157)	II (N = 586)	III (N = 519)	IV (N = 253)	
Picnicking	X				.10
Swimming or to the beach	X				.01
Camping	X				.05
Sailing	X				.01
Water skiing	X				.01
Nature walks	X				.05
Snow skiing	X				.01
Ice skating	X				.01
Tobogganing or coasting	X				.01
Fishing		X			.01
Hunting		X			.05
Bicycling		X			.05
Horseback riding		X			.05
Canoeing		X			NS
Other boating		X			.01
Hiking		X			NS

* The Chi-Square test of significance was used to test for disproportionality between leisure activity and the four levels of occupational prestige. In all cases a 2 x 4 table resulted with a level of significance of .10 or less being reported. The X shown in the analysis tables indicates which prestige level had the highest percentage of persons participating in the particular leisure activity. Persons in other prestige levels may also participate to a lesser degree. For example, all four groupings went picnicking, but Class I's went most often. This format for analysis and presentation follows also for Tables 2 through 6.

leisure might be more active in leisure. Nonrespondents in the present study tended to be older and unemployed.

Except for certain activities, such as canoeing which showed little response, and hiking, which was sometimes taken by respondents to mean simply walking around the block, the statistical evidence strongly suggests that persons in the higher social classes are the major users of outdoor recreation facilities. Picnicking was the most popular of all outdoor activities.

Almost 60 percent of the sample households reported participation at least once during the year, although the percentage was most frequent for Class I persons.

The significant finding for the outdoor recreation activities, with the exception of the large amount on nonparticipation by the two lower occupational prestige classes, is the syndrome of activities associated with the two upper prestige classes. There appears to be a difference based on routinely available and moderately priced recreation versus the more exclusive and expensive. Activities that might be classed as more expensive and less generally available include camping, sailing, snow skiing, water skiing, and tobogganing. Activities which are generally accessible include fishing, hunting, bicycling, and boating.

Urban Activities. Twelve types of urban recreation activity in relation to occupational prestige level are shown in Table 2. With the exception of driving for pleasure, all chi-square relationships were significant.

Table 2 Urban Recreation Activities by Prestige Level Participating Most Frequently

| Activity | Prestige level participating most frequently | | | | Level of significance |
	I	II	III	IV	
Driving for pleasure	X				.10
Walking for pleasure	X				.01
Work in flower garden	X				.01
Play golf	X				.01
Go dancing	X				.01
Attend the movies	X				.01
Attend concerts and plays	X				.01
Play cards	X				.01
Spend time in a tavern, bar, club	X				.01
Attend parties	X				.01
Go bowling		X			.01
Work in vegetable garden			X		.01

Urban leisure activities were most common to persons in prestige level I, with the exception of bowling and working in a vegetable garden, which were characteristic of persons in Class II and Class III, respectively. For persons in prestige level IV, no urban recreation activities were the most popular.

Another term for urban activities might well be after-work activities. Most are readily available within the immediate living environs of urban dwellers. Skill is a limitation only for the golfer and the bowler, although for the casual participant this is not a problem. A more realistic block to participation in some urban activities such as golf might be lack of money or perhaps lack of prior socialization in the activity. As an activity becomes more popular, it would be expected that appeal would increase for persons in all class levels. Bowling seems to be undergoing such a transition, but golf continues to be the exclusive domain of persons in the higher-status occupations.

The findings shown in Table 2 are rather consistent with status expectations. We expected and found that persons in the highest prestige category played golf, went dancing, attended concerts and plays, drank at cocktail lounges and clubs, and attended parties.[5] Some of these activities, such as golfing, spending time in a bar or club, and parties might well be dictated by occupational demands. The surprising finding is that activities such as flower gardening, dancing, attending the movies, and card playing were most common to a greater percentage of persons in the upper prestige levels. This finding appears to indicate that participation in a variety of even the more mundane leisure activities is most common among the higher prestige groups.

The activities of bowling and working in a vegetable garden were found to be common for persons in prestige levels II and III, respectively. Bowling certainly has the connotation of middle class or lower-middle class. While recreational bowling is quite popular, this sport has been sustained by bowling leagues that keep the alleys full during otherwise slack recreational periods. Working in a vegetable garden, while undeniably a relaxing activity, has certain economic value to families on a limited budget. The conclusion that status differences affect the type of gardening and that the importance of gardening for production would increase for lower-status persons appears reasonable.

Sports Activity. Table 3 shows the results of the chi-square analysis between playing certain sports and games and occupational prestige levels. Many of the results are not statistically significant, due to the small number of people who reported participation in some of the sports activities.

The results indicate that playing sports was generally most common to the two highest occupational prestige levels. Playing softball, basketball, and

Table 3   Sports Activity by Prestige Level Participating Most Frequently

Activity	Prestige level participating most frequently				Level of significance
	I	II	III	IV	
Played soccer	X				NS
Played tennis	X				.01
Played badminton	X				.01
Played croquet	X				.01
Played chess	X				.01
Played checkers	X				NS
Target shooting or variation	X				NS
Played baseball		X			NS
Played volleyball		X			NS
Played archery		X			NS
Played miniature golf		X			.01
Played at the driving range		X			.01
Played wrestling		X			NS
Played softball			X		NS
Played basketball			X		NS
Played touch football			X		NS

touch football were common to Class III, with no participation in sports common to level IV.

Although most of the statistical relationships were not significant, a general clustering of sports activity around different prestige levels appears to exist. The sports requiring individual skill and execution appear to be popular for persons in the highest prestige level. Team sports appear to be generally more popular with persons in prestige level III. This relationship, however, is not statistically significant. Persons in prestige level II have an interest in a mixture of team as well as individual sports, although only in the case of miniature golf and the driving range was the relationship significant. The finding that playing miniature golf or frequenting the driving range is a middle class to lower-middle class activity supports the earlier finding that golf—actually playing on a course—is predominantly the domain of higher-income persons.

Table 4   Attendance at Sporting Events by Prestige Level Participating Most Frequently

Sporting event	Prestige level participating most frequently				Level of significance
	I	II	III	IV	
Football games	X				.01
Baseball games	X				.01
Hockey games	X				.01
Zoo	X				.01
Soccer matches	X				NS
Golf matches	X				.01
Horse races	X				.01
Go-cart races	X				NS
Basketball games		X			.01
Stock car races			X		NS
Boxing matches			X		NS
Wrestling matches				X	NS

Attending Sports Events. Attendance at sporting events was compared with occupational prestige levels using chi-square analysis as shown in Table 4. Most of the relationships were significant and indicate that persons in the highest prestige level were the most likely to attend sporting events.

Attendance at sports events follows the popular conception of high and low prestige activities. For example, high-status persons reported minimal attendance at stock car races, or boxing and wrestling matches (with the possible exception of amateur wrestling), but were most likely to watch football, soccer, or golf. Watching basketball was found to be most common to persons in prestige level II. Since the sample area was without a professional basketball team, it can be assumed that attendance was at secondary and collegiate level games.

These results differ radically, but not unexpectedly, from those of other researchers. Clarke found attendance at baseball games and the zoo common to the lowest prestige level, while the present study found these activities to be characteristic of persons in the highest prestige level (Clarke 1956, p. 304). The syndrome of upper middle class activity includes football games, hockey, golf, and betting on the horse races. Most of these sporting events are expensive and admission charges, with the exception of horse races, are enough to exclude lower income groups. Attendance at the zoo could very likely be part of the socialization process of upper middle and middle class persons. Attendance at soccer matches and go-cart races was so small for the entire sample to make comparison almost impossible. The general finding is that persons in the higher prestige categories tend to be the greater participants in spectator sports.

A major finding in this study that runs counter to popular conception regards baseball. Most people have thought, and popular literature supports the notion, that baseball is the working man-laborer sport. According to this study most frequent attendance, and significantly so, is for the highest prestige categories. Data on the number of times respondents attended baseball games was not obtained in the questionnaire. It may be that certain members of the working class attend many games throughout the year and that many persons in the higher prestige classes attend only once a year.

Hobbies. Table 5 shows the results of the chi-square analysis between levels of occupational prestige and participation in hobbies. The results provide many instances of nonsignificance, although this was due in part to the small numbers of persons reporting activity in hobbies. More than half of

Table 5   Hobbies by Prestige Level Participating Most Frequently

| Activity | Prestige level participating most frequently | | | | Level of significance |
	I	II	III	IV	
Sketching	X				.05
Decorating	X				.01
Refinishing furniture	X				NS
Painting	X				NS
Flower arranging	X				NS
Photography	X				.01
Music	X				.01
Reading books	X				.01
Collections	X				.01
Ceramics		X			NS
Carving		X			NS
Woodworking			X		NS
Home improvement			X		NS
Automobiles			X		NS
Motorcycles			X		NS
Cooking				X	.01
Sewing				X	NS

the respondents did not report even one hobby. Persons in prestige level I generally had the greatest variety of hobbies.

Respondents in Class IV indicated cooking and sewing as hobbies. Unfortunately, the analysis did not determine if the cooking was recreational or done from necessity. Gourmet cooking, which is generally classed as a hobby, is popularly thought to be the exclusive domain of the highest prestige individuals. Woodworking, home improvement, automobiles, and motorcycles were found to be common as hobbies to persons in prestige level III. The occupations in this category mostly include persons with some technical skills that were being transferred to leisure use. The hobbies common to persons in Class I require some special talent as well as financial support and educational background.

Other Recreation Activities and Activity Orientations. Table 6 shows the relationship between levels of occupational prestige and certain forms of leisure which are of special interest to persons concerned with the future development of outdoor recreation facilities.

Persons in the higher prestige occupations appear to be among those most interested in private recreation facilities. Those who have fished at a fee fishing lake, would like to fish at a fee fishing lake, would like to hunt at a commercial hunting area, would like to and do rent cottages or cabins, would like to go on a farm vacation, and would like to camp at a private camp-ground, are more likely to come from the highest prestige occupations. These are the same people who took the most vacations and weekend trips. Those in prestige level III, however, were the most likely to have taken a paid vacation at home. Persons in prestige level IV did not have any hobbies, did not participate in sports, and did not attend sporting events.

The analysis indicates that persons in the highest prestige level would be a potential market for any type of private recreation. These persons, however, represent only about 10 percent of the families. Also, it should be remembered that verbalizing a desire and actual participation are quite different; but since persons in Classes I and II, which make up about half of the sample, were the most active in other forms of outdoor recreation, they seem to offer the best prospect for any future private development.

CONCLUSIONS

This paper has examined the relationships between specific leisure activities and levels of occupational prestige as measured by the North-Hatt Occupational Prestige Scale. It was found that persons in the highest occupational prestige level were the most active in all major types of structured leisure. Of

Table 6   Other Recreation Activities and Activity Orientations by Prestige Level

Activity	Prestige level participating most frequently				Level of significance
	I	II	III	IV	
Fished at fee fishing lake	X				NS
Would like to visit fee fishing lake	X				NS
Would like to hunt at commercial area	X				NS
Would like to rent a cabin or cottage	X				NS
Would like to go on a farm vacation	X				NS
Would like to camp at private camp-grounds	X				.01
Took vacation	X				.01
Took overnight trip	X				.01
Took vacation at home			X		NS
No hobbies				X	.01
Played no sports				X	.01
Attended no sports events				X	.01

the 82 specific forms of leisure activity here reported, persons in the highest prestige level were the most active in 57, followed by 17 for level II, 11 for level III, and 3 for level IV. Although some class differences in types of leisure behavior were found, the persons in the highest prestige classes were found to participate in the greatest variety of leisure activities.

For the outdoor recreation activities, winter and water sports, such as snow skiing, water skiing, and sailing, were significantly associated with persons in Class I. Persons in Class II were more likely to be active in such forms of outdoor recreation as fishing, hunting, and bicycling. None of the outdoor recreation activities were related statistically to persons in Classes III and IV.

Urban recreation, with the exception of bowling and working in a vegetable garden, was found to be most common to persons in prestige level I.

Bowling was common to persons in level II and working in a vegetable garden common to level III.

Participating in sports activities was found to have occupational prestige differences based on whether the sport was of an individual or team nature. The higher the occupational prestige, the more likely the person was to engage in individual sports. The finding that golfing (on a golf course) was common to Class I persons with miniature golf and the driving range common to Class II persons suggests that one of the ways people prepare for entrance into a higher social class is to imitate the leisure behavior of that group.

Attendance at sports events followed a rather common-sense pattern. Events such as stock car races, boxing and wrestling matches, which have not enjoyed widespread popularity, were found to be attended most frequently by individuals in the lower prestige occupations. Most other sports events included in this study were attended by persons in the higher prestige occupations.

Hobbies were found to vary by prestige levels. Hobbies that require aesthetic and educational background were common to persons in Class I. Hobbies that require a special occupational skill, such as woodworking and automobiles, were common to the prestige levels that include skilled workers. Finally, hobbies that have a daily, functional application were common to persons in the lowest prestige groups.

Questions concerning the desire to utilize private recreation facilities were analyzed in relation to levels of occupational prestige. Persons in the highest occupational prestige level were the most likely immediate prospects for future participation in private outdoor recreation.

This study indicates that the concept that various forms of leisure or free-time activity are associated with specific social classes should be re-examined. The data presented here show that for almost every type of leisure activity the probability is that, proportionately, the participants will come from the middle or upper classes. Persons in these occupations, while not generally experiencing a decline in the length of the work week, are afforded sufficient income to pursue leisure in their free moments. Another reason for greater participation by the upper prestige occupations is that their life experience opens up a variety of opportunities. Education tends to broaden one's perspective and the income from better-paying jobs allows opportunity to explore a variety of leisure pursuits. Persons in the working or lower occupational groupings tend to have limited education and life experience. They tend to interact with other persons of limited perspective, and they may also feel that many forms of leisure are not open to them simply because of their class position.

By including only "structured" forms of leisure activity in the interview schedule certain types of free-time activity common to persons in lower prestige occupations may have been excluded. It may be that unstructured activity such as "sitting" and "talking" is more common to persons in this prestige level. A detailed investigation focusing on this particular group would be helpful in better understanding their leisure styles.

This paper does not suggest that most structured forms of leisure activity are the exclusive domain of the two highest class levels. Except for the activities of snow skiing, sailing, attending golf matches, and ceramics, some frequency of participation was noted in each activity for each class. The normative styles of persons in Classes I and II suggest, however, that they are the present participants in leisure activity. The long-term trend in American society is for professional, business, and white-collar occupations to increase, and for blue-collar and semi-skilled occupations to decline. It is suggested that the leisure styles found to be associated with Class I and II persons will become more widespread as the occupational composition of American society becomes more like persons represented in this study by Class I and II persons. As the general level of affluency increases, however, leisure and recreation styles may diffuse more rapidly from upper to lower classes.

NOTES

1. Structured leisure refers to that activity which is specifically named and has societal recognition to the extent that persons derive status from the social structure for participating in the activity. Structured leisure is the opposite of activity that is nondescript and provides no specific status for the participant.

2. This definition, with some slight rewording, is similar to that proposed by Lundberg, et al. These researchers noted that "leisure is popularly defined as the time we are free from the more obvious and formal duties which a paid job or other obligatory occupation imposes upon us." George A. Lundberg, Mirra Komarovsky, and Mary Alice McInery, *Leisure: A Suburban Study* (New York: Columbia University Press, 1934), p. 2.

3. The effect of work or occupation on other types of nonwork behavior has not been ignored in sociological thought. Sorokin points out that in a society with a complex division of labor, the occupation exerts influence in the form of occupational selection and in "molding the body, mind, and behavior of its members." On this last position he notes that "the occupation group is one of the most indispensable coordinates for a definition of the sociocultural position in an individual. . . ." See Pitirim A. Sorokin, *Society, Culture, and Personality* (New York: Cooper Square Publishers, Inc., 1962), pp. 211 and 215.

4. See Alfred C. Clarke, "The Use of Leisure and Its Relation to Levels of Occupational Prestige," *American Sociological Review,* Vol. 21 (September, 1956), pp. 301-312. The present study utilized the following ranges in the North-Hatt scores for the four levels of occupation prestige: Class I, 93-75; Class II, 74-65; Class III, 64-54; and Class IV, 53-35. These categories were developed on the basis of the normal curve which ideally places 16 percent of all respondents in Class I, 34 percent in Class II, 34 percent in Class III, and 16 percent in Class IV. However, due to frequent cases of many persons receiving the same score (107 steel workers received the North-Hatt score of 60) it was not possible to achieve these ideal divisions. The empirical categories yielded 10.4 percent of the sample in Class I ($N = 157$), 38.7 percent in Class II ($N = 586$), 34.3 percent in Class III ($N = 519$), and 16.6 percent in Class IV ($N = 253$). This measure of occupational prestige was found to correlate with education +.470, family income +.468, and with a measure of social class—based on social and economic data from census tracts—of +.374.

5. Unfortunately, these data did not distinguish between the separate establishments of taverns, cocktail lounges, and clubs. It might be expected that different status groupings would frequent different surroundings. However, most of the responses to this question came from persons in Class I.

REFERENCES

Burdge, Rabel J., "Occupational Influences on the Use of Outdoor Recreation," Ph.D. dissertation, The Pennsylvania State University, 1965.

Burdge, Rabel J., and others, 1962, *Outdoor recreation research: a pilot study of the economic, sociological and physical aspects of private and public outdoor recreation in a selected Ohio county,* Columbus: The Natural Resources Institute, The Ohio State University.

Clarke, Alfred C., 1956, "The use of leisure and its relation to levels of occupational prestige," *American Sociological Review,* 21: 301-7.

Department of Agricultural Economics and Rural Sociology, The Pennsylvania State University, 1963, "The North-Hatt Scale," mimeographed.

Havighurst, R. J., and Fiegenbaum, K., 1959, "Leisure and life style," *American Journal of Sociology,* 64: 396-404.

Hollingshead, A. B., 1949, *Elmtown's Youth,* New York: Wiley.

Lundberg, George A., Komarovsky, Mirra, and McInery, Mary Alice, 1934, *Leisure: A Suburban Study,* New York: Columbia University Press.

North, Cecil C. and Hatt, Paul K., 1947, "Jobs and occupations: a popular evaluation," *Opinion News* (September).

Outdoor Recreation Resources Review Commission, 1962, *National Recreation Survey,* Study Report No. 19, Washington, D.C.: Government Printing Office.

_____, 1962, *Outdoor Recreation for America,* Washington, D.C.: Government Printing Office.

_____, 1962, *Participation in outdoor recreation: factors affecting demand among American adults,* Study Report No. 20, Washington, D.C.: Government Printing Office.

Reissman, Leonard, 1954, "Class, leisure, and social participation," *American Sociological Review,* **19**: 76-84.

Sorokin, Pitirim A., 1962, *Society, Culture, and Personality,* New York: Cooper Square Publishers.

White, R. C., 1955, "Social class differences in the use of leisure," *American Journal of Sociology,* **61**: 145-50.

THE STUDY OF SPORT AND SOCIAL MOBILITY

John W. Loy, Jr.

Much has been said about the American Creed, the American dream, and the United States as a land of opportunity with an "open" class system. As Leonard Reissman has observed:

> The belief in social mobility holds a strategic place among American values. It is a hub around which much of what Americans believe revolves, whether it is shouted as a platitude or cynically rejected. The creed of egalitarianism means not only that we are social equals, though not economic equals, but even more to the point, that the class structure is open and available. The positions at the top are open to those who have the talents, aptitudes, and whatever else it takes to reach them. At the same time, of course, we must be prepared to accept the corollary: Those who do not reach the top do not deserve to. Americans of all classes have held to this belief and have made it legend. The honor roll is filled with the names of heroes who give substance to the legend, and in every period there is always a fresh example of someone who has gone

John W. Loy, "The Study of Sport and Social Mobility," in Gerald S. Kenyon (ed.), *Aspects of Contemporary Sport Sociology,* Chicago: The Athletic Institute, 1968, pp. 101-133. Reprinted by permission.

from rags to riches. The legend continues to remain alive and real, to the cynics as to the patriots (1959, pp. 293-294).

The rags to riches myth occupies an especially prominent place in the world of sport, for every major sport has its heroes who were recruited from humble social origins and rose to unimagined heights of social success. Thus, we have the rags to riches stories of such sport figures as Willie Mays (Smith, 1954), Mickey Mantle (1967), Bill Russell (1966), Bob Cousey (1961), Johnny Unitas (1965) and Althea Gibson (1958). These stories and others like them have played a major role in sustaining the American dream. But are these individual illustrations of social mobility in sport the exception rather than the rule? In short, to what extent does sport involvement facilitate upward social mobility? This rather simply stated question is an exceedingly difficult one to answer, as a number of problems both theoretical and methodological are associated with it.

PROBLEMS

Dimensions of Mobility

A major reason for the difficulty in determining the degree to which sport participation enhances social success lies in the fact that social mobility is a most complex, multidimensional phenomenon. Conceptually, one can account for the sources of variation in social mobility in terms of seven basic dimensions (see Tumin, 1967, p. 88).

First, there is the dimension of *direction*. As Sorokin long ago (1927) pointed out, "There are two principal types of social mobility, *horizontal* and *vertical*" (1958, p. 133). Horizontal mobility is the transition of an individual from one social position to another across one or more social strata, either upward or downward. Although both dimensions of mobility are important, this paper will address itself largely to the matter of vertical social mobility.

A second dimension of social mobility is that of *distance*. Past research has tended to emphasize total mobility, and only recently has there been a deliberate stress on measuring the degree or distance of mobility (Svalastoga, 1965, p. 123). We have some information concerning the total volume of sons of blue-collar workers who become white-collar employees, but we have little knowledge regarding how far they ascend within the white-collar ranks or what percentage rise even higher.

A third dimension of social mobility is that of *time*. Attention can be centered on *intra*generational mobility, or it can be focused on *inter*generational mobility. In either case, one may ascertain the amount of time it takes an individual to move from one social position to another. Furthermore, one can measure the degree of mobility per unit of time.

A fourth dimension of social mobility concerns the specific kind of *status change*. For instance, one can be primarily concerned with occupational mobility, educational mobility, prestige mobility or some combination thereof. For both theoretical and empirical reasons, most investigations of mobility patterns have emphasized occupational changes, but other status changes might be equally relevant in the sport situation.

A fifth dimension of social mobility is the *unit* of analysis. Does one, for example, study the mobility patterns of individuals, families, peer groups, age cohorts or even larger social groupings?

A sixth dimension of social mobility "concerns the distinction between *objective* and *subjective* changes in status" (Tumin, 1967, p. 88). A change in salary as measured by annual income is an example of the former; while an internally perceived change in psychic gratification as a result of increased salary exemplifies the latter. Objective changes in status have typically received most research attention due to their relative ease of measurement.

Finally, a seventh dimension of social mobility has to do with the social *mechanisms* underlying it. We, of course, are concerned here with sport involvement as a major mechanism of mobility. It is obvious, however, that successful participation in athletics might facilitate upward mobility in a variety of ways. Therefore, analyses of the mobility patterns of sportsmen should attempt to isolate the predominant means of facilitation for given groups of individuals; and if several ways are considered in combination, then some attempt should be made to assess the direct and indirect influences of each.

Measurement of Mobility

The preceding discussion of the several dimensions of social mobility reveals the conceptual complexity of the phenomenon. Moreover, it indicates that its measurement is also a very complex matter. Tumin (1967) observes that in order to simplify the problems of mobility measurement at least eight choices must be made:

(1) *Which aspects* of mobility shall be measured, e.g., economic, educational, or occupational prestige? (2) *Whose experiences* shall be analyzed, e.g., individuals', families', and strata's? (3) *Who* shall be *compared,* e.g., fathers with sons, groups of sons with each other, or groups of persons at one time vs. the same persons at another time? (4) What *starting points* shall be taken, e.g., first job, "best job," job at age 30? (5) What *termination points* shall be taken, e.g., best job, last job, job at a certain

age? (6) What *classifications of jobs* or of other factors, and how many divisions should be employed, e.g., census classifications of occupations; three, four or five divisions of income; blue collar vs. white collar; three, four or five educational levels? (7) If several aspects of mobility are to be measured, e.g., education, income, occupational prestige, etc., shall these be put together into a *combined index* of mobility, and if so, how? (8) Shall the analyses include *objective* and *subjective* dimensions of mobility? If both, how shall mobility be reckoned, i.e., how can different rates of objective and subjective mobility be accurately combined? (p. 89).

Ideally, the choices associated with measurement problems should be made on the basis of some theoretical rationale; but this is easier said than done. Blau and Duncan (1967) have noted, for example, that "the design of mobility research is not suited for the study of the problems posed by stratification theory, for it centers attention not on the institutional differences between societies but on the differential conditions that affect occupational achievements and mobility within any one" (pp. 3-4). In general, measurement choices in past research have been largely made on pragmatic grounds associated with the factors of time, money, assistance and availability of subjects. Hopefully more attention will be given to theoretical issues in future research.

PATTERNS

A Model Study

As a model, the interested investigator of social mobility would not go wrong in referring to the recent work of Blau and Duncan, titled *The American Occupational Structure* (1967). Their inquiry is based on a representative sample drawn in 1962 of over 20,000 American men between the ages of 20 and 64 (p. 1). In addition to its sample, the study is notable for its use of quantitative multivariate techniques. As noted by Blalock, "the Blau-Duncan study provides the first really major empirical application of path analysis to sociological data" (1968, p. 297). Blau and Duncan clearly spell out the major conditions underlying occupational success, show the relationships between family and occupational life, outline the historical changes in the occupational structure, and comment on the causes of social mobility in contemporary society. Perhaps most importantly for the investigator of athletic mobility, they provide normative mobility standards with which results of smaller scale studies of selected groups can be compared.

Some Studies of Mobility Related to Sport

Although no definitive study of social mobility in the sport context has been conducted, numerous social scientists have commented on the role of sport as a mechanism of mobility for lower-class youth. Hodges (1964) states in his text on social stratification that "college football has functioned as a highly effective status elevator for thousands of boys from blue-collar ethnic backgrounds" (p. 167). Surprisingly, Hodges provides not one shred of evidence to support his rather striking statement.

In a similar manner, other social scientists have made rather broad generalizations on the basis of only a modicum of empirical data. For instance, Havighurst and Neugarten, on the basis of a case study, assert that "Athletic prowess combined with education often provides a very good base for mobility in a lower class boy" (1957, p. 45). And Riesman and Denney, on the basis of their cursory examination of early All-American football listings, write:

> There is an element of class identification running through American football since its earliest days, and the ethnic origins of players contain ample invitations to the making of theory about the class dimensions of football. Most observers would be inclined to agree that the arrival of names like Kelley and Kipke on the annual All-American list was taken by the Flanagans and the Webers as the achievement of a lower-class aspiration to be among the best at an upper-class sport (1951, p. 310).

An exception to these expository accounts is Weinberg's and Arond's study of professional boxers (1952). Drawing upon empirical data, they show that nearly all boxers are recruited from low socioeconomic backgrounds. They also show that although a number of successful boxers experience a rather quick economic ascent at a young age, their punitive sports career typically results in an equally swift economic descent.

Other sociological studies of professional athletes, while not directly concerned with mobility patterns *per se,* do, nevertheless, provide some data from which inferences can be made. Information regarding the income and educational levels of major league baseball players, for example, is contained in the works of Gregory (1956), Andreano (1965a, 1965b), and Charnofsky (1967). Moreover, a comparison of the three studies is indicative of changes in the social characteristics of professional ballplayers. As an example, Charnofsky's data when compared with that of Andreano may indicate ". . . an important trend toward increasing college education for major league baseball players" (p. 8). On the basis of data collected from 75 major league players in the summer of 1965, Charnofsky found that "... only 3% of the sample failed to graduate from high school, and whereas only 17% managed to earn a college degree, 58% had attended college ..." for one semester or more (p. 8).

Findings from the few studies of professional athletes, while giving some indication of the social status of certain sportsmen and a hint of their social origins, do not provide a firm basis for generalization concerning mobility patterns; nor do they show the linkage between sport, education and the broader occupational structure of society. Regretfully, research studies regarding the relationships between participation in collegiate athletics, college graduation, and consequent upward mobility are also few in number. On the one hand, a couple of large-scale surveys have been made which illustrate the occupational success patterns of former college athletes in several sports, but they fail to report where the athletes began their social ascent. On the other hand, largely in the form of master theses in physical education, there have been a few studies which indicate the social origin of athletes in several sports, but they fail to show what social heights the athletes have risen to in later life. An early example of the former type of study is the survey made by the National Biographical Society in 1927 and presented in the volume titled *Who's Who in American Sport* in 1928. Questionnaires were mailed to more than 32,000 contemporary or former sportsmen in America, and over 12,000 responded in whole or in part. Data concerning present occupation, educational achievement, and past athletic records are reported for 4,000 of the individuals who returned their questionnaires. In order to gain some small historical insight into the occupational trends of selected sportsmen, the speaker has coded the data for these 4,000 individuals and placed it on edge-notched punch cards to be hand-sorted and analyzed in the near future. Admittedly, the analysis is not likely to produce important findings, since the social origins of the sportsmen are not given in their biographical sketches.

A more modern survey of some scope is that made by the Assistant Athletic Director at the University of Pittsburgh in 1961. He located 1,678 former Pitt lettermen whose performances date from 1900 to 1960. A questionnaire was mailed to each of these former athletes and 1,391 or 83% returned them. The former Chancellor of the University of Pittsburgh, Dr. Edward H. Litchfield, presented some of the findings of the survey in an article written for *Sports Illustrated* with Myron Cope in 1962. They cite several exemplary cases of personal success and report that 37% of the sample had earned advanced degrees. They also record what percent of athletes in each of seven sports (tennis, baseball, golf, track, swimming, football, and basketball) have succeeded in each of eight professions (medicine, law, engineering, education, management, entrepreneurs, sales, and dentistry). A predominant number of golfers were found to have gone into sales work, swimmers stressed engineering, baseball players were prominent in education, and there was ". . . a clear affinity between football and dentistry. Only 8% of former lettermen [had] gone into coaching, of whom three-quarters [were] also teachers" (p. 67). Again, no data were given as to what was the original socioeconomic background of the athletes in the various sports.

An example of an investigation explicitly designed to determine the socioeconomic background of college athletes is that of McIntyre (1959). He set forth two hypotheses: "(1) Differences in socioeconomic levels are characteristic of persons engaging in various types of sports, and (2) individuals who participate in contact or combative type sports, such as football and wrestling, are more likely to have been brought up in a lower social setting than those athletes who participate in non-combative sports" (p. 66). McIntyre tested his hypotheses by determining the socioeconomic background of varsity athletes participating in football, basketball, gymnastics and wrestling at Pennsylvania State University in the 1958-59 academic year. In brief, he found that ". . . football players are characterized by a constellation of socioeconomic factors which are not typical of other athletes"; and "wrestlers seem to fall into a socioeconomic background pattern very similar to that of basketball players and gymnasts" (p. 68). A specific finding underlying his general conclusions is the fact that 69% of the fathers of football players had not completed high school as compared to 35% of the fathers of basketball players and 31% of the fathers of gymnasts and wrestlers (p. 26). Where the athletes of McIntyre's sample are now located in the social structure is, of course, an open question; suggesting that longitudinal studies of athletic mobility are needed.

At this point in the paper I wish to note that all of the guest speakers at this symposium have examined in some manner the relations between sport and social stratification; and three of the speakers have systematically studied aspects of social mobility of sportsmen. Professor Webb (1968a, 1968b), at the National Convention of the American Association for Health, Physical Education, and Recreation held in St. Louis last March, reported his research regarding the social backgrounds and success patterns of college athletes. Professor Schafer and his colleagues have recently presented findings concerning relationships between athletic participation and academic achievement in the *American Journal of Sociology* (Rehberg & Schafer, 1968) and *Trans-Action* (Schafer & Armer, 1968). In brief, the combined findings of their investigations show a positive relationship between participation in interscholastic athletics and high school grades, completion of high school and college plans (Schafer, 1968, p. 7). A particularly striking discovery of their researches is the fact that "... A greater percentage of athletes than non-athletes expect to complete four years of college among working-class rather than middle-class boys; among boys with less, rather than more, parental encouragement; and among boys in the lower rather than the upper half of their graduating class" (Schafer & Armer, 1968, p. 61). They conclude:

> It would seem, then, that interscholastic athletics serves a democratizing or equalizing function. It represents a vehicle for upward mobility, especially of those otherwise not likely to complete college. And the data suggest that, at least as far as participants are concerned, athletics fosters rather than interferes with the educational goal of sending a maximum number of youth to college (Schafer & Armer, 1968, p. 61).

One of the most substantial studies reported in the literature regarding social mobility among sportsmen is that of Professor Lüschen (1963). In an investigation of a sample of 1,880 youth in German sports clubs he found that 14% were upwardly mobile and 7% were downwardly mobile. Moreover, he discovered a number of characteristics which differentiated the two groups of sportsmen. Lüschen found, for example, that approximately half of the upwardly mobile sportsmen occupied leadership positions in the clubs, while not a single important office was held by downwardly mobile sportsmen. Another interesting finding of his study is that sport seems to be an important means of instilling middle-class values in upwardly mobile lower-class youth. A third point of interest is that the lowest status sports in Germany appear to be cycling and boxing followed by soccer, wrestling, and field handball. Finally, it is noted that Lüschen found that downwardly mobile sportsmen showed a preference for boxing and hockey while upwardly mobile athletes preferred sports like track and rowing. These latter findings have certain parallels with findings reported by Meyer (1951) in America.

Meyer attempted to identify certain characteristics related to success in the human relations aspect of work-group leadership. He administered a battery of tests to approximately 200 first line supervisors in a large utility company. Meyer established a criterion of leadership ability and classified supervisors rated in the upper and lower 27 percents on the criterion measure as good and poor supervisors, respectively. Regarding the differences between the two groups, Meyer reports that:

> The most conspicuous of all the differences found was probably the fact that many more of the good supervisors had participated in sports than

had the poor supervisors. In twenty-one of the twenty-five activities listed, more of the good supervisors indicated that they then did or that they had at one time participated in the activities than did the poor supervisors. For most of the popular sports, such as tennis, golf, football, softball, swimming, track, and bowling, the differences were significant at at least the five percent level of confidence. . . . [However] more of the poor supervisors had participated in boxing and wrestling than had the good supervisors (p. 22).

The preference shown for combative sports by poor supervisors raises an interesting problem for the psychologist as well as the sociologist. Two other findings of Meyer which might be of interest to the student of personality are: (1) ". . . poor supervisors indicated that they were more fond of their mother than of their father . . ." (p. 26), and (2) although the poor supervisors of manual workers participated more often in card playing, pool and billiards than did the good supervisors, a greater proportion of the poor supervisors indicated that they never made wagers on their games (p. 26). In conclusion, Meyer states that ". . . the poor supervisors were evidently somewhat defensive about admitting the possession of any reprehensible characteristics" (p. 26). His several findings bring to mind the research of Coopersmith (1967, 1968) and Rosenberg (1965) on self-esteem. It may be recalled, for instance, that Rosenberg discovered that ". . . adolescents who report close relationships with fathers are considerably more likely to have high self-esteem and stable self-images than those who describe these relationships as more distant" (p. 44).

Mobility Mechanisms of Sport

In summary, the several studies cited are suggestive of at least four ways in which involvement in sport as an active participant might facilitate upward mobility. First, early athletic participation may lead to the high development of selected physical skills and abilities which permit entry directly into professional sports. For example, adolescents may become boxers, jockeys or even professional baseball players with a minimal amount of formal education.

Second, athletic participation may directly or indirectly enhance educational attainment. Participation in interscholastic athletics may foster better grades, increase the possibility of graduation, and/or lead to an athletic scholarship from a given college or university. Collegiate sport competition, in turn, may influence the attainment of academic degrees and/or the acquisition of marketable sport skills.

Third, as spelled out by Schafer (1968, p. 3), athletic participation may lead to various forms of "occupational sponsorship." Thus, a successful street fighter may acquire a promoter and be groomed for the Golden Gloves Tournament which in turn may lead to a professional boxing career. Or a wealthy alumnus may sponsor a college sport star through such means as summer jobs and upon graduation give the athlete a position in his corporation. Or the successful athlete may marry into wealth by using his popularity to establish courtship relations with well-to-do coeds (see, e.g., Annarino, 1953).

Fourth, athletic participation may possibly facilitate upward mobility by the fact that sport competition may lead to the development of attitudes and behavior patterns valued in the larger occupational world. For example, Meyer's study suggests that sports experience may conceivably foster leadership ability via the acquisition of human relations skills.

Negative Arguments

A word of caution is perhaps in order at this point. Since the major emphasis of this paper is on sport as a means of upward mobility, we may do well to suggest that in certain cases sport may act as a negative mobility mechanism. Coleman, in his book *The Adolescent Society* (1961), makes the case that athletic participation is detrimental to educational attainment, in that it discourages stress on scholarship, and encourages a diversion of school resources, parental support and student energies away from the mission of academic excellence. Even if one accepts the criticism of Coleman's conclusions by Schafer and his colleagues (Schafer, 1968; Schafer & Armer, 1968; Rehberg & Schafer, 1968) and their counter findings, there is still the question of whether athletic participation is additive in nature. In short, is there a linear relationship between athletic participation and degree of social mobility? An interesting problem for investigation would be to study the mobility patterns among a cohort of outstanding high school athletes who complete a college education but who differ among themselves in the fact that some discontinue athletic participation while others remain involved. A first look at the problem has been made by Sage (1967). He examined the differences between eighty-five undergraduate male college students who had been outstanding high school athletes but forty-three of whom elected not to participate in college athletics. Sage found that the nonathletic subgroup achieved better college grades, were less likely to be fraternity members, and were occupationally oriented rather than socially oriented to their college environment.

Finally, on the negative side of the ledger we mention the most interesting investigation made by Pooley (1968) which examined the question of whether involvement in soccer clubs by immigrants and certain minority group members facilitates or inhibits their assimilation of the core values of American culture. His general conclusion was that sport involvement acts as an inhibiting agent. If the assumption is granted that conformity to the core values of a culture is important for social achievement, then it may be inferred that immigrants and minority group members who retain allegiance to certain ethnic subcultures via sport involvement may limit their chances for upward mobility.

PROSPECTS

Even assuming that overall sport acts as a positive mechanism of mobility, there is still the largely unexplored area of social stratification and mobility within sport. First, information is needed about the status hierarchy of sports in America at both the amateur and professional levels. A worthy thesis problem would be to establish a NORC scale or to develop a Duncan status index for sport. Second, knowledge is needed concerning the differential effects of participation in various sports on upward mobility. Do participants in the higher prestige sports, for example, experience greater mobility than participants in the lower prestige sports? Third, information is needed regarding social mobility within a given sport. Are professional quarterbacks, for instance, more likely to become coaches or general managers than tackles? Fourth, knowledge is needed about the extent to which individuals' social and ethnic backgrounds inhibit or facilitate entry into and mobility within given sports. Brief mention will be made of a few studies which touch on these problems.

On the basis of his analysis of Negro athletes in professional baseball, Blalock (1962) has set forth thirteen theoretical propositions concerning occupational discrimination. It is suggested that the application of his propositions to different professional sports might in large part account for the differential rates of discrimination found in various sports.

A highly interesting investigation of differential sport participation as a function of social background is Eggleston's (1965) study of Oxbridge Blues. For the benefit of the "Yankees" in the audience, the term "Oxbridge" denotes the joint consideration of Oxford and Cambridge, while the term "Blue" corresponds in the main to our concept of a varsity letter. Eggleston investigated the relationship between secondary school origin and the awarding of Blues in soccer, rugby and cricket at Oxford and Cambridge over a ten-year period (1953/4 to 1962/3). Analysis of the awards granted showed that "... the ex-pupils of the maintained grammar schools are at a disadvantage to ex-pupils from the public schools in cricket and rugby, both absolutely and relative to their total representation in the university population" (p. 241). In translation, boys entering Oxford and Cambridge from private secondary schools were more likely to earn varsity letters in cricket and rugby than were boys admitted from public secondary schools.

As concerns mobility within a sport, reference is made to the work of Grusky (1963). He argues that the type of position an individual occupies within an organization greatly influences his acquisition of varying role skills; and further argues that the possession of key role skills is highly related to an individual's chances for assuming a leadership position in an organization. Specifically, Grusky hypothesizes that high interactors are more likely to obtain leadership positions than are low interactors. High interactors are characterized by their occupancy of centrally located positions, performance of dependent tasks, and high rates of interaction with their workmates. Grusky obtained confirmative support for his proposition by finding in the context of professional baseball that high interactors (i.e., infielders and catchers) are more likely to become field managers than are low interactors (i.e., outfielders and pitchers). Loy and Sage (1968) in an extension of Grusky's work found that interscholastic baseball captains are more likely to be from the ranks of high interactors rather than low interactors.

Grusky's work and its extension by Loy and Sage illustrates the usefulness of theory in empirical investigations of changing social statuses among sportsmen. Moreover, although general theories of social stratification have been held to be too abstract for dealing with social stratification and mobility problems at the micro-level, it may, nevertheless, be possible to make certain worthwhile transformations and applications of general theories to specific situations.

The speaker, in conjunction with a colleague, is presently trying to apply Lenski's theory of social stratification (1966) to professional football. Lenski contends that *prestige* is largely a function of *power* and *privilege*. He defines *privilege* as "the possession or control of a portion of the surplus possessed by a social organization" (p. 45); and defines *power* as "the probability of persons or groups carrying out their will even when opposed by others" (p. 44). Two types of institutionalized power are recognized by Lenski: (1) *Authority*, which he defines as "the enforceable right to command others"; and (2) *Influence*, which he defines "as the ability to manipulate the social situation of others, or their perception of it, by the exercise of one's resources or rights, thereby increasing the pressure on others to act in accordance with one's own wishes" (p. 57).

It should not be too difficult to get actual or vicarious football participants to rank, say, the various offensive positions of a team in terms of perceived social prestige. The variance associated with given prestige ranks could then be accounted for in terms of power and privilege. Privilege could be considered in terms of the portion of the economic surplus of the organization possessed by an individual; and thus operationally measured by average annual salary according to team position. The concept of power, however, poses more difficult measurement problems. With respect to authority it is obvious that the quarterback has the greatest legitimate right to command others, but the rank order of other team positions as concerns authority is open for debate. And the amount of influence associated with a given team position is even more difficult to objectively assess.

Since power within a social system is largely associated with the set of structures and processes related to goal-attainment and decision-making, perhaps influence could be examined in terms of the probability of a given player influencing the call of a quarterback. Thus, the suggestion of a halfback is likely to carry more weight than that of a tackle. Alternatively, one might determine the average number of opposing players an offensive player is likely to influence in the course of a typical play or the duration of a game. Thus, a center usually keys on only one or two defensive men, whereas a guard may come into contact with several opposing players. This latter approach to the assessment of influence brings to mind the concept of "territorial control" made so prominent of late by Ardrey in his work *The Territorial Imperative* (1966) (see also Browne, 1968). But let us turn from speculation to summary.

Albeit superficially, I have attempted: (1) to show the conceptual complexity of the phenomenon of social mobility, (2) to indicate the problems associated with its measurement, (3) to suggest a model study as reference for the interested investigator, (4) to review some research related to the mobility patterns of sportsmen, (5) to outline some of the ways in which athletic participation may facilitate upward mobility, (6) to suggest that in certain cases sport involvement may negatively influence mobility, and (7) to illustrate how social mobility might be studied within sport as well as outside it.

The major generalization which can be made from the discussion to this point is that not much is really known about the extent to which athletic participation facilitates upward mobility, if in fact it does. This overall conclusion in conjunction with what has been said herein suggests that at least three basic kinds of studies need to be made. First, we need to determine what in fact are the social backgrounds of athletes in various educational institutions in America at the present time. Second, longitudinal studies of athletes, using appropriate control groups, are needed to determine the effects of athletic participation on their future social and occupational careers. Third, since athletes yesterday may not be similar to athletes today and since changes in the social structure may have differentially affected mobility rates of sportsmen, studies of the mobility patterns of former college athletes are also needed. In the time remaining at my disposal I wish to share with you some preliminary findings of a recent exploratory investigation related to this third type of study.

UCLA Study

As previously pointed out, the major weakness of research bearing on the problem of mobility patterns of college athletes is the fact that investigations have either focused on social backgrounds or on success patterns and have not considered initial and termination points of mobility simultaneously in a given study. In view of this fact I recently made an effort to examine both the social backgrounds and success patterns of a selected sample of college athletes. Specifically, I attempted to ascertain the social origins and present social status of Life Pass holders at the University of California, Los Angeles. In order to obtain a Life Pass, an athlete must have competed at the college level for four years and have earned at least three varsity letters. According to records of the Athletic Department of the University, 1,386 men had received a Life Pass as of last spring. Addresses were obtained for 1,097 of these men, and a six-page questionnaire concerning past and present social statuses was mailed to each individual. Thirty-three questionnaires were discounted because of wrong addresses, in fifteen cases the individual was deceased, and in twenty-eight cases the Life Pass was found to be honorary rather than earned. Thus, 1,021 former Life Pass holders were eligible for response; and of this group 845 or 83% returned their questionnaire. The survey data was coded this past month and is presently being transferred to punch cards to facilitate analysis. Although a full analysis of the survey will not be completed for some months, a peek at the data for purposes of this paper has revealed some interesting findings.

Social Backgrounds. In order to get a general idea of the social backgrounds of athletes in different sports an effort was made to determine the socioeconomic status of their fathers' occupations, the percent of their fathers in blue-collar jobs, and the percentage of their fathers who had less than a high school education. The mean occupational prestige scores of fathers measured by the Duncan socioeconomic status index are shown in Table 1. For purposes of illustration the sports are arbitrarily grouped into six categories. As is evident from the table, the lowest status score is recorded for fathers of wrestlers, followed by scores for fathers of boxers, football players and baseball players. It is interesting to note that three of the four sports placed in the lower-lower and upper-lower categories are combative in nature (i.e., contact sports). In the lower-middle category are found the status scores for fathers of athletes who competed on soccer, rifle, rugby, track and handball teams. While in the upper-middle category are occupational prestige scores for fathers of team managers, gymnasts, volleyball players and basketball players. Within the lower-upper category are found status scores for fathers of fencers, swimmers, tennis players, cricket players, hockey players and oarsmen. Finally, in the upper-upper category we find the sport of golf.

A number of the figures in Table 1 should not be accorded too much significance since they are based on very small numbers of respondents. The only apparent anomaly in the status hierarchy, however, is the sport of ice hockey. It is noted that the sport has not been played since World War II, and all Life Pass holders in the sport were born prior to 1917.

Table 1 Mean Occupational Status Scores of Fathers of Former Athletes in Twenty Collegiate Sports

Sport	N	Status score	Category
Wrestling	(27)	43	Lower-Lower
Boxing	(12)	47	
Football	(192)	48	Upper-Lower
Baseball	(89)	49	
Soccer	(32)	51	
Rifle team	(12)	51	
Rugby	(16)	52	Lower-Middle
Handball	(6)	53	
Track	(119)	53	
Team managers	(34)	55	
Volleyball	(3)	55	Upper-Middle
Basketball	(91)	57	
Gymnastics	(33)	58	
Fencing	(5)	60	
Crew	(64)	62	
Ice hockey	(9)	62	Lower-Upper
Cricket	(17)	63	
Swimming	(78)	64	
Tennis	(50)	64	
Golf	(19)	74	Upper-Upper

Table 2 shows the percent of fathers in blue-collar occupations when their sons entered college. As is evident from the table, nearly half of the wrestlers came from blue-collar homes as did approximately a third of the football players, baseball players and trackmen. About a quarter of the soccer players and gymnasts came from blue-collar homes; while less than a fifth of athletes in basketball, swimming, tennis, and crew came from blue-collar backgrounds.

Table 2   Percent of Fathers in Blue-collar Occupations according to Sport

Sport	N	Blue-collar (%)
Wrestling	(27)	48.1
Baseball	(90)	36.5
Football	(192)	34.6
Track	(119)	30.5
Soccer	(32)	26.3
Gymnastics	(33)	26.3
Basketball	(91)	16.4
Swimming	(81)	13.3
Tennis	(50)	13.3
Crew	(64)	10.4

A somewhat similar rank order is found in Table 3 which presents the percent of fathers having less than a high school education. As can be seen from the table, approximately half of the fathers of football players, wrestlers and baseball players did not complete high school. On the other hand, approximately seventy-five percent of the fathers of tennis players, swimmers, soccer players and oarsmen finished high school.

Table 3   Percent of Fathers not Completing High School according to Sport

Sport	N	Not completing high school (%)
Football	219	51.59
Wrestling	28	49.99
Baseball	94	49.98
Track	131	43.50
Gymnastics	34	38.21
Basketball	107	37.38
Swimming	81	27.15
Tennis	54	25.91
Crew	67	23.87
Soccer	35	22.85

Success Patterns. In order to obtain a general idea of the overall mobility patterns of athletes, the mean occupational prestige scores of their first job upon leaving college and of their present job as of the Spring of 1968 were compared with that of their fathers. Table 4 portrays the differences among fathers and sons associated with a given sport. As concerns present job, there is not much of a difference in occupation status scores among the various groups of athletes. Moreover, the majority of former athletes are employed in occupations having relatively high socioeconomic status. Perhaps the most striking aspect of the table is the great degree of social mobility achieved by athletes whose parents had the lowest socioeconomic status.

Table 4   A Comparison of Fathers' Occupational Status Scores with Those of Sons' First Job and Sons' Present Job

Sport	Fathers' main job	N	Sons' first job	N	Sons' present job	N
Wrestling	43	(27)	70	(24)	77	(27)
Football	48	(192)	63	(192)	74	(206)
Baseball	49	(89)	64	(90)	75	(91)
Soccer	51	(32)	74	(33)	79	(36)
Track	53	(119)	67	(120)	77	(121)
Basketball	57	(91)	69	(92)	77	(100)
Gymnastics	58	(33)	67	(33)	80	(33)
Crew	62	(64)	69	(52)	78	(65)
Swimming	63	(78)	67	(80)	78	(81)
Tennis	64	(50)	70	(51)	75	(55)

Table 5 further illustrates the success patterns of college athletes. For example, nearly forty-four percent of all athletes were found to have earned an advanced degree.

Consequences of Mobility. In summary, the preliminary analysis has resulted in a number of findings which are indicative of the social mobility patterns of college athletes. It is hoped that further analysis will provide firmer ground for generalization. But even assuming that some information is acquired about the past and present social statuses of athletes, there still remains the very important issue of what are the consequences—both positive and negative—of social mobility for given groups of athletes. In short, how are the *life-styles* and *life-chances* of athletes affected by upward mobility?

Although our survey of former athletes cannot directly answer this question, the questionnaire used did contain a number of items related to the

Table 5   Percent of Athletes Holding Advanced Degrees according to Sport

Sport	N	Athletes with adv. degrees (%)
Gymnastics	34	61.75
Soccer	35	54.28
Wrestling	28	50.00
Track	131	45.79
Swimming	81	45.67
Basketball	107	43.91
Tennis	54	40.72
Baseball	94	37.22
Crew	67	29.85
Football	219	29.21
		Average = 43.84

matters of *life-style* and *life-chances*. For example, regarding political preference which is an aspect of life-style, we asked each former athlete whom he
intended to vote for in the coming presidential election. Table 6 shows the
percentage of athletes in each sport favoring a Republican or Democratic
presidential candidate. It is clear from the table that the majority of athletes
favored Republican candidates.

Finally, as an example of a finding related to an aspect of life-chances,
the percent of former athletes who have been divorced at least once are
shown in Table 7. Overall the divorce rate of former athletes is relatively low.

Table 6   Preferred Presidential Candidate of Athletes according to Sport

Sport	N	Preferring a Republican candidate (%)	Preferring a Democratic candidate (%)
Wrestling	28	60.71	25.00
Football	219	55.70	21.91
Crew	67	55.22	20.89
Basketball	107	54.20	22.42
Swimming	81	53.08	29.62
Gymnastics	34	52.94	26.47
Track	131	51.90	29.77
Baseball	94	46.80	23.40
Soccer	35	42.85	42.85
Tennis	54	42.59	31.48

Table 7   Percent of Athletes who Have Been Previously Divorced

Sport	N	Divorced (%)
Tennis	54	16.66
Track	131	16.03
Gymnastics	34	14.70
Football	219	14.61
Soccer	35	14.24
Crew	67	13.43
Baseball	94	11.70
Basketball	107	11.21
Wrestling	28	10.71
Swimming	81	9.87

In conclusion, I hope that this paper will in some small way stimulate several students in the audience to conduct as part of their graduate work, research related to the problem of sport and social mobility.

REFERENCES

Andreano, Ralph, "The Affluent Baseball Player," *Trans-Action* (May/June 1965a) 2(4): 10-13.

Andreano, Ralph, *No Joy in Mudville*, Cambridge, Mass.: Schenkman, 1965b.

Annarino, Anthony A., "The Contributions of Athletics to Social Mobility," *56th Annual Proceedings of the College Physical Education Association*, New York, 1953.

Ardrey, Robert, *The Territorial Imperative*, New York: Dell, 1966.

Blalock, Hubert H., Jr., "Occupational Discrimination: Some Theoretical Propositions," *Social Problems* (1962) 9(3):240-247.

Blalock, Hubert H., Jr., "Book Review of Peter M. Blau and O. Dudley Duncan, *The American Occupational Structure*," *American Sociological Review* (April 1968) 33(2):296-297.

Blau, Peter M. and O. Dudley Duncan, *The American Occupational Structure*, New York: John Wiley & Sons, 1967.

Browne, Evelyn, "An Ethological Theory of Play," *Journal of Health, Physical Education and Recreation* (Sept. 1968) 39(7):36-39.

Charnofsky, Harold, "The Major League Professional Baseball Player: Self-Conception versus the Popular Image," paper presented at the Annual Meetings of the American Sociological Association, August 29-31, 1967 in San Francisco.

Coleman, James S., *The Adolescent Society*, New York: Free Press, 1961.

Coopersmith, Stanley, *Antecedents of Self-Esteem*, San Francisco: W. H. Freeman, 1967.

Coopersmith, Stanley, "Studies in Self-Esteem," *Scientific American* (Feb. 1968) 218(2):96-106.

Cousy, Robert, *Basketball Is My Life*, Englewood Cliffs, N. J.: Prentice-Hall, 1961.

Eggleston, John, "Secondary Schools and Oxbridge Blues," *British Journal of Sociology* (Sept. 1965) 16(3):232-242.

Gibson, Althea, *I Always Wanted To Be Somebody*, New York: Harper & Brothers, 1958.

Gregory, Paul M., *The Baseball Player: An Economic Study*, Washington, D.C.: Public Affairs Press, 1956.

Grusky, Oscar, "The Effects of Formal Structure on Managerial Recruitment: A Study of Baseball Organization," *Sociometry* (1963) 26:345-353.

Havighurst, Robert J. and Bernice L. Neugarten, *Society and Education*, Boston: Allyn and Bacon, 1957.

Hodges, Harold M., Jr., *Social Stratification (Class in America)*, Cambridge, Mass.: Schenkman, 1964.

Lenski, Gerhard, *Power and Privilege (a theory of social stratification)*, New York: McGraw-Hill, 1966.

Litchfield, Edward H. with Myron Cope, "Saturday's Hero Is Doing Fine," *Sports Illustrated* (July 8, 1962) pp. 66-80.

Loy, John W. and John N. Sage, "The Effects of Formal Structure on Organizational Leadership: An Investigation of Interscholastic Baseball Teams," paper presented at the 2nd International Congress of Sport Psychology, November 1, 1968 in Washington, D.C.

Lüschen, Günther, "Soziale Schichtung and Soziale Mobilitat Beijungen Sportlern," (Social Stratification and Social Mobility Among Young Sportsmen), *Kölner Zeitschrift für Soziologie und Sozialpsychologie* (1963) 15(1):74-93.

McIntyre, Thomas D., "Socio-Economic Background of White Male Athletes from Four Selected Sports at the Pennsylvania State University," M.Ed. thesis, Pennsylvania State University, 1959.

Mantle, Mickey, *The Education of a Baseball Player*, New York: Simon & Schuster, 1967.

Meyer, Herbert H., "Factors Related to Success in the Human Relations Aspect of Work-Group Leadership," *Psychological Monographs* (1951) (No. 320) 65(3):1-29.

Pooley, John C., "Ethnic Soccer Clubs in Milwaukee: A Study in Assimilation," M.S. thesis, University of Wisconsin, 1968.

Rehberg, Richard A. and Walter E. Schafer, "Participation in Interscholastic Athletics and College Expectations," *American Journal of Sociology* (1968) 73(6):732-740.

Reissman, Leonard, *Class in American Society*, New York: Free Press, 1959.

Riesman, David and Reuel Denney, "Football in America: A Study in Culture Diffusion," *American Quarterly* (1951) 3:309-319.

Rosenberg, Morris, *Society and the Adolescent Self-Image,* Princeton, N. J.: Princeton University Press, 1965.

Russell, Bill, *Go Up For Glory,* New York: Coward-McCann, 1966.

Sage, John N., "Adolescent Values and the Non-Participating College Athlete," paper presented at the Southern Section CAHPER Conference, December 2, 1967 at San Fernando Valley State College.

Schafer, Walter E., "Athletic Success and Social Mobility," paper presented at the National Convention of the American Association for Health, Physical Education, and Recreation, March 30, 1968 in St. Louis, Missouri.

Schafer, Walter E. and J. Michael Armer, "Athletes Are Not Inferior Students," *Trans-Action* (Nov. 1968) 6(1):21-26, 61-62.

Smith, Ken, *The Willie Mays Story,* New York: Greenburg, 1954.

Sorokin, Pitirim A., *Social and Cultural Mobility,* New York: Free Press, 1959.

Svalastoga, Kaare, *Social Differentiation,* New York: McKay, 1965.

Tumin, Melvin M. *Social Stratification (The Forms and Functions of Inequality),* Englewood Cliffs, N. J.: Prentice-Hall, 1967.

Unitas, John, *The Johnny Unitas Story,* New York: Grosset & Dunlap, 1965.

Webb, Harry, "Success Patterns of College Athletes," paper presented at the National Convention of the American Association for Health, Physical Education, and Recreation, March 30, 1968a in St..Louis, Missouri.

Webb, Harry, "Social Backgrounds of College Athletes," paper presented at the National Convention of the American Association for Health, Physical Education, and Recreation, March 30, 1968b in St. Louis, Missouri.

Weinberg, S. K., and H. Arond, "The Occupational Culture of the Boxer," *American Journal of Sociology* (1952) 57:460-469.

REACTION TO LOY PAPER

Harry Webb

WEBB: Loy's paper is essentially a report on the sometimes interesting and sometimes not so interesting studies that have been done before, particularly with respect to mobility among athletes with some, of course, introductory cautions regarding the definitional and empirical difficulties involved in doing such investigations, but the upshot of the reports is that participation and upward mobility appear to have some connection about which not much is really known. He then mentions two studies which he has underway, the first dealing with the distribution of authority among team members, an interesting problem, given the high degree of rationalization of some activities, but less interesting if that degree is low. He did not cover that part of his paper but it's related to Lenski's distinction between power and privilege and the fact that prestige produces both of them.

Lenski, in a sense, takes this from Weber's distinction between class and status, class based upon occupational background, and status being something which is achieved in a community setting; and that, of course, is a reply to Marx's earlier emphasis on the fact of occupation as the major basis on which different kinds of attitudes and opinions are formed. In that sense, participation in the economic structure not only influences the way individuals think, but the way society is developed too. It's in that sense, as well, that he says that social consciousness is a direct result of social existence. The one then tends to produce the other. Weber goes on in the *Protestant Ethic* and demonstrates—demonstrates brilliantly, I think—the fact that the two are related and possibly in the other direction; and he points out the very great importance of the Protestant influence, the Protestant ethic, in the development of the capitalistic economy.

In any case, from Weber, Lenski makes this distinction between power and privilege based on prestige and, of course, these are institutionalized particularly in terms of power—in terms of authority and influence; and Loy is interested in investigating the degree of authority, the degree of influence, based upon position on an athletic team. He contrasts the way in which, for example, a halfback and a tackle have differential influence in getting the quarterback to take up a certain kind of play. Well, that kind of focus is interesting and productive only so far as the activity itself is rationalized; that is, it has considerable division of labor and so on, to some ranking of the men on the team in terms of the position they play. In other words, distribution of authority is based on the presumed contribution they make; presumably the contribution of the quarterback is greater than that of the offensive guards and the tackles who are protecting them. Ordinarily the quarterback believes it too. Take a look at Joe Namath: he was up there in training camp, it was before he had ever played professional ball, and he had picked up some $600,000 in the process and the people were around in an effort to get his signature on pieces of paper and bar bills and everything else, and he was giving it out and he told them that he was very sorry that he had to leave because it would be too bad for them, they wouldn't be able to get any more signatures, you know, passing it around and saying they had known Big Joe. Well, the emphasis on this is the sense in which the tackle has less confidence in himself in that respect than a guy like Namath, but it in turn depends on the degree of rationalization of the sport itself.

The second piece of research mentioned is the one dealing with the "fact" of upward mobility of athletes. There are some difficulties with which we should talk about. First of all, Loy claims that 83 percent is a good figure on the return. Well, 83 percent is a good figure on the return if the people in the remaining 17 percent do not differ in any major respects from those obtained, for example, in age. Also, the fact that the nature of the economy over those periods of years has changed quite a deal as he tried to point out, and it would affect the way in which these athletes develop their mobility levels, means, or medians or whatever. The 3 percent of cases lost because they couldn't find an address seems small, but they still constitute 3 percent. And when you're operating in terms of relatively high levels of confidence, for example, .05, there is a possibility that the lost 3 percent could influence the result. But they don't bother me half as much as that 17 percent of non-returns does. The fact is, aside from the questions of reliability and validity, survey research must take into consideration the kinds of people who don't answer these questions. That is, who are the lost 17 percent? For example, are they upper-class people? Probably not. They are very likely the people at the bottom. In a study of this kind of thing, based on my own experience, you run into a lot of trouble with guys who haven't made it, and they don't want to reply. Why should they? They have been losers in a system which places an awful lot of emphasis on not only competition but, more important, on getting there, getting the success, and lacking it they don't reply. It's my even bet that the guys who have not replied are the guys who have not succeeded and it's precisely those guys that we are most concerned with. So it would seem at the very best that a genuine effort be made to pick these people up, and that is of course aside from the fact that there is this real question, very serious question, about what that large number of years has done to affect those results and these are a couple of the kinds of things that should be taken up.

I was going to mention that I wanted a more clear-cut emphasis on that question of conservatism and liberalism too; that should be better qualified, as Page points out. Wallace would make a difference and the intention to vote for a man in May in an enormously confused political situation is not a very good indication of what might have been developed there. The other thing, of course, is guess who those guys are? Are they all kids? We really don't know who they are on the basis of age and that's not a criticism because this kind of analysis has not been made yet, but there is a tendency for people as they get older to become politically more conservative and that would mean that if he has older people in that sample, that this would affect the amount of people, the number of people, voting Republican rather than Democratic. This kind of thing would have to be controlled as well. Since, of course, they have all been upwardly mobile themselves, at least from what it looks like there, they would also be expected to be more conservative since that is related as well to education levels on the first hand, occupation next, and income level next, so these kinds of things will have to be handled if the study is to develop what Loy would like it to.

The other kind of thing that is difficult to get at, the thing that substantially contributes to mobility, is whether or not the guy has a college degree. A lot of athletes don't make it, and you have already skewed your results in an obvious direction if you take only those guys who have got degrees. Clearly they are going to succeed as it seems is indicated by those figures. Four years, of course, in college and three years of getting letters is bound to produce a degree—there is a very high level of correlation based on my own work between number of letters achieved and the likelihood of degree—it's about 0.90. So these guys have got degrees and that assists them in this upward drive. The fact that they seem to achieve at about the same level is difficult, of course, to speculate on, because of the things that we have already mentioned, but the difference between father's occupation and son's occupation, that is if all these guys were drawn from a current population, that kind of result could reasonably be expected. The reason for that is because of the change in the occupation market from predominantly blue-collar and agricultural to one in which there is a great deal of emphasis on white-collar activity and you can get there with a high school degree. The occupation variable is not a very good discriminator.

Now if you want to know the difference between these guys, for example, team athletes as opposed to individual athletes on occupation as defined today, that's one thing. But if you want to test the difference between father's occupation in 1920 and somebody else's occupation in 1940, and somebody else's again in 1960, that's very difficult to do, because of this change in the occupation market. Bureau of Census and Bureau of Labor Statistics show that on a conservative estimate some thirty-two or thirty-five thousand jobs a week, blue-collar jobs a week, are being dealt out of the economy because of cybernation; that is, the computer control of productive processes has been affected, in addition, by the fact that there has been a hell of a lot of job retitling going on in our society. In a system which emphasizes success, defined by the kind of occupational status the man has, you can do a lot to level that by simply retitling jobs. So, for example, the girl who works as a secretary and makes fifty-five bucks a week in New York is called a "gal Friday." There are at least 300 such listings in the *New York Times* each Sunday for gal Fridays. What does that imply? Well, she is the big man's right-hand girl, and without her he cannot operate effectively. So she goes off, pretends she's gal Friday and makes $55 a week. The assistant manager, so-called, in a loan company will make $90 to $110 a week and live in a community like East Lansing next to the professor who is making sixty, seventy, eighty thousand—not really of course, but who is making substantially $15,000 and up: but they can live in the same homes because of the way the economy has changed as well. Instead of purchasing things, we buy them on credit. Houses can be purchased on 30-year mortgages and he can buy the same house that a man much higher in status and in income has. The status levels are roughly the same. There is no distinction in that sense. Now, as I say, if you want to compare them then, because of these changes over time within a specific time, that's one thing. But one thing that compounds the difficulty of intergenerational mobility is the change in the occupational market itself. The way things have worked you can expect some increase in job status or occupational status over every generation in spite of things like education and in spite of things like background, that is, as averages, so these are additional kinds of problems. As Loy points out, it's important that more research be done; but it is, as he has also pointed out, difficult to do that research and so far as his own particular research is concerned there are some additional kinds of things he will clearly have to do if these results are to be accepted.

But since we are interested in this thing and it's difficult to get at information, it just so happens, folks, that between the shirts in my suitcase I discovered some of my own data; and so I would like to present some of that to show that there are some similarities between what Loy has got and data obtained elsewhere.

The data that I have is on some three hundred odd, Michigan State athletes. This is part of a brief synopsis of the two papers that were presented in St. Louis this last spring,* neither of which, like everything else I've done, is published. In any case there were some 300 athletes, and they were all on tenders; which means what? Which means they are the best damned athletes money can buy. So that this business of ability is controlled. These athletes came into Michigan State with tenders and they cross a four- or five-year

* Research Symposium on the Sociology of Sport, AAHPER National Convention, March, 1968.

period; there were just a few that came in '57, but they run from '58 to '62. The last bunch is supposed to be out by '63; so in other words these computations, which have been made very recently, involve athletes who have been out of school for at least five years. Their classes have graduated five years ago, so the time is controlled, athletic ability is controlled and other items as well. There are differences, of course, as you cross the country from the PCC to the Big Ten, and to the Ivy League, and those differences should be investigated as well. They also may skew results, as you might expect. In any case they operate at a very high level of point production, time diminution, you know, in terms of the mile and so on—they have some first-rate athletic teams on the Michigan State campus as Wisconsin is well aware and so that one kind of thing is controlled.

Let's take a look just at what some of these background factors are in terms of occupational status, income and so on. The argument is that athletes come disproportionately from disadvantaged families; as Table 1 demonstrates they clearly do not. If you take total family income by fifths (in 100's of dollars), for all U. S. families in 1960, as obtained from the U. S. Census, you find twenty percent of American families earning less than $2790, and twenty percent earning over $9,000; in addition, but not included here, less than 5 percent were over $15,000; so for those of you who think there has been a great deal of income redistribution, at least according to government figures, it hasn't happened. In any case when athletes' families are compared with all U. S. families, you can see that very few of the athletes come from that bottom fifth and not many of them come from the top fifth either. They are middle income kids and they come from middle level, at least as far as

Table 1   Athletes' Families and U. S. Families* Compared on Gross Income

	Total family income (in 100's of dollars)					
	0-27.9	28-47.9	48-64.9	65-89.9	90+	
U.S. families	20[†]	20	20	20	20	100
Athletes' families (n = 253)	6.7	23.3	28.5	29.6	11.9	100
	Chi square = 52.91		$p < .001$			

* Data from U. S. Census of Population: 1960, Final Report PC (1)-1C, General Social and Economic Characteristics, p. 1-226, Table 95. If a "one sample, goodness of fit" test is applied to a distribution of athletes' families on gross income (expected distribution being on fifths as for U. S. families), then $\chi^2 = 52.91$, $p < .001$.

[†] percent

income is concerned, backgrounds. Chi-square for this distribution is greater than 52, which, friends, I can tell you, gives a probability of somewhat less than .001. In other words, athletes come, not from the poorest or the richest fifths, but from the middle income levels.

Well, you say, the hell with that, man, you know − you skewed it, really it's team athletes we are talking about because we know about those guys that are playing fencing, tennis and golf: but if you do the same thing with team athletes only, the argument fails; the same thing happens. (Table 2). The percentages are roughly the same in both cases, 8.4 at the top, 5.4 at the bottom. And if then you say "I didn't mean them at all, I meant the football players": the same thing follows (Table 3), these guys come from middle income levels. Well, that's going to affect mobility already, isn't it? When sport type alone is contrasted on income, it's clear (Table 4) that athletes in "individual" sports are overrepresented at the top and bottom fifths, the latter because of track athletes.

Table 2   Team Athletes' Families and U. S. Families Compared on Gross Income

	Total family income (in 100's of dollars)					
	0-27.9	28-47.9	48-64.9	65-89.9	90+	
U.S. families	20	20	20	20	20	100
Team athletes' families ($n = 166$)	5.4	24.1	28.3	33.7	8.4	100
	Chi square = 51.53			$p < .001$		

Table 3   Football Athletes' Families and U. S. Families Compared on Gross Income

	Total family income (in 100's of dollars)					
	0-27.9	28-47.9	48-64.9	65-89.9	90+	
U.S. families	20	20	20	20	20	100
Football athletes' families ($n = 111$)	4.5	27.0	28.8	31.5	8.1	100
	Chi square = 35.62			$p < .001$		

GREGORY STONE: Are those averages again that you are dealing with?

WEBB: No, this was clearly based upon categories, no mean or anything else is involved here: the first category includes those families earning less

Table 4   Sport Type and Family Income

	Total family income (in 100's of dollars)					
	0-27.9	28.47.9	48-64.9	65-89.9	90+	
Team (n = 166)	5.6	24.1	28.3	33.7	8.4	100
Individual (n = 87)	9.2	21.8	28.7	21.8	18.4	100
	Chi square = 8.84			$p < .07$		

than $2800. At this point chi-square equals 8.92 which gives a probability level slightly higher than .05 which means that you cannot accept or reject the hypothesis but it's quite close as you can see. What is surprising, the team athletes are the kids who are supposed to be from the poor families relative to individual athletes and that does seem to be the case except for the differentiation at the bottom of the category where about 10 percent of the individual athletes originate and about 7 percent of the team athletes. That may be due to Negroes in track. At the top level roughly 20 percent of the individual athletes are up there compared to less than 10 percent of the team athletes. If you then use something like Kruskal-Wallis analysis of variance and get what would amount to the median on each one of these things— analysis of variance is not the distinction between means but calculates a mean or a central tendency for all groups being compared. It's used, of course, when you are comparing more than two groups and then it examines the amount of the variation around that calculated tendency. You can take the scores for each group and rank them and, although this is mentioned somewhere else in the paper, if you were to do this on the basis of calculating means on, in this case, income, the correlation between what's achieved by this and by the other more powerful statistics is something like .9; it's very, very high. In any case at the bottom in terms of income are track, hockey, football, and gymnastics. At the top you might expect fencing and baseball. Wrestling is surprising. It may result from the fact that wrestlers' blue-collar fathers earn more money as you can see in Table 5.

In terms of father's occupational status, again this is significant (see Tables 6 and 7). You have got the explanation of the rank. Sums are divided by n for that value and the results are then ranked. This seems to be an effective method when employed on gross income and then compared to the ranking by means of gross income. In any case the ranking remains relatively the same. At the top you get an idea of where these kids come from; 33 percent of them are from professional technical backgrounds, compared with 10 percent of the team athletes. At the other end of the scheme about 33 percent of the team athletes are from labor backgrounds compared with

Table 5   Sport Rank on Gross Income*

1. Fencing	7. Basketball
2. Wrestling	8. Gymnastics
3. Baseball	9. Football
4. Swimming	10. Track
5. Golf	11. Hockey
6. Tennis	

* Kruskal Wallis H=23.27 for these data, significant at .009 level, indicating a significant income variation between the sports, which tends to hold on a Team-Individual basis, as above (n=263).

Rank sums for each value are divided by n for that value and the results are then ranked. This seems to be an effective method when employed on gross income and then compared with the ranking by means on gross income, Spearman Rho = .94 ($p < .01$). The mean, of course, may only be used with data of at least "interval" level of measurement, and thus not with "occupation."

Table 6   Sport Type and Father's Occupation

	Father's occupation					
	Prof-Tech	Cler-Sales	Trades	Labor	Not home	
Team ($n = 178$)	10.1	12.4	30.9	32.6	14.0	100
Individual ($n = 85$)	32.9	17.7	22.4	16.4	10.6	100
		Chi square = 25.77		$p < .001$		

Table 7   Sport Rank on Father's Occupational Status

1. Golf	7. Gymnastics
2. Fencing	8. Track
3. Tennis	9. Hockey
4. Swimming	10. Football
5. Baseball	11. Basketball
6. Wrestling	

Kruskal-Waylis H = 50.82, $p < .001$ ($n = 268$)

about 16 percent of the individual athletes. Not-home proportions are roughly the same, because of divorce, or the old man took off, and so on. If you consider team and individual athletes in only major sports on gross family income, these proportions remain roughly the same, although there is some diminution of differences (see Table 8), and the same thing of course

Table 8   Team and Individual Athletes by Major Sport on Gross Family Income

	Total family income					
	0-27.9	28-47.9	48-64.9	90+		
Major team (n = 148)	6.7	22.2	26.3	35.1	9.4	100
Major individual (n = 63)	11.1	22.2	28.5	22.2	15.8	100
			Chi square = 5.00		$p > .20$	

goes for comparison on the father's occupational status (see Table 9). Roughly 30 percent of them stay at the top, about 35 percent of the major team athletes at the bottom, so these guys originate in different backgrounds but backgrounds which are dissimilar only at the top and the bottom levels of the income levels of the rest of the population. They tend to come from the middle income ranks.

There is the question then, given what we know about the background; what happens to them when they come to school? What are their success patterns in school? And that was part of that second thing; the fact is first that—let me come back to this for just a minute—what you would like to do, of course, is predict mobility based on some criterion. One of these, of course, is getting a degree. It's difficult to say whether the kid, if he leaves Michigan State, goes somewhere else to get a degree. Roughly 70 percent of the kids entering Michigan State, based upon the best figures we can get, graduate. It may be somewhat higher than that. Based on a study done, I think, down in Ohio three or four years ago, reported in the *American Sociological Review*, the figure goes up to about 75 percent for all kids entering college. Well, 75 percent of them graduate, but they don't graduate with their class. Many of them take two or three years in addition to get out

Table 9   Team and Individual Athletes by Major Sport on Father's Occupational Status

	Prof-Tech	Cler-Sales	Trades	Labor	Not home	
Major team (n = 151)	10.6	12.6	30.5	35.1	11.2	100
Major individual (n = 61)	31.2	13.1	23.0	21.3	11.4	100
		Chi square = 14.65		$p < .01$		

of school. But most of them, that is, roughly three quarters of them, get degrees; but in any case at Michigan State about 70 percent get a degree.

The first part, that is the background, is based upon information obtained from the Big Ten. The parents had to fill out these financial statement forms to make sure the kids could get the dough and then the second part, the business on how well he makes out in school, is not asked of him but is obtained from records in the Michigan State vaults (which by the way are very difficult to get). The third part of the study which is under way now is an attempt to find out how well these kids have done, what are they doing today, and then, of course, contrast this with that occupational background with the same qualifications and conditions that I have mentioned before which apply to this work as well as to Loy's or anyone else's. So, just to see how some of this makes out, here are some other tables (indicating). This contrasts five years later what's happened to these kids; 49 percent of the team athletes have gotten degrees in Michigan State, roughly 51 percent have not; 60 percent of individual athletes have gotten degrees, roughly 41 percent have not. Now if you include in that sample, which you can see down here at the bottom (indicating) 161 and 143, those kids who were not at Michigan State more than two years, that is, they were there less than two years, they had grade point averages at Michigan State of 1.5 out of a four-point system or above—(that means F+ or above); they also sent at least one transcript to another school, which we get from the records as well—of course, they are in the records—and they were at least in the top 70 percent of their high school graduating class. In other words, those kids if they went some place had some bare chance of getting a degree. You have 42 such kids. You add that and get the proportions at the bottom; 67 percent of all athletes graduate, and the way this manipulation of material operates, 33 percent did not.

Team athlete success is determined by number of letters, degree obtained or not obtained, race, white and Negro, and grades. A Negro kid coming to Michigan State is supposed to really have an opportunity; man, he's going to make it. What's Harold Lucas, who was an All-American at Michigan State, an All-American Tackle, and who later played a little professional ball and then dropped out, what's he doing today? He's working in a factory in Detroit. There are several cases of athletes that I can give like this where the success in athletics has been very great in terms of the numbers of letters and athletic honors won. What happens to them in terms of getting a degree? The percentages are at the bottom; 56 percent of white athletes get degrees, 38 percent of Negro athletes get degrees, five years after this group has left school. I think it should be clear that the likelihood that the Negro kid is likely to get that degree later on is much less than that of the white boy.

The following are for white boys only, and here fathers' occupation is related to whether or not the degree is obtained. Professional and technical, kids coming from that group, 49 percent of them graduate, 46 percent from white-collar groups, 56 percent of the kids from blue-collar groups and 70 percent from the families where the father's absent. That would indicate that athletics provides opportunity for lower-class whites. Of course, this business might not fit with lots of schools as well, it has to be taken into mind, and they are likely to get degrees somewhere else. But for those kids at Michigan State five years later the effect of occupations seems to be clear on getting that degree, and that degree is the ticket of admission to white middle level kinds of occupations and middle level income levels. The kid at the bottom level is making it. He clearly is from these figures.

Of course, there's the fact that he's bound to stay at Michigan State too. He is dependent on his athletic financial support. How about the wealthier kid? He can take off because he doesn't need that money. In fact, his folks, based upon upper occupational level income, can afford to pay his way at another school. So this has to be considered as well when you have a look at that figure. Now if you just take the bottom 40 percent, then control also for blue-collar origin against white-collar origin, you get a definition of lower class and upper class, taking whites only. Sixty-four percent of those white kids at the bottom are getting degrees, contrasted with 52 percent of the kids in the upper income and occupational groups. When sport type at the lower level is compared, 68 percent of team athletes compared with 50 percent of the individual athletes obtain degrees, which may mean that the team athletic business ties the kid tighter, more tightly into operating in an associational unit which provides some varieties of support and this may be an explanation of the difference in effect. The individual athlete type on the other hand is operating in strong competition with other kids and if he's not so successful the likelihood of his dropping out, of course, may be much greater.

And then finally come the term categories, and this is the thing that would or could affect the information already presented. This gives for the lower-class kids and the upper-class kids the number of terms they spent at Michigan State—one to three, four to six, seven to nine. We're on the term basis, so that would be less than a year, one year, two years, three years, four years, and five years. Twenty percent of the lower-class kids have been at Michigan State five terms or less, contrasted with 36 percent of those upper-class kids so that there is a tendency based upon occupational background to leave and that, of course, is probably based upon this difference in effect of parents' ability to support the athlete elsewhere. The kid with the higher occupational background because he's independent financially can do that.

Well, there are a great many other things that have to be investigated. One of the things that should have been done here and was not—it hasn't been done because I haven't had the time—is control of that term business, how long these kids are actually in school. In other words, of those kids who are there for four years or more, how many are getting degrees in terms of white-Negro differences and team-individual ones. But the larger question is the possibility of doing this kind of thing beyond the kinds of things we can get from records, where there is very little bias, and that involves question-naires, going out and asking questions about mobility, you cannot get away from it—and the differential interest in answering those questions based upon the degree or the amount of lack of success, so that those questions remain. I suppose with very tight follow-up systems some of them might to some greater or lesser extent be controlled. In any case, the area is an important one and Loy is beginning a contribution in that area.

DISCUSSION

DAN LANDERS: Did you say roughly 50 percent of the athletes at Michigan State did get a degree in '57 and with Loy about 49 percent had advanced degrees?

WEBB: Loy, don't forget, has guys who have been there for at least four years, they have got three letters, that means that they were there for four years, and as I pointed out there is a very high correlation between getting a degree, and number of letters earned: the higher the number of letters the greater the probability of getting a degree. I have everybody, whether they actually got any letters or not, they came to Michigan State and left because they couldn't really make it or they didn't think they could make it. It was that kind of thing.

JOHN ALBISON: I'd like to refer to John Loy's remark on the response to the question asking about letters earned. We recently did a survey of 275 of our graduates at the University of Michigan, interviewing 65 percent of them and surveying the rest with a mail questionnaire. One of the things we asked them was what they did in high school. We went back and checked high school annuals and found out it didn't turn out that way. Also, we asked the people teaching what professional organizations they belonged to (both by interview and on the questionnaire) and we got a great number of organiza-tions. I sent names to the appropriate organization and on reply it turned out that even with professional people there was a significant difference between the organizations they reportedly belonged to and the ones they actually belonged to. Moreover, there was no difference between the questionnaire and the interview responses, they were consistently lying. I think it's an indication of something we have to watch in any kind of a questionnaire. If you can get it some other way, you will be better off.

WALTER SCHAFER: I'd like to first of all congratualte both Mr. Webb and Mr. Loy, because the study of this has been virtually nil until now. Just one further question which I'd like to direct to Mr. Loy. I think we have to be cautious with regard to comparing the athletes' occupations with their fathers' occupations, I think we have to be cautious about concluding anything about an unusual contribution of athletics to occupational outcome. If you looked throughout the country you would find that the average status range of occupations now to be substantially higher because the whole economic structure has moved up. You could take account of that, however, as Duncan did by looking at the descriptions of occupations in 1950 compared to 1925.

LOY: That's a point well taken. I carried out the study last spring with limited funds which ran out in June. Thus, the data reported here were analyzed by hand. However, when I submit my data for computer analysis later this year, I shall attempt to control for the factors you mention as well as several brought forth by Harry. I shall likely use the recent work of Blau and Duncan as a model for my final data analysis. Although I was not familiar with their text when I began my project, I fortunately asked a number of questions identical to those included in their survey. Thus, I can make use of their findings for comparative purposes.

SEYMOUR KLEINMAN: It might be an interesting paper in itself.

LOY: There is no doubt about it. The thing which really needs investigation, however, is the reasons for the extreme secrecy practiced by athletic departments and what means might be the most effective in obtaining relevant materials from athletic files. For example, a number of athletic departments of major universities have carried out their own extensive studies in recent years regarding such matters as grant-in-aids, academic achievement, recruitment, etc., but these studies are difficult to come by. The major problem in my own study was obtaining a list of names and addresses of former athletes at UCLA. I spent a great deal of time discovering that there was such a list and still more time obtaining permission to use it.

JOHN POOLEY: Although in part you've tried to answer the questions just a moment ago by saying that you haven't had sufficient time to look at the data in the way which you would wish, I wonder if you see any indication of possible ethnic background of some of these students. Bearing in mind the paper by Riesman and Denney, there may be some difference according to interest. And a second question, are there any studies going on in any other country that one might compare, or might be relative?

LOY: I obtained information regarding an athlete's religious background, the national origin of his parents and grandparents, whether a language other than English was spoken in the home, and similar questions. Thus, I am sure that I will find ethnic differences among sport groups, but I hesitate to suggest what these might be until I have had a thorough look at my data. However, regarding national origin, I recall that 60 percent of the fathers of soccer players were foreign born and I know that athletes of Japanese descent were most often found in baseball and wrestling. With respect to religion, I was struck by the fact that a third of the gymnasts came from Jewish families, while athletes from Catholic homes were most prominent in football. One odd finding which I recall is that one-third of the grandfathers of cricket players were Russian born.

As concerns your second question about comparative studies, I must reply that the only work which I am aware of is the study I cited conducted by Dr. Lüschen in Germany and the investigation of Eggleston in England.

KLEINMAN: I think the point he has made, is that the Russians invented cricket!

GREGORY STONE: Just a brief observation. I was impressed with what seemed not to be a close fit, but some sort of a fit between some of my data on spectators and the background of these people in your study. I'm just wondering if you can make some wild inference about the socialization process here.

LOY: I, too, was struck by certain similarities between my data, your own results and the findings of Dr. Lüschen. I don't really know what to conject, however, regarding a socialization process. There does seem to be a relationship between contact sports, such as boxing, wrestling, and football and low SES. This fact might be related to past research which reveals that football players and wrestlers tend to come from large families and that boys from large families tend to have higher pain thresholds than boys from smaller families. However, I am not sure how to tie these odd empirical bits into a theory of socialization.

STONE: I don't know what this means, but there must be some sort of a socialization process. I can't go so far as to think of caste development in sports—I don't dare say that—but it's interesting, the similarity.

CHARLES PAGE: You cannot marry the girl when you are in the movies looking at her.

LOY: My cursory analysis of the returns has led me to form a number of hunches about several aspects of sport, stratification and socialization, but I had best remain silent until I've had a closer look. I can't wait to really get at the data, however.

5 / WOMEN AND SPORT

The personal-social aspects of women's life in American society is currently one of the most lively topics in the social sciences. College classes on the Psychology of Women, Sociology of Women, etc. are becoming commonplace, and some colleges have even initiated programs leading to a major in "Women and Society Studies." While the "Women's Liberation" movement has been omnipresent in recent years, there is no area of human activity that has experienced a greater transformation of women's roles than sports.

Until recent years, women have played a minor role in the history of sport. Women were literally excluded from sports in ancient Greece (except in Sparta). Indeed, women were strictly barred from even viewing the Olympic Games, and punishments were prescribed for any woman caught at the Games. The women did, however, create their own program of sports— The Heraea Games, in honor of Hera, the wife of Zeus. These were athletic events, held every four years, for women only. This might be called the beginning of women in sports. But only in the past fifty years, with the emancipation of women from home responsibilities and their securing of equal status with men in most spheres of life, have women begun to take a prominent part in the world of sport.

Several factors account for the insignificant position of women in sports history. First, in most societies, the woman's cultural tasks have been child rearing and "home making." These tasks leave little time for participation in sports. Even the play pastimes of young girls have been largely limited to "playing house"—taking care of dolls, cooking mud pies, and dressing up like mother. Also, girls have been expected to take care of younger siblings, thus limiting their own play time. Second, there has been a deep-seated suspicion that vigorous sports were a health hazard for women. Folklore about how sports might be injurious to the child-bearing ability of women has persisted for centuries. Finally, social mores of masculine-feminine sex roles have been a powerful influence in discouraging women from participating in sports, particularly highly competitive activities. Boys have been encouraged to develop sports prowess, while girls have been restrained from sports activities and urged to act "feminine," that is, to show dignity and charm. This lack of encouragement has, of course, had the effect of destroying interest in sports performance for women.

Prior to 1860 very few women were active in American sports; then in the latter years of the nineteenth century archery, croquet, tennis, golf, and cycling began to attract women. With the rise of sports interest in the United States in the early years of this century, sports enthusiasm of girls and women increased. Interschool sports teams flourished until, by 1930, many of the excesses of men's sports became the excesses of women's sports. Educators and physicians rose to protect women against sports. And protect them they did, not only from the evils of highly organized competition but also from competition itself. For a number of years, school competition in many forms was forbidden for girls and women. New leadership in the physical education and sports fields in the past ten years has caused the pendulum to swing back to a greater encouragement of sports participation for girls and women.

Probably the greatest impetus to women's sports has been the Olympic Games. Women's events first appeared in the modern Olympics in 1912 in Stockholm, Sweden, and were confined to swimming and diving competition. In 1928, women were allowed to compete in track and field events. But the participation of American women in the Olympics remained at a low ebb until success in the 1956 and 1960 Games sparked a widespread enthusiasm for women's sports competition. The interest generated by the Olympics is reflected in other recent developments. The Division of Girls' and Women's Sports of the American Association for Health, Physical Education, and Recreation has begun to actively promote interschool sports programs, and since 1963, has developed policies for competition in girls' and women's sports on all educational levels. An annual schedule of national intercollegiate championships in sports for college women was initiated in 1969.

The reading by Eleanor Metheny represents an effort to develop an understanding of the roles appropriate for women in sports. The author inquires into the underlying reasons for the traditional custom of denying sports opportunities to women. Biological, mythological, and social interpretations of the nature of women in sport are scrutinized. Structural and functional differences in the sexes are noted, but the author emphasizes that the masculine-feminine roles operating in the societies have been a more dominant force in controlling women's sports experiences. She points out that, although the socially sanctioned images of appropriate feminine behavior have changed since the days of ancient Greece, even today semi-codified social sanctions about women's participation in sport exist. The author then discusses the theory that the sports activities in which women choose to participate serve to formulate some conception of the female's role as a significant force within the universe. Several sports activities which the author suggests are inappropriate for women in contemporary sport are now commonly played, thus illustrating the amount of cultural change in just one decade.

The influence of sex differences on play choices is the subject of the reading by Sutton-Smith, et al. They have made extensive investigations into the games activities of boys and girls. On the basis of their studies, they conclude that boys' increased interest in sports is associated with the male sex role in American society, but their findings for girls are not so clear-cut. They discuss some of the factors which cause sex-role confusion in girls.

In the next reading, Dorothy Harris deals with the question of why sports participation has traditionally not been considered a worthwhile experience for girls in America. She notes that stereotypes and myths have typically mitigated against enthusiastic involvement in sport by girls. For example, men and women have propagated the notion for many years that sports participation masculinizes girls. There is no evidence to support this notion but it nevertheless has served as a strong deterrent to girls' sports participation in our society. Harris discusses a variety of other social conse-quences of sports participation which have discouraged girls from engaging in sports. The author does claim, however, that there is currently a revolution in attitudes toward competitive sports for girls.

Carolyn Sherif's major contention, in the final reading, is that contrary to traditional belief females do compete in a variety of ways in our society and therefore do exhibit competitiveness. She describes numerous ways in which women in American society engage in competitive processes each day but she admits that these competitive situations have not been studied to any extent by social scientists. In reviewing the literature on competition in infancy and early childhood, Sherif finds no convincing evidence that there are genetic differences with regard to competitiveness of boys and girls; she suggests that competitiveness develops with age, and consistent patterns of competitiveness do not emerge until after the age of three. In later childhood the author suggests that there are no differences in competitiveness between males and females but there are differences in what the two sexes will compete for. It is during adolescence that females have traditionally withdrawn from sports and this has led to the popular notion that girls are not "naturally" competitive. Sherif convincingly points out that actually females engage in many forms of competitive behavior at this age but not much in sport because our culture socializes them away from sports competition. The author finds much of the literature on achievement motivation irrelevant for females because the structure of the situation and personal meaning are not accorded proper consideration. Sherif concludes that as females' reference groups—especially peers—give high priority to sports the role of women in sport will be enhanced.

SYMBOLIC FORMS OF MOVEMENT: THE FEMININE IMAGE IN SPORTS

Eleanor Metheny

The issues debated in this paper have a very long history. They were raised as early as 776 B.C. by the custom of excluding women from the sacred precincts of Olympia. They were raised in 1896 when women were admitted to competition in some events in the modern Olympic Games, but excluded from others. They are being argued around the world today as every national Olympic Committee makes its own decisions about the inclusion of women in the lists of competitors. This paper is not an attempt to resolve all of these long-standing issues; rather it is an attempt to inquire into the underlying nature of these controversies.

In an earlier paper—"Symbolic Forms of Movement: The Olympic Games"—I have interpreted the Olympic events as symbolic formulations of man's conception of himself as a consequential force within the universe of space, time, mass, and energy. In the present paper I shall pursue that interpretation with reference to some conceptions of roles appropriate for women.

THE BIOLOGICAL BASIS OF THE FEMALE ROLE

At the biological level, arguments about appropriate roles for men and women must be pursued in terms of differences in anatomical structure and function. These sexually significant differences are too well known to need

Eleanor Metheny, "Symbolic Forms of Movement: The Feminine Image in Sports," *Connotations of Movement in Sport and Dance*, Dubuque, Iowa: W. C. Brown Co., 1965, pp. 43-56. Reprinted by permission of the author.

explication here. With reference to sports competition, the important question is: How are these differences related to the ability to overcome the inertia of mass?

In terms of averages, it is a truism that men are larger and stronger than women; but this generalization does not hold for individual representatives of the two sexes. Some women may be very large and strong, and their ability to overcome the inertia of mass may be far greater than that of the majority of men. Similarly, some men may be smaller and less muscular than many women, and in any contest with the inertia of mass they may make a very poor showing—and may, in fact, be bested by the majority of the opposite sex.

To some extent these relationships may be modified by pregnancy, the demands of infant care, and possibly menstruation; and all of these episodes may serve to limit a woman's interest in the kind of training men may undergo in preparation for international competition. But they do not vitiate the biological fact that women appear to be fully competent to engage in a contest with the inertia of mass. In terms of averages, women's achievements may be less spectacular than those of men; in terms of individual achievement, some women may well excel most of the male competitors in any athletic event.

It would seem then that the age-old arguments about whether or not women should be admitted to competition in the Olympic events cannot be pursued in meaningful terms at the strictly biological level of anatomical structure and function.

THE MYTHOLOGICAL IMAGE OF THE FEMALE ROLE

In every culture, men and women play different roles within the social organization. In part, these roles are defined by the relative contribution each sex makes to the reproduction of the species—a biologically-determined contribution which is the same in all cultures. But in larger terms, these roles are established by some less well-defined set of factors not directly related to these biological differences, as evidenced by the fact that they differ from culture to culture. This complex of factors serves to determine the *masculine image* of behaviors appropriate to males and the corresponding *feminine image* of behaviors appropriate to females in each social group.

At the time of the early Olympic Festivals, which date back beyond the first recorded games of 776 B.C., the images of masculinity and femininity within the emerging culture of ancient Greece were clearly delineated. These early Greeks envisioned their gods as persons very like themselves, differing from human beings only in the extent of their personal powers over the natural forces of the universe. Thus, they assigned to their male gods all of the behaviors appropriate to their own image of supermasculinity, while the behaviors of superfemininity were assigned to the female goddesses. A brief review of the characteristics of these gods and goddesses may give us some insight into the fact that women were excluded from the sacred precincts of Olympia.

Among the male gods, Zeus, the hurler of thunderbolts, had dominion over all the forces of earth; and his messenger, Hermes, could overcome both space and time with winged feet. Poseidon, the earth-shaker, had similar dominion over the forces of the sea. Ares, the god of war, was a powerful destructive force; and Hephaestus, the god of the metal workers, could subdue the materials of earth with one powerful blow of his hammer and shape them into forms of his own choosing. Even Apollo, who epitomized the intellectual powers of reason and logic, was pictured as an athlete, well able to overcome the forces of earth by skillful use of his bodily strength as well as by his intellectual prowess.

What an Olympic team the gods would have been! How they would have excelled in every contest in the early Olympic Festivals! And it may be noted that the Olympic Games in which men strove to overcome the forces of the earth in symbolic contests were held in honor of Zeus, the all-powerful father of the gods.

In contrast, the image projected by the female goddesses is almost totally devoid of any suggestion of physical strength that might be used to overcome the forces of earth—or of men.

Demeter, the Earth Mother, is envisioned as the ground in which all life is bred and nurtured. Hera, the wife of Zeus, is pictured as his helpmate, whose own will must ever be subordinated to the desires of her husband. (It may be noted, however, that Hera is never wholly resigned to this role and at times she uses her own female resources to seduce Zeus into doing her will rather than his.) Aphrodite, born of the foam of the sea, has none of these homely virtues. She is the goddess of beauty, infinitely desirable to all men. But if she delights in arousing their sexual desires, she can also be cruel and treacherous. In return for her favors, she demands tribute from her admirers, and men may well be fearful of her vengeance when her need for adoration is not satisfied. We are told that she was an accomplished swimmer, but she appears to have used this skill largely to display her lovely body in attractive poses that lured men to their own destruction.

The fact that these early Greeks could not reconcile feminine desirability with athletic prowess is underlined in the legends of Artemis and Athena. Artemis, the beautiful goddess of the hunt, was fleet of foot, and none excelled her in the use of bow and arrow—but men did not find her lovely body desirable. Or perhaps it was the other way around. At any rate, legend relates that Artemis and her followers rejected the love of men and found delight in the companionship of women. Athena, goddess of wisdom, and of all goddesses the most respected, carried her own spear as she led men into battle, and her most famous statue shows her in full fighting array. But, alas, she too was denied the love of men, her perpetual virginity being commemorated in the Temple of the Maiden called the Parthenon.

Perhaps Artemis might have entered the foot races in the earliest games at Olympia; perhaps Athena might have thrown the javelin as well as the spear—and in fact there were some limited competitions of this type for maidens in some of the festivals attended by women. But even in Sparta, where young girls were encouraged to develop both strength and skill, marriage put an end to such competitive endeavours. For adult women, the virtues demanded were those of Demeter, Hera, and Aphrodite—and the strength, skill and intellect of Athena and Artemis did not fit in this image of feminine desirability.

These are the elements out of which the prototypes of masculinity and femininity were compounded by the early ancestors of Western civilization. But these images were never wholly static. As men learned increasingly to control the stuff of their universe with skill and intellect, rather than with sheer strength of muscle, the masculine image reflected this evolving interpretation of man's role as a consequential force within the grand design. So, too, the feminine image began to change—albeit much more slowly.

The shift from muscle to skill and intellect may be seen in the contrast between Heracles, the legendary hero of pre-Homeric Greece, and Theseus, the later hero who made Athens into the most powerful of all Greek cities.

Heracles, who is sometimes credited with founding the earliest form of the Olympic Games, was a man of incredible strength. Certainly he would have been a formidable competitor in all of the early Olympic events, for no man could excel him in size or in strength of muscle. In all truth, however, he was not very bright, and his great strength led him into all sorts of trouble. He suffered great pangs of remorse for the damage caused by his own ineptitude, but he did not seem to learn much from these destructive episodes.

Theseus, who comes along much later in the story of Greece, presents quite a different picture. He is smaller than Heracles, and he has less strength, but he uses that strength with far greater skill—and is more disposed to forethought than to remorse and vain regret. He is the first king to establish and maintain his right to rule largely by force of intellect, and in his story we find the first recognition of the virtues of cooperation among men and cities.

Heracles might well have bested Theseus in the pancratium and other weight events in the Olympic arena, but Theseus would have excelled in any contest demanding skill and strategy in the use of the lighter implements, and probably in the team games—which were later to demand cooperation as well as competition.

In the time of Heracles, the feminine image projected by Demeter, Hera and Aphrodite was embodied in the legendary first woman, Pandora. She was lovely to behold, her name means "all joys," and she was welcomed as a helpmate—but, alas, she was really very stupid. Allowing her curiosity to overcome her caution, she opened the box that contained all the evils and sorrows of mankind, and let them loose in the world—where they plague men to this very day. But in her one display of good sense, she did slam the lid down just in time to preserve woman's greatest gift to man—the gift of hope.

In the picture of Pandora, there is little to suggest an interest in overcoming the inertia of mass. But Hippolyta, Queen of the Amazons, who won the enduring love of Theseus many centuries later, presents quite a different image.

As a ruler of her own kingdom, Hippolyta was the equal of Theseus in intelligence and skill, although smaller in size and of lesser strength. As they confronted each other in mortal combat at their first meeting, her courage matched his, and she fought bravely and well, neither asking nor offering advantage. In the eyes of Theseus she was both beautiful and desirable, and when he had won her he found new joy in the sexual embrace, for her ardor and skill matched his own. In marriage, she was a faithful helpmate and a devoted mother, and equally she was a good companion, both at home and in the hunt. In the end, she proved her love for Theseus by offering up her own life to save his—and it is said that he mourned her unceasingly for the rest of his days.

The legendary Hippolyta seems to have combined in her own person the skill and intellect of Artemis and Athena, the homely virtues of Demeter and Hera, and the beauty and desirability of Aphrodite. Surely, to Theseus, she was everything a man might hope to find in a woman. Had she been admitted to the lists of the Olympic Games, it seems likely that she would have earned her laurels proudly—not in the pancratium or weight-events, perhaps, but surely in the foot races and the javelin throw. And it seems likely that Theseus would have found pride in her achievements. But for the citizens of Athens, the time for recognition of such womanly feats had not yet come.

Hippolyta was cruelly rejected by the Athenians, both male and female. They could not reconcile intellect, skill and strength with their image of adult female sexuality. In her own life, however, Hippolyta proved them wrong—

and they never forgave her for this. To this day, her name evokes suspicion in the minds of many men and women. Nonetheless, she left her own bright legend for future generations—the legend of a woman who delighted in using *all* of her own personal powers, a woman far ahead of her own time who won and held the love of the most eminent and farseeing man among the citizens of early Athens.

The gods and goddesses of ancient Greek myth have long departed from their home on Mt. Olympus, but their images are still reflected in the connotations of the words *masculine* and *feminine* as we use them today. Historically, as men have moved forward on the path of skill and intellect pointed out by Theseus, they have tended to devalue the virtues of sheer muscular power—but the term *masculine* still suggests the image of Heracles. So, too, it is Pandora's image that is suggested by the term *feminine*. And many of the arguments about the appropriateness of sports competition for women hinge on those connotations.

However, when the modern Olympic Games were established in 1896, the image of Hippolyta was partially cleansed of the slurs that have tarnished it through the years, and women were at long last permitted to seek their own laurels in some events. Today the image of the feminine athlete is still somewhat blurred, but its modern outlines now seem to be emerging in currently sanctioned patterns of sports competition for women.

THE SOCIALLY SANCTIONED IMAGE
OF FEMININE SPORT COMPETITION

The socially sanctioned images of femininity and masculinity are always relative. They differ from era to era, from culture to culture, and from group to group within a given social organization. In broadest general terms, these socially sanctioned images may be described as a composite interpretation of what the members of either sex may be or do without impairing their opportunities for finding a mate within their own social classification.

The social sanctions indicated below were derived from attitudes expressed by college women in the United States. I am indebted to Dr. Laura Huelster of the University of Illinois and Miss Mabel Hart of the University of Southern California for many of the data used here. They must not, however, be held responsible for my interpretation of their findings nor for the extension of these data to international level or Olympic competition.

1   At the international level, some forms of competition appear to be *categorically unacceptable,* as indicated by the fact that women are excluded from Olympic competition in these events.

These forms include: Wrestling, judo, boxing, weight-lifting, hammer throw, pole vault, the longer foot races, high hurdles, and all forms of team games—with the recent exception of volleyball.

These forms appear to be characterized by one or more of the following principles:

An attempt to physically subdue the opponent by bodily contact
Direct application of bodily force to some heavy object
Attempt to project the body into or through space over long distances
Cooperative face-to-face opposition in situations in which some body contact may occur

It may be noted that the excluded team games are generally acceptable to college women in the United States at the level of intramural competition, and these games are popular during the years of adolescence. Some extramural competition is sponsored at the high school level, but this decreases in the college age group, and only a very limited number of college women continue their interest in team games during their adult years.

2   Some forms of competition are generally *not acceptable* to college women in the United States, although they *may be acceptable to a minority group* within the college population.

These forms include: Shot put, discus throw, javelin throw, the shorter foot races, low hurdles, long jump, gymnastics events, and free exercise.

These forms appear to be characterized by one or more of the following principles:

Direct application of bodily force to a moderately heavy object
Attempt to project the body into or through space over moderate distances
Display of strength in controlling bodily movements

Very few college women show any sustained interest in performance in these events, although some may have found them challenging during the early years of adolescence. Among the Olympic competitors from the United States, Negro women are disproportionately represented in the track and field events. In the gymnastic events, there is a preponderance of women of Germanic and Slavic ancestry, most of whom have developed their interests and abilities in ethnically-defined social and athletic clubs rather than in the college setting.

3   Some forms of individual competition are *generally acceptable* to the college women of the United States, and competence in these events does not appear to militate against social acceptance by males within the college population.

These forms include: Swimming, diving, skiing, and figure skating, and such non-Olympic events as golf, archery, and bowling.

These forms appear to be characterized by one or more of the following principles:

Attempts to project the body into or through space in aesthetically pleasing patterns
Utilization of a manufactured device to facilitate bodily movement
Application of force through a light implement
Overcoming the resistance of a light object

In one way or another, all of these sports involve a considerable expenditure of time, money, or both; and participation is accordingly limited to women in the economically-favored groups. Bowling, which is the least expensive insofar as time is concerned, and in which a moderately heavy ball is used, finds greatest favor with middle-class groups. Success in the other events may contribute to upward social mobility in some instances.

4 Some forms of face-to-face competition are also *generally acceptable* to college women of the United States, with no implication of limited social acceptance for successful competitors.

These forms include: Fencing, such non-Olympic sports as squash, badminton, and tennis, and the team-game of volleyball.

These forms appear to be characterized by one or more of the following principles:

Application of force through a light implement
Overcoming the resistance of an essentially weightless object
Maintenance of a spatial barrier that prevents body contact with opponent

Fencing is not acceptable to certain religiously-defined groups, presumably because it symbolizes the destruction of human life. Adult competition in squash and badminton is largely limited to members of private clubs, but these groups include women from the middle as well as the higher socio-economic levels. Tennis, which was once a private club game, is now commonly played by all groups having access to public facilities, but as yet only a few women from the darker-skinned minorities have reached the level of national competition. Volleyball is commonly played as a recreational game with mixed teams including both sexes.

It is of interest to note the difference between squash, which is socially acceptable for women in the upper economic levels, and handball, which is not. Here the distinction seems to rest on the use of a light implement to apply force in the one game and the use of the hand in the other. However, such resistance to hitting an object with the hand seems to be overcome in the growing popularity of volleyball.

Summarizing this analysis, it appears that the socially sanctioned image of feminine sports competition for college women in the United States may be derived from a few general principles:

1.   It is *not appropriate* for women to engage in contests in which:

the resistance of the *opponent* is overcome by bodily contact

the resistance of a *heavy object* is overcome by direct application of bodily force

the body is projected into or through space over long distances or for extended periods of time

2.   It *may be appropriate* for women identified in the lower levels of socioeconomic status to engage in contests in which:

the resistance of an *object of moderate weight* is overcome by direct application of bodily force

the body is projected into or through space over moderate distances or for relatively short periods of time

3.   It is *wholly appropriate* for women identified with the more favored levels of socioeconomic status to engage in contests in which:

the resistance of a *light object* is overcome with a *light implement*

the body is projected into or through space in aesthetically pleasing patterns

the velocity and maneuverability of the body is increased by the use of some manufactured device

a spatial barrier prevents bodily contact with the opponent in face-to-face forms of competition

SPORT AS A SYMBOLIC FORMULATION OF SOCIALLY SANCTIONED FEMALE ROLES

Within the context of the biological, mythological, and social interpretations of the nature of females, we may now examine the theory that the sports in which women compete serve to formulate some conception of the female's role as a consequential force within the universe of space, time, mass, and energy.

At the international level, as represented by the Olympic Games, women are categorically prohibited from any attempt to overcome an opponent by direct application of bodily force. Since this prohibition cuts across all cultural lines, it would seem to be traceable to some biologically-defined difference common to the men and women of all social groups. The clue may lie in the differences between the ways in which males and females may use their own bodily forces in the mutual act of procreation.

For the male, the procreative act may be construed in terms of direct application of bodily forces subject to the male's control. Conversely, the female role must be construed in passive terms as the act of receiving and nurturing new life rather than creating it by personal intent expressed in terms of bodily force. Thus, the male may use his own muscular powers to coerce the female and force her to submit to his will, but the female cannot similarly coerce the male. By extension, then, it may well seem biologically appropriate for the male to force another person to submit to his will by direct application of muscular powers through bodily contact; conversely, it would be biologically inappropriate for the female to coerce or subdue another person by use of the muscular powers of her own body.

This interpretation may be further extended in the roles assigned to men and women in the mortal combat of war. Here, men have long found it possible to justify their own attempts to coerce other men into submission by threat of death; but men have seldom permitted their women to engage in such direct forms of mortal combat. Athena may have carried her spear as she led men into battle, but, insofar as legend relates, she did not personally use her own body to wrestle with the enemy. Hippolyta and her Amazons did, on occasion, engage in hand-to-hand combat—but the most severe charge made against Hippolyta by the Athenians was that she had "fought like a man."

When the resistance to be overcome in a contest is centered in an *object*, rather than in the body of another *person*, the prohibitions against use of bodily force by women are stated in relative, rather than in categorical, terms. Here the issue seems to be: *How much force* may a woman appropriately apply to an object?

At the Olympic level, women are not permitted to lift heavy weights or to throw the hammer. They are, however, permitted to put the shot, hurl the discus, and throw the javelin. Similarly, they are barred from the pole vault, the high jump, the high hurdles, and the longer foot races, but they are permitted to compete in the long jump, the low hurdles, and the shorter races. They are also barred from the more strenuous team games, but in 1964 they were permitted to compete in the milder game of volleyball—the only team game in which there is no possibility of direct body contact between opponents.

The facets of biology provide no logical basis of support for these relative distinctions. The number of women competent to perform in the excluded events may be small—but so is the comparable number of men; and this is generally true for all of the events included on the women's list, with the numbers increasing as the events become less physically demanding.

Socially, however, there appears to be a relationship between participation in such strenuous events and the kinds of work commonly done by the performer's parents. Women from homes in which both the father and mother are commonly employed in some form of manual labor may seemingly use their own muscular forces in athletics without impairing their own marriageability. Here the old fallacy of associating displays of strength with sexual inadequacy seems to be greatly weakened—although it still cannot be wholly dismissed as a factor in the determination of social approval. It must also be noted that even within the manual laborer group social approval tends to decrease as the muscular forces demanded by the events increase.

Within the category of fully-approved events in which the contestant attempts to overcome the resistance of an object, strength is generally far less important than skill. The contested objects in such games as golf, archery, tennis, badminton, and squash are essentially weightless, and the objective of the contest is to move these objects through space by manipulating a light instrument with skill and speed. (The heaviest such instrument is probably the bowling ball, which even very small women can lift without difficulty.) This emphasis on instrumental manipulation is further emphasized in the face-to-face games by either nets or rules that prohibit bodily contact. (Even in fencing, in which the body of the opponent is touched by the instrument, the touch is symbolic rather than forceful.)

All of these games were developed in the later years of human history by men called "gentle"—men whose personal status rested on the presumption of superiority in intellect and skill rather than on their muscular powers. But women did not participate in the early forms of these games. Not until the Industrial Revolution had created new forms of employment for women in industry, and not until women in the more socially-favored classes had begun to claim some measure of personal equality with their husbands, did women begin to participate in these sports reserved for gentlemen.

Significantly, these sports pioneers seldom competed with men directly in any of these games, and there is still strong aversion to this form of competition. Today, the socially-approved forms of competition in tennis, for example, are still man-man, woman-woman, and mixed doubles—in which the marriage relationship is symbolized by a partnership in which a man and woman combine their forces in a contest with another partnership team. Today, styles in double play are changing—but the most common strategy still emphasizes the man's strength of arm, while the woman uses her skill to support his efforts within a smaller part of their common court area.

Thus, in mixed doubles the woman still tends to play the role appropriate to Hera, the helpmate, as she uses the skills of Artemis and Athena and Hippolyta to support the efforts of her male partner, reinforcing his attempts to win the contest rather than threatening his mastery over their common environment. However, it must be noted that side-by-side play is now frequently seen in mixed doubles, particularly when both of the partners are superior players. So it would seem that men who are sure of their own strength and skill are not offended by displays of strength and skill in their mates—particularly when these female forces are combined with their own male forces to their mutual advantage.

Within the category of socially approved events in which the contestant attempts to project her body into or through space, women display a high degree of muscular strength as well as great skill and daring. In swimming, they propel themselves through the water with great speed, but they seldom compete in the longer distances. As Aphrodite noted, however, the water-supported movements of swimming display the female body to advantage, and it is noteworthy that the aesthetically pleasing patterns of synchronized swimming were developed by women, rather than by men. Similarly, women in gymnastics and free exercise have developed their own movement patterns, which emphasize grace and beauty to a far greater extent than do the standard events for men.

Diving, figure-skating, and skiing are also classed as graceful forms of movement, and in these sports personal velocity is greatly facilitated by the use of such manufactured devices as springboards, skates, and skis. The management of the high velocities produced by these devices requires both strength and skill, but it is skill that is emphasized rather than strength.

Today, in the United States, the image of femininity projected by college women and endorsed by their potential mates is a "double image"—with one aspect identified as "woman at work" and the other identified as "woman at home."

As workers, these college women see themselves dealing with the forces of the universe in consequential ways, even as their men do. But neither the men nor the women picture themselves overcoming the resistance of mass, or of other persons, by sheer muscular force of bodily contact. Rather, they are prepared to use their wits in the realm of ideas, and they are adept in the use of lightweight equipment and manufactured devices that call for dexterity and skill rather than strength. On occasion, the men may still feel called upon to demonstrate the age-old conception of masculinity by performing feats of strength; but few college women seek this expression of their own human powers.

As potential wives and mothers, the college women are concerned with expressing their femininity in quite different ways. Recognizing their own biologically-based need for dependence on the male wage-earner, they modify their behavior in ways designed to enhance their own sexual desirability. They may also, on occasion, conceal their own abilities as workers lest the man of their choice might feel belittled by their competence.

Both sides of the image are evidenced in the socially approved list of sports for women. Strength and bodily contact are de-emphasized in favor of skill and grace; force is applied to weightless objects with lightweight implements; and velocity is attained by use of manufactured devices. And there is no serious competition in which women are matched against men. Rather, in those sports in which men and women participate together, they play as partners, with women generally accepting the supporting rather than the dominant role.

Thus, in our own time, it would seem that the college women of the United States have found it possible to combine the sexually-based image of Aphrodite, Hera and Demeter with the personal powers of Athena, Artemis, and Hippolyta, without doing violence to either, within the realm of sports competition. Thus, too, the forms of competition they have chosen may be construed as a dramatic formulation of their conception of the complex roles females may play as consequential forces within the grand design of the universe. Perhaps Heracles and Pandora might have been dismayed by this interpretation of what a woman is and what she can do—but let it be said to the credit of Theseus that he foresaw this picture some three thousand years ago when he described Hippolyta as everything a man might hope to find in a woman—and let us remember, too, that the legend of his love for her has endured, time without end, through the long years of human history.

DEVELOPMENT OF SEX DIFFERENCES IN PLAY CHOICES DURING PREADOLESCENCE

B. Sutton-Smith, B. G. Rosenberg, and E. F. Morgan, Jr.

This paper is one of a series in which the differences between the preferences for play activities of preadolescent boys and girls have been studied. Two of the papers have contrasted the play preferences of children today with those of children 30 and 60 years ago.[10, 16] Other papers have dealt with a masculinity-femininity scale[9] which is derived from this preference data and which predicts a variety of psychosocial correlates. [11, 14, 15] While in previous papers the preadolescent period has been treated as a whole, the present paper is concerned with developmental changes in preference patterns of boys and girls which take place within that period itself, in particular, the changes occurring between the third and sixth grades.

Earlier research with the game and play preferences would lead to the expectation that girls should show increased responsiveness with age to the items on this scale;[10] that girls' preferences would become increasingly like those of boys across these grades;[16] that, at the fifth grade, girls' preferences might tend again to become more feminine, although the evidence in the literature is somewhat inconsistent on this point; [1, 2, 17, 18] and that the changes in girls' preferences may be an indication of sex role confusion, though here again, there are differences of opinion.[1, 3]

PROCEDURE

In order to investigate these questions concerning girls' increased responsiveness, their increased preference for masculine items, their changes in preference patterns at the fifth grade, and their sex role confusion, a play scale composed of 180 items[13] was administered to 928 boys and 973 girls in grades 3 through 6 in 12 midwestern townships. The samples were obtained from small towns, varying in population from 300 (New Middleton, Ohio) to 24,000 (Findlay, Ohio). The schools sampled were predominantly of lower

B. Sutton-Smith, B. G. Rosenberg, and E. F. Morgan, Jr., "Development of Sex Differences in Play Choices During Preadolescence," *Child Development,* 34:119-126 (1963). Copyright © 1963, by The Society for Research in Child Development, Inc. Reprinted by permission.

and middle socioeconomic classification. The number of children responding to the inventory in each grade was as follows:

	3rd Grade	4th Grade	5th Grade	6th Grade
Boys	137	260	245	286
Girls	153	252	278	290

Children respond to this play scale by ignoring items which they do not play or by indicating like or dislike for the items which they do play. Their responses were analyzed for sex differences and age changes. First, the like and dislike choices for the 180 items were subjected to a chi-square analysis for the differences between the sexes at each grade level. Secondly, the same choices were analyzed within each sex for differences between grade levels.

RESULTS

Only items to which 30 percent of the children responded in at least one grade level were included for analysis. One hundred and forty-six items of the 180 met this criterion. Of this 146, 33 showed no significant sex differences throughout, i.e., they did not distinguish between the sexes ("neutral" items).

The first and most important finding is that, if only those items differentiating at the $p = .01$ level or better are considered, girls and boys have approximately equal numbers of items differentiating between them at all grade levels: the boys have 24, and the girls have 24 (Tables 1 and 2). When the number of items differentiating between the sexes is extended to the $p = .05$ level, greater differences between the sexes begin to appear. These differences do not show themselves, however, until after the third grade level, for at that grade the number of items favoring each sex, even at the .05 level, is approximately equal. It is at the fourth grade level that the girls suddenly appear much more responsive to the items on this scale than the boys (i.e., more items differentiate in favor of girls than boys). The numbers of items differentiating between the sexes at the .05 level during these grades are as follows:

	Masculine items	Feminine items
Third grade	31	37
Fourth grade	30	52
Fifth grade	29	60
Sixth grade	34	59

Table 1 Play and Game Items Which Differentiate Boys from Girls at Several Levels of Significance

Differentiating level	Items
All grade levels	
$p = .001$	Bandits, soldiers, cowboys, cops and robbers, space-men, bows and arrows, throwing snowballs, wrestling, football, boxing, hunting, using tools, model aero-planes, toy trains, work machines, build forts
$p = .01$	Cars, marbles, darts, baseball, shooting, fishing, make radio, climbing
$p = .05$	Baseball
*Some grade levels**	
$p = .05$	Blackman (3), fly kites (3), king of the mountain (3, 6), bowling (3), soccer (3, 4, 6), boating (3), ghosts (4), inventors (4), horseshoes (4, 6), racing (4, 6) tug-o-war (5), capture the flag (5, 6), skiing (5), horse riding (5, 6), pool (6), dice (6), handsprings (6)

* The grade level(s) are indicated in parentheses after each item.

When the same preferences are analyzed within the sexes for age level differences, it becomes apparent that the fourth grade is a period of greatly increased responsiveness for both sexes. Examining those items which differentiate the sexes at the .05 level or better, there are 69 significant item increases between the third and fourth grades and only seven significant decreases (Table 3). While the boys show 28 of these item increases, girls show 41. Girls' greater responsiveness, then, is a condition presumably produced by changes that occur between the third and fourth grades.

Inspection of the present data reveals that various types of changes are taking place at this time. The play items in this inventory can be divided into two levels of maturity. At the immature level are the simple pastimes, such as singing games, make-believe, and tagging games which predominate in the play of children up until the age of about 9 years.[12] At the more mature level are the more complex adult recreations (shooting, fishing), hobbies, games, and sports. Games and sports are recreational activities governed by definite rules of procedure. They have stable sides and definite outcomes, which is to say there are winners. Pastimes, by contrast, although governed by rules of procedures, do not have definite outcomes as both the competition and the winners are episodic, and the sides are unstable.[7,8] Inspection of the responses of the girls which increase significantly between the third and

Table 2   Play and Game Items Which Differentiate Girls from Boys at Several Levels of Significance

Differentiating level	Items
All grade levels	
$p = .001$	Dolls, dressing-up, houses, store, school, church, actresses, stoop tag, ring around Rosy, London bridge, farmer in dell, in and out the windows, drop the handkerchief, mulberry bush, hop scotch, jump rope, jacks, Mother, may I?, dance, sewing, cooking, knit
$p = .01$	Actors, crochet
$p = .05$	Red rover, follow the leader, poor pussy, cartwheels
*Some grade levels**	
$p = .05$	I've got a secret (3, 5, 6), roller skating (3, 4, 5), pom pom pullaway (3), muffin man (3, 4, 6), spin the bottle (3, 4, 6), redlight (3, 5, 6), skating (3, 4, 5), draw or paint (3, 5, 6), seesaw (3, 4, 6), cat and mouse (4, 5, 6), puss in corner (4, 5), fox and geese (4, 5), frozen tag (4, 5, 6), huckle buckle (4, 5, 6), hoops (4, 5, 6), crack the whip (4, 5), leap frog (4, 5, 6), name that tune (4, 5, 6), hide the thimble (4, 5, 6), musical chairs (4, 5, 6), statues (4, 5, 6), here I come (4, 5, 6), what time is it (4, 5, 6), pick up sticks (4, 6), scrapbook (4), collections (4, 5), build snowmen (4, 5, 6), clay modeling (4, 5, 6), blindman's bluff (5), wood tag (5, 6), squirrel in tree (5, 6), post office (5), checkers (5), puzzles (5), black magic (5, 6), doctors (6), hide and seek (6), colors (6), dog and bone (6), tiddley-winks (6)

* The grade level(s) are indicated in parentheses after each item.

fourth grades reveals that these responses involve both levels of maturity and are divided almost equally masculine and feminine items.

Thus, the girls show increased preference for the immature masculine items (bandits, soldiers, cowboys, cops and robbers, bows and arrows, toy trains). At the same time, they show increased preference for the relatively mature masculine items (marbles, basketball, boxing, soccer, baseball, skiing, boating). Again, during this period, girls show not only increased preference for the simple feminine pastimes (pom pom pullaway, hoops, black magic, I spy, statues, here I come, what time is it?), but also for the more mature and

Table 3 Number of Items Showing Significant Increases or Decreases in Preference Between Grades for Each Sex*

	Boys				Girls			
	3-4	4-5	5-6	3-6	3-4	4-5	5-6	3-6
Increases in masculine items	8	—	3	8	15	3	1	18
Decreases in masculine items	—	4	3	5	—	1	—	—
Increases in feminine items	6	—	—	5	14	1	—	6
Decreases in feminine items	4	5	19	29	3	6	16	19
Increases in neutral items	14	1	2	16	12	—	1	17
Decreases in neutral items	—	—	—	—	—	—	—	2
Totals								
Increase	28	1	5	29	41	4	2	41
Decrease	4	9	22	34	3	7	16	21

* $p = .05$.

complex feminine games and activities (bingo, crochet, skating). There are indeed some masculine items for which the girls show increasing preference (bandits, cowboys) at the very time the boys are showing decreasing preference for the same items. Though it should be pointed out that, while the trends for the preferences are in opposite directions, there are still great differences between the sexes in their respective percentages of interest. For example, from the third to the sixth grade, the percentage of boys expressing a liking for bandits drops from 87 to 61 percent, whereas the percentage of girls liking bandits increases from 29 to 39 percent. For cowboys, likewise, boys' preferences decrease from 94 to 73 percent, while the girls' preferences increase from 34 to 52 percent. As these continued differences between the boys and girls are typical, we should not exaggerate the extent to which girls become like boys, even though they do become more like them than before. Boys' increases from the third to fourth grade, on the other hand, are without exception for male items of only the second and more mature game and activities categories (e.g., shooting, horse riding, boating, soccer, darts) and for a few feminine items also of the more mature level (e.g., dance, skating, checkers). In sum, the greater responsiveness of girls in the fourth grade is produced by their choice of both masculine and feminine items on both levels of maturity.

In the fifth and sixth grades there is a reversal of the trend which occurred between the third and fourth grades. Instead of a marked expansion of preferences for items on the scale, there is a marked contraction. Between the fourth and fifth grades, there are 16 significant decreases and only five increases. Between the fifth and sixth grades, there are 38 decreases and only seven increases. For boys there are no great changes in their preferences for the male items already established in the fourth grade, but there are 19 significant decreases in their preferences for female items. For girls also, changes through the fifth and sixth grades involve mainly decreases of interest in female items. There are 16 such decreases. Thus, while the pattern of girls' choices was dissimilar to that of boys in the fourth grade, in the fifth and sixth grades it shows considerable similarity. A further test of these changes was made possible by a two-phase longitudinal study involving the masculine-feminine scales derived from the play scale.[10] Scores were available for a group of children in the fourth grade and for the same children in the fifth grade. Similarly, there were scores available for a group in the fifth grade and subsequently in the sixth grade. In this study, there was a significant decrease in the girls' scores on the femininity scale between the fourth and fifth grades ($t = 2.59$, $p = .05$), but no other significant changes for boys and girls. This finding is consistent with the present inquiry, but limited by the much smaller number of items used in the Mf scale and the fact that it was standardized only on the fourth through sixth grades. This study is reported more fully elsewhere.[6]

The present data do not show the fifth grade or the sixth grade as a turning point towards greater femininity as some writers have suggested. If there is such a trend, it is not revealed by any changes in children's responses to play items. There is rather an accelerated decrease in responses to feminine items. As we shall note in the discussion, this lack of change towards increased preference for feminine items at the fifth grade is most probably attributable to the nature of the items.

DISCUSSION

While the results of this study document the changes that occur in children's play and game preferences, there are certain important limitations to drawing broader conclusions from them. From puberty onwards, playing games and sports is predominantly a masculine phenomenon in this culture. Boys proceed from pastimes into games, but girls by comparison do not. Games and sports are positively associated with the male sex role, but negatively associated with the female sex role.[4] The marked changes in play preferences at the age of 8 to 9 years which have been recorded here are an indication, we believe, of children's dawning awareness of this fact. The boys' shedding of pastimes and their increased interest in sports would seem to indicate such a change in attitude. The generalized choices of the girls are, however, something of a puzzle. If, at the age of 9, they perceive that games are not to be of great importance in their future feminine role, the reasons for their increased responsiveness to many items on this scale are not immediately apparent. While this undirected responsiveness can be interpreted as a sign of confusion, it can be argued with some cogency that this responsiveness is rather an indication of greater role flexibility. Thus, the boys' specialization can be seen as a response to a clear-cut role prescription, the girls' diversity as a response to a lack of such prescription. The girls are free to choose in whatever way they wish, and they do so in much more idiosyncratic terms than the boys. It can be argued, for example, that those girls who increase their responses to the more immature Mf items may well be expressing a response to the domestic aspects of the female role, which involve playing with younger children, being interested in them and nurturing them, or at the very least, not being defensive about this when called upon to do it. It can be argued also that girls who show greater interest in mature masculine items may be merely more active, for which only masculine items are appropriate; or that they may be acting as tomboys which girls are free to do; or that they may be showing an awareness that, although girls may not be as generally participants in boys' sports, they are expected to be interested in them as part of their adolescent sex partner role.

Yet despite all these arguments, there is evidence from associated research by these authors[5] that the fourth grade period is one of peak anxiety for girls (as measured by the Children's Manifest Anxiety Scale) and that this is significantly related to girls' perceiving themselves as "tomboys" rather than "little ladies" at this age level (items from the Juddenham sociometric[18]). After the fourth grade, however, those girls who show a trend away from tomboyish sociometric attributions towards ladylike attributions are the ones who show a decrease in anxiety. This is perhaps not an unnatural finding as relations have earlier been demonstrated between the CMAS and sex role identification.[14] This evidence certainly raises the question as to whether the girls' more generalized responsiveness at the fourth grade level is a product of greater role flexibility or is actually a defense against a sex role anxiety that occurs at that time. Such anxiety would presumably have its source in the lack of prescription for girls' activities and in the greater prestige given to the activities of boys.[1]

SUMMARY

A play inventory of 180 items was administered to approximately 1900 children in 12 midwestern townships in grades 3 to 6. The responses were subjected to chi-square treatment for sex differences and differences between the grades. The results indicate that girls are more responsive to the items on this inventory than are boys and also show an increasing interest in masculine items throughout these grades. The major part of these changes occur between the third and fourth grades. At this time, boys show an increasing interest mainly for the more mature items, whereas girls show an increased interest in both immature and mature masculine and feminine items. There is no evidence of a change back towards an increased preference for feminine items during the fifth grade. It is suggested that, if this occurs in other aspects of girls' behavior, it may not occur with play activities because these are negatively related to the female sex role. The present paper does not contribute definite evidence as to whether or not the generalized responses of the girls at the fourth grade are an index of sex role confusion at that time, although this possibility is indicated.

NOTES

1. Brown, D. G., "Sex role preference in young children," *Psychol. Monogr.,* 1956, 70, No. 14.

2. Gray, S. W., "Perceived similarity to parents and adjustment," *Child Development,* 1959, 30, 91-107.

3. Hartley, R. E., "Children's concepts of male and female roles," *Merrill-Palmer Quart.,* 1960, 6, 83-91.

4. Moss, H. A., and Kagan, J., "Stability of achievement and recognition seeking behaviors from early childhood through adulthood," *J. Abnorm. Soc. Psychol.,* 1961, 62, 504-513.

5. Morgan, E., Rosenberg, B. G., and Sutton-Smith, B., "Anxiety as a function of change in sex role," paper presented at Midwest. Psychol. Assn., Chicago, May 5, 1961.

6. Morgan, E., Sutton-Smith, B., and Rosenberg, B. G., "Age changes in the relation between anxiety and achievement," *Child Development,* 1960, 31, 515-519.

7. Roberts, J. M., Arth, M. J., and Bush, R. R., "Games in culture," *Amer. Anthrop.,* 1959, 61, 597-605.

8. Roberts, J. M., and Sutton-Smith, B., "Child training and game involvement," *Ethnology,* 1962, 1, 166-185.

9. Rosenberg, B. G., and Sutton-Smith, B., "The measurement of masculinity and femininity in children," *Child Development,* 1959, 30, 373-380.

10. Rosenberg, B. G., and Sutton-Smith, B., "A revised conception of masculine-feminine differences in play activities," *J. Genet. Psychol.,* 1960, 96, 165-170.

11. Rosenberg, B. G., Sutton-Smith, B., and Morgan, E., "The use of opposite sex scales as a measure of psychosexual deviancy," *J. Consult. Psychol.,* 1961, 25, 221-225.

12. Sutton-Smith, B., *The Games of New Zealand Children,* University of California Press, 1959.

13. Sutton-Smith, B., and Rosenberg, B. G., *Play and Game List,* Bowling Green State University, IBM Form I.T.S. 1100 A 6140.

14. Sutton-Smith, B., and Rosenberg, B. G., "Manifest anxiety and game preferences in children," *Child Development,* 1960, 31, 515-519.

15. Sutton-Smith, B., and Rosenberg, B. G., "Impulsivity and sex preference," *J. Genet. Psychol.,* 1961, 98, 187-192.

16. Sutton-Smith, B., and Rosenberg, B. G., "Sixty years of historical change in the game preferences of American children," *J. Amer. Fokl.,* 1961, 74, 17-46.

17. Tryon, C. M., "Evaluations of adolescent personality by adolescent," *Monogr. Soc. Res. Child Develpm.,* 1939, 4, No. 4 (Serial No. 23).

18. Tuddenham, R. D., "Studies in reputation: III. Correlates of popularity among elementary school children," *J. Educ. Psychol.,* 1951, 42, 257-276.

THE SPORTSWOMAN IN OUR SOCIETY

Dorothy V. Harris

Why is it that sports participation generally is not considered a very worthwhile or exciting experience for girls? Can we logically explain why sports make up such a small part of the lifetime activities of most women? What is the effect of sports participation on the psychological and social development of females? Does competition have a positive or negative effect on the female? In short, what role does participation in physical activities play in the development of the behavior patterns of girls and women?

While a review of the literature produced no evidence to support the notion that active participation in competitive sports may harm the healthy female, there appears to be an unwritten decree that only certain sports have a desirable effect on the feminine image. Stereotypes, prejudices, and misconceptions have served to curtail the participation of females in vigorous, competitive physical activities for too many years.

Dorothy V. Harris, "The Sportswoman in Our Society," *DGWS Research Reports: Women in Sports,* Washington: American Association for Health, Physical Education, and Recreation, 1971, Chapter 1. Reprinted by permission.

One of the main criticisms is that sports participation tends to masculinize the behavior of girls; however, there is no evidence of this. The traits necessary for high-level participation often correspond to the traits that are admirable in the male: aggressiveness, tough-mindedness, dominance, self-confidence, and the willingness to take risks. Yet these same qualities are often necessary for the female to be successful in competitive life situations. Nevertheless, the young woman who participates in physical activities risks her feminine image. The stereotype frequently associated with females who enjoy vigorous activity poses such a threat that participants bend over backwards to counteract it. Examples can be seen in numerous situations: the blond, bouffant, sprayed hairdos of female track teams, the ruffles on the tennis outfits, the mod apparel worn by many women golfers; the ski togs that flatter the feminine figure, the fancy swim caps and suits, etc. All of these artifacts of femininity assist in reducing the threat of sports participation to the revered feminine image.

In spite of such efforts, the "girl jock" or the "Amazon" stereotype persists, particularly when a female chooses to participate in vigorous physical activity. In this case, she is "laying on the line" everything she represents as a female much the same as the first gal to smoke in public, or the first to appear in public wearing pants, or the first to join a profession that had been the sole domain of the male. The female who has the courage of her convictions and no doubts about her femininity is still taking a risk when she wins a tennis match from her male opponent or dares to out-perform any male whether it be in athletics, business, or a predominantly male profession. Athletics, especially competitive sports, are still primarily the prerogative of the male in our society. In general, females who take the risk and participate in such sports are either secure in their role as a female so that participation does not strike them as a threat, or they do not care, and thus have "nothing to lose." It is those in the latter category who have produced the stereotype of the "girl jock." These females can be observed in almost any competitive situation.

For most females, the avoidance of all participation in physical activities becomes the easiest route to follow. Once little girls become aware of the "socially acceptable" feminine image, the majority choose to conform, hiding behind the claim that it isn't "ladylike" to play. However, many are actually afraid of the risk, of discovering that they cannot meet the threats involved.

Whether or not a particular sport is considered feminine depends mostly on the point of view of the beholder. Since the feminine image, or what is considered feminine, is determined by the male population, educating them with regard to the values and rewards of participation for both sexes would appear to be a logical next step. It is inconceivable that anyone would want to make the joy of participation in physical activity accessible only to males, yet for the most part that has been the accepted pattern.

Among the biggest problems faced by the girl who chooses to become involved in physical activity is that of not being understood. Most people still do not think athletics and girls go together. Lendon H. Smith, the pediatrician who wrote the best seller, *Your Child and Mine,* expressed his concern in this manner in his *McCall's* magazine column: "I worry about a girl becoming a great athlete—especially a runner. She might run so fast she'd never get caught by a boy." In the same way a suburban mother watches her 16-year-old daughter easily win the 400 meters race and worries about her femininity. She is afraid that her daughter will like the idea of winning and never attract a boy because of her interest in track.

Sports Illustrated reported in an article on cross-country skiing that the interest in this type of skiing had grown very slowly among women partly because most Americans have a warped concept of the femininity of the sport. Martha Rockwell, one of the young women training for the U.S. cross-country team, said, "No boy likes a girl with biceps. The only problem with any of this [training for cross-country skiing] is that you just have to wait for a boy who loves to run before you get a very active social life. Most of them don't understand what we're doing."

Willye White, a U.S. long-jumper, said that "If a girl is feminine, anything she does is feminine." The coach of the Tennessee Tigerbelles, Ed Temple, feels that his track stars are young ladies first and athletes second. He is a firm advocate of the philosophy that "girls should be girls" and they should be willing to concede long-term sports participation to the male. He suggests that his girls hang up their track shoes after college.

Sportswriters have done nothing to change this attitude of disrespect for the female athlete; if anything, they have perpetuated it. After watching the U.S. Women's Olympic Track Team work out in Mexico City, a prominent Dutch sportswriter said, "Girls are for laughs, no? Not for sports." John Pennel, the good-looking pole-vaulter, said, "If a woman is really grunting and groaning and sweating, how can she be feminine?" Traditionally, men have been unimpressed by women's athletic ability, and have had little appreciation for the skill and beauty of movement women exhibit as they compete in sports. Even though society encourages exercise, the dedicated girl athlete faces many obstacles. Lack of understanding on the part of men is paramount; they do not understand why any girl would want to become an athlete and sacrifice time from the activities they feel girls should be involved in.

Some sportswomen quietly withdraw from the mainstream of social life. A college psychology teacher who is also a physical education instructor recently suggested that many good female athletes are almost pre-adolescent because of their narrow interests and their uncomfortable feeling around boys who are not active in sports. She suggested further that they frequently are over-devoted to their fathers and are domestic in quaint, old-fashioned ways. Underneath, she contends, they are insecure "little girls." Supporting data for these conclusions were not given, however. This type of comment is a rather sweeping generalization and there are many examples that do not fit.

Now that we are beginning to study the female athlete and the effects of participation so that we will have a greater understanding of these experiences, what about all of the girls who do not participate or who are eliminated from the teams? If we find that there are many values to be derived from participation, shouldn't we give all of our students the benefit of these experiences? Ogilvie shared some concerns about competition in a paper presented at the University of California at Los Angeles in March 1969. He found in working with young competitors that those who have the greatest need for these experiences are the ones who are being excluded. These youngsters are the least inclined to be emotionally stable, are introverted and sensitive, lack tough-mindedness, and tend to over-respond to failure. He raised a rather profound question when he asked, "Are most competitive programs really constructed to enhance the positiveness of people who are already well put together emotionally?" It appears that the youngsters who have the most to gain from the experiences of competition have the least possibility of being a part of competitive programs. We need to reconsider our value system if we are promoting a situation where only the "rich get richer" while we fail to serve the needs of the majority.

At present, without question, athletic opportunities for female participation have increased; more girls are participating and are doing so more frequently. A revolution in attitudes concerning athletic competition for girls has begun in spite of all the problems involved. It will be some time before society accepts the girl athlete as readily as her brother, but genuine concern on the part of each and every individual interested in physical activity will speed up this acceptance. We have the opportunity to test the values derived from participation when we provide competitive experiences for all skill levels. Until then, we cannot evaluate the outcomes of these experiences without bias.

REFERENCES

Blyth, Myrna, "Girl Athletes: What Makes Them Skate, Fence, Swim, Jump, Run?" *Cosmopolitan,* Nov. 1969.

Cheska, Alyce, "Current Developments in Competitive Sports for Girls and Women," *Journal of Health, Physical Education, Recreation,* 41:86-91, March 1970.

Maccoby, Eleanor E., "Woman's Intellect," in Seymour M. Farber and Roger H. S. Wilson (eds.), *The Potential of Woman,* New York: McGraw-Hill Book Co., 1963.

Ogilvie, Bruce C., "The Unanswered Question: Competition, Its Effect Upon Femininity," address to Olympic Development Committee at Santa Barbara, Calif., June 30, 1967.

Phillips, Madge, "Women in Sport: Socio-Culture," address to the National Convention of American Association for Health, Physical Education, and Recreation at Boston, Mass., April 1969.

Ulrich, Celeste, "The Land O' The Leal," address to Division of Girls' and Women's Sports Convention on Sports Programs for College Women at Estes Park, Colo., June 1969.

———, "Bio-Psychological Aspects of Play and Sport for Girls and Women," address to the American Association for the Advancement of Science Symposium at Dallas, Texas, Dec. 1968.

Weiss, Paul, *Sport: A Philosophic Inquiry,* Carbondale, Ill.: Southern Illinois University Press, 1969.

FEMALES IN THE COMPETITIVE PROCESS

Carolyn Wood Sherif

I am a female; one of the some nine percent of all full professors who are female; one of the five percent females among those in this country who earn $10,000 or more a year (which includes all those rich widows) (Bird, 1971); one of about 42 percent of women Ph.D.'s who is married and has children; and I learned recently in an official publication of the American Psychological Association that I am among some 130 or so women in the country who call themselves social psychologists. I guess that I must be a competitive woman, and that is a "bad" thing to admit.

If you are feeling magnanimous, you can ease my confession by pointing out that I am an exception. Factually, you are quite correct. I raise the issue because each of us, by admitting an exception, is referring to more than

Carolyn Wood Sherif, "Females in the Competitive Process," in Dorothy V. Harris (Ed.), *Women and Sport: A National Research Conference,* Penn State HPER Series No. 2, The Pennsylvania State University, 1972.

statistical fact. Our feelings of discomfiture reflect the widespread conviction that females in our highly competitive and individualistic culture do not compete, that it is unfeminine to compete, and therefore probably either unattractive or abnormal. An exception merely confirms this stereotyped view or, if we happen to like or admire the exception, suggests that the woman in question has some unique ability that other mortals do not possess.

The logic in how we deal with exceptions reminds me of a story told at another research conference by Professor Otto Klineberg. It seems that a man was convinced that he was dead. His family offered all possible evidence to the contrary and finally took him to a psychiatrist. The psychiatrist also tested the belief, to no avail. Almost despairing, the psychiatrist suddenly thought of an ultimate test. "Listen," he said, "do dead men bleed?" "No, of course not," replied the man. The psychiatrist seized his hand and pierced it with a letter opener, saying, "You see, you bleed, so you can't be dead." The man looked at the blood as if he could not believe his eyes. "What do you know," he muttered. "Dead men *do* bleed!"

Contrary to the stereotyped notion, I am convinced that females do compete. The conditions of our culture are such that many compete in different ways, for different ends and with different standards than males, particularly after childhood. My reading of the research literature has strongly convinced me that, by and large, we have conceptualized the problem in ways such that our research methods tell us very little about what we want to know and what we need to know, if our intention is practical methods for developing human potentiality through sports, or anything else for that matter. My remark applies to competitive processes involving males as well, some of who are telling us today, I think, that prevalent methods are not contributing much to their well-being either.

Lest you think my stance too extreme, let us note that I am not alone. In her book on *Psychology of Women,* Bardwick (1971) inserted a footnote relating the reaction of her colleagues to seminars on that topic. "There is no psychology of women," they exclaimed, to which she replied, "There will be." Or, consider the jolt I received when reading an article by a young Harvard Ph.D., Naomi Weisstein (1971), with the title "Psychology constructs the female, or the fantasy life of the male psychologist." Its central thesis was as follows: "Psychology has nothing to say about what women are really like, what they need and what they want, essentially because psychology does not know" (p. 70). I have to admit that Dr. Weisstein is correct, but add that in the scattered literature on sex differences, social development and social processes, we can glean and assemble material to answer certain more specific questions.

My thesis and the directions it will take us can be summed up briefly: In one sense all normal human beings compete after early childhood, even in societies where individualistic competition for recognition is not prized as it is in our society. Research on competition often misleads us by identifying the directions, the standards, the goals, and the realistic circumstances that limit goal achievement with competition itself. Competition is not a specific kind of behavior; it is not a unitary motive aimed unerringly at certain specific goals; it is not a specific standard or level of performance.

Competition is a *social process* that occurs when the person's activities are directed more or less consistently toward meeting a standard or achieving a goal in which performance, either by the individual or by the group, is compared and evaluated relative to that of selected other persons or groups. Females are part of such processes every day—whether their activities are toward serving better food than other members of their club; enhancing their appearance; getting the most desirable husband; having a cleaner house; doing a better job in office or factory; improving their ability to get along with other people; contributing to the progress of their club, bowling team, political party; sewing a fine seam; or accommodating themselves with the greatest submission to the plans and desires of husbands, hence being an "ideal wife." If these kinds of competition have not been studied much, the fact certainly tells something about the social sciences, namely that they are not interested in studying such activities. It does not tell us that women are noncompetitive.

Perhaps I can clarify what I mean by saying competition is social process by referring to cooperation, which is often taken as the polar opposite of competition. In fact, cooperation refers to the structure of *activity,* not to specific behaviors at all. Cooperation can occur whenever there is division of tasks or labor in an activity to which individuals contribute differently for a common end. The fact that this is so is readily seen when we consider that no one can cooperate alone. Sport teams, for example, have to cooperate in order to play the game, and they have to cooperate in some degree with another team in order to compete (Lüschen, 1970).

Competition, as I have defined it, does not require the presence of others, as a person can direct activities toward meeting a standard or achieving a goal that she sets herself, as in practicing a skill; but it is still a social process. Such rehearsal implies the evaluation of behavior by other persons or groups, and the standards tend to reflect those set by important reference persons or groups. Cheating at solitaire is cheating because it violates the rules by which others evaluate performance in the game. To the extent that such evaluations are totally lacking, the process ceases to be competitive. However, the evaluation or comparison of performance in competition is not made by just *any* other person, but by *selected* persons, who may be official judges or referees, members of a peer group, or power figures who are capable of handing out the goodies for meeting or exceeding the standard.

If competition is, as I have stated, a social process rather than specific forms of behavior, it follows that to study females competing, we have to study female behavior in the context of other persons who are competitors, standard-setters, judges or evaluators, and even determiners of what activities are valuable enough to the person that she does compete. Very little research of this kind has done so, particularly where females are concerned.

Thanks to Dr. Smith's paper on females and aggression, I do not cover the research in that area, which in any case is appropriately related to competition only under certain circumstances and in certain kinds of activities. All competition is not exemplified by the movie clips now on television showing the gorgeous body of Raquel Welch roller skating in a race with another gorgeous body, while simultaneously in the process of committing mayhem.

EARLY CHILDHOOD WITHOUT COMPETITION

As consistent patterns of activity directed toward competitive performance, competition is simply nonexistent in infancy and early childhood. The genetic code predetermines differences between the sexes before birth, and these include structural and biochemical differences that could affect competition in specific kinds of activities or at different developmental periods. However, girl and boy babies are altogether equal in one respect: both are incapable of competition.

I may add that, at present, there are not sufficient data available to connect genetic differences with very much of the behavioral variation in infancy, according to Maccoby, who has surveyed studies of infants comparing the sexes (1966; revision in progress). Even more seriously, as she points out (1972), the few differences suggested by available data are linked to social behavior in later childhood only by the most tenuous theoretical leaps, and with great difficulties owing to differences in measures and research methods used at different ages. For example, Maccoby has spelled out the tenuous evidence, in some cases lack of support, for data summaries presented by Bardwick (1971) in tabular form as support for the supposedly greater sensitivity of six-month girls to stimulation. Bardwick attributes the supposed greater sensitivity of older girls to social stimuli to this shaky evidence, and finally the supposedly superior empathy, imaginativeness and fantasy life of women. Unfortunately, the infant data do not even support clear sex differences at six months. For such reasons, I believe that at present we are on very shaky grounds when assigning genetic determination to the few fairly well documented sex differences in social behavior of infants, namely the trend toward more aggressive activities by boys and greater dependence of girls (Maccoby, 1966). Data on parental treatment clearly indicate that differential learning experiences are also involved, a fact which in itself does not vitiate genetic accounts. However, the linkage between the sorts of childhood behaviors assigned these labels and important kinds of adult aggression or dependency relationships is so weak as to cast doubt on the usefulness of the knowledge beyond childhood anyway.

The best longitudinal comparisons of the same individuals from birth through adulthood that bear on competitive behavior come from the Fels Research Institute's study from 1929 to 1959 comparing various measures of achievement and of recognition (Moss and Kagan, 1961). Significant though not impressively large correlations with adolescent or adult ratings appear with measures taken in the age ranges we would expect on the basis of other evidence, namely 6-10 years for boys and somewhat earlier for girls. As the measures were heavily weighted for intellectual activities, the somewhat earlier ages for girls are in line with the early sex differences in cognitive development favoring girls. Perhaps I should add that the well-known Terman study of genius also studied boys and girls through adulthood, reporting a relationship for men between IQ and adult achievement occupationally and professionally, but not for women, for reasons that should be too obvious to belabor.

Observations of children's play reveal at first a predominance of side-by-side activity (once the baby gets over the discovery that other children have eyes and mouths) then parallel play before simple role playing and rule following occur (Parten, 1932-33; Salusky, 1930). Competition, however, involves the child's experience of her own performance, the performance of others, and their relationship in a single pattern. This complex attainment requires, as Piaget (1932) pointed out, the ability to compare oneself to others, as well as to appreciate rules of conduct that govern winning or losing, success in some degree, or failure.

According to several studies in different countries, children do not exhibit consistent patterns of competitiveness until around age four, with middle-class American children competing somewhat earlier than working-class children (e.g., Greenberg, 1932; Leuba, 1933; Hirota, 1953). As concrete evidence that competitiveness is not the bipolar opposite of cooperativeness, note in addition that just at this time (around 3-5 years) cooperative play becomes a predominant form (Parten, 1933; Salusky, 1930), consistent patterns of cooperativeness are reported (Berne, 1930), and children begin to respond consistently and appropriately with sympathy to others in distress (Murphy, 1937). Somewhat later, children begin to be consistently responsible for their own behavior and, by five or six, to set fairly consistent standards for their own performance (Gesell and Ilg, 1943; Goodenough, 1952).

To add to the apparent mystery, it is around 4-5 years of age that children in settings that discriminate by skin color also start to make invidious comparisons according to skin color (Clark and Clark, 1947; Goodman, 1952). Their gender identity, which Money (1970) believes is established in rudimentary form well before three years, is also becoming elaborated into rather consistently feminine and masculine patterns of behavior (Murphy, 1947), including preference in toys and games (e.g., Sutton-Smith *et al.*, 1963) in which boys tend to be more masculine than girls are feminine.

What does all of this mean? It means that competition, like a host of other social-psychological processes, develops only with age, in which the child's conceptual development as well as his experiences are basic (Piaget, 1952). Such consistencies are signs of the developing self system—a system of interrelated attitudes linking the person conceptually and emotionally to others, to activities, objectives and concepts in the social world (Sherif and Cantril, 1947).

CONSISTENCIES AND DISCONTINUITIES FROM CHILDHOOD THROUGH ADOLESCENCE

The search for *patterns* in behavior consistencies in a variety of respects is, I believe, the only hope for making sense out of research data focused on behavior in more specific respects, such as competitive activities. Such conjunction of evidence on consistent patterns of behavior constitutes the basis for the concept of a self system, which is aroused situationally and regulates activities through selective perception and attention, giving the directionality, heightened intensity and focus that are typical of any motivated behavior (*cf.* Sherif and Sherif, 1969, Chapter 19).

The formation of the self system in early childhood is enormously accelerated and forever afterward transformed by the acquisition of language. As a system of rules and categories for differentiating among stimulus events and contrasting their differences, on one hand, and for defining similarities through assimilating slight differences, on the other, language also bears heavy loads of cultural value defining what is self and not self, what one should and should not be, what activities and objects are more and less desirable for one's self and what are definitely to be avoided. With language acquisition, the self system is transformed into a categorical system for relating self and social world, the categories both defining self-other relationships and becoming ranked or structured in terms of their priority or importance.

It is precisely these features—*viz.* the interrelationships among different aspects of the self system and their priorities within the system—that make the problem of social motivation so extraordinarily difficult and complex. For one thing, these features change over time, so that the physical maturation and social transitions of adolescence or aging alter both the relationships and the priorities of various aspects of the self system. In addition, at different ages and times, society itself presents different opportunities and demands upon the person.

Unless we tackle these problems, I believe that theory and research on the development of motives related to competition, achievement, recognition, and the like are bound to remain a hopeless muddle. In the process, we have to recognize the extent to which sex comparisons are simply flooded by mythology.

Two such myths can be typified with reference to Sigmund Freud, who by no means originated them, but who is identified with them owing in part to his capacity for synthesizing and the extraordinary clarity of his writing. The first myth that has permeated many quarters of society through Freudian influences revolves around presumed pathology in female development. Such attribution is only a bit more sophisticated than simple declaration that women are inferior. Freud himself was very frank in such attribution, which he blamed on biology, even though he still confessed that women remained a mystery to him.

Recently, research on personal traits rated by both college students (Rosencrantz *et al.*, 1968) and by clinicians with degrees in psychiatry or psychology (Broverman *et al.*, 1970) as typical of males and females yielded convincing evidence of the prevalence of the myth of pathology. Males were accorded the most favorable traits by both students and clinicians who, incidentally, did not disagree seriously. Females were pictured by a cluster of traits which, while containing a few redeeming positive traits of the kind we assign even to our worst enemies, can only be characterized as pathological. Both men and women characterized women as tending to be *not at all* resourceful, intellectual, competent, or realistic and being immature, subjective, submissive, easily influenced and wracked with inferiority feelings.

It is disturbing that the myth is so readily accepted by women; however, that merely shows how readily females learn the prevalent cultural myths. Apparently, the readiness with which the myth is accepted has very little to do with actual events in early childhood that are supposed to lead to pathology. It is very much related to social role learning by female children through observation and value dictums. Hartly (1970) reports that both boys and girls, ages 8–11, painted a very conservative picture of what women do and are supposed to do, even when their own mothers were working. Similarly, American men agree that marriage and children are the most important aspects of a woman's life, although they are considerably more generous in assessing their ideal woman than American women anticipate they will be. For example, men rejected a subservient woman and accepted activity, creativity, and equality of female opinions (Steinman and Fox, 1966).

Couple the pathological image with the fact that many instruments, particularly the so-called projective tests, are highly susceptible to biased interpretation. Without labels on the cases, qualified clinical judges cannot differentiate accurately test results produced by psychotics or neurotics from normals (Little and Schneidman, 1959) or homosexuals as compared to heterosexuals (Hooker, 1957). We have a situation in which a great deal of sand can be thrown in a great many eyes. This pathological and negative view of women continues even though by almost all social indicators of disturbance (including suicide, alcoholism, drug addiction, and crimes of violence), males lead the parade. Of course, the male statistics call forth floods of explanation in terms of specific pathologies in male development, but without affecting the basic splendor of the male image. Such speculative explanations do violence to males as well, since the probability of their being wrong is exceedingly high.

The second myth permeates social life far beyond psychology and psychiatry, for it insists that human personality is formed basically and irrevocably in very early childhood. Echoing Freud in assigning supreme importance to parental treatment during the very early years, this myth has produced a research literature focused on parent-child relationships to the exclusion of the rest of the social world that the child discovers very early.

I can illustrate the focus through the writing of a non-Freudian who is keenly sensitive to effects of social learning but, as noted earlier, committed to the basic premise of genetic and developmental continuity in personality development. In *The Psychology of Women,* Bardwick wrote: "Perceived in the most general way, the broad reactive tendencies of children, their original response proclivities to the world, seem to form a consistent life style, although specific behaviors will clearly reflect the sophistication and abilities of a particular stage of development. The extraverted, impulsive, motoric child will tend to continue to respond to the world that way—and such a child is not likely to engage in intellectual pursuits when he or she is older" (1971, p. 103) and so forth. Of course, in one sense, this statement tells us nothing specific, as it is framed "in the most general way" about "general reactive tendencies." In another sense, it tells us precisely where to look for solution to the puzzle of human personality, namely in infancy. Therefore, it effectively perpetuates the second myth without generally acceptable scientific evidence.

Such exclusive focus on early childhood ignores another whole body of data having to do with changes in physiological functioning and social roles during adolescence. Without embracing *other* myths about that period, for example, that it is always or necessarily a stormy crisis or rebellion against adults, we must recognize that adolescence involves body changes signaling the arrival of sexual maturity and in modern societies a prolonged transition from childhood to adult status as a full-fledged male or female. These changes require changes in the self system and confront the person with problems that can affect personality enormously. Furthermore, the adolescent period faces the girl or boy with some striking cultural discontinuities, in the sense that the relative importance of various activities for achievement, sexual behavior and conceptions of self as male or female are markedly different from those of childhood.

I know of no evidence that boys and girls differ in competitiveness during the period of so-called middle childhood (roughly the grade school years) except in what they readily compete *for.* Overall, in our culture, girls exceed boys in competing scholastically, while boys at this period compete more readily in active sport and games (Maccoby, 1966). However, despite these average trends, the great majority of boys are competing successfully in school (otherwise I suspect schools would be closed) and girls are by and large active physically, with their games including both male and female typed activities.

Sutton-Smith and Roberts (1970), reporting that games of skill tend to reflect the power structures and struggles of a culture, have ventured to predict that for this reason boys will be more likely to be involved in games of skill than girls, who they suggest are therefore more prone to games of chance. (Are there more female than male gamblers?) I believe that this extrapolation from cultural analysis to the social-psychological level of choice is apt to be an oversimplification. After all, tradition is a very strong force toward choice of male or female activities, and opportunity is another. I am reminded of a summer camp for boys in western Massachusetts where we conducted research a few summers ago. Even for 8–10 year olds and prominently for older boys, the favored sports were tennis and sailing. One simply has to appreciate the affluent upper-middle-class background of these boys to understand these choices. Similarly, in individual sports, opportunity for females is paramount within the bounds traditionally defined as feminine, which now include swimming and diving, figure skating, tennis and gymnastics.

No matter how smooth the middle childhood years may be, the bodily changes and increased growth rate before and after pubescence are, in themselves, powerful impetus for changing the self system. Such changes do not occur in isolation, for the young person is confronted on all sides from mass media, schools and example with images of the changes required in conception of self, increasingly toward adult maleness or femaleness.

It is very easy in describing the adolescent predicament of girls to exaggerate, and to fail to recognize the increasingly flexible, alternative patterns that may be available to individual girls. On the other hand, it is easy to emphasize the flexible alternatives to the point of neglecting the overriding fact that the image of the female and the future that are offered her are sexual and sexually linked, to the point that in the myth a future without marriage and children is a special hell reserved for the unattractive, noncompetitive, unachieving, miserable exceptions. As symbolic of what happens, we find in the research literature that the girl who was once active becomes absorbed in nonathletic contexts, her physical performance in running, jumping, and throwing levels off or drops from ages 12–16 (Horrocks, 1969, p. 445); both IQ and academic performance level off or decline during the same years that boys' levels are increasing, on the average (Horrocks, 1969; Kagan and Moss, 1960; Moss and Kagan, 1961); and she discards most of the unusual and/or "masculine" choices of occupations from her earlier childhood to focus on preparation for catching a mate (a competitive activity) and marriage, or preparing for those occupations defined as feminine or at least offering opportunities for female employment (Seward, 1946; Bird, 1968).

This is not a very attractive picture and, without the age specified, might sound like a decline due to aging. Of course, the girls are attractive as they bloom into sexual maturity, taking care of their appearance at least superficially and throwing themselves wholeheartedly into the activities of their peer world. They compete in matters that touch the heart of the psychological pocketbook. Like boys of their age or a little older, they are finding the people who are in the same boat as they and hence can really understand them—those in their own age range.

The exclusive focus on parents or nuclear family as a source of social learning and motivations is nowhere more absurd than during the adolescent period. Conversely, I believe that the genuine importance of the family constellation during adolescence can be understood better if viewed within the context of the adolescent's relationships with peer groups and related institutions. That is why, I believe, so much research investigating quite reasonable hypotheses about family relationships and adolescent behavior produces so few findings of interest. For example, it was quite reasonable to suppose that girls with older brothers might be more likely than girls only with older sisters to be committed to sport participation. Surely, interests expressed in the family are important in channeling adolescent interests. Yet Landers (1970) tested the sibling hypothesis and found it unsupported. He found that girls with *younger* sisters were underrepresented among college girls committed to sports but that older sisters or brothers or birth order had no important effect.

Some of our own research on adolescent girls with Kelly suggests that the best way to predict sports involvement is to observe who the girl regularly associates with in and out of school. In fact, this is also a pretty surefire way to predict many other behaviors at this time, such as participation in athletic booster clubs, school leadership activities and somewhat illegal participations with older boys after school hours (Sherif *et al.,* in press).

Research on peer culture indicates pretty clearly that for girls, joining the active sport enthusiasts is not exactly the best way to achieve recognition from other girls and especially boys. Such recognition goes to girls who are popular and are school leaders (e.g., Coleman, 1961). There are two strikes against every teacher or coach of sport activities insofar as they desire to involve adolescent girls in their programs. Research on adolescence with regard to aspirations for education and occupation also shows that the student composition of particular schools, the school programs and extra-curricular activities form a powerful pattern whose characteristics can together override the effects of parental direction, training and preference (Sherif and Sherif, 1964).

The importance of the peer associations is further shown in research on the various sources adolescents rely upon for advice and decisions. Of course, parents do have influence, particularly in those matters where their authority, financial resources or expertise as adults is of great importance (*cf.* Brittain, 1963; Gecas, 1972). However, where parental authority cannot intervene, or in matters where peer and parental standards differ but closely concern peer life, reference groups of peers come to be the most potent source of influence on adolescents' decisions (Kardel and Lesser, 1969; Thomas and Weigert, 1970; Emmerich *et al.*, 1971). Here, as in the entire area of adolescent behavior, the value of the activity in the self system is a crucial determinant of whose word will count. For this reason, the call of some researchers on achievement motivation (e.g., Moss and Kagan, 1961) for differentiation in terms of achievement for *what* is certainly appropriate.

It follows from this discussion that it is terribly important for an analysis of adolescent competition to know something about the specific brands of peer culture in which the male or female is immersed, for these do differ (e.g., Sherif and Sherif, 1964; Gottlieb, 1964; Coleman, 1961). It is equally important to know the specific reference groups of peers whose standards become so important in defining success or failure. Perhaps it is not really surprising that we know much more about reference groups of adolescent boys than we do girls (Sherif and Sherif, 1964, 1967), for boys' groups are sometimes associated with pressing social problems such as delinquency. What is surprising are the genuine contradictions reported in the literature about girls' groups.

For example, the California Growth Study (reported in Sherif and Cantril, 1947) presented sociometric data indicating that at the junior high school level, girls' informal groups of friends were more tightly knit and closed than those of boys of the same age. Yet Horrocks (1969) has reported that girls' associations were smaller and more transient, a conclusion that Bardwick echoes in her book (1971). On the other hand, contrary to the California study, there is considerable evidence that boys' groups from about 13-14 years of age are very closely knit and relatively stable through the high school years (*cf.* Sherif and Sherif, 1964).

In plain truth, we simply do not know enough about girls' friendships and groups to draw firm conclusions. Furthermore, the obvious fact that boys and girls form, at times, cross-sex groups of great importance to members has been virtually neglected. We do know that when adolescent girls have had very poor relationships with their families, their peer groups of other adolescents and young adults become utterly pivotal in maintaining their psychological identity as a person, as Konopka (1965) has related so compellingly in studies of unwed mothers and delinquent girls. The absence of such ties with a reference group, Konopka found, amounts to a spiral into pathology and even suicide.

Because female groupings are so important in affecting standards of activity and the relative importance of various activities to participants, I believe that the lack of research on female groups is the most serious gap in the literature. Their importance is attested by our own research (Sherif *et al.*, in press) in which we found that by observing girls' behavior and activities as they associated with each other, we could make quite accurate predictions about judgments made individually by group members outside of their groups and in situations where group membership was not mentioned at all. It is such impact of the person's group on individual behavior, even apart from the group's immediate influence, that makes the study of groups so significant psychologically.

Thus, I believe that research on sport offers a very important opportunity to study the structure and dynamics of female groups, including their relationship to competitive behavior. Such research would contribute signally to knowledge about females and sports and would help to fill a near void in the social-psychological research literature.

DYNAMICS OF COMPETITIVENESS AND ACHIEVEMENT MOTIVATION

My reading of the literature on achievement motivation in females convinces me that we can understand the competitive process only if we determine the priority of the activity in the self system, find *whose* standards count for the person in assessing performance and the level of that standard relative to what the person can accomplish. William James wrote years ago that success or failure was experienced in relative terms that could be expressed as a ratio between the person's actual performance and his pretensions or aspirations in that field of activity. Furthermore, observing that aspirations vary with the importance of the activity for the person, he noted that he cared a great deal what other psychologists thought of him as a psychologist but not a whit what Greek scholars thought about his proficiency in Greek.

Following James' insights, Kurt Lewin and others pursued research into conditions governing the setting of levels of aspiration and the experiences of success and failure (Lewin *et al.*, 1944). I will summarize some of the main findings with relevance for competition of females.

1. The level at which standards of performance are set is governed by standards prevailing in one's reference groups and relative to other groups with whom the reference group compares itself. For example, when female college students were told that their reference groups (in this case Christian or Jewish) tolerated less pain than a comparison group (Jews for the Christians, Christians for the Jews), the women responded by tolerating more pain than their counterparts who had not received such instructions, as though they

must prove the sturdiness of their reference group (Lambert, Libman and Poser, 1960). Instructions that their reference group could tolerate more pain also increased pain tolerance for Jewish women and had a phenomenal effect on the Christian women, as though they had been told "Go ahead, you're a winner!" If, on the other hand, the comparison offered is one of a group clearly above one's own, through expertise or skill in the task at hand, knowledge of performance by that comparison group leads to lowering one's own level of aspiration (Chapman and Volkmann, 1939; Hansche and Gilchrist, 1956). There is little doubt that in many activities the stereotyped notions of male vs. female abilities coupled with exclusively male examples of success produce a lowered level of aspiration for females, whether the activity be intellectual, mechanical, political, or athletic.

2.   When an activity is very important to the person, there is a tendency to maintain a fairly high and inflexible level of aspiration, even though actual performance fluctuates. Two possible consequences come to mind: First, this relative rigidity of aspiration level means that the person has to learn to tolerate the experience of failure as she competes and to persist in the activity despite it. Although speculative, my belief is that our training of females demands considerably less of them in this respect than the training of boys, who are expected to persist and try again in the face of temporary setbacks. Second, this rigidity of aspiration also occurs when one is personally involved with the performance of others, as witness the tears of female cheering sections when their team is losing. In a study I conducted several years ago, I found that mothers were particularly likely to invest themselves in high and rigid aspiration levels for their children's performance (reported in Sherif, 1948). Since females are in fact barred from achievement in a good variety of activities, I would expect them to be particularly prone to such vicarious competition and experiences of success or failure. The schoolteacher in the *Corn is Green* who was determined to get her young Welsh miner into the university is a good example.

3.   The effects of continuing experiences of success or failure have been documented, beginning with the research of Pauline Sears. When accustomed to success, a child is able to tolerate occasional failure without breaking up over it. But persistent experiences of failure to meet the expected standards means that almost every drop in performance is soul shattering. Over time, the aspiration level for performance is set lower and lower until pretensions may vanish altogether. This finding would seem to be particularly relevant for female competition in sports, especially if the female follows the trend from late childhood of stabilized or decreased performance levels while standards get higher because she is older. Of course, there is no irrevocable physical

reason why these decreases should have occurred, but if they have, the encouragement of sports competition has to take the ensuing experiences of failure into account. The same caution is urged in encouraging reentry of older women into activity programs.

The key concept in understanding level of aspiration and performance findings is the degree of personal involvement in the activity. Neglect of this concept has, I believe, produced one of the so-called puzzles in research findings on the achievement motive inspired by the conceptions of McLelland *et al.* (1953) and Atkinson (1958). The puzzle arose because the great bulk of research was conducted with men, which is not at all atypical when the world is viewed as a man's world and which it certainly is from the viewpoint of power, authority and the great social problems of our day. In brief, the puzzle arose when female subjects did not behave in the ways predicted by the theory and supported by research on males.

The achievement motive is postulated as a "stable, enduring personality characteristic" formed through experiences in early life that set the basic level of the motive. However, says the theory, in specific situations the effort that will be expended in an activity and the aspiration level set depends upon the motive being aroused, the probability that the person foresees of success, and how important the activity is to the person. Neglect of the last variable has been crucial to the so-called puzzle.

The puzzle was not that females revealed a lack in the achievement motive, for their responses in college samples were typically as high or higher than males. It was that these responses had very little to do with females' actual behavior or competitiveness in concrete situations. Much of the puzzle has turned out to hinge on the failure to specify the importance of the activity to the female. For example, educated Brazilian (Horner, 1970) and Filipino females (Licuanan, 1972) do compete when placed in achievement situations that arouse male competition, as do high-achieving American females when competition involves only other females (Lesser, Krawitz and Packard, 1963). Thus, individual differences in proneness to compete have to be studied relative to the degree of the individual's involvement in the activity at hand (*cf.* Stein *et al.,* 1971).

Working within the McClelland-Atkinson formulations, Matina Horner (1970) developed a new motive largely for females which presumably is also a "stable, enduring personality characteristic." The female's achievement motive, she said, is stifled by "fear of success." She presented brief story lines to college women, typified by the following: "After first-term finals, Anne finds herself at the top of her medical school class." Males received the same verbal lead, except that John was substituted for Anne. Then she assessed the achievement motive through the Thematic Apperception Test (TAT), which involves telling a story about pictures presented to the subject. The assumption is that their fantasy in the story is a projection of their motives, in this case the achievement motive. She found, however, that about 65 percent of the females, as compared with less than 10 percent of the males, told stories that simply could not be scored as achievement motivation. One group of such stories included social rejection and unhappiness for Anne; another group dubbed Anne abnormal, neurotic or physically unattractive; a third group denied that the story line was true, by absolving Anne of responsibility ("it was luck"), inventing a male who got higher grades, or regarding Anne as a hoax created by medical students to fool their instructor. Horner further studied the reactions of students whose fear of success scores put them in the upper or lower fourth of the distribution by assessing their performance in noncompetitive situations and in situations involving competition with males. Those who scored higher in fear of success performed better in a noncompetitive situation (13 out of 17 women), while those who scored low performed better in the competitive situation (12 out of 13). In addition, however, those who scored high in fear of success imagery also rated the importance of doing well on the tasks as less than those who scored low in fear of success.

Horner's findings are both important and provocative; however, I must confess doubts about the usefulness of positioning another motive such as fear of success. Horner says females learn that competition in traditionally male activities is widely believed to require sacrifice of feminine attractiveness and sex appeal that attracts males. Add to that the documented fact that success in medical school is sufficiently demanding to require sacrifice of many other activities and is unlikely for females in the United States owing to barriers placed on entrance (Rossi, 1965). You have, I think, stories about Anne that merely reflect acceptance of prevailing stereotypes about women who succeed in the medical field and recognition of the improbability of the story. The females who responded may not have feared success, but have accepted the cultural truism that you can't have your cake and eat it too.

Related evidence suggests that the female responses interpreted as fear of success may be reflections of such stereotyped views of female achievement. Studies show that identical written passages or abstract paintings are rated higher when attributed to a male (John) than to a female (Joan) (Goldberg, 1968; Peterson et al., 1971). Horner's findings might, therefore, be explained most parsimoniously by the statement that females who accept stereotyped conceptions of male superiority reveal those conceptions in stories by attributing other kinds of failure to successful females or denying the success as an improbable event. Owing to their stereotype, they neither regard activities involving competition with males as so important nor do they try to perform well in competition with males.

A CRITICAL VIEW OF RESEARCH METHODS

Despite disclaimers to the contrary, the entire line of research that relies upon the TAT or similar projective tests for measurement of competitiveness or achievement motives is open to criticism based on the fact that reliability of the measures is distressingly low (Entwisle, 1972). What this means is that measures obtained at different times or based on different pictures are not highly correlated, suggesting that persons are responding to specific features in the different research situations rather than revealing their motives.

Now I should not like to suggest that the more or less enduring attitudes and motives of the person are not important. Nevertheless, the highly individual-centered ideology of our culture contains a pitfall, *viz.* our tendency to rectify the importance of personality measures when, in fact, all they can do is indicate some consistencies in response in given situations. The remedy is not to throw out personality variables, but to assess them over time in a variety of situations and to look for cross-situation and cross-time consistencies.

It is likely that the folklore of our culture attaches too much weight to the determination of behavior by personality and sex role variables, particularly in situations that are highly compelling and well structured. Milgram's research on obedience to authoritative commands to administer increasingly strong electric shocks to another person in a learning experiment (1965) illustrates the point quite well. One would think that mature males would be somewhat reluctant to administer electric shock to a fellow male even when ordered to by a scientific researcher. A sample of psychiatrists in fact predicted that less than one-tenth of one percent would deliver the maximum shock. In fact about 65 percent of the males did deliver what they thought was the maximum shock on the experimenter's orders, although changes in the situation—such as putting the shocker and the victim very close together—reduced that percentage considerably. Although everything that we read in the literature about females might suggest that they would be less likely to deliver such shocks, Milgram (personal communication) found that they were not, as did Larsen *et al.* (1972) more recently. Larsen *et al.* also reported a great under-estimation of the shock that would be delivered by college students to whom the procedures were described. The only significant sex differences were that females administered shock over 60 trials for a total time about 10 seconds less than the males and the maximum shock they administered was about 30 volts less on the average. It is noteworthy, however, that none of five personality tests given to these subjects correlated significantly with behavior in the shock situation. (It should be added that no one in this experimental set-up actually receives shock. The victim behaves as though he had been shocked.)

Another fiction about female personality that has been perpetuated by too little attention to the impact of the situation is that females are, by virtue of their cultural role training, more compliant or conformist than males. This fiction is stated by Gergen and Marlowe (1972) as follows: "Social-psychological folklore has it that women should be used as subjects when one wants easily persuaded or conforming subjects." After discussing the research literature, they concluded: "Perhaps we simply know less about women and why they behave as they do because in psychology, as in most professions, it's a 'man's world' " (p. 32).

In fact, a reading of research on compliance to social influence or persuasion reveals very clearly that sex differences appear when the situation is not well-structured but ambiguous and without clear guides for behavior. Then the attempt to influence behavior is apt to be more effective for both males and females. Typically the matter at hand is not very important or personally relevant in such studies (Sherif and Sherif, 1969). In addition, there is no battery of tests or performances that can predict female or male compliance generally in a variety of specific situations (Allen and Newston, 1972; Beloff, 1958; Hollander, 1960; Miller *et al.,* 1965). For example, Tittler (in Sherif *et al.,* in press) repeated an earlier study on persuasion from which it had been concluded that females could be persuaded more easily and consistently than males, a difference attributed to social role training. In addition to the topics used earlier, which had included such topics as General von Hindenburg's place in history and the probable success of a fictitious TV comic, Tittler included topics related to male and female sex roles. All subjects were persuaded easily to change their opinions about von Hindenburg and the comic, and females and males were equally resistant to persuasion on the sex role issues.

The structure of the situation itself and its personal meaning are thus so significant that a great many blanket generalizations have to be reconsidered. For example, quite contrary to theory on the achievement motive, male students who were high achievers on both college aptitude test scores and academic grades were not significantly less influenced by fictitious group performance standards than high-achieving females when the instructions were designed to arouse the achievement motive. They were more influenced than females when told that the group had been chosen so that the values of individuals were very similar, even though it was stressed that performance was not very important in the task at hand (Wyer, 1967).

A body of literature that bears directly on our topic, namely the choice of competition vs. cooperation in games of strategy, seems to indicate that the structure of the game itself is overwhelmingly important in affecting competitive behavior. The rules of the game, the number of players, the way rewards are or can be distributed and (although this may sound silly when compared to real life) whether or not the players can communicate with each other are examples of such structural properties. For example, in the prisoner's dilemma game the strategy choices are to take a long chance on winning individually, cooperating and losing, or following the surefire cooperative strategy which does not penalize either player. Rappaport and Chammah (1965) reported that in over 300 trials female pairs adopted the surefire cooperative strategy less frequently than males. This finding has been interpreted (Bardwick, 1971, p. 132) as indicating that when faces are hidden, females are really more competitive and aggressive than males, although why they should feel aggressive toward unknown females is not altogether clear. Other research (e.g., Swingle and Santi, 1972) indicates that the crucial fact here is not that faces are hidden but that no communication is permitted. When communication is either permitted or required, female pairs predominantly choose the cooperative strategy.

While the female tendency to cooperate in such games of strategy does vary markedly according to the structure of the game and the situation, the research literature does suggest that males are more likely than females to interpret such game situations as tests of themselves as individuals, and to follow individually competitive strategies more frequently than females (Wrightsman *et al.,* 1972; Grant and Sermat, 1969). This tendency is particularly pronounced when the game includes the opportunity to decide how rewards (usually small sums of money) are to be divided (Vinacke, 1959). While males are more likely to attempt a winner-take-all approach or to form an alliance with another player against a third, females playing together, more often than males, adopt strategies and divisions of reward that divide the rewards equally among the three players. Since I know of no evidence that money is less highly regarded by females than males, the explanation seems to lie in the greater challenge in the activity itself to males than females, as a means of proving himself. I would not expect males to compete so individu-. alistically if the activity was, let us say, baking a cherry pie, nor would I expect females to be so cooperative if the stakes were really high in her eyes.

The importance of such findings is two-fold. First, they suggest that in activity structured so that cooperation is a feasible strategy to win and share rewards, females are if anything more prone than men to cooperate. If such cooperation is aimed at competition with another team, it is, of course, a much better situation than one in which individuals on teams seek stardom at the expense of team cooperation, a tendency reinforced for males by the reward systems prevailing in sports. Second, such research findings suggest feasible approaches to research and planning on female competitive sports, namely systematic consideration of structures of different games and team competitiveness. To this I should add that we should include properties sorely neglected in research on strategy games, such as the group properties (leader-follower relations, norms, solidarity and goals that develop over time). Such systematic examination would greatly expand our knowledge of effective team functioning and may suggest feasible alternatives in building new sport programs.

CLOSING REMARKS

The most honest way to sum up this paper is to say that we have very few firm conclusions to suggest that females are less competitive than males, but that we have a great deal of evidence that competition depends upon the importance of the activities in question to the person, upon whose words and standards count to the person in assessment of performance, and upon the level of the standards as these relate to actual performance capability or potential. We know that in some societies women compete to be submissive and in others they compete to be dominant, as Margaret Mead's anthropological research has shown (1949). We suspect that in a country like the Soviet Union, where 75 percent of the doctors are women, females would compete to be successful and respected doctors. We have every reason to suspect that the same conditions govern competition in sports.

In the United States, something has gone awry in the relationships between sports for females and the reference groups of adolescents and many adult females. Even though there is nothing incongruous at all in sports participation and being physically attractive (in fact, quite the opposite is more likely), the prevailing sentiment among the female adolescents who are likely to be most prestigious is that females who indulge regularly in sports programs are oddballs. In the case of the most popular and feminine sports, outstanding performers are viewed as exceptions whose devotion and performance is to be admired but not emulated. There are many signs that such sentiments are changing, as indicated for example by a revived and widespread interest among adolescent and college-age females in being outdoors, in hiking and camping. It is also perfectly respectable and desirable to be able to hold one's own at tennis, swimming, and in other sports as well.

What I am saying seems more applicable to team play in the more active games. I suspect that one reason females shrink from competitive team play against females may be that it strikes them as caricature of male team play. Yet, so far as any evidence available, there is no reason to believe that the motivating effects of female groups are any less than those of males. For example, like young males, females in research compete so intensely that blockage of their group goals brings exactly the same sort of hostility that is aroused among boys' groups (Avigdor, 1952; Sherif and Sherif, 1969, Chapter 11). However, the competition in that research involved putting on a play, not sports.

The preferable time to do something about this state of affairs is not adolescence, for pre-pubescent and pubescent girls are among the most conventionally feminine in our population (*cf.* Seward, 1946; Hartley, 1970). In fact, although the female sex role is more flexible among high school students than it once was, only a couple of years ago the high school was a hotbed of reaction against attempt to change the role (Farley, 1971). Nevertheless, while I believe that the age to start changing the state of affairs for girls and sports is in grade school and before, the transition to high school must still be made and this transition is likely for a long lime to be marked by considerable discontinuity from the role image prevailing for the earlier period. Therefore, I will make some comments that seem to be warranted by the evidence.

First, the alternatives considered by high school and young adult females are likely to continue in the direction of greater flexibility of the female role concept and in the perception of more alternative styles for being female. This projection is based on the probable increased effects of the revived woman's movement as they filter down through colleges to high schools and the larger changes in outlook about identity and worthwhile goals that have already affected many youth and are likely to affect more. The implication is that the current period is probably the most fertile for innovation in female sports programs of any since it was deemed desirable that they exist at all.

Second, particularly since the dominant mythology of female success will continue to be centered on sexual attractiveness and femininity both in securing a mate and in employment, attempts to increase interest in sports competition individually or in teams that place any but the most outstanding female participant in direct competition with males or that produce weak carbon copies of male programs are not likely to make any more headway than they ever have. Here, the catchwords might well be not to imitate, but to innovate. By expanding the concepts of sports competition to include enjoyment in building and strengthening the body with companionship while doing so, I believe that many females could be involved in sports not traditionally included in athletic programs.

The competitive process, which is really essential for maintaining *élan* and improving performance, does not have to be modeled on either the individualistically oriented winner-take-all model or the varsity-team-is-our-hero model. Competition can occur in activity structures where rewards intrinsic to the activity and rewards for team effort do not hinge on aggressive destruction of the opponents. If there is reluctance for competition with males but a reasonable desire for integrated sports, why not introduce activities in which males and females compete together against others? I am not proposing a female tackle on every football team, but instead the addition of activities in which males and females can appropriately cooperate in competing with others. Research-oriented programs of this kind would be extremely valuable.

Finally, the most fruitful soil for developing and innovating new sport structures and heightening the value of sports is females' reference groups— those whose standards do count and whose encouragement or discouragement is personally important. Here sports programs share with all other adult sponsored or controlled activities the urgent problem of involving youth and being involved *with* youth in the problems that actually move them. The increasingly bureaucratic and compartmentalized structures of large public schools and universities, their increasing divorce from the real problems of youth, and youthful reactions in the form of both protest and mechanical apathy in doing what is required of them, all militant against such involvements. However, if there are determined efforts to give youth, including females, genuinely cooperative roles in planning and execution, I believe that we shall find females and males actively competing to participate in setting new standards for performance that both can genuinely respect because they are their own.

REFERENCES

Allen, V. L., and Newston, D., "Development of conformity and independence," *Journal of Personality and Social Psychology*, 1972, 22, 18-30.

Atkinson, J. W. (ed.), *Motives in Fantasy, Action, and Society,* Princeton, N.J.: Van Nostrand, 1958.

Avigdor, R., "The development of stereotypes as a result of group interaction," Doctoral dissertation, New York University, 1952.

Bardwick, J. M., *Psychology of Women. A Study of Bio-Cultural Conflicts*, New York: Harper and Row, 1971.

Beloff, H., "Two forms of social conformity: Acquiescence and conventionality," *Journal of Abnormal and Social Psychology*, 1958, 56, 99-104.

Bem, S. L., and Bem, D. J., "Training the woman to know her place: The power of a nonconscious ideology," in Garskof, M. H. (ed.), *Roles Women Play: Readings Toward Women's Liberation*, Belmont, Calif.: Brooks Cole Publishing Co., 1971, 84-96.

Berne, E. V. C., "An experimental investigation of social behavior patterns in young children," *University of Iowa Studies in Child Welfare*, 1930, 4, No. 3.

Bird, C., *The High Cost of Keeping Women Down*, New York: David McKay, 1968.

Bond, J. R. and Vinacke, W. E., "Coalitions in mixed-sex triads," *Sociometry*, 1961, 24, 61-75.

Brittain, C. V., "Adolescent choices and parent-peer cross-pressures," *American Sociological Review*, 1963, 28, 385-391.

Broverman, I. K., Broverman, D. M., Carlson, F. E., Rosencrantz, P. S., and Vogel, S. R., "Sex-role stereotypes and clinical judgments of mental health," *Journal of Consulting and Clinical Psychology*, 1970, 34, 1-7.

Chapman, D. W. and Volkman, J., "A social determinant of the level of aspiration," *Journal of Abnormal and Social Psychology*, 1939, 34, 225-238.

Clark, K. B. and Clark, M. K., "Racial identification and preference of Negro pre-school children," in T. M. Newcomb and E. L. Hartley (eds.), *Readings in Social Psychology*, New York: Holt, 1947.

Coleman, J. S., *The Adolescent Society*, Glencoe, Ill.: Free Press, 1961.

Emmerich, W., Goldman, K. S., and Shore, R. E., "Differentiation and development of social norms," *Journal of Personality and Social Psychology*, 1971, 18, 323-353.

Entwisle, D. R., "To dispel fantasies about fantasy-based measures of achievement motivation," *Psychological Bulletin*, 1972, 77, No. 6, 377-391.

Farley, J. T. T., "Women on the march against the rebirth of feminism in an academic community," Doctoral dissertation, Cornell University, 1970.

Gecas, V., "Parental behavior and contextual variations in adolescent self esteem," *Sociometry*, 1972, 35, No. 2, 332-345.

Gergen, K. J. and Marlowe, D., (eds.), *Personality and Social Behavior*, Reading, Mass.: Addison-Wesley, 1970.

Gesell, A. and Ilg, F. L., *Infant and Child in the Culture of Today*, New York: Harper, 1943.

Goldberg, P. A., "Are women prejudiced against women?," *Trans-Action*, 1968, April, 28-30.

Goodenough, F. L., *Developmental Psychology*, New York: Appleton Century, second edition, 1945.

Goodman, M. E., *Race Awareness in Young Children*, Reading, Mass.: Addison-Wesley, 1952.

Gottlieb, D., and Ramsey, C., *The American Adolescent*, Homewood, Ill.: Dorsey, 1964.

Grant, M. J., and Sermat, V., "Status and sex of others as determinants of behavior in a mixed-motive game," *Journal of Personality and Social Psychology*, 1969, 12, 151-158.

Greenberg, P. J., "Competition in children: An experimental study," *American Journal of Psychology*, 1932, 44, 221-248.

Hansche, J., and Gilchrist, J. C., "Three determinants of the level of aspiration," *Journal of Abnormal and Social Psychology*, 1956, 53, 136-137.

Hartley, R. E., "American core culture: Changes and continuities," Chapter 6 in Seward, G. and Williamson, R. (eds.), *Sex Roles in Changing Society*, New York: Random House, 1970, 126-149.

Hirota, K., "Experimental studies in competition," *Japanese Journal of Psychology*, 1951, 21, 70-81, abstracted in *Psychological Abstracts*, 1953, 27, 351.

Hollander, E. P., "Competence and conformity in the acceptance of influence," *Journal of Abnormal and Social Psychology*, 1960, 61, 365-369.

Hooker, E., "Male homosexuality and the Rorschach," *Journal of Projective Techniques*, 1957, 21, 18-31.

Horner, M. S., "Femininity and successful achievement: A basic inconsistency," Chapter 3 in Bardwick, J. M. *et al.*, *Feminine Personality and Conflict*, Belmont, Calif.: Brooks Cole Publishing Co., 1970, 45-74.

Horrocks, J. E., *The Psychology of Adolescence Behavior and Development*, Boston: Houghton Mifflin, third edition, 1969, Chapter 14, Adolescent groups and group membership; Chapter 15, Friendship and interpersonal adequacy; Chapter 20, Physical functioning and efficiency.

Kagan, J., and Moss, H. L., "The stability of passive and dependent behavior from childhood through adulthood," *Child Development*, 1960, 31, 577-591.

Kandel, D. B., and Lesser, G. S., "Parental and peer influences on educational plans of adolescents," *American Sociological Review*, 1969, 34, No. 2, 213-223.

Konopka, G., *The Adolescent Girl in Conflict*, Englewood Cliffs, N.J.: Prentice Hall, 1965.

Lambert, W. E.; Libman, E.; and Poser, E. G., "The effect of increased salience of a membership group on pain tolerance," *Journal of Personality*, 1960, 28, 350-357.

Landers, D. M., "Siblings, sex, status and ordinal position effects on female's sport participation and interests," *Journal of Social Psychology*, 1970, 80, 247-248.

Larsen, K. S., Coleman, D., Forbes, J., and Johnson, R., "Is the subject's personality or the experimental situation a better predictor of a subject's willingness to administer shock to a victim?," *Journal of Personality and Social Psychology*, 1972, 22, 287-295.

Lesser, G. S., Krawitz, R., and Packard, R., "Experimental arousal of achievement motivation in adolescent girls," *Journal of Abnormal and Social Psychology*, 1963, 66, 59-66.

Leuba, C. J., "An experimental study of rivalry in young children," *Journal of Comparative Psychology*, 1933, 16, 367-378.

Lewin, K., Dembo, T., Festinger, L., and Sears, P. S., "Level of aspiration," in J. McV. Hunt (ed.), *Personality and the Behavior Disorders*, New York: Ronald, 1944.

Licuanan, P. B., "The impact of modernization of Filipino adolescents," Manila: Ateneo de Manila University, *IPC Papers No. 10*, 1972, 1-28.

Little, K. B., and Schneidman, E. S., "Congruences among interpretations of psychological and anamestic data," *Psychological Monographs*, 1959, 73, 1-42.

Lüschen, G., "Cooperation, association, and contest," *Journal of Conflict Resolution*, 1970, 14, 21-34.

McClelland, D. C., Atkinson, J. W., Clark, R. A., and Lowell, E. L., *The Achievement Motive*, New York: Appleton-Century-Crofts, 1953.

Maccoby, E. E. (ed.), *The Development of Sex Differences*, Stanford: Stanford University Press, 1966.

Mead, M., *Male and Female*, New York: Morrow, 1949.

Milgram, S., "Some conditions of obedience and disobedience to authority," in Steiner, I. D., and Fishbein, M., (eds.), *Current Studies in Social Psychology*, New York: Holt, Rinehart and Winston, 1965, 243-262.

Miller, N., Doob, A. N., Butler, D. C., and Marlowe, D., "The tendency to agree: Situational determinants and social desirability," *Journal of Experimental Research in Personality*, 1965, 2, 78-83.

Milton, G. A., "Sex differences in problem solving as a function of role appropriateness of the problem context," *Psychological Reports*, 1959, 5, 705-708.

Money, J., "Sexual dimorphism and homosexual gender identity," *Psychological Bulletin*, 1970, 77, 6, 425-440.

Moss, H. A., and Kagan, J., "Stability of achievement and recognition-seeking behaviors from early childhood through adulthood," *Journal of Abnormal and Social Psychology*, 1961, 62, 504-513.

Murphy, G., *Personality*, New York: Harper and Row, 1957.

Murphy, L. B., *Social Behavior and Child Personality*, New York: Columbia University Press, 1937.

Parten, M. B., "Social participation among pre-school children," *Journal of Abnormal and Social Psychology*, 1932, 27, 243-269; "Social play among pre-school children," *ibid.*, 1933, 28, 136-147.

Perterson, G. I., Kiesler, S. B., and Goldberg, P. A., "Evaluation of the performance of women as a function of their sex, achievement and personal history," *Journal of Personality and Social Psychology*, 1971, 19, 114-118.

Piaget, J., *The Moral Judgment of the Child*, London: Kegan Paul, 1932.

Piaget, J., *The Origins of Intelligence in Children*, New York: International Universities Press, 1952.

Rosenkrantz, P., Vogel, S., Bee, H., Broverman, I., and Broverman, D., "Sex-role stereotypes and self concepts in college students," *Journal of Consulting and Clinical Psychology*, 1968, 32, 287-295.

Rappaport, A., and Chammah, A. M., "Sex differences in factors contributing to the level of cooperation in the prisoner's dilemma game," *Journal of Personality and Social Psychology*, 1965, 2, 831-838.

Rossi, A. S., "Barriers to the career choice of engineering, medicine or science among American women," in Mattfeld, J. A., and Van Aken, C. G., (eds.), *Women and the Scientific Professions*, Cambridge: MIT Press, 1965, 51-127.

Salusky, A. S., "Collective behavior of children at a preschool age," *Journal of Social Psychology*, 1930, 1, 367-378.

Seward, G. H., *Sex and the Social Order*, New York: McGraw-Hill, 1946.

Sherif, C. W., with Kelly, M., Rodgers, L., Sarup, G., and Tittler, B., "Personal involvement, social judgment and action," *Journal of Personality and Social Psychology*, 1973, 27, 311-328.

Sherif, M., *An Outline of Social Psychology*, New York: Harper, 1948.

Sherif, M., and Cantril, H., *The Psychology of Ego Involvement*, New York: Wiley, 1947.

Sherif, M., and Sherif, C. W., *Reference Groups: Conformity and Deviation of Adolescents*, New York: Harper and Row, 1964.

Sherif, M., and Sherif, C. W., *Social Psychology*, New York: Harper and Row, 1969.

Stein, A. H., Pohly, S., and Mueller, E., "The influence of masculine, feminine and neutral tasks on children's behavior, expectancies of success and attainment values," *Child Development*, 1971, 42, 195-208.

Steinman, A., and Fox, D. J., "Male-female perceptions of the female role in the United States," *Journal of Psychology*, 1966, 64, 265-276.

Sutton-Smith, B., and Roberts, J. M., "The cross-cultural and psychological study of games," in G. Lüschen (ed.), *The Cross-Cultural Analysis of Sport and Games*, Champaign, Ill.: Stipes Publishing Co., 1970, 101-108.

Sutton-Smith, B., Rosenberg, P. G., and Morgan, E. F., "Development of sex differences in play choices during pre-adolescence," *Child Development*, 1963, 34, 119-126.

Swingle, P. G., and Santi, A., "Communication in non-zero sum games," *Journal of Personality and Social Psychology*, 1972, 23, 54-63.

Thomas, D. L., and Weigert, A. J., "Socialization and adolescent conformity to significant others: A cross national analysis," *American Sociological Review*, 1972, 33, 305-326.

Vinacke, W. E., "Sex roles in a three-person game," *Sociometry*, 1959, 22, 343-360.

Watson, G., and Johnson, D., *Social Psychology. Issues and Insights*, New York: Lippincott, 1972, Chapter 11.

Weisstein, N., "Psychology constructs the female, or the fantasy life of the male psychologist," in Garskof, M. H. (ed.), *Roles Women Play: Readings Toward Women's Liberation*, Belmont, Calif.: Brooks Cole Publishing Co., 1971, 68-83.

Wrightsman, L. S., O'Connor, J., Baker, N. J. (eds.), *Cooperation and Competition: Readings on Mixed Motive Games*, Belmont, Calif.: Brooks/Cole, 1972.

Wyer, R. S., "Behavioral correlates of academic achievement: Conformity under achievement and affiliation-incentive conditions," *Journal of Personality and Social Psychology*, 1967, 6, 255-263.

6 / RACE AND SPORT

It is often argued that sports have been the most responsive of the many integrating social agencies in American society for enculturalizing and providing personal-social opportunities to the polyethnic and multiracial groups in it. Indeed, sport is frequently called the greatest democratizing institution in this country. In this regard, Boyle (1963) states:

> Sport has often served minority groups as the first rung on the social ladder. As such, it has helped further their assimilation into American life. It would not be too far-fetched to say that it has done more in this regard than any other agency, including church and school (p. 100).

Riesman and Denney (1951) in their classic paper on the role of football for cultural diffusion suggest that the linkage between football and various ethnic groups has been pronounced since the 19th century. They say, with reference to football:

> . . . its rationalization as a sport and as a spectacle has served to bring out more openly the part it plays in the ethnic, class, and characterological struggles of our time—meaning by "Characterological struggle," the conflict between different styles' of life. The ethnic significance of football is immediately suggested by the shift in the typical origins of player-names on the All-American Football Teams since 1889. In 1889, all but one of the names (Heffelfinger) suggested Anglo-Saxon origins. . . . After 1895, it was a rare All-American team that did not include at least

one Irishman. ... By 1927, names like Casey, Kipke, Oosterbaan, Koppisch, Garbisch, and Friedman were appearing on the All-American list with as much frequency as names like Channing, Adams, and Ames in the 1890's (pp. 309-310).

Although individuals and groups from a variety of origins have been prominent in American sports — DiMaggios and Pepitones of the Italians, Nagurskis of the Poles, Greenbergs and Koufaxs of the Jews, Joe Lewis and Willie Mays of the Blacks — it would be highly inaccurate to describe the sports world as completely equalitarian. The most infamous example of racial discrimination is professional baseball which excluded blacks for over 50 years (see Robert Peterson's book, *Only the Ball Was White*, for an account of this).

Racial prejudice against blacks has been with us since slaves were imported into this country. But even in the days of slavery, several sports were open for black participation. Boxing was generally open to blacks; horse racing had many black jockeys in the nineteenth century; and blacks were prominent in the early years of professional baseball up to 1888, when an unwritten law of professional baseball barring blacks was introduced. This law was effective until 1945, when Jackie Robinson became the first modern black to sign an organized baseball contract.

Although racial discrimination has always been incompatible with the ideals of American sports, widespread sports opportunities for the black emerged only when discrimination became incompatible with good financial policy. In those team sports in which the profit motive has come to dominate, the contribution of outstanding black athletes to winning championships and holding public interest has opened up opportunities to blacks in college and professional sports. Sports more social in nature and with less spectator interest have been slow to attract and integrate the black.

In the past 20 years the black has assumed a remarkably prominent role in American sports. In 1956, 14 percent of the professional football players were blacks; today more than 30 percent of all players in the NFL are blacks. In baseball's major leagues, about 33 percent of the players are blacks. And a recent count of professional basketball teams shows that blacks represent 56 percent of the total players. Thousands of blacks are playing on college athletic teams, and today the basketball teams of many high schools, especially in the big cities, often have five nonwhites in the five starting positions.

American black athletes have dominated recent Olympic Games in the short races and the jumping events. Moreover, blacks are champions in most boxing weight classifications.

Sports opportunities have undoubtedly improved for blacks in the past two decades, but discrimination appears to persist, albeit in a more subtle form. Rosenblatt (1967) reported that an analysis of Major League batting averages over two different three-year periods (1958-61 and 1962-65) showed that the black ballplayer, to be treated equally, must be better. Loy and McElvogue (1969) reported apparent racial segregation, based upon the positions which they play, for both professional football and baseball players.

The black's success in sport has led many to seek an explanation for this phenomenon. Some have claimed that the black possesses physical characteristics which are advantageous for athletic performance (see Kane, 1971). Anthropologists have identified several structural differences in blacks and Caucasians, but no proof has been given that these differences actually do provide motor skill advantages, and investigations of various physical factors comparing blacks and Caucasians have yielded inconclusive results.

Many social scientists are of the opinion that sociological and psychological factors are the primary reason for the black's rise to eminence in sports. They note that most black athletes come from the low socioeconomic classes; here recreational outlets for the young are mainly sports, so many hours are spent playing in the streets, recreation centers, and playgrounds (see Axthelm, 1970). Furthermore, it has been emphasized that excellence in sports provides an opportunity for blacks to escape from the slums and ghettos. Thus, the desire to escape from their childhood environments seems to have caused many black youths to approach sport with greater motivation to excel than is found in middle-class whites.

In the first reading, Harry Edwards forcefully attacks the notion that blacks have physical advantages which enable them to excel in sports. He suggests that in fact the propagation of the notion that blacks are physically superior to whites is a racist guise to advance the old stereotype that blacks are not as phylogenetically advanced as whites, that they are closer to lower animals. Edwards warns those who accept the notion of the genetic theory of black physical superiority that they are falling into the trap set by white racists. For Edwards, the conditions which are responsible for the current black prominence in American sports are mainly social. Since a great majority of blacks are in the lower social classes, and since there are only one or two avenues for upward social mobility based on personal achievement—one being sports—these conditions produce a strong motivation among young blacks to achieve and excel in sports.

The second reading by Yetman and Eitzen is concerned with a form of racial discrimination which is far more abstruse than that which we look for in everyday life. There is no doubt that blacks are contributing more than their proportional share of athletes to American sports. This fact has led many to believe that racial discrimination does not exist in sport, and indeed the overt, flagrant, racial abuses do not exist as they once did. However, recent research (Rosenblatt, 1967; Loy and McElvogue, 1969) seems to indicate that a subtle and insidious form of racism does exist at several levels of sport; i.e., college, professional. The unique focus of the research which Yetman and Eitzen report in this reading is on the proportion of black players in starting roles on college and professional basketball teams versus the proportion of black players in nonstarting roles. Their data show that black players in both collegiate and professional basketball are found disproportionately in starting roles. Of course, there are a number of explanations which might be advanced to explain these conditions. The authors examine several of these in some detail. They conclude that, although there are alternative explanations, their findings have probably uncovered a form of subtle racial discrimination.

In the third reading, Hare portrays the plight of the black boxer, using personal experiences and interviews with fighters as his means of data collection. Although reminiscent of Weinberg and Arond's (1952) classic study of the subculture of boxers, Hare's study focuses specifically on black fighters and the unique sociocuture problems with which they have to contend. The author notes that black boxers are products of the racial tensions of the larger society and that black-white rivalry is manifested through the special significance which black fighters place on beating white opponents. It is also displayed in whites seemingly endless search for a "White Hope" to win championships possessed by blacks. The role of social class and role modeling is well exemplified in Hare's findings about why black fighters became involved in the sport. His sample of boxers were overwhelmingly from the lower classes, with many having little family structure to bind the family together. Idolatry of successful boxers, membership in community-sponsored boxing programs, and success as a street fighter served as agents for socializing most black fighters into the sport. Most fighters start with the notion that boxing will be an avenue for upward social mobility but of course only a very few achieve wealth, and those who do frequently lose it quickly. Boxing does not develop skills which can be used after retirement; most fighters are poorly educated, and very few have money to invest in occupational ventures. So for most black fighters retirement means a return to the degradation of the slums.

The reading by Paul Hoch is a far-ranging essay on racism in sport. The author briefly reviews the history of the black's treatment in American sport. He notes that while greater opportunities are available in sports today there are still many positions in sports in which blacks are excluded and he suggests that black athletes are still mistreated in sports. He reviews the racial flare-ups and protests at the collegiate, Olympic, and professional levels in which blacks have been involved and describes the conditions which produced the incidents.

REFERENCES

Axthelm, P., *The City Game,* New York: Harper & Row, 1970.

Boyle, R. H., *Sport: Mirror of American Life,* Little, Brown, and Company, 1963.

Kane, M., "An Assessment of 'Black is Best,' " *Sports Illustrated,* 34 (January 18); 72-83, 1971.

Loy, J. W., and McElvogue, J. F., "Racial Segregation in American Sport," paper presented at the International Seminar on the Sociology of Sport, Macolin, Switzerland, September, 1969.

Peterson, R., *Only the Ball was White,* Englewood Cliffs: Prentice Hall, 1970.

Riesman, D., and Denney, R., "Football in America: A Study of Culture Diffusion," *American Quarterly,* 3:309-319, 1951.

Rosenblatt, A., "Negroes in Baseball: The Failure of Success," *Trans-Action,* 4 (September): 51-53, 1967.

Weinberg, S. K., and Arond, H., "The Occupational Culture of the Boxer," *American Journal of Sociology,* 57 (March): 460-469, 1952.

THE MYTH OF THE RACIALLY SUPERIOR ATHLETE

Harry Edwards

While there can be little argument with the obvious fact that black performances in sports have been and continue to be superior, on the whole, to
those of whites, there is room for considerable debate over the identity and
character of the factors that have determined that superiority and contributed to its perpetuation.

The myth of the black male's racially determined, inherent physical and
athletic superiority over the white male rivals the myth of black sexual
superiority in antiquity. While both are well fixed in the Negrolore and folk
beliefs of American society, in recent years the former has been subject to
increasing emphasis due to the overwhelmingly disproportionate representation of black athletes on all-star rosters, on Olympic teams, in the various
"most valuable player" categories, and due to the black athletes' overall
domination of the highly publicized or so-called "major sports"—basketball,
football, baseball, track and field. But seldom in recent times has the myth of
racially linked black athletic prowess been subject to so explicit a formulation
and presentation as in the January 18, 1971 issue of *Sports Illustrated*
magazine.

In an article entitled "An Assessment of 'Black is Best'" by Martin Kane,
one of the magazine's senior editors, several arguments are detailed, discussed

---

Harry Edwards, "The Myth of the Racially Superior Athlete," *Intellectual
Digest*, 2:58-60 (March 1972). Originally published in *The Black Scholar*,
3:16-28 (November 1971). Copyright © by *The Black Scholar*. Reprinted by
permission of *The Black Scholar* and *Intellectual Digest*.

and affirmed by a number of widely known medical scientists, athletic researchers, coaches and black athletes. In essence, the article constitutes an attempt to develop a logical and scientifically defensible foundation for the assertion that black athletic superiority in sports is due to racial characteristics indigenous to the black population in America but not generally found within the white population.

Clearly there is no argument that black society is contributing more than its 11% share of athletes and star-status performers to professional sports. And where blatant racism and discrimination do not keep blacks from participation almost completely—such as in the Southeastern Conference—a similar pattern of black domination prevails in colleges and at other amateur levels where major sports endeavors are pursued.

Attempting to explain this disproportionate representation, Kane mentions, almost in passing, the probable influences of contemporary societal conditions and then launches into a delineation and discussion of the major factors giving rise to black athletic superiority. They are:

Racially linked physical and psychological characteristics:

1. Proportionately longer leg lengths, narrower hips, wider calf bones and greater arm circumference among black athletes than among whites.

2. A greater ratio of tendon to muscle among blacks, giving rise to a condition typically termed "double jointedness," a relatively dense bone structure.

3. A basically elongated body structure among black athletes enabling them to function as more efficient heat dissipaters relative to whites.

Race-related psychological factors:

1. The black athlete's greater capacity for relaxation under pressure relative to the capacity of the white athlete.

Racially specific historical occurrences:

1. The selectivity of American slavery in weeding out the hereditarily and congenitally weak from among those who came to be the forebears of today's black population.

Let us now turn to a general consideration of these major factors.

RACIALLY LINKED PHYSICAL
AND PHYSIOLOGICAL CHARACTERISTICS

Kane's attempt to establish the legitimacy of this category of factors as major contributions to the emergence of black athletic superiority suffers from two basic maladies—one methodological, the other arising from a dependence upon scientifically debatable assumptions and presumptions concerning differences between the "races" of men and the impact of these differences upon capacity for physical achievement.

Simply stated, one grossly indefensible methodological tactic is obvious in virtually every case of "scientific" evidence presented in support of a physical or physiological basis for black athletic superiority. *In no case was the evidence presented gathered from a random sample of subjects selected from the black population at large in America.* Thus, supporting data, for the most part, were taken from black athletes of already proven excellence or from blacks who were available due to other circumstances reflective of some degree of uncontrolled social, political, or otherwise contrived selectivity. Therefore, the generalization of the research findings on these subjects to the black population as a whole—even assuming the findings to be valid—constitutes a scientific blunder of the highest magnitude and invalidates the would-be scientific foundations of this component of the author's argument.

With regard to the alleged physical traits supposedly characteristic of black athletes, the question can justifiably be posed, "What two outstanding black athletes look alike or have identical builds?" One of Kane's resource persons answers this question: "Lloyd C. 'Bud' Winter makes it quite obvious that black athletes differ from each other physically quite as much as whites do." He notes that Ray Norton, a sprinter, was tall and slender with scarcely discernible hips, that Bobby Painter, a sprinter, was squat and dumpy with a swayback and a big butt, that Dennis Johnson was short and wiry, that Tommy Smith was tall and wiry, and so on.

Further evidence is plentiful: What physical characteristics does Lew Alcindor have in common with Elgin Baylor, or Wilt Chamberlain with Al Attles, etc? The point is simply that Wilt Chamberlain and Lew Alcindor have more in common physically with Mel Counts and Henry Finkel, two seven-foot white athletes, than with most of their fellow black athletes.

Even excepting the hyperbolic illustrations just documented, what emerges from any objective analysis of supposed physical differences between so-called races is the undeniable fact that there exist more differences between individual members of any one racial group than between any two groups as a whole.

Recognition of this essential fact precludes the type of incredible qualification that Kane is forced to make when faced with exceptions that do not fit the framework he has developed. A case in point is his assertion that the physical differences between white and black racial groupings predispose blacks to dominate the sports requiring speed and strength while whites, due to racially linked physical traits, are predestined to prevail in those sporting events requiring endurance. When confronted with the fact that black Kenyans won distance races and defeated highly touted and capable whites in the 1968 Olympic Games, the author makes the ridiculous post hoc assertion that (the Kenyans) Keino and Bikila have black skin but a number of white features.

RACE-RELATED PSYCHOLOGICAL FACTORS

The academic belief in the existence of a national or a racial "character" was supposedly disposed of by scholars decades ago. Their persistence among the ranks of coaches and other segments of the American population only indicates the difficulty with which racial stereotypes and caricatures are destroyed or altered to comply with prevailing knowledge. Kane and his resource persons, mostly coaches, recreate a portrait of the black athlete as the happy-go-lucky, casual, "What—me worry?" Negro made so familiar to Americans through history books, Stepin Fetchit movies and other societal outlets. But besides the fact that the overall portrayal is inappropriate, not even the psychological traits attributed to black athletes are substantiated.

Kane quotes Lloyd C. Winter, former coach of a long line of successful black track and field athletes, as stating: "A limber athlete has body control, and body control is part of skill. It is obvious that many black people have some sort of head-start motor in them, but for now I can only theorize that their great advantage is relaxation under stress. As a class, the black athletes who have trained under me are far ahead of whites in that one factor—relaxation under pressure. It's their secret."

In data collected by Bruce C. Ogilvie and Thomas A. Tutko, two athletic psychologists whose work was ironically featured in the same issue of *Sports Illustrated* in which Kane's article appears, a strong case is made for the fact that black athletes are significantly less relaxed than white athletes in the competitive situation. (I am intimately familiar with this data as a result of my Ph.D. dissertation, *Sport in America: Its Myths and Realities.*) Using an Institute for Personality and Ability Testing (IPAT) test that is generally considered to have a high degree of reliability in both cross-cultural and simple comparative investigations, the following findings emerged when the psychological orientations of successful black and white athletes were compared:

1. On an IPAT test, successful black athletes showed themselves to be considerably more serious, concerned and "uptight" than their white counterparts as indicated by their relative scores on the item "Sober/Happy-

go-lucky." Blacks had a mean stern score of 5.1 as compared to a mean score for whites of 5.5 (level of significance of differences between scores is .01; N = 396 whites, 136 blacks).

2.   On the IPAT item of "Casual/Controlled," successful black athletes indicated a more controlled orientation. Blacks had a mean stern score of 6.6 as compared with the whites' mean score of 6.2 (level of significance of differences is .01; N = 396 whites, 136 blacks).

Sociologically, this pattern of differences among black athletes is perhaps to be expected, given the fact that they are aware that they operate at a decided disadvantage competing against whites for highly valued positions and rewards in an admittedly white racist society. Furthermore, sports participation holds the greatest promise of escape from the material degradation of oppressed black society. Thus, the assertion that black athletes are more "relaxed" than white not only lacks scientific foundation but is ludicrous as even a commonsense assumption.

RACIALLY SPECIFIC HISTORICAL OCCURRENCES

Kane states that "it might be that without special breeding the African has a superior physique." The statements of Kane and his resource persons evidence confusion as to the scope of characteristics involved in the selectivity process as it has affected mankind. Natural selection or "the survival of the fittest" has been predicated upon relative strength and physical attributes to a lesser degree in mankind than in any other form of animal life. This has been due largely to man's tremendously developed mental capabilities. The same would have held for the slave. While some may have survived as a result of greater physical strength and toughness, many undoubtedly also survived due to their shrewdness and thinking abilities.

The major implication of Kane's argument for the black population at large is that it opens the door for at least an informal acceptance of the idea that whites are *intellectually* superior to blacks. Blacks, whether athletes or nonathletes, must not give even this passing credence to the possibility of white intellectual superiority. By a tempered or even enthusiastic admission of black physical superiority, the white population of this racist society loses nothing. For it is a simple fact that a multitude of even lower animals are physically superior, not only to whites, but to mankind as a whole: gorillas are physically superior to whites, leopards are physically superior to whites, as are lions, walruses and elephants. So by asserting that blacks are physically superior, whites at best reinforce some old stereotypes long held about

Afro-Americans—to wit, that they are little removed from the apes in their
evolutionary development.

On the other hand, intellectual capability is the highest-priced commodity on the world market today. If in a fit of black identity, or simple
stupidity, we accept the myth of innate black superiority, we could be
inadvertently recognizing and accepting an ideology which has been used as
the justification for black slavery, segregation and general oppression.

What then are the major factors underlying black athletic superiority?
They emerge from a complex of societal conditions. These conditions instill a
heightened motivation among black male youths to achieve success in sports;
thus, they channel a proportionately greater number of talented black people
than whites into sports participation. Our best sociological evidence indicates
that capacity for physical achievement (like other common human traits such
as intelligence, artistic ability, etc.) is evenly distributed throughout any
population. Thus, it cuts across class, religious, and, more particularly, racial
lines. For race, like class and religion, is primarily a culturally determined
classification. *The simple fact of the matter is that the scientific concept of
race has no proven biological or genetic validity.* As a cultural delineation,
however, it does have a social and political reality. This social and political
reality of race is the primary basis of stratification in this society and the key
means of determining the priority of who shall have access to means and thus,
valued goods and services.

Blacks are relegated in this country to the lowest priority in terms of
access to valued goods and services. This fact, however, does not negate the
equal and proportionate distribution of talent across both black and white
populations. Hence, a situation arises wherein whites, being the dominant
group in the society, have access to *all* means toward achieving desirable
valuables defined by the society. Blacks, on the other hand, are channeled
into the one or two endeavors open to them—sports, and to a lesser degree,
entertainment.

Bill Russell once stated that he had to work as hard to achieve his status
as the greatest basketball player of the last decade as the president of General
Motors had to work to achieve his position. The evidence tends to indicate
that Russell is quite correct. In short, it takes just as much talent, perse-
verance, dedication and earnest effort to succeed in sports as to become a
leading financier, business executive, attorney or doctor. Few occupations
(music and art being perhaps the exceptions) demand more time and dedication than sports. A world-class athlete will usually have spent a good deal of
his youth practicing the skills and techniques of his chosen sport.

The competition for the few positions is extremely keen and if he is fortunate he will survive in that competition long enough to become a professional athlete or an outstanding figure in one of the amateur sports. For as he moves up through the various levels of competition, fewer and fewer slots or positions are available and the competition for these becomes increasingly intense because the rewards are greater. Since the talents of 25 million Afro-Americans have a disproportionately higher concentration in sports, the number of highly gifted whites in sports is proportionately less. Under such circumstances, black athletes naturally predominate. Further, the white athletes who do participate in sports operate at a psychological disadvantage because they believe blacks to be inherently superior as athletes. Thus, the white man has become the chief victim of his own lie.

BLACK AMERICANS IN SPORTS: UNEQUAL OPPORTUNITY FOR EQUAL ABILITY

Norman R. Yetman and D. Stanley Eitzen

Since 1947, when Jackie Robinson broke the color line in the "national game" of baseball, the idea that organized sport has escaped the pervasive effects of racism has become one of the most cherished myths in American life. According to this myth, which is confirmed for most Americans by the prominence of Willie Mays, a Kareem Abdul-Jabbar, or a Gale Sayers, collegiate and professional athletics have provided an avenue of mobility for blacks unavailable elsewhere in American society and thus have "done something" for black Americans. However, an increasing number of social scientists, journalists, and black athletes have challenged this myth, charging that black athletes are exploited and that discrimination pervades the entire sports establishment. According to these critics, the existence of racism in collegiate and professional sports is especially insidious because the promoters of and commentators on athletics have made sports sacred by projecting an image of it as the single institution in America relatively immune from racism.

Norman R. Yetman and D. Stanley Eitzen, "Black Americans in Sports: Unequal Opportunity for Equal Ability." Reprinted from *Civil Rights Digest,* Volume 5, Number 2 (August, 1972), pp. 20-34. Copyright © Norman R. Yetman and D. Stanley Eitzen. Reproduced by permission.

Several aspects of the athletic world have been alleged to be racially biased—recruitment policies, the assignment of playing positions, performance expectations, and rewards. One of the best documented forms of discrimination in both the college and professional ranks is the unequal distribution of blacks by playing position. This phenomenon, popularly known as "stacking," refers to situations in which minority group members are relegated to specific team roles and excluded from competing for others. The consequence is often that intra-team competition for starting roles is between members of each race (e.g., those competing as running backs are black while those competing as quarterbacks are white). Aaron Rosenblatt, for example, noted that while there were twice as many pitchers on a baseball team as there were outfielders, in 1965 there were three times as many black outfielders as black pitchers.[1]

An interesting interpretation of the stacking phenomenon has been advanced by John W. Loy and Joseph P. McElvogue. To explain the racial segregation that occurs in sports by position, they combined Oscar Grusky's notions about the formal structure of organizations (i.e., some organizational roles are more "central" to the organization than others because of their social interaction potential) and H. M. Blalock's proposition that the greater the degree of social interaction on the job, the greater the degree of discrimination.[2] Thus the more central a position to the action, the more likely it was that whites would be found in the position.

Their data for 1968 substantiated the hypothesis. For baseball, 83 percent of the persons listed as infielders were white, while 50 percent of the outfielders were white. The proportion of whites was greatest (27 of 28, or 96 percent) in the position of catcher, the most central position in baseball. In football, the positions most central on the offensive unit (center, guards, and quarterback) were 96 percent white in 1968. Our own analysis of the 1971 rosters of the National Football League (NFL) demonstrated that this strong relationship between role centrality and race has persisted. We found, moreover, that the greater the number of years in the league, the higher the proportion of white players in central positions (among those players in the league 1 to 3 years, 82 percent were white; 4 to 6 years, 90 percent white; 7 to 9 years, 96 percent white; and 10 or more years, 97 percent white. (This may be a consequence of the league having a smaller proportion of black players in the past. A better analysis would be to follow a cohort through their playing careers.)

This evidence demonstrates clearly that blacks are the victims of discrimination. The effects are more devastating than just limitation to certain positions, however, because playing in non-central positions has additional penalties. First, for the 17 of 26 teams returning the information to us, approximately three-fourths of all advertising slots (radio, television, and newspapers) allotted to pro football players in 1971 went to those in central positions. Second, non-central positions in football depend primarily on speed and quickness, which means in effect that playing careers are shortened for persons in these positions. For example, only 5.8 percent of the players listed in the *Football Register* in the three predominantly black positions—defensive back, running back, and wide receiver (62 percent of all black players)—were in the pros for 10 or more years, while 10.4 percent of players listed in the three predominantly white positions—quarterback, center, and offensive guard—remained that long. The shortened careers for non-central players has two additional deleterious consequences—less lifetime earnings and limited benefits from the players' pension fund, which provides support on the basis of longevity.

According to the Loy and McElvogue interpretation, the paucity of blacks in central team roles reflects the impact of wider societal stereotypes of blacks. Since it is widely assumed that blacks are intellectually inferior and incapable of leadership and that tension will be generated by placing them in leadership positions, blacks in sports are relegated to positions where the requisite skills are speed, strength, and quick reactions, not thinking or leadership ability. However, Barry McPherson has challenged the notion of "centrality," asserting that the unequal racial distribution of players occurs through a process of self-segregation; black male youths select those positions in which black sports heroes, who are among their leading role models, are most prominent.[3]

Although McPherson produces no empirical support for his explanation, it is conceivable that socialization variables contribute to the racial stacking patterns in baseball and football as noted above. Our own position is that this interpretation is plausible if socialization for sports roles is conceived to include negative, as well as positive, perceptions. That is to say, given discrimination in the allocation of playing positions (or at least the belief in its existence), young black males will consciously avoid those positions for which opportunities are (or are believed to be) low (e.g., pitcher, quarterback) and will select instead those positions where they are most likely to suceed (e.g., the outfield, running and defensive backs). As quoted by Jack Olsen in "The Black Athlete" (*Sports Illustrated,* Part IV, July 22, 1968), Gene Washington, all-pro wide receiver of the San Francisco Forty-Niners, was a college quarterback at Stanford through his sophomore year, then switched to flanker. Washington requested the change himself. "It was strictly a matter of economics. I knew a black quarterback would have little chance in pro ball unless he was absolutely superb. . . ."

Another form of discrimination that allegedly occurs in professional sports is the discrepancy between the salaries of white and black players. At first glance such a charge appears to be unwarranted. Black players rank among the highest paid in professional baseball (seven of 10 superstars being paid more than $100,000 in 1970 were black), and the mean salaries of black outfielders, infielders, and pitchers exceed those of whites. However, Scully reanalyzed data employed by Pascal and Rapping in an earlier study, and found substantial salary discrimination against blacks when performance levels were held constant, i.e., blacks earn less than whites for equivalent performance.

An obvious case of monetary discrimination becomes apparent if one takes into account the total incomes of athletes (salary, endorsements, and off-season earnings). Pascal and Rapping, for instance, citing the Equal Opportunity Commission Report of 1968, related that black athletes appeared in only 5 percent of the 351 commercials associated with New York sports events in the fall of 1966.[4] Our own analysis of the advertising and media program slots featuring starting members of one professional football team in 1971 revealed that eight of 11 whites had such opportunities while only two of 13 blacks did. Blacks also do not have the same opportunities as whites when their playing careers are finished. This is reflected in radio and television sportscasting where no black person has had any position other than providing the "color."

Officiating is another area that is disproportionately white. Baseball has had only one black major league umpire in its history. Professional basketball has only recently broken the color line in officiating. The same is true of football, which provides another case of racial "stacking." Blacks are typically found in the head linesman role—seldom in the role of head referee.

Although the percentage of black players in each of the three most prominent American professional sports (baseball, football, and basketball) greatly exceeds their percentage of the total population, there is ample evidence that few opportunities are available to them in managerial and entrepreneurial roles. For example, the data from 1971 sources (*The Baseball Register, Football Register,* and *National Basketball Association Guide*) show that of the 24 major league baseball managers and of the 26 National Football League head coaches, none was black. Three of the 17 head coaches (18 percent) in the National Basketball Association (NBA) were black.

The virtual dearth of black coaches in professional sports is paralleled at the college and high school levels. Although many predominantly white colleges and universities have, in response to pressures from angry black athletes, recently made frantic efforts to hire black coaches, these have been almost exclusively as assistant coaches, and seldom has a coaching staff included more than one black. As of this writing not a single major college had a black head football or track coach, and only four major colleges (Arizona, Georgetown, Illinois State, and Washington State) had head basketball coaches who were black. This same pattern has characterized American high schools. Blacks, historically, have found coaching jobs only in predominantly black high schools. And, although the precise figures are unavailable, it would appear that the movement toward integration of schools during the 1960's would have had the effect of eliminating blacks from coaching positions, as it has for black principals and for black teachers in general.[5] So anomolous is a black head coach at a predominantly white high school in the South that when, in 1970, this barrier was broken, it was heralded by feature stories in the *New York Times* and *Sports Illustrated,* the latter in adaptation of a book on the subject.[6] And the situation would appear to be little different outside the South, where head coaches are almost exclusively white.

As for blacks in high executive positions in sports organizations, the evidence again points to discrimination. In 1971 no black held a high executive capacity in any of the 24 baseball organizations. There was one black in the baseball commissioner's office and one held an executive position in the NBA league office. Again it was a noteworthy event when former NBA star Wayne Embry was recently named general manager of the NBA Milwaukee Bucks, thereby becoming the first black to occupy such an executive position in professional sports.

A final form of discrimination in sport—one we will explore more fully—is unequal opportunity for equal ability. This means that entrance requirements to the major leagues are more rigorous for blacks—therefore, black players must be better than white players to succeed in the sports world. Rosenblatt was one of the first to demonstrate this mode of discrimination. He found that in the period from 1953 to 1957 the mean batting average for blacks in the major leagues was 20.6 points above the average for whites. In the 1958 to 1961 time period the difference was 20.1 points, while from 1962 to 1965 it was 21.2 points. He concluded that:

> ... discriminatory hiring practices are still in effect in the major leagues. The superior Negro is not subject to discrimination because he is more likely to help win games than fair to poor players. Discrimination is aimed, whether by design or not, against the substar Negro ball player. The findings clearly indicate that the undistinguished Negro player is less likely to play regularly in the major leagues than the equally undistinguished white player.

Since Rosenblatt's analysis was through 1965, we extended it to include the years 1966-1970. The main difference between blacks and whites persisted; for this 5-year period blacks batted an average of 20.8 points higher than whites.

The existence of racial entry barriers in major league baseball was further supported by Pascal and Rapping, who extended Rosenblatt's research by including additional years and by examining the performance of the races in each separate position, including pitchers. They found, for instance, that the 19 black pitchers in 1967 who appeared in at least 10 games won a mean number of 10.2 games, while white pitchers won an average of 7.5. This, coupled with their findings that blacks were superior to whites in all other playing positions, led them to conclude that: ". . . on the average a black player must be better than a white player if he is to have an equal chance of transiting from the minor leagues to the major." Moreover, Scully's elaborate analysis of baseball performance data has led him to conclude that ". . . not only do blacks have to outperform whites to get into baseball, but they must consistently outperform them over their playing careers in order to stay in baseball."

The findings of Rosenblatt, Scully, and Pascal and Rapping indicate that in major league baseball, at least, there is an unequal opportunity for blacks with equal ability. An obvious question is whether this type of discrimination is found in other sports at the professional and collegiate levels as well. The thrust of the research reported here is to assess the allegation that black athletes are disproportionately overrepresented in the "star" category and underrepresented in the average or journeyman athlete category on collegiate and professional basketball teams. Whether the distribution of the races on basketball teams has changed over time also will be considered.

METHODS

A primary value of using sport as the focus of sociological research is that team and individual performances can be determined with relative precision and that the performance records are public information and easily accessible. Three sources of data were employed in this study. Information on college scoring averages of 4,120 players on 417 racially integrated teams was obtained from sports information directors of National Collegiate Athletic Association (NCAA) member schools. The racial identification of the players was derived by examining the photographs in team press brochures and the *Converse Basketball Year Book,* which is published annually by Converse Sporting Goods. Finally, records for the NBA were found in the 1971-72 *National Basketball Association Guide.*

In a previous study we analyzed performances of players on 246 integrated NCAA 1970 basketball teams and discovered that two-thirds of the black players were starters. This situation was constant regardless of region, size, and type of school (whether private, denominational, or public) and NCAA classification ("university" or "college" division).[7]

For the present study we wished to obtain a historical perspective on the presence of blacks in organized basketball and to determine whether there have been changes in the positional patterns of black players over time. Consequently, we extended our analysis to include NCAA teams at 4-year intervals from 1954, the year of the Supreme Court's *Brown v. Board of Education* decision that declared segregated educational institutions unconstitutional, to 1970. Prior to 1954, blacks were almost totally excluded from collegiate basketball squads at predominantly white institutions and from the National Basketball Association.

Since our earlier analysis had demonstrated that the positional patterns of black athletes were virtually identical on NCAA university and college squads ("large" and "small" schools), and because major colleges were more consistently pictured in the *Converse Basketball Year Book,* we restricted our historical analysis to 126 *major* colleges that had an integrated team pictured in the *Yearbook* for the following years: 1953-54, 1957-58, 1961-62, and 1965-66. 1969-70 data were derived from our previous study. As we had done before, we requested final team and individual player statistics from a school's sports information director for those years in which team pictures were available. Consequently, data were not requested for 4 years from all 126 schools; for a given year the data were requested only if the school's team had been pictured in the *Yearbook* and if it were integrated. Returns were received from 95, or 75 percent, of the schools. Of these, 86, or 67 percent, provided some useful information.

The first question that we wished to investigate concerned the extent to which basketball teams—collegiate and professional—were integrated during the period of 1954-1970. As in football and baseball, basketball was largely a segregated sport until the 1950's. Although there are records of black players on teams from predominantly white schools as far back as 1908, such instances were rare. In the professional game, the National Basketball Association remained an all-white institution until 1950, three years after Jackie Robinson had broken the color line in modern major league baseball and four years after blacks re-entered major league football after having been totally excluded since the early 1930's.[8]

Tables 1 and 2 document the striking changes in the racial composition of basketball since 1954. From the immediate post World War II situation

Table 1   Racial Composition of NCAA Basketball Teams, 1948-1970

Year	Number of NCAA teams pictured in Converse Yearbook	Number of black players	% of teams with blacks	Black players as % of total	Avg. no. of blacks on inte-grated squads
1948	182	25	9.8 (18)	1.4	1.4
1954	184	83	28.3 (52)	4.5	1.6
1958	201	182	44.3 (89)	9.1	2.0
1962	239	241	45.2 (108)	10.1	2.2
1966	235	381	58.3 (137)	16.2	2.8
1970	253	685	79.8 (202)	27.1	3.4

(1948) when less than 10 percent of collegiate squads were integrated, to 1970, when nearly 80 percent contained members of both races, there was a substantial and impressive move toward integration. Not only were more schools recruiting blacks, but the number of black players being recruited at each school increased dramatically. The most substantial increase among collegiate teams was during the period between 1966 and 1970, which can be partly attributed to the breakdown of previously segregated teams through-out the South.[9] The changes in the professional game are even more marked, for blacks have clearly come to dominate the game—both numerically and, as we shall note more fully below, statistically. Although blacks comprise approximately one-tenth (11 percent) of the total U.S. population, they account for more than one-fourth (27 percent) of the Nation's collegiate

Table 2   Racial Composition of Professional Basketball Teams, 1954-1970

Year	Number of teams	Number of black players	% of teams with blacks	Black players as % of total	Avg. no. of blacks per total team
NBA:					
1954	9	4	44 (4)	4.6	.4
1958	8	11	87 (7)	11.8	1.3
1962	9	34	100 (9)	30.4	3.8
1966	9	57	100 (9)	50.9	6.3
1970	14	94	100 (14)	54.3	6.7
ABA:					
1970	11	80	100 (11)	57.3	7.3

basketball players and more than one-half (54 percent) of the professional players. The percentage composition of black players on college basketball teams is even more striking when, according to the *Chronicle of Education* (October 4, 1971), blacks comprised only 6.9 percent of undergraduate students in 1970 and that nearly half (44 percent) attended predominantly black institutions. Therefore, as contrasted to nearly two decades ago, organized basketball—on both the college and professional levels—has eliminated many of the barriers that once excluded blacks from participation.

Having determined that black players are disproportionately over-represented on collegiate and professional basketball teams relative to their distribution within the general population, we wanted to examine more systematically the roles blacks played on these teams. Specifically, we wanted to determine whether they have been found disproportionately in the first five ranks (starters) and whether their average position ranking on a team has been higher than that of whites. We also wished to utilize historical data to determine whether the positional patterns had changed significantly in the years during which the percentage of black players had increased so dramatically.

We have operationally defined the top players according to their offensive productivity as measured by their scoring average. The five players with the highest scoring averages will be referred to hereafter as the top five, first string, top players, or starters. We believe that this method represents the best single measure that could be obtained, and that there is no appreciable bias involved in its use.

FINDINGS, COLLEGE BASKETBALL

The three tables below provide an answer to the question of whether blacks have been disproportionately represented in starting roles in college basketball. Table 3 presents the data, by year, on the percentage of players who were black for each of the 10 positions. Although the situation in 1954 is ambiguous, perhaps because of the small number of cases, there is a clear trend in each of the other years for starting positions to be overrepresented by blacks. Although there are a few minor deviations, for each year studied there is a progressive decline in the percentage of blacks occupying a position as scoring percentage declines. This is most marked in the distribution of black players in the Number 1 and Number 10 positions, respectively. While the black players comprised no more than 29 percent of all the members of integrated teams during the years 1958-1970, in each of these years nearly half of the leading scorers were black. Conversely, blacks were disproportionately under-represented in the Number 10 position.

Table 3   Percentage of Blacks at Each Scoring Rank, 1954-1970

Scoring Rank	1954 % Black	N*=17	1958 % Black	N=35	1962 % Black	N=56	1966 % Black	N=61	1970 % Black	N=248
1	18	(3)†	46	(16)	48	(27)	52	(32)	47	(117)
2	18	(3)	29	(10)	34	(19)	46	(28)	42	(105)
3	18	(3)	25	(7)	27	(15)	39	(24)	40	(98)
4	12	(2)	29	(10)	18	(10)	26	(16)	36	(90)
5	12	(2)	11	(4)	36	(20)	26	(16)	26	(64)
6	30	(5)	17	(6)	11	(6)	16	(10)	27	(66)
7	6	(1)	14	(5)	13	(7)	20	(12)	18	(45)
8	6	(1)	11	(4)	14	(8)	13	(8)	20	(49)
9	6	(1)	11	(4)	7	(4)	18	(11)	17	(41)
10	12	(2)	6	(2)	7	(4)	7	(4)	17	(39)

* Refers to the total number of integrated teams.

† Refers to the number of black players at each position.

Because of their overwhelming numerical superiority during the years examined, whites, comprising at least 70 percent of the total player population, dominate in each position (although in 1966 more than 50 percent of the Number 1 players were black). However, these data can be presented in another way—the distribution by rank for each race separately. Thus, rather than looking at the percentage of players in a specific rank who were blacks, we examined the percentage of black players (and white players) who were found in each rank. When examined in this manner, the linearity noted above remains; for blacks the percentage found in each rank position decreased as it became less valuable, for whites the percentage increased. Rather than presenting the data for all 10 ranks, we have organized Table 4 according to the distribution in the Number 1 rank and the total percentages of black players

Table 4   Percentage of Players in Leading Scoring Ranks, by Race, 1954-1970

	1954	1958	1962	1966	1970
% of the blacks on the starting five	57 (13)	69 (47)	76 (91)	72 (116)	66 (474)
% of the blacks in leading rank	13 (3)	24 (16)	23 (27)	20 (32)	16 (117)
% of the whites in leading rank	10 (14)	7 (19)	7 (29)	7 (29)	8 (131)

Table 5 Percentage of Black Professional Players in Starting Roles, 1958–1970

	1958 % N	1962 % N	1966 % N	1970 % N
Total number of blacks in NBA	55(6) 11	56(18) 32	55(27) 49	50(43) 86

found in starting roles. These data reveal that between 1958 and 1970 no less than two-thirds—and as high as three-fourths—of the black players were starters. Moreover, black players consistently appeared most frequently in the leading player rank and, again with the exception of 1954, were more than twice, and often three times, as likely as whites to be found in that position. These data present solid evidence that, at least since 1958, blacks have been found disproportionately in the top five positions on college basketball teams and have been disproportionately underrepresented on the second five.

PROFESSIONAL BASKETBALL

Nowhere else in professional sports have blacks come to dominate the game so completely as in professional basketball. As the data in Table 2 indicate, however, this has not always been the case. Table 5 reveals that, although in 1962 and 1966 blacks were slightly overrepresented in starting roles, the differences are not so pronounced as they were among college teams. Indeed, it would appear that any differences that may have occurred in the past are diminishing.

Since the number of players and teams is much smaller than was the case for collegiate basketball, the data for professional basketball have been organized somewhat differently. Following Rosenblatt's approach in analyzing major league baseball teams, we compared the scoring averages of black and white players for 1957-58, 1962-63, 1965-66, and 1969-70 (data for the scoring averages of all players in the league were unavailable for 1953-54). Although scoring averages were identical for both races in 1957-58, blacks outscored whites in the remaining years by an average 5.2, 3.3, and 2.9 points, respectively. It is apparent that since 1962 the magnitude of these differences has declined as the percentage of black players in the league has increased.

In Table 6 these data are presented according to the scoring quartiles in which the players were ranked, looking at each race separately, with the goal of obtaining a percentage distribution for each quartile or half by race. It is

Table 6   Percentage of NBA Players by Race in Each Scoring Quartile

	black		white		difference	
1957-58						
Upper quartile	25.0 ⎱	66.7	27.7 ⎱	49.4	− 2.7 ⎱	+17.3
Upper middle	41.7 ⎰		21.7 ⎰		+20.0 ⎰	
Lower middle	8.3 ⎱	33.3	26.5 ⎱	50.6	−18.2 ⎱	−17.3
Lower quartile	25.0 ⎰		24.1 ⎰		+ 0.9 ⎰	
	100.0		100.0			
1961-62						
Upper quartile	32.4 ⎱	70.6	21.8 ⎱	41.0	+10.6 ⎱	+28.4
Upper middle	38.2 ⎰		19.2 ⎰		+19.0 ⎰	
Lower middle	23.5 ⎱	29.4	25.6 ⎱	58.9	− 2.1 ⎱	−28.5
Lower quartile	5.9 ⎰		33.3 ⎰		−27.4 ⎰	
	100.0		100.0			
1965-66						
Upper quartile	29.8 ⎱	57.9	20.0 ⎱	41.8	+ 9.8 ⎱	+16.1
Upper middle	28.1 ⎰		21.8 ⎰		+ 6.3 ⎰	
Lower middle	24.6 ⎱	42.1	25.5 ⎱	58.2	− 0.9 ⎱	−16.1
Lower quartile	17.5 ⎰		32.7 ⎰		−15.2 ⎰	
	100.0		100.0			
1969-70						
Upper quartile	30.5 ⎱	55.8	17.9 ⎱	42.3	+12.6 ⎱	+13.5
Upper middle	25.3 ⎰		24.4 ⎰		+ 0.9 ⎰	
Lower middle	25.3 ⎱	44.2	24.4 ⎱	57.7	+ 0.9 ⎱	−13.5
Lower quartile	18.9 ⎰		33.3 ⎰		−14.4 ⎰	
	100.0		100.0			

here that the distribution of black players among the leading scorers is most marked. It is shown that in each year the percentage of black players in the league who were in the top half of league scorers was greater than for whites. Again, however, there appears to have been a progressive but significant decline from 1962 to 1970. This would indicate that as the NBA becomes increasingly dominated by blacks it has also become increasingly egalitarian. Although the pattern of preference for white players persists, the differentials have narrowed substantially. This is in contrast to the situation in professional baseball, where the mean batting average for blacks has remained 20 points greater than the average for whites for nearly two decades.

One reason why the initial NBA scoring averages in 1957-58 were equal may be that, except in extraordinary cases where players (primarily big men such as Wilt Chamberlain and Kareem Abdul-Jabbar) have dominated the game as rookies, few players have achieved stardom immediately. Most players have to acquire considerable professional experience before becoming league leaders in scoring. In 1958, blacks were relatively new to the league, the 11 blacks then in the NBA having played an average of only 2.5 previous seasons. In several instances those blacks who were later to become superstars were, because of their inexperience, well down the ranks of scoring (e.g., Sam Jones, who in 1970 was one of 10 players voted to the silver anniversary NBA all-star team, averaged 4.6 in his rookie season, ranking 74th of 92 players in the league).

CONCLUSIONS

Although the patterns are not so strong among pro as among college teams, these data have consistently shown that black players in organized collegiate and professional basketball have been found disproportionately in starting roles. Several possible explanations for this phenomenon have been advanced. First, it has been suggested that blacks are naturally better athletes and their predominance in starting roles can be attributed to their innate athletic superiority. As sociologists, we are inclined to reject interpretations of black athletic superiority as genetically or physiologically based, although our stance must be an agnostic one, since there is too little evidence on the question. What is important to note here, however, is that although a genetic interpretation is a logical (if not entirely convincing) explanation of the disproportionate percentage of blacks found on college and pro teams, it cannot explain their prevalence in starting roles. Even if blacks possessed genetically based athletic superiority, they should not be systematically overrepresented in starting positions, but should still be randomly distributed throughout the entire team. As Jim Bouton, a former major league baseball player who has challenged the racial composition of major league baseball teams, has written, "If 19 of the top hitters are black, then almost two-thirds of all hitters should be black. Obviously it is not that way."[10] An interpretation based on the natural superiority of blacks must, therefore, be rejected.

A second possible explanation is discrimination in recruiting practices. Harry Edwards has charged that college coaches, in their recruitment of blacks, seek to obtain only those players who are almost certain to be starters.

> A black athlete generally fares well in athletic competition relative to other incoming athletes at a white-dominated college. The cards are somewhat stacked for him, however, because few black high school athletes get what are typically classified as second-and-third string athletic grants-in-aid. One simply does not find black athletes on 'full-rides' at predominantly white schools riding the bench or playing second-or-third team positions. Second-and-third team athletic grants-in-aid are generally reserved for white athletes.[11]

This appears to be a plausible explanation of the data for both college and professional players. On the one hand, the coach may be consciously or unconsciously prejudiced and may find the idea of having black team members repugnant, but nonetheless he may recruit black "star" players because their presence will enhance his team's performance. In this situation the black player who is capable, but not outstanding, is liable to be overlooked, while his white counterpart is not. In addition, coaches are sensitive to criticism of their coaching policies by powerful alumni, booster organizations, and fans. In a situation where these groups are perceived by a white coach as bigoted, even if he himself is not, it is likely that his recruitment of black players will be calculated to minimize criticism of his coaching policies. Therefore, black team members are more likely to be outstanding athletes, for the performance of average ballplayers would be inadequate to counterbalance the criticism their presence would create. For many years a "quota" system, limiting the number of black starters, operated informally in both college and professional basketball.[12]

The selective recruitment of only those blacks certain to be starters may be undertaken consciously or unconsciously, but it would appear seldom to be acknowledged by a coach. However, one of the nation's most highly successful college coaches, one who has been acclaimed as a recruiter adept at communicating with young black ballplayers, has advanced a sophisticated rationale for the reason three of the four blacks on his 1970-71 squad were starters. "The ghetto environment of the black demands that he be a star, if he is to participate at all," he explained. "He could never justify an understudy's role to himself or to the brothers he left behind in the playground. Thus there is no point recruiting blacks who will not start."[13] Whether this impressionistic theory of black sport role socialization is valid or merely a justification for selective recruitment must be more fully assessed.

Another explanation that has been advanced to explain the disproportionate number of black starters is that of structural inequalities—especially educational and economic—that are found in the larger society and have disproportionate effects on black, as contrasted to white, athletes. Thus, athletic ability, talent, and associated skills are not the only criteria by which a potential college athlete is selected. Academic ability is also a crucial factor to be weighed in the decision of whether or not to award an athletic scholarship. One of the major problems in the recruitment of an athlete to compete for a college or university is that he may be academically unqualified for the academic demands that a college athlete must face. Since the quality of elementary and secondary education received by blacks has been demonstrated to be inferior,[14] a greater percentage of potential black athletes would tend to be marginal students.

Moreover, most universities reflect a white middle-class cultural bias that represents a substantial hindrance to students from backgrounds other than white and middle class. Thus, while a coach may offer a scholarship to an outstanding player who is a marginal student or to a marginal player who is an outstanding student, he will most likely hesitate to offer a scholarship to a marginal player who is also a marginal student. These factors are important ones for the college coach to weigh, and, although racial factors may not enter into these calculations directly, the *effects* of these kinds of policies will be felt disproportionately by blacks.

This appears to be a plausible interpretation of the data and, indeed, there are undoubtedly situations in which these kinds of considerations have operated. Fortunately we possessed some data that enabled us to test how significant a factor this may have been in explaining our earlier findings. As part of our original request of sports information directors, we requested information on the grade-point averages (GPA's) of the players. We received information on all members of 110 integrated teams. If the argument that academic potential is a significant variable influencing the relative recruitment of marginal black players is valid, then one would conclude that the GPA's of second-string black players would be higher than those of first-string blacks, for whom the academic considerations would be a less crucial factor.

We found that the average GPA's of the 106 starting blacks in our sample was 2.26 (on a 4-point scale), whereas the average of 98 second-string players was 2.33. Although this slight difference is in the predicted direction, it did not even approach statistical significance. Thus, although these considerations may have been operative in specific cases, they must be dismissed as factors in substantially influencing the distribution of the data.

The limited access of blacks to institutions of higher learning may also be instrumental in contributing to the patterns described above in another way. Each competing educational institution has only a limited number of athletic scholarships to dispense each year and these are awarded to outstanding players. However, often a squad will have players from the student body— "walk-ons"—who have not been recruited by the coach but who "try out" for the squad and make it. Because blacks comprise an extremely small proportion of the student bodies at predominantly white institutions, most such non-scholarship athletes will be white. Thus, a team may be composed of several outstanding black and white players on scholarship and several mediocre players who are white.

A final explanation of the disproportionate black prowess in both college and professional basketball resides in the structural limitations to which black children and adults are subjected. Since opportunities for vertical mobility by blacks in American society are circumscribed, athletics may become perceived as one of the few means by which a black can succeed in a highly competitive American society; a male black child's and adolescent's primary role models are much more likely than a white's to be athletic heroes.[15] And the determination and motivation devoted to the pursuit of an athletic career may therefore be more intense than for the white adolescent whose career options are greater. Jack Olsen, in his *The Black Athlete,* quotes a prominent black coach:

> People keep reminding me that there is a difference in physical ability between the races, but I think there isn't. The Negro boy practices longer and harder. The Negro has the keener desire to excel in sports because it is more mandatory for his future opportunities than it is for a white boy. There are nine thousand different jobs available to a person if he is white.

On the other hand, James Green of the University of Wisconsin, Green Bay, has questioned whether the lure of a professional career completely explains the strong emphasis on athletics among blacks. He argues that the explanation that blacks manifest a "keener desire to excel . . . because it is mandatory for his future . . ." simply reflects the commentator's own future orientation. An alternative explanation of strong black motivation, according to Green, is the positive emphasis in black subculture that is placed on the importance of physical (and verbal) skill and dexterity. Athletic prowess in men is highly valued by both women and other men. The athletically capable male is in the comparable position of the hustler or the blues singer; he is something of a folk hero. He achieves a level of status and recognition among his peers whether he is a publicly applauded sports hero or not.

Whatever the factors operating, the conclusion that black athletes encounter discrimination in collegiate and professional basketball seems inescapable. Despite the myth to the contrary, equality of opportunity for those of equal skills is not operating. This conclusion has implications that extend beyond the sports world. If discrimination occurs in so public an arena, one so generally acknowledged to be discrimination free, and one where a premium is placed on individual achievement rather than upon ascription, how much more subtly pervasive must discrimination be in other areas of American life, where personal interaction is crucial and where the actions of power wielders are not subjected to public scrutiny.

NOTES

1. Aaron Rosenblatt, "Negroes in Baseball: The Failure of Success," *Trans-Action*, 4 (September 1967), pp. 51-53. Anthony H. Pascal and Leonard A. Rapping, *Racial Discrimination in Organized Baseball* Santa Monica, California: Rand Corporation, 1970; and Gerald W. Scully, "The Economics of Discrimination in Professional Sports: The Case of Baseball," paper prepared for a Brookings Conference on Government and Sports Business (December 1971).

2. John W. Loy and Joseph F. McElvogue, "Racial Segregation in American Sport," *International Review of Sport Sociology*, 5 (1970), pp. 5-24; H. M. Blalock, Jr., "Occupational Discrimination: Some Theoretical Propositions," *Social Problems*, 9 (1962), pp. 240-243; and Oscar Grusky, "The Effects of Formal Structure on Managerial Recruitment: A Study of Baseball Organization," *Sociometry*, 26 (1963), pp. 345-353.

3. Barry D. McPherson, "Minority Group Socialization: An Alternative Explanation for the Segregation by Playing Position Hypothesis," a paper presented at the Third International Symposium on the Sociology of Sport, Waterloo, Ontario, August 22-28, 1971.

4. See also Ira Berkow, "Advertisers Shun Black Sport Stars," NEA news release (July 22, 1969).

5. *New York Times*, March 19, 1971, p. 1.

6. *New York Times*, May 18, 1970, p. 31; Pat Jordon, "The Man Who Was Cut Out for the Job," *Sports Illustrated* (October 11, 1971), pp. 19-22; Pat Jordon, *Black Coach*, New York: Dodd, Mead, 1971.

7. Norman R. Yetman and D. Stanley Eitzen, "Black Athletes on Intercollegiate Basketball Teams; An Empirical Test of Discrimination,"

Majority and Minority: The Dynamics of Racial and Ethnic Relations,
Norman R. Yetman and C. Hoy Steele (eds.), Boston: Allyn and Bacon,
Inc., 1971, pp. 509-517.

8. A. S. Young, *Negro Firsts in Sports,* Chicago: Johnson Publishing
    Company, Inc., 1963, pp. 238-250.

9. Cf. Frye Gaillard, "Crumbling Segregation in the Southeastern Con-
    ference," *The Black Athlete*—1970, Nashville, Tennessee: Race Relations
    Information Center, 1970, pp. 18-40.

10. Jim Bouton, *Ball Four,* New York: World Publishing Company, 1970, p.
    302.

11. Harry Edwards, *The Revolt of the Black Athlete,* New York: The Free
    Press, 1969.

12. William F. Russell, "Success is a Journey," *Sports Illustrated* (June 8,
    1970), pp. 81-93.

13. Quoted by Robert Lipsyte in the *New York Times* (March 1, 1971), p.
    37.

14. James S. Coleman, *Equality of Educational Opportunity,* Washington,
    D.C.: U.S. Department of Health, Education, and Welfare, 1966.

15. The prominence of sports stars among role models of black adolescents
    has been suggested by Joseph Himes, "Negro Teen-Age Culture," *Annals,*
    1961.

A STUDY OF THE BLACK FIGHTER

Nathan Hare

Fighters occupy a peculiar position within the realm of the professional
athlete. They emerge from the most oppressed strata within the major cities
and excite widespread attention as the most exploited group within the
athletic world. Currently, most (more than 70 percent) are black, and the
"white hope" syndrome is so intense as to enter into fights between two
blacks.

When the late Sonny Liston was preparing to fight Floyd Patterson, the
NAACP and Ralph Bunche both made public statements that victory for

Nathan Hare, "A Study of the Black Fighter," *The Black Scholar,* Volume 3
(November, 1971), pp. 2-8. Reprinted by permission.

Liston would strike a serious blow for the black struggle for equality.[1] When Muhammad Ali joined the black muslims, Martin Luther King remarked that he had become "a champion of racial segregation." Ali responded that he was "an example for the youth of the whole world."[2] Today, when Ali fights, blacks and whites of a variety of political persuasions will regard him and his fight as a political force.

Fighters as a group are:

> . . . set apart in the public mind by the fact that the object of their sport is to inflict bodily injury. Thus to some people they represent brutality and degradation; to others, virility and courage. . . . They are very human individuals, equipped with all the human reactions and emotions. Most fighters know the natural fear of getting hurt. Most of them do not enjoy hurting their opponents and feel a compulsion to rationalize this as a business necessity. Although they are all looking for financial reward, the greatest number are impelled even more by the desire for recognition and prestige. They long for the approval of the fans and for public understanding and acceptance. In their private lives they have a number of special problems, and when they retire they find it difficult to adjust to routine life.[3]

For the black fighter, these and other problems are intensified. I know this to be true for two main reasons. One is that I was a boxer myself.[4] Although I boxed mainly as an avocation and never attained great heights as a fighter, I did have thirty-six fights, both amateur and professional. In my last professional fight on December 5, 1967 in the Washington, D.C. Coliseum, I knocked out my opponent in two minutes and twenty-two seconds of the first round. In all, I won twenty-eight and lost eight and was never knocked down or badly beaten.

In the process, I came to know personally hundreds of fighters and retired fighters, including Muhammad Ali and Bobby Foster, the light heavyweight champion, with whom I frequently sparred in the days when he was still an up-and-coming fighter.

However, my observations on professional fighters go beyond my daily contacts with them. For my master's thesis at the University of Chicago, I conducted a systematic study of fifty-eight professional fighters, some active, some retired, and nearly all of them black. I sought to discover what forces lured them into the boxing ring and what happened to them after retirement.

During months of canvassing gymnasiums, I witnessed the inter-ethnic conflict, rivalries and other private emotions the fighters expressed. I saw ethnic groups stealing the towels of another group and listened to their hostile racial jokes. I saw that it was a particular comedown for a black fighter to lose to a white fighter. Many black fighters relieve racial hostility in their fights with white fighters. Whenever a black fighter has a fight scheduled with a white fighter, his comrades kid him with the query as to whether he is "afraid of white folks," a fear which has been said to motivate even Muhammad Ali in part.

A Louisville friend, who had known Ali since childhood, once observed:

> Even when he's talking about race—when he says, "I don't want to be bombed, I don't want to be set on fire, I don't want to be lynched or have no dogs chase me"—he's expressing more of a general fright than he is a real racial attitude. I think he finds it safer to be with Negroes, his own kind. It allays his fear of all those things his father used to tell him the whites'd do to him. He keeps this tight little Negro group around him and he's scared to death to venture away from it.[5]

Fighters are products of the racial hostilities and socioeconomic conflicts in which they live. Professor Kirson Weinberg, of Chicago's Roosevelt University, has found that professional boxers reflect changes in the ethnic composition of the lower strata of the urban slums. In the early part of the century the Irish predominated. By 1928 Jewish fighters had replaced them; by 1936 the Italians succeeded them. Since 1948 the blacks have dominated.[6] Currently, seven of the eleven best heavyweights in the world are black Americans.[7] Except for the four years Rocky Marciano was champion, and the year Ingemar Johannsen borrowed the title briefly from Floyd Patterson, blacks have held the heavyweight championship since 1936. In recent years, Tampa, Florida barred professional boxing because, the commission's report read in part, "boxers no longer represent a cross-section of America."[8]

> A "natural" to the fight mob connotes any fight which pits a white man against a Negro, although the Madison Avenue boys who have moved into the promotional forefront of the sport would seek a euphemistic definition. By any definition it brings loot. ... It has been traditional that any "white hope" is matched against a colored champion, a natural is in the making. It appeals to all that is primitive and basic in this most primitive and basic of all sports.[9]

Because of this premium placed on white fighters, black fighters feel that they must fight them harder in order to get ahead. Black fighters especially are forced to seek in boxing the financial security and the social esteem denied them outside the ring, not to mention the gnawing resentments built up from a lifetime of abuse suffered at the hands of white supremacists. Joe Louis was so enraged by Max Schmelling's pre-bout boasts that Germans are superior to blacks, he attacked the Nordic with a fury that left him hospitalized. In this reaction, Louis was not unique.

Most black persons do not become fighters, however. To find out why some turn to boxing, I went to the origins of the fighters in my sample. From the Illinois State Athletic Commission I obtained the address from which each fighter applied for his first professional license. I visited each dwelling and noted the economic need of their family origins. Only 35 percent had working fathers at home when they turned professional. All the working fathers were laborers, except one who operated a small laundry. Twenty-nine percent said their fathers had deserted the family, and five percent said their fathers had died.

Since most poor boys do not become fighters either, I sought out the specific reasons why those in my group had entered the ring. Thirty-one said they first became interested in boxing because a relative, friend or neighbor (a role model) was a fighter. Thirteen traced their interest to natural ability discovered in street fights. Fourteen gave other reasons such as childhood membership in an organization sponsoring boxing or a fondness for sports in general and boxing in particular.

One interesting point was that only five percent of the scientific boxers attributed their initial interest to street fighting, whereas 48 percent of the sluggers gave this reason. My survey findings are borne out by the cases of various well-known fighters. Sluggers such as Sonny Liston and Henry Hank had much success in street fights. It was different with scientific boxers like Ray Robinson and Ezzard Charles.

Robinson, who used to run from street fights as a child, started to box because he lived in the same Detroit neighborhood as Joe Louis, and often carried Louis' bag to the gym. Charles first became interested when, near his home in Cincinnati one day, he saw Kid Chocolate, the featherweight champion, in an expensive car, and heard Chocolate tell of his sizeable wardrobe.

Boys in the black slums take note of these and other benefits a boxing career can offer, and are moved to use this means of escaping slum deprivation. Joe Louis, after his humiliation of Max Schmelling, became a hero for blacks all over the nation; and nonwhites throughout the world also were able to take him for a model.

Many fighters, far from being "born" fighters, had to learn fighting to get by as boys in their tough slum environments. Professor Weinberg even found fighters who took up fighting because as boys they suffered insults to their manliness.[10] The girlish name of one, for instance, attracted the jeers of playmates. The boy eventually altered his name to make it manly sounding, and set out to learn boxing to back up his new name. He was soon able to convince his jesters that he was at least as manly as they.

This problem also has plagued well-known fighters. At the weighing-in ceremonies before the bout in which champion Benny Kid Paret was fatally injured a few years ago, Paret called Griffith a "woman," apparently because Griffith used to be a choirboy and is now a designer of ladies' hats. Paret's widow, Lucy, blames this insult for the "bad blood" between the fighters and the savage fury of Griffith's punches.[11]

Although almost all fighters start with the idea of making money, 45 percent in my sample told me that after three or more years they liked the recognition and prestige even more than the financial rewards. Joe Law, a lightweight, expressed it this way: "A guy knocks you down. You get up and put up a good fight and the crowd cheers you. Drop into a night club and people recognize you. The emcee says, 'We got a celebrity in the house,' and shines the spotlight on you. I'm telling you, it makes you feel good."

Sonny Liston explained:

I never had a dime to my name before I became a fighter. I never had friends before, or respect. Now when people see me on the street, they turn around and say, "ain't that Sonny Liston, the fighter?"[12]

Muhammad Ali has said: "I started boxing because I thought this was the fastest way for a black person to make it in this country."[13]

Most fighters begin with an exaggerated idea of the prestige and money to be made. They read about the huge purses received by the Alis and Louises and Robinsons and have little understanding of how much must be deducted for taxes, expenses and manager's share. Of the forty-eight retired fighters I questioned, none said they had saved most of the money they earned in fighting. Two out of three had saved little, and 25 percent had saved none at all.

"My manager was like a father to me," said a lightweight who won forty-six of his sixty-three fights, "but you've still got expenses and a lot of friends. Everybody wants to have a good time off your money. Once I made $5,000 in a fight in California, but by the time I got home I only had about $500."

"The higher a fighter goes in the fight game, the higher the class of people he runs around with," another fighter told me. "He's got to spend money to keep up with the crowd. His manager won't let him keep on livin' on State Street, payin' cheap rent, because it won't look right. A boxer comes from the bottom. He ain't been used to nothin' or he wouldn't be fighting in the first place."

In the effort to squeeze the most from the fighter as a commodity, managers must seek to extract a viciousness and disdain for suffering in the fighter. Trainers assist them in conditioning the fighter to taking and giving punishment. "This ain't no baby game. You got to be mean. You got to be tough," trainers repeatedly tell their fighters. "You got to try to kill that guy; he's going to try to knock your head off. Try to kill him. Try to knock his eye out. He's going to knock yours out if he can."

The fighter who succeeds best is thus able to suppress his emotions sufficiently to sustain a "killer instinct" and take advantage of his opponent. Questioned after his fatal injury of then featherweight champion Davey Moore, Sugar Ramos remarked: "As long as a man keeps hitting me back I know I have to hit him back." After fatally injuring Art Doyle, Sugar Ray Robinson said simply that "hurting people is my business."

To force him to fight harder, Jonny Bratton's manager used to bet his fighter's purse on the outcome of his fights, leaving Bratton broke and wanting whenever he lost.[14] In the exploitation of the boxer by his handlers, it is necessary to exercise intensive control and constraint over the fighter's thinking and behavior, to dominate the fighter and his total mood. Manager Cus D'Amato was said to receive a "sadistic delight in keeping Floyd Patterson under his hypnotic spell." He would tell Floyd over and over again: "The entire world is against you, trust no one but me."[15]

At the same time, a fighter cannot always count on his manager's good intentions. While most fighters are black, almost all managers are white. One manager I know bet against his fighter, then secured a woman for the fighter shortly before the fight to weaken him for defeat.

Beyond this, many fighters feel resentful that a fighter's success depends too little on what he knows and too much on whom his manager knows. "You have to be in a clique," a former fighter insisted to me. "You take some guys that are fighting in the preliminaries, and if they had the right backing they could get somewhere. It used to be that when you lost three or four fights you dropped in the ratings. Now some fighters lose three or four and then fight for the title."

Further evidence of the exploitation and racism of promoters is that today, when most fighters are black, most fight clubs still pay their preliminary fighters what they paid them thirty years ago when prices and tickets were cheaper.

The financial exploitation of the fighter compounds the special strain which his career places upon marriage. Forty of the fifty-eight I talked to were, or had been, married. Among the forty-eight retired fighters in the group, twenty-five were still married, but the wives of ten others had deserted them.

The glamor of boxing and, in the case of successful fighters, the huge sums of money they make, enables boxers frequently to marry women from higher social classes. Joe Louis, for instance, who did not complete high school, is married to a prominent attorney. Thus, many fighters encounter class conflict in their marriages.

"A fighter starts at the bottom," one told me. "Every notch you move up in boxing, you move up a notch with the big shots. That's how come a lot of fighters marry women too high for them. Or if they don't do that, they get their wives too used to luxury and prestige. Then after you quit, and can't keep it up, she gets where she can't stand you and leaves."

I found this fighter in his room in a third-class hotel. He had missed a previous appointment with me because, he explained, he had been drunk. He told me that he had taken to alcohol after his wife had left him. "I'd be the happiest man in the world," he said, "if I could just find her and get her back."

Another fighter, who had become close enough as a friend to invite me to be the best man in his wedding to a Washington, D.C. school teacher, told me that some individuals were telling him that to continue fighting would degrade his wife's profession.

"No wife, I mean no wife, approves," one fighter told me. "All wives like the glory, but they also got to see you come in with your face all beat in—see you nursing your face at night."

Many wives grow impatient with a fighter's financial progress. "I'm like you," I once heard a young fighter confide to another in a Chicago dressing room. "My wife's getting tired of me not being able to keep a job more'n six months at a time. I get money from a fight and I give it to her, but I don't get that too regular, so all the time she's buying the groceries. She just bought nineteen dollars' worth of food last Saturday and that's all gone. I made the mistake of asking her for a dollar—I caught hell before I got that dollar. She's tired of it," he said. "You know, living with her peoples and they know whenever we get in an argument, and I ain't fucking her or nothing trying to get in shape for a fight."

A common reason for marriage failure among fighters is the enforced separation that their training rules demand. Managers and trainers caution fighters to limit their sexual relations as much as possible. But many fighters find it hard to "hold out" against their women, wanting to end long sexual vacations before a fight. Some trainers will go so far as to sleep with their fighters before an important bout in order to keep them out of trouble with their wives. Sixty-two percent of the fighters in my sample told me, however, that they often broke one rule or another in their relationships with women. In general, fighters feel that about two weeks of celibate living before a fight is sufficient—three said only one day—but all who had experienced marriage named this as a major problem.

"You got to keep up your homework," a middleweight told me one night in a Chicago tavern frequented by fighters and ex-fighters. "If you don't, somebody else'll be doing it for you. A fighter fights in so many different cities it's best for him not to have a wife, because she'll cheat on him. It's a mental disturbance to leave, knowing she'll cheat. You can't box if your mind is split on something else."

In spite of all this, only ten of thirty-four who had an opinion on the subject thought marriage was bad for a fighter. Managers and trainers, on the other hand, are almost unanimous in believing that fighters should not burden themselves with marital responsibilities.

"It's better to leave your wife at home," a trainer told me in Washington, D.C. "Of course, if she was rooting for you, she'd come unbeknownst to you. But it's better to leave her home." Later, he told a young fighter not to bring any of his relatives because he might try to "show off" and end up doing worse than ever.

Most of the fighters I studied had launched their careers with the approval of their families. Only about one-sixth of the fathers disapproved, and only two-fifths of the mothers. A fighter's relations with his family generally change, however, during his career and immediately following it. His family's admiration for him fluctuates with his success and usually wanes when his career is ended.

One of the most pathetic examples was a former welterweight—now in his thirties and unemployed—who said he had made enough money during his career to send his sister through college. I found him living with his mother in a third-floor walk-up apartment on Chicago's South Side. He was dressed in a shirt and old slacks. I suggested that we go out for a beer.

"My sister's a schoolteacher. My brother's got a good government job," he told me in the tavern. "I'm the bum in the family. My mother wouldn't allow my youngest brother to become a fighter, and he was a natural. I wasn't—I had to develop my skill. My mother can't stand the sight of a fighter, especially me. I had a birthday last month, and I didn't get one present from my family."

At that point he fell silent, and a friend of his entered the bar and walked over to him. "Your mother wants you to come home and clean out the cellar," he said. "I got to get out of this," the former fighter said to me.

Another put his brother into business, but they soon fell into periodic fights in which he beat his brother. Finally his brother took out a warrant for his arrest and won't speak to him or give him money now that he is broke.

Such factors lead most fighters to long to return to the ring. Almost 70 percent of the retired fighters at one time or another got the urge to resume, and 40 percent actually did make one or more comeback attempts. This indicates the difficulty most fighters experience in trying to adjust occupationally and otherwise after their ring careers end. The problems of physically and mentally impaired ex-boxers have been widely publicized, but it seems to me that too little attention has been paid to the more common problem of maladjustment.

Fighters come mostly from urban slum areas where there is a lower standard of living and a higher prevalence of mental and physical disease. Professional boxing fails to equip its graduates for other work. In fact, it tends to prejudice them against it. Managers and trainers are opposed to having their fighters learn other trades or work at other jobs during their careers. They want a fighter to devote himself completely to boxing. They also feel that a fighter who has no other means of support and no other skills will train harder and, when the going in the ring gets rough, fight harder.

There is no way in which a fighter can use his special skills after retirement, unless he becomes a trainer of fighters. He finds it hard to accept the routine, time-clock nature of most jobs, and he has become used to receiving his pay in comparatively large, lump sums, rather than in small, fixed amounts at regular intervals. In the partnership of boxer, manager and trainer, the fighter rightfully is the important party. He loses and misses this sense of importance when he embarks upon another line of work.

"I ain't going to do no hard work," an ex-fighter who had tried nine jobs in six months told me. "Look. Feel my hands. I never had a callus in my life. When I was boxin' I wasn't used to havin' a boss and workin' all day. Oh, before I'd steal I'd work for a while, but I'd do it where nobody could see me. I'd die if somebody saw me."

White boxers typically do better in post-career life because of greater benevolence on the part of their managers (c.f. Rocky Marciano and Joe Louis). Also, for small-time fighters (by far the majority) there are better jobs available to whites after retirement.

Thirty-seven of the forty-eight retired fighters I visited did have steady jobs, but 60 percent of those said they would be happier in different work. Most of them were unskilled or semi-skilled laborers. Four operated small taverns or restaurants, one was a jazz musician and one ran a dry-cleaning establishment.

I found that scientific boxers adjusted to post-career life slightly better than the sluggers. The unsuccessful scientific boxers adjusted best of all, and the successful sluggers experienced the most difficulty. Half of all the retired fighters, however, told me that they would need more than an additional $100 a week to live the way they wanted.

We may conclude, then, that boxing does not leave all its scars on a fighter's face. The tragedy of the fighter's life is that when his career comes to an end in his late twenties or early thirties—an age at which most young men are just approaching their prime—he feels that the best years of his life are already behind him. For too many this is the unfortunate truth.

In the gyms, I watched the active fighters working and waiting for the lucky break which, they believed, would take them to the wealth and glory of a championship. In the taverns and poolrooms, I listened to the former fighters reliving their own fighting careers, boasting to sustain their pride, dissatisfied now with their present lot and trying to call back in conversation the youth and skills that had once been theirs.

Three years after winning the welterweight championship, Johnny Saxton was charged with two burglaries and held in a New Jersey jail. There he tried to take his own life and had to be confined for a while in the New Jersey State Mental Hospital. "I used to be somebody," the ex-champ explained, "but now I'm nobody. I wish the police had shot me."

I have seen ex-fighters trying to borrow carfare with no avail and, in the case of a blind ex-fighter, doing calisthenics and shadowboxing nightly in his hotel room. One night I found a fighter who retired about thirty years ago after sixteen years in the ring, but whose name still evokes memories for fight fans who go back that far. I found him living with his wife in a transient-hotel room in a slum area, reminiscing about the days when he was the National Boxing Association middleweight champion, boxing throughout this country and in Paris, and she was a professional dancer.

Boxing is good for some black men, allowing them to escape the deprivation of the slums; but for most, it merely reflects and aggravates their basic oppression.

NOTES

1. Barry Gottenhrer, "How Great is Sonny Liston?" *Boxing Yearbook,* 1964, p. 11.

2. Jose Torres, *Sting Like a Bee,* New York: Abelard-Schuman, 1971, pp. 138-139.

3. Nathan Hare, "What Makes a Man a Fighter?" ed. by W. C. Heinz, *Saturday Evening Post* (March 8, 1958), p. 27.

4. "Dr. Nathan Hare: Black Power Professor with a Punch," *Sepia* (April, 1968), pp. 50-54. Bernard Garrett, "Fired Howard University Teacher Returns to Boxing Career," *Jet* (October 26, 1967), pp. 16-21.

5. Jack Olsen, *Black is Best: The Riddle of Cassius Clay,* New York: Dell, 1967, p. 93.

6. S. Kirson Weinberg and Henry Arond, "The Occupational Culture of the Boxer," *American Journal of Sociology* (March, 1952), p. 460.

7. "Boxing Illustrated's World Boxing Ratings," *Boxing Illustrated* (August, 1971), p. 16.

8. Nathan Hare, "White Supremacy Backfires in Boxing," *Flamingo* (September, 1962), p. 42.

9. Jack Zanger, "Here Comes Ingo . . . Again," *Boxing Annual,* 1963, p. 10.

10. Aronds and Weinberg, *op. cit.,* p. 461.

11. Hare, *op. cit.,* p. 44.

12. Alexander Berger, "Best Bet for the Big Title," *Boxing Illustrated* (August, 1959), p. 35.

13. Torres, *op. cit.,* p. 83.

14. George Puscas, "Child of Tragedy," *Negro Digest* (April, 1962), p. 42.

15. Wendell Smith, "Patterson—The Recluse," *Boxing and Wrestling* (January, 1962), p. 41.

THE BATTLE OVER RACISM

Paul Hoch

When you are the anvil you bend. But when you are the hammer you strike.

> A black "rioter" at Attica state prison in New York.

It's insulting to me that I don't see more black coaches . . . any black managers in baseball, any black head coaches in football playing the game. It's insulting to me when I look around and see Alabama and Mississippi playing on television and Chris Schenkle comes on and makes the statement: "And these two teams epitomize the spirit of sport and fair play and brotherhood in America."

> Harry Edwards, from National Educational Television's film,
> *Take Me Out of the Ball Game.*

Racism is everywhere in America—in the streets, in the factories, in schools, on the media, everywhere. If it is closer to the surface in sports, this may be because the sexual anxieties that provide so much of the motive force for racism are closely related to the cult of masculinity and machismo which permeates the sports world. (The argument goes that the black man must be kept in his place—otherwise he'll be after "our" women. And by this standard the black athlete, being a potential black "Superman," must be even more carefully watched and kept in his place. Hence—the exaggerated racism of the sports world.)

The racial stereotype has been, for some time, that the black is a good athlete. Today, with more and more black faces turning up on college and professional teams, it is hard for many people to imagine that these blacks are being discriminated against. But what we forget is that almost every new group of immigrants that came to America (and found itself stuck in urban ghettos and excluded from jobs) predominated in professional sports for a time. This being one of their few outlets, they had to. But this does not mean the athletes themselves weren't exploited financially by ruthless promoters and owners. Nor does it mean that they were allowed their full share of human dignity simply because they became athletic performers. This was as true of the "brawling Irish" of John L. Sullivan's day as the black athletes of today. But the race problem in sports is further complicated by the institutionalizing of racial prejudice in Western society generally that dates from a colonization of Africa at least four centuries old.

We have previously seen how the all-white character of our team sports as they developed in nineteenth-century England was intimately related to the main function of these schools and their sports—to knit together an imperialist elite which would rule over workers at home and men of color abroad. Obviously you could not have blacks in these schools or in these sports at that point because they couldn't become part of the elite. So racism in sports—as with racism generally—was part and parcel of imperialism against men of color abroad. (Much later on when it became fashionable—and absolutely necessary—to have a black puppet elite to help run the colonies, it became permissible for chiefs' sons to study at English universities and play ball with their white collaborators.) Sports was part of the system of ruling-class identification. Ruling-class people played ruling-class sports. (Soccer was finally appropriated by the English working class after a struggle lasting around six centuries—for a great deal of this time there were royal edicts against serfs kicking a ball around or taking part in games.) And, similarly in America, right down to the early fifties (and—in many sports, many schools and many parts of the country—right down until *today*) the policy of racial apartheid in sports reigns supreme, as part and parcel of the mechanisms by which white supremacy is enforced in society generally. "The essential attitude," writes Jack Olsen in *The Black Athlete: A Shameful Story* (New York: Time-Life Books, 1968), "is that these are white men's games, as indeed they are." He notes that all the blacks playing football when Paul Robeson was smashing through the line at Rutgers would not have been enough to fill a "colored only" waiting room in a small hick town in Georgia. Until less than twenty years ago, blacks who wanted to play "professional basketball" had only the option of being professional clowns (in red, white, and blue uniforms) with the Harlem Globetrotters.

At first the lack of black athletes in many sports (from which they were excluded) was pointed to as clear evidence of their "inherent inferiority." But even when blacks began to dominate certain sports like track and field, they fared no better. For example, USC track coach Dean Cromwell wrote, ". . . the Negro excels in the events he does because he is closer to the primitive than the white man. It was not long ago that his ability to sprint and jump was a life-and-death matter to him in the jungle." (*Championship Technique in Track and Field,* New York: McGraw-Hill, 1941, p. 6.) In a racist society, the black man is damned if he wins, and damned if he loses. The game is rigged against him. If today we can no longer exclude the black man from "white" sports entirely, then we introduce him into them in a gradualistic and token fashion, with appropriate quotas to protect team popularity. (In a racist society it's difficult to have too many blacks on the first team—the audience might be offended.) At any rate, you can pretty much keep him out of the "thinking" positions—football quarterback, middle linebacker, center and guards, as well as coaching and managerial jobs. "The Negro may be permitted to help out," adds Jack Olsen (*op. cit.*), "but his role is clearly defined: he is a hired performer, and he has a job only so long as he knows his place in the white game and stays in it."

How many black referees, umpires, judges, and linesmen have you seen in professional sports? In big-time college sports? How many black announcers? (A recent token has been the creation of what amounts to an "assistant announcer" post for blacks. It is a sad thing to see a Bill Russell acting as back-up to a white announcer who knows maybe a tenth as much about basketball as he does.) How many black members on the United States Olympic Committee? (That brotherhood-serving body.) On the board of the New York Athletic Club? How many black sports owners?

In one generation the situation has gone from one of virtual exclusion of blacks from American sports to what is today sometimes called the "plantation system." The contemporary situation resembles a plantation in that almost all of the overseers are white (except for the now-standard black *assistant* coach in basketball) and almost all of the top players are black. Moreover, when the professional basketball playoff games roll into town, we are faced with the odd situation of predominantly black teams playing before predominantly white suburbanite audiences. (It is again highly reminiscent of the Roman amphitheater gladiator contests in which African and Greek slaves performed for the predominantly Roman audiences.)

Even today you can pretty well keep blacks out of the elite sports—like tennis or golf or polo or even ice hockey. And if you have to have them, you have them room separately from the whites. You discourage inter-racial dating. (It's bad for the image.) And perhaps most of all you have to crush quickly the "uppity" blacks—otherwise they will all be getting out of hand.

Jack Johnson was an "uppity nigger." Worse still, he was heavyweight champ, could beat the pants off of any white around, and laugh in their face to boot. He fucked white women. So they caught him taking a white girl across state lines, and hit him with a criminal conviction for supposedly transporting her for purposes of prostitution. He was forced into exile, stripped of his title, and eventually, he claims in his autobiography, he had to make a deal to take a dive in exchange for a reduction on his jail sentence. His story is told in the play and movie *The Great White Hope*. (The title speaks for itself.)

Muhammed Ali is another "uppity" one. First he offended the white racist sportswriters by having too much to say, by not showing proper respect. He kept saying, "I am the greatest," he announced he was a black nationalist, and to top it off he changed his name (to this day the most racist sportswriters refuse to call him by his Muslim name). But his supreme heresies were to call America a racist country and to refuse to be drafted to kill other men of color in Vietnam. Obviously, he did not know his place. So just as soon as he refused to be drafted, and long before his case was decided in the courts—he was eventually acquitted—the self-appointed crusaders for Truth, Justice and the American Way on the boxing commissions decided that "Clay" was guilty until proven innocent, stripped him of his heavyweight title and refused to allow him to fight for three and a half years. (By comparison, recent boxing champions adjudged as "fit" to hold their titles included professional union-buster and assaulter Sonny Liston, convicted mugger Joey Giardello, panderer Jake LaMotta, army deserter Rocky Graziano, and as a "fit" top challenger—felony murderer Ruben Carter!) The sportswriters jumped in gleefully, landing cheap shots left and right (mostly Right). The New York *Daily News'* patriotic columnist Gene Ward contrasted Ali with Joe Louis, the latter a credit to his race and one who dearly loved his country. Ali was not the first uppity black to get the can. But the thing they never have, and never can, forgive him for is that he fought back.

Just before the 1968 Olympics, Professor Harry Edwards tried to organize an Afro-American boycott of the Games on the grounds that their participation would be used to bolster America's image abroad while they continued to be treated like second-class citizens at home. One of those to join the boycott was basketball's most outstanding player, Lew Alcindor. He was interviewed on television by that patriotic sportscaster Joe Garagiola. With his usual bluntness Joe told this uppity black man that, if he didn't like things in this country, he could just get out.

Meanwhile, the Olympic establishment was having a fit over the boycott. After all, they were fighting hard to keep white racist Rhodesia and South Africa in the competition. And they had been threatened with a boycott of black African and east European countries if they did that. So eventually they had to drop their South Africa cronies just to keep the show on the road. Luckily for them, the black American boycott waned. But then when sprint champions Tommy Smith and John Carlos gave their famous black power salute during the playing of the United States National Anthem, the

Olympics establishment screamed bloody murder that the blacks were "injecting politics into sport" (i.e., opposing the white supremacist politics of their bosses) and ejected them from the Games. After some stiff questioning from a *Ramparts* reporter at a subsequent press conference, the U.S. Olympic Committee's press officer demanded to see the reporter's credentials. "You're on the nigger side, aren't you?" he said. Most American and British sportswriters wrote that Smith and Carlos had been soundly booed. In fact, according to *Ramparts* sports editor Jack Scott who was there, virtually the only boos to be heard came from these same writers! Also, although the Western media did their damndest to minimize the fact, a good many *white* Olympians stood solidly with the blacks. American hammer-throwers Hal Connolly and Ed Burke joined with various blacks on the U.S. team in threatening to withdraw from the Games after the Smith-Carlos suspensions (Scott, *op. cit.*, p. 87). Martin Jellinghaus, wearing the button of Harry Edwards' Olympic Project for Human Rights, noted after his team's bronze finish in the 1,600-meter relay, "I am wearing this medal because I feel solidarity not only for them as persons, but for the movement, the human rights movement." Peter Norman, the Australian sprinter who shared the victory stand with Smith and Carlos and fully supported their gesture, likewise appeared wearing the Human Rights medal (and was sternly reprimanded by the Australian sports establishment). The Harvard crew team likewise supported Harry Edwards' boycott movement almost every step of the way and was repeatedly harassed by U.S. sports officials. So at least some of the white sportsmen were waking up to the way the Establishment uses racism as a weapon to divide and conquer.

It is interesting to review the records of some of the men who accused the blacks of playing politics. Once before these men had been confronted with a boycott threat. The incident is described by Richard D. Mandell in his book on *The Nazi Olympics* in Berlin in 1936. At that time the issue was that Hitler's German team discriminated against Jews. The Olympic establishment repeatedly claimed that this wasn't so, or if it was, it was irrelevant. Eventually, as the movement to boycott the Olympics gathered momentum in America, they sent General Charles Sherrill (a member of the American and International Olympic committees) to Berlin to negotiate with the Nazis. Sherrill vigorously opposed the boycott and, upon his return, discussed the reasons for his mission:

> I went to Germany for the purpose of getting at least one Jew on the German Olympic team and I feel that my job is finished. As for obstacles placed in the way of Jewish athletes or any others in trying to reach Olympic ability, I would have no more business discussing that in

Germany than if the Germans attempted to discuss the Negro situation in the American South or the treatment of the Japanese in California. (New York *Times*, October 22, 1935).

He also claimed that he knew many Jews who opposed a boycott and who feared that "it would be overplaying the Jewish hand in America as it was overplayed in Germany before the present suppression and expulsion of the Jews were undertaken." The next day, Frederick Rubin, then Secretary of the American Olympic Committee, announced his position: "Germans are not discriminating against Jews in their Olympic tryouts. The Jews are eliminated because they are not good enough as athletes. Why there are not a dozen Jews in the world of Olympic caliber." (New York *Times*, October 23, 1935.) General Sherrill later appeared before the Italian Chamber of Commerce in New York and praised Mussolini as "a man of courage in a world of pussyfooters," adding, "I wish to God he'd come over here and have a chance to do that same thing." (New York *Times*, November 27, 1935.)

The President of the American Olympic Committee (and close colleague of Sherrill and Rubin) was Avery Brundage. He has remained at the top of the Olympic establishment ever since, and is presently head of the International Olympic Committee. He opposed the anti-Nazi boycott just as he was later to oppose the black boycott. He opposed exclusion of Germany in 1936, of Japan in 1940, and of Rhodesia and South Africa in 1968. In 1936, according to Mandell, "Brundage and his supporters posed as being far above petty chauvinism—a position that did not prevent them from occasionally praising the visible accomplishments of the Nazis and from slurring the adherents of (the boycott) Committee on Fair Play as being Reds or even Communists."

In May 1968 *Ramparts* reported that Brundage had told an AAU National Convention that the German Jews were "satisfied" with their treatment under the Nazis. Was this just a hastily thought-out view based largely on ignorance? Apparently not. For even after Brundage made the trip to Nazi Germany with the 1936 American Olympic team, he returned to a packed rally of 20,000 at Madison Square Garden with heady praise for the Nazi establishment. According to the October 3, 1936, New York *Times*, Avery Brundage "brought his audience to their feet cheering in an outburst of enthusiasm when he paid tribute to the Reich under Adolf Hitler." He told them, "We can learn much from Germany. We, too, if we wish to preserve our institutions, must stamp out communism. We, too, must take steps to arrest the decline of patriotism."

"As recently as August 1940," *Ramparts* reported, "Brundage was serving as head of Citizens to Keep America Out of War, a group now known to have been Nazi-supported." It came as no great surprise that the only two Jews on the American track and field team, Sam Stoller and Marty Glickman, were mysteriously dropped from the 400-meter relay team just before the start of the Berlin Games.

Whenever college athletes become "rebellious"—and even more especially whenever *black* college athletes become rebellious—some coach or sports-writer will inevitably come out with the old garbage about how "the college has given these athletes a free education for which they should be grateful." The argument goes that the sports teams were the first things on campus to be integrated, and "if it wasn't for sports they'd still be back in their ghettos." (This is like a boss who tells his striking employee, "if it wasn't for me you wouldn't have a job.") First of all, is it not curious that the first college sport to be "integrated," namely football, is also the sport that makes the most money? Is it not curious that the "integration" of college basket-ball, especially at some of the Big Ten schools, has come along only in the last decade? That college baseball is still 98 percent lily white? That schools such as the University of Texas at El Paso which were eager to welcome black athletic crowd-pleasers onto their campus with open arms took quite awhile to extend the same admission to non-athletic black students? "The black athlete in the predominantly white school," says Harry Edwards in *The Revolt of the Black Athlete* (New York: Free Press, 1969), "was and is first, foremost, and sometimes only, an athletic commodity." But, you say, at least he gets an education. Yes, an "education" composed mostly of courses in things like phys ed and basket weaving. He's expected to give most of his time to the "team." And after his athletic eligibility ends, so does his scholarship. Most never even graduate. They end up right back in the ghetto.

Lately, with the exception of the lily-white teams of the deep South, as more and more black faces are seen on the playing fields, some white sports fans have been getting more and more impatient. During the 1969 Notre Dame-Michigan State basketball game at South Bend, the Notre Dame coach committed the extreme *faux pas* of having five black faces on the court at the same time. Never mind that they were his best players. The overwhelmingly white "Fighting Irish" student body at Notre Dame field house nearly had a fit. Hoots and boos rang through to the rafters whenever the five black players were on the court together. The black players resigned and did not rejoin the team till they received a public apology from the president of the Notre Dame student body. The mask of white liberalism was wearing very thin, and the racism was increasingly showing through. A few years earlier, Dick Harp, the basketball coach at Kansas had resigned in disgust at the abuse he had received from fans and alumni for starting four black players during the 1963-64 season.

No doubt the exploitation of the white athlete is almost equally ruthless. He too gets his share of junk courses. Gives his all for the team, while the college collects the profits. He, too, a large part of the time never graduates. But he also has a lot of job opportunities that his black teammate does not. He has not been so thoroughly coaxed into believing that sports is his best chance to "make it" in life. Jack Olsen points out that although sports has led a few thousand blacks out of the ghetto, for hundreds of thousands—maybe millions—of others, "it has substituted a meaningless dream. It has helped to perpetuate an oppressive system." Though sports may also have provided an arena in which blacks vicariously acted out their aggressions against whites by cheering on their heroes, it did little to deal with the grievances that caused such aggressions. Hence, even integrated sports have been used as a racial opiate.

At times the use of black athletes in college sports resembles nothing so much as a modern version of the slave trade, in which coaches send their scouts out looking for quality black horse flesh to reel in the trophies (and the cash), only to be thrown back in their ghetto cages when the game ends. "The whites call the Negro football players cannibals," said UTEP (University of Texas at El Paso) basketballer Willie Worsley, "and the basketball players [who in 1966 won the NCAA Championship] animals. You play basketball and that's it. When the game's over they want you to come back to the dormitory and stay out of sight." His athletic director George McCarty replies, "Four of our colored alumni are playing pro basketball right now . . . and you can't just say that we got a bunch of cattle in here and milked them. It was profitable both ways." And who says they aren't still being "milked" in the pros? "You know those junkyards along the highways in Jersey?" says former Cleveland Indians outfielder Larry Doby, who was the first black to be allowed into the American League. "Well, they have scrap heaps just like that for athletes—most of them black. Black athletes are cattle. They're raised, fed, sold and killed. . . . Baseball moved me toward the front of the bus, and it let me ride there as long as I could run. And then it told me to get off at the back door." (Jack Olsen, *op. cit.*) "They look upon us as nothing but animals," said Olympic sprinter John Carlos. "Low animals, roaches, and ants. . . . They give us peanuts, pat us on the back and say, 'Boy, you did fine.' " Behind all the outrage that blacks are not more grateful for "the chances we've given them" lies the old apartheid attitude that, after all, blacks don't really belong on "our" sports fields and colleges; they are only there because we "gave" them something. As if anything that great were happening on the football fields and colleges! The main thing happening in football is that a lot of guys are being injured so that others can make big profits. As for the colleges, the main things they are teaching are the top-down view of the world, contempt for all those not in college, and absolute obedience to the administration. (Happily, many students have other ideas.)

But times are changing, and black athletes are getting the message. In 1965 black members of the American Football League All-Star teams banded together and refused to play the game in racially biased New Orleans, Louisiana. The AFL's Commissioner had to move the game to another city. (Unfortunately, as a direct result of this incident, the AFL's two top black running backs, Abner Haynes and Cookie Gilchrist, were promptly traded and were soon seen riding the bench on their new teams.)

Two years later the season's opening football game between San Jose State College and UTEP had to be cancelled when black San Jose student activists threatened they would break it up as a protest against racism on their campus. (There were also rumors that if the game were played, SJS's stadium would be "burned to the ground.") November 1967 brought the start of the Olympic boycott campaign. It was strongly supported by Lew Alcindor:

Everybody knows me. I'm the big basketball star, the weekend hero, everybody's All-American. Well, last summer I was almost killed by a racist cop shooting at a black cat in Harlem. He was shooting on the street—where masses of black people were standing around or just taking a walk. But he didn't care. After all we were just niggers ["Doc" Ellis and Willis Reed would have similar experiences.] . . . Somewhere each of us has got to make a stand against this kind of thing. (Harry Edwards, *op. cit.*)

February 1968 brought a black boycott of the New York Athletic Club's games in protest against the club's membership bar against blacks:

The intransigence of the N.Y.A.C. in its refusal to even admit the problem of racism in its ranks, much less take steps to rectify it, is, we believe, indicative of the present demeanor of White America toward taking real steps to deal with racism in this society. We see, through this protest, that it isn't just racist *individuals* we are up against. It's a racist conspiracy involving many of the would-be-great institutions of the Society. (From the boycotters' press release.)

The same month black athletes at the University of California's Berkeley campus threatened to boycott, picket, and disrupt all the school's athletic competitions unless the athletic director and the basketball coach were replaced, black coaches were hired, more black students were recruited, more black studies courses included in the curriculum, and the treatment of blacks on campus was greatly improved. They won all of their demands including the replacement of the athletic director and football coach. (Similar boycott threats or protests were made at, among other places, Michigan State University, Western Michigan University, Marquette, Kansas, San Francisco State, Washington, and Princeton. Some token Negro coaches were promptly hired to cool things down.) All in all, there were racial revolts on the teams of no less than thirty-seven major college campuses in the year 1967-68 alone.

There were also serious racial flare-ups on the St. Louis Cardinals and Cleveland Browns pro football teams. In St. Louis a lot of the dissension was caused by the attitude of white players and coaches toward interracial dating. "They won't have our respect," one white Cardinal said about his black teammates, "as long as they keep getting caught with white women. To me that's the worst offense there is—dating white girls." Roy Shivers tells about the time he ran into the fiancée of a white friend from his college days. A couple of Cardinal coaches promptly came up "and gave us the funny look." Then there was some advice from an older Negro player: "The coach wants you to cool it, be a bit more discreet." According to running back Johnny Roland, the coaches "set a tone that the white racist guys just follow. Some of the coaches treat us like animals, so why shouldn't the players do the same." Bernie Parrish writes that to Cincinnati Bengals and former Cleveland Browns head coach Paul Brown the players were just his "animals." "When Jim Brown ripped off a good gain or two early in a game," says Parrish, "Paul would rub his hands together and whisper to John Wooten, one of his messenger guards [and black], 'The animal's runnin' today—the animal's ready today.' " (Parrish, *op. cit.,* pp. 95-96.) And Paul Brown was no fly-by-night fill-in coach. For more than twenty-five years he has been at the very top of the professional football coaching profession. Similarly, with Alvin Dark. It's now about ten years since he made his famous remarks about black and Latin American baseball players being not as bright as whites, lazy and lacking in team spirit to boot. Although Dark was fired that year (for getting on the wrong side of his owner) he returned to the majors and soon had one of the longest managerial careers in baseball.

"There are definite signs of quotas and definite signs that black players are stacked at certain positions," continued the Cardinals' Johnny Roland.

"It isn't enough for a Negro to be good to make this team. He's got to be better than good." Similarly in baseball.[1] Aaron Rosenblatt's statistical survey in *Trans-Action* showed that in the seasons 1962-65 inclusive, the average black major leaguer hit 21.2 points higher than the average white, and that approximately the same percentage held for the preceding nine years.

"It's a sad thing to face," said Cardinal fullback Prentice Gautt, "but racial prejudice is almost a tradition in sports." He remarks that black athletes could be telling other blacks that there is no need to rebel. "But what kind of hypocrites would we be to go back and tell them a better day is coming, when that day isn't even in sight on the playing field?"

Carl Brettschneider, a former player and front-office man with the Detroit Lions, told Bernie Parrish, "The Lions, while I was personnel director, they practically ordered me to draft more colored guys than white guys. You know why? Cheaper, they sign cheaper." When Parrish asked him if it was correct that black players are paid less than white players of comparable ability, he replied, "Oh, I think so, sure, sure." (Parrish, *op. cit.,* pp. 149-50.)

In his autobiography, *Confessions of a Dirty Ballplayer* (New York: Dell, 1971, p. 85), Johnny Sample tells the story of the problems he had getting a just raise after he first made All-Pro cornerback. "I know you had a great year, Sample," said his coach. "But black athletes just don't deserve that kind of money and I won't pay it." (The coach in question had his personal elderly black valet "Bootsy," who would wake him up in the morning, spit-polish his shoes, get him his coffee, etc., "for which he was paid next to nothing and treated like a dog.") In 1963, John Nisby of the Redskins and John Henry Johnson, the top fullback for the Steelers, started writing a book on racism in the NFL. They wrote to every black player in the league for information. According to Sample, Chicago Bears owner-coach George Halas somehow got a copy, called up all the other owners "and all hell broke loose." Sample says, "John Nisby was quickly ousted." (*Ibid.,* pp. 214-15.) Johnson was one of the top rushers in the league; so he was allowed to stay for a while. But in 1965 he injured his leg and got the heave-ho. "This kind of thing will continue," says Sample, "until black players get together and put a stop to it."

Parrish gives another interesting example. Clifton McNeil, the wide receiver who led the NFL in pass receiving with seventy-one catches in 1968, had the boldness to insist on a substantial raise for his successes. Not only was it refused, but according to Parrish, "he was disciplined for having the temerity to ask by being benched through most of the next season . . . and at the end of the year he was traded to the Giants as damaged goods." (Parrish, *op. cit.,* p. 152.) He managed to catch fifty passes for the Giants in 1970, but early the following year he was suddenly shipped to the Redskins.

Walter Roberts, one of the Redskins' outstanding flankers of 1970, had previously gone to New Orleans in the expansion draft. "After one season," writes Parrish, "Tom Fears [the New Orleans coach] suspected Walt of organizing the black players, so he made a deal with Detroit to take Roberts for a little while, then drop him and blackball him from the league." (*Ibid.*, p. 179.) Walt Roberts had to sit out of pro football for a year. Bob Brown, an All-Pro offensive tackle with the Los Angeles Rams, was suddenly shipped to the Oakland Raiders. "You've really got trouble there," the San Francisco *Chronicle* says the Raiders' general manager was told. "It's funny," said Brown much later. "If you speak up for your rights, you're a troublemaker, and if you're a black athlete who speaks up, you're really bad." All-Pro tight end John Mackey had the reputation of being a fairly mild fellow until he took over as president of the NFL Players' Association and led them through the 1970 strike. After that he was often referred to as a "Bolshevik." A year later he found himself playing second string. "You have to have the right 'attitude' or you can't play," noted Baltimore Colts All-Pro tackle Jim Parker. "At Ohio State I had a friend who I thought could play a good game, but the coach said he didn't have the right [Right?] 'attitude,' so he sat on the bench for four years. Even in pro football you look at a guy and you think he can play, and then one day he's on the train going home; something to do with his 'attitude.' You worry about it, but you don't ask any questions because you have a family to feed." (Olsen, *op. cit.*)

During the 1970 college football season at least seventy-nine black athletes boycotted or were suspended from their teams over charges of racism. Possibly the most serious flare-up was at Syracuse University where eight blacks boycotted the squad and two more dropped off for "medical" reasons.

Ben Schwartzwalder, the Syracuse coach, is probably one of the best known and most successful coaches in college sports. He has won bowl games, been named "Coach of the Year," and has had top black players like Jimmy Brown, Floyd Little, and the late Ernie Davis.

As the 1969-70 academic year drew to a close, racial tensions on the Syracuse football squad headed toward the boiling point. It was said that black players had been addressed by coaches as "Hey, boy!" and "nigger." That blacks, such as Richie Bulls, had received tongue lashings for being seen around with white girls. That coach Schwartzwalder seemed unduly keen about blacks shaving off their mustaches. Afro hair styles were absolutely taboo. Later, at a basketball game at the Syracuse field house, the coach jumped hard on blacks who refused to stand for the National Anthem:

With all the crap we were going through at the school, and with this country fostering apartheid here and in South Africa, killing Asians who are Black, adding to the oppression of Arabs in the Middle East, I didn't think that I should stand and salute a flag of a country that is not mine. The United States has never taken into account the welfare of Blacks in any of its economic policies. In fact they foster unemployment among Blacks as a tool to fight inflation. They keep Blacks in a poverty spectrum. Why should I stand and recognize this flag? (Defensive back Duane Walker, quoted in *Black Sports,* June 1971.)

Schwartzwalder told them he didn't want any "commies" on his team. They would either stand for the Anthem or get out. (Eventually black players would stay in their locker rooms during the playing of the Anthem.)

Then there were the hundred and one intangible things that convinced the black athletes that the coaches and the school regarded them as "super-niggers," good enough to beat their brains in on the field for the Ole Alma Mater, but not much good for anything else. They decided that they wanted a black coach—he at least might have some understanding about their griev-ances—and put their point of view to the head coach. After the university came up with nothing, the players suggested that a black professional be hired to stick with the squad for the thirty-day 1970 spring training session. The coaches eventually came up with Floyd Little, the Denver Broncos pro who, in his days at Syracuse, had bitterly opposed a petition from other black athletes against games with schools with proven records of racial discrimi-nation. According to linebacker Jeff Logan, Little's participation in spring training consisted of little more than walking out onto the field for an hour one day, and then disappearing. The black players figured they had been had (*Black Sports,* June 1971).

The fourth day of spring training they boycotted practice. They were immediately suspended, and even threatened with being kicked off campus (though, as the publicity glare flooded the university, they were eventually allowed to stay). When the administration suggested that the suspensions be lifted, the white jocks unanimously voted against it. (A year earlier when the blacks had first asked for a black coach, the whites had unanimously voted that they would not play for one.)

Nothing could have shown more clearly the ability of the system to use racism to divide the people against each other. One of the black's main complaints had been inferior medical attention—being sent back onto the field to risk permanent disability when you were really too injured to play. "I've got calcium deposits in my knee," declared one white jock, "but that's my problem. I'm not going to complain about it." Then, too, not only had coaches called some players "nigger," they had called others "wop," "polack," "dirty kraut," and so on. Most important, both white and black players had been subject to the same vicious authoritarianism. Only the whites thought that they had to take their football complete with a dictatorship, and that was that. The blacks were trying to do something about it. But the whites thought that the color of their skin gave them more in common with their bosses than it did with their black fellows. (Of course a lot of this response was manipulated by the coaches.)

Eventually with the football season about to get under way the Chancellor of the University appointed a committee of trustees, administrators, professors, and students to look into the situation:

> The Committee concludes that racism in the Syracuse University Athletic Department is real, chronic, largely unintentional, and sustained and complicated. unwittingly by many modes of behavior common in American athletics and longstanding at Syracuse University ... The definition of the spring boycott merely as an issue of violating coaching authority, and the penalizing of black athletes without taking into consideration the broader context of their protest was an act of institutional racism unworthy of a great university. (From the Committee's Report.)

The Chancellor allowed as how he found the findings "fair," but did nothing to discipline the coaches. The Committee called for the suspended players to receive an additional year of football eligibility, and for the running of the athletic programs to be taken out of the hands of the administration and put under the control of a committee representing different segments of the (so-called) university community. Instead of a pledge to obey the coach—as the administration had demanded—they recommended a sort of "bill of rights" for athletes, guaranteeing them the same rights of dress, hair length, and political involvement as are allowed other students. A kind of jock liberation.

Naturally the report was, for the most part, quietly shelved. Committee reports not backed by any threat of militancy are seldom worth the paper they are written on. Indeed, a short time later some Syracuse alumni gave Schwartzwalder a testimonial dinner at the Hotel Americana, and *congratulatory* messages arrived from Governor Rockefeller and President Nixon.

Coach Jim Harding of the University of Detroit is not unlike a good many other coaches. Where he is almost unique is that in November 1970 his entire team simply refused to play for him anymore. In a letter signed by the thirteen black players and three whites who made up the varsity basketball squad, Harding was accused of "failure to recognize us as human beings with human feelings." When informed that he had a team without any players, the coach remained unperturbed. "If that's what they said," he told the wire services, "then they won't remain on the team long. *I* am the head coach and will be here for the next three years." (Face-saving gestures were made, and the players eventually returned.)

In December 1970 four blacks on the University of Washington football team turned in their cleats, charging that the racial practices of the coaches "have forced us to the point where we no longer can tolerate the playing conditions imposed upon us." Charges of racism had previously been leveled at Washington football coaches for more than two years, beginning with spring practice 1968. As at other schools, one of the main issues was interracial dating. Junior Coffey, later a fullback in the NFL (where various teams said he had a bad "attitude") suddenly found himself benched in college. When he asked his assistant coach at Washington why, he was told, "You're dating this white girl and I'd advise you not to do it. I think it would be detrimental to your future, and it could be a reflection on other Negro players." He says it was even hinted that the University would stop recruiting black athletes altogether if he did not knuckle under. At the time Junior Coffey was the *third leading rusher in the nation.* And he never started another Varsity game!

"It has also been discrimination," Charlie Sifford told a reporter for *Black Sports* (June 1971), "that has kept the black golfer ten to fifteen years behind." And yet, we are supposed to weep huge tears when blacks protest the appearance of South Africa's Gary Player at tournaments like the Master's that most black Americans still don't get into. But the anti-apartheid forces are not exactly taking it lying down. In addition to the welcomes for Gary Player, there were disruptions of the games of the South African Springboks cricket and rugby tours in Britain, Ireland, Australia, and New Zealand. (The cricket tour had to be cancelled in Britain because, it was said, black nationalists were "using" the issue to set back race relations some twenty years. Presumably they threatened to have more *equal* race relations.) Nor have South African tennis players been ignored. There have been sit-ins on the courts, hecklings, even aerial bombardments. And in British swimming, Olympic team captain Tony Jarvis greeted the appearance of Prime Minister Edward Heath at the 1970 Commonwealth Games by brandishing a placard proclaiming: "Heath. South African Arms Dealer." In the most faithful traditions of British racist sports, Jarvis was threatened with debarment from the European championships and forced to sign a "no politics" pledge.

In recent years there has also been a growing chorus of protest about the racist stereotypes of American Indians encouraged by the names and emblems of many American professional teams. Names like the Redskins, Indians, Braves and so on—often with emblems showing a hook-nosed, racist stereotype of an Indian—have come under increasing attack both in the United States and Canada.

At the Oakland Coliseum Arena, meanwhile, pentathlon star Sam Goldberg was back in competition. A year earlier he was kicked off the track team at the University of Kansas and lost his scholarship, after he announced that he was dedicating a victory medal to the Black Panthers. He finished a close second in the Oakland meet to the 1970 AAU decathalon champion and beat out a member of the U.S. Olympic team. "I'm dedicating the medal I won tonight," said the blond-haired Goldberg, "to Bobby Seale." He said he was running for an organization whose existence the AAU would rather not face up to—Woodstock International:

> The idea behind Woodstock is a combination of the Black Panther Party's concept of community involvement, and that of progressive working class—in short, it's sports for the people. Let's face it, man. Because of the conservative element in our society, sports have become political. We're competing for the flag, the country, and everything else. My event, without going on an ego trip of what I've done, is for the people. My participation, and everyone competing for Woodstock, is dedicated to America's getting out of Vietnam and the Black Panther Party and anyone else that's getting ripped off.

He added that, when he runs in the big meets, he wears high-top gym shoes, "like the brothers in the ghetto, because like them I can't afford those twenty-dollar jogger shoes." (*San Francisco Examiner,* February 13, 1971.)

NOTE

1. It is also worth noting that except for a few outstanding players there have been very few Jewish major leaguers. Dave Oliphant, a Connecticut businessman formerly the property of the New York Yankees, gave Curt Flood some clues as to why. He was sent to a farm club "whose manager, a rabid anti-Semite ostracized him—except when threatening to get rid of 'that Jewboy.'" He eventually asked for his release; but to get it, his father had to *buy* back his contract. With things like this going on, it's disgusting to see blacks and Jews in places like New York fighting each other for crumbs, while the racists who are screwing them both get the cake. (*The Way It Is,* p. 199.)

7 / SOCIAL CHANGE AND SPORT

Every society possesses stable and permanent structures and functions but they are always subject to change through time; indeed change seems to be universal among societies. In observing change within societies, there are some which seem hardly to change at all while others change rapidly and dramatically. Social change, then, might be viewed as a continuum from static to revolutionary. The contemporary world seems to have very few static societies, a few revolutionary societies, with the great bulk of societies between these two extremes. However, worldwide change seems to be occurring more rapidly than at any time in human history.

There are a number of factors which affect the acceptance of social change. Perceived need for change is one factor. Material inventions or innovations are more readily accepted than changes in basic values and beliefs because they typically reduce human labor or enhance lifestyles. Values and beliefs of various kinds are commonly based upon religious foundations about truth, good, salvation, etc., and are therefore less amendable to modification. Another factor with regard to acceptance of change is the extent to which the proposed change is different from current practices or conditions. A small change is more readily accepted and assimilated into human actions than a dramatic change. The structure of a society is a third factor which affects the acceptance of change. Societies which vest authority in the older members and which adhere to immutable laws of a "supreme" being are likely to be highly resistant to change. Thus, we see the Amish sect in Pennsylvania practicing a way of life reminiscent of centuries ago.

Every society is characterized by forces which make for stability and forces that make for change. Resistance to change comes from various sources. Older members of a society tend to resist change. They often feel that their cultural heritage is being taken from them when change occurs. The wealthy in a society tend to resist change; in most societies the wealthy are the most conservative group. These persons are threatened by change because they have the most to lose if the change fails or if it produces a new group of wealthy persons, since the new may weaken the economic status of the old. Where vested interests are involved, there is a tendency to resist change. Those who have vested interest in a certain area wish to maintain the advantage they have. Change tends to transform or redistribute resources and this is opposed by the vested interests. Those in authority positions, the powerful, tend to resist change, especially if it is initiated from subordinates. In some societies there is enormous respect for authority; persons who hold leadership positions are expected to be obeyed without question. Of course, social change is quite threatening to authority figures because they feel that change may bring about a reduction in their authority and indeed perhaps even their demise. Furthermore, those in powerful positions often feel that their authority has been conferred by some "higher being" or has been earned because of their special abilities and talents; therefore, for a subordinate to suggest change is blasphemous, or at least rude and insolent. Change, when and if it is to come, authority figures often believe, will be properly initiated and controlled by them.

Historically, sport has played a prominent role in social change in Western civilization. The extreme asceticism which was promoted by religious groups such as the early Catholic church and later by the Puritans was gradually modified as people insisted that they be allowed to participate in sports. Sports came into direct conflict with some religious mores and it was the religions which had to be modified, as people violated religious customs in order to engage in sports.

Sport has often been responsible for breaking down social class lines, racial and ethnic barriers, and sex role stereotypes. Sport often is the common denominator for members of different social classes—they may use sport as a focus for conversation or may band together to participate or support a sport team. Thus members of different social classes may unify in the cause of sport. Although sport has not been as equalitarian as some idealists believe, it nevertheless has played a prominent role in American life in assimilating different races and ethnic minorities into American culture. Racial and ethnic integration appeared in sport before it was accepted by the general society. The liberation of the female has its linkage with sport. The bicycle and tennis craze of the later 19th century broke the fad of long skirts and confining undergarments. Bare legs for women were first displayed in sports and then became acceptable in everyday life. The short tennis skirts appear to have been the prelude to the miniskirt. Sport seems to have brought about considerable changes in lifestyles within the past generation. With increasing affluence and leisure, people have come to build a large part of their waking hours around sports involvement. The American weekend has become a time for watching college and professional sports on television or, for the doer, a time to play tennis, golf, etc., go fishing, boating, skiing, or any number of things that are now available. Finally, sport has played a role in bringing about a breakdown in national barriers. Sportsmen have been used as goodwill ambassadors and have brought about changed relations between countries, the "Ping Pong" diplomacy between the United States and China being the most recent example.

Sport is a microcosm of any society and therefore reflects the mores, values, and general culture of a society. The similarities between the evolution of sport and the development of American society are evident to even a casual observer. The traditional American cultural values are pretty generally the values which have been prominent in sports. Indeed, educators and businessmen have agreed that sports participation is an excellent medium for socializing youth into the adult world of America. So the relationship between sport and the promotion of cultural values and behaviors have been mutually supportive.

Within the past decade, the United States has undergone a staggering attack upon its cultural heritage. Several factors have been responsible for this: the race issue, the Vietnam war, pollution and overcrowding in the cities, disillusionment of youth with traditional values and customs, among others. These conditions have spawned riots, assassinations, sit-ins, boycotts, and general social upheaval in recent years. The old culture, and the things for which it stood, have been attacked and a "counterculture" has been proposed as a substitute. The tenets of this counterculture are grounded upon "the absolute worth of every human being—every self." It "rejects the whole concept of excellence and comparative merit that is so central to 'the old culture.' Each person has his own individuality, not to be compared to that of anyone else." It requires that each person "be wholly honest with others, use no other person as a means" (Reich, 1970: pp. 242-244).

The social change occurring throughout American society has invaded the sports world and produced considerable soul-searching, and even turmoil. Authority is being challenged in all spheres of sports life, and tyrannical control is particularly being attacked. Since athletic coaches have one of the most powerful positions in any social institution in American society, this authority is being challenged throughout sports—from the Little Leagues to the professional ranks. This challenge is coming from the athletes themselves because they believe some coaches are oppressive. They also believe that coaches tend to assume too much control over the functioning of the sports team. Criticism of coaches is also coming from social reformers who regard the coach as a symbol of the old cultural values which, they believe, need to be changed.

Although the initial reaction of coaches to these attacks has been resistance, and in some cases counterattacks, coaches are changing. Events in the past few years give evidence that coaches are capable of making significant changes because rules on grooming, training, and general social behavior have been relaxed and some coaches are giving greater responsibilities for the team's functioning to the players.

In the first reading, Crase notes that critics of organized sports came initially from individuals extrinsic to sports but more recently the challenges have been issued from within the athletic community itself. The author identifies several current problems which confront sports programs, such as crowd control, racial grievances, fiscal concerns, drug abuse, educational dimensions of interschool athletics, behavior of coaches, and athletic policies. He discusses each of these problems and suggests some solutions for each.

Stern, in the next reading, discusses how the changing culture in the broader society is affecting sports, focusing particularly upon the coach-athlete relationships in educational institutions. He suggests that sport is undergoing a cultural crisis because the traditional behavior of coaches is not in tune with the needs and interests of today's young athletes. The author discusses several ways in which athletes conceive the purpose and nature of sport much differently than their coaching mentors. These differences are perceived by some coaches and athletes as being irreconcilable but the majority of both groups are gradually working toward accommodation, with the coaches making most of the changes. Stern identifies several sources of the cultural crisis between coaches and players and suggests ways for resolving each area of conflict.

In the third reading Sage discusses the rise of humanistic psychology and the emergence of a "counterculture." He compares the underlying ideas of these two movements and shows their similarities. At the foundation of both is the notion of humane relationships between persons and the need for social experiences which promote personal growth and self-actualization. Sage discusses the conflict between these movements and traditional values in American sports. He concludes the presentation by suggesting courses of action which might resolve the conflict between traditional practices and contemporary values, and he discusses research strategies which have promise for assessing the outcomes of sports participation, particularly with regard to promoting personal growth and self-fulfillment.

In the final reading Sage discusses leadership style in coaching. He suggests that American coaches have generally adopted the Scientific Management leadership style which was advanced by Frederick Taylor in the early years of the 20th century. This style of leadership makes several assumptions about human nature and motivation. Man is viewed as basically lazy, needing extrinsic rewards to get him to perform. An alternative to this leadership style is what is known as Human Relations management. Sage notes that the Human Relations management approach has gained enormous support in industry in the past 20 years and he recommends that this approach be adopted more widely by coaches. This leadership style treats group members more humanely and gives members a greater share in determining their own destiny and in setting goals and means for achieving the goals of the organization.

REFERENCE

Reich, C. A., *The Greening of America*, New York: Bantam Books, 1970.

ATHLETICS IN TROUBLE

Darrell Crase

For some time now critics of "big time" athletics have been predicting that problems and tensions, germane to the instability of competitive athletics, would surface during the decades of the seventies and eighties. From many indications it appears that these claims have reached some form of fruition. Jack Scott, director of the Institute for the Study of Sport and Society in Oakland, California, and perhaps the most outspoken critic of athletics today, says in his latest book, *The Athletic Revolution,* that "college athletics as we enter the 1970's is facing its most severe crises." Most observers and students of competitive programs would agree that today an athletic revolution is simmering.

There have been others who for some time have been predicting the collapse of professionalized competitive athletics. These persons cover the gamut of sporting goods economists, college and university professors, university presidents, sports writers and coaches. Some of these critics have even taken overt steps toward the debasement or elimination of athletics. Thus, the "new" attacks today may or may not be alarming or threatening depending on one's vantage point and his willingness to contemplate the issues.

Attacks which have germinated in past years have been fabricated primarily by those persons extrinsic of the athletic community. These have usually taken the form of verbal outblasts by university professors, education critics, and a few college and university presidents (all of whom question the educational value of athletics). Competitive athletics, along with other social

Darrell Crase, "Athletics in Trouble," *Journal of Health, Physical Education, and Recreation,* 43:39-41 (April 1972). Reprinted by permission of the American Association for Health, Physical Education, and Recreation.

institutions, has had its share of sporadic problems throughout this century which have produced temporary "set-backs" and cast some doubt as to the efficacy of athletics as an educational endeavor. These incidents have ranged from serious organizational squabbles between the Amateur Athletic Union and the National Collegiate Athletic Association to sport scandals involving team members, and in a few cases, coaches. Such developments have temporarily damaged the athletic image, but not to a lasting extent. It appears now, however, as we move into the seventies that attacks on organized athletics, particularly at the college and university levels, are germinating within, and are indigenous to, the athletic community. Thus, the questions, doubts, and apprehensions being raised may have far wider implications than at any other time in the history of American athletics.

Some of the current issues which threaten to debase athletics are those of crowd behavior, racial grievances, monetary problems, drug abuse, educational accountability, internal ferment among participants and coaches, and behavior of coaches and policies of athletic departments.

The immense problem of *crowd control* during athletic contests has been intensifying in numerous school districts across the country. Unruly behavior of spectators is evidenced both within the athletic arena and in near-by areas. As a result, educators have been working extremely hard to find ways of controlling emotionally aroused crowds. To work toward a solution of a problem of this magnitude will require an accelerated educational campaign to improve the behavior and sportsmanship of spectators, players, and coaches during athletic contests. Other adjustments such as an increased liaison between police and school authorities, careful scheduling of events, and the reduction of week-end games will be necessary. Perhaps coaches, players, and administrators have been somewhat remiss in performing their roles as models and/or mediators. Crowds must be controlled if athletics are to continue as a spectator sport. Otherwise, many contests cannot be held and loyal spectators will be kept away from games in anticipation of unruly behavior.

The problem of *racial equality* in athletics reached levels of temporary explosion within the past five years. For some time there was talk about inequities among black members of athletic squads, but it was not until Jack Olsen undertook the momentous task of exposing the shameful story of the black athlete in *Sports Illustrated* that the black athlete began to be heard. It has become obvious to the public that racial problems have and do exist within the athletic community.

It is imperative that better lines of communication be established between the administrative personnel and black players, equal playing and coaching opportunities be guaranteed for blacks, and equitable behavior codes be established and enforced which will permit individual expression within a meaningful context.

Can we continue to *finance* athletics? There is a perpetual cycle in athletics in that winning brings on more fans, thus larger gate receipts which leads to program expansion (larger arenas, more money for recruitment), to more scholarships for more athletes, and more and better athletes leads again to winning. Somewhere along this cycle loopholes are being discovered— coupled with inflation and the shrinking purchasing power of the dollar—and more than a few high schools and universities have found themselves in the red financially. Accordingly, major football programs have been discontinued in more than a few colleges and universities in recent years and countless public school athletic programs are financially handicapped.

Another contributing factor to the shrinking budget may be the rapid expansion of professional athletics to every major city in the country. The professional teams in turn take away monies which conceivably would be earmarked for support of interscholastic and intercollegiate contests.

What about *drug abuse* in athletics? Jack Scott stated that "One of the most critical issues the athletic world must face as we enter the 1970's is the problem of drug abuse. Athletes on the high school and college level as well as in the pros are being given steroids, amphetamines, pain killers, and most any other drug that seems to aid their performance with little or no concern being shown for the dangerous side-effects of these drugs." Newspapers have presented numerous examples of drug abuse among college and professional athletes. Dave Meggyesy in *Out of Their League* has spoken of the widespread use of various drugs in football and by his former professional football team in particular.

The entire drug scene for athletes—what drugs to use? when? how much? legality? ethics involved?—is an enigmatic phenomenon and one in dire need of some strong guidelines. Indiscriminate drug use is apt to further weaken the athletic community.

Are athletics *educational?* The worth of athletics from an educational viewpoint has long been discussed. Typically, such lofty claims have been made as the development of sportsmanship, socialization for specific roles, social mobility, a way of learning many of the lessons of life, controlling of tensions, the building of character, and so on. Usually these claims go unchallenged. Not until recently have sport psychologists and sport sociologists taken on some of these claims. When they have, some interesting conclusions have been drawn. For example, two prominent psychologists, Bruce C. Ogilvie and Thomas A. Tutko, who have been studying personality traits of athletes for a long time, have now taken on the role of "spoilers" by publishing in *Psychology Today* that competitive sports do not build character. Social integration has been assumed to be an educative adjunct through athletics. The concept that athletics facilitate social (upward) mobility is also commonly accepted. These notions have raised some reservations in recent studies.

Today, the pendulum seems to be swinging in the direction that professionalized competitive athletics are serving mainly as public entertainment and not as an educational tool. High school and college athletics must be controlled by educators and can be justified only as long as they continue to be valid instruments of the educative process. When this function becomes invalid, athletes as well as the lay public should cry aloud for accountability. Athletics are for athletes and any other rationale for their being becomes superfluous. Accordingly, a coach's first and foremost responsibility, and his only real reason for existence, is to enhance an athlete's achievement through a program of educational athletics.

The *internal ferment* being manifested within athletic squads and brought out into the open by certain athletes has caused much consternation relative to existing athletic policies. Within the past six years students on college and university campuses have gained a long-awaited privilege by becoming involved in decision making regarding those matters pertinent to a student's education. Thus today there are student representatives on most official committees which govern and give direction to educational change. The right of students to become involved as decision makers has not been won overnight.

In athletics, however, the authoritarian coaching staff continues to make most decisions based on policies established by the coaches for the behavior of athletes. And, for the most part, athletes have not had much input relative to decision making nor are they usually outwardly vociferous when it comes to expressing discontent.

In a speech to coaches and physical educators, Louis E. Alley, ex-coach, current chairman of the Physical Education Department of the University of Iowa, and the 1971-72 AAHPER president, made some succinct observations relative to the internal ferment in athletics. One reason for internal problems, he believes, is the rebellion of the athletes themselves against what they will grow to regard as a dehumanizing, authoritarian system that is more concerned with monetary gains than with the mental, physical, and social development of the individual athlete. Alley feels that this movement will continue unabated as long as athletic contests are "regarded as games to be won rather than as potent tools for educating youth—players and spectators alike."

Coaches and their staffs are in a predicament in that they are held accountable to the various publics, some of whom control much of the finances that support athletics. The usual yardstick of accountability of the coaching staff is the number of games won and not the number of football players graduated. As long as this situation exists, and as long as athletics serve primarily to entertain, it is the coach whose future is jeopardized after a losing season and not the player's status. This sort of unfortunate dichotomy minimizes player input relative to decision making and stymies self-expression and self-actualization. Thus, dissension and internal bickering in the 1970's are apt to continue unabated, though not for the betterment of athletics.

It is time for a fresh, new look into the mechanics of athletic administration. The muscle fiber of athletic empires is being tested, and whatever voices need to be heard and actions heeded in order to make athletics a more viable, educational experience for athletes and student bodies alike should be reflected in a democratic process of governance. As indicated above, the responsibility for much of the dissidence being witnessed today in competitive athletics rests primarily with the coach and his subordinating staff and secondarily with athletic directors, principals, college and university presidents. It is the coach, however, who still enjoys a relatively high position within the social status hierarchy, who must emerge to the forefront in a most persuasive and cogent fashion in order to cure some of the internal problems and curtail many of the tensions indigenous to athletics today.

The intent of this article has not been to place any blame on the coach or to praise him; instead, it has been an attempt to articulate to the coach, in a fairly cogent manner, the urgency for careful introspection of the mechanics of educational athletics, and to present a brief list of contemporary articles and books which speak eloquently about the current turmoil evidenced in some aspects of competitive athletics.

In order to become more knowledgeable and to establish some rationale for decision making regarding the matters discussed above, it is strongly recommended that the coach carefully peruse the articles and books listed here. They should be read, not in a hostile climate, but in a receptive and analytical context. These sources represent a compendium of carefully formed opinions, personal observations, and empirical research which is representative of a growing body of knowledge becoming available to athletes, coaches, and sport sociologists.

REFERENCES

Beisser, Arnold R., *The Madness in Sport*, New York: Appleton-Century-Crofts, 1967.

Bouton, Jim, *Ball Four*, New York: Dell Publishing Co., 1971.

_____ , *I'm Glad You Didn't Take It Personally*, New York: William Morrow & Co., 1971.

Boyle, Robert H., *Sport—Mirror of American Life*, Boston: Little, Brown & Co., 1963.

Edwards, Harry, *The Revolt of the Black Athlete*, New York: The Free Press, 1969.

Hart, M. Marie, (editor), *Sport in The Socio-Cultural Process*, Dubuque, Iowa: Wm. C. Brown Co., 1972.

Jordan, Pat, *Black Coach*, New York: Dodd, Mead & Company, 1972.

Kenyon, Gerald S., (editor), *Sociology of Sport*, Chicago: Athletic Institute, 1968.

Loy, John W., Jr., and Gerald S. Kenyon (editors), *Sport, Culture, and Society*, London: Macmillan Company, 1969.

Lüschen, Günther, ed., *The Cross-Cultural Analysis of Sport and Games*, Champaign, Ill.: Stipes Publishing Co., 1970.

Meggysey, Dave, *Out of Their League*, Berkeley: Ramparts Press, 1970.

Merchant, Larry, *...And Everyday You Take Another Bite*, New York: Doubleday & Co., 1971.

Miller, Donna Mae, and Kathryn R. E. Russell, *Sport: A Contemporary View*, Philadelphia: Lea & Febiger, 1971.

Ogilvie, Bruce C., and Thomas A. Tutko, *Problem Athletes and How to Handle Them*, London: Pelham Books, 1966.

Olsen, Jack, *The Black Athlete: A Shameful Story*, New York: Time-Life Books, 1968.

Parrish, Bernie, *They Call It A Game*, New York: Dial Press, 1971.

Raiborn, Mitchell, *Financial Analysis of Intercollegiate Athletics*, Kansas City, Mo.: The National Collegiate Athletic Association, 1970.

Sage, Geroge H., (editor), *Sport and American Society*, Reading, Mass.: Addison-Wesley, 1970.

Scott, Jack, *Athletics for Athletes*, Oakland, California: Other Ways, 1969.

_____ , *The Athletic Revolution*, New York: Free Press, 1971.

Shecter, Leonard, *The Jocks*, New York: Bobbs-Merrill, 1969.

Weiss, Paul, *Sport: A Philosophical Inquiry*, Carbondale, Ill.: Southern Illinois University Press, 1969.

Magazine Articles

Drake, Edwin, "What Are They Doing with the Sacred Game of Pro Football?" *Sports Illustrated*, October 25, 1971.

Gilbert, Bill, "Three part series on drugs in sport," *Sports Illustrated*, June 23, June 30, July 7, 1969.

Kane, Martin, "An Assessment of 'Black is Best,' " *Sports Illustrated*, January 18, 1971.

Ogilvie, Bruce C. and Tutko, Thomas A., "Sport: If You Want To Build Character, Try Something Else," *Psychology Today*, October 1971.

Rapoport, Roger, "Pro Football's Dropouts," *Sport*, September 1970.

Russell, Bill, "Success Is a Journey," *Sports Illustrated*, July 8, 1970.

Ryan, Pat, "A Grim Run to Fiscal Daylight," *Sports Illustrated*, February 1, 1971.

Wolfe, Dave, "The Growing Crisis in College Sports," *Sport*, June 1970 and July 1970.

THE CULTURAL CRISIS IN AMERICAN SPORTS

Barry E. Stern

This article attempts to understand the cultural crisis in American sports. It emphasizes the changing coach-athlete relationship in educational institutions as the dimension of the dilemma which most accurately reveals the new directions which school and university athletics must take if they are to maintain their prominent place in American youth culture. Once the true dimensions and causes of this dilemma can be identified, it can be dealt with directly. Until the present, unfortunately, society has chosen to concern itself with the symptoms of the problem rather than eliminate the causes.

What, then, is the problem? The answer to this question depends on whom you ask. Most coaches perceive their dilemma with athletes in the same

Barry E. Stern, "The Cultural Crisis in American Sports," *Journal of Health, Physical Education, and Recreation*, 43:42-44 (April 1972). Reprinted by permission of the American Association for Health, Physical Education, and Recreation.

way that parents perceive their problems with their children. Some blame their misfortunes on permissive child-rearing practices and the subsequent lack of discipline in youth. Others cite the interracial strife which has gripped this country, or the war in Vietnam. In my own view, the nature of the dilemma transcends the race issue or the war issue, and the resolution of conflict between student athletes and coaches is more than a matter of strict versus permissive disciplinary action.

Simply put, the problem is that student athletes perceive a conflict between the sports culture in which they operate and the larger culture which values (or at least pays lip service to) the principles of participatory democracy and achievement on the basis of merit. Students raise questions concerning the limits of coaches' power and authority in governing sports competition. As in other areas of student life, students are requesting—in fact, demanding—greater voice and vote in making decisions which directly affect their lives. The fact that the "student power" movement affects so popular a part of student life as interscholastic and intercollegiate athletics should not surprise us. Considering the close relationship that coaches have traditionally had with students, athletes or not, it is somewhat surprising, however, that this movement has been resisted, if not ignored, by the great majority of coaches.

Perhaps the reason for their intransigence is that the basic assumptions made by the coaching profession about organized athletics are being challenged. Many coaches reason that if these assumptions are effectively challenged, their survival as coaches—moreover, the survival of organized athletics as they have organized them—is in jeopardy. In a way, they are right. The question remains, as it does for so many adult authority-figures in our society today, whether running scared to preserve the status quo is the answer, or whether the nature of coaching and athletics can be changed sufficiently to adapt to a changing society.

One assumption made by coaches that is being challenged is that team members must consider team loyalty above all else. Players and coaches are beginning to disagree more and more as to how much team loyalty is enough. Just what is a 100% commitment to an athletic team? Can one be committed to the team while he is committed to his manhood, the improvement of the human race, his studies, his girl friend? I interviewed one black player who said, "Look, I'm committed to a lot of things, not the least important of which is the survival of my race. If there's a late meeting of the black caucus and it's important that I be there, I will go even though I know I might have to break curfew to attend. Now that's not a 100% commitment to football, but I feel I should play in the game if my 75% is better than someone else's

100%. Of course, if I really did not feel fit enough to contribute to a winning cause, I would feel obligated to tell the coach. He has the right to know if I was at an all-night meeting, as he would if I didn't get sufficient sleep because of a variety of other reasons."

What many coaches have failed to appreciate is that an increasing number of students, athletes or not, want to make their own choices, choosing among alternatives which they have created for themselves. Coaches are teachers (their athletes are merely advanced students of sport), and teachers should welcome this desire for autonomy and independence as a sign of emotional maturity and growth. If a student has loyalties and commitments which compete for his attention, all the coach can do is to make his program as attractive as possible so that it will be given higher priority by these students. Moreover, both he and the players should agree on the kinds of competing loyalties and commitments which do not detract from one's performance on the team. Just as a classroom teacher should be willing to negotiate with his students to determine "what's fair," the coach must negotiate with his athletes.

In the name of developing a winning attitude in their charges, coaches over the years have seen fit to establish for players rules which govern a number of their outside-of-athletics activities. Some of these are training rules, e.g., refrain from smoking, drinking, and consuming certain foods. Others refer to social life, e.g., when a player can go out on dates, and occasionally, who he can date and who he cannot. And still others refer to comportment in public, e.g., not to engage in loud or raucous behavior, to refrain from swearing, to abstain from associating with individuals who engage in, or who have been engaged in, delinquent acts, etc. Some coaches have even prohibited team members from joining political pressure groups, reasoning that this would somehow cause dissension amongst team members.

CULTURAL SENSITIVITY AND SOCIAL MATURITY

Obviously, some of these rules are reasonable and others are not. The point is that all should be considered negotiable. A boy of Latin American descent, for example, is oftentimes accustomed to drinking alcoholic beverages at a party. He does not necessarily get drunk and it will probably have no discernible effect on his athletic performance. Does the coach have the right to ask that boy to refrain from moderate drinking, or even to refrain from attending the party itself? Yes, he has the right to ask, to persuade, and to suggest. Whether or not he has the right to demand abstinence from this kind of behavior is debatable. I would like to suggest that the rules regarding outside-of-school activities should accommodate rather than penalize team members from minority group backgrounds and that the coach make every effort to acquaint himself with the family and cultural background of each player. Being culturally sensitive helps a coach determine which rules are reasonable and which are not.

As always, "reasonable" depends on the context. What is right for a college athlete may not be appropriate for a professional. And a high school student need not be treated as an elementary school child. Indeed, it seems to me that the most manly way for a coach to handle his team is to allow the players to help determine the rules by which they will live. Once coach and players alike have agreed what the rules shall be and what the consequences of breaking them will be, then all can be expected to abide by them. Participation in rule-making is a valuable lesson in growing up. If rule-making is the sole prerogative of the coach, the athlete becomes dependent on him for the development of his own moral ideology, hence delaying the achievement of social maturity. On the other hand, if an individual is encouraged to investigate the reasons for rules and is assured a voice in their development, he will be given a chance to grow and to obtain his independence. Developing social maturity in his players should be as much an objective of the coach as winning.

Coaches, for the most part, do not want to keep their players docile and dependent. On the contrary, the coach, perhaps more than any other professional working with youth, is actively attempting to facilitate social and emotional growth in them. Many, however, overreact to what appears to be rebellion against their authority by athletes. Many coaches perceive athletes' questions about the reasons for one team rule or another as personal attacks. They should instead understand that young people, for better or for worse, want more autonomy, a greater feeling of mastery over their environment and hence their lives. Young people are searching for good reasons for accepting the rules they are asked to live by. The pressure they are putting on coaches is no more and perhaps much less than the pressure applied to school and college administrators. Coaches have an excellent opportunity to channel this desire for increased participation into socially acceptable and responsible directions.

A noticeable result emerging from confrontations in athletics, however, is that *those students who choose not to conform are no longer choosing athletics as a form of self-expression.* There seems to be enough circumstantial evidence to postulate that non-conforming types do indeed shun athletics. In the San Francisco Bay Area, for example, it seems that the highly politicized high schools and universities (i.e., the ones with the greatest degree of student political activism) have the greatest student apathy toward athletics.

To be sure, many students regard athletics as one of the most important school activities and the father-figure coach is still admired and often worshipped by millions of our nation's young people. While the coach still serves as one of our society's ideal male role models, there is an increasing number of young people with whom he has not been able to establish any rapport whatsoever, particularly those from the radical, anti-establishment, long-haired, and militant minority groups. In fact, the indifference to organized athletics found in many of these groups is beginning to change to outright hostility. What is ironic about this is that these turned-off individuals are not turned off by the physical or non-verbal aspects of human experience. Indeed, many of these young nonconformists are seriously exploring such things as sensory or bodily awareness (something that the physical education profession has known about for years), and they really dig such things as hiking, camping, and outdoor living. Why, then, are they not turned on by athletics?

The answer to this question could well be that these youngsters identify organized athletics with those elements of American "establishment" culture that they no longer respect. What are these elements?

NONCONFORMITY AND RELATIVE ACHIEVEMENT

For one thing, our nonconforming youth disagree with the notion that a person ought to be judged or evaluated on the basis of how he appears—his clothing, hairstyle, etc. Rather, they feel, an individual should be evaluated on the basis of what he can do and does. In most schools and colleges, however, athletes must conform to strict grooming regulations; naturally the nonconformist becomes less interested in athletics when the appearance issue becomes as important, if not more important, than the individual's measurable achievement. They perceive quite correctly that in athletics *especially* individuals should be evaluated on the basis of relative achievement.

Another cultural value which is being questioned by many young people is the principle of majority rule, especially when that rule is applied to such a degree that minority or culturally different groups become disenfranchised. While many segments of our society are beginning to accept the shift toward political as well as cultural pluralism (the right of different social, racial, or ethnic groups to be different so long as they do not infringe upon the rights of other groups), the coaching profession has tended to "stand firm" against this change, demanding conformity, as it were, because the majority prefers conformity. Inasmuch as the nonconformist tends to agree that a shift toward pluralism is necessary (the "do-your-own-thing" philosophy), he is not likely to want to participate in a system (organized athletics) which still operates under the assumptions about democracy which are concomitant with too much majority rule.

DEMOCRACY VS. PLURALISM AND
DISCIPLINE VS. WINNING

Some coaches are perpetuating the myth that democracy and pluralism on the one hand and discipline and winning on the other are incompatible. Their notion of discipline has alienated a great number of students from athletics. In the name of discipline and preparing oneself to win, many coaches demand behavior on the part of athletes which denies them their individuality, even outside the team context. Why should individualism off the field mitigate effective teamwork on the field? This outlook is becoming obsolete; hopefully, coaches will modernize.

In microcosm, then, we see in the controversies over athletics many of the issues which confront our democracy today: pluralism vs. majority rule, student power vs. teacher power, selection on the basis of merit vs. selection on the basis of something else, individualism vs. conformity, etc. The forces which are bringing stress and strain to the coaching profession are the ones bringing stress to the society as a whole. Coaches are reacting in very different ways to their dilemma. Some are becoming more flexible in their approach to athletics and hence are putting up with more diversity and individualism than they have in the past. Many coaches, on the other hand, are saying that the more ground you give, the less chance you have of surviving.

Such statements, I feel, reveal a lack of understanding of what is happening in our society today. Anthropologists would call it "cultural lag," meaning that although the athletic programs in the United States were harmoniously integrated with the rest of our culture at one time in our history, these same programs are not accommodating themselves to the cultural change that our society is undergoing at present.

At this point, I am sure that many readers are taking sides for or against the so-called athletic establishment (i.e., the coaches, administrators, alumni, and athletes who support the present system of organized athletics). But to take sides is to avoid the real issue, for organized athletics should have something to offer any student no matter what his political beliefs or behavior. And *that* is the issue: whether or not present-day athletic programs can be made flexible enough to accommodate *all* students who desire to benefit from them.

What can be done to achieve this? First and foremost, a definite attempt should be made to limit and possibly reduce the power of the coaching establishment in the organization of school and particularly college athletics, ceding much of this power and authority to the group which presumably benefits the most from athletics, namely, the students (athletes).

Coaches are probably correct when they foresee a change in their role, but not all of their fears are well-founded. In spite of what some coaches say, no one is trying to tell them "how to coach" or "who to play at what position." In other words, no one is trying to usurp the professional tasks of the coach. Athletes invariably agree that the teaching and training tasks should be left to the coach. However, a significant number do resent the power which coaches have over the nonathletic aspects of their lives if they desire to participate on teams. Rather than striving for conformity—same haircuts, street clothing, social contacts, etc.—coaches should emphasize pulling together in such a way that common team goals can be achieved without sacrificing too much in the way of individuality. Perhaps the most salient advice for coaches who seek a solution to their dilemma with students and athletes is to become aware of the changing youth culture and its values and to modify their own behavior and programs accordingly.

REASONABLE RULES AND SOCIAL EQUALITY

More athletes, including competent athletes, will try out for athletic teams when they perceive the management of these teams to be governed by sensible and democratically arrived-at rules. These athletes will be respected as persons as well as students. The coach will finally be allowed to be the professional teacher. As a result of the new status of the athlete, the coach can concentrate upon the physical skills, mental developments, and teaching phases of the sport. He no longer need be the father, psychiatrist, minister, and watchguard over the athlete. Finally, the greater participation of students and athletes in the governing of athletics will make the distasteful and often dishonest task of recruiting less necessary. The coach will become what any teacher ought to be—a human resource for the students who wish to take advantage of his expertise.

The greater social equality between the athlete and coach, as between student and teacher, will make for more honest and fruitful human relationships. Historically the coach, either through choice or circumstance, has been forced into roles with athletes which, in many instances, never should have been his responsibilities. The athlete too often has used the coach as a crutch for his whims and desires, for his failures, and sometimes his successes. Now they will be in a position to respect each other as individuals both on and off the playing field.

The coaches' dilemma, in conclusion, reflects our country's social dilemma. If the issues raised here can be resolved effectively and ethically within the confines of organized athletics, perhaps the experience will serve as an example for the larger culture which must somehow reverse present trends toward social disorganization and alienation. Those of us involved in athletics have a very exciting opportunity to help lead our culture through peaceful change. We should be the first ones, not the last, to understand the youthful desire for increased participation.

HUMANISTIC THEORY, THE COUNTER-CULTURE, AND SPORT: IMPLICATIONS FOR ACTION AND RESEARCH

George H. Sage

I. DEVELOPMENT OF HUMANISTIC PSYCHOLOGY

There is a revolution taking place in the social sciences and there is a related social revolution occurring in the general society. Radical activities in psychology, sociology, economics, political science, and anthropology, as well as a growing interest in phenomenology and existentialism, provide powerful evidence of a humanistic trend in these fields. Concurrently, many aspects of our society are experiencing a transformation from traditional values of corporate organization and the Protestant Ethic to a new and different moral and ethical system embracing a "counterculture" ideology. These activities are particularly affecting occupations in education, business management,

George H. Sage. Revision of a presentation made at the Allerton Conference, North American Society for the Psychology of Sport and Physical Activity, Monticello, Illinois, May, 1973.

social work, as well as many other fields in which there is frequent inter-personal experiences.

The "humanistic" approach to human personal-social behavior has recently made a dramatic impact in psychology, where it has become a third force transcending the limitations of the two main approaches to psychology—behaviorism and psychoanalysis. This alternative to behaviorism and psychoanalysis goes under several names: humanistic psychology, perceptual psychology, existential psychology, neo-Freudianism, or sometimes "third force psychology." Regardless of the name, it definitely provides a unique alternative to the other two perspectives. In *Toward a Psychology of Being* Maslow (1968), one of the major theorists of humanistic psychology, says that the humanistic perspective is a true social revolution in that it brings about "new ways of perceiving and thinking, new images of man and of society, new conceptions of ethics and of values, new directions in which to move . . . [p. iii] ."

Behaviorism and Freudianism emphasize man as he is; humanistic psychology emphasizes what man can become—the emphasis, then, is not only on actualities, but upon potentialities as well. While the first two forces in psychology view man as *re*active to the events in the environment or the psyche, humanistic psychology views man as being active and as having the capacity to choose between a set of alternatives. Humanistic psychology recognizes that the environment and culture influences behavior, but it insists that the ultimate effect of culture and environment is to a large extent determined by the individual's unique view and perspective of these factors. Thus the emphasis is on the individual's own perception of the world, not on the perceptions of others (Bruce, 1966). According to Maslow (1968) humanistic psychology is "a viable third alternative to objectivistic, behavioristic (mechanomorphic) psychology and to orthodox Freudianism [p. iii] ."

Humanistic psychology is not a total rejection of Behaviorism or Freudianism. Indeed, Maslow (1966) said, with regard to Behaviorism: "I believe mechanistic science (which in psychology takes the form of Behaviorism) to be not incorrect but rather too narrow and limited to serve as a general or comprehensive philosophy." With regard to Freud, Maslow (1968) said: "Freud's picture of man was clearly unsuitable, leaving out as it did his aspirations, his realizable hopes, his godlike qualities. . . . Freud supplied to us the sick half of psychology and we must now fill out with the healthy side."

Humanistic psychology has gained recognition through the writings of Maslow, Rogers, Lewin, Bugental, and Jourard and its central concern is with the dignity and worth of man and the development of human potentialities. Indeed, the root of the humanistic approach is a fundamental concern for the human person as an entity having a measure of autonomy, choice, and self-determination.

The disciples of humanistic psychology include: the Gestalt, or field theorists, who emphasize man's interaction with his environment as a unitary function; the neo-Freudians whose perspective is on man as primarily a social and cultural, rather than biological or instinctive, organism; the organismic psychologists, who, like the Gestaltists, focus on the individual as a whole; and the perceptual and existential psychologists, who emphasize the uniqueness and integrity of the individual and of his personal and unique interpretation of his life and environment (Bruce, 1966).

II. THE COUNTERCULTURE MOVEMENT AND ITS RELATIONSHIP TO HUMANISTIC PSYCHOLOGY

Accompanying and supporting a great deal of the theoretical structure of the humanistic perspective is a social revolutionary movement which, in global terms, goes under the name of the "counterculture."[1] The roots of this movement reside in a strong disillusionment with traditional values and interpersonal relations as manifested in corporate organizational values and behavior and the Protestant Ethic. It began with the youth groups in colleges across the country and spread to subcultures of "beatniks" and "hippies" of the 1960's and '70's. It has spawned a substantial body of literature, but two writers, Philip Slater (1970) and Charles Reich (1970) are probably two of the best known of the counterculture writers. It is to their work that I will refer in characterizing the counterculture ideology.

From the viewpoint of the counterculturist, it is important to recognize that differences between the "old culture" and the counterculture cannot be resolved simply by some type of compromise or "golden mean" approach. A culture normative system is a dynamic whole, resting on processes which tend to accelerate to the point at which the system becomes self-sustaining. Social change must, therefore, affect the motivational roots of a society or it is not change at all. Thus, the counterculturist suggests that, since the old culture is dysfunctional and cannot merely be modified as a solution, an entirely new culture, with a new motivational system, must be adopted (Slater, 1970).

The ways in which the old culture and the new culture, or counterculture, may be differentiated are enumerated by Slater (1970):

The old, when forced to choose, tends to give preference to property rights over personal rights, technological requirements over human needs, competition over cooperation, violence over sexuality, concentration over distribution, the producer over the consumer, means over ends, secrecy over openness, social forms over gratification, Oedipal love over communal love, and so on. The new counter-culture tends to reverse all of these priorities (p. 100).

Reich (1970) develops a similar conceptualization of old and new cultures by his three categories of "Consciousness." Consciousness I is ". . . the harsh side of self-interest, competitiveness, suspicion of others. . . . Underlying this attitude was the assumption that 'human nature' is fundamentally bad, and that a struggle against his fellow men is man's natural condition [p. 23]." Consciousness II is linked to the corporate state and the individual's role in it. "One of the central aspects of Consciousness II is an acceptance of the priority of institutions, organizations, and society and a belief that the individual must tie his destiny to something of this sort, larger than himself, and subordinate his will to it [p. 71]." The "new culture" of Slater is Consciousness III for Reich and is characterized in this way:

> Consciousness III postulates the absolute worth of every human being— every self. . . . Consciousness III rejects the whole concept of excellence and comparative merit that is so central to Consciousness II. III refuses to evaluate people by general standards, it refuses to classify people, or analyze them. Each person has his own individuality, not to be compared to that of anyone else. . . . A third commandment is: be wholly honest with others, use no other person as a means (pp. 242-244).

Basic to both humanistic psychology and the counterculture is the conviction that "best" individuals are those who possess a positive self-concept and accept themselves in an appreciating way. Both groups believe that one cannot function to his fullest capacity without believing in and accepting the totality of himself. As one humanistic psychologist says:

> An essentially positive view of the self permits adequate people to be effective without the worry about conformity or nonconformity. . . . It provides a kind of security that permits the owner a freedom he could not have otherwise. . . . This permits him to be creative, original, spontaneous. . . . Feeling he is much more, he has much more to give (Combs, 1962, p. 59).

And Reich (1970) says Consciousness III "declares that the individual self is the only true reality [p. 242]."

The acceptance of one's self is also expanded into feelings of oneness with one's group. Both humanists and counterculturists confirm that this feeling is necessary to their conceptions of the adequate person. Combs (1962) states:

> Truly adequate people have a greatly expanded feeling of self. . . . It is a feeling of unity or oneness, a feeling of sharing a common fate, or striving for a common goal . . . most adequate men and women . . . seem to reach a point where they identify with great blocks of mankind, with 'all' mankind, without reference to creed, color or nationality (p. 54).

Similarly, Reich writes: "The Consciousness III idea of community among people is another aspect of the new culture [p. 271]."

Finally both points of view posit an expanded awareness, a willingness to accept all facets of reality and perception. Maslow (1970) suggests: "Self-actualizing people have the wonderful capacity to appreciate . . . freshly and naively, the basic goods of life, with awe, pleasure, and wonder, and even ecstasy, however stale these experiences may have become to others . . . [p. 163]." In this vein, Reich (1970) says: "It is the essence of the thinking of the new generation that man should be constantly open to new experience, constantly ready to have his old way of thinking changed, constantly hoping that he will be sensitive enough and receptive enough to let the wonders of nature and mankind come to him [p. 284]."

III. TRADITIONAL SPORTS VALUES AND PRACTICES AND RELATIONSHIPS TO "FIRST TWO FORCES" IN PSYCHOLOGY AND THE "OLD CULTURE"

The American sport tradition is very much related to the older psychological perspectives and to Reich's Consciousness I and II. The emphasis on competition and a "winning is the only thing" ideology is grounded in the idea that we must struggle against others to get ahead. A fundamental tenet of the old culture is scarcity; there is the assumption that the world does not contain the wherewithal to satisfy human needs. Thus people must compete for the scarce resources and those who win the largest share of these resources are said to be "successful." If they have to be ruthless and unscrupulous in accomplishing this, well, tough, the important thing is beating out the opposition. The idea that we are inherently bad and must be trained to be good through a system of rewards and punishments is also fundamental to much of sport practice as well as the old psychologies and the old culture practices.

Leadership practices in American sport are firmly based on the older psychologies and especially on Consciousness II. There is an acceptance of the priority of institutions and organizations and a belief that the individual must subordinate his will to them. An established hierarchy and the implementation of efficiency procedures are seen as necessary and inviolable, and the domination of man and environment by technology is a central ideology. Life is seen as a fiercely competitive struggle for success and the leader therefore is expected to provide the wherewithal to produce success for the organization. This leadership model is reflected in the "Scientific Management" approach proposed by Frederick Taylor in 1911 and owes much to the old culture values and the first two forces in psychology.

It is clear that the dominant approach in current institutionalized sport is an authoritarian, product-oriented enterprise. The basic concern is with athletes subjecting themselves to the will of the coach whose primary concern is with winning athletic contests. The rise of increasingly institutionalized and codified sports teams has caused many coaches to view team members as objects in a machine-like environment who need to be conditioned to perform prescribed, fragmented tasks as instrumental to team performance. Thus the players become the instrument of another man (the coach), and are used to reach the objectives and goals of the organizational collectivity; they are reduced to cogs in the organization's machinery. The individual player is expected to do his best to fit himself into functions which are needed by the organization. This is vividly exemplified in the popular locker room slogan: "There is no I in team." A system of incentives and rewards, i.e., letter awards, helmet decals, etc., is instituted to "motivate" athletes to perform. It may be seen that in this approach decisions are made by management (the coach), after a thorough cost efficiency analysis, and the players are expected to carry out the will of the coach for the accomplishment of organizational goals (Sage, 1973).

The most important foundation of both American sport and corporate organization is authority. In both realms rigid and bureaucratized hierarchy controls more and more aspects of the workers', and athletes', lives both on and off the job or, in the case of sports, the field of play. As Hoch (1972) says:

> In football, like business . . . every pattern of movement on the field is increasingly being brought under the controls of a group of nonplaying managerial technocrats who sit up in the stands . . . with their headphones and dictate offenses, defenses, special plays, substitutions and so forth to the players below (p. 9).

IV. RECONCILING HUMANISTIC PSYCHOLOGY
AND THE COUNTERCULTURE WITH SPORT

The ideology of both humanistic psychology and the counterculture concerning ideal human function are basically in accord. This ideal includes a positive self-concept, an empathetic identification with others, an openness to experience, and an acceptance of a wide and rich perceptual field for information from which to draw. The person who possesses these qualities is considered a "healthy person." The importance of these viewpoints for sport are particularly related to coaching and management methods which most effectively facilitate these goals.

In increasing instances, the Scientific Management model, with its emphasis on relatively rigid structure, direction and control exercised through a formal hierarchy of authority—with the coach as the all-powerful authority figure—a fixed system of rights, duties, and procedures, and relative impersonality of human relationships, is proving dysfunctional to the contemporary realities in sport, as exemplified in the new culture. No matter how much emphasis is placed on such other qualities in coaching as coaching technique, technology, equipment, and facilities, the humanity of the coach is the vital ingredient if athletes are to learn self-identity, self-responsibility, self-direction, and self-fulfillment. Most coaches define coaching as analogous to sculpturing—making the players what the coaches want them to become. Thus we have two sport psychologists labeling athletes who will not be molded in the way coaches wish as "problem athletes" (Ogilvie and Tutko, 1966). The humanistic psychologist views the coaching experience as gardening—helping athletes grow and find what they want to be.

According to the Third Force in psychology and the counterculture, the goal of school sports, and in fact of all education, must be the production of increasing uniqueness and independence, and this cannot be achieved in an autocratic atmosphere in which all decisions are made by the coaches while players are relegated to being passive followers of orders. A common-sense principle of school sport, then, is that it should promote the fulfillment of the individuals engaged in and influenced by it; thus the real goal of sport, or any educational venture, is seen to encompass nothing less than the fulfillment of the student. In the sense I am using it here, fulfillment implies the actualization of the full potentialities for growth latent in the individual.

The contemporary society requires self-directing, responsible adults who are capable of independent behavior. Even the armed forces, the most authoritarian social institution, has discovered this fact and for the past ten years has been increasing the degree of responsibility and direction to even the lowest ranks.

While humanism and the counterculture give preference to cooperation over competition, they do not necessarily reject competition in a sport context. Reich (1970) states: "Competition, within limits of a sport like tennis or swimming, is accepted for its own pleasure, although even as athletes III's are far less competitive ... [p. 242]." Thus, except when carried out as fun, there is a belief that intense "competition generates conditional self-worth, role-specific relationships, goal-orientation, excellence based on competitive merit, self as a means, and subjection of self to external control—all of which are to be avoided (Schafer, 1971)." In this regard, Reich (1970) says: "Instead of insisting that everyone be measured by given standards, the new generation values what is unique and different in each self; there is no pressure that anyone be an athlete unless he wants to; a harpsichord player is accepted on equal terms [p. 243]."

Miller (1970) suggests that individuals who play games to win are actually not "playing" games; they are working at them. Thus they do not win anything of value. In a society which is ends-oriented, the game is for winning; in the means-oriented society, the game is the game: it is for playing. In the first society, the player cannot be happy unless he is winning and is successful whereas in the second, if one is satisfied and happy with the play, he is successful. In this second society the expressive nature of sport is emphasized, and "sport needs no other justification than that it provide a setting for sociability and fun (Ingham and Loy, 1973, p. 7)."

Although space does not permit a full explication of this topic, it seems clear that humanism and the counterculture have great potential for transforming sport from a product-oriented, Gesellschaft, conservative, authoritarian emphasis toward exploring possibilities and alternatives for improving the sport experience, individual human growth, and perhaps society as a whole. We only need to understand and appreciate the enormous scope of human potentialities which are possible to develop through sport.

V. RESEARCH APPROACHES: EFFECTS OF THE HUMANISTIC PERSPECTIVE ON SPORT

The Humanistic Research Perspective

Perhaps Jourard's (1968) tongue-in-cheek problem may serve as a preface to a description of the humanistic psychologist's position on research:

> If I complain I have no will of my own, that people are influencing me in subtle and mysterious ways, you'll accuse me of being paranoid, and direct me to a psychotherapist.

If I put on a white laboratory coat, and assert that you have no will of your own, that your action and experience can be manipulated, predicted, and controlled, then I am recognized as a scientific psychologist, and honored.

This is most peculiar.

Since the humanistic image of man is different than older, traditional images which conceptualize man as an organism comparable to rats, pigeons, and monkeys, different strategies are used as guides to theory, research, and application. The humanistic commitment is not a worship of science but a humane concern for man. As Glass (1971) emphasizes: "What is argued for is an enlarged view of science, beyond the narrow goals of control and prediction, of studying only what is quantifiable or measurable, away from the behavioristic, positivistic, and technicist ethos borrowed from the hard sciences [p. 179]." Moreover, Maslow (1970) in his excellent chapter "Problem Centering vs. Means Centering in Science" suggests that a commitment to normative zeal (to do good, to help mankind, etc.) is compatible with scientific objectivity and perhaps promotes better science through a wider-ranging scope than exists now when it tries to be value neutral. He relates "that many of the weaknesses of orthodox science and particularly of psychology are consequences of a means-or-technique centered approach to science." By means centering, he refers "to the tendency to consider that the essence of science lies in its instruments, techniques, procedures, apparatus, and its methods rather than in its problems, questions, functions, goals [p. 11]."

Humanist psychology asks: What is a human being, and what might man become? Jourard (1968) suggests that in this context humanistic psychology is similar to industrial psychology or the psychology of mental health or of advertising. Thus a series of questions such as what variables affect morale, or the output of workers, or the maintenance of wellness, or the purchasing behavior of customers are appropriate. But humanistic psychology also asks: What are the possibilities of man? This leads to the issues of what is optimum man, from among the possibilities, and what conditions account for attainment and maintenance of these optima?

Humanistic Pyschology Research Strategies

For humanistic psychology, the beginning and ending point—the essence—of human life is the self, and the theoretical framework of this perspective has come to be known as "Self-theory." Maslow (1970), Seeman (1959), Rogers (1961), Fitts (1970), and other humanistic psychologists have formulated self-theory as pertaining to the realization and development of human potential. Maslow emphasizes "self-actualization," Seeman "personality integration," Rogers the "fully functioning person," and Fitts "interpersonal competence." While all of these theories deal with the continuum of personal adjustment, they go beyond and elaborate such things as the conditions which are essential for self-actualization and other self-fulfilling conditions, and they all agree that "self-actualized, or fully functioning" persons are happier, more productive, and that they more fully develop their human potentialities.

Self-theory is based upon the principle that man reacts to his phenomenal world in terms of the way he perceives it, and probably the most salient feature of each person's phenomenal world is his own self—the self as perceived and experienced by him. This is the individual's self-concept. The self-concept is defined as what constitutes the person's attitudes and feelings about himself and as the group of psychological processes which govern behavior and adjustment. The first part of the definition is thought of as self-as-object while the second feature defines the self-as-process (Hall and Lindzey, 1970).

There is a general agreement that the self-concept does not exist at birth. Kinch (1963) states: "The individual's conception of himself emerges from social interaction and, in turn, guides or influences the behavior of that individual [p. 481]." The basic postulates of self-theory are: The individual's self-concept is based on his perception of the ways others are responding to him, the individual's self-concept directly influences his behavior, and the individual's perception of the responses of others toward him reflects the actual responses of others toward him (Fitts, 1971).

With self as the central concern, the humanistic psychologists have focused their research efforts on elucidating self, formulating theories on the development of self-concept, and attempting to measure the effects of various variables on self-concept. These efforts have taken place in clinical as well as experimental situations.

The term "healthy personality" has emerged from humanistic theory and is related to Maslow's highest need, which is self-actualization. Self-actualization refers to the desire of humans for self-fulfillment—to become actualized in what we are potentially; in Maslow's words: ". . . to become everything that one is capable of becoming [p. 46]." Study of the healthy personality has opened the way for research along several related lines, only two of which will be mentioned here: self-disclosure and self-actualization.

Jourard (1964, 1968) has suggested that accurate and authentic portrayal of the self to others, self-disclosure, is an identifying criterion of a healthy personality while neurosis is related to inability to know one's "real self" and to make it known to others. The relationship between self-disclosure and healthy personality is, Jourard (1964) says, "both a symptom of personality health and at the same time a means of ultimately achieving healthy personality [p. 24]." In saying that self-disclosure is a symptom of personality health, Jourard means that a person who displays many of the other characteristics of a healthy personality will also display the ability to make himself fully known to other persons. Clinical study and written questionnaires are typically employed for collecting information about this dimension of personality.

In Maslow's (1970) hierarchy of needs, the need for self-actualization rests at the top. It is this need which uniquely identifies humanity, and it is the fulfillment of this need which produces the best of what mankind is capable of becoming. In Maslow's chapter on "Self-Actualizing People: A Study of Psychological Health" he reports on his study of selected persons "who have developed or are developing to the full stature of which they are capable [p. 150]." Maslow collected case histories of friends and personal acquaintances as well as public and historical figures and developed global or holistic impressions with regard to their degree of self-actualization and the characteristics of self-actualized persons. More recent researchers have developed questionnaires for ascertaining information about this aspect of psychological health.

Humanistic Pyschology Research Instruments

A good many humanistic psychologists have been specialists in counseling and psychotherapy and a substantial body of research has been collected from the clinical setting, especially by Rogers and his associates (see, for example, Rogers and Dymond, 1954). In clinical psychology, the content analysis method, which consists of formulating a set of categories by means of which the verbalizations of a client can be classified, has been frequently used by humanistic psychologists as an instrument for research. Of interest is whether the client, from a content analysis of his comments in therapy, becomes more accepting of himself, and, if so, if he becomes more accepting of other people as well.

The Stephenson Q-technique provides an excellent instrument for investigating the self-concept by the single case method. In the Q-technique a person is given a packet of statements and is asked to sort them into a prearranged distribution along a continuum from those most characteristic of the person doing the sorting to those least characteristic of him. This method may be used for studying systematically the perceptions of a person about himself, and it may be used not only for discovering how the person perceives himself at the present time but also how he would like to be, or how he was at an earlier age, or how he thinks others perceive him. The possibilities for obtaining information about a person's perceptions of himself are quite large.

The most prolifically used measurement instruments for humanistic psychology research are the self-concept scales. Robinson and Shaver (1969) say that there "are now perhaps two-hundred such scales in the literature [p. 45]." Some of the more frequently used instruments of this type are: "Self-Concept Semantic Differential Scale" of Schwartz and Tangri; "Self-Concept Semantic Differential Scale" of Pervin and Libby; "Inventory of the Self-Concept" by Sherwood; "The Tennessee Self-Concept Scale" of Fitts; and the "Self-Esteem Scale" by Rosenberg.

Jourard (1964, 1968) has been the most prominent theorist and researcher on self-disclosure. He and others have developed instruments to measure this aspect of behavior, and there is a substantial body of research in which self-disclosure instruments have been employed.

Recently, the *Personal Orientation Inventory* was developed by Shostrom (1966) and is designed to measure values and behavior believed to be important in the development of self-actualization. The instrument was developed for use in therapy as well as in empirical research. The POI has been used in studies reported in over 50 published articles and 70 unpublished reports and dissertations involving a wide variety of subjects and research procedures.

Notwithstanding the wealth of measurement tools for the use of humanistic psychological research, many conceptual and theoretical problems beset this field of study, not the least of which is the operationalization of the key concepts themselves. For those who use the terms "hard" and "soft" when referring to scientific research, they would probably consider the humanistic research among the "softest" of the soft sciences.

The Humanistic Perspective and Research Problems in Sport

Although at present there is enormous interest in the humanistic perspective among sports psychologists, sports sociologists, and physical educators— indeed it is almost at the tidal wave point—little research has been published that relates humanism to sports variables. And certainly nothing like a substantial causal study has been published.

There are several ways that the humanistic research approach may be used in sport. A humanistic research approach might focus on the study of the values held in the sport context, not only as preached but as practiced, and the personal and social consequences. Moreover, one might study the degree to which specific values, and sports based on those values, facilitate or hinder the development of self-concept, self-actualization, self-disclosure, and other personal qualities related to the healthy personality. A humanistic perspective would enable researchers to develop theories and research that study the consequence of the sport experience from the standpoint of human growth and self-fulfillment, rather than in terms of social adjustment and performance criteria alone, which is the viewpoint prevalent at present. In sport there are almost no studies which focus on creativity, joy, self-fulfillment, or on sport organizations which facilitate these.

Interpersonal relationships are widespread in sports, and in terms of the helping relationship those who enhance the self-development of individuals with whom they associate tend to be persons who become involved in the *lives* of those associates. How do athletes remember their coaches? How do athletes perceive coaches in terms of their encouragement of personal growth?

Humanistic psychology research has shown that external cues are not a good source for cues about interpersonal relationships which exist between individuals. Rather cues of how an individual feels about his role in a group, other persons, etc. are better cues. In light of what recent critics have said about overt coaching behavior, it might be interesting to ascertain whether athletes perceive the coach the same way outsiders do.

Hopefully, in the coming years these questions and many others which are related to the outcomes of sports experiences will be answered through appropriate research. At present, the surface has not even been scratched and it is a shame since sport is such a pervasive activity in our society.

NOTE

1. I am indebted to Tom Fauquet for the general theme of ideas which are discussed in this section. See his paper "Reich, Combs and the Open Classroom," *Colorado Journal of Educational Research*, Volume 12, No. 1, Fall, 1972.

REFERENCES

Bruce, P., "Three Forces in Psychology and their Ethical and Educational Implications," *The Educational Forum*, 30:227-235, 1966.

Combs, A. W., "A Perceptual View of the Adequate Personality," in Combs, A. W., (Ed.), *Perceiving, Behaving, Becoming*, ASCD Yearbook, Washington, D.C., 1962.

Fitts, W. H., *Interpersonal Competence: The Wheel Model,* Dede Wallace Center Monograph, Nashville, Tennessee, 1970, No. 2.

Fitts, W. H., *The Self-Concept and Self-Actualization,* Dede Wallace Center Monograph, Nashville, Tennessee, 1971, No. 3.

Glass, J. F., "The Humanistic Challenge to Sociology," *Journal of Humanistic Psychology,* 11:170-183, 1971.

Hall, C. S., and Lindzey, G., *Theories of Personality,* (2nd Edition), New York: John Wiley and Sons, 1970.

Hoch, P., *Rip Off The Big Game,* Garden City, New York: Doubleday and Company, 1972.

Ingham, A. G., and Loy, J. W., "The Social System of Sport: A Humanistic Perspective," *Quest,* Monograph XIX, January, 1973, pp. 3-23.

Jourard, S. M., *Disclosing Man to Himself,* New York: Van Nostrand Reinhold, 1968.

Jourard, S. M., *The Transparent Self,* Princeton: N.J.: D. Van Nostrand Company, 1964.

Kinch, J. A., "A Formalized Theory of Self-Concept," *American Journal of Sociology,* 68:481-486, 1963.

Maslow, A. H., *The Psychology of Science,* New York: Harper and Row, 1966.

Maslow, A. H., *Toward a Psychology of Being,* (2nd Edition), New York: Van Nostrand, 1968.

Maslow, A. H., *Motivation and Personality* (2nd Edition), New York: Harper and Row, 1970.

Miller, D. L., *Gods and Games: Toward a Theology of Play,* New York: World, 1970.

Ogilvie, B., and Tutko, T. A., *Problem Athletes and How to Handle Them,* London: Pelham Books, 1966.

Reich, C. A., *The Greening of America,* New York: Random House, 1970.

Robinson, J. P., and Shaver, P. R., *Measures of Social Psychological Attitudes,* Ann Arbor, Institute for Social Research, 1969.

Rogers, C. R., and Dymond, R. F., (Eds.), *Psychotherapy and Personality Change; Co-Ordinated Studies in the Client-Centered Approach,* Chicago: University of Chicago Press, 1954.

Rogers, C. R., *On Becoming a Person,* Boston: Houghton Mifflin, 1961.

Sage, G. H., "The Coach as Management: Organizational Leadership in American Sport," *Quest,* Monograph XIX, January, 1973, pp. 35-40.

Schafer, W. E., "Sport and Youth Counter-Culture: Contrasting Socialization Themes," paper presented at Conference on Sport and Social Deviancy, State University of New York, Brockport, December 10, 1971.

Seeman, J., "Toward a Concept of Personality Integration," *American Psychologist,* 14:633-637, 1959.

Shostrom, E. L., *Personal Orientation Inventory,* San Diego: Educational and Industrial Testing Service, 1966.

Slater, P., *The Pursuit of Loneliness,* Boston: Beacon Press, 1970.

THE COACH AS MANAGEMENT: ORGANIZATIONAL LEADERSHIP IN AMERICAN SPORT

George H. Sage

Leadership is the process of influencing the activities of an organized group toward goal setting and goal achievement (Stogdill, 1950). For most American sports teams the coach is the appointed leader. While it really is not known to what extent the success or failure of a team is due to the leadership competence of the coach, there is little doubt that it is an important factor in team performance and the coach, as the leader, is held responsible for the team's performance. Thus, the coach serves a function that is similar to management leaders in the business world.

Many aspects of our society are experiencing a transformation from traditional values of corporate organization and the Protestant Ethic to a new and different moral and ethical system. Accordingly, athletic coaches are being forced into reassessing their current beliefs concerning interpersonal relations, especially in a leadership context, and many are seeking ways of developing more effective personal relationships with the young athletes on their teams. Several recent critics from within and outside the sports setting have claimed that traditional sports practices and values are dehumanizing and brutalizing and that coaches are insensitive and autocratic (Scott, 1971; Meggyesy, 1971; Ogilvie and Tutko, 1971). They are calling for a counter-culture in sport, based on individuality, human values, and self-actualization.

George H. Sage, "The Coach as Management: Organizational Leadership in American Sport," *Quest,* Monograph XIX, January 1973, pp. 35-40. Reprinted by permission.

THE SCIENTIFIC MANAGEMENT
AND LEADERSHIP STYLE

The fundamental complaint of those who attack athletic coaches is directed toward the leadership style which is employed by many coaches. Tutko and Richards (1971) suggest that as leaders most coaches believe in strong discipline, rigidity of rules, extrinsic motivation, and an impersonal attitude towards their athletes, and they characterize most coaches as being hard-nosed or authoritarian. This leadership strategy bears a strong resemblance to that employed by the so-called Scientific Management movement which emerged from the studies and writing of Frederick W. Taylor (1911a,b) in the early years of the 20th century, a time of population growth and industrial expansion. Taylor's managerial methods were based on cost efficiency. He suggested that an organization could achieve its production goals only when it could achieve an optimal cost-efficiency ratio. Taylor's primary propositions were: (1) Use time and methods study to find the one best way of performing a job. By the best way is meant the way that permits the largest average rate of production over the day. (2) Provide the employee with an incentive to perform the job in the best way and at good pace. In general, do this by giving him a specified bonus over regular rates if he meets the standard of production. (3) Use specialized experts to establish the various conditions surrounding the worker's task. Scientific Management treated man as a means by assuming that he would cooperate and work only when forced to do so. This arrangement reduced man to an instrument of the organization who functions under a hierarchical authority relationship. The climate of inter-personal relationship under the Scientific Management approach was at a low level. Relations between leaders, or managers, and workers were closed and inflexible; there was little opportunity for change initiated by the workers.

The underlying notion implicit in the Scientific Management approach with regard to the nature of man is that he is bad, lazy, and incentive-oriented. This notion has firm historic roots. Machiavelli (1952), in *The Prince,* suggested that man is by nature uncooperative and rebellious and must be ruthlessly controlled. He said: ". . . men in general . . . are ungrateful, voluble, dissemblers, anxious to avoid dangers, and covetous of gain [p. 98]." Hobbes, Darwin, Freud, and more recently Ardrey have all held pessimistic assumptions about the nature of man.

American business enthusiastically adopted Taylor's approach to management leadership, and this leadership style has frequently been used by various non-business organizations such as schools, the military, and sports.[1] While research which began in the late 1920's and extended to the present has shown that the basic assumptions of Scientific Management with regard to worker performance has questionable validity, nevertheless some segments of American organizational life still adhere to the propositions and methods of Scientific Management.

One sphere of American organizational life in which this leadership style has traditionally been utilized is in athletic coaching.[2] With the rise of increasingly institutionalized and codified team organization, many coaches have tended to view team members as objects in a machine-like environment where emphasis is on instrumental rather than consummatory behaviors. Thus, the players become another man's (the coach) instrument, and are used to reach the objectives and goals of the organizational collectivity; they are reduced to cogs in the organization's machinery. Accordingly, coaches have structured coach-player relations along authoritarian lines; they have analyzed and structured sports team positions for precise specialization of the performers, and they have endeavored to control player behavior not only throughout practice and contest periods but also on a round-the-clock basis, e.g., grooming rules, training rules, dating behavior, etc. Furthermore, for incentives and rewards, a system of letter awards, newspaper stories, locker room posters, helmet decals, etc. have been used. An observer at many athletic team practice sessions might believe that he was viewing a factory assembly-line work shift. Indeed, the coaches punctuate the air regularly with shouts of "work, work, work."

The organization in this case is the team and the players under this form of leadership are the instruments for the fulfillment of organizational goals. In most cases, they have not been consulted about the organizational goals (it is assumed that they want to be champions and that they are willing to pay the price to be winners). They have not been consulted about team membership, practice methods, team strategy, or any of the other dynamic functions of a team. The assumption has been made that they have nothing to contribute toward identifying group goals and the means for achieving them. Decisions are made by management (the coach), after a thorough cost efficiency analysis, and the players are expected to carry out the will of the coach for the accomplishment of organizational goals.

HUMAN RELATIONS MANAGEMENT
AND LEADERSHIP STYLE

Over forty years ago social research began to throw serious doubt on the validity of Scientific Management versions of human nature and leadership functions. The research of Elton Mayo (1933) at the Western Electric

Company's plant in Chicago initiated what became known as the Human Relations school of management leadership. This was followed by the research of Kurt Lewin (1935, 1936, 1948) in the 1930's and 1940's in social psychology; various writers and researchers built upon Lewin's work and by the 1960's McGregor (1960) formulated a definitive work on leadership for executives which he called the Theory Y form of management. Finally, Abraham Maslow (1954, 1965) indirectly contributed to Human Relations leadership theory through his writings in psychology which have fostered what has become known as Third Force Psychology.

Mayo and his colleagues found in their studies at the Hawthorne plant of Western Electric in Chicago that formal and informal personal relations are critically important to productivity and job satisfaction. In *Human Problems of an Industrial Civilization* (1933), Mayo concluded that his extensive research showed that workers do not respond as isolated individuals, but as members of a group. More specifically, he suggested that there is a social system consisting of established informal relationships between particular persons in any live organization, and this system invariably has important consequences for achievement. Improvement of the organization's achievement will be either impossible or extremely difficult if informal relationships are not taken into account.

Building upon Mayo's work, Kurt Lewin, one of the most prominent social psychologists, suggested several implications of his research for organizational leadership. Most importantly he suggested that the willingness of a person to cooperate in a program of activities depends on his perception of the environment and his own place in it. Moreover, groups with a democratic atmosphere, whose members participate in determining their own goals, will have higher morale and more commitment to the organization than those directed by authoritarian leaders. Under some conditions, the amount of participation will determine the group's level of achievement.

Maslow developed an intriguing and persuasive theory of human motivation which touches on every aspect of human behavior. His theory challenged some of the basic premises that have dominated American social theory during the early 20th century. Maslow's theory is centered on man himself—his needs, his goals, his achievements, and his success. He saw people as able to make their own decisions and deal with their own crises; he saw them as trustworthy, dependable, and possessing a dignity and an integrity which must be respected; finally he held that people are capable of being creative, dynamic, and active participants with their environments.

McGregor's work is in the tradition of the Human Relations approach and the Theory Y style of management which he proposed draws heavily from Mayo, Lewin, and Maslow. The viewpoint underlying Theory Y is summarized by McGregor (1960) as follows:

1. The expenditure of physical and mental effort in work is as natural as play or rest. The average human being does not inherently dislike work. Depending upon controllable conditions work may be a source of satisfaction. . . .

2. External control and the threat of punishment are not the only means for bringing about effort toward organizational objectives. Man will exercise self-direction and self-control in the service of objectives to which he is committed.

3. Commitment to objectives is a function of the rewards associated with their achievement. The most significant of such rewards, e.g., the satisfaction of ego and self-actualization needs, can be direct products of effort directed toward organization objectives.

4. The average human being learns, under proper conditions, not only to accept but to seek responsibility. Avoidance of responsibility, lack of ambition, and emphasis on security are generally consequences of experience, not inherent characteristics.

5. The capacity to exercise a relatively high degree of imagination, ingenuity, and creativity in the solution of organizational problems is widely, not narrowly, distributed in the population.

6. Under the conditions of modern industrial life, the intellectual potentialities of the average human being are only partially utilized [pp. 47-48].

McGregor (1957) suggests that if employees are lazy, indifferent, unwilling to take responsibility, intransigent, uncreative, uncooperative, their behavior is due to the traditional bureaucratic assumptions and methods of organization and control.

The Human Relations approach to leadership differs from Scientific Management in that it emphasizes men in contrast to positions; that is, it is deeply concerned with attitudes, values, and emotional reactions of individual group members. This viewpoint sees man as only minimally controlled by the carrot-and-stick principle; instead effective control is viewed as developing from within the individual. External control will not motivate men to apply all of their talents in behalf of group goals. The emphasis is on nonauthoritarian styles of leadership, member participation in group decision making, and encouragement of organization activities in the service of individual needs. In short, this approach permits individual autonomy, presumably maximizing task involvement and intrinsic motivation. Individual goals and organizational goals become the same.

The conceptions of human nature and personality are quite different within these two systems of thought. Scientific Management holds these assumptions about man: He is inherently self-centered, lacks ambition, dislikes responsibility, prefers to be led, is indifferent to group needs, resistant to change, and is by nature an indolent creature who works as little as possible. Thus, strong leaders must be responsible for organizing the elements or goal accomplishments; they must direct, motivate, and control the workers' actions, modifying their behavior to meet the needs of the organization. The leader's task is to persuade, reward, punish, and control member behavior. The leader must get things done through the members. The Human Relations approach holds these assumptions about man: He is not by nature passive or resistant to group needs, he has become so as a result of experience in organizations; the motivation, the capacity for assuming responsibility, and the readiness to direct behavior toward group goals are all present in people. This approach has as its foundation the notion that man's tendency toward good can be made to prevail, if given the opportunity, and that he can make sound decisions concerning himself and in cooperation with others engage in constructive and supportive performance. Accordingly, it is the responsibility of leaders to make it possible for people to recognize and develop their human characteristics for themselves. Leaders must arrange organizational conditions and procedures so that people can achieve their own goals best by directing their own efforts toward organizational objectives.

ORGANIZATIONAL LEADERSHIP AND THE COACH

This second approach is more in keeping with contemporary values and ethics which emphasize individuality and freedom from capricious autocratic control. Today, the task of the coach is to enhance his players' potential and enable them to enjoy what they are doing, derive joy and satisfaction from their sports participation, and thus achieve self-fulfillment. In applying Human Relations leadership to sports, the coach will not assume without question that the total team program takes precedence over the needs and desires of team members. Preferences of the individual will be given equal consideration with those of the team. Team objectives and methods of reaching them will be accomplished by consultation with all team members. The coach will restrict his own authority to essentials, not imposing his arbitrary will upon the players. The old arrangement by which the athletes are instruments of the coach will give way to a mutuality in which each functions to the advantage of the other.

This is not to suggest that directive and dynamic leadership is to be abandoned to a form of obsequious equalitarianism. Many persons assume that strong, directive leadership is always bad, overlooking the fact that there are psychologically healthy leaders whose motives are for the good of their group members and the good of the organization. Indeed, in Maslow's opinion the great leader is one who has just the right combination of humility and flexibility while at the same time possessing the strength of character to stand alone when an important principle is involved. Maslow (1965) says: "The kind of person who must be loved by all probably will not make a good leader [p. 130]." He implies that there are circumstances when the leader must say no, be firm, strong, and courageous. But the excellent leader takes pleasure in seeing his group members grow and self-actualize under the necessary restraints of group membership. It is nonsense to suppose that every step in coaching can be democratic. It is obvious that in task-oriented groups, such as one finds in sports, where decisions frequently have to be made quickly and on the basis of experience, a pure democratic leadership system cannot effectively prevail. That a leader may have to unilaterally make decisions for the group does not necessarily diminish his sensitivity and humanism for the members.

The coach and athlete are in need of each other; team goals cannot be accomplished without both. The emphasis here is that coach and player need each other and benefit by mutual accommodation of objectives and goals. Leadership significantly affects the personal development of those who are led and it is often a critical factor in an individual's attitudes about the group and human relations in general. The coach needs to seek new ways of relating to players; he needs to become more aware and sensitive to other people. An increased sensitivity to others' unique humanness will enhance individual actualization and may lead to better performance. The coach can reflect in his leadership behavior a willingness to have confidence and trust in his players, for this creates a foundation for building individual confidence and security. In applying a leadership style of this kind the coach will be raising the level of interpersonal relations in the athletic world. Team membership will become inherently interesting and gratifying, and sports participation will become a genuine cooperative venture for coach and players and its rewards will be what Maslow calls "peak experiences" in personal-social living.

NOTES

1. In *Education and the Cult of Efficiency* (1962), R. E. Callahan has argued that Scientific Management was one of the most important historic forces to shape the administration of public schools in America.

2. Riesman and Denny (1951) in their classic paper on cultural diffusion and American football discuss the relation between Taylor's writings and the development of American football.

REFERENCES

Callahan, R. E., *Education and the Cult of Efficiency*, Chicago: The University of Chicago Press, 1962.

Lewin, K., *Dynamic Theory of Personality*, New York: McGraw-Hill, 1935.

Lewin, K., *Principles of Topological Psychology*, New York: McGraw-Hill, 1936.

Lewin, K., and Allport, G. W., (eds.), *Resolving Social Conflicts*, New York: Harper, 1948.

McGregor, D., "The human side of enterprise," *The Management Review*, 1957, 46, 22-28, 88-92.

McGregor, D., *The Human Side of Enterprise*, New York: McGraw-Hill, 1960.

Machiavelli, N., *The Prince*, New York: Mentor Books, 1952. (Translation of the book first published in 1532.)

Maslow, A., *Motivation and Personality*, New York: Harper, 1954.

Maslow, A., *Eupsychian Management*, Homewood, Illinois: Irwin-Dorsey, 1965.

Mayo, E., *The Human Problem of an Industrial Civilization*, New York: The Macmillan Co., 1933.

Meggyesy, D., *Out of Their League*, New York: Ramparts Press, 1971.

Ogilvie, B. C., and Tutko, T. A., "Sport: If you want to build character, try something else," *Psychology Today*, 1971, 5 (Oct.), 61-63.

Riesman, E., and Denny, R., "Football in America: A study of cultural diffusion," *American Quarterly*, 1951, 3, 309-319.

Scott, J., *The Athletic Revolution*, New York: The Free Press, 1971.

Stogdill, R., "Leadership, membership, and organization," *Psychological Bulletin*, 1950, 47, 1-14.

Taylor, F. W., *The Principles of Scientific Management*, New York: Harper, 1911a.

Taylor, F. W., *Shop Management*, New York: Harper, 1911b.

Tutko, T. A., and Richards, J. W., *Psychology of Coaching*, Boston: Allyn and Bacon, 1971.

8 / SPORT AND THE SCHOOL

The elaborate organization of interschool sports is a uniquely American phenomenon. In most countries of the world there is very little sport in the school systems. School sports, or athletics as they are often called, provide countless Americans with excitement and entertainment, and any serious proposal to curtail them is immediately met with a barrage of rebuttals. School teams are the mobilizing force of morale and esprit de corps for school and community, and the athletes are the folk heroes of the subculture of the educational world.

The emphasis on school sports originally developed in the first half of the nineteenth century and began at colleges that were attended mostly by students living away from home. Games and sports were a diversion from the boredom of classroom work. The students played a variety of sports, first as unorganized and impromptu games and later as organized intramural and interclass activities. As the number of colleges and their geographic proximity increased, the next logical step was for the students of one college to challenge the students of a nearby school to a sports contest. The first officially recorded intercollegiate sports contest was a rowing race between Harvard and Yale in 1852. At the beginning, school sports were organized by the students, usually over faculty objection. In time, with increased organization and the proliferation of sports teams, faculties assumed administrative control over sports. Today this control is manifested in national organizations—such as the National Collegiate Athletic Association—which derive their authority from the colleges and universities.

American high schools mimicked the colleges in the development of sports. Following basically the same pattern as the colleges, high schools initiated interschool sports programs, and by 1900 several states had established high school athletic associations. In 1922 the National Federation of State High School Athletic Associations was founded, indicating the nation-wide scope of high school sports.

American school sports have been praised as the most important factor in the evolution of national character by some and assailed as the "poison ivy" of the schools by others. Supporters of school sports have cited their potential as a developer of better health, socialization, and the learning of moral lessons. Sports critics, on the other hand, have claimed that sports contribute nothing whatsoever to education and that they simply divert the attention and energy of the students and community from the main purpose of education and use up valuable time. For these critics, school sports have become the "tail that wags the educational dog."

The first reading is by James S. Coleman, a sociologist who has conducted extensive research on the values of high school students. He asserts that his investigations show conclusively that success in school sports is valued far more highly among high school students than is academic achievement. To support his claim, he discloses the results of an investigation which compared the popularity and status of athletes with that of scholars at ten high schools. He believes that the high status of athletes in high school is a function of the entire social system—parents, peers, and community. All provide rewards and recognition to the athletes, and since recognition and respect are fundamental needs of students, sports is the best avenue for attaining these in high school. Although Coleman recognizes the various beneficial values of school sports, he believes that sports, as now constituted, create numerous problems for the schools. He suggests that the dominance of sports be diminished by the development of game experiences in various subjects in the curriculum.

Richard Rehberg and Walter Schafer, in the next reading, agree with Coleman that high school athletics are a central feature of the schools, but whereas Coleman implies that athletics have a detrimental effect on the educational objectives of the school, Rehberg and Schafer examine the question of whether athletics have a positive influence on the participants, at least in one dimension—the expectation of going to college. The purpose of their study was to ascertain whether participation in school sports influenced the participant's educational aims. From their review of the literature, they hypothesize that there is a higher proportion of athletes who expect to go on to college than nonathletes with this objective. They also hypothesize that the strength of the positive relationship between sports participation and educational expectations for college is greater for boys from working-class homes than for those from middle- and upper-class homes. Both hypotheses are sustained.

In the third reading, John Phillips and Walter Schafer review the pertinent findings of studies which show that high school athletes tend to exceed nonathletes in their educational expectations and in their achievement of educational goals. First, they review the literature on the relationship between athletic participation and high school academic achievement. They indicate that the research evidence tends to suggest that athletes achieve better grades than nonathletes, notwithstanding the belief of many that athletes are poor students. Second, they review the literature on college expectations and report that the evidence on this topic indicates that athletes aspire to and succeed in attending college more than do nonathletes. Third, they examine the relationship between athletics and delinquency and suggest that athletic participation may be a deterrent to delinquent behavior. Next, they suggest that high school athletics may serve as a means for upward social mobility, especially for athletes from blue-collar backgrounds. Finally, the authors employ the concept of subculture to explain the processes intervening between athletics and various behavioral outcomes.

In the final reading, Snyder conceptualizes the coach as a "significant other" for high school athletes. He examines the role of the coach in advising and counseling players about their educational and occupational aspirations. Snyder reports that high school coaches are indeed influential persons for assisting athletes in forming their educational and occupational goals. Coaches are more influential with athletes from lower social class backgrounds than with athletes from upper social class backgrounds.

ATHLETICS IN HIGH SCHOOL

James S. Coleman

Abstract

Research—based on the visibility of athletic stars, on most desired achievement, on the composition of the leading crowd, on status criteria in leading-crowd membership, on popularity—demonstrates conclusively that athletics is far and away more important as a value among high school students than intellectual achievement. And the school itself seems to encourage rather than to discourage this relative evaluation. There must be basic reasons for these phenomena, and these may be discerned in the functions performed by athletics not only in the school but also in the community. Among boys, for example, it has been found that athletics has a democratizing effect, breaking up organization based on background and reconstituting it on the basis of common activity or achievement. Athletics serves an important function in motivating students. It generates strong positive identification with the school; without athletics the school would be lifeless for the student, deficient in collective goals. With athletics, it is possible for all students to identify with their school through their teams. Not only schools but whole communities depend upon the collective enthusiasm generated by their local high school athletic teams. The problem for the school is to find a way to have the functions now performed by athletic teams performed in ways more conducive to the intellectual aims of the school. Debate used to serve this function, music contests may also, as well as drama contests, and mathematics

James S. Coleman, "Athletics in High School," *Annals of the American Academy of Political and Social Science*, 338:33-43 (November 1961). Reprinted by permission.

tournaments. It is possible that social and economic games played by means of complex computers may come to perform, on a far more intellectual level, the integrating function now performed almost exclusively by athletics.

The role of interscholastic athletics in high schools is a controversial one. Athletics is castigated as the antithesis of scholastic activity by intellectuals—many of whom have never taken part in interscholastic sports. It is defended and praised as the builder of men by coaches and athletes—most of whom have a vested interest in this proposition.

It is characteristic of athletics to provoke violent and lasting controversies, for it occupies a very special position in high schools. The amount of attention devoted to athletics would be most striking to an innocent visitor to a high school. A visitor entering a school would likely be confronted, first of all, with a trophy case. His examination of the trophies would reveal a curious fact: The gold and silver cups, with rare exception, symbolize victory in athletic contests, not scholastic ones. The figures adorning these trophies represent men passing footballs, shooting basketballs, holding out batons; they are not replicas of "The Thinker." The concrete symbols of victory are old footballs, basketballs, and baseballs, not works of art or first editions of books won as literary prizes. Altogether, the trophy case would suggest to the innocent visitor that he was entering an athletic club, not an educational institution.

Walking further, this visitor would encounter teen-agers bursting from classrooms. Listening to their conversations, he would hear both casual and serious discussions of the Friday football game, confirming his initial impression. Attending a school assembly that morning, he would probably find a large segment of the program devoted to a practice of school yells for the athletic game and the announcement of a pep rally before the game. At lunch hour, he would be likely to find more boys shooting baskets in the gymnasium than reading in the library. Browsing through a school yearbook, he would be impressed, in his innocence, with the number of pages devoted to athletics.

Altogether, this visitor would find wherever he turned, a great deal of attention devoted to athletics. As an impressionable stranger, this visitor might well suppose that more attention is paid to athletics by teen-agers, both as athletes and as spectators, than to scholastic matters. He might even conclude, with good reason, that the school was essentially organized around athletic contests and that scholastic matters were of lesser importance to all involved.

To be sure, his impression would vary from school to school—but, perhaps surprising to him, it would vary little by the social origins and destinations of the adolescents served by the schools. In ten schools recently studied by the author, athletics was about as dominant, by any of several criteria, in middle-class schools with a high proportion of their graduates going to college as in working-class schools.[1]

Considering his impressions, such a visitor to American high schools might ask himself two questions: First of all, why is it this way? He had assumed, naively, that schools were for learning, yet his impressions led to a different conclusion. He had talked with educators about curriculum, new academic programs, and scholastic standards. Yet, upon visiting the schools, he found the adolescents' attention on athletics, and all the excitement and enthusiasm he found was focused around athletic contests. Why the discrepancy?

The visitor might ask another question: What are the consequences of the attention devoted to athletics? What are the consequences within the school itself, and what are the long-term consequences for these adolescents when they have become adults?

It is to these two questions, the question of consequences and the question of sources, that this paper is directed. The examination will be based upon evidence collected during a study of ten high schools in 1957-58. These high schools were located in the Middle West. Five were small-town schools with 500 or fewer students; one was a parochial school of 750 boys in a large city; there was a working-class, suburban school of 1,000 students; two small-city comprehensive schools were included of 1,400 and 2,000 students respectively; there was an upper-middle-class, suburban school of 2,000 students. Unless otherwise noted, the generalizations mentioned below apply to all schools.[2] In fact, a striking discovery in this study was the similarity of all schools in the importance attached to athletics. Greater similarity among schools was found in this than in any other dimension of the research.

CONSEQUENCES

The more difficult question concerns the long-term consequences of attention to athletics. On this question, the study has no evidence, since adolescents were studied only during one year in high school, and there seems to be no systematic evidence on the matter available elsewhere. However, evidence from the research does show some of the short-term consequences, those manifest in the school itself.

Impact on Freshmen

The attention focused upon athletics in high schools directly affects the impact of the schools upon their incoming freshmen. Football, which is played in the fall as school begins, is especially important. A major element in the impact of athletics is the visibility of the athletic stars. A boy who achieves something, however creditable his achievement, can be a model to emulate only if that achievement is made visible by the structure of activities in the school.

Some idea of the relative visibility of scholastic achievement and athletic achievement can be gained through a finding from the survey of the ten schools. About six weeks after school opened in the fall, each boy in every school was asked to name the boy whom he saw as the best student in his grade and the boy who was the best athlete. This can be a difficult task for freshmen, but it is less difficult in those areas for which school activities focus attention on achievement. Thus, a comparison of the proportions of boys able to answer the questions provides some guide to the relative visibility of scholastic and athletic achievements in each of the four years of school.

Table 1 shows this comparison. The data indicate, in general, that the best athletes are more visible than the best scholars. The difference is greatest for the freshmen—the best athlete is known 10 percent more often than the best scholar in the small schools and 14 percent more often in the large schools. Only in the junior and senior years does the visibility of the best scholars catch up with that of the best athletes. Thus, for the impressionable freshmen, the achievements that stand out most are those of the athlete, not those of the scholar.[3]

Table 1 Comparative Visibility of Best Athletes and Best Scholars to Their Classmates

	Freshmen	Sophomores	Juniors	Seniors
Small schools				
Percent naming best athlete	68%	75%	88%	85%
Percent naming best scholar	58%	66%	83%	88%
Number of cases	317	292	214	205
Large schools				
Percent naming best athlete	54%	56%	48%	72%
Percent naming best scholar	40%	47%	57%	68%
Number of cases	635	1,049	749	557

Note: Percentages are based on the nine public schools.

Assuming adolescents desire to be successful, known, and recognized, one consequence of the visibility of achievement in athletics or scholarship would be the desire to achieve in these particular areas. Does the environment and climate of opinion in the school affect these desires? Boys were asked, in the fall shortly after school had started and again in the spring toward the end of the school year, how they would most like to be remembered at school—as a brilliant student, an athletic star, or most popular. One would suppose, if schools focus attention on scholastic endeavors, that the effect of the school year would be to increase the strength of the brilliant-student image relative to that of the athletic-star image. Yet, for the freshmen and sophomores of the schools surveyed, matters are quite different. Of all those responding either "brilliant student" or "athletic star," 44 percent in each grade responded "brilliant student" in the fall and only 37 percent gave this response in the spring.[4] Rather than increasing in strength over the school year, the brilliant-student image declined in strength relative to that of the athlete. It appears, then, that the very functioning of the school itself tends to reduce the initial interest of the adolescent in being seen as a brilliant student, or tends differentially to increase his interest in being seen as an athletic star.

Another effect of athletics upon the incoming freshmen concerns the "leading crowd" in school. Most high schools, other than the very smallest, have a leading crowd in each grade though schools larger than about 2,000 in enrollment may have more than one. This crowd is recognized by other students and by its own members, and most students can name members of the leading crowd in their grade. This, in fact, was what they were asked to do in the research discussed above. In addition, all boys were asked to name their friends, so that it was possible to reconstruct the actual crowds or cliques in the school. Then, by identifying which of the cliques had as members boys frequently named as members of the leading crowd, it was possible to identify objectively the leading clique or crowd in each grade of each school. Having done this, the question then was asked: What do these boys, who constitute the leading crowds in their grades, have in common?[5]

Among the freshmen in each of the four schools studied for leading cliques, the one attribute shared by every boy in every leading clique—twenty-three boys in all—was being out for either football or basketball. Most of the twenty-three were out for both. No other attribute—in background, activities, or attitudes—so sharply distinguished the leading cliques. In the later years of school, the leading cliques were found to be less uniformly athletic, but, among freshmen, they were found to be totally so.

Athletic participation as a basis for membership in the leading clique is not, of course, characteristic of every freshman class in the country, but it seems likely that the general tendency is widespread. Athletic teams provide a basis for intensive and prolonged association, more than any other activity in school. Thus, the foundation is laid, from the very beginning of high school, for a cohesive, tightly-knit group. This, together with the attention directed toward athletic contests and athletic stars in high school, makes it very likely that the athletes will constitute the leading crowd among freshmen. Later, when other activities develop in school and groups form on other bases, there is less dominance of the athletic crowd. But, in the crucial first year, when a boy's aims and aspirations in high school are established, the athletic crowd dominates.

Altogether, then, athletics is a particularly important factor in the impact of the high school upon its freshmen. Through the several mechanisms discussed above, the freshmen get a picture of the school focused even more toward athletic achievement than it actually is.

Athletics in the Status System

One of the most important aspects of any social system is its distribution of status: the way status attaches to different persons and to different activities. The importance of the distribution of status lies partly in its effect as a motivating device, for it motivates people toward those activities which confer status upon them. To the extent that adolescents are concerned with status among their peers—and every indication suggests that the great majority of them are so motivated—their motivations and aspirations in various activities are shaped by the distribution of status.

It is important, then, in assessing the consequences of the attention to athletics in high schools, to examine the position of athletics in the adolescent status system. In the present research, this was done by several means.

Each boy was asked to assess what was required in his school to be a member of the leading crowd, and he was asked to rank various attributes for making a boy popular.

In response to the first question, the two attributes most often mentioned were personality—mentioned by 23 percent of the boys—and a good reputation—mentioned by 17 percent. Next in order, however, was athletic ability—mentioned by 16 percent. This was followed by good looks and success with girls—mentioned by 14 percent—and good grades or "brains"— mentioned by 12 percent.

In ranking attributes for their effect in making a boy popular, six attributes were available to be ranked from first to sixth. These attributes, with their average rank in all schools, were the following:[6]

Being an athletic star	2.2
Being in the leading crowd	2.6
Leader in activities	2.9
High grades, honor roll	3.5
Having a nice car	3.9
Coming from the right family	4.5

These answers show the great value that boys attribute to athletic achievement in gaining popularity. It is ranked considerably above any other item and far above good grades, which is fourth among the six.

In addition to these subjective estimates, it is also possible to determine which boys have highest status. In this research, it was done by asking each boy to name another boy he would like to be like, one he would like to be friends with, and who were members of the leading crowd. The status of a boy was determined by the number of such choices he received. Another question had made it possible to identify the boys seen as the best athletes and the best scholars. By comparing the likelihood of the best athletes to receive the status choices with the likelihood of the best scholars to receive such choices, it is possible to examine the objective status of athletic achievement. Table 2 shows the average number of choices on these criteria received by the best athletes, the best scholars, and all other boys in the schools studied.

As in various other tests, athletics scored higher than scholarship, although both athletes and scholars far outdistanced other boys. Stated another way, the star athletes, only 6.6 percent of the schools' male enroll-

Table 2 Average Numbers of Choices Received by Athletes, Scholars, and All Other Boys on Status Criteria

	Be friends with or be like	Member of leading crowd	Number of cases
Athletes	5.6	7.8	272
Scholars	3.4	4.9	278
All other boys	0.4	0.8	3,598

Note: "Athletes" and "scholars" are those named two or more times as best athlete or best scholar in their respective grades by other boys. Percentages are based on the nine public schools.

ment, received 47.4 percent of the "be friends with" and "be like" choices and 36.5 percent of all the leading crowd nominations.

According to all evidence, then, the status of athletic achievement in the schools surveyed is exceedingly high, considerably higher than that of scholastic achievement. Thus, the attention paid to athletics in American high schools, which would so puzzle an innocent visitor, is paralleled by the status of athletic achievement among adolescents.

Other Studies

Other research shows that these facts are not limited to the ten schools surveyed nor even to high schools in the Middle West.

In a large, predominantly Jewish, middle-class high school in New York City, Abraham Tannenbaum studied evaluations of stereotyped, fictitious students.[7] These fictitious students were distinguished in short descriptive statements on the bases of intelligence, athletic ability, and studiousness. Juniors in the high school were then asked to ascribe traits—some desirable, some undesirable—to each of the eight fictitious characters. Tannenbaum devised a mean acceptability rating from the ascribed traits, and the fictitious students fell in the following order of acceptability, from high to low:

1.   Brilliant nonstudious athlete

2.   Average nonstudious athlete

3.   Average studious athlete

4.   Brilliant studious athlete

5.   Brilliant nonstudious athlete

6.   Average nonstudious nonathlete

7.   Average studious nonathlete

8.   Brilliant studious nonathlete

As the order shows, all athletes had higher acceptability ratings than any nonathlete. Brilliance apparently had little effect in increasing acceptability, and studiousness reduced acceptability. Thus, in a school in which, because of its location and student body, one would expect to find brilliance or studiousness outdistancing athletics, the results are otherwise—and consistent with the results in the ten midwestern high schools.

These data on the status of athletic achievement in schools of widely varying types raise even more insistently the question of why there is such a dominance of athletics. Athletics is wholly outside the focus of attention of many educators in schools of education, for whom curriculum variations have over-riding importance. Yet athletics is central to the attention of adolescents, far more so than curriculum variations. And, despite educators' professional disinterest, athletics is an activity promoted by the schools themselves—not an outside interest like cars and dates. These inconsistencies and paradoxes all lead to the question: Why does athletics hold a place of such high importance in the high schools?

Athletics, Democracy, and Legitimacy of the System

The effect of athletics in forming leading crowds among freshmen was examined earlier; the formation of leading crowds among girls was left unexamined. The cliques of girls among freshmen reflect, much more than for boys, associations from earlier grades. Girls who travel together in the lower grades maintain their cliques in high school and often present an impregnable front to outsiders. Presumably as a result, the leading crowds for girls among freshmen are more completely middle class in background than for boys.

In effect, athletics provides for boys an interruption of this pattern, breaking down the organization based on common background and replacing it with organization based on common activity or achievement. Perhaps as a consequence, boys are more willing than girls to accept the status system of the school and view it as more legitimate. When asked to agree or to disagree that "There are a few who control things in this school, and the rest of us are out in the cold," 43 percent of the girls agreed with the statement in the fall, and the number increased to 48 percent by the next spring. Only 34 percent of the boys agreed that the statement was true in the fall, and their number decreased to 32 percent by spring.

Such a democratizing mechanism is particularly important for boys, who, to begin with, are less involved in school than girls and get poorer grades. If it were not for interscholastic athletics or something like it, the rebellion against school, the rate of dropout, and the delinquency of boys might be far worse than they presently are. This can only be a matter of conjecture. It does seem clear, however, that athletics introduces an important democratizing factor in the status system for boys in high school by undercutting social background as a basis for status.

SOURCES

Clearly, a part of the importance of athletics for adolescents lies in its compatibility with teen-age energy, enthusiasm, and explosive spirits. Were it not for this basic compatibility, the avidity with which teen-agers follow sports contests would be difficult to explain.

But the compatibility does not explain the special place that athletics holds in the activities of a school. As an innocent visitor might observe, the institution itself often seems more oriented toward athletic goals than academic ones. This can hardly be explained by the interests of teen-agers alone, for teen-agers are interested in many things—popular music, cars, dates—which have relatively little place in the high school structure of activities. Nor can the interests of teen-agers explain the fact that, in the ten schools surveyed, the strength of the athletic-star image increased during the school year and, apparently, decreased over the summer.[8]

Athletic contests in schools seem to serve an important function for the institution. Every institution depends for its survival upon capturing a certain portion of the energies of its members. In business organizations, this is done by pay, including incentive pay, and by opportunity for promotion. Among some members of an organization, identification with the achievements of the organization provides additional motivation. In unions, motivation derives from the common goals of the members, which can only be gained through concerted, collective effort.[9]

Schools, however, provide no comparable motivating devices for their students. Students are forced by family and by law to attend school, but this insures only their physical presence, not their involvement in school activities. The necessary motivation for the expenditure of effort in school arises naturally only for those students whose backgrounds and aspirations make good grades important for them. For some students, that is, grades are comparable to pay for workers in a factory. The crucial difference is that grades are important for only a part of the school population. For many adolescents, high school only delays their access to adult freedoms and pleasures and does not offer any unique and necessary benefits.

But, even for students with the right backgrounds, grades are a poor motivating mechanism, because they are unique to the school and useful only in comparison with grades of fellow students. This generates invidious comparisons, sets each student in competition with his fellows, and is a powerfully divisive force among the students. Direct incentive pay, or piece work, in factories produces the same effect and has sometimes been consciously used by employers to keep employees divided against each other.[10]

In the long run, this is a dangerous mechanism, as the history of incentive pay has shown. Under many conditions, it encourages informal norms restricting production—against the "rate-buster"—just as grade systems in high schools promote informal action against too much studiousness—against "the curve-breaker" or the "D.A.R.," Damned Average Raiser. Finally, piece work systems in factories have led to organized collective activity against the companies, unless the workers feel strongly identified with their companies.[11]

A much more successful mechanism of control in an institution is one which generates strong positive identification with the institution. Churches employ such mechanisms with their revival meetings and special holy day services. Associations and groups of all sorts do the same with rallies and collective events. But schools—apart from their athletic contests and similar activities—are peculiar institutions. There are no collective goals which the students share, and the institution is lifeless. There are only individual goals, individual scholastic achievements, made largely at the expense of the other students.

Athletic contests with other schools provide, for these otherwise lifeless institutions, the collective goals that they lack. The common goals shared by all make the institution part of its members and them part of it, rather than an organization outside them and superimposed upon them. The results are evident to any observer: The adolescent social system is centered at the school, not at the drugstore; the name by which the teen-agers identify themselves is that of the school ("Those are East High kids; I'm from Tech."); the teen-agers think of the school, the team, and the student body as one and use the pronoun "we" in referring to this entity ("We're playing Parkville Friday.").

Such effects are evident as well in the bases of alumni loyalty to many private preparatory schools and colleges. Athletic competition as a basis of loyalty is so dominant that the stereotypical alumnus is a man cheering wildly at a football game, waving a school banner in his hand. Colleges which dropped interscholastic athletics, like University of Chicago, or which never depended on them, like Johns Hopkins, thereby sacrificed the attention and support of many alumni.[12] Historians have noted that colleges in the United States, before the introduction of organized sports, were beset by student violence directed at both the college and other students. Sports seemed to transform the disorganized and explosive student body into a close-knit community with strong common goals.

Thus, the importance of athletic contests in both high schools and colleges lies, at least in part, in the way the contests solve a difficult problem for the institution—the problem of generating enthusiasm for and identification with the school and drawing the energies of adolescents into the school.

In the study of the ten high schools upon which much of this paper is based, all students were asked, "If school were not compulsory and it were completely up to you, would you stay in school until graduation, leave school before graduation, or are you undecided?" Very few students, only 3.6

percent, responded that they would leave, and only 9.3 percent were un-decided. It is hard to imagine that the great body of adolescents in our society which has been brought into high school in such a short period could be so positively oriented to school without some mechanism such as athletic contests for providing common goals.[13]

Lack of Common Community Goals

A force which strengthens the emphasis upon athletics in the high schools comes from outside the schools themselves. Except in the very largest cities, a high school is a community or neighborhood institution. Many communities have only a single high school, whose name is the name of the town. In those cities with several high schools, each school usually represents a community area within the city and often carries the name of that community.

Communities, like schools without interscholastic games, have few common goals. They fight no wars, seldom engage in community rallies, and are rarely faced with such crises as floods or tornadoes that can engender a communal spirit and make members feel close to one another by creating collective goals. One of the few mechanisms by means of which this can occur is that of games or contests between communities. Sometimes these games are between professional teams representing the communities.[14] More often, there are high school games, and these contests serve the purpose admirably. The community supports the team, and the team rewards the community when it wins. The team is a community enterprise, and its successes are shared by the community, its losses mourned in concert.

The results of this are evident in many ways. One striking evidence is teacher salaries. The school board characteristically pays more to athletic coaches than to other teachers and, occasionally, to keep a winning coach, may pay more than to the principal. When a new principal is to be found among the ranks of teachers, the pattern is common for the athletic coach to be promoted to the job.[15]

Another indicator is buildings. It is often easier to obtain funds for a new gymnasium—especially in "basketball territory"—than for other buildings. In Paris, Illinois, for example, where the high school team won the state basketball tournament a few years ago, the community voted funds for a large new gymnasium, while the high school remained without a library. In one of the ten schools included in the survey, the author found, returning in 1961, that a new gymnasium and a new reading room had been built. Funds for the gymnasium had been donated by a member of the community; the reading room had been added by means of school building funds.

SUBSTITUTES FOR ATHLETICS

It is indisputable that the interscholastic sports function to give the school and the community a collective identity. Few principals would seriously consider dispensing with these games. Yet, it is also indisputable that athletic contests create serious problems for schools. Perhaps the most serious problem is the change they engender in the institution itself. Their very importance to the life of the school transforms the school from an institution devoted to learning into an institution focused, at least partly, on athletics.

It is useful to wonder whether another mechanism might not give the school collective goals without effecting this transformation. Completely to replace athletic contests between schools with something else would possibly have ill effects. To reduce the dominance of athletics in high schools, however, clearly would be desirable. The most obvious course is to keep the game but to change the content in the direction of educational goals. Although it is true that athletics fits especially well with the interests and energies of adolescents, other games could fit equally well.

There is some experience with games and contests other than athletics, the most extensive being with debate. In a number of areas where debate leagues have flourished, these contests have generated some of the same community and school enthusiasm and involvement that is evident with athletic games. In a few states, interscholastic leagues promote competition in other fields than athletics: music, drama, mathematics. Although the effects of these contests have not been adequately evaluated, they do provide examples of what might be done.

There has very recently been another development which promises to make games truly educational in many areas. These are social and economic games which use a complex environment provided by electronic computers. The first to be developed were management games which involve teams of decision-makers representing competing firms. These games have been used by business and are coming to be used in graduate business schools. A political game, with teams representing political candidates in competition for votes, has been programed for a computer and is used in a college course at Johns Hopkins. At least one economic game has been developed—at Washington University in St. Louis—for teaching the course in principles of economics. Experience with these games shows that they generate a high degree of involvement and interest among players and spectators. It is possible that the most valuable use of machines in education will come to be their use for games, rather than programed learning.

These examples indicate that it is possible to change the content of games in an educational direction yet to maintain some of the values athletics provides for school. To do this, however, would require more than sporadic contests. To gain attention and involvement, leagues, schedules, and tournaments would be necessary. Through such means, it might be possible to transform schools back into the educational institutions they were intended to be. An innocent visitor to such an institution, upon examining the trophy case, listening to student conversation, and examining a yearbook, might well conclude that the institution was one devoted to learning.

NOTES

1. See James S. Coleman, *The Adolescent Society,* Glencoe: The Free Press, 1961, pp. 70-71, 88-90.

2. In certain cases, random variation due to the small number of students in the smallest school prevents separate conclusions about it.

3. Other areas of achievement were included in the questionnaire, for example, knowing about cars and being most attractive to the girls. The visibility for both of these was far below that for athletes or scholars.

4. The number of cases was over 800 in each grade, so the difference reported is significant beyond the .001 level.

5. This question was studied only in four of the five smallest schools; technical problems prevented it in the large schools, and the smallest school had no distinct crowds.

6. The ranks average to 3.3 rather than 3.5 as they should, because not every boy assigned all ranks.

7. Abraham J. Tannenbaum, "Adolescents' Attitudes Toward Academic Brilliance," unpublished Ph.D. dissertation, New York University, 1960.

8. For further discussion of this point, see Coleman, *op. cit.,* p. 303.

9. When a union becomes merely a business union, no longer actively fighting for collective worker benefits, it survives in name, but it can no longer depend upon its members for active support. This, in fact, is the fundamental problem of many unions at the present time.

10. This can be illustrated by the story, perhaps apocryphal, of the employer who paid every second worker on an assembly line a higher rate, so that every worker's neighbors received rates different from his own. A similar mechanism has been documented in department stores, where clerks are given marginal differentiations in title and pay to keep them divided. See Carl Dreyfuss, "Prestige Grading: A Mechanism of Control," in R. K. Merton and Others, *Reader in Bureaucracy,* Glencoe: The Free Press, 1952, pp. 258-264.

11. One of the important reasons that incentive pay, in the form of commissions, has always worked well for salesmen is that their active work in selling the company products to doubtful customers generates in them a

positive identification with the company. Another reason, of course, is that they are usually dispersed, not in contact with one another.

12. This is not to say that the absence of athletic emphasis in these institutions has principally bad consequences. Many colleges have, rather, compromised their original goals through the power and interest of their athletically involved alumni. But the withdrawal from interscholastic athletics without the substitution of other bases for institution-inspired pride and identification leaves the institution weaker and less likely to survive.

13. This suggests that high schools in Europe, which are coming to enroll larger and larger proportions of adolescents, will increase the emphasis upon athletic contests, unless they find another mechanism to accomplish the same end.

14. The sense of shock and disbelief in Brooklyn when the Dodgers moved to Los Angeles is a measure of Brooklynites' identification of the team with their community. On the other side, it has been said that Los Angeles ceased to be a collection of suburbs and became a city for the first time when "their" Dodgers won a pennant.

15. This pattern is being replaced by a pattern of promoting assistant principals or guidance counselors, who have administrative training in schools of education. There is no evidence that they make better principals than coaches do.

PARTICIPATION IN INTERSCHOLASTIC ATHLETICS AND COLLEGE EXPECTATIONS[1]

Richard A. Rehberg and Walter E. Schafer

Abstract

Data from 785 male seniors from six urban Pennsylvania high schools are used to evaluate the relationship between post-high-school educational expectations and participation or nonparticipation in interscholastic athletic activities. A zero-order γ of .28 indicates that expectations and participation

Richard A. Rehberg and Walter E. Schafer, "Participation in Interscholastic Athletics and College Expectations," *The American Journal of Sociology,* 73:732-740 (May 1968). Copyright © 1968 by the University of Chicago. Reprinted by permission.

are positively associated. The possibility that this association is spurious is tested by statistically controlling three potentially confounding variables: social status, academic performance, and parental educational encouragement. A third-order net partial association of .24 suggests that the association is not spurious, that the positive relationship between expectations and participation is a result of the socialization experiences of athletics rather than of differential selection into high school sports. Further analyses indicate, however, that the positive association between expectations and participation is not constant over relevant categories of the control variables but that the relationship is an interactive one; specifically, that the positive association between expectations and participation is strongest for those categories of respondents least positively disposed toward a college education and weakest for those categories of respondents most disposed toward a college education.

INTRODUCTION

James Coleman has remarked that a stranger in an American high school might well suppose, by looking and listening, that "more attention is paid to athletics by teenagers, both as athletes and as spectators, than to scholastic matters."[2] Certainly, the vast amounts of spectator and participant time and energy devoted to athletic teams attest to the importance of high school sports, both to the students themselves and to their communities.

Given this importance, the question can be raised as to what effect, if any, interscholastic athletics has upon the educational objectives of the high school. One of these objectives is the preparation of students for college. The question examined in this paper is whether participation in interscholastic sports exerts a positive or a negative influence on boys' educational expectations.

Since literature on the athletic participation-educational expectation relationship is virtually nonexistent, we cannot approach the construction of hypotheses directly but must do so circuitously, namely, by noting the findings of those studies which have investigated the relationships between athletic participation and those variables linked with educational expectations.

One set of such studies is concerned with athletic participation and academic performance, and academic performance and educational expectations. A positive association between participation and performance has been reported by several investigators, including Eidsmore, Schafer and Armer, and indirectly, Coleman.[3] In his study of participants and nonparticipants in varsity football teams from twenty-four of the top thirty Iowa high school teams for the year 1962, Eidsmore reported that "the total grade-point average of the 592 players in all subjects carried was 2.523, whereas the grade-point average of their nonparticipating classmates was 2.085."[4] And, while the tone of Coleman's *The Adolescent Society* suggests that athletic participation is detrimental to educational pursuits, the data of the study suggest otherwise. An inspection of the appropriate tables reveals that in six of the ten midwestern schools surveyed athletes, at least "top athletes," had higher scholastic averages than the male student body as a whole.[5]

Without controls for relevant antecedent variables, it is possible that the grade-point differences reported by Eidsmore and Coleman are spurious. Evidence that such differences are not spurious comes from Schafer and Armer's study of 585 boys from two Middle Western high schools. In that study, controls were invoked for five relevant variables: year in school, measured intelligence, father's occupation, previous grade-point average, and curriculum. While these controls reduced an initial zero-order difference of .52 points on a four-point scale (athletes = 2.35, non-athletes = 1.83) to a fifth-order difference of .11 points (athletes = 2.35, non-athletes = 2.24), the direction of the data still showed a positive association between academic performance and athletic participation.[6]

A positive association between academic performance and educational expectations has been reported in several studies. Berdie and Hood, for example, reported correlations between these two variables averaging about .36.[7]

A second set of relevant studies are those concerned with athletic participation and peer group membership and with peer group membership and educational expectations. One of Coleman's clearest findings was the relationship between athletic participation and membership in the leading crowd. He writes: "The relationship is striking. Going out for football is related to being a member of the various elites more than any other variable in this study."[8] As to the social background of such elites, he reports that "there is a tendency toward control by the higher-educated, more middle-class students in the school, [although] this tendency is sharply diminished when such students become a small minority in the system."[9] Concerning the educational expectation of these elites, Coleman states that "the elites more often intend to go to college than do the students as a whole."[10]

That educational expectations of peer groups are positively associated with the expectations of the adolescent himself has been reported by Alexander and Campbell, Krauss, Rehberg, and others.[11]

Given these two sets of findings relating athletic participation to educational expectations via academic performance and membership in college-oriented leading crowds, we suggest that the proportion of athletes expressing expectations to enroll in a four-year college is greater than the proportion of non-athletes expressing such expectations.

Returning to the Schafer-Armer study, it is important to note their finding that athletic participation made a greater positive contribution to the grade-point averages of those athletes "less-disposed" toward high academic achievement (that is, blue-collar, low intelligence, non-college preparatory students) than it did to the averages of those athletes "more-disposed" toward high academic achievement (that is, white-collar, high intelligence, college-preparatory students).[12]

This finding raises the possibility of a similar interaction with respect to the expectation-participation relationship. We have suggested two possible linkages between expectations and participation, and there is reason to believe that each may lead to a stronger association between expectations and participation among those less disposed toward college than among those more disposed. First, if there is a positive association between expectations and participation, and if that association is mediated by higher academic performance resulting from participation, and if, as Schafer and Armer found, the performance-participation relationship is especially strong among boys less disposed toward high performance, we should expect a similar interactive association between expectations and participation. Second, if the expectation-participation relationship is mediated by membership in the leading crowds, an interactive relationship is also probable for the following reason. A more disposed boy, namely, one from the middle classes, has a good chance to associate and identify with other college-oriented boys by virtue of his status background or his current interests or performance. A less disposed boy, namely, one from the working class, however, is less likely to associate and identify with middle-class, college-oriented friends. But, if a working-class or other less disposed boy participates in sports, and especially if he is successful in such participation, then he is more likely than comparable nonathletes to enter the leading crowd or at least to associate with college-oriented students, thereby becoming exposed to college-attending norms. Thus, the difference in exposure to college-oriented peers is likely to be greater between less disposed athletes and less disposed nonathletes than between more disposed athletes and more disposed nonathletes. We therefore suggest that the strength of the positive relationship between educational expectations and athletic participation is greater among boys less disposed toward college than among those more disposed toward college.

DESIGN AND DATA

In the spring of 1965, questionnaire data were gathered from 785 senior males from three public and three parochial schools in three middle-sized Pennsylvania cities. Information for the independent variable, participation or nonparticipation in interscholastic sports, was secured with an item which requested each respondent to list all of his extracurricular activities for his senior year. The dependent variable, educational expectations, was measured with a fixed-response item which requested each respondent to indicate how far he actually *expected* to go in school.[13] The relevant categories for this variable are: (1) expect to enroll in a four-year college, and (2) do not expect to enroll in a four-year college.

RESULTS

Expectations and Participation: A Zero-Order Analysis

Table 1 presents the data for the zero-order relationship between athletic participation and educational expectations. Consistent with the first hypothesis, 62 percent of the athletes expect to enroll in a four-year college compared with 45 percent of the nonathletes. The strength of the association is indicated by a γ value of .28.

This finding does not eliminate the possibility, however, that the relationship is spuriously produced by one or more variables associated with both the independent and the dependent variables. Consequently, the second step in the analysis requires a control for potentially confounding variables.

Expectations and Participation: N-Order Partial Analysis

Data were gathered for three variables which could theoretically produce a spurious relationship between expectations and participation. The first of those, social status, was measured with the Hollingshead Two Factor Index of Social Position.[14] A positive association between this variable and expectations has been reported consistently in a large number of studies.[15] The findings on the relationship of participation with status are not so consistent, however. Hollingshead implied no association when he wrote: "Athletics attracts boys from all classes in about the same proportion."[16] Schafer and Armer, however, reported a positive association between the two, with 33 percent of white-collar boys participating compared with 22 percent of blue-collar boys.[17] Temporally, we assume that this control variable precedes the independent variable in any kind of causal sequence.

Consistent with virtually all previous studies, expectations and status are positively associated (γ = .50). The association between status and participa-

Table 1   Percentage of Respondents Reporting Specified Educational Expectations, by Athletic Participation (Zero-Order Association)*

Athletic participation	Educational expectations (in years)				Total	N
	16 or more	14	12 or less	No response		
Yes	62	20	17	1	100	284
No	45	30	24	1	100	490
No response	73	9	9	9	100	11
Total	52	26	21	1	100	785

*$\gamma = .28$.

tion, minimal as it may be, is indicated by a γ of .04, suggesting that for this sample the relationship is more like that reported by Hollingshead than that reported by Schafer and Armer. Partialling out status from the expectation-participation relationship with Rosenberg's test factor standardization technique has no effect on the magnitude of association (for example, both zero- and first-order gammas are .28).[18]

The second potentially confounding variable is academic performance, measured with rank in graduating class. Again, positive associations have been reported in previous studies between performance and participation and between performance and expectations. Consistent with previous research, educational expectations and academic performance are highly related ($\gamma = .73$). However, performance and participation are virtually unrelated in this sample ($\gamma = -.02$).[19] As a result, the removal of the effects of academic performance leaves the magnitude of the relationship between expectations and participation virtually unchanged (first-order $\gamma = .29$).

The third control variable is parental educational encouragement, measured according to the respondent's indication of how frequently each parent encourages him to continue his education beyond high school.[20] Kahl, Bordua, Cohen, and Rehberg and Westby have reported moderately strong correlations between expectations and encouragement.[21] We are unaware, however, of any studies which have investigated the relationship between athletic participation and parental encouragement. As anticipated, expectations and encouragement are rather strongly related in this sample ($\gamma = .58$). Encouragement and participation are moderately associated, with a γ of .28. Removing the effects of this control variable reduces the association between expectations and participation from a zero-order coefficient of .28 to a first-order coefficient of .22.[22]

Parental educational encouragement, then, is the only one of the three control variables which is more than minimally associated with both the independent and the dependent variables. Therefore, it is not surprising that the strength of the original relationship between expectations and participation as displayed in Table 2 is only slightly reduced in a third-order partial analysis, that is, from a zero-order gamma of .28 to a third-order γ of .24. This finding thus renders tenable the proposition that athletic participation exerts an independent positive effect on the educational expectations of high school boys.

The Expectation-Participation Relationship—Invariant or Interactive?

It was suggested previously that the effect of athletic participation on educational expectations may be stronger for those boys who are less disposed toward college and weaker for those who are more disposed toward college. Since each of the three control variables—social status, academic performance, and parental encouragement—is an established correlate of educational expectations, each is used as a "dispositional" variable, with the high level indicating those boys who are more disposed toward college and the low level indicating those boys who are less disposed toward college.[23]

Table 3 indicates that the magnitude of the relationship between expectations and participation is indeed stronger in the less disposed levels of each of the three control variables. Thus, the γ value for the expectation-

Table 2   Percentage of Respondents Reporting Specified Educational Expectations by Athletic Participation, with Social Status, Parental Educational Encouragement, and Academic Performance Controlled (Third-Order Association, Standardized Table)*

Athletic participation	Educational expectations (in years)				Total	N
	16 or more	14	12 or less	No response		
Yes	61	19	18	1	99	284
No	46	30	23	1	100	490
No response	70	20	9	1	100	11
Total	52	26	21	1	100	785

*γ = .24.

participation relationship is .38 for those of low status and .27 for those of high status; .40 for those reporting low encouragement and .25 for those reporting high encouragement; and .51 for those of low academic performance and .26 for those of high performance.

An interaction does appear to exist, then, between expectations and participation with respect to the dispositional variables. That this interaction persists at the third-order level is evident from Table 4. As the appropriate γ's excerpted from Table 4 and displayed in Table 5 indicate, there is a continuing tendency for the magnitude of the association between the dependent and the independent variables to be stronger in the less disposed levels of each of the three control variables than in the more disposed levels.

Two additional aspects of these interactions merit comment. First, the positive association between expectations and participation all but vanishes in the three conditions where at least two of the three dispositional variables are high. To some extent, this may be attributable to a "ceiling" effect. Since the percentage of adolescents expressing college expectations in these categories is already very high (75-96 percent), participation in sports probably adds little or nothing to the determination of educational goals.

Second, the interaction effect appears to be cumulative. That is, the degree of positive association between expectations and participation is

Table 3 Interaction Effects of Educational Expectations and Athletic Participation: Percentage of Respondents Reporting Educational Expectations to Four or More Years of College (First-Order Relationships)

Disposition variable		Athletic participation				γ^*
		Yes		No		
Name	Level	%	N	%	N	
Social status	High[†]	78	90	67	144	.27
	Low	55	194	36	346	.38
Parental encouragement	High	68	208	56	298	.25
	Low	45	66	26	164	.40
Academic performance	High	85	116	78	205	.26
	Low	46	164	21	280	.51

* Because of the attrition of cell N's in tabular partialling, these γ values have been computed for a 2 x 2 table, i.e., athletic participation—non-participation crossed with four-year college expectations—non-four-year college expectations. The "no responses" have been omitted from the computations.

[†] This level refers to the middle status category, but for consistency of nomenclature the designation "high" is employed.

greater for boys less disposed on three than on two, on two than on one, and on one than on none of the three dispositional variables. Thus, the mean weighted γ value for the expectation-participation relationship is .64 for those adolescents less disposed on three of the control variables, .46 for those less disposed on two of the control variables, .15 for those less disposed on one of the control variables, and -.18 for those less disposed on none of the three control variables.

In brief, the data suggest that the effect of athletic participation on educational expectations is greater among boys less disposed toward college and weaker among boys more disposed toward college.

Table 4 Interaction Effects of Educational Expectations and Athletic Participation: Percentage of Respondents Reporting Educational Expectations to Four or More Years of College (Third-Order Relationships)

Disposition variables			Athletic participation				γ^*
			Yes		No		
Social status	Parental encouragement	Academic performance	%	N	%	N	
High	High	High	95	40	96	57	-.18
		Low	68	31	49	45	.37
	Low	High	75	8	75	16	.00
		Low	67	6	11	18	.88
Low	High	High	85	52	84	73	.04
		Low	45	82	25	121	.44
	Low	High	69	13	50	46	.38
		Low	26	38	7	82	.64

*Computed with 2 x 2 cross-classification, i.e., four years of college—less than four years of college, athletic participation—non-athletic participation, to enhance statistical reliability.

Table 5 Selected Expectation-Participation Gammas: High and Low Levels of Three Control Variables (Third-Order Partials)

HiSES, HiPEE,	HiAcPer.= -.18	LoSES,	HiPEE, HiAcPer.	=.04
	LoAcPer.= .37		LoPEE,	=.38
HiSES, LoPEE,	HiAcPer.= .00	LoSES,	HiPEE, LoAcPer.	=.44
	LoAcPer.= .88		LoPEE,	=.64

SUMMARY AND CONCLUSIONS

These data have shown that a greater proportion of athletes than nonathletes expect to enroll in a four-year college, even when the potentially confounding variables of status, academic performance, and parental encouragement are controlled. This relationship is especially marked among boys not otherwise disposed toward college, that is, those from working-class homes, those in the lower half of their graduating class, and those with low parental encouragement to go to college.

Since the sample of this study is nonrandom and all extraneous variables have not been controlled, conclusions about the generality and causal direction of the relationship must be drawn with caution. We suggest, however, that the positive relationship between educational expectations and athletic participation is probably not spurious, that is, not produced by "selection" variables but, rather, is "true," that is, reflects the socialization consequences of participation in interscholastic sports.

Earlier in the paper, two processes were identified that might mediate between expectations and participation and thereby account for the hypothesized socialization consequences. The first, higher academic performances resulting from participation in sports, does not appear to be operative in the data reported herein, since there is virtually no difference in class rank between athletes and nonathletes. This linkage cannot be entirely dismissed, however, since dropouts who are nonathletes and are disproportionately low achievers are excluded from the sample.

The second suggested mediating linkage is involvement in the leading crowd. Since we have no data on peer associations, it remains plausible that athletes more often expect to enroll in college because, compared with others, they more often enter the leading crowd and thereby become subjected to its achievement influences. This linkage also remains a plausible interpretation of the stronger relationship between expectations and participation among less disposed boys, since, as argued earlier, they stand to gain the most from exposure to the achievement influences of the leading crowd.

Further research should explore the two preceding interpretations as well as several others which might operate independently or simultaneously. First, it is possible that in sports the emphasis on hard work, achievement, self-improvement, present preparation for future competition, persistence, etc., carries over from the playing field, thereby increasing motivation and aspirations in other areas, including post-high-school career orientations. Second, social-psychological theory suggests that level of aspiration is partly determined by self-esteem and that self-esteem results partly from positive appraisals from significant others. It is likely, then, that the prestige and popularity enjoyed by athletes (especially successful athletes) enhance their self-esteem, which in turn results in higher career goals. Third, because of their increased visibility in both the school and the community, it is plausible that athletes receive a quantity and quality of career counseling and encouragement superior to that received by nonathletes.[24] Fourth, some athletes who otherwise would not go to college probably desire to go primarily to continue their athletic careers. Fifth, some athletes who otherwise would not enroll in college may do so essentially because of athletic scholarships.

One or more of these alternative mediating linkages may not only account for the overall relationship between expectations and participation but also for the interactive relationship alluded to earlier. For example, it might be that all athletes receive more college counseling, encouragement, and sponsorship but that this is especially true for athletes from working-class strata.

To the extent that future research substantiates the relationships reported here, interscholastic athletics will have been shown to be one channel for upward mobility, insofar as mobility is contingent on a college education. Perhaps this paper will stimulate further inquiry and that such studies will succeed in identifying and confirming those variables which serve to link educational expectations with participation in interscholastic sports.[25]

NOTES

1. The research reported herein was supported by an initial grant from the Cooperative Research Program of the Office of Education, U. S. Department of Health, Education and Welfare, and a subsequent grant from the Center for the Advanced Study of Educational Administration, the University of Oregon. This paper is a revised version of an earlier draft presented at the annual convention of the American Sociological Association, August, 1967, held in San Francisco.

2. James S. Coleman, "Athletics in High Schools," *Annals of the American Academy of Political and Social Sciences, CCCXXXVIII* (November, 1961), 33-43.

3. Russell M. Eidsmore, "High School Athletes Are Brighter," *School Activities* (November, 1963), pp. 75-77, Walter E. Schafer and J. Michael Armer, "On Scholarship and Interscholastic Athletics," *Trans-Action* (in press) (a longer version will also appear in Gregory P. Stone [ed.], *Sport, Play, and Leisure,* Indianapolis: Bobbs-Merrill, in press); and James S. Coleman, *The Adolescent Society,* Glencoe, Ill.: Free Press, 1961, especially pp. 252, 274, and 275.

4. Eidsmore, *op. cit.* (see n. 3 above), p. 76.

5. Coleman, *The Adolescent Society* (see n. 3 above).

6. Schafer and Armer, *op. cit.* (see n. 3 above). GPA's based on all major courses over the high school career.

7. Ralph F. Berdie and Albert B. Hood, *Trends in Post High School Plans Over an Eleven-Year Period,* Minneapolis: Student Counseling Bureau, University of Minnesota, 1963 (Cooperative Research Project No. 951), pp. 56-57.

8. Coleman, *The Adolescent Society* (see n. 3 above), p. 131.

9. *Ibid.,* p. 109.

10. *Ibid.,* p. 115.

11. C. Norman Alexander and Ernest Q. Campbell, "Peer Influences on Adolescent Educational Aspirations and Attainments," *American Sociological Review* (August, 1964), pp. 568-75; Irving Krauss, "Sources of Educational Aspirations among Working-Class Youth," *American Sociological Review* (December, 1964), pp. 867-79; and Richard A. Rehberg, *Adolescent Career Plans and the Impact of Chronic Economic Distress upon Adolescent Educational and Occupational Expectations and Aspirations,* University Park: Pennsylvania State University, 1965, Cooperative Research Project No. S-119.

12. Schafer and Armer, *op. cit.* (see n. 3 above).

13. Expectations constitute the *realistic* level of a career orientation as distinguished from aspirations which constitute the *idealistic* level. For a further discussion of this conceptual distinction as well as a consideration of specific theoretical and empirical implications, see Richard A. Rehberg; "Adolescent Career Aspirations and Expectation: An Evaluation of Two Contrary Stratification Hypotheses," *Pacific Sociological Review* (Fall, 1967).

14. August B. Hollingshead, "The Two Factor Index of Social Position," New Haven, Conn.: Yale University, 1957, mimeographed.

15. The number of such studies is too long to enumerate. For a rather comprehensive bibliography of these studies, see William Kuvleksy and George W. Ohlendorf, *A Bibliography of Literature on Educational Orientations of Youth,* College Station: Texas A. and M. University, 1965.

16. August B. Hollingshead, *Elmtown's Youth,* New York: John Wiley & Sons, 1949, p. 194.

17. Schafer and Armer, *op. cit.* (see n. 3 above).

18. Leo A. Goodman and William H. Kruskal, "Measures of Association for Cross Classifications," *Journal of the American Statistical Association* (September, 1954), pp. 732-64; Morris Rosenberg, "Test Factor Standardization as a Method of Test Interpretation," *Social Forces* (October, 1962), pp. 53-61.

19. One possible explanation for the discrepancy between our finding and that reported by Schafer and Armer is that their sample included adolescents who later dropped out of school. Dropouts, of course, tend to

receive lower grades and participate less in interscholastic sports. The sample used for this study includes only students who were still enrolled during their senior year. Had this sample consisted of sophomores, as did Schafer and Armer's sample, we too probably would have found a positive association between academic performance and athletic participation.

20. The question read: "Which ONE of the following statements is most true about continuing your education beyond high school?
   "1. My father [mother] *never* urges me to continue my education.
   "2. My father [mother] *sometimes* urges me to continue my education.
   "3. My father [mother] *often* urges me to continue my education.
   "4. My father [mother] *constantly* urges me to continue my education."
   The question was asked separately for each parent. Ordinal scores of 1-4 were assigned to the response for each parent (1 = never and 4 = constantly), then added, and from the total the integer of one was subtracted, yielding a score range of 1-7. Low encouragement consists of scores of 1-4; high encouragement consists of scores of 5-7.

21. Joseph A. Kahl, "Educational and Occupational Aspirations of 'Common-Man' Boys," *Harvard Educational Review* (Summer, 1953), pp. 186-203; David T. Bordua, "Educational Aspirations and Parental Stress on College," *Social Forces* (March, 1960), pp. 262-69; Elizabeth G. Cohen, "Parental Factors in Educational Mobility," *Sociology of Education* (Fall, 1965), pp. 404-25; Richard A. Rehberg and David L. Westby, "Parental Educational Encouragement, Occupation, Education, and Family Size: Artifactual or Independent Determinants of Adolescent Educational Expectations," *Social Forces* (March, 1967), pp. 362-74.

22. The positive association between parental educational encouragement and athletic participation is analogous to the finding reported previously by the senior author of this paper that parental educational encouragement correlates positively not only with adolescent educational orientations but with occupational orientations as well. This suggests that educational encouragement represents a form of achievement socialization somewhat more diffuse than that pertinent to educational orientation only (see Rehberg and Westby, *op. cit.* [see n. 21 above]).

23. For consistency of nomenclature, middle status respondents are referred to as "high" status respondents.

24. For a discussion relevant to the increased "visibility" of athletes, see Coleman, *The Adolescent Society* (see n. 3 above).

25. The authors currently are engaged in a four-year longitudinal panel project involving 3,200 adolescents. One of the major objectives of that research is the investigation of the relationship between adolescent ambition and participation in interscholastic athletics.

CONSEQUENCES OF PARTICIPATION IN INTERSCHOLASTIC SPORTS: A REVIEW AND PROSPECTUS

John C. Phillips and Walter E. Schafer

Very few sociological studies on the role of athletics in high schools appear to have been done prior to 1960. Since that time, a considerable amount of work has appeared, with generally consistent findings on certain aspects of high school athletics. The research the authors are presently doing involved an effort to explain one of those consistent findings—the fact that athletes tend to exceed comparable nonathletes in their achievement of educational goals. In this paper, we will review the evidence on the academic achievement of high school athletes, discuss our efforts to employ the concept of subculture to explain the advantage that athletes enjoy and, finally, speculate on possible broader applications of the kind of work we have been doing.

ATHLETES AND ACADEMIC ACHIEVEMENT

As information about high school athletes has grown more and more plentiful, a number of popular myths about the effects of athletic participation have been supplanted. Perhaps the best example of factual information replacing myth is the relationship between athletic participation and high school scholastic achievement. Athletics has been considered an anti-intellectual influence by some authors (Henry, 1963; Coleman, 1960, 1961, 1966), but there is compelling evidence that athletes get slightly better grades than do comparable nonathletes. Schafer and Armer (1968) found that high school athletes got slightly better grades than nonathletes in their matched sample. Athletes from blue-collar homes and boys who were not in a college-preparatory program got even better grades than their nonathlete counterparts. Bend (1968) found substantially the same pattern. Athletes got slightly better grades and the advantage of athletes was most pronounced among "low-endowment" (low-IQ, low-SES) boys.

"Consequences of Participation in Interscholastic Sports: A Review and Prospectus," by John C. Phillips and Walter E. Schafer, is reprinted from *Pacific Sociological Review*, Volume 14, No. 3 (July 1971), pp. 328-338 by permission of the Publisher, Sage Publications, Inc.

The fact that "low-endowment" athletes showed the most pronounced difference in achievement could be important to our interest in subculture as an explanation of these differences. Could it be that athletes are put under special pressure to perform well in the classroom? Perhaps the low-endowment athletes do better than low-endowment nonathletes because they experience pro-educational influences similar to those experienced by middle-class boys.

There is strong evidence to indicate that athletes aspire to and succeed in attending college more than do nonathletes. Bend found that 81.8% of his sample of superior athletes compared to 56.1% of the nonathletes aspired to at least some college education. The figures for low-endowment superior athletes and nonathletes was 39.8% and 13.3% respectively. Over 71% of the superior athletes actually attended college, while 50.0% of the nonathletes attended. Figures for low-endowment athletes and nonathletes were 14.8% and 6.9%. Bend's large sample, longitudinal design, and the fact that the relationship between athletic participation and educational achievement increased as degree of athletic involvement increased inspire confidence in his results. Rehberg and Schafer (1968) and Schafer and Rehberg (1970a, 1970b) found similar patterns in aspirations and expectations for college attendance.

Again, we see blue-collar athletes far exceeding comparable nonathletes in aspirations for college attendance and in the achievement of college attendance. We contend that this difference can be attributed, at least in part, to their experiences as athletes.

Schafer (1969) provides data that indicate that athletes are less likely to be deviant than comparable nonathletes. Again, blue-collar athletes were markedly less likely to be delinquent than blue-collar nonathletes, while the relationship is virtually eliminated among white-collar boys. Schafer argues that, unless some selection factor is working, there must be some influences in athletics that deter boys from engaging in delinquent behavior. We will argue that if potentially delinquent boys were being selected out of athletic participation, then white-collar as well as blue-collar delinquents would be selected. Thus, the negative relationship between athletic participation and delinquency would hold for boys from all socioeconomic backgrounds, not just for lower blue-collar boys.

With the association between athletic participation and educational success especially marked among blue-collar boys, one has firm grounds for expecting more upward social mobility among athletes than among comparable nonathletes. Schafer and Stehr (1968) suggest that, since blue-collar and white-collar athletes are more likely than are nonathletes to associate with the white-collar, college-bound "leading crowd" in high schools (Coleman, 1961:

35-50, 145-151), their mobility chances are enhanced. In a later paper, Schafer and Rehberg (1970a) found that athletes, compared with non-athletes, are more likely to report having been encouraged by teachers and counselors to go on to college. This relationship grows stronger as aspirations for going on to college diminish. Thus it appears that athletes not only attain higher educational achievement, but those who are not disposed toward furthering their education receive special encouragement or sponsorship to do so.

Phillips' (1965) study of college athletes has suggested another possible source of upward mobility among athletes. Phillips found that athletes tended to interact with one another much more than did nonathletes. He argued that this high interaction reduced what Hodges (1964) has termed "the psychic cost of mobility." By having a ready circle of middle-class friends, a blue-collar athlete might better develop the manners, mannerisms, attitudes, and social contacts that facilitate upward mobility. This tendency for athletes to choose other athletes as friends has also been found by Schafer and Rehberg (1970b).

Schafer and Rehberg (1970b:12) also found that athletes "tend to have close friends who are more positive in educational attitudes, aspirations, and behavior than the close friends of non-athletes." While the nature of their data prohibits firm conclusions, they do suggest the possibility that the differences between athletes and nonathletes can, at least in part, be attributed to their greater exposure to pro-educational peer influences.

We may summarize the evidence on differences between high school athletes and nonathletes as follows:

1.   Athletes generally receive slightly better grades and are more likely to aspire to and attain more education than comparable nonathletes. This is especially marked among athletes from blue-collar homes.

2.   There is some evidence to indicate that athletes are less likely than nonathletes to become delinquent. We do not know whether this relationship is due to selection factors or due to some deterrent effect of athletic participation.

3.   Athletes from blue-collar backgrounds are more likely to be upwardly mobile than nonathletes. This can be explained to a great extent by their greater educational attainment, but other factors such as sponsorship and association may also bear on this mobility.

What are the sources of these differences? Schafer and Armer (1968) suggest several possible explanations. First, athletes may receive special assistance in academic matters from teachers, peers, or coaches. Athletes might simply be graded more leniently. Second, there may be certain organizational requirements that might motivate athletes to perform better than non-athletes. Most high schools require a minimum grade-point average for participation. Athletes may work not only to achieve good enough grades for participation, but to qualify for entry into a college to continue their athletic careers. Third, athletes may be favored by "spillover" of certain qualities they have developed through sport. Higher peer status due to the generalization of their athletic status to other areas of social participation may enhance the athletes' self-esteem and, hence, their motivation to succeed in school work. Values of hard work, excellence, and persistence may be developed in sports activities and applied to academic and other activities. Practice and training regimens may influence athletes to use their study time more efficiently. Fourth, it is possible that conforming, ambitious, able boys tend to go out for sports more than do boys who are less "in tune" with the expectations of the school authorities. That is, athletics selects good students and tends to reject bad students (Schafer, 1969).

One recent article has examined the several possible sources of the educational advantages of athletes. Jerome and Phillips (1971) note the evidence of greater attainment of educational goals by athletes in American high schools. They point out the fact that sports programs in American and Canadian high schools are very similar, but that in Canada athletic participation does not receive the same status and esteem it does in American high schools. The authors argue that if good students, more than poor students, tend to go out for and be selected for athletic teams, the educational advantages of American athletes should exist among Canadian athletes as well. Likewise, if values and habits developed in athletics are applied to one's studies, the Canadian athletes should enjoy the same educational advantages that the American athletes enjoy.

Since the Canadian athletes do not appear to be better than their nonparticipating classmates in the achievement of educational objectives, Jerome and Phillips argue that the source of the American athletes' greater achievement lies not in "spillover" or selection but in one or more of the other explanations suggested by Schafer and Armer. These explanations (see above) center on *special experiences that are encountered by athletes* but not by nonathletes.

THE ATHLETIC SUBCULTURE

The evidence that athletes in American high schools appear to have certain special experiences, coupled with evidence of differences of behavior between athletes and nonathletes, has led us to the concept of subculture as a possible explanation of the processes intervening between athletic participation and various behavioral outcomes.

We should note here that two of the crucial conditions for the emergence of a subculture exist among athletes—special experiences and high rates of interaction (Phillips and Schafer, 1970). According to Cohen (1955) and Cohen and Short (1958), persons in like circumstances sharing like experiences should tend to develop values, norms, and beliefs (i.e., a subculture) favorable to those in the special circumstances. Our findings indicate that athletes, who experience special rewards in school, tend to develop a pro-school subculture (Phillips and Schafer, 1970).

In two recent papers, Phillips and Schafer (1971, 1970) have tried to develop a conceptual and methodological approach to the study of sub-cultures. We follow the thinking of Vander Zanden (1970) in conceiving of subculture as values, beliefs, symbols, and norms that are shared among some people but not by the general population. Thus, a subculture exists to the extent that a number of people differ in the norms, values, beliefs, and symbols that they share.

Wolfgang and Ferracuti (1967) point out the problems in measuring the elements of subcultures and point to the salient importance of measuring norms of conduct if we are to study subcultures at all. We contend that, since culture tends "to form a consistent and integrated whole" (Vander Zanden, 1970:35), we can gain an understanding of all the elements of a subculture by studying any single element—in this case, norms. The return potential model for the measurement of norms (Jackson, 1966, 1960) appears to provide a solution to many of the problems that Wolfgang and Ferracuti cite as impediments to the study of subcultures.

Our recent investigations have been concerned with determining the extent to which there exists a distinguishable subculture shared by inter-scholastic athletes, and the extent to which such a subculture might account for the differences between athletes and nonathletes reported earlier in this paper.

In a preliminary study of one high school, we found that athletes interact with other athletes much more than do nonathletes, and, while athletes appear to expect the same kinds of conduct from their friends, the norms shared by the athletes are much more intense and more likely to regulate behavior. That is, athletes appear to be under greater pressure to conform to conventional school standards than are nonathletes (Phillips and Schafer, 1970). This greater pressure to conform to conventional standards of behavior is reflected from time to time in newspaper stories depicting often sharp controversies regarding the misbehavior of athletes (albeit not high school athletes). Few college students need fear reprisals for wearing beards or mustaches, but one can read about athletes being removed from their team rosters for even so minor a transgression.

We are also interested in the role of the coach as a link between the official school culture and the athletic subculture, which, as we have discussed above, reflects the official school culture. We believe that coaches affect not only the norms shared among athletes but the individual athletes themselves. To the extent that we find the official school norms, values, and beliefs being transmitted through the coach to the athletes, and the norms, values and beliefs they share, we will be able to explain the tendency of athletes to conform to the official school goals of academic achievement and conventional conduct.

While we have emphasized the positive outcomes of interscholastic athletics, we are interested in some of the criticisms of highly competitive interscholastic athletics as well. Could it be that the more conventional athletes tend toward intergroup and interpersonal intolerance, uncritical acceptance of existing systems, and a disinterest in public affairs? Since they are rewarded by the "system," athletes may well resist change and reform. We know of one recent incident where high school athletes joined together to suppress an effort by certain other students to challenge a number of school rules.

FURTHER RESEARCH

Until now, we have discussed only the possible existence of subcultural influences on American high school athletes and how those influences might produce the differences we have observed between athletes and nonathletes. We have paid little attention to collegiate athletes, club athletes, and professional athletes. Neither have we sought to investigate the possible impact of the game itself on the participant. These questions promise to be interesting and important if the existing literature is any indication. Weinberg and Arond (1952), Charnofsky (1968), and Scott (1968) respectively provide us with insights on the occupational culture of boxers, baseball players, and jockeys. They discuss the role of superstitions, norms regarding physical courage, beliefs about how one might best win, the athletes' image of themselves, and other matters that suggest the presence of an occupational subculture and, perhaps, certain shared norms, values, beliefs, and symbols that stem from the participants' common interest in the game, but extend to matters external to sports.

Another focus on subcultures in sport might involve participants' commitment to the official value system of a given sports organization or movement. Hans Lenk (1964) has investigated athletes' commitments to the traditional and official aims and values of the Olympic games. He has also examined the implications of the postwar tendency of German athletes to be committed to their clubs only in the realm of sport, not in other aspects of their lives (Lenk, 1966). We would expect the degree of athletes' commitment to sports organizations to strongly influence the degree to which the official organizational norms regulate the behavior of club athletes.

It is possible that a national sports movement might enhance certain government efforts toward social change. Wohl (1969a, 1969b) discusses how sports clubs have helped to reduce certain traditional hostilities based on social and geographical origins, as well as replacing certain backward peasant traditions with more open, modern modes of behavior. We would hope to someday examine the condition of peasant and worker sports club participants and nonparticipants to determine if patterns exist that are similar to those we have observed in American high school athletes.

A final aspect of sports that might play a role in the generation of subcultural influences is the meaning of the game to the participants. Webb (1969) discusses the way in which attitudes toward sport are "professionalized." While young children tend to just play at their games, older children appear to place an increasing emphasis on skill and winning. Heinila (1969) employs a similar notion of playing for the sake of a "good match" and playing to win. Whether a team emphasizes the game (good match) or the game outcome (winning) may determine the nature of the interpersonal and organizational relationships among members of the team. These relationships may, in turn, influence the development of subculture among the participants.

In summary, we have convincing evidence that American interscholastic athletes achieve educational goals more than do comparable nonathletes. We have some preliminary evidence that indicates that the athletes share norms that exert a strong pro-school influence on them, and that these norms appear to fit our concept of subculture. We are still investigating the sources and content of this apparent athletic subculture. In the future, we hope to investigate whether subcultures develop among athletes in certain sports, or among members of sports clubs or organizations. We also hope to employ the concepts of professionalization of and commitment to sports and determine their impact, if any, on the development of subcultures in sport. If athletes collectively or individually continue to exert the influence they have in the recent past, the nature of any athletic subculture could take on an increasing importance that extends beyond the world of sport.

REFERENCES

Bend, Emil, *The Impact of Athletic Participation on Academic and Career Aspiration and Achievement*, New Brunswick, N.J.: National Football Foundation and Hall of Fame, 1968.

Charnofsky, Harold, "The major league professional baseball player: self-conception versus the popular image," *International Rev. of Sport Sociology*, 3:39-55, 1968.

Cohen, Albert K., *Delinquent Boys: The Culture of the Gang*, Glencoe, Ill.: Free Press, 1955.

_____ , and James F. Short, Jr., "Research in delinquent subcultures," *J. of Social Issues*, 14:20-37, 1958.

Coleman, James S., "Adolescent subculture and academic achievement," *Amer. J. of Sociology*, 65 (January): 337-347, 1960.

_____ , *The Adolescent Society*, New York: Free Press, 1961.

_____ , "Peer cultures and education in modern society," pp. 266-269 in T. M. Newcomb and E. K. Wilson (eds.), *College Peer Groups: Problems and Prospects for Research*, Chicago: Aldine, 1966.

Heinila, Kalevi, "Football at the crossroads," *International Rev. of Sport Sociology*, 4:5-30, 1969.

Henry, Jules, *Culture Against Man*, New York: John Wiley, 1963.

Hodges, Harold M., Jr., *Social Stratification: Class in America*, Cambridge: Schenkman, 1964.

Jackson, Jay, "Structural characteristics of norms," pp. 136-163 in *The Dynamics of Instructional Groups*, Yearbook of the National Society for the Study of Education, Chicago: Univ. of Chicago Press, 1960.

_____ , "A conceptual and measurement model for norms and roles," *Pacific Soc. Rev.*, 9 (Spring): 63-72, 1966.

Jerome, Wendy C., and John C. Phillips, "The relationship between academic achievement and interscholastic participation: a comparison of Canadian and American high schools," *C.A.H.P.E.R.J.*, 37 (January/February): 18-21, 1971.

Lenk, Hans, *Werte, Ziele, Wirklichkeit der Modernen Olympischen Spiele (Values, Aims, Reality of the Modern Olympic Games)*, Scharndorf bei Stuttgart: Karl Hoffmann, 1964.

_____ , "Total or partial engagement? Changes regarding personal ties with the sports club," *International Rev. of Sport Sociology*, 1:85-108, 1966.

Phillips, John C., "Motivation for participation in athletics: an exploratory study," M.A. thesis, San Jose State College, 1965.

_____ , and Walter E. Schafer, "The athletic subculture: a preliminary study," presented at the annual meetings of the American Sociological Association, Washington, D.C., 1970.

_____ , "Subcultures in sport: a conceptual and methodological model," in Publication 2 of the Research Institute of the Swiss Federal School of Gymnastics and Sport, Basel: Birkhauser, 1971.

Rehberg, Richard A., and Walter E. Schafer, "Participation in interscholastic athletics and college expectations," *Amer. J. of Sociology,* 73 (May): 732-740, 1968.

Schafer, Walter E., "Participation in interscholastic athletics and delinquency: a preliminary study," *Social Problems,* 17 (Summer): 40-47, 1969.

_____ , and J. Michael Armer, "Athletes are not inferior students," *Trans-Action* (November): 21-26, 61-62, 1968.

Schafer, Walter E., and Richard A. Rehberg, "Athletic participation, college aspirations, and college encouragement," University of Oregon (unpublished), 1970a.

_____ , "Athletic participation, peer influences, and educational aspirations: toward a theory of the athletic subculture," University of Oregon (unpublished), 1970b.

Schafer, Walter E., and Nico Stehr, "Participation in competitive athletics and social mobility, some intervening social processes," presented at the meetings of the International Committee on Sociology of Sport, Vienna, Austria, 1968.

Scott, Marvin B., *The Racing Game,* Chicago: Aldine, 1968.

Vander Zanden, James W., *Sociology: A Systematic Analysis,* New York: Ronald Press, 1970.

Webb, Harry, "Professionalization of attitudes toward play among adolescents," pp. 161-178 in Gerald S. Kenyon (ed.), *Aspects of Contemporary Sport Sociology,* Chicago: Athletic Institute, 1969.

Weinberg, S. Kirson, and Henry Arond, "The occupational culture of the boxer," *Amer. J. of Sociology,* 57 (March): 460-469, 1952.

Wohl, Andrzej, "Integrational functions of sport," in Publication 2 of the Research Institute of the Swiss Federal School of Gymnastics and Sport, Basel: Birkhauser, 1969a.

_____ , "Engagement in sports activity on the part of the workers of large industrial establishment in peoples Poland," *International Rev. of Sport Sociology,* r:83-127.

Wolfgang, Marvin E., and Franco Ferracuti, *The Subculture of Violence,* London: Tavistock, 1967.

HIGH SCHOOL ATHLETES AND THEIR COACHES: EDUCATIONAL PLANS AND ADVICE

Eldon E. Snyder

Data gathered from high school basketball coaches and players indicate that the coach is a significant other in advising players about their future educational and occupational plans. Moderate positive correlations exist between advice given by the coach about whether and where to attend college and the players' educational plans after high school. Additionally, many players perceive their coach as influential to them, but this influence is primarily a function of the coach's advice.

A number of investigators have studied the influence of socialization agents upon adolescents. For example, considerable evidence has accumulated to indicate a congruency between parental and children's attitudes, particularly in regard to educational and occupational aspirations. Evidence for parental and familial influences has been presented in the research of Aberle and Naegele (1952); Kahl (1953); Bordua (1960); Straus (1962); Ellis and Lane (1963); Rehberg and Westby (1967); Sewell and Shah (1968); Campbell (1969); and Kandel and Lesser (1969). The importance of the peer group as a socializing agency among adolescents has been emphasized by Coleman (1961) in his study of adolescent behavior and value orientations in ten midwestern high schools; additional studies of peer influence include Haller and Butterworth (1960); Alexander and Campbell (1964); Krauss (1964); and Duncan, et al. (1968). Other socializing agents frequently cited include teachers (Warren, 1968), ministers, family friends, and other adults (Ellis and Lane, 1963; Herriott, 1963; Clausen, 1968; Campbell, 1969; Sewell, et al., 1969; Sewell, et al., 1970; for similar research data on reference groups of Middle Eastern students see Tomeh, 1968, 1970).

Noticeably absent in the above studies, however, are empirical data related to athletic coaches as socialization agents. The objective of this paper is to cite socializing agents influential in the high school athlete's educational

Eldon E. Snyder, "High School Athletes and Their Coaches: Educational Plans and Advice," *Sociology of Education,* 45:313-325 (Summer 1972). Reprinted by permission of the American Sociological Association.

and occupational plans, with an emphasis on the importance of the coach in the constellation of reference persons, and also to analyze the player's decision on college attendance as related to: (1) the coach giving advice about whether or not to attend college, (2) the coach giving advice about where to attend college, and (3) the player's perception of his coach's influence on him.

Although empirical data have been lacking, several investigators have noted the theoretical relevance of the coaching role in socialization. Strauss (1959:110-118) has dealt with the function of the coach in the socialization process; more recently, Kenyon (1968) has suggested that physical education and sports provide the necessary conditions for socialization with the existence of agents and models. Elsewhere, Kenyon (1969) has discussed the degrees and types of involvement by participants in a sport and the variations of reference groups that are likely to be important to them. Page (1969:200) has cited the function of coaches as reference persons and educational advisors: "When the kid who at fifteen or sixteen has tremendous promise, coaches are apt to think in career terms: 'you go to Michigan State, we have connections with such and such pro team' [sic]. In this way, coaches become career specialists."

The influence of the coach in the socialization process for athletes is particularly important when several dimensions of the coach-player relationship are analyzed. Since participation in high school athletics is a highly-prized prestige-granting activity, the coach has considerable control—through his use of power and authority—in selecting players and granting rewards and punishments. The players, in turn, voluntarily submit to the coach's control and influence. Brim (1966:27) has noted that "this procedure of selection helps to assure that those who enter the organization [or activity] will not present difficult problems for the socialization program." Additional characteristics of the coach-player relationship that are likely to result in effective socialization include the high degree of participant involvement by players and coaches and the probability that the relationship will be expressive and affective (Snyder, 1970).

The importance of the coach as a reference person is supported by Kemper's (1968) approach to reference groups. He has suggested that there are three types of reference groups: the normative which defines the role the individual is to assume; the role model with whom the actor can compare his performance; and the audience to whom the actor attributes certain values that serve as his behavioral guides. For many athletes, the high school coach embodies all three types of reference groups; he provides normative expectations, a role model, and he promotes value orientations the player uses as guides for his behavior.[1] Kemper (1968:40-41) has noted that the coincidence of these three types of reference groups potentiates the most effective type of socialization.

METHODOLOGY

In the spring of 1969, with the cooperation of the Ohio Association for Health, Physical Education, and Recreation, a sample of 270 Ohio high schools participating in basketball was selected. This sample consisted of one-third of the high schools affiliated with the above association and was a representative cross-section of the schools that participated in the sport. A questionnaire was sent to the basketball coach and to two varsity team members for each of the 270 schools. Since the focus of the study was on the coach-player relationship, the age of the players was a potential extraneous source of variation, particularly with dependent variables such as educational or occupational plans. While variations in the players' ages and the length of time the coach-player relationship had existed may have been valuable data, the present study was limited to varsity players whose reported ages indicated they were likely to be juniors or seniors (96 percent of the players who responded to the sample were juniors or seniors). The response rate to the questionnaires was 64.5 percent for the coaches, 50 percent for the players.[2]

FINDINGS

Influential Socializing Agents

Since educational and occupational plans are likely to be associated with parental socioeconomic status, this variable was controlled.[3] Table 1 presents the players' responses to the question: "Which of the following persons has been the most important influence on your thinking about your future education and/or occupation?"

In all socioeconomic classifications of players, the coach ranked third in importance. This ranking indicated that for students in the athletic subculture, the coach was a significant other. However, players of lower socioeconomic status were more likely than players of higher status categories to indicate the coach was the most important person in their educational/occupational plans. Additional analysis of the data based on mother's educational background likewise showed that the coach ranked third in importance across all educational status categories, though the percentage of players who ranked the coach first was less in the case of players from higher educational backgrounds. The data in Table 1 also suggest that the nonfamilial reference

Table 1 Reference Persons Cited by Players as Most Important Influence in Their Thinking about Educational and/or Occupational Plans, by Socioeconomic Status of Father (Percentages)

Persons cited as most important	Education of Father			Occupation of Father		
	Less than high school N=80	High school N=145	Some college or more N=64	Semi-skilled, unskilled N=58	Clerical, sales skilled, farm N=153	Professional, executive, proprietor N=68
Mother	33	31	23	22	35	19
Father	21	36	53	26	37	44
Coach	19	9	13	19	12	10
Classroom teacher	10	6	3	9	7	3
Girlfriend	9	6	0	7	5	3
Brother	3	5	3	7	0	9
Minister or priest	3	3	0	3	0	4
Sister	1	1	0	2	1	0
Other relative	1	3	3	3	1	6
Boyfriend	1	0	2	2	0	1

persons, including teachers and coaches, may be more important for players of lower than of upper socioeconomic status backgrounds.

The coaches' responses to a parallel question regarding reference persons who were important in their educational and/or occupational plans are presented in Table 2. For coaches who came from lower socioeconomic status backgrounds, their own coach was their most prominent reference person. Anticipatory socialization may explain this response; the coach served as a role model. As was true of the players, the importance of the coach as an educational/occupational influence declined for the coaches from higher socioeconomic status backgrounds. When the reference persons of coaches were analyzed by mother's educational background, the coach still ranked first (39 percent) in the "Less than High School" category but declined to third (9 percent) in the "Some College or More" group.

In the sample of coaches, as with the players, the percentage of non-familial reference persons was greater for the respondents of lower rather than higher socioeconomic status backgrounds. These data may be partially explained by the likelihood that middle and upper status players had fathers present with educational and occupational achievements that the players admired and sought to emulate, while the lower status respondents turned to other reference persons, including their coach, for guidance.[4]

The importance of the coach to the lower socioeconomic status player suggests that the coach represents a reference person who promotes social mobility. This finding provides supportive data for several recent studies (Rehberg and Schafer, 1968; Schafer and Armer, 1968; Rehberg, 1969; Snyder, 1969) that have shown that participation in high school athletics and activities is associated with educational aspirations and achievement. However, the coach's influence is only one of several possible explanations of the social mobility function of athletics (Rehberg, 1969).

Player's Decision Concerning College Attendance, Coach's Advice About College Attendance, and the Player's Perception of His Coach's Influence

A player's college plans may be associated with (1) the coach giving advice about whether or not to attend college, (2) the coach giving advice about where to attend college, and (3) the player's perception of his coach's influence.[5]

The gamma matrix of Table 3 summarizes the intercorrelations between educational plans, the advice given by coaches about whether and where to attend college, the player's perception of his coach's influence, as well as the additional variables of father's education, occupation, and the player's

Table 2   Reference Persons Cited By Coaches as Most Important Influence in Their Thinking about Educational and/or Occupational Plans, by Socioeconomic Status of Father (Percentages)

Persons cited as most important	Education of Father			Occupation of Father		
	Less than high school N=83	High school N=52	Some college or more N=38	Semi-skilled, unskilled N=46	Clerical, sales skilled, farm N=75	Professional, executive, proprietor N=50
Coach	36	31	13	30	37	18
Mother	27	23	26	26	24	28
Father	19	29	58	20	28	46
Brother	5	2	0	0	4	4
Classroom teacher	4	4	0	6	1	2
Sister	2	0	0	2	1	0
Other relative	2	4	0	2	1	2
Girlfriend	2	2	3	9	0	0
Boyfriend	2	4	0	4	1	0
Minister or priest	0	2	0	0	1	0

Table 3 Gamma Correlation Matrix of Variables Used in the Analysis of the Player's Decision on College Attendance, Coach's Advice on Whether and Where to Attend College, and Player's Perception of his Coach's Influence

	(2)	(3)	(4)	(5)	(6)	(7)
1. Father's education	.720	.239	.032	.033	-.163	.328
2. Father's occupation	. . . .	.199	.058	.065	-.070	.311
3. Reported grades		. . . .	.167	.080	.058	.579
4. Coach gave advice: whether to attend college			. . . .	.654	.387	.315
5. Coach gave advice: where to attend college				. . . .	.306	.237
6. Player's perception of coach's influence					. . . .	.150
7. Player's decision on college attendance						. . . .

reported grades.[6] The last three variables were analyzed since their association with educational plans for college provided a potential extraneous influence in examining the relationships between the independent variables and educational plans.

Father's education and occupation were positively associated with a player's plans to attend college; however, these variables showed little or no association either with the coach's advice about whether and where to attend college or the player's perception of his coach's influence. Thus, the player's socioeconomic status did not seem to be influencing the relationships between the coach's educational advice or the player's perception of his coach's influence and the player's college plans. Reported grades did, however, show a slight positive relationship with the coach giving advice about whether to attend college (.17). Rosenberg's (1962) test factor standardization technique was used to determine whether the relationship between this advice and educational plans was independent of reported grades. With reported grades standardized, the relationship was reduced from .31 to .27, still a significant relationship.

The coach's advice about whether to attend college and his advice about where to attend college were positively associated with the player's decision concerning college attendance; advice about whether to attend college showed approximately the same relationship to educational plans as did the player's socioeconomic background. The two advice variables also were associated (.39 and .31) with the player's perception of his coach's influence; however, the latter variable showed a relationship of only .15 with plans to

Table 4 Player's Decision on College Attendance, Coach's Advice on Whether and Where to Attend College, and Player's Perception of His Coach's Influence (Percentages)

A. Coach gave advice on whether to attend college and player's decision on college attendance

Player's decision on college attendance	Coach gave advice on whether to attend college		
	Often (N=116)	Seldom (N=107)	Never (N=64)
Definitely will attend	78	64	58
Probably will attend	18	20	19
Definitely will not and probably will not attend	4	16	23

Gamma = .31, original relationship
Gamma = .16, with coach's advice on whether to attend college standardized
Gamma = .30, with player's perception of his coach's influence standardized

B. Coach gave advice on where to attend college and player's decision on college attendance

Player's decision on college attendance	Coach gave advice on where to attend college		
	Often (N=66)	Seldom (N=124)	Never (N=97)
Definitely will attend	75	73	59
Probably will attend	17	16	23
Definitely will not and probably will not attend	8	11	18

Gamma = .24, original relationship
Gamma = .20, with coach's advice on where to attend college standardized
Gamma = .24, with player's perception of his coach's influence standardized

C. Player's perception of his coach's influence and player's decision on college attendance

Player's decision on college attendance	Player's perception of his coach's influence		
	Great (N=136)	Some (N=121)	Little, None (N=31)
Definitely will attend	71	69	55
Probably will attend	19	18	19
Definitely will not and probably will not attend	10	13	26

Gamma = .15, original relationship
Gamma = .06, with coach's advice on whether to attend college standardized
Gamma = .12, with coach's advice on where to attend college standardized

attend college. The data in Table 4 display these variables utilizing Rosenberg's (1962) standardization technique as a means of examining their independent effects on the decision to attend college.

Panel A of Table 4 indicates that the advice coaches gave players about whether to attend college was not independent of the advice they gave about where to attend college. When advice about where to attend college was controlled, the correlation between advice about whether to attend college and college plans was reduced from .31 to .16. (Note also the correlation of .65 between these two variables in Table 3.) Likewise, panel B shows that the association between the coach's advice about where to attend college and college plans was reduced from .24 to .20 when the coach's advice on whether to attend college was standardized.

The player's perception of his coach's influence had no effect in reducing the associations between the advice variables and the player's educational plans. However, an examination of panel C indicates that advice variables reduce the relationship between the player's perception of his coach's influence and college plans. These data suggest that because the coach is providing advice about going to college, and perhaps making arrangements with colleges and coaches for visitations, he is perceived of as influential by the player.

In summary, these data demonstrate moderate positive relationships between the advice coaches give about whether or not to attend college, where to attend college, and the player's decision on college attendance. However, the two advice variables are not entirely independent in their effects on educational plans. Additionally, while many players perceive their coach as influential, this influence is diffuse (see footnote 5); when examined with regard to educational plans, it seems to be primarily a function of the coach's advice.

SUMMARY AND CONCLUSIONS

In reference group theory, emphasis usually has been placed on the importance of parents, peers, teachers, and other persons and groups. These significant others vary in primacy and salience depending upon the age of the individual. Brim (1966:8) has referred to "the emergence of a series of 'self-other systems' in which the child is oriented toward the role of prescriptions and evaluations of significant others in his environment." The high school coach is not necessarily an important reference person for most high school students, though he probably is a role model for more male students than merely the actual players on his team; however, he is an important reference person for the athletes under his control and influence.

The data presented in this paper indicate that high school coaches are influential reference persons in athletes' future educational and occupational plans. The coach was reported to be influential in these plans by more players from lower than from upper socioeconomic backgrounds; also, the number of reference persons cited was greater for the lower than for the higher status players. This finding seems to support the thesis of Inkeles (1968:121-122) who has pointed out that there is less of a consistency of role models for lower-class than for middle-class youth.

The advice that coaches give their players regarding educational plans beyond high school is positively associated with the players' decisions to attend college. Furthermore, this advice is independent of either parental socioeconomic background or grades. Many players see their coach as influential, but this influence only has a low relationship to educational plans; it is partially a function of the advice given by coaches.

The exploratory findings of this paper suggest that the coach-player relationship is a fruitful area for future research. This relationship usually contains both instrumental and expressive characteristics. The coach's advice to the player often represents a genuine concern and desire to help him. Inherent within the same situation, however, is the potential for self-aggrandizement by the coach. A coach will receive recognition when his athletes continue to receive rewards beyond high school, particularly if they continue their education and participate on a prestigeful college team (many college athletic brochures include the high school from which the players graduated and their high school coaches). A coach's success and self-esteem reflect not only his win-loss record but the number of outstanding athletes he has produced that have continued to distinguish themselves after high school graduation.

NOTES

1. In the present study, 70 percent of the players indicated that their coach gave them advice about personal problems. Additional advice given by coaches, as reported by players, included: whom to date—22 percent, how often to date—49 percent, manner of dress—73 percent, swearing—84 percent, and hair style—88 percent. See footnote 5 for the ways players felt their coaches were influential.

2. While the rate of return for players was not high, an analysis of the early and late returns indicated no significant differences on the following variables that are relevant to the study: (1) players' plans to attend college ($\chi^2 = 1.38$, 1 d.f.); (2) the coach having given the player advice on whether or not to attend college ($\chi^2 = 3.05$, 2 d.f.); (3) the coach having given

advice on where to attend college ($\chi^2 = .21$, 2 d.f.); (4) the player's perception of his coach's influence ($\chi^2 = 2.07$, 2 d.f.). In response to the question: "Would you be willing to continue participation in a follow-up study?" 87 percent of the players who responded indicated their willingness to do so. This datum might be interpreted as a high degree of interest in the study and probable care in answering the items. The research was handicapped by not having access to the players' home addresses. The questionnaires were sent to the players at their respective high schools and it is likely that the letters were not always delivered promptly to the players. Furthermore, the questionnaires were sent during the last month of the school year when the end of school activities might have interfered with answering the questionnaires. In general, the factors that seem to best explain the rate of return appear to be randomized rather than reflecting a response bias.

3. The occupational level was operationalized by asking: "What sort of work does your father (or stepfather) do? If retired or dead, what sort of work did he generally do when he was working?" Responses were trichotomized as in the tables. The educational level was operationalized by the question: "How much formal education does your father or stepfather have?" and categorized as in the tables.

4. Incidental to the present study is the relative influence of the parents presented in Tables 1 and 2. The greater importance of the mother than the father among the lower status respondents is apparently a function of using the father's educational and occupational background for classification. Such a classification may be unrealistic for lower status respondents. When the respondents (both players and coaches) were classified by their mother's educational background, the father's influence was equal to, or greater than, the mother's influence at all educational levels.

5. These items were operationalized by the following questions: "Have you decided whether or not to go to college? Definitely decided to go . . . .; Definitely decided not to go . . . .; Not decided, but probably will go . . . .; Not decided, but probably will not go . . . ." For statistical analysis, players were classified on educational plans as: Definitely will attend college; Probably will attend college; Probably will not; and will not attend college. "Does your basketball coach ever give suggestions or advice about whether or not you should go to college? Often . . . ., Seldom . . . ., Never . . . ." "Does your basketball coach ever give suggestions or advice about where you might go to college? Often . . . ., Seldom . . . ., Never . . . ." "Has your basketball coach been an influence to you? Great deal of influence . . . ., Some influence . . . ., Little or no influence . . . ." "If he has been an influence, in what ways?" The percentage distribution of the players' perceptions of their coaches' influence was: (a) a great deal of influence—47 percent, (b) some influence—42 percent, and (c) little or no influence—11 percent. To illustrate the breadth of influence, the answers to the open-ended question on the ways the coach had been influential yielded the following categories: helped with personal prob-

lems, helped develop basketball proficiency and discipline, taught pride, teamwork, and sportsmanship, showed the value of hard work, accepted me as an individual, and provided understanding. Three percent of the players indicated the coach had been a negative influence.

6. Reported grades were operationalized by the question: "What would you say is your average grade in high school subjects? Mostly A's . . . ., Mixed A's and B's . . . ., Mostly B's . . . ., Mixed B's and C's . . . ., Mostly C's . . . ., Mixed C's and D's . . . ., Mostly D's . . . ." For analysis, the grades were trichotomized into the categories: (1) Mostly A's, Mixed A's and B's, and Mostly B's, (2) Mixed B's and C's, and (3) Mostly C's, Mixed C's and D's, and Mostly D's.

REFERENCES

Aberle, D. F., and K. D. Naegele, "Middle-class father's occupational role and attitudes toward children," *American Journal of Orthopsychiatry,* 22 (April): 366-378, 1952.

Alexander, C. N., Jr., and E. A. Campbell, "Peer influences on adolescent educational aspirations and attainments," *American Sociological Review,* 29 (August): 568-575, 1964.

Bordua, D. J., "Educational aspirations and parental stress on college," *Social Forces* 38 (March): 262-269, 1960.

Brim, O. G., "Socialization through the life cycle," pp. 3-49 in Orville G. Brim, Jr. and Stanton Wheeler (eds.), *Socialization After Childhood: Two Essays,* New York: John Wiley and Sons, 1966.

Campbell, E. Q., "Adolescent socialization," pp. 821-859 in David Goslin (ed.), *Handbook of Socialization Theory and Research,* Chicago: Rand McNally and Company, 1969.

Clausen, J. A., "Perspectives on childhood socialization," pp. 132-181 in J. A. Clausen (ed.), *Socialization and Society,* Boston: Little, Brown and Company, 1968.

Coleman, James S., *The Adolescent Society,* New York: The Free Press, 1961.

Duncan, O. D., et al., "Peer influences on aspirations: a reinterpretation," *American Journal of Sociology,* 74 (September): 119-137, 1968.

Ellis, R. A., and C. Lane, "Structural supports for upward mobility," *American Sociological Review,* 28 (October): 743-756, 1963.

Haller, A. O., and C. E. Butterworth, "Peer influences of levels of occupational and educational aspirations," *Social Forces,* 39 (May): 287-295, 1960.

Herriott, R. E., "Some social determinants of educational aspiration," *Harvard Educational Review,* 33 (Spring): 157-177, 1963.

Inkeles, A., "Society, social structure, and child socialization," pp. 74-129 in Clausen, J. A., (ed.), *Socialization and Society,* Boston: Little, Brown and Company, 1968.

Kahl, J. A., "Educational and occupational aspirations of 'common man' boys," *Harvard Educational Review,* 23 (Summer): 186-203, 1953.

Kandel, D. B., and G. S. Lesser, "Parental and peer influences on educational plans of adolescents," *American Sociological Review,* 34 (April): 213-223, 1969.

Kemper, T. D., "Reference groups, socialization, and achievement," *American Sociological Review,* 33 (February): 31-45, 1968.

Kenyon, G. S., "Sociological considerations," *Journal of Health, Physical Education, and Recreation,* 39 (November-December): 31-33, 1968.

————————— , "Sport involvement: a conceptual go and some consequences thereof," pp. 77-84 in Gerald S. Kenyon (ed.), *Aspects of Contemporary Sport Sociology,* Chicago: The Athletic Institute, 1969.

Krauss, I., "Sources of educational aspirations among working class youth," *American Sociological Review,* 29 (December): 867-879, 1964.

Page, C. H., "Symposium summary, with reflections upon the sociology of sport as a research field," pp. 189-209 in Gerald S. Kenyon (ed.), *Aspects of Contemporary Sport Sociology,* Chicago: The Athletic Institute, 1969.

Rehberg, R. A., "Behavioral and attitudinal consequences of high school interscholastic sports: a speculative consideration," *Adolescence,* 4 (Spring): 69-88, 1969.

Rehberg, R. A., and W. Schafer, "Participation in interscholastic athletics and college expectations," *American Journal of Sociology,* 73 (May): 732-740, 1968.

Rehberg, R. A., and A. Westby, "Parental encouragement, occupation, education, and family size: artifactual or independent determinants of adolescent educational expectations," *Social Forces,* 45 (March): 362-374, 1967.

Rosenberg, M., "Test factor standardization as a method of interpretation," *Social Forces,* 41 (October): 53-61, 1962.

Schafer, W. E., and J. M. Armer, "Athletes are not inferior students," *Trans-Action,* 6 (November): 21-26, 61-62, 1968.

Sewell, W. H., et al., "The educational and early occupational attainment process," *American Sociological Review,* 34 (February): 82-92, 1969.

————————— , "The educational and early occupational status attainment process: replication and revision," *American Sociological Review,* 35 (December): 1014-1027, 1970.

Sewell, W. H., and V. P. Shah, "Social class, parental encouragement, and educational aspirations," *American Journal of Sociology,* 73 (March): 559-572, 1968.

Snyder, E. E., "A longitudinal analysis of the relationship between high school student values, social participation, and educational-occupational achievement," *Sociology of Education,* 42 (Summer): 261-270, 1969.

_____ , "Aspects of socialization in sports and physical education," *Quest,* 14 (June): 1-7, 1970.

Straus, M. A., "Work roles and financial responsibility in the socialization of farm fringe, and town boys," *Rural Sociology,* 27 (September): 257-274, 1962.

Strauss, A., *Mirrors and Masks,* New York, The Free Press, 1959.

Tomeh, A. K., "The impact of reference groups on the educational and occupational aspirations of women college students," *Journal of Marriage and the Family,* 30 (February): 102-110, 1968.

_____ , "Reference-group supports among middle-eastern college students," *Journal of Marriage and the Family,* 22 (February): 156-166, 1970.

Warren, R. L., "Some determinants of the teacher's role in influencing educational aspirations: a cross-cultural perspective," *Sociology of Education,* 41 (Summer): 291-304, 1968.